WHY THE CONSTITUTION MATTERS

WHY THE CONSTITUTION MATTERS

SELECTED SPEECHES

JUSTICE
D.Y. CHANDRACHUD

VINTAGE
An imprint of Penguin Random House

VINTAGE

Vintage is an imprint of the Penguin Random House group of companies whose addresses can be found at global.penguinrandomhouse.com

Published by Penguin Random House India Pvt. Ltd
4th Floor, Capital Tower 1, MG Road,
Gurugram 122 002, Haryana, India

Penguin Random House India

First published in Vintage by Penguin Random House India 2025

10 9 8 7 6 5

ISBN 9780143476184

Typeset in Adobe Caslon Pro by Manipal Technologies Limited, Manipal
Printed at Replika Press Pvt. Ltd, India

The author's proceeds from this book are dedicated to his alma mater, Campus Law Centre, University of Delhi, to be utilized in memory of his distinguished teachers Dr B. Sivaramayya, Dr Lotika Sarkar and Dr Mool Chand Sharma.

www.penguin.co.in

To Kalpana,
whose quest for ethical living continues
to enrich our love and companionship

Contents

Introduction

In early 1880, Oliver Wendell Holmes, Jr was a thirty-nine-year-old, mostly known—if at all—as his famous father's son. Recognition had largely eluded him. With a none-too-distinguished career thus far, Holmes penned a book review of a contract law casebook assembled by Christopher Columbus Langdell, who presided as the dean at Harvard Law School. While critiquing the book's approach to the law of contracts as excessively rigid, Holmes introduced a resounding sentence: 'The life of the law has not been logic: it has been experience.'[1] This sentence shaped the course of legal history. Far from becoming epoch-making, Holmes's dictum would have remained tucked away in small print, had he not decided to place it as the fourth sentence of the first paragraph on the first page of his book titled *The Common Law*, which was published a year later. Touted as 'the most famous sentence [Holmes] ever wrote', it acquired significance as a symbol of legal modernism and the Central truth of legal thought. That single sentence became the bone and sinew of legal thought—a statement of timeless, enduring principle.

Holmes's statement refuses us the comfort of thinking about law as an abstract doctrine. It provides a framework that perceives the law as enmeshed with human lives, emotions, aspirations, conflicts and societal evolution. It is an ongoing conversation across generations, an animating force. This dialectic—between fixity and fluidity, past and present, principle and experience—remains law's essential charge. For me, Holmes's dictum has remained a companion—not merely an abstract ideal but a working guide—throughout my own years as a lawyer and a judge. The Central value of law lies in its engagement with human lives.

The law in statute books may appear as an abstraction. When a law is framed, the cumulative weight of human experiences is formulated in legal doctrine. Stories of suffering and injustice are reduced to their bare bones. Human stories become transformed into the purpose of each law, which judges use to interpret the law. But the law is not just comprised of the sterile architecture of canon and logic. If that were to be the case, an algorithm or a computer programme would prove to be an effective and efficient way of applying the law to the vagaries of human existence. In actuality, the law is a living system—a complex, organized entity capable of maintaining its own existence through self-sustaining processes, fuelled and furthered by a near-constant interaction with the environment that surrounds it. Just as a teeming colony of microbes living in the earth's oceans thrives through homeostasis, responsiveness, energy, growth, evolution and reproduction, legal systems also contain vitalistic, adaptive qualities. They acquire their lifeblood and form through their quest for stability and predictability. The quest for a stable legal order is embodied in concepts such as stare decisis or precedent. Kelsen, as a legal philosopher, developed the concept of Grundnorm, which represents the basic normative truth underlying each system of law. The law has evolved over age and time through collective human experience, reason, debate and because of the friction between established doctrine and new social understandings.

During my years on the bench, I have attempted to explore this relationship through my judgments. Judges lead a lonesome existence, closeted away from social contact to maintain their impartiality. There is a danger that the isolation of judges can create a 'virtual' reality of its own. A judicial career runs the risk of being confined to the contact of peers with little insight into the reality of the world around. I believe that the role of a judge comes with a responsibility to engage with citizens, within ethical bounds. To whom does a judge speak and for whom does a judge write? I believe in the significance of the outreach to the community for whom the law exists. Individual citizens are impacted by justice and injustice. Hence through their work on and off the bench, judges need to share the nature of the judicial role, the constitutional normative structures that impact judicial decisions and the process of reasoning that underlies decisions on complex legal concepts. Reaching out to those for whom courts exist as institutions in a democratic polity serves to foster civic understanding and public trust. Over the course of my career as a judge, there were invitations to participate in the dry discourse of legal issues and principle. Some were inevitable. Beyond this, there was an invigorating dialogue with civic institutions, universities and policy forums. There were visits to art and music festivals which provided insights into facets of law and life which remain hidden in the dry pages of legal pleadings.

Judicial opinions are constrained by case specifics, precedent and collective negotiation. Engaging in public forums has allowed for broader reflection. It has provided historical context, philosophical exploration and a personal perspective on the enduring values that guide decision-making in the larger project of the law.

Over the course of my judicial career spanning over two decades, I have paused to think about what Holmes said, when faced with a legal quandary that seemed incapable of being resolved by statutory and precedential canons or the tools of doctrinaire logic.

The law is founded on the enduring belief in the power of words and ideas. Our words reshape beliefs, awaken responsibility and touch the soul. Judges are tasked with more than rendering decisions. They work upon the words of the written constitution. They are interpreters not merely of law but of the values that animated the act of founding. This book takes its impetus from the belief that the moral and pedagogical responsibilities of judging are as important—if not more—than the doctrinal basis of their work. One reflection on the potency of language reminds us that, 'Words have energy and power with the ability to help, to heal, to hinder, to hurt, to harm, to humiliate and to humble.'[2] In a culture of relentless acceleration, we risk forgetting how a timely, well-chosen word can start movements or recast a nation's ethical horizon. The story of democracy—in India and elsewhere—is a story not only of statutes and ballots but of moments when words transcended events and pointed to an unformed future.

In 1963, Martin Luther King, Jr spoke from the steps of the Lincoln Memorial. Sharing his ideas in 'I Have a Dream', he broke from the text to invoke a dream 'that my four little children will one day live in a nation where they will not be judged by the color of their skin but by the content of their character'.[3] His speech was not a ruling on law but a summons to justice. Though not written into the law of the time, the address transformed the law. His words spoken to faith, courage and to the possibility of change awakened the soul. In doing so, the words redefined the quest of the nation and the Constitution.

I begin this collection not with a formal invocation but with an openness to initiate a conversation. These pages will I hope unravel the social project that transcends judicial rhetoric in a way similar to the path in which a speaker intertwines responsibility and dissent, resilience and belonging, liberty and dignity.

Ideas arrive clothed in words which are our gateways. In *Harry Potter and the Prisoner of Azkaban*, J.K. Rowling encapsulates a universal truth: 'Happiness can be found even in the darkest of times if one only remembers to turn on the light.'[4] The work of a judge is unfulfilled if it does not come face to face with injustice. The dry words of the law are animated by real stories of injustice, suffering and discrimination. It is in the narration of those stories that the law fulfils its mandate of being of relevance to life.

My endeavour in speaking to audiences has been to begin with a discussion of law or principle but to have this dialogue quickly grow into something more, a call to think about justice, citizenship and the values that guide us. My motto, if I were speaking to a graduating class, would be: 'Be curious. Be humble. Understand that citizenship is more than rights, it is a responsibility. That dissent is not disobedience, and that mercy and justice must walk together.'

Our Constitution demands to be seen as a living text, urging us to bring the principles out of courtrooms and into classrooms, workplaces, neighbourhoods and daily conversation. This anthology would have served its purpose if it initiated a dialogue—a sense that the idea has alighted somewhere in the life of the listener, awaiting its own work.

The aspiration is not to conclude but to invite: to foster reflection, to pose questions, to share the solemnity of concepts whose edges have to be clarified. For me, these pages are liberated from the formality of court.

Having traced the power of the word, it is necessary to reflect on its purpose. Why gather these addresses into a single volume? What does it mean to the reader, citizen, interlocutor?

When a judge pens a judgment, it is an exercise in formal resolution: a direction issued to parties, the legal community and the embedded institutional order. The aim is to settle, to declare, to interpret. When a judge speaks outside the courtroom—particularly at public forums, ceremonies or lectures—the audience is enlarged. The words are meant not only for the law or to those in conflict, not just for lawyers and judges but for citizens. They may have little value as a precedent but address the possibilities inherent in the engagement of law and society.

In curating these addresses, I was reminded of a work that has shaped my own understanding: *My Own Words* by American Supreme Court Justice Ruth Bader Ginsburg.[5] Justice Ginsburg weaves together decisions, lectures and reflections. She reminds us that:

> A constitution, as important as it is, will mean nothing unless the people are yearning for liberty and freedom.[6]

The vigour of the Constitution, she reminds us, depends on its dwelling in the moral imagination of the people. In this collection, whether addressing law students, discussing constitutional values or reflecting on inclusivity, dissent and gender, I have sought to bring those aspirations to the fore: speech as ethical action, not mere display; invitation, not finality.

This volume is also my response to a persistent question—one voiced most often by the young: What does it mean to be a 'constitutional citizen' today? This collection does not venture on the path of offering easy answers. I seek to encourage an open, plural, ongoing encounter with constitutional meaning—one that lives, thrives and is questioned beyond the courts; in schools, streets, and in the everyday dealings of individuals with one another.

In this book, the reader will find that I have included some of the convocation addresses that I was invited to deliver, over the years. Convocation addresses are often dismissed as ceremonial footnotes to academic life. I see them differently. I regard them as civic appeals, as points of inflection where law reinforces its compact with the emerging citizen.

Many of these talks are reflections on my own life—its uncertainties, losses, dreams and ideals. These ideas have developed in numerous conversations with my spouse, away from the demands of a public life. Her impatience for change, commitment to gender equality and compassion towards every sentient being in the pursuit of a vegan lifestyle continue to animate my own thoughts. That she is critical more than occasionally is the surest symbol of an abiding bond of friendship between us. Some of the ideas embody the ethos of my mother, whose home-grown strength of character provided care and nurture over the years. My father's strong belief in public service influenced my early interactions with the Constitution. This collection reflects the teachings of my instructors, the lived wisdom of my colleagues and the insights gleaned from generations of students, law clerks and interns from whom I have had the opportunity of learning. Law, in my experience, is lived as much as learned. My law clerks have over the years provided me with insights into the emerging world, ensuring that the isolated work of a judge did not result in mental desuetude.

I hope these speeches invite the reader into reflection, debate and—above all—a sense that our democracy, like our Constitution, remains a living, striving work in progress. Progress arises not from isolation but from dialogue, not from recitation but from engagement across our many differences. Our plural culture is our founding and continuing strength.

The animating conviction here is that the Constitution is a discourse—unfolding, interactive, contested and reimagined through the moral imaginations of the people. The Constitution evolves through living conversations. Our conversations refuse to fossilize the constitutional text. Our stories, including the embellishments they gather over time, breathe life into principle.

The Constitution, in its original design, anticipated debate, contestation and growth. In his 1912 campaign speech, later published in 1913 as 'What Is Progress?' in *The New Freedom*, Woodrow Wilson argued that:

> Society is a living organism and must obey the laws of life, not of mechanics; it must develop. All that progressives ask or desire is permission, in an era when 'development,' 'evolution,' is the scientific word, to interpret the Constitution according to the Darwinian principle; all they ask is recognition of the fact that a nation is a living thing and not a machine.[7]

One speech that has remained etched in my conscience is Justice M. Hidayatullah's 'Lest We Forget'.[8] His address reflects on the essence of judging. The worth of a judicial life lies in the duties undertaken, knowledge sought and a willingness to differ when conscience requires. Such a view is necessary for the continued credibility and vitality of the bench. He claims that an enduring judicial tradition stems not from the number of decisions handed down (or cases disposed of) but from 'a judge's sense of his own duties', the relentless pursuit of knowledge and the moral courage to disagree. 'A dissent,' he recalls Chief Justice Hughes saying, 'is an appeal to the brooding spirit of the law, to the intelligence of a future day'.[9]

According to Locke's *Second Treatise of Government*, legitimate civil society occurs when individuals 'consent to make one Community or Government',[10] forming a unified body whose authority rests on the will and determination of the majority. Rousseau's concept of the general will promotes civic participation, debate and self-definition, allowing citizens to act collectively for the common good and legislate for themselves. More recently, John Rawls's *A Theory of Justice* envisioned justice as fairness, with each citizen in an equal position behind a 'veil of ignorance', a thought experiment in constitutional discourse.

From Locke's *Second Treatise*, which grounds political society in the consent of the governed, through Rousseau's 'general will', to Rawls's 'veil of ignorance', we encounter constitutionalism not as fiat but as the result of ongoing participation, dispute, reflection—a conversation in which the many become one and yet still remain many. These speeches seek to investigate the conscience of a republic rather than simply comment on the legality of the issues that confront it.

In one of my addresses, I spoke of the 'we' in 'We the People' as ever expanding, a move towards an inclusive constitutional identity that allows many forms of belonging, particularly for those formerly marginalized. The verdicts providing equality of entry for women in the armed forces; on viewing disability as a social rather than medical construct; and regarding merit itself as a notion which must transcend acquired social and cultural capital have been written to be more than just outcomes. They initiate dialogues with society, with oneself and with the concept of the person in law. In those reflections, I have attempted to demonstrate that the law must recognize the autonomy of the individual not in isolation but in relation to others and the institutions that shape their lives.

Constitutional discourse extends beyond the courts. It reverberates throughout art, journalism, education and public memory. One of my addresses alludes to how 'the newsprint voiced the aspiration of the soul, a yearning for freedom'. I recalled how a single editorial, blank in protest on the outbreak of the Emergency in June 1975, could speak louder than pages of text. My own experiences as a young student in Delhi University during the Emergency years provided a grim reminder that the Constitution could be reworked in street protests, newsrooms and the dissident voices of students. The media's ability to 'speak truth to power' is a vital expression of constitutional conscience.

In another convocation speech, I addressed feminism not as a slogan but as a method for reimagining power, agency and equity. Future lawyers, I urged, should read the Constitution with the conscience of citizens, not technicians. I have contended that the law must be attentive to stories, especially those that have been silenced. Law, like literature, is a custodian of memory—a responsibility best undertaken with humility and a realization of our own fallibility. At its peak, the Constitution is a narrative of struggles past and visions as yet unrealized. This collection, then, is an invitation—a hope that each reader will meet the Constitution as a relationship, not just a code; as a text to live by, not just to interpret.

Each of us, in our way, is an intrinsic part of the social project that seeks to define liberty, equality and fraternity anew. The Constitution speaks through its words and silences. So must we listen with honesty, respond with responsibility, act with optimism and survive in the hope that each individual life matters.

1

The Sounds and Silences of Our Constitution[1]

Words and texts occupy an important place in the idea of law. The expression of ideas in terms of precise words is supposed to bring certainty and permanence to the law. Words become even more important when they take the form of a 'constituent' act. As Laurence Tribe, Professor Emeritus, Harvard Law School, and one of the foremost scholars of American constitutional law, put it in his Tanner Lecture, the idea that 'words can somehow infuse a government with structure and impose limits on that structure—that language can directly power the ship of state and chart its course'[2]—has played an important role in what we understand of constitutions.

The dependence on words for constituting nations manifests itself best in the history of Indian constitution-making. In November 1948, some members of the Constituent Assembly objected to the bulky nature of our Constitution. They preferred a constitution that did not carry administrative details. While Dr B.R. Ambedkar agreed that administrative details should find no place in the Constitution, he also believed that since we had not yet imbibed 'constitutional morality', it was important to lay down administrative rules in words.[3] This idea of stating values explicitly in the words of the Constitution has given us the world's longest written constitution.

More than 1,46,000 words, 400 articles and 100 amendments later, this bulky constitution has charted the course of our nation. This so-called 'lawyers' constitution', as Sir Ivor Jennings, a British lawyer and academic, widely regarded as an authority on the British Constitution, would disapprovingly pronounce it,[4] has survived with the nation, albeit not to complete satisfaction. Is this precision of our Constitution (or verbosity as some would say, depending on the eyes of the beholder) a vice or a virtue? Has our Constitution succeeded *because* of its bulkiness or *despite* it? These are recurring questions. However, it is clear that in our 'constituent' act, words occupy a special place. As Pratap Bhanu Mehta, prominent Indian academic and public intellectual, known for his work on political theory and constitutional law, puts it, 'There was a self-conscious sense that in writing a text, India was finding a way to resolve debates on norms and values.'[5]

As much as we may relate words with precision and certainty, our exercise of laying down constitutional values in words is replete with ambiguity. These ambiguities of the text may be a result of either the open texture of language or of the drafter's inability to anticipate the future, or of both.[6] Or, as James Madison, the founding father and architect of Constitution of the United States, would put it, 'no compositions which men can pen, could be formed, but which would be liable to the charge of ambiguity'.[7] Constitutions struggle with them, too. Amidst what may seem a chaotic ocean of uncertainty affected by political climate change, tools of constitutional interpretation are islands of reprieve. There is a rich debate on how judicial review *infuses* and *should* infuse certainty in this vagueness. Professor Philip Bobbitt, American legal scholar and political theorist, provides a typology of constitutional arguments. According to him, there are six kinds of constitutional arguments: textual (the present sense of the language of the document); structural (the institutional relationships created by the Constitution); prudential (the understanding that constitutional doctrines are best advanced by practical wisdom); historical and ethical (based on a certain constitutional ethos).[8]

The relative reliance on these different kinds of arguments depends on where one finds oneself in the spectrum of constitutional theory. In the United States, we have witnessed invigorating debates on how constitutions should be interpreted. There is no singular theory of constitutional interpretation that completely captures the 200 years of constitutional jurisprudence. Leave aside any one unifying theory, there is neither any definitive list of theories, nor any agreement on how such theories should be applied.[9] However, the debate is primarily occupied by two broad schools of constitutional interpretation. On the one hand, we have originalism, which emphasizes the original meaning or original intent; on the other hand, we have what is metaphorically called the 'living tree' theory.

There is a strong disagreement between various scholars and judges as to what originalism means. For instance, Judge Robert Bork argues that originalism is about the original intent of the drafters. According to him, interpreters need not determine what the founding fathers would have felt about a particular application but need to state a core value that the framers intended to protect, and then apply that core value to the issue at hand.[10] Some other originalists, such as Justice Antonin Scalia, believe that originalism is about the original *meaning* of a word and *not what draftsmen originally intended*.[11] The determination of original meaning is based on how a reasonable person belonging to the historical context in which the constitution was made will construe the words in that constitution.[12] Thus, according to this theory, the meaning of a constituent word is historically fixed.

Similarly, living constitutionalism sees constitutions as evolving organisms; they evolve as society develops. It calls for a reasonably flexible interpretation of the constitution so that it suits the changing needs of society. The theory finds its justification in the presence of 'majestic generalities' in the language of constitutions; for example, 'equality before law' or the phrase 'life and liberty'. As Justice Oliver Wendell Holmes Jr put it:

> When we are dealing with words that also are a constituent act, like the Constitution of the United States, we must realize that they have called into life a being the development of which could not have been foreseen completely by the most gifted of its begetters. It was enough for them to realize or to hope that they had created an organism; it has taken a century and has cost their successors much sweat and blood to prove that they created a nation.[13]

According to living constitutionalism, though the courts cannot disregard constitutional text, they apply text in the current context, instead of the context in which it was enacted.[14] For example, the terms 'equality before the law' and 'equal protection of laws' should be imbued with the context prevalent in the present day, not the context of the 1950s as set out by the judgment *A.K. Gopalan* (where the Supreme Court advanced a restrictive interpretation of the equality clause).[15] Obviously, living constitutionalism does not mean a rule by fiat based on judges' whims and fancies. Structure, history, text and 'legal culture' limit the seemingly expansive space of living constitutionalism.[16] As Professor Jack Balkin,[17] American legal scholar and professor at Yale Law School, puts it, 'the great engine of constitutional evolution has not been judges who think they know better than the American people. It has been the evolving views of the American people themselves about what rights and liberties they regard as most important to them'.[18]

What I have spoken about, originalism and living constitutionalism, is only a flash of this debate that has illuminated constitutional theory for several decades. Amidst the potpourri of constitutional theories, it is important to go back and ask: What do these theories tell us about 'silences'? Are silences fixed in time? Do silences also evolve as words? Can the judges instil in silences whatever sounds they wish?

There is an important distinction between sounds and silences. While there is a way to communicate words, silence is not easily communicable. Understanding 'what is said' is not sufficient to understand 'what is not said'. When we have to understand silence, the interpretation of words will only take us so far.

In his famous novel *Siddhartha,* Hermann Hesse gets the protagonist to say to his friend, 'Knowledge may be communicable, wisdom is not.' He says that 'everything that is thought and expressed in words is one-sided, only half the truth; it lacks all totality, completeness, and unity'.[19] As much as the 1,46,000-plus words that the Constitution contains matter, they do not complete the story of our constitutionalism. The essence of a constitution lies not merely in its text but in how it is interpreted, lived and constantly reshaped by institutions, courts and the people over time. Constitutions are as much about what is unsaid as they are about what is said. At several moments in our constitutional history, we have found ourselves in a situation where we have had to deal with what the constitutions do not say, i.e. constitutional silences. These silences permeate all of constitutional law, as much as, if not more than, words.

In a crude sense, constitutional silence is essentially about gaps or omissions in an otherwise seamless constitution. However, not all silences are the same. As Professor Tribe puts it, there are as many reasons to be silent as there are to speak'.[20] Similarly, 'there are as many ways of hearing silences. In the remaining part of this speech, then, I seek to draw a map of various kinds of silences.

I. DOOR-CLOSING SILENCES

1. Silences in Ordinance-Making Power

Some silences perform what Professor Tribe contends are 'door closing functions'.[21] Recently, I was faced with a significant constitutional question about the interpretation of Article 213 of the Constitution, which deals with the ordinance-making power. Article 213 (2) (a) states that if an ordinance lapses or is disapproved by the legislature, it shall 'cease to operate'. The question that we were faced with is: What happens to the actions taken before the ordinance ceased to operate? Simply put, does the phrase 'cease to operate' save the actions taken under the ordinance before its lapse or disapproval? 'Can an ordinance, which by its very nature has a limited life, bring about consequences for the future which will endure beyond the life of the ordinance?'[22] Unlike other provisions, which use the phrase 'cease to operate', there was no savings provision in Article 213.[23] This is a classic case of constitutional silence. We had to first hear the silence, i.e. what this constitutional silence conveys, *and* then provide sounds to that silence, i.e. what constitutional rule emanates from what this silence conveys. The sound we provided to this silence upheld an important constitutional value—'legislative control over ordinances'.

> The *silences of the Constitution must be imbued with substantive content by infusing them with a meaning which enhances the rule of law.* To attribute to the executive as an incident of the power to frame ordinances, an unrestricted ability to create binding effects for posterity would set a dangerous precedent in a parliamentary democracy. The court's interpretation of the power to frame ordinances, which originates in the executive arm of government, cannot be oblivious to the basic notion that the primary form of law-making power is through the legislature.[24] (Emphasis added)

The actions before the ordinance lapses or is disapproved cannot continue to be valid. In doing so, we closed the doors on the 'savings' of past actions taken under an ordinance that has lapsed or is disapproved by the legislature. This is an example of a 'door-closing' silence.

2. Silences in the Scope of Article 32

In 2004, Zee Telefilms moved the Supreme Court claiming a fundamental rights violation by the Board for Control of Cricket in India (BCCI, a society that regulates the sport of cricket in the country). The court rejected their claim, holding that '[the] prerequisite for invoking the enforcement of a fundamental right under Article 32 is that the violator of that right should be a State'.[25] Since the BCCI is not 'State', Article 32 is not applicable.

Article 32, which is commonly described as 'the heart and soul of the Constitution', provides the right to move the Supreme Court for the enforcement of the rights conferred by Part III, spanning Articles 12 to 35. However, it is silent about *who* such rights can be enforced against. The text of Article 32 does not even mention the term 'state'. Further, while some fundamental rights, such as Article 14, specifically deal with 'state' violations, other fundamental rights such as Article 15 (2) or Article 21, at least textually, are not restricted to 'state' (what may be called 'horizontal fundamental rights'). If one just sees the silences as they are, one may argue that a person can move the Supreme Court even if a non-state actor violates a horizontal fundamental right.

Article 226, on the other hand, is categorical in its prescription of who writs can be issued against, unlike Article 32, which is silent on this point. Under Article 226, writs can be issued 'to any person or authority'. This sound of Article 226 provides a new sound to the silence of Article 32. Silence in Article 32 meant that the doors of the Supreme Court are closed for horizontal violation of fundamental rights. Ordinarily, unless provided otherwise (as in Article 226), constitutions are concerned with 'state action'—a command that the court has 'heard' in the sounds of constitutional silence.

3. Silences and the Doctrine of Occupied Field

Our Constitution has a Concurrent List, which contains certain subjects on which both Parliament and state legislatures have concurrent power to make laws. If a law made by the state legislature is in conflict with a law made by Parliament, such a law will be repugnant, unless the President gives assent to the state legislature.[26] But the Concurrent List does not take the complete share of conflict between the Central and state legislatures. Certain entries under List II are subject to certain entries under List I. For example, Entry 24, List II (Industries) is made subject to Entry 52, List I, which provides that Parliament may *declare*, by law, that the control of a certain industry by the Union is in the public interest. Entry 23, List II (Mines and Mineral Development) is made subject to Entry 54, List I. This means that while states can legislate on mining and mineral development, their power is limited by the extent to which the Union Parliament declares such regulation and development to be in the public interest. Unlike the Concurrent List and Article 254 (which is only for the Concurrent List), the Constitution is silent on how to understand those items under List II, which are subject to items in List I. In the case of *State of Orissa v. M.A. Tulloch*,[27] the court provided sounds to constitutional silence with the doctrine of 'occupied field'. The doctrine of occupied field postulates that for those entries in List II which are subject to certain entries in List I, the state legislature would not have the competence to enact any law in the first place, even if it is not contradictory to Central legislation. As the court put it, this is 'not because of any repugnance between the two statutes but because the State Legislature had no jurisdiction to pass the law'.[28] Therefore, the silences of the phrase 'subject to' under List II are provided sound by the doctrine of 'occupied field'. This is also another unstated command of the Constitution that 'closes doors' for state legislatures to enact laws under those specific entries.

In all the examples I have discussed earlier, 'silences' close doors—silence equates absence. However, silences do not always equate with absence. At times, they also open doors.

II. DOOR-OPENING SILENCES

Professor Tribe says that some silences of the Constitution open the door to a desired constitutional interpretation. They are, in other words, an open invitation to read into the text of the Constitution something that has not been explicitly stated.[29] Our constitutional history is replete with instances where courts have opened the doors in the process of providing sounds to the silences of the Constitution.

Article 13(2), falling in Part III of the Constitution of India, provides:

> The State shall not make any law which takes away or abridges the rights conferred by this Part and any law made in contravention of this clause shall, to the extent of the contravention, be void.

However, it is *silent* as to whether the articles in the Constitution are mutually exclusive while dealing with specific subjects and instances of rights' violation. More importantly, there is *silence* as to the test or yardstick to be applied for determining whether a statute infringes a particular fundamental right. These two questions came up early for adjudication before the Supreme Court within a few months of the Constitution coming into force in 1950.

Mutual Exclusivity of Fundamental Rights

In *A.K. Gopalan v. State of Madras*,[30] the Supreme Court was confronted with a habeas corpus petition under Article 32, where the petitioner challenged his detention and the governing statute as violative of the rights under Articles 19, 21 and 22. The court dismissed the petition and declared only Section 14 to be *ultra vires*, but preserved the constitutional validity of the rest of the enactment.

In the process, the court closed doors to both the silences mentioned earlier. The majority concluded that Article 22 being a complete code relating to preventive detention, the validity of an order of detention must be determined strictly according to the terms and 'within the four corners of that Article' and that its validity cannot be tested against Articles 19 and 21. In other words, fundamental rights were not a continuous stretch of entitlements but isolated pockets of discrete rights. While the majority closed the doors to an interpretation that the articles were not codes in themselves and were not to be read independently, Justice Fazl Ali gave a different voice to the *silence*. He observed:[31]

> To my mind, the scheme of the Chapter dealing with the fundamental rights does not contemplate what is attributed to it, namely, that each article is a code by itself and is independent of the others. In my opinion, it cannot be said that articles 19, 20, 21 and 22 do not to some extent overlap [with] each other. The case of a person who is convicted of an offence will come under articles 20 and 21 and also under article 22 so far as his arrest and detention in custody before trial are concerned. *Preventive detention, which is dealt with in article 22, also amounts to deprivation of personal liberty which is referred to in article 21 and is a violation of the right of freedom of movement dealt with in article 19(1)(d).* That there are other instances of overlapping of articles in the Constitution may be illustrated by reference to article 19(1)(f) and article 31 both of which deal with the right to property and to some extent overlap each other. (Emphasis added)

Subsequent decisions followed *A.K. Gopalan,* and it took the Supreme Court two decades to reopen the door they had closed earlier. In *R.C. Cooper v. Union of India,*[32] the petitioner challenged the nationalization of banks as infringing his rights guaranteed under Articles 14, 19 and 31. The court overruled the mutual exclusivity theory of *A.K. Gopalan*, and held that Part III does not seek to enunciate distinct rights, but it *weaves a pattern* of guarantees on the texture of basic human rights in a single thread.

Test to Determine Constitutional Infringement

On the question of the test to be applied to determine whether a statute infringes the Constitution, the court in *A.K. Gopalan* held that the protection of the guarantee of a fundamental freedom must be adjudged only in the light of the object and form of state action in relation to the right of the individual. This theory, applied in subsequent cases, closed the doors for considering the incidental, immediate or direct implications of the actions on the enjoyment of rights.[33] It was not until the newsprint cases that the door closed by *A.K. Gopalan* was attempted to be reopened when the Supreme Court considered the possibility of testing the statute on the touchstone of its direct and inevitable consequences, which were in the contemplation of the legislature.[34] The door was unlocked in *R.C. Cooper*, where the court said that it is the effect and direct operation of the law and of the action upon the right, which attract the jurisdiction of the court to grant relief.

Thus, we see that the court followed a door-closing policy while providing sounds to the *silence* of Article 13 to begin with but over time opened the door. In doing so, it heralded an era of expansive interpretation of rights.

Constitutional Interpretation and Unenumerated Rights

Treating silences as door openings has allowed courts greater latitude in interpreting particular phrases and articles in the Constitution. An excellent instance is the recent case where the court had to decide the validity of the actions of the Governor of Arunachal Pradesh which culminated in the dismissal of the chief minister.[35] Article 163(1) of the Constitution reads:

> There shall be a Council of Ministers with the Chief Minister at the head to aid and advise the Governor in the exercise of his functions, except in so far as he is by or under this Constitution required to exercise his functions or any of them in his discretion.

The Constitution is *silent* on the meaning of 'discretion' in Article 163(1), and it fell upon the court to decide the same. Based on an analysis of precedents, the court concluded that it meant: *first*, a constitutional provision expressly requiring the Governor to act at his own discretion; *second*, where the intent to grant a discretionary power emerges from a legitimate interpretation of the concerned provision, and this cannot be construed otherwise, and *third*, situations where the court has declared that the Governor should exercise the particular function on his own and without aid or advice because of the impermissibility of the other alternative, by reason of a conflict of interest.[36] Yet again, we see that the court has provided workability to the Constitution by giving sounds to the silence.

Another area where the courts have spoken for the Constitution is unenumerated rights. On several occasions, they have read in a right that has not been provided for explicitly in any provision of the Constitution. The foremost example of same is the right to privacy, which does not find a mention in the text of the Constitution. However, after the decision in *Kharak Singh*[37] and *Gobind*,[38] the right to privacy was established as constituting an essential ingredient of 'personal liberty' under Article 21. It is interesting to note that in both these decisions, the court placed reliance on international jurisprudence, international covenants and the scheme of the Constitution to fill the void in the document. This issue has now been referred to a constitution bench to be revisited.[39]

However, the most significant outcome of these door-opening silences has been the power it vests in the court to utilize multiple explicit rights to declare unenumerated rights to be within constitutional protection. In *PUCL v. Union of India*,[40] the question before the court was whether phone tapping is a violation of constitutional rights. The court analysed the provisions of the statute and concluded that the right against phone tapping could be located in Article 19(1)a and Article 21. Unregulated surveillance meant that the right to express one's opinion as well as the right to privacy was violated. In coming to this conclusion, the court did something similar to the Supreme Court of United States when it had said that '[the] right of marital privacy is protected as being within the protected penumbra of specific guarantees of the Bill of Rights'[41]. In that case, the court located the right to marital privacy in five different amendments to the Constitution of the United States and in a similar vein, the court in the People's Union for Civil Liberties (PUCL) case located the right against phone tapping in the penumbra of Articles 19(1)(a) and 21.

III. SILENCES IN WHAT IS SAID ABOUT THE CONSTITUTION

The Supreme Court of India decides thousands of cases every year. In a significant percentage of cases, it decides questions on issues on which the Constitution is silent. However, while deciphering these silences, it is often the case that the court is silent on what it says about the Constitution.

In *Kesavananda Bharati*,[42] the only instance of thirteen judges of the Supreme Court deciding a case, the court had to decide if there were any additional limitations on the amending power of Parliament than those prescribed in Article 368. The genesis of this question lies in the attempt of Parliament to abolish the zamindari rights. This action was questioned as a violation of the right to property which was a fundamental right then. The Constitution was *silent* on this aspect and in two earlier cases, the court held that the Constitution could be amended so as to take away the fundamental rights.[43] However, subsequently in *Golakh Nath*, the Supreme Court provided a different meaning and held that no amendment could abridge or take away the fundamental rights.[44] *Kesavananda Bharati* changed the wavelength of this sound by holding that there had to be limitations on the amending power. Justice H.R. Khanna noted:

> The word 'amendment' postulates that the old Constitution survives without loss of its identity despite the change and continues even though it has been subjected to alterations. *As a result of the amendment, the old Constitution cannot be destroyed and done away with; it is retained though in the amended form. What then is meant by the retention of the old Constitution? It means the retention of the basic structure or framework of the*

> *old Constitution* . . . Provision regarding the amendment of the Constitution does not furnish a pretence for subverting the structure of the Constitution nor can Article 368 be so construed as to embody the death wish of the Constitution or provide sanction for what may perhaps be called its lawful harakiri. Such subversion or destruction cannot be described to be amendment of the Constitution as contemplated by Article 368. The words 'amendment of this Constitution' and 'the Constitution shall stand amended' in Article 368 show that what is amended is the existing Constitution and what emerges as a result of amendment is not a new and different Constitution but the existing Constitution though in an amended form. The language of Article 368 thus lends support to the conclusion that one cannot, while acting under that article, repeal the existing Constitution and replace it by a new Constitution. (Emphasis added)

Thus, he concluded:

> The power of amendment under Article 368 does not include power to abrogate the Constitution nor does it include the power to alter the basic structure or framework of the Constitution. Subject to the retention of the basic structure or framework of the Constitution, the power of amendment is plenary and includes within itself the power to amend the various articles of the Constitution, including those relating to fundamental rights as well as those which may be said to relate to essential features. No part of a fundamental right can claim immunity from amendatory process by being described as the essence or core of that right. The power of amendment would also include within itself the power to add, alter or repeal the various articles.[45]

In this process, the court gave voice to one great silence and created another great silence. While the court attempted to define what constitutes the basic structure,[46] the decision on *whether a particular feature constitutes a part of the basic structure* was left to be determined by the court in appropriate cases. It is interesting to note that different judges in *Kesavananda Bharati* had different lists of what they considered to be parts of the basic structure. The new silence had multiple echoes since its birth.

In an endeavour to read this silence in what was said about the constitutional silences, later cases have included features such as the rule of law,[47] equality and the right to life[48] as part of basic structure.

Since *Kesavananda Bharati*, the doctrine of basic structure has been a regular player in constitutional cases. Interestingly, it is not just that the basic structure has evolved, but the features have themselves evolved over time.

Article 124 (2) of the Constitution provides:

> Every Judge of the Supreme Court shall be appointed by the President by warrant under his hand and seal after consultation with such of the Judges of the Supreme Court and of the High Courts in the States as the President may deem necessary for the purpose and shall hold office until he attains the age of sixty five years: Provided that in the case of appointment of a Judge other than the Chief Justice, the Chief Justice of India shall always be consulted.

The Three Judges cases dealt with questions relating to the interpretation of this article in the context of appointment of judges to the higher judiciary.

In the First Judges Case,[49] independence of judiciary came to be recognized as a part of the basic structure. It was noted:

> . . . independence of judiciary is doubtless a basic structure of the Constitution but the said concept of independence has to be confined within the four corners of the Constitution and cannot go beyond the Constitution . . .

Later, in the Second Judges Case, the court observed:[50]

> Rule of law is a basic feature of the Constitution which permeates the whole of the constitutional fabric and is an integral part of the constitutional structure. Independence of the judiciary is an essential attribute of rule of law.

However, the contour of what constitutes the independence of the judiciary has itself changed over time. Arguably, after the Second Judges Case and more recently, the Fourth Judges Case (NJAC judgment),[51] it is believed that primacy to the judiciary's opinion in the process of appointment of judges is an integral part of the independence of the judiciary and thus, a part of the basic structure in itself.

In this way, the silence in the *Kesavananda Bharti* case as to what constitutes 'basic structure' was provided sounds by expanding the doctrine in later cases.

Silences in Unwritten Constitutional Principles (Brexit)

The phenomenon of constitutional silence is not merely a trouble for the polities with a definitive constitutional document. Unlike India and the US, the United Kingdom (UK) does not have a constitution in the sense of a single coherent code of fundamental law which prevails over all other sources of law. Perhaps, this is why constitutional scholar Professor A.V. Dicey described the British polity as 'the most flexible polity in existence'.[52] Even in such a flexible constitutional system, silences have their own constraining force. In 2020, we witnessed one of the most important constitutional upheavals in the UK: Brexit. The referendum, albeit with a close margin, ruled in favour of 'leav[ing]' the European Union. Article 50 of the Treaty of Lisbon (2009) stipulates, 'Any Member State may decide to withdraw from the Union in accordance with its own constitutional requirements.' However, it is silent on what 'constitutional requirements' mean, albeit intentionally so as it may differ from member to member.

As the dissenting judge puts it, the silence lies *between two 'undisputed' rules* of the UK constitutional law—Rule 1: The executive cannot change law made by Act of Parliament; and Rule 2: The making and unmaking of treaties is a matter of foreign relations within the competence of the executive.[53]

The dispute was about how the Supreme Court of the United Kingdom fills the silence that lies between these two undisputed rules, i.e. what happens if the withdrawal from an international treaty (which is conventionally an executive act) also changes domestic laws made by Parliament (which is conventionally a legislative act)? The court provided the sound in the form of an important principle.

> [I]f, as we consider, what would otherwise be a prerogative act would result in a change in domestic law, the act can only lawfully be carried out with the sanction of primary legislation enacted by the Queen in Parliament.[54]

Providing sounds in this case was not a result of any textual or structural analysis. Rather, it was an exposition of an important value of the UK Constitution: that of parliamentary supremacy. This case explains to us that constitutional silences do not need 'texts'; they may also linger between flexible principles and values.

CONCLUSION

We have explored the various ways of providing sound to silences. However, at this point, we need to reverse our gaze and ask: Should we *always* provide sound to silences? Or are there certain silences that *ought not* to be provided with sound? Perhaps we need not get overenthusiastic about providing sounds to silences. I will end on a note of caution. As Michael Foley, a British political scientist, argues, 'constitutional government seems always to depend upon a space of the unsaid, of tacit understanding, of recognizing that "discretion" means being discreet, means casting a veil or a dustsheet over the things which cannot be said'.[55] He calls such situations constitutional abeyances, where a constitution tries to avoid certain controversies by not speaking about them. By doing so, it preserves the legitimacy of a constitutional order. Certain features of the constitution remain integral because of their 'inherent resistance to explicit expression' and therefore, they remain in a state of constant unsettlement. In that sense, while we discuss how to provide sounds to silence, the dignity of some silences is better protected if they remain silent.

2

Indian Environmentalism[1]

In 1973, a group of peasants in a remote Himalayan village stopped a crew of loggers from felling a patch of trees. This led to the inception of the Chipko Movement, and through it developed an important phase of Indian environmentalism, which opened up the perception of conflict between protecting the environment and pursuing economic development.

The Chipko Movement was:

> . . . representative of a wide spectrum of natural resource conflicts in the 1970s and 1980s—conflicts over forests, fish, and pasture; conflicts about the siting of large dams; conflicts about the social and environmental impacts of unregulated mining. In all these cases, the pressures of urban and industrial development had deprived local communities of access to the resources necessary to their own livelihood. Peasants saw their forests being diverted by the state for commercial exploitation; pastoralists saw their grazing grounds taken over by factories . . . artisanal fisherfolk saw themselves being squeezed out by large trawlers.[2]

Evidently around the same time, the spirit of Indian environmentalism was highlighted by the then Indian prime minister, Mrs Indira

Gandhi, who, in her famous speech at the UN Conference on the Human Environment (UNCHR), delivered on 13 June 1972, said that 'the inherent conflict is not between conservation and development but between environment and the reckless exploitation of man and earth in the name of efficiency'.[3]

The debate around development and the environment is still continuing. On one side are those who argue for faster economic growth since that alone will generate more jobs, and at the same time, and on the other side are those who argue against the preservation of our rivers, lakes, mountains and wonderful biodiversity in its myriad forms. As observed, these 'two groups are not talking to each other', but 'are talking at each other and with every passing day, the gap seems to be widening'.[4]

This takes us to the call for sustainable development, which was given to India as early as 1928, by none other than the father of our nation, Mahatma Gandhi, who had said: 'God forbid that India should ever take to industrialization after the manner of the West. The economic imperialism of a single tiny island kingdom (England) is today keeping the world in chains. If an entire nation of 300 million took to similar economic exploitation, it would strip the world bare like locusts.' Perhaps, what Gandhiji and later environmentalists, such as the leading figure of the Chipko Movement, Chandi Prasad Bhatt, had asked 'was not a return to the past, but for the nurturing of a society, and economy, that meets the demands of the present without imperilling the needs of the future'[5].

The new modern India, therefore, has to look at environmental issues not only from the perspective of those who benefit from development but also from the perspective of those who are affected by it. A higher standard of living for the impoverished people of the earth has to be achieved without alienating them from their heritage, 'without despoiling nature of its beauty, freshness and purity so essential to our lives'.[6]

Our Constitution has recognized the need for a clean and pollution-free environment. Article 48A, which was added by the Forty-Second Amendment to the Constitution of India, places a duty on the states to ensure the protection and improvement of the environment. The amendment also added Article 51A, which imposes a duty on each citizen to protect and improve the environment. Articles 48 and 51A use the phrase 'protect and improve'. Protecting the environment requires its preservation. Improving the environment requires positive steps to enhance the quality of the environment. This phrase places a positive obligation on the government to improve the quality of the environment. The affirmative duty of the government goes beyond merely preserving the environment, in whatever degraded form that it exists. The citizens also must appreciate the importance of a safe environment and must also contribute towards a pollution-free environment.

SUSTAINABLE DEVELOPMENT AND THE SUPREME COURT

Sustainable development is in the spirit of Indian environmentalism. This spirit was highlighted by the Supreme Court, exactly three decades ago, in *M.C. Mehta v. Union of India* (1987) 4 SCC 463, by recalling the proclamation adopted at the UN Conference on Human Environment at Stockholm in June 1972:

> A point has been reached in history when we must shape our actions throughout the world with a more prudent care for the environmental consequences. Through ignorance or indifference we can do massive and irreversible harm to the earthly environment on which our life and well-being depend. Conversely, through fuller knowledge and wiser action, we can achieve for ourselves and our posterity a better life in an environment more in keeping with human needs and hopes. There are broad vistas for the enhancement of environmental quality and the creation of a good life. What is needed is an enthusiastic but calm state of mind and intense but orderly work. For the purpose of attaining freedom in the world of nature, man must use knowledge to build in collaboration

> with nature a better environment. To defend and improve the human environment for [the] present and future generations has become an imperative goal for mankind—a goal to be pursued together with, and in harmony with, the established and fundamental goals of peace and of worldwide economic and social development.[7]

About a decade later, in 1996, the Supreme Court in *Indian Council for Enviro-Legal Action v. Union of India* (1996) 5 SCC 281, had stated:

> Both development and environment must go hand in hand, in other words, there should not be development at the cost of environment and vice versa, but there should be development while taking due care and ensuring the protection of environment.

In *Essar Oil Ltd. v. Halar Utkarsh Samiti,* AIR 2004 SC 1834, the Supreme Court observed that 'the objective of all laws on environment should be to create harmony between [development and environment] since neither one can be sacrificed at the altar of the other'.

'Survival of mankind', thus, depends on the realization of sustainable development 'in letter and spirit'.[8]

INCEPTION OF THE NGT

The discussion of environmental problems at the historic first United Nations Conference on Environment and Development (UNCED) in 1992 had led to a series of administrative and legislative measures in both developed and developing countries. 'The environmental renaissance, which saw the development of global conferencing technique at Stockholm (1972), Rio de Janeiro (1992) and Johannesburg (2002), has brought about worldwide phenomenal growth in environmental awareness, policies, legislation and institutions. The importance of this development lies in the fact that [the] enforcement of global regulatory measures has to take place at the national level.'[9]

However, at the national level, the problem is essentially with administrative structures. Explicitly, a credible environmental policy and an adequate set of laws and rules are already in place, and the problem is with implementation. If the judiciary has stepped in, it is primarily because of a weak executive at both the Central and state levels, having limited capacity for environmental regulation.

The lack of trained professional staff and reach across the country to undertake the work of environmental clearances, scrutiny and monitoring has been a major issue. Indeed, the lack of capacity has been a weakness that plagues the monitoring bodies in most states.

This led the Supreme Court of India in a number of cases, such as *M.C. Mehta v. Union of India*[10] (1986), *Indian Council for Environmental Legal Action v. Union of India*[11] (1996) and *A.P. Pollution Control Board v. Professor M.V. Nayudu (Retd)*[12] (1999) to highlight the need for the setting up of special environmental courts.

Later, in 2003, the Law Commission of India took cognisance of the Supreme Court's suggestion and undertook a detailed study on the need for the establishment of environmental courts. In 2003, it released a comprehensive proposal for constituting environment courts. It was believed that technical knowledge and expertise were needed in dealing with environmental law issues. Additionally, not only did these cases require speedy disposal but also continuous monitoring. Hence, the setting up of green tribunals was imperative, as it would have been difficult for regular courts to give sufficient time to environment cases while ensuring speedy disposal.

In 2010, the National Green Tribunal (NGT) was established by the National Green Tribunal Act, 2010, for the 'effective and expeditious disposal of cases and also to reduce the pressure on the regular courts'.[13]

The composition of the NGT is unique, as it comprises an equal number of judicial and expert members. This balanced composition has led to the emergence of NGT as a specialized institution that has exercised its expertise in dealing with environmental cases involving multidisciplinary issues. For example, for assessing the impact of the activities of the big multinational corporations, the tribunal has not only looked at the pollution of natural resources but also evaluated the impact on the local communities with respect to livelihood, health and employment.

The NGT has been making efforts in ensuring speedy and effective justice. As of 31 August 2017, almost 22,948 cases have been filed before the NGT since its inception.[14] A total of 19,638 cases have been disposed of, with 3310 cases pending.[15] Reportedly, in 2016, the number of pending cases at the Western Zone was 268 as against 812 filed cases.[16]

The NGT has been lauded for delivering detailed and comprehensive judgments. The landmark judgment of the River Ganga rejuvenation delivered by a five-judge bench is an example of how the tribunal is willing to devote sufficient time in ensuring that a detailed action plan is framed for controlling pollution.[17] The tribunal thoroughly examined the waste composition of each water stream that discharges effluents into the Ganga. Specific directions were issued as to how to tackle pollution in these streams. Further, the tribunal declared an area of 100 metres from the edge of the river as a 'No-Development Zone' and prohibited waste dumping within 500 metres of the river.[18]

The tribunal also ensured that the need for economic development does not infringe upon the rights of marginalized people and communities, and pollute the environment. In the POSCO case, the tribunal acted as the custodian of the rights of the local communities by suspending the establishment of a 12 million tonne per annum steel plant, which would have adverse environmental impact, thus affecting the daily lives of the people.[19] The Western Zone Bench in a case held that even though there were defects in the pleadings and the format of the application filed by fishermen's association, the bench accepted the pleadings and fined the respondents to the tune of Rs 30 crore payable to the aggrieved families for the destruction due to developmental activities.[20]

The NGT has not only concerned itself with going after the big corporations but also paid heed to the problems of the people in their daily lives. In the case of *Dileep B. Nevatia v. Union of India*[21] (2014), it ordered the Ministry of Road Transport and Highways, Government of India, to lay down the standards for sirens and multi-tone horns used by different vehicles. The NGT has also played an important role in the reduction of pollution in Delhi. According to a Delhi Environment Department report submitted to the NGT, annual PM2.5 levels decreased from 128 $\mu g/m^3$ in 2018 to 106 $\mu g/m^3$ in 2023, and PM10 levels dropped from 277 $\mu g/m^3$ to 216 $\mu g/m^3$ during the same period.[22] The NGT has been instrumental in improving Delhi's air quality by enforcing tougher regulations on vehicle emissions, dust control measures, stubble-burning penalties and industrial checks—and by ordering agencies to take prompt action. Its efficacy is demonstrated by the quantifiable decrease in fine particle matter and the increase in days with healthy air. In the case of *Vardhaman Kaushik v. Union of India*[23] (2014), the tribunal directed a committee to prepare an action plan and, in the interim, ordered that the vehicles that are more than fifteen years old would not be allowed to ply or be parked on the roads.

The Western Zone Bench has also been liberal in deciding who can approach the tribunal. In a landmark order, the Western Zone Bench decided that even foreign nationals are allowed to approach the tribunal and their application would not be invalid.[24]

ENVIRONMENTALISM, AWARENESS AND TRANSPARENCY

An article[25] in the *Economic and Political Weekly* (*EPW*) observed that whenever environmental concerns were first publicly voiced, access to environmental information was considered to be critical so as to address the concerns. In stating so, the following reasons were summarized:

- First, environmental degradation was taking place at a scale impossible to comprehend without aggregated information of the sort usually available with governments and scientific institutions.
- Second, many of the pollutants that threatened human health or the environment could not be identified without the sort of scientific instrumentation usually not available to common citizens.
- Third, adverse environmental effects were often a result of activities that were geographically (and sometimes temporally) far removed from the impact.

'There is also the paradox that, often, people do not even know that they are living in polluted conditions or being poisoned and, consequently, they do not feel the need to seek information till it is too late.'[26]

The failure of adequate accountability on the part of the governments led to civil society groups' movements seeking pertinent environmental information, which had its effect.

'In recent decades, most governments around the world, bowing to sustained pressure from civil society organizations, have either legislated on or signed up to a broader universal convention promising access and transparency on environmental matters. These struggles have been varied . . . the struggle for assuring freedom of information has had the added benefit of raising awareness levels, even of those considered illiterate. As environmental deterioration threatens the very future of the world, what is required is global action that could facilitate the free flow of information across borders and nations.'[27]

This trend of transparency and environment has been endorsed by the NGT as well. In *Save Mon Region Federation v. Union of India*[28] (2016), the Save Mon Region Federation (SMRF), on behalf of the

Monpa indigenous community of the Tawang and West Kameng districts of Arunachal Pradesh, challenged the environmental clearance granted for the construction of a hydroelectric dam on the Naymjang Chhu River. The federation pointed to faults in the environmental impact assessment (EIA) procedure and a lack of close scrutiny of the project by the expert appraisal committee (EAC).

The proposed location of the dam is one of two wintering sites for the endangered black-necked crane (*Grus nigricollis*), which is revered by the local Monpa community as the incarnation of His Holiness the Sixth Dalai Lama, Tsangyang Gyatso, who was born in Tawang. This material information was not revealed in the scoping process and, accordingly, was not discussed or evaluated in the EIA or properly considered by the EAC. The EIA also lacked any discussion of the cumulative impacts of other projects being proposed within the river basin.

The NGT concluded:

> It is true that hydel power project provides eco-friendly renewable source of energy and its development is necessary, however, we are of the considered view that such development should be 'sustainable development' without there being any irretrievable loss to environment. *We are also of the view that studies done should be open for public consultation in order to offer an opportunity to affected persons having plausible stake in environment to express their concerns following such studies. This would facilitate objective decision by the EAC on all environmental issues and open a way for sustainable development of the region.* (Emphasis added)

The NGT suspended the environmental clearance until the Ministry of Environment, Forest and Climate Change (MoEFCC) undertook an environmental flow study to determine how to protect the black-necked crane and its habitat. As is practice, all studies must be provided to the public for consultation. Thereafter, the EAC was expected to make a fresh appraisal of the dam project, with the new information and public comments in mind.

Environmental decision-making processes, particularly in developing countries, have generally been found to be 'opaque and inaccessible'. 'India's experience [of NGT] in striving to improve its processes may thus provide useful lessons for other jurisdictions.'[29]

CHALLENGES AND CONCERNS BEFORE THE NGT

While the NGT has acted as an 'effective deterrent' to violations of environmental norms, recent challenges to its decisions in courts are a matter of growing concern. A recent article titled 'Impact of the National Green Tribunal on Environmental Governance in India: An Analysis of Methods and Perspectives'[30] states:

> Another growing concern has been that in recent years, the NGT decisions have been challenged in various High Courts under Article 226 . . . Other High Courts like the Bombay High Court have also started entertaining appeals against the NGT orders and have asserted the superiority of a High Court over the NGT, saying 'High Court is a constitutional body while NGT is a statutory body'.

According to the NGT Act, its decision can be challenged before the Supreme Court, but petitioners have been invoking Article 226 (power of High Courts to issue certain writs) to challenge decisions before the High Courts.[31] The Supreme Court is yet to decide on what decisions of the NGT can be challenged before the High Courts, and on what grounds. The paper also raises the concern that in cases where the NGT's decisions are not complied with, it was pointed out that its decisions were 'not feasible to implement within a given timeframe'.[32]

The biggest challenge people face is access to justice. In Jharkhand's Chaibasa municipality, the Bindrai Institute for

Research Study and Action (BIRSA), along with the Occupational Health and Safety Centre (OHSC), had approached the NGT over abandoned asbestos mines at Roro in the same municipality. BIRSA highlighted that while their role was to raise awareness about the harmful effects of asbestos, only activists based in metropolitan cities had the access and the means to approach the NGT on the issue. It was stated by the convenor of BIRSA that: 'We do not have much knowledge about NGT. For a tribal activist based in a remote location, it is extremely difficult to travel to Kolkata and find accommodation there.'[33] Perhaps the strongest and most simple critique about NGT's inaccessibility comes from Dayamani Barla, known as the Iron Lady of Jharkhand, a tribal leader who has led campaigns against displacement and mining. It was lamented by her: 'I do not know about NGT.' She questions why someone should travel all the way to Kolkata to fight a legal case. She added that, 'A green tribunal should have been based in a place that has the highest forest cover or large mineral deposits. That is where the dispute is and that is where the extremely poor live.'[34]

The NGT is located in only five big cities spread across India. Once the tribunal started operating, lower courts were barred from taking up environmental cases. This has meant that poor and disadvantaged communities living in remote parts of the country have to go to NGT benches in their respective zones to get justice. For a tribal individual trying to stop pollution from an iron ore mine in Bastar, this means filing and fighting a case in Bhopal. For a villager affected by oil pollution in Nagaland, this means coming to Kolkata and hoping to be heard quickly, which is 'neither easy nor affordable'.[35] It would be a welcome move if the number of benches could increase and be also located in affected areas, thus ensuring access to justice to everyone.

Therefore, many improvements are still required to make accessible, speedy and effective resolution of environmental disputes a practical reality. The fight for **Environmental Justice** is also a fight for **Social Justice**.

CLIMATE CHANGE AND THE IMPOVERISHED

One has to be alive to the social justice aspect of environmental degradation. Mostly, the discourse that we have around the possible solutions to environmental problems is a one-size-fits-all approach. There's an unspoken belief in policy discussions that governance that benefits businesses and elite groups is automatically assumed to benefit everyone, even the poor and marginalized, without questioning whether that's actually true. What is often lacking is the acknowledgement that the intensity of impact that environmental degradation has in everyday lives is heightened in the case of the most marginalized, disadvantaged and vulnerable sections of society.

Climate change could effectively negate India's economic progress, pushing 45 million Indians into extreme poverty over the next fifteen years, according to a World Bank report.[36]

While the recognition of common but differentiated principle at COP21 (UNFCCC Conference of Parties) is an important step to ensure that an undue burden in not placed on developing countries, it's time we shifted our focus on making our domestic environmental laws more equitable towards the poor and marginalized communities which have traditionally borne a disproportionate share of the harmful effects of pollution or environmental hazards because they lack economic or political clout.

The relationship between poverty, environment and development in India is quite complex and not amenable to easy generalization. Poverty is often seen as a cause of environmental degradation, and the poor are not in a position to use natural resources sustainably. However, there is another aspect to the relationship that must not be ignored. One must also look at poverty as the effect of environmental degradation. This is because of the fact that in developing or relatively poor countries, the poor depend directly on the natural resource environment for their livelihood. Climate-related shocks also affect those who are not poor but remain vulnerable (non-poor vulnerable people) and can drag them into poverty.

The poor suffer the most as a result of floods and droughts.[37] They lose their productive assets, sometimes through a distress sale, which adversely affects their capacity to resume normal economic operations when normalcy is restored. Even disasters that look temporary may have a lasting, debilitating impact on the economy of the poor. Man-made ecological disasters such as the poisonous gas leak in Bhopal in India in December 1984 have affected the poor the most. Some 3500 people were killed and 2 lakh were injured in the Bhopal tragedy. Most of them were poor. If the possibility of such disasters is not drastically reduced, poverty aggravation is inevitable.

The impoverished and marginalized sections are also among the worst affected by environmental pollution and degradation. Those living in vulnerable areas with the fewest resources find it difficult to recover quickly from shocks. For example, the effect of floods, tsunamis, droughts and other natural disasters is felt the most by communities with an already fragile infrastructure. They often lack safe housing, live in overcrowded cities or very rural villages and have little access to health and other services.

Changing temperatures and rain patterns, particularly droughts, have detrimental effects on farmers and can cause food insecurity. Agriculture as a sector is one of the most sensitive to climate change given its dependence on weather conditions, both in terms of the direct impact that shifts in climactic patterns have on agricultural yield and on account of climate-dependent stressors (pests, epidemics and sea-level rise). Unfavourable weather can lower crop yields and decimate livestock. This means that income declines for farmers and their families, sending people further into poverty. It can also cause massive food shortages, increasing food prices. Higher food prices can be devastating for the poor.

Another health-related impact of climate change is access to clean water. Shrinking sources of fresh water, droughts, changes to the water cycle and fewer resources for purifying water, all detrimentally impact access to clean water and sanitation.

Coastal flooding is becoming more prevalent because of rising sea levels. Flooding can contaminate water sources, increasing the transmission of water-borne diseases, such as typhoid and cholera. Like rising food costs, diseases also disproportionately affect people with lower incomes who pay more out of pocket for healthcare.

The reasons why poor people are more at risk point to possible policy solutions. Ending poverty will not be possible if climate change and its effects on poor people are not accounted for and managed in development and poverty-reduction policies. This means, in part, providing poor people with social safety nets and universal healthcare.[38] Conversely, we must also ensure that climate change policies contribute to poverty reduction. In other words, we must strive to create a situation where climate change policies contribute to poverty reduction and poverty-reduction policies contribute to climate change mitigation and resilience building.

In India, as in many parts of the world, climate change has hit indigenous communities especially hard. Their dependence on the surrounding environment for their everyday life makes them important stakeholders in climate change protection. The intimate knowledge that these communities have of their surrounding environment also makes them crucial partners in the battle against climate change.

GENDER AND ENVIRONMENT

Although it may appear that the relationship between human society and the physical environment is seemingly gender-neutral, affecting both women and men in indistinguishable way,[39] this is not entirely accurate. Men and women have different relations to the environment, and environmental changes affect the lives of men and women differently.[40] Some of these differences arise on account of biological factors, as in the case of pregnant women who have been found to attract malaria-carrying mosquitoes twice as much as non-pregnant women. Due to climate change, these mosquitoes have increased in numbers, but an even more common explanatory factor to differentiated linkages with the environment than biological differences is gender differences.[41] Gender may be defined as 'a social construction organised around biological sex. Individuals are born male or female but they acquire over time a gender identity, that is, what it means to be male or female'.[42] Historically, the construction of masculine and feminine roles has been based on, and has led to further asymmetries in social and economic power, often with men having more power than women, and the social roles that women and men play usually have a profound effect on the use and management of natural resources.[43] It has been noted that women are uniquely vulnerable to environmental degradation due to different susceptibilities to toxic chemicals,[44] and disproportionate burden of environmental hazards and disease falling upon them.[45] For example, women's responsibilities in household work mean that women are more exposed to toxic chemicals found in products used for cleaning, personal care and pest control, and to pesticides and house-building materials stored at home. In rural areas, indoor pollution affects women more than men, as women are more exposed to smoke from burning fuel.[46] This is also true as regards the environmental consequences of waste disposal, where the vast majority (up to 80 per cent) of waste pickers in India are women, who collect, sort and recycle waste by hand.[47] Since women or girls are overwhelmingly responsible for fetching water, sanitation and maintaining a hygienic home, women bear a disproportionate burden of deteriorating water quality and availability in rural and urban areas. Lack of access to water decreases women's contributions to agricultural production and their economic opportunities.[48] The adverse impacts of environmental degradation can be aggravated by various factors, including age, socio-economic status, geographical location and other vulnerabilities.[49]

It was in this light that the UN's Fourth World Conference on Women held in Beijing in 1995 identified environment as one of the twelve critical areas for women. Section K of the Beijing Declaration and Platform for Action[50] is worth quoting extensively. The section noted that through their management and use of natural resources, women provide sustenance to their families and communities, and women's contributions to environmental management, including through grassroots and youth campaigns to protect the environment, have often taken place at the local level, where decentralized action on environmental issues is most needed and decisive. Thus, as consumers and producers, caretakers of their families and educators, women play an important role in promoting sustainable development through their concern for the quality and sustainability of life for present and future generations.[51]

However, due to gender power relations, women's knowledge and contributions are often overlooked.[52] Take forest management, for example. In general, men's use of forests causes more environmental degradation. For example, men often collect firewood by felling and processing trees, while women use fallen branches and thus have a less damaging impact on the environment and to a larger extent than men, women use products such as berries, herbs and honey. Nonetheless, women have less land rights and access to forests, and participate less in forest management and decision-making in spite of research showing that women's involvement has a positive impact on sustainability, regeneration and conflict management.[53]

Considering these issues, a gender analysis of environmental management is necessary, looking at gender aspects of the use of natural resources, consumption of services and goods and experiences of environmental degradation.[54]

This necessity has been underlined in Principle 20 of the Johannesburg Declaration on Sustainable Development (2002),[55] which committed to ensure that women's empowerment and emancipation, and gender equality are integrated in all activities encompassed within the Millennium Development Goals (MDGs). Following this, the UN Commission on Sustainable Development at its eleventh session in 2003 decided to make gender a cross-cutting issue in all its work on sustainable development,[56] thereby acknowledging that the contribution of women to economic development, social development and environmental protection, which are mutually reinforcing components of sustainable development, should be recognized and supported, and that there is need for a clear gender perspective in environmental management since, unless the contribution of women is recognized and supported, sustainable development will be an elusive goal.[57]

So, gender mainstreaming for environmental protection is necessary to promote equal opportunities for men and women as its participants and beneficiaries of environmental protection. This requires that the key differences in their knowledge and positioning be factored in. This includes producing and disseminating information about environmental protection, reaching out to both women and men, and recognizing their different roles and priorities in relation to the environment[58] and ensuring opportunities for women to participate in environmental decision-making at all levels[59]—including, I might add, in adjudication of environmental disputes.

GENERAL REMARKS

In an article published in the *India Together* magazine, Prahlad Shekhawat presented an alarming statistic concerning India's per capita resource consumption rates.

> [It has been estimated] that India's population will reach 1.7 billion by 2050. In that case, the country is likely to face a widening ecological deficit even if its current per-capita levels of resource-consumption remain the same. Therefore, for Indian society to continue to prosper in an increasingly resource-constrained world, business and government leaders must work actively to protect the natural capital on which India's economy, and all human life, depends.[60]

Shekhawat added:

> In national and international debates on Sustainable Development Goals (SDGs), the interests and livelihood of the poor and tribal people, which depend largely on access to common resources such as forests, water bodies and grazing

> lands, are woefully neglected. The commons, on which these sections depend often for their very survival, cannot be allowed to fall prey to pollution and the pursuit of unregulated private profit. India has to first put its own house in order before it can lead the developing world.[61]

Thus, the arithmetic of India's demographic future presents us with a formidable challenge. This projection of India's future confronts us with an inescapable ecological reality.

Sunderlal Bahuguna, a key leader in the Chipko movement, outlined the steps necessary to ensure that the skewed impacts of climate change on women are mitigated. He stressed the need to empower women by ensuring that their status as citizens is elevated, by ensuring access to education and securing their livelihoods.

> Women, while continuing to perform their traditional domestic roles are increasingly involved in earning livelihoods. In many poor households they are often the principal or the sole breadwinners. A major thrust at the policy level is necessary to ensure equity and justice for them. Literacy and a basic education are essential for enabling the poor to access the benefits offered by development initiatives and market opportunities. Basic education is therefore a precondition for sustainable development. A sizeable proportion (about 60 per cent according to some estimates) of the population is not integrated into the market economy. Ensuring the security of their livelihoods is an imperative for sustainable development.[62]

Technology plays a significant role in today's world. Therefore, the transfer, development and use of technology

> . . . must be informed by an understanding of its implications in the social, economic and environmental contexts of the receiving societies. Technologies must be usable by and beneficial to local people. Where possible, existing local technologies must be

> upgraded and adapted to make them more efficient and useful. Such local adaptations should also lead to the upgradation of local technical skills. Local innovations and capacity building for developing and managing locally relevant and appropriate technologies must be encouraged and supported.[63]

India is the world's largest democracy. In a democracy, development must be in tune with human rights and basic democratic principles. Development means the realization of basic human freedoms; those social, political and economic freedoms, which define the object and purpose of development.

Knowing the destination and the road to follow is not enough. We need the commitment to keep us going. A greener future will not be decent by default but by design and planning.[64]

The magnitude of this challenge shapes what we might call India's ecologically fraught existence in the twenty-first century. Unlike previous eras of human development, where environmental constraints could be overcome through geographical expansion or technological substitution, the current century presents us with planetary boundaries that are both finite and non-negotiable. This universality of participation reflects the recognition that sustainable development, to be genuinely sustainable, must be comprehensive in its reach and inclusive in its processes. The interconnectedness of environmental, social and economic systems means that exclusions and inequities anywhere in the system can undermine the stability and sustainability of the whole.

3

The Indian Legal Profession in the Age of Globalization[1]

Good evening! It is always a pleasure to reconnect with my alma mater, Harvard Law School. The book that we are here to discuss today, *The Indian Legal Profession in the Age of Globalization: The Rise of the Corporate Legal Sector and Its Impact on Lawyers and Society*, is an outstanding example of the pioneering research that continues to be carried out at Harvard Law School.

At the outset, I congratulate all who were involved in this impressive collection of essays. Hitherto, there have been very few empirical studies in India on the legal profession. The book provides the first comprehensive analysis of the impact of globalization on the Indian legal profession. Relying on original empirical data that has been painstakingly collected by a multinational and multidisciplinary team over a long period of six years, it explores in great depth the emergence of the new corporate legal sector in India and its impact on other parts of the Indian legal profession, including legal education, the development of pro bono and corporate social responsibility, the regulation of legal services, and gender, communal and professional hierarchies within the legal profession.

In 1991, the world's largest democracy embarked on a journey of moving from a closed, state-controlled economy to an open economy that welcomed foreign investment, commonly known as liberalization—a journey that had a significant impact on the legal sector in the country. There was a need for new laws and regulations to operate in this new economic landscape, and which gave rise to a demand for lawyers who could navigate through this new legal and regulatory environment. While the development of this new legal sector, known as the corporate legal sector, has been influenced by the Anglo-American model to an extent, the Indian corporate legal sector is not simply the product of the adoption of Western practices but rather to quote a phrase from the book itself, a 'hybridized corporate legal ecosystem'. As the book demonstrates, in spite of the influence of US and UK law firms on the corporate legal sector in India, India's most influential law firms have developed their own identity, characterized by some values that are deeply connected to India's history and culture. For example, and I'm sure I am not sharing any family secret, family and communal ties are very important to some of the most influential Indian law firms.

I now move on to how the growth of this corporate legal sector has affected the legal profession at large. The most significant impact has been on legal education in India, due to the increasing number of law graduates (particularly from the elite law schools) who choose to work in law firms. The prospect of high-paying corporate jobs at the end of the law course has changed who applies to law school, the choice of law schools, the educational experience at law school and also how much students are willing to pay for legal education.

Prior to the emergence of the corporate legal sector, jobs available to graduating lawyers were mostly limited to assisting as junior advocates to senior lawyers in the profession; jobs that paid little or nothing. Law was thus not always a viable profession for students who did not have families that could support them for a long period of time. The late 1980s and 1990s in India saw the setting up of 'national law schools' with the objective of supplying well-trained lawyers to the bar and bench so that access to justice is enlarged and the quality of justice for the common man is improved and strengthened.[2] At the same time, the 1990s were also a milestone in the Indian economy, and the landscape of a liberalized Indian economy created a demand for lawyers who could provide legal advice in a completely new terrain. This led to the growth of a corporate legal sector. The high pay packages that are offered at law firms, even at the entry level, have now made law as a whole a more lucrative and alluring profession, leading to a dramatic increase in the number of students pursuing law as a career option.

The demand of corporate law firms for law graduates and the exceedingly high supply of law graduates have significantly altered the landscape of legal education. Since the most influential law firms that offer high-paying jobs at the entry level are known to recruit from only a handful of the top law schools, students interested in securing these jobs scramble to gain admission into one of these select law schools. Further, prospective law students and lawyers are willing to pay much more and even take loans to attend law schools that offer highly remunerative jobs. The financial return from working in a law firm comes much sooner than it does in litigation, making the investment in legal education a less risky investment.[3] The quest for a high-paying job at a law firm does not end with gaining admission into law school. Students interested in gaining employment in the corporate legal sector fashion their choice of courses, their extracurricular activities, as well as the internships they pursue in a manner that would make them attractive candidates for recruitment—a 'corporatization of education'.

At this point, it is important to mention that these elite law schools, roughly a dozen in number, represent only a small fraction of the nearly 1390 law colleges recognized by the Bar Council of India as of 2013. The corporate legal sector is known to recruit only from the topmost law schools (a single-digit number). Unfortunately, some law firms are also known to discriminate between graduates at the same position or level by offering lower salaries to graduates of what are considered tier-two or tier-three law schools. This elitism and discriminatory practice must be condemned because it is antithetical to the principles of fairness and equality upon which the practice of law is founded. Not only do these practices deprive meritorious students of opportunities, but they also deprive the corporate legal sector of the talented legal minds that are found in most Indian law schools and colleges.

A top firm also discriminates in salaries on the basis of your grades in law school. If you were in the top ten ranks of your batch, your salary would be roughly Rs 1 lakh more per month as compared to your peers. While this may be some way to reward academic excellence, it is time we moved away from recognizing merit only through grades and universities, given that the Indian legal education system is far from perfect. The fact that legal education is now being viewed only as a means to secure a job in a high-paying law firm is evident in the manner in which law schools are ranked, recruitment by the corporate sector being the most important factor in determining law school rankings. This approach of viewing legal education as only a means to an end and not an end in itself is highly problematic and is leading to our young lawyers missing out on the true value of education in our lives.

At this point, I would like to reiterate that the national law schools were set up largely to encourage talented Indian students to enter government service or to provide access to justice for India's millions of poor citizens. In a developing country like India, the Constitution enjoins the legal system to facilitate the eradication of poverty, inequalities in status and of opportunity, and to ensure justice to all in social, economic and political spheres. However, an overwhelming majority of the top students in India's best legal institutions now work in the corporate sector. Members of the bar and bench frequently lament the corporatization of legal education, due to which the objectives with which national law schools were created are not being met.

It is definitely heartening that the recruitment of law graduates in the corporate legal sector has empowered law students by increasing social and economic mobility and in overcoming some of the barriers that exist in litigation. But there is a flip side to this trend: the impact on the growth of the bar and the bench, and therefore on the quality of justice delivered. Since national law schools were set up, in 1986, there has been only one National Law School graduate who has made it to the higher judiciary—a development that has only taken place this year, when a 1996 alumnus of the National Law School of India University, Bengaluru, Shekhar Saraf, was elevated as a judge of the Calcutta High Court. At the same time, in 2014, 26 per cent of the partnerships of the top six corporate law firms in India were occupied by graduates of the same National Law School. Therefore, the disparity between the base of the pyramid and the tip of the pyramid is evident for all to see.

The Indian legal market is set to continue to grow in a big way in the coming decade, given the rate of growth achieved consistently over the last two decades. This is bound to impact the way the profession is organized and the way legal services are delivered. When you consider the number of talented graduates that the National Law School system has churned out over the last two-and-a-half decades, there is much to reflect on about the system and the factors that motivate the choices of our young lawyers. This is definitely a matter of concern for those in charge of ensuring the delivery of equal justice to all under a democratic constitution. Instead of lamenting the growth of this corporate legal sector and the potential loss of legal talent in litigation, we must look at how we can address the factors that impede young lawyers from joining litigation.

Young lawyers who were interviewed during the research being carried out as a part of this book have reported that at the outset of their careers, they had considered litigation but thought the field would be too difficult to break into, given the social position and connections that were perceived to be a prerequisite for success in litigation. They believe that law firms provide a more professional and meritocratic environment. Family connections and religious and ethnic social networks are considered important for a successful litigation practice since these provide the infrastructure and resource support required in the early years of litigation and also help in acquiring clients. These barriers do not operate at the point of entry but rather determine the survival of litigators once they have entered the profession. We cannot blame our talented graduates for taking up attractive, well-paying jobs in the corporate sector, as the inequalities and initial hardships that accompany the practice of litigation, which young juniors have to bear, cannot be denied. Young juniors entering litigation today are paid little or nothing as compared to their corporate peers. The unfortunate effect of this is that it makes litigation an exclusive domain and the privilege of only a chosen few who have families with the means to support them through the difficult initial years. What is most disheartening is that litigation as an option is closed to those who might have been truly passionate about it and would have made great future counsels or judges in our country, simply because it is not possible for them to continue on meagre salaries when they have spent significant sums on their education and have families to support. I can understand why young lawyers would not want to deal with the inequalities perpetuated by the system, the pendency of cases and trials that stretch over decades, when they have a more lucrative option available. Therefore, the need of the hour is for the entire legal community to collectively work towards reforms that not only make jobs in the litigation sector attractive but also viable and rewarding.

WOMEN IN INDIA'S LAW FIRMS

This discussion on the litigation sector brings me to an unfortunate realization that one half of Indians face much greater obstacles to entering the litigation sector than the other half. The Indian legal profession has been predominantly male-dominated. A brief look at statistics shows that there are much fewer women in positions of power as well as there being fewer women in general who are practising in the litigation sector. As of 2012, only five out of 294 lawyers who have been promoted to the position of senior advocate in the Supreme Court of India have been women—an abysmal 2 per cent. Similarly, in the sixty-three-year-old history of the Supreme Court, out of 204 judges, only five have been women, at a poor 2.5 per cent. Recently, there has been a promising change in these metrics. In February and August 2024, twenty-two females were designated as senior advocates by the Supreme Court of India. Together, these designations were more than the cumulative number of females designated as senior advocates by the Supreme Court since its inception. After 2012, there has been an addition of six female judges to the Supreme Court. This includes Justice B.V. Nagarathna, who is slated to become the first female Chief Justice of India in 2027. Across many states in India, in fresh recruitments to the judicial service, over 50 per cent of the fresh recruits are females. In some states, nearly 70 per cent of the new recruits to the district judiciary consist of females. These statistics indicate that females continue to excel where a level playing field is provided in selection of judges, including through competitive examinations. With the passage of time, these female judges recruited to the district judiciary would occupy positions as district judges, High Court judges and eventually, as judges of the Supreme Court. This trend needs to be replicated in making direct appointments of female lawyers drawn from the bar to the High Courts. In a significant measure, these trends reflect the evolving nature of legal education. Across India, a significant proportion of students admitted for the study of law are females; in some colleges, over half of the students admitted are females. Transactional law firms have attracted huge numbers of female lawyers and gradually, the same trend is witnessed in court-oriented practice as well. This provides an opportunity and a challenge. The increasing strength of females in the legal profession would bring diversity and social transformation. The challenge lies in creating equal opportunity for the growth and success of females in the law as a career choice.

In stark contrast to this depressing picture, the gender dynamics in elite corporate law firms seem to offer some hope. Women in corporate law firms seem to be entering and succeeding at par with their male peers at all levels of advancement, including partnership. These seemingly gender-neutral trajectories in elite law firms are very encouraging given the general inequalities in the workplace. In particular, we must question to what extent the corporate legal sector has been able to challenge entrenched power structures and hierarchies. How many women are in positions of power in the corporate legal sector as managing partners and equity partners?

At a global level, research suggests that there are more women than ever graduating from law schools and entering the legal profession, and while the situation has definitely improved, there continues to be some evidence of gender biases and gender-based discriminatory treatment both in legal education and in the legal workplace.

LACK OF PRO BONO CULTURE IN INDIA'S LAW FIRMS

One of the most thought-provoking chapters in the book, for me, as a judge, was 'Pro Bono and the Corporate Legal Sector in India', which is the first qualitative empirical study of pro bono practices of elite corporate law firms in India. It is common knowledge that Indian law firms lack an institutionalized pro bono culture, unlike Western law firms, which has also been reaffirmed through the findings of this empirical study.

It appears that litigation-based pro bono work forms the smallest constituent of the overall pro bono work done by law firms, and corporate law firms have participated in only a handful of court cases on a pro bono basis. When asked about their preferred mode(s) of performing pro bono work, it appears that almost all law firms chose 'providing their regular transactional services to not-for-profit/social entrepreneurial clients for free/at reduced rates' over 'participating in litigation matters involving those in need.' Given the lack of pro bono culture in India, there is little empirical research at present to explain this choice. One of the reasons given by the President of the Society for Indian Law Firms to explain this trend is that the mandate to provide pro bono legal services is entrusted to the National Legal Services Authority (NALSA).

The corporate legal sector must realize that the existing national network of the legal service providers, including various NGOs, is unable to meet the needs of India's disadvantaged populations today, and most organizations face significant resource constraints. Unfortunately, in practice, only a few of these organizations are able to deliver these services effectively, often relying on the Public Interest Litigation (PIL) mechanism to provide legal aid. Private lawyers in India are not mandated to do or report pro bono work, and despite progress being made by a few leading law firms, most law firms do not have mandatory pro bono programmes or pro bono requirements for their associates. Though individual lawyers may contribute time to pro bono activities, the work tends to be ad hoc. Moreover, in what is an extension on the prohibition on foreign law firms, foreign-qualified lawyers cannot directly engage in pro bono work in India, even if they are interested in doing so. However, they can partner with local organizations in the capacity of different supporting and advisory functions.

The legal profession cannot live in ignorance of the reality of India—a burgeoning population and a society that is characterized by massive inequalities and injustice. The problem of access to justice is deep and pervasive in India and has affected the ability of the legal system and judicial process to respond to injustices. Compounded with the grave problem of pendency of litigation in India, which has engulfed the Indian legal process, there is an urgent need for reforms at various levels, including the involvement of all stakeholders.

I personally believe that lawyers for whom the legal profession has been extraordinarily profitable have a special responsibility and commitment to address the problem of access to justice in India. Those who have benefited financially from our legal culture need to invest in its roots and more could—and should—be done by the most successful in the legal profession to help protect access to justice for all. While speaking about the access to justice issue in the US, American jurist and retired US Circuit Judge David S. Tatel had remarked: 'If the nation's richest and most powerful law firms *donated a mere one-quarter of one percent of their revenues*—these lawyers would still be quite rich. This increased giving would more than double the amount of money that they donate to legal aid groups and make a world of difference to the poor who need lawyers' (emphasis added).

Pro bono is essential not only because of the enormous need for legal aid in our country but is also beneficial for the corporate legal sector. Studies conducted on pro bono practices at leading law firms in the US have shown that what makes good moral and ethical sense, often makes good business sense too. Pro bono work gives young lawyers an opportunity for hands-on training and puts them in real-life situations that firms often cannot provide. It becomes an efficient and inexpensive method for firms to professionally develop the skills of lawyers. Moreover, pro bono work plays a huge role in impacting the firm's brand value and reputation itself, both within the legal community and in the public eye. This, in turn, helps make the law firm more attractive to clients. In the US, which has a structured pro bono model, there are a number of firms that enjoy an established national reputation for pro bono work. On the other hand, there are many firms that have also discovered how a lack of attention to pro bono has disadvantaged them in the legal market, both in terms of serving commercial clients and also in terms of the recruitment of young lawyers, who prefer to join law firms that have established their commitment to serving the community. Pro bono work also benefits lawyers on a personal level, as it gives them the chance to work with clients on a one-on-one basis, which fosters a sense of connectedness and satisfaction which lawyers do not always gain from corporate jobs. Justice Ruth Bader Ginsburg of the US Supreme Court has also remarked 'a lawyer will gain large satisfaction when he or she is not simply a fee-charging artisan, but a contributor to the public good',[4] emphasizing how pro bono work may provide a partial answer to the career fatigue of law firm associates. One of the impediments faced in effective pro bono work being carried out by law firms is the information asymmetry between those seeking legal advice and representation and those carrying it out. Undoubtedly, some firms do engage in several pro bono activities. The need of the hour is to move from an ad-hoc basis to an institutionalized culture of pro bono work. I am glad to say that small but assured steps are being taken in this regard. A few months ago, the Ministry of Law and Justice, Government of India, announced a very novel initiative on behalf of the government, in an effort to channel free legal aid to the poor and marginalized sections of society. Called the 'pro bono legal services' or 'Nyaya Bandhu' programme, it involved the creation of a web-based platform on the Department of Justice website, where interested lawyers could register themselves to volunteer pro bono services to underprivileged litigants and which provided registered lawyers with various professional incentives to engage in pro bono work.

TECHNOLOGY AND LAW

Speaking about this web-based platform brings me to the remarkable and perhaps even unfathomable ways in which technology is going to influence the practice of law, including the corporate legal sector. In today's expanding information technology (IT) landscape, the pervasive role of the internet and technology cannot be ignored. In such an information-centric world, where cloud computing, information processing, machine learning, knowledge processing and speech synthesis are the mainstay, organizational boundaries are being realigned and are continuously shifting to new directions to meet these emerging realities. Artificial intelligence (AI) systems find increasing relevance and usage in fields and industries, including finance, healthcare, education, transportation and more.

Despite such giant leaps in various sectors of the economy, the legal profession has generally been slow to adapt to technological changes. Disruption averse, our law firms and corporate legal sector continue to be driven by inefficient practices and dependency on manual systems, a far cry from the increasingly automation- and innovation-driven world. However, this practice will inevitably change in the future. There is increasing competition and focus on efficiency in the global markets. As markets open to the world, specialization is necessary for firms to gain an advantage over their competitors. The clients seek better and cheaper services, and this drives firms to innovate and reduce costs, so that they remain competitive and continue to derive profits. Thus, technology and the internet play a major role in innovation and in transforming the legal landscape by shaking off entrenched conventional habits of lawyers and firms. Some of these potentially groundbreaking changes include the adoption of practices and technology platforms, such as automated document assembly, connectivity, electronic legal marketplace, e-learning, online legal guidance, legal open-sourcing, workflow and project management, online dispute resolution, intelligent legal research, big data and AI-based problem-solving, to name just a few. On the one hand, these systems increase output by streamlining the information systems and reducing duplication of work and on the other hand, they improve quality due to specialization and focussing.

MENTAL HEALTH

In the last segment of my speech, I would like to discuss an issue that is neglected and rarely discussed in the legal profession, which is mental health. Lawyers' jobs can often be very stressful, making them more prone to addiction and mental health issues, such as depression, at higher rates than the general population. This is supported by findings of various research studies in the US and Australia, which conclude that lawyers suffer from significantly lower levels of psychological and psychosomatic well-being than other professionals.[5] Comparable to US lawyers, 37 per cent of 384 lawyers in an Australian study indicated moderate to extremely severe depression, 31 per cent reported similar levels of anxiety and 49 per cent showed high levels of stress.[6] Various law firms abroad have now started taking mental health issues very seriously. They are offering on-site psychologists and incorporating mental-health support alongside other wellness initiatives.

There are no empirical studies in India regarding the mental health of legal professionals due to the general stigma in Indian society regarding mental health issues. However, the steep increase in the number of suicides in India's premier legal institutions is indicative of the systemic flaws. Of late, efforts have been made by made by law colleges and their students, such as the Gujarat National Law University (GNLU) or the National Academy of Legal Studies and Research (NALSAR) in Hyderabad, to recognize the need for addressing these concerns and provide avenues for students to reach out within the institution. In comparison to these recent initiatives by law schools, the legal profession, including the corporate legal sector, is doing woefully little. Law firms in India definitely need to be more sensitive to their employees' concerns about unsatisfactory work culture and a complete lack of work-life balance. Since many issues specific to the legal profession are responsible for the heightened level of stress that most of us have felt, general empathy and sensitivity to understand mental issues must be accompanied by the knowledge of the idiosyncrasies of this profession. As lawyers, we must collectively work to create a healthier work environment. Change on an institutional level requires the creation of support structures, a massive change in our attitude and destigmatization of mental-health issues amongst members of the profession.

CONCLUSION

On a concluding note, I am confident that the book will be of immense interest to academics, lawyers and policymakers who are invested in the critical role that a rapidly globalizing legal profession is playing in the legal, political and economic development of important emerging economies such as India, and how these countries are integrating into the institutions of global governance and the overall global market for legal services. The book provides some important insights at a time when crucial decisions are being made regarding the future of the legal services sector, particularly regarding further liberalization of the legal services market to allow the entry of foreign law firms in India.

It must be remembered that the corporate legal sector still forms a minuscule fraction of the legal profession in India, in terms of the number of legal professionals. While the size of this sector is going to increase in the coming years, traditional lawyers in the litigation sector will far outnumber corporate lawyers for years to come in the near future. I sincerely hope that similar extensive research will be carried out by the Harvard Centre for the Legal Profession on this part, which forms the majority of the legal profession in India, in order to catalyse reform initiatives.

4

The Rule of Law in India

Past and Present[1]

> 'In a world divided by differences of nationality, race, colour, religion and wealth[,] [the rule of law] is one of the greatest unifying factors, perhaps the greatest, the nearest we are likely to approach to a universal secular religion.'
>
> —Lord Tom Bingham

The concept of the rule of law in India has a long history. The material on this subject is so vast that it would not be possible for me to cover everything. Yet, I will make a modest endeavour to present a broad picture of how the modern conception of the rule of law evolved in India.

THE RULE OF LAW IN ANCIENT INDIA

There were two sources of law in classical Indian traditions: the texts of law (the Shastras and Smritis,[2] as they were called, such as Manu-smriti, or the Laws of Manu) and custom. In Hindu religious traditions, Shastras and Smritis are collections of texts that guide religious and social life. Shastras are treatises on specific fields of knowledge, while Smritis are remembered or recorded traditions, often dealing with law, ethics and conduct. The sacred texts were sources of written law, customs and unwritten laws. The actual juridical administration was carried out by the law of the courts. In the administration of justice, the king was the highest appellate court. The classical law of India continued for many centuries, and even after Muslim rule began in India, the fundamental structures of the classical law of the country were not altered. Islamic law, brought by Muslim rulers, was applied only to the believers, while Hindus were ruled by the Shastras. In both Hindu and Islamic laws, custom held a significant role.[3] Law supported by custom permitted social discrimination on the basis of caste and gender. Such discrimination was considered a part of the natural scheme of things.[4] Sociologist André Béteille has observed in this regard:

> Hindu law in particular took a tolerant view of such diversity, and, where there was divergence between the classical (or shastra-based) law and custom, it often allowed the latter to prevail.[5]

The rule of law in this period thus meant the rule of customs. What a custom constituted was generally agreed upon by most of the adult male members of society.[6]

A major transition in law and society took place when Indian society was subjected to British colonialism. The colonial era had a deep influence on the legal traditions in Indian society and laid down the foundations of modern law. The influence of colonial rule continues to determine the relationship between law and society even in contemporary India.[7]

THE RULE OF LAW IN THE ERA OF COLONIALISM

In the initial years of its rule, the British administration was hesitant to interfere with social customs, such as those related to caste and gender. The British did not have any general or specific plan to bring about a change in the Indian society and in the conception of law.[8] The colonial administration soon realized that law and custom in the Indian society were 'intertwined in the most complex and confusing manner'.[9] Assistance was sought from native experts not only in interpreting the law but also in codifying and systematizing it.[10] Their main objective was to maintain law and order and stability, which could lead to efficient administration. Lord Thomas Macaulay, a member of the first Law Commission established in 1834 by the British government, played a crucial role in this task of codification and formalization. His important and lasting contribution to Indian law and jurisprudence was the establishment of the Indian Penal Code, 1860. Macaulay famously said:

> Our principle is simply this; uniformity where you can have it; diversity where you must have it; but in all cases[,] certainty.[11]

The British brought with them a new idea of the 'Rule of Law', which did not have any counterpart in any of the legal systems prevalent in India at the time. The doctrine of the rule of law is ascribed to A.V. Dicey, who in his book in 1885 on the British Constitution, titled *The Law of the Constitution,* gave the following three implications of the doctrine of rule of law:[12]

1. **Absence of arbitrary power,** that is, no man is punished except for a breach of law.
2. **Equality before the law,** that is, equal subjection of all citizens (rich or poor, high or low, official or non-official) to the ordinary law of the land administered by the ordinary law courts.
3. **The primacy of the rights and liberties of the individual,** that is, the constitution is the result of the rights of the individual as defined and enforced by courts of law.

Dicey had stated that the above three features existed in the British Constitution. The British Constitution is judge-made, and the rights of the individual are part of the Constitution, as these are secured by the courts.[13] The broad emphasis of the doctrine of the rule of law is the absence of any centre of unlimited or arbitrary power.

Beteille has observed that this idea of the rule of law must be counted as a 'permanent legacy of the British rule in India'.[14]

THE RULE OF LAW UNDER THE INDIAN CONSTITUTION

When the Constituent Assembly of India met at the time of Independence, its main task was to build a new social order based on the rule of law.[15] The framers of the Indian Constitution incorporated the basic components of the rule of law into the Constitution. The leaders of the Indian freedom struggle rejected the idea of the rule of law under the Dharmasastras, which formed the basis of classical Indian law.[16] Democracy and the rule of law were advanced to achieve a new society in India, which would be based on an egalitarian social order. The democratic features of the Indian Constitution, which promote the rule of law, can be summarized as: representative government with adult suffrage, fundamental rights providing for equality under the law and personal liberty, an independent judiciary, and other provisions to assist the underprivileged and marginalized to better their condition in society, by ending blatant oppression.[17]

As a basic component of the rule of law, rights and liberties of the individuals were specifically incorporated under the Constitution, in the form of fundamental rights[18] and directive principles.[19] Affirmative action protected the rights of marginalized communities. Granville Austin, a leading commentator on the framing and working of India's Constitution, has observed:

> The Constitution, by its very existence, was a social revolutionary statement. It was to be a modernizing force. Social revolution and democracy were to be the strands of the seamless web most closely related. Democracy, representative government, personal liberty, equality before the law, were revolutionary for

> the society. Social-economic equitableness as expressed in the Directive Principles of State Policy [under the Constitution] was equally revolutionary. So were the Constitution's articles allowing abolishing zamindari and altering property relations and those allowing for compensatory discrimination in education and employment for disadvantaged citizens.[20]

The journey towards a nation based on the rule of law has been long and arduous. The founders of the Indian Constitution hoped for the best and had set the conception of the rule of law in motion by establishing its essential features and institutions through the Constitution, albeit without explicitly stating the term 'rule of law'. Their successors (the elected representatives and the judges) had to cope with the challenges that were to come.

THE RULE OF LAW AS INTERPRETED AND EXPANDED BY THE INDIAN SUPREME COURT

The law laid down by the Supreme Court is binding on all courts throughout the territory of India.[21] The Supreme Court of India has invoked the rule of law several times[22] in its pronouncements to emphasize upon certain constitutional values and principles. An online search of the Supreme Court's reportable judgments delivered between 1 January 1950 and 1 January 2010 resulted in 1299 hits for the term 'rule of law'.[23]

The first prominent use of the term was when Indian judges crafted an innovative doctrine, called the basic structure of the Constitution, which is composed of those 'essential features' of the Constitution, which could not be taken away even by the constituent power of the legislature. The Indian Supreme Court, in its thirteen-judge bench decision (largest bench constituted till date in Indian legal history) in *Kesavananda Bharati v. State of Kerala*[24] proclaimed the 'rule of law', 'equality', 'fundamental rights', 'secularism', 'federalism', 'democracy' and 'judicial review' to be the essential features of the basic structure of the Constitution.

Taking this approach of promoting the rule of law further, in his celebrated dissent, Justice H.R. Khanna of the Supreme Court of India, in a case titled *Additional District Magistrate, Jabalpur v. Shivakant Shukla*,[25] referred to the 'rule of law' as the 'antithesis of arbitrariness'. The said case pertains to the time of the proclamation of the Emergency by the Union government. A presidential order was issued that barred anyone detained or arrested from seeking any relief through a habeas corpus or any other writ filed in the High Court. The question before the Supreme Court was: Whether a High Court, despite the presidential proclamation, could entertain a writ of habeas corpus filed by a person challenging his detention. Justice Khanna invoked the conception of the rule of law to hold that the State does not have the power to deprive a person of his life or liberty, even during the period of Emergency.[26] Justice Khanna held:

> Rule of law is now the accepted norm of all civilised societies . . . [E]verywhere it is identified with the liberty of the individual. It seeks to maintain a balance between the opposing notions of individual liberty and public order. In every State the problem arises of reconciling human rights with the requirements of public interest. Such harmonising can only be attained by the existence of independent courts which can hold the balance between citizen and State and compel Governments to conform to the law.[27]

Unfortunately, at that time, Justice Khanna's view espousing the rule of law was a part of the minority judgment. However, the *New York Times* (on 30 April 1976) praised Justice Khanna in the following words:

> If India ever finds its way back to the freedom and democracy that were proud hallmarks of its first eighteen years as an independent nation, someone will surely erect a monument to Justice H.R. Khanna of the Supreme Court.[28]

In 2017, a nine-judge bench[29] of the Supreme Court (the majority opinion in this case was authored by me) upheld Justice Khanna's view and overturned the decision of the majority in the *ADM Jabalpur* case.

These judgments also make it explicit that judicial review is an essential component of the rule of law. Judicial review involves the determination not only of the constitutionality of the law but also of the validity of administrative action. In a constitutional democracy, every exercise of power is subject to constitutional control. It is the mandate of constitutional supremacy that every institution of governance is subject to the norms embodied in the constitutional text. No institution, which has been created by the Constitution, has absolute power. Separation of power between different institutions acts as a check and balance among the institutions and promotes the rule of law to ensure that no institution can act in an arbitrary manner. Judicial review as part[30] of the basic structure of the Constitution and as an essential component of the rule of law and separation of powers, is intended to ensure that every institution acts within its bounds and limits.

In a recent decision, *Kalpana Mehta v. Union of India*[31] (delivered on 9 May 2018), a constitution bench of the Supreme Court emphasized on a new interpretation of separation of powers which focuses upon 'inter-institutional assistance and aid towards the joint enterprise of good governance'. The court held:

> The current view on the doctrine of separation of powers also seeks to incorporate mutual supervision, interdependence and coordination because the ultimate aim of the different branches of the government, through their distinct functions is to ensure good governance and to serve public interest, which is essential in the background of growing social and economic interests in a welfare state.

The emerging view is different from the earlier version of the doctrine of separation of power, which sought to compartmentalize and isolate the different branches of the government from one another, with limited permissible exceptions. The new view, the court held, is relevant to the Indian Constitution, as it envisages that the Indian society must move 'from the culture of authority and submission to the law, to one of justification and rights under the law'. This view, though recognized now, has been in practice for decades. The Supreme Court of India has played an active role in creating new ways to promote the rule of law. One such way has been that of public interest litigations (PILs), by virtue of which anyone can approach the constitutional courts in public interest, highlighting the violations of fundamental rights of citizens.

Professor Upendra Baxi in his article titled 'The Rule of Law in India' has observed that the Indian Supreme Court devised an extraordinary form of jurisdiction, called Social Action Litigation (SAL)—Baxi's coined term for 'Public Interest Litigation'—to accomplish a list of impressive results, which include:[32]

- a radical democratization of the doctrine of *locus standi*;[33] every citizen may now approach courts for vindicating the violation of human rights of co-citizens;
- the 'de-lawyering' of constitutional litigation in the sense that petitioners-in-person with all their chaotic forensic styles of argumentation are being admitted;[34]
- the establishment of new styles of fact-finding via socio-legal commissions[35] of inquiry to assist adjudicatory resolution;
- the generation of a new adjudicatory culture;[36]
- the SAL/PIL jurisdiction is conceived not as adversarial but as a collaborative venture between citizens, courts and a recalcitrant executive;
- the invention of continuing jurisdiction through which courts continue to bring about some minimal restoration of human rights in governance practices;[37] and
- the fashioning of new ways of judicial enunciation of human rights, a complex affair in which the Supreme Court especially brings back to life rights deliberatively excluded by the

constitution makers (such as the right to speedy trial[38]), creates some component rights to those enunciated by the constitutional text (such as the right to livelihood,[39] privacy,[40] education[41] and literacy, health[42] and environment[43]), rewriting the constitution by way of invention of new rights (such as right to information,[44] the right to compensation,[45] etc).

In this way, the Indian Supreme Court has developed the conception of the rule of law by evolving a 'new social movement aspiring to re-democratize the Indian State and governance'.[46] The rule of law in India has thus brought more and more areas of the Indian social life within its ambit.

THE RULE OF LAW IN PRACTICE: THE PRESENT

As discussed above, the Indian conception of the rule of law is also seen as an integral part of good governance. Questions are, however, raised as to the extent to which the constitutional promise of the rule of law matches with the actual realities in India.

The United Nations (UN) has defined the term 'rule of law' in a comprehensive way:[47]

> The term 'rule of law' refers to a principle of governance in which all persons, institutions and entities, public and private, including the state itself, are accountable to laws that are publicly promulgated, equally enforced and independently adjudicated, and which are consistent with international human rights norms and standards. It requires, as well, measures to ensure adherence to the principles of supremacy of law, equality before the law, accountability to the law, fairness in the application of the law, separation of powers, participation in decision-making, legal certainty, avoidance of arbitrariness and procedural and legal transparency.

In 2017, India celebrated seventy years of Independence—a significant milestone in a long journey of realizing its constitutional goals. While Indian democracy has withstood the last seven decades of social, economic and political developments, there remain numerous challenges to democratic governance. One of the greatest challenges is that the rule of law is still not sufficiently protected in Indian society. In this regard, a number of challenges to the rule of law continue to undermine Indian democracy and pose grave threats to governance.

India is one of those countries which, at least on paper, has a long tradition of upholding the rule of law, setting it apart from many of its autocratic peers and similarly situated countries. This tradition is enshrined in India's Constitution and the ensuing legislations, held together by democracy and free elections and protected fiercely by the courts.

Yet, it is pertinent to also analyse the efficacy of the rule of law in practice, and that is where India fares poorly. According to 2017 World Justice Project data,[48] which measures rule of law adherence in 113 countries and jurisdictions worldwide based on more than 1,10,000 household and 3000 expert surveys across eight factors, which are: constraints on government powers, absence of corruption, open government, fundamental rights, order and security, regulatory enforcement, civil justice and criminal justice, India ranks sixty-second. The unfortunate conclusion to be drawn from the dataset on India is that the country has laws, but there is a great deal of uncertainty about how those laws are implemented.

There is a distinction between the formal and substantive contents of the rule of law. The procedural legitimacy of law and institutions demands that laws are prospective, well-drafted, properly implemented and independently reviewed. It is critical that we realize that the rule of law is not a single entity but a spectrum of activities. At the upstream end of this chain is the structure of the laws and statutes that govern any society and the lawmakers who write them. Next come the investigative arms of the state, followed by the prosecutorial agencies. The judiciary and penal system constitute the downstream end. Each component of this chain influences the strength and quality of the preceding step(s).[49]

In India, the entire rule of law supply chain has become deeply dysfunctional. Furthermore, the very lawmakers who write the laws are hardly exemplars of the rule of law themselves, with many state and national legislators facing criminal charges. This shocking fact has a negative influence on the credibility of the entire rule of law supply chain, from law-making to enforcement.[50]

Moving further down the chain, the police and prosecutorial systems also need an overhaul. However, the judiciary in India has many bright spots: The Supreme Court of India, for instance, is one of the country's most widely respected public institutions. Whether one agrees or disagrees with aspects of the Supreme Court of India's sixty-eight years of constitutional adjudication, two points are clear. First, the court undeniably has played a major role in protecting and sustaining democratic governance and the rule of law in India; and, second, its jurisprudence is so rich, so varied and its institutional history so dramatic, that it can justly lay claim to being one of the most interesting and important constitutional courts in the world.[51] Yet, even the courts, on the whole, face challenges, from vacancies to backlogs and weak internal processes of self-regulation.

One of the greatest problems is India's archaic laws, many of which were enacted in the colonial era, with very different circumstances from the ones persisting today. Marc Galanter has noted:

> Contemporary Indian law is, for the most part, palpably foreign in origin or inspiration[,] and it is notoriously incongruent with the attitudes and concerns of much of the population which lives under it. However, the present legal system is firmly established[,] and the likelihood of its replacement by a revived 'indigenous' system is extremely small. The modern Indian legal system, then, presents an instance of the apparent displacement of a major intellectual and institutional complex within a highly developed civilization by one largely of foreign inspiration.[52]

India does not require the expiration of certain laws after a fixed period of time, and historically, the country has always favoured enacting new laws without repealing or amending the existing ones. The result is a multitude of laws on the statute books, with many unsuited to the times. Various states often have their own laws to regulate different activities, and the multiplicity and complexity of laws make compliance, deterrence and enforcement difficult. Potential solutions include empowering the Law Commission of India and granting it the resources to undertake the mammoth task of revising, repealing and updating old laws, while also placing a greater emphasis on precise and targeted legislative drafting to reduce future litigation.

There are also problems with the police and prosecutors. In India, the primary objective of policing remains the maintenance of law and order instead of the prevention of crime, which is another colonial relic that needs reform, given that in the modern welfare state, the mandate of the police is centred on public good. Outdated colonial era laws and inter-service rivalries between the forces, coupled with the politicization of police institutions, are also factors that have hindered the police force, which is also afflicted by the lack of resources, as it is not armed with the technological capabilities required to perform quality investigations. As a result, it is often understaffed and undertrained, and demoralized, which in turn, contributes to the low conviction rate, casting a poor light on both the police and the judiciary. These challenges ought to be addressed for the actual realization of the rule of law in India.

A RESPONSE TO CRITICISM OF THE RULE OF LAW DOCTRINE IN INDIA: LESSONS FROM THE PAST

One of the criticisms of the rule of law doctrine in the Indian context is that it has not been able to completely eradicate harmful social customs.[53] In many parts of India, social institutions still govern the conduct of citizens.[54] Therefore, the challenge lies in tackling this conflict between the rule of law and the rule of social customs in contemporary India. At this point, I would like to refer to two ancient conceptions of India: (i) *Dhamma*, and (ii) *Niti-Nyaya*.

Coming to the first, the term 'Dhamma', which is a conception of law inspired by morality, became popular when Gautama Buddha turned the wheel of social order in the religio-philosophical sphere. Buddha gave the call for Dhamma against the unequal social order prevalent in India. Manu-smriti has been an important source of law in the traditional Indian society. The text supported distinctions of caste and gender in law. The so-called upper castes were considered to be the superior class. As such, they had in law and in fact privileges and prerogatives not held by other sections of Hindu society.[55] In that sense, the concept of Dhamma becomes much more imperative, as it took a diversion from the established social order in India. The question is: What is the takeaway from this ancient conception of Dhamma?

In his illuminating article, political theorist Rajeev Bhargava discusses the situation, when in a democracy, the rule of majority can become arbitrary, when the power is exercised by popular whim rather than by predictable, stable norms emanating from collective reflection. The key takeaway, Bhargava suggests, is that the citizens owe to each other two things: (a) an impartial rule of law which checks abuse of popular power and saves the people, from acts that we might come to regret later and that binds even those we have temporarily chosen to govern us; and (b) something like Dhamma, a constitutional morality—justice, tolerance, freedom, equality and civic friendship—that guides us all, the ruler and the ruled.[56]

The above takeaway is also reflected in Nobel laureate Amartya Sen's work *The Idea of Justice*, where he discusses the Indian conceptions of *niti* (rules) and *nyaya* (justice). Sen has observed:

> Among the principal uses of the term *niti* are organizational proprietary and behavioural correctness. In contrast with *niti*, the term *nyaya* stands for a comprehensive concept of realized justice. In that line of vision, the roles of institutions, rules and organization, important as they are, have to be assessed in the broader and more inclusive perspective of *nyaya*, which

> is inescapably linked with the world that actually emerges, not just the institutions or rules we happen to have.[57]

Interpretation of the laws, therefore, should be in accordance with the contemporary needs and challenges. The rule of law is not all about *niti*, which is the Sanskrit word for rules. It is also about *nyaya* (justice),which entails the enforcement of law in a manner that is just.

The rule of law would be able to overcome social customs only when it is accompanied by favourable circumstances, which could be achieved by Dhamma- or nyaya-based social policies and by a change in public opinion about customs.

Further, in contemporary times, it is often stated that the rule of law is routinely trampled upon by those in power.[58] In many parts of India, social institutions (such as khap panchayats) still have influence over the conduct of citizens. The above-discussed conceptions of Dhamma and nyaya require that our elected and unelected representatives owe it to us that they be not merely rulers but moral exemplars, faithful adherents themselves of the rule of law and constitutional morality.[59] Rule of law has a certain internal morality as a part of which it embodies fundamental notions of justice and fairness.[60]

CONCLUSION

The rule of law is 'the hallmark' of Indian democracy. Though this is the ideal scenario or benchmark, India's mixed performance when it comes to the enforcement of the rule of law must be acknowledged. As the country undergoes massive economic and social change, improving India's rule of law institutions must become a priority. The social and economic progress achieved by various democracies has been shaped by their efforts to successfully protect the rule of law. Democracy and the rule of law are inextricably connected with each other.[61] The onus lies on India's democratic regimes to take urgent steps not only to protect its rule of law society in India but also to enhance the credentials which form the fundamentals of the rule of law.

Dr Rajendra Prasad, India's first President, while moving the motion for adoption of the Constitution in the Constituent Assembly, had said:

> . . . Whatever the Constitution may or may not provide, the welfare of the country will depend upon the way in which the country is administered. That will depend upon the men who administer it. If the people who are elected, are capable and men of character and integrity, they would be able to make the best even of a defective Constitution. If they are lacking in these, the Constitution cannot help the country. After all, a Constitution like a machine is a lifeless thing. It acquires life because of the men who control it and operate it, and India needs today nothing more than a set of honest men who will have the interest of the country before them . . . *It requires men of strong character, men of vision, men who will not sacrifice the interests of the country, at large for the sake of smaller groups and areas and who will rise over the prejudices which are born of these differences. We can only hope that the country will throw up such men in abundance* . . .[62] (Emphasis added)

Has the 'hope' been realized? If not, it has to be done soon. The future of the rule of law in India will depend upon the commitment of those who hold the fate of our institutions.

5

The Rule of Law in a Constitutional Democracy[1]

It is truly an honour for me to speak at the National Law University, Delhi (NLU, Delhi). This is my very first visit to NLU, Delhi. I have meant to visit this esteemed institute for quite some time, but the demands of my judicial docket as a judge of the Supreme Court—having to deal with seventy special leave petitions that get listed before us on Monday mornings and then another seventy on a Friday, followed by about fifteen odd special leave petitions on all other days of the week—have meant that I have had to keep to my chambers. But I was just thinking to myself, *in token of my exhilaration of visiting your institute, I am going to pinch that little notepad which says 'NLU Delhi' as a keepsake*. Though I never got the opportunity to study at NLU, Delhi, that notepad will be a fond reminder of my first visit here.

I am nineteenth on the list of a galaxy of speakers who have previously graced this lecture series. Seeing their names, I thought to myself: I have indeed a formidable task to discharge this morning, coming to speak after such illustrious names and in particular because the lecture series is dedicated to the memory of such a distinguished judge, Justice Bodh Raj Sawhny.

As I begin, let us collectively recount the lives of the people who devoted themselves to the cause of our freedom before Independence, whose lives are thus closely associated with the Indian freedom movement and as a consequence, with the founding moments of our Constitution, in which were forged the values that have shaped our Constitution. This contemplation is one of the very reasons I have chosen a theme today that transcends the strict boundaries of legal theory, one which is not just restricted to the rule of law. If I were to only speak about the rule of law today, I would address you on the Albert Venn Dicey's conception of the rule of law, retrace my steps to 1979 to the lecture halls of Delhi University, where I was taught his theory, and probably conclude my speech.

It is, however, the element of constitutional democracy that imparts a different texture to the theme that I will be speaking on this morning. This lecture is not just about what the rule of law is; it is also about how the rule of law finds specific meaning in our constitutional democracy and how it produces a theory of adjudication unique to the ethos of our legal system. The third facet that I will cover in my lecture is about the limitations of the role of the judiciary in creating the rule of law and of adjudication itself. That is where I will speak about the importance of associating non-judicial institutions in enhancing the rule of law.

While speaking about the rule of law, I begin with a simple question that was posed by the renowned political theorist Stephen Holmes: Why do people with power accept limits to their power? An even more pointed formulation of this query is: Why do people with guns obey people without guns, without the might of the state? An economic twist to this argument would be: Why would the well-endowed ever voluntarily part with a portion of their wealth or resources? In legal theory, a parallel question is: Why do politicians sometimes hand over power to judges? We see that happening in the Supreme Court every day. We saw that while dealing with the case in which Section 377 of the Indian Penal Code, 1860, was under challenge.[2] During the course of the hearing, we posed a query to the additional solicitor general (ASG) appearing on behalf of the

Union government in an attempt to glean its stance on the validity of the provision. In response, we were told that the government was leaving this to the 'wisdom of the court'. This was too enticing a principle for me not to respond, and so I did. I am not sure whether you have seen that, as it is a fairly obscure part of the judgment. In my opinion, I have stated: 'All that the stand of the Government indicates is that it is to the "wisdom" of this Court that the matter is left. In reflecting upon this appeal to our wisdom, it is just as well that we as Judges remind ourselves of a truth which can unwittingly be forgotten: flattery is a graveyard for the gullible.'[3] This brings me back to the question I posed to you all earlier. Why do politicians allow judges, who control neither the purse nor the sword, to overturn and obstruct their decisions and sometimes even send officeholders to jail? These questions are overbroad and considerably vague to be answered with any degree of certainty or comprehensiveness. What they do provide us, in the absence of any definitiveness, nonetheless, is a starting point, to pry loose some of the salient insights about the origins, evolutions and the limitations of the rule of law in a constitutional democracy like ours.

The rule of law subserves various important constitutional values, including legality, certainty, accountability, efficiency, due process and access to justice. So, at a Central level, the rule of law discharges a very formal function, one that brings to mind Lon Fuller's 'internal morality of the law'.[4] When we speak of the system of 'internal morality of the law', we refer to concepts such as the *generality* of the law, *publicity* of the law, *prospectivity* of the law, *intelligibility*, *consistency*, *practicability*, *stability* and *congruence*. When contrasted with the realities of how the law exists in practice, we see that the law is not necessarily general, it is not as public as it should be and it may not necessarily be prospective. Let us take the example of the *Vodafone International Holdings BV v. Union of India* case. Vodafone International Holdings had entered into a bilateral agreement with an entity situated in Hong Kong. The Indian government, invoking its income tax regime, demanded payment of taxes by Vodafone for the acquisition of the stake of the offshore company. The Supreme

Court in its judgment[5] sided with Vodafone and quashed the order demanding payment. In response, Parliament decided to enact a statutory amendment[6] to the Income Tax Act. This amendment was retrospective in nature, with effect right from the year 1962, meant to cover scenarios such as Vodafone's case. This created a huge furore in the international business regime.

The law is not necessarily intelligible, consistent, practicable or stable. This is for the simple reason that different judges respond differently to the needs of the law, and the law may not be congruent. But apart from the formal concept associated with Lon Fuller, there is a more procedural concept of the law. This procedural concept was propounded by Dicey and consisted of the following set of requirements or notions, viz. (i) that you should be *heard* by an impartial or an independent tribunal, (ii) where you have a right of representation, (iii) a right to confront, (iv) the right to reason the argument and (v) the right to a reasoned dialogue between various stakeholders in the adjudicatory process. There is a third and overarching element which is the substantive element, which is that the content of the law will be determined or evaluated in order to determine whether the law is compatible with the moral rights or the natural rights that citizens possess.

I think all of us, at least the judges of my generation, have grown up with Dicey's formulation of the rule of law. His postulate was essentially based on the principle of parliamentary sovereignty and on the rule of law. In fact, when he propounded his formulation of the theory of the rule of law in the nineteenth century, he described how foreign observers who visited England around that time were astounded by the distinguishing mark it bore—the fact that it was under the rule of law. As per Dicey, when Voltaire, the French Enlightenment philosopher, visited England, the predominant sentiment of his age was that he had passed out from the realm of despotism into a land where the laws may have been harsh, but it was one where men were ruled by law and not by caprice. Thus, in its original configuration, the rule of law conception was consistent with this—there were laws which were very well unjust and harsh, but the fact that there existed, as an overarching, abiding imposition, a normative legal framework in the ether of the legal system from which judges, politicians and society at large were able to draw a sense of authority provided a justification for the concept itself. From this portrait of Dicey's times—where these supposedly harsh and constricting laws existed alongside the rule of law—one thing is made manifest: that Dicey did not equate *the rule of law* with the notion of a *good* law. Nor did he contend that in order to qualify as a law, a particular norm of law must necessarily conform to the standards of fairness, reasonableness or be just. This begs the question, what did Dicey mean by the rule of law? To answer this question: There were three overlapping concepts which Dicey propounded. These were: *First*, that there should be a control on the exercise of discretionary power; *second*, that there should be no punishment without a pre-existing law; and *third*, that all power must be authorized and exercised through ordinary courts of law.

Dicey's second principle—and that's where I will depart from Dicey and his conception and segue into a notion of equality—involved what he referred to as the equal subjection of all individuals to a legal regime, of all classes to one law administered by the ordinary courts. Dicey's primary concern was that public officials should not have special immunities or privileges, and they should be held accountable by ordinary private causes of action before regular courts of law for their official conduct, no different from anyone else.

When we look at how the rule of law has been shaped in a constitutional democracy, no understanding or explanation of the subject would be complete without referring to the context in which it has emerged and evolved. This social and political context adds an additional layer to the existing theoretical discussion on the rule of law in our constitutional democracy. That is my postulate this morning, and I am going to speak about some of our recent cases as we go along. The first is: What is the law in a constitutional democracy intended to achieve? The *first* and basic premise which I want to place before you is the transformative role of the Constitution. What is it that the Constitution seeks to achieve in terms of the rule of law?

The crucial element therein, to my mind, is that the Constitution itself is intended to transform society.

To excavate this better, we must briefly visit the context in which the Constitution was enacted. There were inherent tensions in the drafting process in the Constituent Assembly between social reformation and the preservation of a long-standing status quo of a purely feudal and essentially patriarchal society. So, the process of constitutional draftsmanship reflects, first and foremost, a movement for political freedom. The Constitution was essentially drafted in the context of the freedom movement; a movement whose key objective was that people should have civil and political liberties, and rights. But parallel to the freedom movement that was taking place before the advent of the Constitution, another parallel social movement was well underway. This social movement was reflected in the work of people like Dr B.R. Ambedkar, as well as those who preceded him, like Jyotirao Phule or Savitribai Phule in Maharashtra. These were people essentially battling against a society founded on prejudice, on immutable features and on discrimination against several marginalized groups that it comprised. So, when one looks at the Constitution, it can be seen that there is an unmistakable emphasis on a commitment to a transformation of sociopolitical relations: the relations between the individual and the state and between the individuals themselves. This transformative vision of our Constitution underlies its working and interpretation. The rule of law in this background enjoins the recognition of these tensions and a vision of a society which is headed towards dignity, liberty and equality. Soon after the Constitution was enacted, you find in our rule of law approaches to the interpretation of constitutional rights, a palpable divide between the formal and the substantive.

Dicey's theory is characteristic of the formal perspective of the rule of law doctrine. However, for a period of time, the divide between the formal and the substantive aspects of law was lost to the process of constitutional interpretation itself in India. Take, for instance, the theory of classification, as it emerged after *Anwar Ali Sarkar*[7] and the series of cases that followed it. Equality, as an overarching principle of Part III of our Constitution, was reduced to a formula in *Anwar Ali Sarkar*. By being reduced to a formula, the doctrine of equality would be satisfied (as per the classical formulation) simply by the presence of intelligible differentia, and second, if there was a rational relationship between the intelligible differentia and the object of the law. However, the theory of classification reduced the substance of the rule of law to merely its form. By exclusively emphasizing on classification aspect of the doctrine of equality between 1952 [with *Anwar Ali Sarkar*] up to the case of *E.P. Royappa*[8] in 1974—a judgment that marked a turning point by shifting focus from formal classification to a broader understanding of equality as antithetical to arbitrariness—our jurisprudence tended to focus on the formal nature of the adjudicatory process as opposed to exposing the real substantive underlying values which layered the foundation of all constitutional adjudication.

Let us turn to the notion that emerged after *A.K. Gopalan*[9]—that each fundamental right was independent of the other, existing in silos, never interacting or intersecting with one another. This generated in law a formalistic doctrine of constitutional jurisprudence; for instance, by the standards in *A.K. Gopalan*, an order for preventive detention will be tested with reference to Article 22; the impact of that order on other rights like Article 19 or Article 21 was not up for inquiry. Such a theory of rights being essentially disconnected, of the rights being disjunctive, of rights not being holistic, gave rise to artificial definitions in constitutional law. It gave rise to an approach towards constitutional law that missed the Central aspect of the human personality itself—that the human personality is holistic, it is one. So, whether an individual exercises the right of free speech, or asserts an entitlement to be treated equally or a right under Article 21 to retain the core of her privacy, it is one individual or a human who contains multitudes within herself. Moreover, individuals often exercise composite rights—rights which are in conflict with each other even when a single individual is exercising them. The rights which interact with each other or have an interface with each other are not necessarily only the interactions with the State or interactions with other individuals but are also interactions within the personality of an individual. Each of us is exercising at any one given point of time a multitude of composite rights which give rise to a multitude of identities.

In understanding the interface between the rule of law and constitutional adjudication, we need to understand the real limits of the jurisprudence of the Supreme Court as it evolved until the post-Emergency years, because we tended to miss the Central connection of rights between individuals and within individuals, in the evolution of the human personality. In *Kesavananda Bharati*,[10] the formulation that the doctrine of the rule of law is a part of the basic structure was propounded. Justice Khanna, in his seminal dissent in the *ADM Jabalpur*[11] case posed the question: If there were no law, could we imagine a situation where no rights exist at all? This question highlights a Central issue in the rights discourse: Are rights created by the Constitution, or does the Constitution merely formally recognize rights that inherently belong to individuals, independent of it?

If there is no law that seeks the protection of rights or if there is no constitutional superstructure that provides for the protection of rights, does that mean you have a society without rights at all? In my opinion, this is what Justice Khanna was referring to in his dissenting opinion quoted above. Before the advent of both *Kesavananda* and *ADM Jabalpur* cases, came the classical pronouncement by one of our most liberal judges, Justice K. Subba Rao in the *I.C. Golaknath* case.[12] In *Golaknath*, Justice Subba Rao sought to establish the balance between the egalitarian facets of the Constitution, the social welfare entitlement doctrines contained therein and doctrines pertaining political liberties. This brings us to Justice Krishna Iyer's declaration in *Bar Council of Maharashtra v. M.V. Dabholkar*,[13] when he said that the rule of law cannot lay claim to be built on the ruins of democracy. These four emergent premises from the era leading to the Emergency—which surface from *Golaknath*, *Kesavananda*, *ADM Jabalpur* and Justice Krishna Iyer's decision in *Dabholkar*—

reveal many a doctrinal fundamental regarding the close interface between the rule of law and democracy; and within a democracy, the close interface between rights of a political nature and rights of a socio-economic nature.

Now, let us turn to the issues that have emerged before us in the last few years. I want to dwell on a few such judgments to tell you about the substantive verses, the formal aspects and how there is this constant tension in the mind of a judge, and in the craftsmanship of the judge, in seeking to craft a decision that seeks to preserve both the formal as well as the substantive element of the rule of law in the working of democracy.

First, let us examine the decision we handed down on the ordinance making powers that are contained in the Constitution. As you must be aware, Article 123 and Article 213 give powers to the Governors in the states and to the President at the Centre to formulate ordinances at the time when the Parliament and the state legislatures are not in session, and when an extreme situation has arisen, warranting the exercise of the ordinance-making power. Essentially, ordinances are *exception*s to the rule of law. The Constitution tells us that the ordinance-making power shall be treated as a power of law-making (and the ordinance-making power does satisfy the formal notions of the rule of law). By virtue of a deeming fiction, the Constitution also provides legal recognition to ordinances by recognizing these to be 'law' for the purposes of Article 13.[14] Nonetheless, there is a substantive element which is lacking in the ordinance-making power. There is an institutional connection between ordinances and the rule of law. It is this: In a diverse, constitutional democracy like ours a *law* must be framed by the legislature because the legislative process involves a high degree of circumspection and reflection. This occurs particularly during committee deliberations, where a range of stakeholders participate—often bringing conflicting interests that challenge or counter the government's position. It is through this process that law-making becomes more balanced and representative. This process also consists of committees making a law, committees that are set up for this very purpose, and a key component of this process in particular is that you have a variety of stakeholders who participate in the process and assert interests which may be contrary to the self-interests that the government seeks to further through enactment of the law. Thus, what the ordinance-making power essentially does is that it deprives a diversity of stakeholders in society of the opportunity to represent and contribute variegated perspectives to the discourse. These perspectives are essential to the process of making laws in any diverse and democratic society. Moreover, Articles 123 and 213 do not explain how the subjective satisfaction of the President or the Governor—when they believe that circumstances justify the use of their law-making power—should be evaluated. This raises an important question: Can such satisfaction be examined through judicial review? This is the next important aspect: What happens when the government seeks to lay down the consequences for the future through an ordinance that extend beyond the lifetime of the ordinance itself? The life of an ordinance is limited to six months and six weeks. This is because the Parliament has to be convened within an interval of six months, and an ordinance has to lapse no later than six weeks after the legislature is convened. But what happens when the legislature, in the course of framing an ordinance, lays down consequences for the future that outlast even the life of the ordinance?

So, in the course of exercising a law-making power which is essentially transient, can the legislature leave us with consequences that will bind us for posterity?

Can we alter the rights discourse in our society? Technically, and using a formal rule of law notion, that is possible. However, in *Krishna Kumar Singh*,[15] which was delivered by a bench of seven judges last year (in 2017), we attempted to balance the formal perspective of the rule of law with a more substantive perspective of the rule of law. *First*, the decision of the President or the Governor in regard to the satisfaction on whether the ordinance-making powers were required to be utilized, would not be final. It would be subject to judicial review. In *A.K. Roy*,[16] the Supreme Court stated that as a result of the Forty-Second Amendment of the Indian Constitution, such decisions might not be final and might be subject to judicial review. However, by the time *A.K. Roy* was decided, the National Security Ordinance (whose validity had been up for consideration before the court) stood replaced by the National Security Act and thus, the five-judge bench left the question of permissibility of judicial review open. When the seven-judge bench took up *Krishna Kumar Singh* for decision, we aimed to make it clear that the President's or Governor's satisfaction can be reviewed by the courts. After all, if ordinances are meant to operate only when the legislature is not in session, how can the executive, using this exceptional power, create lasting changes, like altering rights or imposing obligations, which go beyond that temporary period? Hence, we held that unless a situation arises where the rule of law or public interest warrants it, we will not accept a situation where consequences for posterity are laid down beyond the life of an ordinance. By way of illustration, let us consider a simple case. Suppose the government enacts an ordinance and says every illegal structure in Delhi is regularized. Suppose the government enacts an ordinance and says every ad-hoc employee is regularized, though they have all come in through the back door, in violation of Article 16. Can such an ordinance have an effect that lays down such consequences for posterity? The answer to that is a categorical no. This is because doing so would be to trump the formal notions of the rule of law with the more substantive notions of the rule of law. Or take the second example that I want to highlight this morning—the entire debate around the issue of euthanasia. On the one hand, you have statutory provisions in the Indian Penal Code (IPC) which make an attempt to commit suicide unconstitutional and illegal. An attempt to commit suicide is a penal offence and therefore necessarily a violation of the law. But you also have a situation where individuals have a right to live with dignity. You have the Mental Healthcare Act, 2017 today, which has made a quantum difference to the entire regime on mental health and particularly in relation to the attempt to commit suicide. What the Act does is that it sees an individual who attempts suicide as not a violator but essentially as a victim—a victim of social circumstances, a victim of economic circumstances, a victim of a variety of things that afflict individual lives. So, one of the key issues that came up before the court when we dealt with the case in *Common Cause v. Union of India*,[17] was simply this, something that takes me back to what Justice Khanna spoke of in his dissent in *ADM Jabalpur*. There was no specific law in place that regulates passive euthanasia. Insofar as active euthanasia is concerned, the law that would stand applicable is section 309 of the IPC. There are several other provisions in the IPC that also come into play—starting with Section 300 (which defines murder), followed by Section 302 (which prescribes the punishment for the offence of murder) and then Section 304 and others that deal with related offences.

But insofar as passive euthanasia is concerned, does an individual not have the ability to refuse medical treatment? Does an individual not have the right to postulate for the future that should my situation so evolve in future as to deny me the right to live a dignified existence, I will lay down in advance the course of action that ought to be followed? In our judgment, we laid down that the active–passive divide, i.e. the divide between passive and active forms of euthanasia is, in itself, extremely problematic. Active euthanasia may be something that is contrary to the law on our statute books, as it stands. But we ruled that passive euthanasia, and in an incident of passive euthanasia, the right of an individual to make an advance would have to be upheld in a law, and in laying down the norms for advance wills, we relied on several provisions of the Mental Healthcare Act, 2017. Thus, upon examining the contours of the court's judgment and approach to the issue of legalizing some forms of euthanasia, it can be seen that euthanasia is another area where the court is engaged in a deep evaluation of the formal versus the substantive notions of the rule of law. What is it that you really want to protect? Do you want to create a society for the future in which individual dignity, individual autonomy, where the individual's right of choice has any significant bearing? This brings me to the theme that emerged from *Puttaswamy*,[18] which was exactly about a year ago (in 2017).

I am not going to deal with *Puttaswamy* specifically because I am going to deal with the decision in *Navtej Singh Johar*. Take the third illustration, the decision on whether recourse can be taken to reports of Joint Parliamentary Committees in judicial proceedings. The argument that was urged before the court was that reliance on the report of a Joint Parliamentary Committee in the course of an adjudication, particularly of a social interest litigation, would infringe upon parliamentary privilege. The submission before the court was that as the Parliamentary Committee submits its report only to Parliament and not to the court, while being subject to internal control by Parliament, there can be no evaluation of or a challenge raised to a Parliamentary Committee report in a court of law. This, again, represented the formal versus the substantive dichotomy. Take the idea of the 'formal', for example—in the famous bribery case,[19] where someone tried to challenge an MP's vote in Parliament, the Supreme Court held that you can't question in a court of law why a member of Parliament voted a certain way. In regard to this, you cannot hold an individual member of Parliament accountable, who speaks either before a committee or before Parliament in a court of law. That was intended to subserve the purpose of freedom of expression in Parliament. But more significantly in *Kalpana Mehta*[20] (a decision concerning the evidentiary value of Parliamentary Committee Reports), what we really had to deal with was that the notion of separation of powers has traditionally been associated as an integral element of the rule of law. The manner in which the doctrine of separation of powers has evolved in India, as part of the basic feature of the Constitution, has long been assumed to be a one-institution one-function approach. What this doctrine means to us is this: Parliament will legislate, the executive will administer the law and the judiciary will adjudicate the dispute of rights under the law. But is this notion of the rule of law and separation of powers, which postulates this one-institution one-function approach, a correct approach when we are speaking of a rights discourse? What does a Parliamentary Committee do? Let us assume that a Parliamentary Committee is enforcing authority for the Mahatma Gandhi National Rural Employment Guarantee Act (MGNREGA), or that the Parliamentary Committee is exploring the impact of the food security law. The Parliamentary Committee is essentially trying to exact accountability on the part of the government in discharging its responsibilities under social welfare legislations. What is the function that the court is exercising? When the court exercises its power of judicial review, the court is exacting a sense of accountability on the part of the executive in discharging its duties towards first, the Directive Principles of State Policy, but more significantly, in terms of the rights that individual citizens have in terms of access to education, to healthcare, to clean water and a whole host of other social welfare entitlements.

In *Kalpana Mehta*, the court tried to fuse these two institutional areas: If we see Parliament's role in holding the executive accountable, and the judiciary's role in ensuring accountability through judicial review as complementary functions, then there should be no constitutional objection to the Supreme Court relying on reports of Joint Parliamentary Committees. This was something which was so well assumed for the last thirty or forty years that when the issue came up, it really had us thinking about what we should be doing.

Take the December 2023 judgment in the *National Capital Territory (NCT)*[21] case. This case involved a whole host of constitutional amendments. A separate chapter has been created concerning the National Capital Territory (NCT). The Sixty-Ninth Constitutional Amendment Act of 1991 granted special status to the National Capital Territory (NCT) of Delhi by introducing Articles 239AA and 239AB into the Indian Constitution. While the NCT retains its character as a Union Territory, it is not a state. While retaining its character as a Union Territory, however, the NCT lies in two very significant areas where the constitution has made a change. First, NCT has an elected legislature, and whether there *should* be an elected legislature is not left to the will of Parliament by law to decide. The Constitution provides that there *shall* be a legislature for the NCT, which is elected by direct representation. Second, it also says that NCT would be administered by a lieutenant governor, acting on the 'aid and advice' of the council of ministers. At the same time, it says that if there is a difference of opinion between the lieutenant Governor and the council of ministers, that difference will be referred to the President of India, and the lieutenant Governor will be bound by the view that is taken by the President of India on the point of difference. Now, what does the term 'difference' mean in such a context? The Constitution does not tell you what the differences are all about. Textually, it simply indicates that if there is a difference between the lieutenant Governor and the elected council of ministers in the NCT, that difference would be referred to the President of India and the lieutenant Governor and the government would be bound by the determination of the President. How do you answer these points? Are there certain constitutional values that must infuse the process of adjudication? Now, this is not purely a rights discourse. I gave you earlier, examples of the issues that arose in relation to the rights discourse in the euthanasia case and of those arising, albeit indirectly, in *Kalpana Mehta's* case through a rights discourse. Here, there is no rights discourse taking place except the right of the difference of the residents of the NCT to be governed by a government that they directly elect. In that sense, tangentially, it is a rights discourse but not in terms of usual rights that crop up in such discourses as contained in Article 21, 14 or 19. Now while trying to give meaning to the concept of a 'difference' between the lieutenant Governor and the elected head of government, we thought that we must give this constitutional amendment a value that aligns with the principles of democracy, viz., the importance of political representation and accountable governance, where real power rests with the elected government rather than with a non-elected figurehead like the Head of State. Our polity comprises an asymmetrical federal structure. So, we construed this amendment, which brought in a special arrangement for governing the NCT, as an arrangement which enhances the basic features of the Constitution. The basic structure doctrine has been used particularly in the context of the rule of law as imposing a restraint on the exercise of the constituent power. But in the *National Capital Territory* decision, we used the basic structure doctrine in its converse by regarding an amendment to the Constitution to mean something which essentially enhances those basic features of the Constitution, namely, a republican form of government, of democracy itself, of representative governance, an interpretation that is in line with what the amendment itself was intended to achieve.

I will dwell briefly on the Section 377 decision. The judgment in *Navtej Singh Johar*, at its heart, represented the battle between laws of a colonial origin and laws that must truly represent constitutional values. That was the first layer of the value. If you see the judgment, you will find that in every one of the opinions that it comprised, there really was a layered argument unfolding. At a certain level, the judgment reflects this concern about the need to harmonize pre-Independence or colonial laws with the emerging ethos of constitutional jurisprudence. The second level at which the judgment operates, which I think is perhaps the more significant, is the level where we try and supply to individual dignity, the autonomy, the choice, the liberty of an individual, some substantive content. Therefore, you find that though in some judgments such as in *Navtej Singh Johar,* there is a reference to the fact that '*I am as I am, let me be as I am*', there are other judgments that do not regard this right to be as 'I am and or let me be as I am', as something that is immutable. If you read Amartya Sen's work,[22] for instance, you find that many of our identities, though they are seemingly immutable, may not be as immutable as they appear to be, if seen through a very disjunctive lens. In that sense, is gender an identity that is not shaped by our social milieu? If it is (as I believe all identities are) shaped by our constant interactions with each other, with society and with our own selves, you cannot postulate that there is any one identity that an individual possesses which is constant, over time, or in relation to society or that individual himself or herself. I believe that it is important for us to recognize these fluidities of human experience, including the fluidities of sexual experience. So much of *Navtej Singh Johar* in that sense is about trying to answer what we tried to explain as the binarities or the polarities of gender and sex.

What Section 377 of the IPC did essentially was to say that well, this is how a man should be, this is how a woman should be. This is not what a man is or this is not what a woman is. And I think by bringing focus on the binarities, the polarities of gender, Section 377 was deeply offensive to the ethos of a liberal constitution.

A very crucial issue in deciding the Section 377 case was: How do you deal with sexual orientation and the expression 'sex', in Article 15? Does sexual orientation emerge from sex under Article 15? Personally speaking, I interpreted Article 15 in a slightly different manner than what the NALSA judgment[23] had, by speaking of Article 15 not so much in terms of sexual orientation being a part of sex, but as much as by speaking about Section 377 as imposing deep prejudices in terms of gender stereotypes, which was found to be offensive to Article 15. Now Article 15, as you know, also uses the word 'only' ('The state shall not discriminate *only* on the grounds of religion, race, caste, sex or place of birth or descent'). What does the word 'only' mean? If you follow a very formalistic rule of law approach, 'only' means that the moment you have discrimination on the grounds of sex plus something else, that discrimination is valid, which is the test of Article 14 as per the view taken in the *Nergesh Meerza* case.[24] But is that really a correct assessment? What if the legislature ostensibly uses something apart from sex to discriminate where the impact is disproportionately on sex or what if the legislature decides to use something apart from religion to cause discrimination and the impact is on your right to religion? Would that pass muster using the *Nergesh Meerza* test or the world 'only' (if you give the word 'only' a very literal meaning)? It would pass muster. But in *Navtej Singh Johar*, we thought we must really explore these boundaries of our constitutional law by postulating the intersectional nature of discrimination. It is my belief and hope that what constitutes these intersectional aspects of discrimination would be evaluated in future cases as we evolve in our constitutional jurisprudence.

But above all I think *Navtej Singh Johar* emphasizes the need for equal citizenship. *Navtej Singh Johar* also emphasizes one critical ingredient of the rule of law, which I think we need to emphasize today more than ever, which is that the rule of law, if it has to flourish in a constitutional democracy, has to flourish in a society that is based on a diversity of cultures, in a diversity of ideologies, in a plural society where individuals must be free to draw and flourish and be enriched and perhaps sometimes be poorer by their own experiences. I am sure all of us have had our own experiences. Some of them are fantastic, some of them which have left us a little poorer. But I think being poorer in terms of your experience of life and living is intrinsic to your ability to develop as you grow. I think my favourite part of writing the judgment in *Navtej Singh Johar* was that I was able to incorporate these lyrics from Leonard Cohen and Bob Dylan (from Leonard Cohen's song titled 'Democracy'), whom I idolize. I found this obscure lyrics from this song I frequently listen to, and it says:

> Democracy, it's coming through a hole in the air, it's coming from the feel that it ain't exactly real, or it's really, but it ain't exactly there. From the walls against disorder, from the sirens night and day, from the fires of the homeless, from the ashes of the gay, democracy is coming.

We also need to understand that when we talk about the rule of law and about democracy and the position of the rule of law therein, we need to understand that in recognizing the rights of others in terms of our constitutional discourse, we are not just empowering those whose rights we recognize. We are not just recognizing the entitlements of others. I think more or equally important is the effort of the Constitution to transform ourselves when we recognize the freedoms of others. Too often we believe in our own freedoms and we don't dwell on the importance of recognizing the freedoms of others. It is in recognizing the freedoms of others that society is constantly being transformed and society is then evolving. That's why I felt that if we don't make an answer, or even if we don't ask very difficult questions about the forms and substances of injustice in our own society, we risk being not merely the inheritors of an unjust society but the *causes* of it as well.

To conclude, when we speak of the rule of law, there is a tendency to overemphasize the importance of the adjudicatory function. Particularly with judges and lawyers, we always believe in the importance of the work which we do. But I think the message that I will leave with you is that every day of our lives as judges, we also learn of the limitations of the work which we do—in terms of its ability to answer if justice is achieved. Which means that we need to create social structures. We need to create individuals like you, individuals who would, in that sense, further constitutional values.

One of my law clerks mentioned to me just yesterday that helping me with the research on these aspects and my judgments has proven to be an enormous source of motivation and has been life-changing. This is because it is not so much about the doctrine that we discuss or write, but it is about the many ways in which that doctrine transforms us in our hopes of transforming others.

So much as we as law students, lawyers and judges focus on the rule of law and the importance of the adjudicatory institutions of the states in enhancing the rule of law, we need to realize that there is so much of life beyond the law and we understand the law when we understand the life which exists beyond the law.

6

Feminist Lawyering and Feminist Judging[1]

Q1: What, if anything, does feminism add to the task of judging?

What feminism adds to the task of judging is an acknowledgement of the value of the female experience, which facilitates inquiry and reflection. It is an intervention into the legal space that seeks to challenge the ongoing exclusion of women from legal subjectivity, 'whether as the authors of legal decisions and doctrine, or as the subjects upon whose knowledge, experience, activities and concerns law is founded'.[2]

It has been argued by feminist scholars that 'law does not simply operate on pre-existing gendered realities, but contributes to the construction of those realities, often in a constraining or damaging way'.[3] A feminist perspective on the laws essentially aims to disrupt this process of gender construction and to introduce different accounts of gender that might be less limiting for women.

Feminist judgments provide additional 'social framework' material that places the particular facts of the case and/or the legal issues involved in a broader context.[4] In *The Gender of Judgments*, Reg Graycar has questioned the sources of judges' knowledge of the world and suggested that such knowledge is '(masculine) gendered'.

Feminist judgments are an endeavour to correct this imbalance.[5] It represents an attempt to tackle the power and authority of the law and its impact on the lives of women, not from the distance of academic critique but on its own ground through an alternative judgment method.

One of the most important contributions of feminist thought to the process of judging is the form of addition of fresh perspectives.

The Importance of Diversity: Erika Rackley,[6] a legal scholar, whose research focuses on judicial diversity, explains that diversity 'acts as a catalyst for disruption; impacting upon the legal monotony, destabilising its taken-for-granted assumptions and uncovering alternative ways of seeing, understanding, and judging'.[7] In this way, sex is only one point of difference, as women judicial officers often bring a diverse set of backgrounds, experiences and perspectives to the role as compared to their 'benchmark' male counterparts.[8]

In addition to the laws, judicial decisions are inevitably influenced by the judges' personal values and perspectives.[9] A rich body of feminist scholarship, including feminist theories and methods, has helped shape the feminist approach to judging. Feminist literature does not dictate specific results but rather provides valuable procedural suggestions on how feminist judging can take place in practice. Though the substantive decision reached depends largely on the meaning of the term 'feminism' to the particular judge, there are various methods adopted by judges[10] to promote the substantive goal of feminism—the achievement of equality in society. These include:

a) **Challenging the gender bias in legal doctrine**, which includes taking efforts to identify and overcome gender bias in legal principles. It also involves recognizing that the law is an inherently gendered framework. Correcting this imbalance involves questioning the current legal construction of the term 'woman', and intervening to challenge and confront sexism, racism and gender bias.

b) **Asking the woman question(s)**, which involves identifying the gender implications of rules which appear to be neutral. Asking this question also leads to discussion about other forms of exclusion (based on religion, race, etc.) that may be operating in a particular case. (Such intersectionality in India, for example, would mean a Dalit woman or a Muslim woman.)
c) **Contextualization**, which involves an exercise in feminist practical reasoning, which entails a reasoning from context that focuses on a woman's lived experience. This aids a judge in making an individualized rather than an abstract decision.[11]

In terms of the outcome of the case, a feminist judge is likely to be concerned about making decisions that improve women's lives, correct perceived injustices and promote substantive equality. Although the extent of the feminist approach that can be employed will depend on the unique nature and facts of the case, the potential of reasoning in a manner that promotes substantive equality is much greater in cases that raise questions of equality and discrimination.[12] Similarly, there is also greater scope for feminist reasoning in cases that require a judge to exercise his discretionary powers (*Hadiya*'s case,[13] for example). Discretion, however, cannot be unconstrained and must be exercised within the bounds of law. Nonetheless, judges who engage in discretionary decision-making are often guided by their values, experiences or by predispositions towards liberalism, the states or particular institutions.[14] Similarly, judges are also guided by their commitment to feminist reasoning.

Research indicates that a feminist perspective brings about the much-needed diversity and balance to judicial decision-making. A study of three-judge federal appeals court panels in the US has shown that panels of judges with the same outlook tended to lean towards a more extreme position in decision-making in line with that outlook, whereas the presence of a single judge with a different outlook had a marked moderating effect. The positive influence of having judges who express different judicial philosophies and varied personal experiences on a 'hard case' is described as thus in the words of Lord Justice Etherton:

> It makes it more likely that the decision, and the reasoning that underpins it, will reflect the evolving values and institutions of the community, and that relevant arguments are not overlooked or brushed aside, and that insupportable preconceptions are challenged.[15]

The Feminist Judgment Project can also be understood as an initiative contributing to global constitutionalism, which is an understanding that the principles of constitutionalism, including equality, and the institutions that exist to implement them, should be used to further the legitimacy of the international legal order and the welfare of the global citizen. Global constitutionalism and the feminist movement share values of equality. The rewriting of judicial opinions from a feminist perspective is a transnational movement that holds appeal, systems of jurisprudence and areas of law. Moreover, the unique approach and outcomes of the project contribute to judicial decision-making in a number of ways.

First, since it involves a rewrite, this is the first project that actually demonstrates rather than just describes how cases could have been decided differently if they had been informed by a feminist perspective. (As judges, we often find that while it's easy for others to criticize our decisions, it's important to understand what it's like from our perspective—making tough calls with limited material and complex choices before us.)

As Diana Majury, feminist legal scholar and an advocate for women's rights, reports, the inspiration for the first Feminist Judgment Project, known as the Women's Court of Canada, was a feeling of despondency, which in turn sparked action and energy with the revelatory question: 'So why don't we show them how it could have been done? . . . Why don't we rewrite these decisions that are so wrong?'[16]

Second, the rewritten feminist judgments adopt judicial language and tone and successfully showcase the transformation of feminist thought and theory into legal language. In doing so, the opinions collectively create a body of feminist judicial language. This feminist judicial language that is employed shows how careful attention to issues of gender, sexuality and race can be incorporated into judgments, while still adhering to precedent. Lastly, reading the shadow judgments provides an opportunity for self-reflection for the judges and challenges them to consider influences different from their own.[17] In the words of one of the judges who participated in the English Feminist Judgments project:

> Reading the rewritten opinion should be [a] chastening experience for any judge who believes himself or herself to be both true to their judicial oath and a neutral observer of the world.[18]

Feminist sociologist Carol Smart has written that it may seem as if feminist 'legal theory' is immobilized in the face of the 'failure of feminism to affect law and the failure of law to transform the quality of women's lives'.[19] Given the broad goals of feminism, reforming the law cannot be an exclusive strategy, but so long as women interact with the law and law continues to have material effects on women's lives, feminism's engagement with the law must continue.

Lately, there has been increasing support for the view that the gap between judgments and academic writing is beginning to narrow because of developments in the form of judgments. The use of headings, cross-referencing, footnotes, appendices, academic literature and so on is now commonplace. It means that judges are increasingly 'producing what to all intents and purposes amount to academic articles, mini-treatises, on the point at issue'.[20] The quality of both good judgments and good academic writing is determined first and foremost by the substantive merits of their arguments. 'Both rely on effective communication of this argument through the strategic deployment of various rhetorical or literary techniques. The qualities of good academic writing—clear prose and persuasive argument—are also characteristics of a good judgment.'[21]

Q2: Should judges identify themselves as feminists? Is feminism compatible with the task of judging?

Put simply the query is: 'Should judges be feminists?', and 'Can judges be feminists?'

For many people, including judges across the world, the answer to both these questions would be 'no' because the 'law' is portrayed as a 'gender-neutral' framework and judges are trained to be detached, neutral, independent and dispassionate in order to apply the law fairly.[22]

The extent of feminism's compatibility with these tenets of judging depends largely on how we understand feminism. Feminism can be understood as 'a movement and perspective historically grounded in politics, and one that motivates social, legal and other battles for women's equality'.[23] As feminist scholarship has evolved, it has become apparent that there exists not one feminist theory but multiple feminist theories and methods that have all matured under the umbrella of 'feminist legal theory'.

As the book *Feminist Judgments: From Theory to Practice* states: '"feminism" is far from monolithic. Liberal feminists, radical feminists, cultural feminists, postmodern feminists, postcolonial feminists, critical race feminists, sex-positive feminists and so forth are likely to take different positions on or approaches to different issues.'[24]

> . . . a single, token woman judge cannot possibly represent the range of women's perspectives on a particular issue, but further, a single, token feminist judge cannot possibly represent the range of feminist perspectives on an issue. Much broader representation, not only of women but of feminisms, among the appellate judiciary is required before anything approaching true judicial diversity could be said to have been achieved.[25]

The beauty of feminism lies in the fact that it encompasses and tolerates a range of approaches. There are no unitary feminist methods or reasoning processes.[26] This lends itself to an acknowledgement that feminists can disagree but can still be feminists in their own right.[27]

The answer to this question becomes easier once we acknowledge the inherent flexibility of 'feminist thought'. *It is an individual's personalized understanding of 'feminism' that necessarily informs answers to these questions.* Judges are not and cannot be expected to be blank slates. Judging is realistically inflected by a judge's philosophical, religious and political beliefs, which may also include a commitment to feminism.[28] These are all valuable perspectives that inform a judge's decision-making process. According to me, there is no problem in incorporating these perspectives in judicial decision-making as long as the judge does not allow himself/herself to prejudge the issue or to be biased against particular parties or particular arguments. A feminist approach must always be subordinated to judicial norms, and feminist judgments must therefore necessarily develop within the limits of judicial framework. But even within these constraints, there is considerable scope for various feminist interpretations of the law.

Due to the complexities of modern-day adjudication, judges often find themselves in a position where the existing legal rules do not lead to a clear decision. In such cases, they are still required to reach a decision, and they do so by turning to 'their own sense of justice'.[29] This 'sense of justice' is guided by the judge's own life experiences, perspectives and personal values, and may or may not be influenced by the consideration of feminist values.

Therefore, there is a clear need for judges to bring a gendered sensibility to their decision-making.[30] The gendered nature of the law reinforces the need for a judge to *be* a feminist. However, is it necessary for a judge who engages in feminist judging to *identify* as a feminist? I think there is an important distinction between these two propositions. One school of thought advocates that feminist judges *must* identify themselves as feminists:[31] Rosemary Hunter states that some judges insist that they are not feminists, alluding to the social construction of feminism as a biasing influence or as something negative or dangerous, perpetuating this negative perception of feminism.[32]

The second school of thought is a more balanced view—feminist judging is not the exclusive domain of judges who openly identify as feminists. Judges may be unable to identify as feminists due to judicial constraints, or due to their preference for appearing neutral; as judges, we risk losing our credibility completely if we appear biased. These are choices that must be respected. It is indeed inappropriate to require feminist judges to self-identify as feminists; instead, feminist legal scholars can identify feminist judges by their feminist adjudication. Once we understand that feminist judges and feminist scholars have distinctive professional cultures, this understanding comes with an acceptance that therefore, they may also choose to reveal their feminism in different ways. Thus, feminist legal scholars should study feminist judges on their own terms. Additionally, self-identification is also fraught with the dangers and pressure to meet the expectations of feminist judges in all situations.[33] As Hunter argues:

> Self-identification gives rise to expectations that feminist judges must meet expectations about their commitment to women, to challenging the treatment meted out to women by law and the state, to promoting women's equality rights, and generally to their recognition of the need to disrupt [mainstream] power.[34]

These are certainly pressures that a judge can do without, especially given that there is no such pressure on judges who do not identify as feminists.

Moreover, judicial history is replete with examples of judges who did not explicitly identify as feminists but who are celebrated as exemplars of 'feminist judging'.[35] This category includes Justices Bertha Wilson, Claire L'Heureux-Dubé of the Supreme Court of Canada and Chief Justice Sian Elias of New Zealand, judges who did not identify as 'feminist judges' but have nonetheless behaved like them.[36] Indeed, as Justice L'Heureux-Dubé had aptly stated, 'making a difference' should be the only guiding consideration for judges, and it should not be the responsibility of only female judges or judges who were openly feminist. She remarked:

> Everyone in a position of power should take responsibility for understanding different perspectives and reflecting them in law, and all judges should develop an increased sensitivity to the diverse human experiences which are presented to courts on a daily basis.[37]

Therefore, it becomes clear that all feminist judging requires are judges with self-identified feminist consciousness. Neither does it necessitate that all feminist judges must be women, nor does it require a feminist judge to explicitly identify as a feminist. In reality, 'it cannot be assumed that a judge who identifies as a feminist will necessarily incorporate feminism into all her judgments (for a variety of reasons), nor that a judgment reflecting feminist concerns would necessarily be written by a judge who thought of herself (or himself) as a feminist'.[38]

This leads me to the second part of the question: Is feminism compatible with the task of judging? I firmly believe it is.

Feminist legal scholarship is characterized by its criticism of the liberal notion of formal equality, which means treating likes alike. Formal equality establishes the male norm as the benchmark for treatment. Therefore, it has limited purchase in addressing women's inequalities in the multitude of circumstances in which women are historically, biologically and socially unlike men. Thus, many feminists instead 'prefer the goal of substantive equality'. This view seeks to 'accommodate difference, address historical disadvantages, and incorporate women's experiences into the norms by which equality is judged'.[39]

(A classic example of this: a policy of granting monthly menstrual leave might violate formal equality between men and women but might be in furtherance of substantive equality since it accommodates a 'difference' that can significantly impact women's lived experiences.)

I believe the unique similarities between the guiding values of feminism and justice render them compatible. The dispensation of justice by the judiciary is guided in large part by a sense of securing a more egalitarian society. Similarly, feminism has substantive goals, in particular the achievement of equality and justice for women in society. The extent to which feminism is compatible with the task of judging is determined primarily by the 'meaning of feminism' to the judge in question. The process of feminist judging requires the consideration of various factors such as 'asking the woman questions', 'noticing the gender implications of apparently gender-neutral rules' and 'challenging the gender bias' rather than dictating a specific result.[40]

It must be understood that feminist judging does not simply involve 'deciding for the woman', nor does it constitute a singular programme. Rather, feminist judging is adjudication that is informed by feminist theories and an understanding of gendered experience that is then manifested in various approaches to judicial decision-making.[41]

We have the benefit of the example of numerous members of the judiciary around the world who have demonstrated the possibility of integrating judging and feminism in practice. Well-known role models of feminist judging include Baroness Brenda Hale of the Supreme Court of the United Kingdom, Justice Ruth Bader Ginsburg of the US Supreme Court and Justice Mary Gaudron of the High Court of Australia.[42] The Supreme Court of India[43] has also seen many noteworthy instances of feminist judging, including some very recent ones. Moreover, the global Feminist Judgment Project itself provides empirical evidence of the successful fusion of judging and feminism. The outcomes of the project have demonstrated that a feminist judgment can be a perfectly legitimate legal judgment and that the legal method is not impervious to the feminist approach.[44] As Lady Hale had stated, the UK Feminist Judgements book was the best objective evidence that a 'different perspective can indeed make a difference' to the outcome of cases.[45]

A feminist judging perspective is more likely to cause a judge to make decisions within context, to take into account detailed individual facts about a case and to consider more broadly how the decision will impact women and other historically disadvantaged groups. Broadly, the incorporation of a feminist understanding of issues may inform the characterization of facts, the interpretation of statute and precedent, the development of doctrine and the exercise of discretion. The aim of feminist judging is not to reach a predetermined conclusion or to change the decision; rather it is to bring a particular set of sensibilities to judging that will seek to enhance the decision-making process. There is ever-growing evidence that feminist legal theory is informing legal practice, and feminist legal practice is contributing to feminist legal theory.

Q3: How might feminist lawyering impact the ability of the judiciary to deliver gender-just decisions?

1) **The influence of feminist legal theory on lawyering**: The last few decades have seen the growth of a rich and diverse body of scholarship under the label of 'feminist legal theory'. This literature also includes different approaches to feminist legal methods and theories. Feminist lawyering can benefit by accounting for some of these methods, which include:

   a) Feminist practical reasoning: Feminist practical reasoning involves a recognition that what counts as a problem and the effective resolution of that problem largely depends on the unique factual context. It rejects the notion that there is a monolithic source of reason and values, which is the approach followed by traditional legal reasoning. It seeks to identify sources of legal reasoning by drawing on the perspectives of 'outsiders', or those who are not included in the popular dominant culture. The aim of this method is to improve decision-making by accounting for diverse perspectives.[46]

   Lawyers can incorporate this approach in their arguments before the court. Situating the facts in a broader context and bringing in diverse viewpoints will provide the court with more perspective and positively impact the ability of the court to render gender-just decisions.

b) Narrative feminist method: Closely related to feminist practical reasoning is the use of the narrative to illuminate the effect of the law on individual plaintiffs. While feminist practical reasoning looks to situate the facts of the case in a broader context in which the law is applied, the narrative feminist method focuses on presenting the facts of a case as a story. A story is Central to the law, and lawyers can build on a narrative in a manner that humanizes the law. Ingenious narrative lawyering can play a role in drawing the attention of the court to the actual people who have come before the court, instead of abstract rules and ideals.[47]

c) Another closely related concept is *contextualization*, which I have discussed earlier. Judges are human, and judges' world view, which is shaped by their own experiences and values, influences decision-making. They exert a significant, if difficult to see, influence on the interpretation and application of the law. Contextualization involves focusing on the reality of a woman's lived experience in each situation. Feminist lawyering should aim to deliver this account of a woman's experience to the court in a vivid manner. This will help the court produce a decision that is individualized rather than abstract. The objective of lawyering should be to present the case in such a manner as to broaden the perspectives of the decision makers. This directly impacts the ability of the judiciary to deliver gender-just decisions.

2) **Promoting equality**: Lawyers and judges both have an equally crucial role to play in helping to achieve a more egalitarian society, which is one of the substantive goals of feminism. Lawyers who engage in feminist lawyering can assist the court in furthering this aim. They can do so by founding their arguments in evolving feminist scholarship and by drawing the attention of the judges to it. In doing so, they might be encouraging the court to look at the matter in a different light, which it would not have done if the particular feminist argument had not been presented to the court. Similarly, compelling feminist scholarship which

is brought to the attention of the judge might become the legal basis for a court's opinion.

Q4. Has there been any case where feminist insights have aided in your reaching what you thought was a just/more just decision or where feminist insights led you to re-evaluate how you looked at a prior decision?

I think I will reiterate what I have previously said about the overlaps between a commitment to the constitutional goal of equality and feminism. When feminism is understood as substantive equality, it complements our job as judges and interpreters of the Constitution. But I'd like to elaborate on some examples:

1 Privacy: On the aspect of the feminist criticism of privacy, while feminist insights did not affect my conclusion that the right to privacy was a constitutionally protected right, the discussion on the feminist position was important because the recognition of that right was in furtherance of liberty and dignity. Given that it was a nine-judge decision[48] and is significant in terms of its value as a precedent, it was important to write a word of caution to ensure that the right to privacy is not interpreted as a shield to protect actions that adversely affect the liberty and dignity of women within the 'private sphere'.

2 The euthanasia case: The right to bodily privacy itself became one of the grounds to legalize euthanasia. There were complex moral issues at play in the adjudication of the case, but I did not think there was a feminist perspective until I read a perspective that was developed by Ratna Kapur, a feminist legal scholar and former director of the Centre for Feminist Legal Research, New Delhi, in her critique of the *Aruna Shanbaug*[49] judgment.

In her article, Kapur explains that the brutal attack on Aruna Shanbaug in KEM Hospital indicated that the hospital had failed to be a safe workspace. However, despite this fact, the staff of the same hospital were given Aruna Shanbaug's guardianship.

This was especially concerning given the fact that the dean of the hospital at the time of the incident had refused to allow a complaint of sodomy to go forward, as he was more concerned about the reputation of the institution.

Kapur points out that Aruna's case was not used to bring out the reform that it should have—stating that it should 'have been a leading case on women's rights where "caring" extended beyond the physical support for the individual who was harmed, to taking active steps to improve the working conditions for women, including addressing pervasive and systemic sex discrimination and sexism'.[50]

She also makes us think about the choices Aruna may have made, had she not been reduced to a permanent vegetative state. Kapur questions whether she would have chosen to remain in the same hospital for her treatment after the violent and brutal sexual assault she experienced there. Or would she have chosen to be treated elsewhere? Would she have sued the hospital for failing to provide her with a safe working environment?

Kapur states that it is tragic that Aruna was denied the right to bodily integrity in life and the right to self-determination in death. Her life was viewed from various lenses, all but her own, ranging from those of the 'carers', to the medical and legal professionals and their views on euthanasia. The unfortunate consequence was that she 'became nothing more than a spectre in her own story'.

3 More recently, Section 377, adultery and the *Sabarimala Temple Entry* case: Given the inequality inherent in the laws in all these cases, the striking down of unequal laws as unconstitutional was perhaps expected. But as a judge (and I may be biased because this is what I do for a living), I believe that a judgment is a lot more than just the conclusion, and that the approach taken to arrive at the conclusion also has its own value. Given the deeply unequal and gendered nature of many of our laws, I endeavour, where possible, to explore the transformative potential of the Constitution to fulfil what I understand to be the constitutional vision of equality. Such

an approach to interpreting the Constitution is often celebrated by feminists because of its emancipatory potential. The decision decriminalizing Section 377[51] was a recognition of social oppression of certain groups and that even facially neutral laws are illegal if they perpetuate existing oppressions and hierarchies based on sex. I also adopted the anti-stereotyping analysis of the *Anuj Garg*[52] case to disrupt the law's reinforcement of gender roles for men and women in my judgments decriminalizing Section 377 and adultery. I am told that my judgment in the adultery case[53] has been celebrated by feminists for treating women as equals in matters of sexual autonomy.

However, all judgments cannot incorporate feminism because in my opinion, some issues of law are not about gender. I have disagreed with my brother and sister judges when I did not find that a particular case involved a feminist issue as seen in certain cases. Take for example my dissenting opinion in the video-conferencing case:[54] Chief Justice Dipak Misra's opinion made it about women's dignity, but in my view, whether the Family Courts Act, 1984, allows or prohibits video conferencing has nothing to do with gender.

In custody cases, when lawyers representing the mother base their argument on the mother as the 'caregiver', aren't we perpetuating gender stereotypes and unequal roles and responsibilities in parenting?

CONCLUSION

- Alternative judicial practice: While feminist legal theory has long warned against over-investment in the law—particularly judge-made law—as a site within which progressive social or political transformation might begin, feminist judgments are increasingly regarded not only as advancing critique of legal judgment, rules and doctrine but also as uniquely accessible and powerful models of alternative judicial practice.
- The project is a significant step in establishing feminist judging as a new and legitimate critical legal method. I hope that

it also contributes as a facet of legal practice, and just as this groundbreaking project has been inspired by sister projects, our model also inspires feminist judgment projects in other jurisdictions.

- As the legal scholar Professor Margaret Davies[55] observed in her review of the English Feminist Judgments Project:

> In the end, the law (as opposed to individual laws) is not going to be changed by theory, it is not going to be changed by specific reforms or by individual judges, and it is not going to be changed by critique. All of these interventions have an influence, of course. But the only way the identity of law—in its ethos, its culture, its fundamental attachments, its boundaries, and its metaphysics—has ever changed, and the only way it ever will change, is through sustained critical-mass practices which bring new meanings, and new directions to legal culture. For this reason, it is the collective effect of this book rather than individual pieces or any theoretical rationalisation, which most contributes to legal change.[56]

7

Justice as a Narrative[1]

When I first received an invitation to speak at today's conference, I thought a great deal about the theme. I wondered as to how far removed the world of storytelling is from the law. And what must a judge, who seemingly deals only with cold facts and dry texts, have to say about the human enterprise of storytelling? The more I reflected on the same, the more I felt that the two shared a rather compelling connection. The intertwining of the worlds can be best illustrated with a story.

The tale of the Speluncean explorers is a fictional creation of the American legal scholar Lon Fuller.[2] The Central characters were five individuals who were caught in a rather cruel situation. While on an expedition, they found themselves trapped in the interior of a cave due to a landslide. Without any food necessary for their survival, the explorers did the unimaginable on the twenty-third day of their entrapment: They consumed the flesh of one of their companions to avoid death by starvation. Huge efforts were made to rescue the explorers, and ten people lost their lives in the process. The explorers only managed their escape on the thirty-second day of their entrapment.

Upon their rescue, the four explorers were tried and convicted for the offence of murder by the trial court. The statute was worded as thus: 'Whoever shall willfully take the life of another shall be punished by death.' As per the defendant's testimony, it was the deceased explorer who had suggested the arrangement that involved selection by a roll of dice but got cold feet at the last minute. But as luck would have it, he was chosen for the sacrifice as per the arrangement.

Their appeal lay before five judges of the fictional Supreme Court of Newgarth. Through five brilliantly crafted divergent opinions, Fuller brought into focus the different choices that the judges were confronted with, describing them as 'permanent problems of the human race'.[3] Each judge acted on their moral impulses and relied on a philosophy they believed to be applicable to the circumstances. Each judge attributed different identities to the explorers—some saw them as practical survivors, ruthless murderers or even moral transgressors, while to others, they were cold-blooded murderers or sinners. I will briefly dwell on each of the judgments to illustrate how, when presented with the same facts, each judge constructed a different narrative of the characters and facts before them, coloured by their own understanding of the purpose of law and how it governs individuals.

The first judge lamented that the explorers found themselves to be in a 'tragic situation' and acknowledged that the unfortunate circumstances entitled them to clemency. However, he could not be the one granting it, as the law clearly called for a conviction. Instead, he opined that it was a case that was suited to receive a pardon from the chief executive to mitigate the 'rigors of the law'.

The second judge undertook a rather creative interpretation of the law and facts before him. In the narrative constructed by him, the men found themselves not in a 'state of civil society' but in a 'state of nature'. He held that they drew a new charter of government appropriate to the situation in which they found themselves, and the law of the Commonwealth was not applicable to the explorers. The judge further reasoned that a man whose life is under threat will repel his aggressor, whatever the law may say, and the legal exception of self-defence was squarely applicable to the explorers.

The third judge stated that a conviction for their actions would have been an absurdity in light of the ten heroic lives laid down in rescue operations. He vacillated between being sympathetic towards the explorers and feeling disgust at the 'monstrous nature' of their act.[4] Unable to ignore these contradictory emotions and to come a determinate answer, he withdrew from the case.

The fourth judge gave primacy to the wording of the law and did not dwell on the narratives arising out of the case. He held that the exception of self-defence would not apply as the deceased bore no threat to the lives of the explorers and confirmed the sentence.

The fifth judge observed that the judiciary is likely to lose touch with the common man, and in the process of applying legal principles, facts and narratives are generally turned to dust. He decided to read through all the legalese and rely on common sense. He noted that the four men had endured more humiliation than most men in a thousand years and held that the explorers ought to be acquitted of the charges.

As the Supreme Court was evenly divided, the sentence of death was affirmed. The case of the Speluncean explorers is telling of how the same set of facts can yield different narratives, which played a crucial role in determining the reality the judges constructed. The narratives the judges chose to create and rely on shaped their idea of what a just outcome would be in the given set of circumstances.

As novelists shape the narratives of the characters in their stories, judges rely on the facts before them to craft a narrative they believe to be the most probable in the given circumstances. Like writers, judges are intuitive reasoners, and a lot of our creative thinking is unconscious. A novelist writes a story in a certain way because it feels right, but the same has to be supported with a plot and well-constructed characters. Likewise, judges often have a strong sense of which way a case should be decided, but good judges must always explain their decisions.

Judges, I daresay, may be considered artists in their own right. Like artists, judges employ craftsmanship with creativity in creating judicial opinions. The craftsmanship of the judge as well as that of the novelist depends largely on their ability to employ a relevant set of facts and articulate through words. Stories as well as judgments serve as forms of dialogue, which require their respective authors to effectively engage with their audiences and resonate with their lived experiences.

Ronald Dworkin, the American jurist, draws an interesting analogy between law and stories: He states that the law is like a chain novel—successive interpreters and composers of novels all work on subsequent chapters and build on what has already been written. After an author writes the first chapter, the second elaborates on the first chapter and follows its plotline. In this manner, the discretion with each subsequent chapter is reduced. Similarly, precedents serve to form a chain of coherence which are purported to limit the discretion that each judge has as the body of precedents grow.

However, this view sees law as static and unwilling to change. When a judge is presented with a question of law, they may look at history and construct a story completely different from another judge. One judge may view the Constitution as a clear break from a colonial past and question colonial legislation, while another may find continuity in such laws. In the same vein, judges are specifically conferred with the discretion to break away from precedent in order to ensure complete justice. Article 142 of the Constitution thus allows the Supreme Court to pass any order required to do complete justice.

If the law that is constructed is to operate as more than just an expression of power, the understanding of law must involve coming to terms with competing narratives of reality.[5] This is not just limited to resolving disagreements but must be accompanied by a deeper understanding of the nature of the realities out of which the disagreements arise. These multifaceted realities constitute the social life that the law, in its application, mediates and constructs.

A narrative construction of reality allows a fuller understanding of the plurality of social lives that are negotiated by law. Employing narrative in forming responses to conflicts between the plurality of social lives allows for a just negotiation of conflicts and to gain a holistic understanding of the reality of different lives. It provides a nuanced approach to the role of law in saying 'what happened'.

As Anthony G. Amsterdam, law professor, and Jerome Bruner, psychologist, put it:[6]

> Law lives on narrative, for reasons both banal and deep . . . Clients tell stories to lawyers, who must figure out what to make of what they hear. As clients and lawyers talk, the client's story gets recast into plights and prospects, plots and pilgrimages into possible worlds . . . If circumstances warrant, the lawyers retell their clients' stories in the form of pleas and arguments to judges and testimonies to juries
> . . . Next, judges and jurors retell the stories to themselves or each other in the form of instruction, deliberations, a verdict, a set of findings, or an opinion. And then it is the turn of journalists, commentators and critics. This endless telling and retelling, casting and recasting is essential to the conduct of the law. It is how law's actors comprehend whatever series of events they make the subject of their legal action.

Which brings me to the next question: Given the role of narrative in shaping the character of justice, how must a judge construe varying narratives of identity, experiences and circumstances to further the cause of justice?

As illustrated in the case of the Speluncean explorers, any factual scenario throws up a multiplicity of narratives. However, engagement with each narrative does not in any way take away from the objectivity and determinacy of the law. It is true that the rule of law privileges legal determinacy and generality, wherein the consistent application of prior rules stated must prevail.

However, the rule of law is not—and must not be—understood as something divorced from individuals and their lived experiences. Legal determinacy must not be accorded a weight that leads to it discounting completely the lived experiences of those it seeks to govern. Substantive justice is thus necessarily contextual.

James Boyd White, the pioneer of the law and literature movement, says:

> Law is not, at heart, an abstract system or scheme of rules, as we often think of it; nor is it a set of institutional arrangements that can be adequately described in a language of social science; rather, it is an inherently unstable structure of thought and expression, built upon a distinct set of dynamic and dialogic tensions. It is not a set of rules at all, but a form of life. It is a process by which the old is made new, over and over again.[7]

To view law in this holistic sense is to acknowledge the contribution of human elements of thought and expression in the development of legal structures. The legitimacy of the rule of law will also depend largely on whether the law, in its application, does not obscure the experiences of those that it seeks to govern and particularly the less-privileged communities. In that sense, the judge must be circumspect to ensure that less-dominant narratives, which are not as vociferously presented, do not get lost.

In her seminal paper titled 'Poets as Judges',[8] Martha Nussbaum underscores the relevance of literary imagination in judging, which allows engagement with narratives of individuals with empathy. She cites the example of *Bowers v. Hardwick*, a case in which the American Supreme Court upheld a Georgian state law criminalizing all forms of sodomy, to illustrate how adjudication bereft of narrative is problematic. Nussbaum noted that the majority opinion maintained a distance from the facts of Hardwick's case. Hardwick was being prosecuted under the anti-sodomy law. The distancing language expresses a refusal to think about how Hardwick's personhood is affected. She notes that the events are not described with a sense of familiarity and there is a concerted effort to keep the human story at a distance. A more empathetic consideration of the situation might not have altered the judgment in terms of its reading of precedents, but it would have led to a thorough consideration of the violation of the right to privacy.

Individual, concrete human voices and laws, when viewed in isolation, often conflict. Written laws are often worded as general and impersonal in nature, and as students of the law, we are trained to treat like cases alike and to define relevant similarities generally. However, this focus on only the text of the laws leads to the invalidation of individual experiences. Must we privilege logical consistency and predictability over compassion and substantive justice?

Law, and the narratives which unfold before it, must be viewed as concrete human stories and take into account the myriad human voices. How does a court dealing with racial segregation understand its consequences without recounting the lived experiences of those who suffer racial discrimination? How does a court understand the plight of manual scavengers without taking into account the social exclusion and boycott they face?

These experiences and stories illuminate the law with meaning. In *Navtej Singh Johar*,[9] we struck down Section 377 of the Indian Penal Code, which criminalized consensual sexual relations between persons of the same sex. This judgment highlights the importance of recording human experiences in order to understand the true impact of law. In my separate opinion, I recognized the identities of the petitioners and recounted the experience of one person in the submissions before the court. One argument for the retention of Section 377 was that there were a minimum number of prosecutions under the provision. However, the effect of Section 377 was not in its criminalization of an act but in its silencing of a specific set of identities. It was recognized that the retention of the provision perpetuated a certain culture, which is antithetical to our constitutional values. This culture and stereotype fostered by the provision silenced the identity and lived experiences of numerous individuals and perpetuated homophobic attitudes, making it almost impossible for victims of abuse to access justice.

This discriminatory effect could only be captured by taking into account the lived experiences of people. Without that, the facially neutral provision may have escaped constitutional scrutiny. As seen clearly in this case, justice was a function of the narrative. It tells us that within the tapestry of legal scholarship and advocacy, empathy, storytelling and different voices must be woven in.

If one looks closely enough, the text of our laws has its own stories.

For example, the constitutional moment is portrayed as representing triumph and victory of the decades-long struggle towards freedom. It consists of stories of struggle and a nationalist fervour to give India her independence. But are there narratives of Partition that didn't find their way into the mainstream narrative of triumph, glory and freedom—stories of separation, sexual savagery and violence?

Urvashi Butalia, in a historical account titled *The Other Side of Silence*, revisits the experiences of women during Partition. The book captures the layered emotional terrain of India's birth, marked by a sense of hope and idealism coexisting with the brutal realities of violence and displacement.[10] The notion of women as property, as belonging to their respective families, communities and men, has led to routine violation of their rights.

Let me give you an example. In 1947, the Government of India and Pakistan signed the Inter-Dominion Treaty, which spoke of both governments recovering what they termed 'abducted women'. The Abducted Persons (Recovery and Restoration) Ordinance was transformed into an Act in 1949. The Indian government set up an implementation machinery to arrive at a definition of 'abducted women'. A set of individuals who were also displaced by Partition were post-abduction children.

Complicated questions presented themselves: How does one decide whether someone was abducted? What if a person went on their own free will? How does one propose to find these women? Would the 'recovered' woman be accepted by conservative families upon her return? What about the fate of children whose families were torn apart?

For an impersonal agency, it was easier not to account for these questions and lived experiences and set a time, date and figure to solve the problem. As the violence in Punjab had, by some accounts, started in 1947, any woman living with, in the company of or in a relationship with a man of the other religion after 1 March 1947 would be presumed to have been abducted. All marriages and conversions after this date would not be recognized by the two governments.

When the law assumed force, the narrative of women and children—no matter what they said, no matter how much they protested or how 'real' the relationship was—was destroyed. The Act was silent about couples who had conceived. There were two kinds of post-abduction children: those born to 'abducted' Muslim women in India and subsequently recovered, and children born to 'abducted' Hindu women and then recovered. In most cases, the children stayed on with their fathers, the 'abductors'.

The stories of separated families are gut-wrenching. There are numerous stories of women who protested. How could they trust these men willing to take them away? What of the atrocities carried out in the process? What of the stories of the separation of children from their mothers? Here, the State agenda was carried out on the body of the woman. Recovered women were not seen as free adults who could exercise their own agency but as missing members of a community.[11] They were viewed as repositories of family, community and national honour.

The law here was built on its violence to the narrative of women and children by silencing their story of forced separation. To deny narrative is to deny identity. Multi-faceted identities are produced by association with different groups, societies and cultures, each of which subsumes a distinct narrative. Justice as a narrative compels us to give recognition to voices and experiences that are lost in the process. We must remember that to ignore the narrative on which the law is built is to further the violence meted out in its inception.

Our Constitution itself is built on various narratives; it carries the hue of the hopes and aspirations of a populace that has known oppression and is hopeful of a new freedom. This is reflected in the broad contours of rights enunciated in the Constitution.

The narrative of our Constitution is meant to be/is a vision of transformation—to obliterate practices and values that are antithetical to the values of liberty and dignity; to galvanize social reform. As Justice Vivian Bose put it in 1955, the Constitution:

> . . . blotted out in one magnificent sweep all vestiges of arbitrary and despotic power in the territories of India and over its citizens and lands
>
> . . . the past was obliterated except where expressly preserved; at one moment of time the new order was born with its new allegiance springing from the same source for all, grounded on the same basis: the sovereign will of the peoples of India with no class, no caste, no race, no creed, no distinction, no reservation.[12]

The text and silences of our Constitution reflect this and is to be borne in mind in the reading and interpretation of it.

The oppression faced by the citizens of our nation in the colonial era led the makers of independent India to strive for an egalitarian society for her future citizens, devoid of all forms of oppressive discrimination. In furtherance of this, the drafters of the Constitution included a provision to counteract the social malaise of untouchability, which plagued Indian society. About sixty-eight years after its enactment, in the *Sabarimala Temple Entry* case, the Supreme Court was tasked with interpreting the provision in light of the indignity suffered by women as a result of a long-standing belief that menstruation is impure. Taking into account the history of exclusion faced by women, I held in my separate opinion that the treatment of menstruation as a form of impurity amounted to the practice of untouchability.

Until now, it was largely believed that the interpretation of untouchability as contained in Article 17 was limited to practices relating to caste-based exclusion. The narratives of women who have faced exclusion due to the stigma attached to menstruation have seldom been acknowledged. In fact, in many sections of society, menstruation is never discussed, thus relegating a part of the reproductive experience of the woman to non-existence, a suppression of their experiences. The taboo on menstruation is an ugly stain on the story of social change as envisaged by the Constitution. Through my interpretation in *Sabarimala Temple Entry* case,[13] I held this social malpractice to be unconstitutional.

The story of the Constitution has been written by multiple actors. Notwithstanding the contributions of the drafters of the Constitution, the Constitution as it exists today is a product of continuing interactions between three elements: the text, the courts, and above all, 'the people'.[14] It is the people of this nation who, in recognizing their rights, come before the courts, compelling a reconsideration of narratives—some pre-existing, some newly emerging and some disregarded so far. In that sense, it allows a revisiting of narratives.

Every interpretation of the Constitution is a retelling of its story, shaped and heavily influenced by the social context of its time. The reading of the Constitution, being a dynamic process, it must take into account new challenges which confront society and evolve to accommodate newly formed social and political identities that are a necessary by-product of social churning. The spirit of the Constitution is captured by Dr Ambedkar when he says:

> [The] Constitution is not a mere lawyer's document, it is a vehicle of life, and its spirit is always the spirit of age.

The letters of the Constitution are written in the language of emancipation—from economic, social and political injustices. The spirit of the Constitution, in essence, is the spirit of social progress—a spirit that is also captured in the values of the Increasing Diversity by Increasing Access (IDIA). The IDIA programme is structured towards changing the narrative of law schools and the legal profession—by postulating hard-hitting questions about privilege and increasing access to legal education. In doing so, it is dismantling social structures that exclude a vast section of society from being represented in the legal profession. It is my belief that granting representation will also ensure a fresh infusion of experiences and narratives offered by these individuals into the legal profession, and it is the profession that will be richer for it.

With a legal education, each of you scholars has the potential to impact society. Of course, you will be armed with knowledge and objectivity, but stories teach each of us that empathy and compassion find a significant place in this profession. As I end this lecture, I hope I have left you with some thoughts to reflect on, for the purpose of a storyteller is not to tell you how to think but to give you questions to think upon.

8

Why Does the Constitution Matter?[1]

It is a great honour for me to address this august gathering at the Justice K.T. Desai Memorial Lecture; not just because this is my parent court and some of my most treasured moments associated with the profession have been in these premises but also because this lecture has been organized in the memory of an individual whose contributions to public life provide beacon to judges and lawyers who continue in that tradition. Justice Desai (or Kantibhai, as he was fondly called) was born in May 1903 in Mumbai. He cleared two really difficult examinations—Bombay Incorporated Law Society's Solicitors examination in 1928 and the examination to qualify as an advocate entitled to practise on the original side of the High Court of Bombay in 1930—a rare achievement in those times. He practised on the original side of the Bombay High Court and was considered an eminent draftsman. Invited to the bench by Chief Justice M.C. Chagla of the Bombay High Court, Justice Desai accepted judgeship with the knowledge that he had only six years at the bench, leaving a lucrative practice at the bar.[2] Judges of his genre firmly established the foundations of commercial law, shaping its development in Mumbai and influencing its evolution far beyond.

Justice Desai possessed a great sense of humour—at the bar dinner hosted to felicitate him, he famously remarked that he was conscious of the fact that justice must not only be done but must also be seen to be done and hence a cushion must be placed under his seat.

Justice Desai's daughter, Justice Sujata Manohar, has carried forward his legacy in public service—having been appointed the first female judge of the Bombay High Court as well as its first female Chief Justice. She was subsequently elevated to the Supreme Court, a court that she served with distinction, independence and an unwavering sense of personal integrity.

I am extremely grateful to her for inviting me to speak today on a subject that is close to my heart—the Indian Constitution. Although it does give me some leeway to conclude or at least put forth an adverse view—that constitutions do not or perhaps may not matter. This would mean, first, facing the dangers of our constitutional democracy collapsing, and second—for me personally—the risk of being out of a job. Let me begin by stating which side of the line I stand on. Our Constitution does indeed matter.

The Indian constitutional project did not commence in December 1946 when the Constituent Assembly sat in New Delhi for its first session. It first echoed in the battlefields of Bengal in the 1857 Rebellion. Bal Gangadhar Tilak, whose famous trial took place in this very courtroom,[3] was amongst the first to call for *purna swaraj* (meaning 'complete independence'). For many decades prior to the coming into force of our Constitution, the Indian self-rule movement was a mass movement and encompassed many sections of the society. The call was simple—a governing document of the people, by the people and for the people.

The constitutional culture in India predated the coming into force of our Constitution. Before the advent of our Constitution, a well-known demand had emerged to establish, through the participation of the people, basic rules and principles of behaviour which would constitute universally binding legal norms. The Constitution was to mark a transfer of power to steward the destinies of its citizens.

The Constitution was to put in place an organic structure that would sustain the country's independence and freedom, equipped with the tools for 'social revolution', as noted historian Granville Austin called it.

This potential of a constitutional document, in steering the course of the society it governs, lends it paramountcy in comparison to statutory law. A quote by writer and jurist Carl Schmitt comes to mind—'the essence of the constitution is not contained in a statute or a norm but in a prior and fundamental political decision by the bearer of the constitution-making power. In a democracy . . . this is a decision by the people'.[4]

A constitutional culture is based on the understanding that a constitution unifies a population beyond those in one's immediate sphere of acquaintance and that, whatever our differences, this is something we have in common.[5] When the Constitution was adopted, there was a consciousness that in writing its text, India was finding a way to resolve major substantive debates and disputes over norms and values.[6] In granting people power over their own destiny, the Constitution placed the individual at its heart to guide the functioning of the democratic institutions it put in place.

Our history of constitutional drafting is replete with anecdotes that illustrate that there was an attempt by the framers to stake ownership over the document. They did not place the Constitution for approval before the British Parliament. Following the Irish precedent, Article 395 of the Constitution of India repealed the Indian Independence Act, 1947. The framers repudiated the source that authorized them to enact the Constitution. This was a symbolic denial of Indian Independence being a benevolence of the imperial Parliament.[7]

These actions of the framers ensured that the chain of constitutional validity did not extend to the Crown-in-Parliament. They delivered a completely 'autochthonous Constitution', 'home-grown' and rooted in our soil.[8] The Constitution owed its validity and authority to its own people rather than to the fact of enactment by a foreign legal process. In this transformative manner, we, the people, through the members of the Constituent Assembly, came to be the 'source' of authority of the Constitution, rather than the Indian Independence Act enacted by the British Crown-in-Parliament.

This is important because not all constitutions are always an expression of the will of the people or a product of it. For example, the events that gave rise to Israel's constitutional structure did not come about as a result of a constitutional convention, referendum, civic mobilization or any other deliberate process that characterizes traditional constitution-making. Instead, the country went from being one with no written constitution or judicial review to having a full-blown constitutional regime overnight[9] after a single pronouncement by their Supreme Court in the *United Bank Mizrahi Bank v. Migdal Cooperative Village* case[10] where the court held that the basic laws passed since the inception of the state did, in fact, constitute the making of a constitution.[11] The gradual evolution of the constitutional process in India has ensured its durable strength.

The advent of the Indian Constitution thus marked the coming together of a population, the culmination of a desire for self-governance. It represented a bottom-up approach where the *people* granted to themselves their structures of governance. In lawyer and jurist Nani Palkhivala's words: 'The Constitution represents the charter of power granted by liberty and not [the] charter of liberty granted by power. Liberty is not a gift of the state to the people; it is the people enjoying liberty as the citizens of a free republic who have granted power to the legislature and executive.'[12]

The Constitution was required to take into account multiple conflicts: freedom of expression and national integrity, personal liberty and political stability, special treatment for some segments of society and equality for all, property rights and social revolutionary needs. Those in positions of authority may go terribly wrong, as when we jail a cartoonist for sedition or when jail, instead of bail, is given to a blogger critical of religious architecture. In the wisdom of her people, however, the Constitution trusts. The trust is broken at our peril. The most fundamental struggle was between Parliament and the Supreme Court over the custody of the Constitution, the Central issue being whether Parliament's power of amendment was complete and unrestrained.

In the initial decade of the nation's independence, a stronger Central government with far-reaching powers had assumed importance in order to drive socio-political revolution. The nation was born into what Granville Austin described as a state of 'emergency', a moment marked by deep crisis, uncertainty, and the urgent need for constitutional transformation. Two decisions immediately fuelled a change in the Constitution. The decision of the Supreme Court in *Romesh Thapar v. State of Madras* striking down the Madras Maintenance of Public Order Act, 1949,[13] and in *Brij Bhushan v. State of Delhi*[14] striking down the East Punjab Public Safety Act, 1949, immediately prompted the need to insert the word 'reasonable' in Article 19(2) of the Constitution as well as new grounds of 'public order', 'friendly relations with foreign states' and 'incitement to an offence' in order to allow the states to regulate free speech.[15]

One other article inserted into the Constitution reflected the Centre's concern to Centralize power through the Constitution and enact property legislation. By the First Amendment, Articles 31A and 31B were also added to the Constitution, which expressly saved laws providing for the acquisition of estates from being void on the ground that they are inconsistent with fundamental rights. Acts and regulations specified in the Ninth Schedule would be immune from the operation of Article 13.

In keeping with the tense atmosphere into which India was born, the operation of the preventive detention law brought into focus a jurisprudential position by the court which was deferential to the states. This was at its most evident in *A.K. Gopalan v. The State of Madras*,[16] where the majority held that Article 22, being a complete code relating to preventive detention, the validity of an order of detention must be determined strictly according to the terms and 'within the four corners of that Article', and that its validity cannot be tested against Articles 19 and 21. In other words, fundamental rights were not a continuous stretch of entitlements but isolated pockets of discrete rights.

The working of the Constitution in the first decade of its existence, in the context of a newly born nation looking to consolidate national unity, was characterized by deference to the state agenda. To the exigencies of the time, the Constitution adapted and endured.

A developing body of comparative constitutional studies, which studies the resilience of constitutions, has indicated that there are three features that exert an overwhelming bearing on their endurance: inclusiveness, specificity and flexibility.[17] The Indian Constitution serves as an outstanding example of durability, in no small part due to the formal power of constitutional amendment granted to Parliament through Article 368 of the Constitution. The power of amendment is the foremost expression of flexibility and has been exercised to reflect the march of time and the evolving needs and values of society. It indicates, above all else, the ability of the Constitution to adapt to changing circumstances. Since the enactment of the Constitution in 1950, Article 368 has been used extensively. As of October 2018, there have been more than 100 amendments to the Constitution, with these amendments both frequent and wide-ranging. However, the flexibility is balanced by the need to protect its character as the supreme law, insulated from the whims of the government of the day.[18] This was achieved by virtue of the basic structure doctrine developed in *Kesavananda Bharati*[19] in 1973 and the jurisprudence of the Supreme Court that followed, which placed limits on the plenary amendment power of Parliament, thus safeguarding principles that form the bedrock of the Indian constitutional order. As a result, the procedure for amendment today is reflective of a finely struck balance: It is neither too rigid nor too flexible, blending pragmatism and adaptability with carefully designed safeguards.

Indian constitutional history has borne witness to a number of landmark constitutional amendments. What was formerly the 'fundamental' right to property enjoys the unique distinction of being the most amended provision in the Indian Constitution. It was protected as a fundamental right until the enactment of the Forty-Fourth Constitutional Amendment in 1978, the right to property was thereafter deprived of its fundamental status to reflect the growing realities of a conflict between the protection of existing property rights and the desire to move towards a more egalitarian society, which would involve a redistribution of land.[20] The Sixty-First Constitutional Amendment of 1988, passed in recognition of the political consciousness of the country's youth and the desire to integrate them into the political process, reduced the voting age from twenty-one to eighteen years for elections to the Lok Sabha and state legislative assemblies.[21] The Seventy-Third and Seventy-Fourth Amendments, through the insertion of Part IX and Schedules Eleven and Twelve of the Constitution, provided a major boost to the protection and recognition of the local self-government model in India, by supplying a constitutional status to panchayats (rural self-governments) and municipalities (urban self-governments). The Eighty-Sixth Amendment of 2002 recognized the primacy of education for the nation's youth and, through the insertion of Article 21A, made free and compulsory education between ages six and fourteen a fundamental right and the responsibility of the states.

The underlying philosophy of constitutional amendments has been dealt with in great depth by erudite judges who delivered the decision in *Kesavananda Bharati*. For example, Justice A.K. Mukherjee in *Kesavananda Bharati* speaks about how constitutions are expected to endure and must necessarily be elastic: 'The society grows, its requirements change. The Constitution and the laws may have to be changed to suit those needs. No single generation can bind the course of the generation to come.'[22]

Justice S.M. Sikri, on the other hand, states: 'The expression "amendment of this Constitution" does not enable Parliament to abrogate or take away fundamental rights or to completely change the fundamental features of the Constitution so as to destroy its identity.'[23]

The makers and interpreters of the Constitution were confronted with various tensions, which ultimately shaped its character. The Constitution of India is a text that governs over 1.45 billion people, in twenty-nine states, speaking twenty-two constitutionally recognized languages (not to mention hundreds of dialects) and practising virtually every mainstream religion of the world.[24] Indian constitutionalism has been described as a boisterous and contentious enterprise that strives to endow the largest, most diverse and complex democracy with legal form.[25] The sheer diversity of the persons it governs threw up challenges in the nature of religious, cultural and linguistic differences. Significantly, this diversity has led to contradictions in the Constitution, which were often in the form of a grant of a different status to a community, identity or territorial region to preserve the plural social fabric of the nation.

Rivalling the importance of a social revolution to be fostered by a transformative constitution were the goals of national unity and stability, considered as prerequisites for a social renaissance.[26] The framing and working of the Constitution can be described as an attempt to balance the contradictions of a multicultural and multi-ethnic society, which, among other things, involves reconciling a secular state with a fundamentally religious society.

Though the phrase 'secular State' was introduced in the Constitution only in 1976, specifically through the Forty-Second Amendment, the secular nature of the Indian state was affirmed by the Constituent Assembly. During the framing of the Indian Constitution, a significant question arose as to whether religious and other groups should have separate and distinct political representation in electoral processes.[27] While the Government of India Act of 1935 contained provisions for communal representation in electorates, the policy of communal representation was rejected by the Minorities Sub-Committee and the Advisory Committee. Finally, communal representation was done away with. Article 325 of the Constitution provided that '. . . no person shall be ineligible for inclusion in any . . . electoral . . . roll nor claim to be included in any special electoral roll for any such constituency on grounds only of religion, race, caste, sex or any of them'. The only exceptions were made for special electorates for India's Scheduled Castes and Scheduled Tribes and the Anglo-Indian community.

The draft of the Constitution was a declaration of social intent.[28] While rejecting political fragmentation on the basis of religion, the Assembly granted certain autonomy to religious minorities.

The chapter on fundamental rights is based on the principle of non-discrimination.

Article 15 applies it to 'religion, race, caste, sex or place of birth'. The 'freedom of religion', located within the chapter, is expressed in four articles (Articles 25 to 28). The Centrality of secularism in the constitutional system was reinforced by the Indian Supreme Court assigning it, in the decision in *S.R. Bommai v. Union of India*,[29] the value of a 'basic feature of the Constitution'.

The Indian Constitution contains a panoply of instruments for the protection of minorities, based on an innovative combination of individual and group rights.[30] Thus, religious differences were reconciled with an assurance of equal political representation. The 'religious rights' granted in Articles 25 to 28 reflect an acknowledgement of the diverse religious identities existing within the country. Another important aspect of the chapter on fundamental rights is contained in the grant of 'cultural rights', declared under Articles 29 and 30.

The Constitution does not limit minority rights to the recognition and protection of their culture but also recognizes the right to establish and administer educational institutions of their choice as a corollary of their cultural freedom. Finally, Articles 350A and 350B reinforce this right but with an ambit limited to linguistic minorities, providing that 'it shall be the endeavour of every State and of every local authority within the State to provide adequate facilities for instruction in the mother tongue at the primary stage of education to children belonging to linguistic minority groups . . .'

The Indian Constitution is a multicultural document that provides political and institutional measures for the recognition and accommodation of the country's diversity.[31] In India, cultural and religious minorities are not considered as 'external' elements but as actors participating in the construction of a common plural identity and as basic elements of the constitutional system.[32] Cultural heterogeneity celebrates precisely those plural values that would seem to contradict the unity required for successful democratic constitutionalism.[33]

Another contradiction to be addressed is asymmetric federalism, which is a means to provide recognition to the multiple identities and nationalities across the breadth of its territory. Jammu and Kashmir is the only state in the Union which negotiated special terms of entry to the union at the point of accession and has its own Constitution.[34]

The Constitution recognizes our diversity when it provides special measures for governance in areas inhabited by 'indigenous communities' or 'Scheduled Tribes' under the Fifth and Sixth Schedules. The Fifth Schedule grants the Union government greater powers to intervene in the interests of the socio-economic development of Scheduled Tribes. The Governor has the power to declare certain acts of Parliament or state legislature as not applicable to the Scheduled Tribes, as well as regulate land sales and the operation of moneylenders. In the areas covered under the Sixth Schedule in the North-east, extensive powers of self-governance are granted to Autonomous District Councils. At the inception of the Constitution, councils were established for the 'hill tribal' communities in Assam. However, due to the reorganization of northeastern states, they are now found in Assam, Meghalaya, Tripura and Mizoram.

These constitutional balances reconcile social, political or cultural differences. The Constitution embraced these differences. In doing so, it has fostered a heterogenous cultural and social fabric that recognizes different identities. The multicultural identity of our country is an ode to its strong democratic values, which do not compel homogeneity.

This brings me to the topic of 'constitutional identity', which encompasses concepts as broad as the features and provisions of the document itself, to the relation between a Constitution and the culture in which it operates, and to the relation between the identity of the constitution and other relevant identities, such as national, religious or gender identity. In his seminal book *Constitutional Identity*, Gary J. Jacobsohn argues that a constitution acquires an identity through experience—from a combination of the aspirations and commitments that express a nation's past and the desire to transcend that past. He acknowledges the complexity of constitutional identity by stating that just like identity is not fixed in the distinctive make-up of the infant who first emerges from the womb, the identity of a constitution is only 'imperfectly knowable' through the provisions promulgated during its adoption.[35] Yet, it is the most obvious starting point for commencing an examination of constitutional identity,[36] and the first step on the 'long and winding road from political design for collective identity to a socially embedded institution that actually fosters such identity'.[37]

Modalities of legal subjectivity, identity and citizenship are rapidly shifting in the context of contemporary globalization. While state nationalism remains a strong force, there are concurrently many other modes of connection that are shaping people's sense of personal and collective identities. A range of new legal relations are

> . . . brought about by new labor markets, new industries and commodities, new forms of secular and religious violence, new cultural and sexual politics, new reproductive technologies, new materialist understandings of agency, and a rethinking of the autonomous subject/citizen with increasing attention being given to a blurring of conventional divides between the human and non-human.[38]

Emerging changes in science and technology pose a challenge to our legal and constitutional values by disrupting conceptions of the very definition of personhood and identity. The burgeoning of multifaceted and intersectional identities accompanied by an acknowledgment of the inherent fluidity in various identities lends immediacy to the need that our Constitution keep pace with them.

Increasingly so, the Constitution recognizes diverse identities of its citizens. An important example is the recognition of different gender and sexual identities. While the break from a heteronormative framework has been gradual, the courts have played an important role in recognizing the autonomy of individuals within the Constitution to determine their orientation as well as gender identity.

It was my belief while writing the Section 377 judgment,[39] that the 'we' in 'We, the People of India' in our Preamble must be an ever-inclusive, expansive 'we'. The 'we' is not prefixed by 'only', stating 'only we' or any other such prefixes connoting religious, caste, class, sex, political or ideological affiliation. It is a simple and obvious interpretation, but as George Orwell said, 'The work of intelligent people is to restate the obvious' because the devil is very often in the details. As people in the field of law, we would agree that the limits of our words are the limits of our world.

The shift in our jurisprudence that came with *R.C. Cooper v. Union of India*[40] was crucial. The court overruled the earlier view from *A.K. Gopalan* that each fundamental right stands alone. Instead, it held that the rights in Part III of the Constitution form a single, interconnected framework for protecting basic human freedoms. Viewing constitutional rights as overlapping opened new avenues to the court to realize the emancipatory power of the Constitution. This issue presented itself before us in the *Sabarimala Temple Entry* case. Article 25 of the Indian Constitution protects the equal entitlement of all persons to a freedom of conscience and to freely profess, protect and propagate religion. Article 26 preserves the right of denominations to manage their affairs in matters of religion. However, Article 26 does not embody the additional stipulation found in Article 25(1), which subjects it to other provisions of Part III.

But does that by itself lend credence to the theory that the right of a religious denomination to manage its affairs is a standalone right uncontrolled or unaffected by the other fundamental freedoms? It is the shift in our jurisprudence that grounds Article 26 not as an independent silo but among a large cluster of freedoms which the Constitution has envisaged as intrinsic to human liberty and dignity. Hence, the dignity of women, which emanates from Article 15 and is a reflection of Article 21, cannot be disassociated from the exercise of religious freedom under Article 26. A conversation within the Constitution between religion, dignity and morality is aided by such a shift.

The Constitution of India is a transformative document. It was to usher in a radical transformation from a colonial regime to a liberal constitutional democracy. It sought to empower the individual, who it placed at the very heart of society and polity. The promise of substantive equality in Parts III and IV was truly revolutionary for it gave many the language to articulate, voice and agitate moral indignations. Citizen interpretive practices remain diverse, conflicted and contradictory. These articulations are a litmus that test the successful functioning of the Constitution. At the heart of the learnings and unlearnings of the Constitution lies its basic unit—the individual.

We must not lose sight of the fact that the judiciary comes from the citizenry. The text of the Constitution, while the obvious starting point for interpreting the Constitution, was not intended to be the end of the interpretive task. The subjects of the Constitution—citizens of this country—have assumed new and diverse social and political identities since its inception—and the text of the Constitution has embraced these identities. The text is infused with meaning every time the court is called upon to interpret the Constitution. So, when the court does take upon this task, the question is: Should it ignore the underlying values of the Constitution? Should it not attempt to ensure that the Constitution is a living document that remains relevant to the needs of a constantly evolving society? Should it overlook the transformative vision of our Constitution?

For instance, the Bombay High Court in 2010 initiated a suo motu PIL on the basis of an article in the newspaper *Mumbai Mirror* describing the condition of children in a state-aided mentally deficient children's (MCD) home situated near Mumbai. I was a part of the bench with Chief Justice Mohit Shah, which commenced proceedings in this matter, and the matter was taken forward by successive benches headed by Justice V.M. Kanade, Justice Abhay S. Oka and myself. In the first hearing, the court acknowledged that the fundamental rights of these children had been violated. In the sixty-seven hearings that have taken place as of May 2018, wide-ranging directions have been issued—pertaining to victims, witness protection, physical and mental health of children living in MDC homes. This case is a wonderful example of the culmination of the actions of various agents—the people, the judiciary and significantly, the text of the Constitution—in furthering the cause of justice and changing the landscape of child-rights jurisprudence.

Citizen interpretive practices are essential to realizing the democratic ideals of the Constitution. Public interest litigations characterized by a 'collaborative approach, procedural flexibility, judicially supervised interim-orders and forward-looking relief',[41] served to bring 'the people' into judicial discourse. Usha Ramanthan,[42] human rights activist and independent legal researcher, argued that the PIL jurisprudence led to an 'explosive jurisprudence of constitutional relevance and the rejection of the redundancy of the peoples'. *People's Union for Democratic Rights (PUDR) v. Union of India*[43] is a shining light in this regard. It involved *the* non-implementation of labour laws on construction projects for the Asian Games and the non-payment of minimum wages. Given the relaxed locus standi of the PIL jurisprudence, PUDR's petition was held to be maintainable. Justice P.N. Bhagwati, interpreting Article 23 of the Constitution, held that the phrase 'forced labour' included not only physical coercion but economic compulsion as well. Another instance where accountability by the democratic institutions grounded by the Constitution is realized is the active use of the Right to Information (RTI). The active use of the RTI has the power to transform the way the government functions and is a symbol of hope for a more transparent government.

The guarantees of the Constitution must be assessed for the social change they can engender, which depends heavily on the working of institutions. Without a judiciary and citizenry that truly recognizes the transformative potential of the Constitution, it will remain an empty promise—doing mere lip service to the laudatory goal of achieving an egalitarian, liberated society. Professor Upendra Baxi's view on citizen participation[44] is that: 'Constitutions are not arenas of practice of state power, they also provide registers of interpretive practices of active citizenry.'[45] The Constitution, if it is truly transformational, is so because of the people who work it. The Constitution is worked on a daily basis by the courts, legislators, citizens, civil society and the media. The same document can be a charter to destroy human freedom, or it can be a document that pushes society in the direction of recognizing the inherent value in human dignity. As a former US secretary of State noted: 'Here the illegal we do immediately; the unconstitutional takes a little longer.'

The working of the Indian Constitution, in and out of courts, bears an intricate relationship with societal change. It is through the working of the Constitution that we give meaning and therefore, life to the Constitution. And by giving life to the Constitution through interpretation, we determine who we are as a people governed by it. Thus, the working of the Constitution has the power to change lives.

> The ultimate question must be what do the words of the text mean in our time? For the genius of the Constitution rests not in any static meaning it might have had in a world that is dead and gone but in the adaptability of its great principles to cope with current problems and current needs. What the constitutional fundamentals meant to the wisdom of other times cannot be their measure to the visions of our time. Similarly, what those fundamentals mean for us, our descendants will learn, cannot be the measure of the vision of our future.[46]

But what of the future of the Constitution? There are emerging questions that the drafters of the Indian Constitution did not envisage and to which the text of the Constitution provides no clear answer. For instance, technological advances have radically changed how we conduct our lives, interact with people and communicate ideas. These changes have seeped through how the law governs, how the courts carry out their procedures and how the state chooses to identify us as citizens. While facilitative and enabling in a manner, these advances also have the potential of disrupting conceptions of basic principles that we have long been familiar with—be it free speech, privacy, right against self-discrimination, personal liberty or the very definition of personhood. As we, as a population, become increasingly adept at using newer modes of technology, the Constitution will have to keep pace in order to continue being relevant. The rise of technology also raises potential questions of who *personhood* can be attributed to. With advancements towards AI and robo-mechanics, where do concepts such as negligence and tortious liability lie? Constitutional interpretation will again require the court to mould the text to apply constitutional principles to emerging technologies, so that values of security and personal liberty can be protected.

The Constitution is an instrument which lives and breathes. It is not a static manuscript but a framework crafted to evolve over time. A Constitution which cannot adapt to changing times risks irrelevance. What gives our Constitution an enduring value is the ability to respond to changing realities. Democracy is not confined to the act of casting a vote or the holding of free elections. It is a continuing process, shaped by competing interests, negotiated by compromises, and moulded by institutions entrusted with the function of governance. At its core, democracy is sustained by reflection, challenge and renewal. The drafters of the Constitution were prophetic: They foresaw that the questions that confront Indian society would change over the years. However, the answers would always be found in the enduring spirit of the Constitution to adapt and its effectual working by the people it seeks to govern, which is why the Constitution matters.

The ideals laid down long ago still govern us today and are the foundation of what a better future might look like—a future that must be affected by us collectively as a democracy and as a people. This sentiment is captured by the words of Dr Ambedkar: 'However good a constitution may be, it is sure to turn out bad because those who are called to work it happen to be a bad lot. However bad a constitution may be, it may turn out to be good if those who are called to work happen to be a good lot.'[47]

The Constitution works even if you don't believe in it or even if it doesn't matter to you—it has been working all this while. An anecdote from the physicist Niels Bohr's life explains this. Surprised at seeing a horseshoe above the door of Bohr's country house, a fellow scientist visiting him exclaimed that he did not share the superstitious belief regarding horseshoes keeping evil spirits out of the house, to which Bohr snapped back: 'I don't believe in it either. I have it there because I was told that it works even when one doesn't believe in it at all.' And that is why the Constitution matters—because it works even for those who don't believe in it.

9

The Rainbow above Kala Ghoda[1]

It is indeed an honour to be invited to the Kala Ghoda Arts Festival, which truly captures the soul and essence of the city. Mumbai, a melting pot of distinct cultures and identities, is represented in all its cosmopolitan splendour in this festival. Coming back to Mumbai evokes an odd feeling—a mix of belonging and not estrangement, for every time I visit the city, I feel like it's rapidly changing—in some ways beyond recognition. And the inevitable question is always posed: Do I identify as a Mumbaikar, or am I a Dilliwallah now? To be honest, I feel like one of the lost flamingos that flock to the city of Bombay periodically, scrambling for and managing to find familiarity in the city.

But at the same time, certain aspects of the city remain unaltered. Though there are new shops and restaurants mushrooming throughout the city every day, I believe that Mumbai has managed to retain its soul and quintessential character. Kala Ghoda as well as the festival it hosts, are a part of the glorious heritage and history of Mumbai.

Today, as we gather here to celebrate the completion of two glorious decades, the Kala Ghoda Festival has blossomed into a world-renowned immersive, inclusive cultural celebration, one that enjoys both a distinct cultural and visual identity. Housed in the Kala

Ghoda Art district—home to one of the finest collections of heritage structures the country has to offer, the Kala Ghoda Arts Festival has gone from strength to strength, incorporating an eclectic mix of visual arts, theatre, dance, literature, lectures and workshops. The festival draws its visual identity from the array of architectural masterpieces in our city, including the Jehangir Art Gallery, the Prince of Wales Museum (renamed Chhatrapati Shivaji Maharaj Vastu Sangrahalaya), Elphinstone College, the National Gallery of Modern Art and our hosts for today, the David Sassoon Library. The energy in the streets today is infectious. The vivacity of the festival and the artists who participate in it resonate with the pulse of our fast-paced city.

As I reminisce, looking back to when I began my practice as a lawyer in Mumbai in the 1990s, and the twelve years I spent as a judge at the Bombay High Court, the rich cultural experiences that Mumbai offers have had a huge influence in shaping me into the individual I am today. I am reminded of a few lines from one of my favourite films, *Dead Poets Society,* by Robin Williams—an actor I am sure many of us dearly miss:[2]

> . . . We don't read and write poetry because it's cute. We read and write poetry because we are members of the human race. And the human race is filled with passion. And medicine, law, business, engineering, these are noble pursuits and necessary to sustain life. But poetry, beauty, romance, love, these are what we stay alive for.

I believe that the life of the law cannot be divorced from these human elements. At its heart, the judgment in the case concerning Section 377 was about the primordial instinct to love. The verdict merely restored to members of the LGBTQIA+ community the long-overdue access to the experience of full citizenship.[3] It acknowledged that in a society as diverse as ours, tolerance for different forms of life and acceptance of different ways of being, are 'the warp and the weft of the fabric of our plural culture'.[4] To some of us, embedded in our own social and cultural milieus, some of these ways of being may be strange at first, and even frightening.[5] Put in the words of the eminent law scholar Gautam Bhatia: 'Our Constitution is the bridge that allows us to meet each other above the abyss of prejudice and intolerance. The building blocks of that bridge are Article 14 (equal protection of laws), Article 15 (non-discrimination), Article 19(1)(a) (freedom of expression) and Article 21 (life and personal liberty).'[6]

The legal foundation was laid over a decade ago when the Naz Foundation petitioned the courts seeking that Section 377 of the Indian Penal Code be declared unconstitutional. That even the journey of that legal challenge in our legal institutions has taken this long is only a sobering reminder of how long it can take to redress injustices of the gravest kind.[7] And decriminalization is only a first step—legal change must be followed by a change in societal and moral values. Our work must merely begin so that we may not be the cause of injustice from having once been its inheritors. It is only then that we will truly be able to unlock our true transformative potential. The approach of transformative constitutionalism must go beyond 'who we are' to 'who we can be'—both to ourselves and to each other, and also how we can use constitutional morality as a transformative power to address the myriad forms of inequalities that divide all of us.[8]

In his seminal book *Constitutional Identity*, Gary Jacobsohn argues that a constitution acquires an identity through experience—from a combination of the aspirations and commitments that express a nation's past and the desire to transcend that past. He acknowledges the complexity of constitutional identity, stating that just like identity is not fixed in the distinctive make-up of the infant who first emerges from the womb, the identity of a constitution is only 'imperfectly knowable' through the provisions promulgated during its adoption.[9] Yet, it is the most obvious starting point for commencing an examination of constitutional identity, and the first step on the 'long and winding road from political design for collective identity to a socially embedded institution that actually fosters such identity'.[10] Modalities of legal subjectivity, identity and citizenship are rapidly shifting in the context of contemporary globalization.[11] While State nationalism remains a strong force, there are concurrently many other modes of connection that are shaping people's sense of personal and collective identities. These new range of legal relations are 'brought about by new labor markets, new industries and commodities, new forms of secular and religious violence, new cultural and sexual politics, new reproductive technologies, new materialist understandings of agency, and a rethinking of the autonomous subject/citizen with increasing attention being given to a blurring of conventional divides between the human and non-human'.[12] Emerging changes in science and technology pose a challenge to our legal and constitutional values by disrupting conceptions of the very definition of personhood and identity. The burgeoning of multifaceted and intersectional identities, accompanied by an acknowledgement of the inherent fluidity in various identities, lends to the indispensable requirement of a constitution that keeps pace with these identities. Increasingly so, the Constitution is recognizing the diverse identities of its citizens. While the break from a heteronormative framework has been gradual, the courts have played an important role in recognizing the autonomy of individuals within the Constitution to determine their orientation as well as gender identity.

Identities are contextual; they do not exist as abstract entities. The conception of every citizen as a constructed idea of a person who is both free and equal is bereft of meaning without the recognition of the pluralities of identity. In some cases, the social, cultural and economic contexts serve as impediments to the realization of the identity envisaged by the Constitution. The court is then tasked with the decimation of social constructs and the reinvention of identities. For instance, in *Joseph Shine v. Union of India*,[13] the Supreme Court acknowledged how legislation perpetuated restrictive gendered identity on the country's female citizens. When the impact of these identities was understood by the court, the patriarchal leanings of the law on adultery stood completely exposed. Constitutional discourse was instrumental in reinventing not just the identity of the married woman as an individual imbued with sexual agency but also how it is manifested in the conception of marriage as a sacrament 'between equals'.

In my judgment on Section 377,[14] I also recognized that the effect of Section 377 was not limited to its subjection of adults engaging in consensual intercourse to criminal liability. In effect, Section 377 also pushed the identities of these citizens into obscurity and oblivion. As text is dependent on context, and as the context is subject to transformation over time, constitutional discourse is integral to invent and reinvent identity.[15] Constitutional discourse also creates a narrative. The court, in acknowledging diverse identities and their impact on the lives of its citizens, built a narrative of sexual autonomy and equal citizenship.

While constitutional discourse may be used to decimate the construct of identities that are antithetical to constitutional values, it also operates to create a conducive space in which diverse identities can exist and flourish. The Constitution has embraced differences and fostered a heterogeneous cultural and social fabric that recognizes different identities. The multicultural identity of our country is an ode to its strong democratic values, which do not compel homogeneity. It was my belief while writing the Section 377 judgment that the 'we' in 'We, the People of India' in our Preamble needs to be understood as an ever-inclusive, expansive 'we'. The 'we', as you will notice, is not prefixed by the word 'only', so as to indicate 'only we' or any other such prefixes connoting religious, caste, class, sex, political and ideological affiliation.

Abhijit Naskar, in his book titled *Either Civilized or Phobic: A Treatise on Homosexuality*, writes: 'Discriminations are never a sign of a civilized society. What makes us civilized is our act of liberated kindness with other people beyond the man-made primitive citadels of gender, race, religion and sexual orientation.'[16] I firmly believe that as human beings, all of us deserve an environment in which we have the opportunity to attain our fullest potential—factors such as who you choose to love cannot be a reason to deny that.

I also had the occasion to deal with the issue of identity in the technological era in the *Aadhaar* case. In my opinion, the Aadhaar

Act 2016 reduced the rich complexity of individual identity to merely their biometric data. The myriad forms of expressing identity were pigeonholed into just biometric information. The concept of identity was 'flipped' so that identification through identifiers became the only form of identity in the time of database governance. This involved a radical transformation in the position of the individual. In holding the Aadhaar Act to be unconstitutional, I held that identity includes the right to determine the forms through which identity is expressed and the right not to be identified. When the Constitution protects our right to be and to be what we are, it creates a space where the individual is immune to interference. By recognizing our liberty as autonomous persons, the Constitution recognizes our ability to preserve and shape our identities in interactions with others. In the context of a living constitution, moreover, constitutional identity is the product of a dynamic process that is always open to further elaboration and revision.[17]

Speaking at this forum has given me the opportunity to think about the relationship between art and law, and I take the liberty to share my musings:

For the legally trained mind, the first thought on the intersection of law and art is often law's role in regulating art. This includes the legal, public policy and ethical issues that concern artists and all those comprising the world of art, such as the rights of artists (including copyright, resale royalties, moral rights and freedom of expression issues, how the market in art functions. This also includes questions such as whether the special character of art distinguishes it from other tangible property and justifies different treatment under the law in terms of ownership, protection, regulation and funding.[18]

But there is more to the intersection between art and the law than what is glimpsed through the lens of intellectual property law. One of the greatest playwrights of all time, George Bernard Shaw, had famously remarked that: 'Without art, the crudeness of reality would be unbearable.' While art does make some harsh realities of inequality and injustice a little more palatable, there is also a larger instrumental power at play. Both art and the law are immense transformational tools. Actor and activist Ossie Davis says that, 'Any form of art is a form of power; it has impact, it can affect change—it can not only move us, it makes us move.'[19]

I think most of us have at some point of time in our lives experienced the feeling of being moved by a work of art—a painting, a song, a play, a poem, a story, a painting or a spatio-temporal experiment.[20] We are transported to a new place and become aware of a feeling that is perhaps not completely unfamiliar to us but which we did not actively focus on before.[21] This experience of engaging with a good work of art can connect us to our senses, body and mind and make the world *felt*.[22] And this *felt* feeling holds the potential to spur thinking, engagement and even action.[23]

Our lived experience dictates the narrow bandwidth of our map of possibilities and determines the decisions we make in our lives. It is not surprising that artists, cultural leaders and, more importantly, their ideas have together played an integral role in a wide range of social movements.[24] Martin Luther King's inspirational speech about civil rights begins with the imagery of a *dream*. Imagination invites one to envision possibilities other than the status quo and impacts our heart, mind and dreams. Artists and activists both envision and enact 'possibilities other than the status quo',[25] push us to think radically and interrogate the world as it is, and to imagine how it could be, thus engendering us to work towards social change.[26]

Scholars have opined that the reason art and social justice seem to be intrinsically linked is that art not only creates feelings of *possibility*, it also engenders feelings of *empathy*. One of the great challenges we face today is that we often feel untouched by the problems of 'others'—problems we do not experience ourselves (for example, effects of global warming are felt differently by different people). We do not feel strongly enough that we are part of a global community, part of a larger *we* as compared to our parochial view of 'we'. Who we allow the freedom to speak and be heard, and at whose cost, is crucial to both art and law. It brings to mind a beautiful poem by the tribal poet Waharu Sonawane:[27]

We did not go on to the stage,
Neither were we called.
We were shown our places,
told to sit.
But they, sitting on the stage,
went on telling us of our sorrows,
our sorrows remained ours, they never became theirs.

While the advent of science and technology has revolutionized the speed at which information is disseminated, mere access to data can leave people overwhelmed and disconnected, not connected and poised for action.[28] Art helps convey not only knowledge but also feelings. In doing so, art can mitigate the numbing effect created by the glut of information we are faced with today and motivate people to transform thought into action.

Art is the bridge that transports us from an us-and-them and other-ing mentality to a broader idea of *we*. It influences society by changing opinions, instilling values and translating experiences across space and time.[29] Research has shown that art affects the fundamental sense of self.[30] Art preserves what fact-based historical records cannot: how it felt to exist in a particular place at a particular time.[31] Art in this sense is communication; it allows people from different cultures and different times to communicate with each other via images, sounds and stories.[32] Art is often a vehicle for social change. It can give voice to the politically or socially disenfranchised.[33] Viewed this way, art touches people everywhere. I am reminded of John Lennon's soulful song 'Imagine', which has captured the imagination of generations, with the possibility of an unfragmented, undivided world:

Imagine all the people
Living life in peace
You, you may say I'm a dreamer
But I'm not the only one

The contemporary art world can be viewed as a microcosm reflecting significant aspects of the larger world in which we live, including all its nuances. As women have become more a part of the contemporary art world, they have found myriad ways of expressing many facets of their identity through their work. Several female artists of diverse backgrounds in terms of ethnicity, religion, sexual orientation and other aspects of individuality have woven the threads of their identity into their work.[34] Much before the law of our courts may have acknowledged binaries, works of art (literature and sculpture) since time immemorial have challenged the idea of the gender binary. Artists have been at the forefront of these changes, creating works that question the normative assumptions of what our bodies should look like or do while drawing from a variety of perspectives on the subject.[35] Artistic explorations of sex and gender are not a modern phenomenon; such inquiries have transcended time and place, reflecting their complexity and fluidity across cultures and eras.[36]

Further, engaging with art and culture also has a greater symbolic value. Art and culture represent one of the few areas in our society where people can come together to share a transcendental experience, even if they see the world in radically different ways.[37] In art and other forms of cultural expression, disagreement is not only accepted but even celebrated as an essential ingredient. Works of art can thus make us more tolerant of difference and teach us to embrace diversity, transcending the polarizing populism and 'othering' of people, which is sadly so endemic in public discourse today.[38] This personal engagement with art—and with others over art—can help us identify with one another, expanding our notions of *we*.[39]

Art also encourages us to cherish intuition, uncertainty and creativity, as well as to search constantly for new ideas. Artists in their pursuit often find unorthodox ways of approaching contemporary issues.[40] I think as judges we also like to think of ourselves as artists—the materials before us are our artistic tools and the judgment our artistic expression. The Constitution is a promise to empower individuals to reach their fullest potential, uninhibited by arbitrary categories. Like art, it nudges us to transcend our saturated psyches and imagine a society where everyone can equally enjoy the richness of living beyond the margins that the brutality of civilization confines some classes of people to. Like art, the Constitution is a unifying document that binds us and equips us with a language to realize concretely the amorphous promise of that imagination. By interpreting a constitution, we breathe life into it, and by breathing life into that constitution, we decide who we are as a people governed by it. Like writers, judges are intuitive reasoners, and a lot of our creative thinking is unconscious. Novelists write a story in a certain way because it feels right, but the same has to be supported with a plot and well-constructed characters. Likewise, judges often have a strong sense of which way a case should be decided, but good judges must always explain their decisions. Like artists, judges employ craftsmanship and creativity in creating judicial opinions. The craftsmanship of the judge as well as the novelist depends largely on their ability to employ a relevant set of facts and articulate through words. Through their distinct forms of art, both seek to resonate with the experiences of their respective audiences.

I would like to recall some lovely lines from Judge Albie Sachs's book titled *The Strange Alchemy of Life and Law*:[41]

> In the beginning and in the end, is the word, at least as far as the life of a judge is concerned. We pronounce. We work with words, and become amongst the most influential story-tellers of our age. How we tell the story is often as important as what we say. The voice we use cannot be that of a depersonalized and divine oracle that declares solutions to the problems of human life through the enunciation of pure and detached wisdom. Nor dare we seek to imitate the artificial sounds of a computer that has been programmed to produce inexorable outcomes. We speak with the living voices of real protagonists who are immersed in and affected by the very processes we deal with.

And just like differences in artistic expression are celebrated, law grants judges the agency to express differing viewpoints through dissent.

As the curtains draw on the celebration of two decades of the Kala Ghoda Arts Festival, I take great pride in observing how much the festival has come to represent, not only to those fortunate enough to have been touched by its magic but also to the wider community. The festival is built on firm values and a clear vision—an undying commitment to protect our common heritage. Year after year, it serves as an outstanding example of the potential of an idea to be an engine that drives transformative social change. As the country's only urban museum, it brings together individuals from all walks of life and infuses them with a collective spirit of diversity, creativity and inclusion. While synonymous with Mumbai, the Kala Ghoda Arts Festival is a microcosm of something larger. It represents something much larger. The festival is a yearly, living exercise in Indian democratic values. At its heart, it is a vibrant celebration of diversity, plurality, fraternity and the fundamental rights of expression, liberty and cultural freedom—values that are the fabric of our nation.

10

Inventing and Reinventing Constitutional Identity[1]

It is a great honour for me to speak today at a lecture organized in memory of a lawyer who has left an indelible impact on the country's constitutional landscape, Mr M.K. Nambyar. Having started his practice in a district court in Mangaluru, he went on to become one of the most prominent advocates of our country. In the words of another legal luminary who has been a mentor to me, Soli Sorabjee: 'There have been many great Indian lawyers. However, there can be no doubt that Mr Nambyar was one of our greatest constitutional lawyers. On account of the farsightedness and the vision involved in his arguments regarding the interpretation of constitutional provisions, especially fundamental rights, he paved the way for and stimulated constructive juristic thinking.'[2]

While it would be impossible for me to cover the breadth of Nambyar's contributions to the law within the time given to me to deliver this lecture, I would like to recount a few of his many significant contributions: Nambyar appeared in *A.K. Gopalan v. the State of Madras*,[3] one of the first cases of the Supreme Court dealing with the interplay and interpretation of fundamental rights. One of Nambyar's key arguments was that a narrow interpretation of the phrase 'except according to procedure established by law' in Article

21 of the Constitution—should not be read literally in the sense that the court only has to ascertain whether there is a procedure and it is established by law. Instead, he contended that this expression must be read to include elements of procedural due process and natural justice.[4] B. Sen, former advocate general for the state of West Bengal, known for his key role in the formative years of the Supreme Court and his contributions to Indian constitutional law, recounts:

> The case I remember best was one that was heard in the very first months of the court. *A.K. Gopalan v. Province of Madras.* The question of detention without trial was at issue and that involved interpretation of Articles 14, 19, 21 and 22 of the Constitution. The constitutional questions raised were new, both to the judges and lawyers, and when M.K. Nambyar appearing for the detenu expounded his arguments, day after day, citing case law from all over the globe with comparisons between the Indian, the Irish and American Constitutions, the entire courtroom seemed to be completely spellbound. There were no interruptions nor questions, the all-pervading silence broken only by Nambyar's voice and the rustling of the pages of the law reports.[5]

The majority of the Supreme Court in *A.K. Gopalan* did not accept Nambyar's argument. It was only after twenty-eight years that the Supreme Court differed from *A.K. Gopalan* as to its interpretation of Article 21 and ruled in the case of *Maneka Gandhi*[6] that the expression in Article 21 'except according to procedure established by law' means a procedure which is fair, just and reasonable.[7]

His erudition shone again in *Golaknath*, where he contended that Article 368's amending power is not absolute but inherently limited.[8] It was later in 1973, in the *Kesavananda Bharati* case,[9] that this stand was adopted, which led to the basic structure doctrine. How the basic structure doctrine is an integral part of our constitutional identity is something that I will reflect upon in the course of this lecture. It is only indicative of the imprint that Nambyar's contributions have left on the identity of our foundational document.

Nambyar has also appeared in many leading cases involving important questions of constitutional law, including for the petitioners in the *Privy Purses* case,[10] wherein the Supreme Court held the abolition of privy purses guaranteed in the Constitution as unconstitutional, signifying that the mandate of the Constitution cannot be sacrificed at the altar of political expediency,[11] and for the petitioners in the *Bennett Coleman* case,[12] where the Newsprint Policy of 1972–73 which, amongst others, limited the number of pages per newspaper to a maximum of ten pages, was struck down holding that the 'freedom of the press is both qualitative and quantitative' and 'freedom lies both in circulation and in content'. The case safeguarded the latitude with newspapers and marked a clean departure to the 'direct effect' test, which laid emphasis not on the object of the state in enacting a legislation but its effect on fundamental rights.

Coming now to the topic before us, the term 'identity' has a long history in the field of philosophy to address perennial questions of stability amidst change, and unity amidst diversity.[13] But the widespread usage of the term may be said to be a more recent phenomenon—today identity is understood as how we understand and define ourselves,[14] which, in turn, can be said to impact our values, our choices and lived experiences. Given the subjective nature of the elements that comprise the term 'identity', it is unsurprising that there are warnings against conceptualizing 'all affinities and affiliations, all forms of belonging, all experiences of commonality, connectedness and cohesion, all self-understandings and self-identifications'[15] into the undifferentiated vocabulary of identity. And yet, the paramount importance of this term in our polity and society cannot be undermined. In light of the fact that 'identity' has become the dominant grammar of politics, some even go as far as stating that all politics is identity politics since all political activity is 'to define or to defend who I am, or we are, or you are, or hope to be or hope to be seen to be'.[16]

Postmodern scholars argue that the identities of subjects are constructed relationally through a variety of discursive practices. To quote:

> Our identities are culturally mapped by a series of discourses, some of which are more fluid than others . . . our identity arises in response to a number of sometimes conflicting factors, including the identities imposed upon us by the dominant discourses, as well as those which are an attempt to mediate, resist or recreate those dominant discourses. The result is a complex identity . . . situated sometimes on the fringes and sometimes closer to the center of mainstream.[17]

The Constitution is one of the discursive sites where identity is mapped. The conception and understanding of the term 'constitutional identity' remains one of the most elusive and widely debated questions in modern constitutionalism.[18] While discussed by academicians and courts alike, there is no agreement over the 'meaning' and content of constitutional identity. It encompasses concepts as broad as the features and provisions of the document itself, the relation between the constitution and the culture in which it operates, and the relation between the identity of the constitution and other relevant identities, such as national, religious or gender identity.[19]

By virtue of its complex, transient nature, constitutional identity is an ever-evolving concept. Crucially, however, while the ambit of 'constitutional identity' divides opinion, its significance does not—for the understanding of constitutional identity is fundamental to constitutional theory.[20] It is the gateway to *the* Central question that lies at the heart of constitutional theory: How do constitutional systems come into being and change over time?[21] One of the most noted scholars on 'constitutional identity', Gary Jacobsohn, argues that a constitution acquires an identity through experience—from a combination of the aspirations and commitments that express a nation's past and the desire to transcend that past. He acknowledges the complexity of constitutional identity by stating that just like identity is not fixed in the distinctive make-up of the infant who first emerges from the womb, the identity of a constitution is only 'imperfectly knowable' through the provisions promulgated during its adoption. Yet, it is the most obvious starting point for commencing an examination of constitutional identity, and the first step on the 'long and winding road from political design for collective identity to a socially embedded institution that actually fosters such identity'.[22]

The writings of intellectuals and freedom fighters such as Raja Ram Mohan Roy, Vivekananda, Sri Aurobindo, Mahadev Govind Ranade, Gopal Krishna Gokhale, Rabindranath Tagore and Mahatma Gandhi articulated varying narratives of a national identity, but the broad consensus was that 'the Indian civilisation was plural, and included different currents of moral and philosophical thought ranging from polytheism to atheism and from crude materialism to the highest form of idealism'.[23] In 1948, Sri Aurobindo said:

> India . . . has always been the home of a peculiar people with characteristics of its own recognisably distinct from all others, with its own distinct civilisation, [and] way of life . . . It has absorbed all that has entered into it, put upon all the Indian stamp, [and] welded the most diverse elements into its fundamental unity.[24]

But India's diversities also gave its people many particular attachments that led to scepticism about its possibility of being a nation—this was also the premise of the British colonial rule in India.[25] Israeli academic and author, Ornit Shani, in *How India Became Democratic* speaks of how the Universal Adult Franchise became the foundation of the world's largest democratic experiment even before the advent of the Constitution. The Universal Adult Franchise, unlike many other vestiges of colonial rule that permeated into independent India, was no legacy of colonial rule and represented one of the starkest acts of decolonization.[26] While electoral institutions existed even prior to Independence, they functioned to strengthen the colonial state and the power of the ruling elites.[27] Individuals were not viewed as individuals in their own right but as members of communities and groups, and seats in electorates were based on religious, community and professional lines, on a limited franchise.[28] This resulted in the deepening of divides and impeded national unity.[29] Under the last colonial framework governing India (the Government of India Act, 1935), suffrage was extended to roughly only one-fifth of the Indian population.[30] Unlike the process of framing the Constitution, the Universal Adult Franchise provided an opportunity to *every single Indian* to participate in this democratic experiment and to contribute in their own individual capacity, leaving imprints on the identity of the post-colonial democratic state.

At the time of its promulgation, the Indian Constitution was laboured with the charge of being 'un-Indian' and that it was not a Constitution suited to the country's needs.[31] Sixty-nine years later, we see that the Indian Constitution has not just endured, it has become a part of the nation's identity.[32] Political freedom involves not just a choice between available alternatives but also imaginatively creating new ones.[33] When India attained independence, there existed marked hierarchies in the Indian society on the basis of caste, class, gender and religion. Some of these hierarchical structures even predated colonial rule. As part of the Indian democratic project, the Constitution was to recognize these many peculiarities in fundamentally altering the structure of the Indian society in the organization of liberty.[34] In the words of Dr Ambedkar:

> For a successful revolution it is not enough that there is discontent. What is required is a profound and thorough conviction of the justice, necessity and importance of political and social rights.[35]

The Indian constitutional project, though inspired from constitutions around the world, ensured a context-specific application that suited its cultural diversity and recognized its vision of social transformation. In defending a migration of constitutional ideas with modification suited to the Indian context, Dr Ambedkar, in addressing the Constituent Assembly, opined that 'there was nothing to be ashamed of in borrowing . . . Nobody holds the patent rights in the fundamental ideas of a constitution'.[36]

Thus, in determining the character of the document, notwithstanding its external influences, the question of its representativeness is of crucial importance.[37] This entails an inquiry into how far the Constitution can be regarded as Indian in terms of ideas, values and social aspirations. For it is the underlying philosophy of the Constitution that determines its character. Though the makers of the Constitution drew inspiration from constitutions across international frontiers, the project of Indian independence sought to achieve an autochthonous constitution of the United States, one that Indian people gave to themselves. Thus, provisions that appear to have been borrowed on their face have also been adapted and tinkered with, taking into account Indian particularities.

Part IV of the Indian Constitution deals with Directive Principles of State Policy—a device borrowed from the Irish Constitution—which plays a far greater role in Indian constitutionalism than was envisaged in Ireland.[38] Though the scheme of fundamental rights was inspired by the US Bill of Rights, it was designed with regard to the unique needs of the Indian society. Provisions on affirmative action sought to address a social inequity that is particular to Indian society—caste-based discrimination. Social justice was to be construed in a 'seamless web' where the values act in harmony[39]—a unique exercise undertaken by the Indian Constitution. In my minority opinion in *Abhiram Singh*,[40] I have elucidated on this attempt to balance individual liberty with the need to redress historical injustices:

> 111 . . . In numerous provisions, the Constitution has sought to preserve a delicate balance between individual liberty and the need to remedy these histories of injustice founded upon immutable characteristics such as of religion, race, caste and language. *The integrity of the nation is based on a sense of common citizenship. While establishing that notion, the Constitution is*

> *not oblivious of history or to the real injustices which have been perpetrated against large segments of the population on grounds of religion, race, caste and language.* (Emphasis added)

Thus, while clause (1) of Article 15 of the Constitution prohibits discrimination on the grounds of religion, race, caste, sex, place of birth or any of them, clause (4) permits the State to make special provisions for the advancement of socially or educationally backward classes or for the Scheduled Castes and Scheduled Tribes. Similarly, clause (1) of Article 16 guarantees equality of opportunity for all citizens in matters relating to public employment, and clause (2) contains a guarantee against discrimination on the grounds of religion, race, caste, sex, descent, place of birth, residence or any of them. However, clause (4) of Article 16 empowers the State to make provisions for the reservation of appointments or posts in favour of any backward class of citizens which is not adequately represented in the services under the State. In a distinctive form of adjudication, the apex court has held prima facie clashing values in the constitutional text to be in perfect harmony with each other.[41]

Vital to the project of Indian constitutionalism has been the reconstruction of the social structure in which the family is embedded. As Jacobsohn puts it: 'The transformative nature of Indian Constitution's identity is implicit in the reach of the powers granted to public authority as well as the rights that are withheld from the ambit of constitutional protection; thus, one of the world's longest constitutions does not contain language mandating state guarantees for the family.'[42]

The Constituent Assembly debates were rich with dialogue on provisions and features that were migrated with modifications to the Indian context. Hence, to an assembly well versed with looking across national frontiers, the absence of such language was arguably not accidental. Thus, though the Irish Constitution was an important source of ideas, the same was not emulated in respect of its explicit protection of the family. The emphasis on the family had different constitutional implications for both countries. The

Indian Constitution's explicit targeting of caste was a manner in which entrenched familial notions could be challenged. This was where a constitutional silence facilitated societal reconstruction and reinforced the particulars of constitutional identity.

Though the Constitution allowed personal law and family law to be determined in accordance with the specific community, the exercise of this freedom was to be in consonance with the equality code. The introduction of an egalitarian notion into the practice of religious freedom and family law was to serve as the springboard to initiate social reconstruction of oppressive familial notions. The explicit outlawing of caste-based discrimination in Article 15 of the Constitution and the prohibition on the practice of untouchability in Article 17 demonstrated a deep understanding of the inequalities particular to the Indian society and an explicit commitment to address them.

The goal of social reconstruction would remain but a writ in sand if the State did not confront itself with religion. The notion of secularism in the West, which was confined to the separation of the church and state, takes on a different form in the Constitution of India.[43] Religion's penetration within Indian life was so entwined that the reconfiguration of social structures and the move towards a democratic polity meant that the State would have to confront itself with questions of religion.[44] This balance is inscribed in several constitutional provisions that express the limits and possibilities of secularism in India.

The aspiration of Indian secularism is embodied in Article 25, which, after providing for religious freedom, declares that the State shall not be prevented from 'regulating or restricting any economic, financial, political or other secular activity which may [be] associated with religious practice'. 'Providing for social welfare and reform' is explicitly included within the parameters of the guaranteed freedom. As Subrata Mitra, an academic and political scientist, noted: 'India, is virtually alone among post-colonial states in Asia to have adopted secularism as a key feature of her constitution and the cornerstone of her strategy of nation building.'[45]

Also crucial to the constitutional project was the goal of national unity, which the drafters believed would require tweaking of the Western notion of federalism to suit the Indian context. For example, while the American model of federalism was ill-suited for the purpose of unifying a country with cultural and linguistic sub-differences, our Constitution adopted a model that by its very design was meant to adapt itself to the needs of the situation—what Professor K.C. Wheare calls a quasi-federal model.[46] Thus, Indian federalism was an 'outcome of our own historical process and a recognition of ground realities'.[47]

In times of emergency, the structure of governance could be unitary in order to ensure national unity. However, the federal structure was designed in a manner that preserved the spheres of both the Centre and the states. This was given force by the Supreme Court in *S.R. Bommai v. Union of India*,[48] where it was categorically held that the power of the President under Article 356 is to be employed only in 'rare' cases as an 'exception'. It was held that states have an independent constitutional existence and are 'neither satellites nor agents of the Centre'.[49] Justice K. Ramaswamy, who was part of the constitution bench in *S.R. Bommai*, opined that: 'Federalism implies mutuality and common purpose for the process of change with continuity between the Centre and the states which are the structural units operating on a balancing wheel of concurrence and promises to resolve problems and promote social, economic and cultural advancements of its people.'[50]

Though the constitutional moment indicates the commitment to a certain identity, the measure of a constitution may be deduced by how well it balances entrenchment and change.[51] As every political order is created with the clear aim of self-preservation, unamendable provisions are designed to preserve the primary constitutive values of the constitutional order.[52] Hence, constitutions contain explicit as well as implicit limitations on amending power.

Legal scholar Michel Rosenfeld remarks that the establishment of a constitutional identity over time requires the weaving together of the 'past of the framers, one's own present, and the future of unborn generations'.[53] Since the past and future are both uncertain and open to conflicting possibilities, unearthing threads of continuity involves several complications.[54] For even if the framers' actual intent were accessible, their relevance and ability to bind future generations could always be disputed.[55] Rosenfeld notes that since the framers' intent can be construed at several levels of abstraction, it provides room for the reinterpretation and reconstruction of one's constitutional identity.[56]

Unamendable provisions seek to protect an inviolable core, vital to the stability and permanence of the constitution. They are designed to preserve the document from changes that might annihilate its essential nucleus or disrupt the constitutional order itself.[57] Ulrich Preuss, professor emeritus of law and politics at the Hertie School of Governance, has highlighted the Centrality of unamendable provisions to the identity of the document:

> [Unamendable provisions] define the essential elements of the foundation myth. In other words, they define the collective 'self' of the polity—the 'we the people.' If the 'eternal' normative stipulations were changed, the collective self or identity of the polity as embodied in the Constitution would collapse.[58]

This enduring normative vision led the Supreme Court to declare 'the Constitution is a precious heritage; therefore, you cannot destroy its identity'.[59] This identity found expression in one of the most unique features of our constitutional heritage: the basic structure doctrine. The doctrine was evolved in the *Kesavananda Bharati* case, which held that no constitutional amendment would stand the test of judicial review if it went so far as to modify the 'basic structure' of our Constitution.

The basic structure doctrine has, since its inception, often been criticized.[60] The strongest criticism against the doctrine has been that 'it gives unelected judges the power to restrict the activity of an elected legislature, thus encroaching upon its activity, and violating the doctrine of separation of powers'.[61] Described as an 'imprecise' and 'elastic' concept,[62] it is opined that there is no unanimity regarding the components of the basic structure. This led the constitutional law expert and renowned commentator H.M. Seervai to lament that, 'a precise formulation of the basic features would be a task of greatest difficulty and would add to the uncertainty of interpreting the scope of Art. 368'.[63]

However, at its core, the doctrine is a dialogical representation of the identity of our Constitution,[64] where, while flexibility is necessary, certain features cannot be eroded because that would take away from the basic premise or value on which the constitutional identity was created. Some examples include the supremacy of the Constitution, the separation of powers, federalism and secularism. This is similar to 'eternity clauses' found in many constitutions of other jurisdictions, which are often framed around their own unique experiences. The Norwegian Constitution, for example, dating back to 1814, has one that protects the very spirit of the Constitution.[65] The French Constitution protects the 'republican' form of government, a testament to their contested history with the monarchy.[66] The German Constitution reinforces their commitment 'to promote world peace as an equal partner in a united Europe' which highlights their own history of the Nazi regime.

Unamendable parts of a constitution present a 'shorthand record' of the memories and hopes of their makers.[67] If a constitution 'reflects the triumphs and disappointments of a nation's past and embodies its hope for the future', this is captured, in part, in its unamendable provisions. Ulysses and the Sirens is often the metaphor used to illustrate the concept of unamendability as a safeguard against majoritarian populism:

> [W]hen Ulysses bound himself to the mast and had his rowers put wax in their ears, it was to make it impossible for him to succumb to the song of the sirens.[68]

The basic structure is not about imposing the wisdom of one generation upon another, but the acknowledgement that a constitution has a coherent moral vision and an identity.[69] It represents a fixation in Indian constitutional jurisprudence, which lay recognition to those features of the Indian polity that were to mark a fixed point of reference for the constitutional path on which the country set out.

Our Constitution articulates a vision of what it means to be Indian, but it is its working that best captures the conflict of identities within India and this conflict for what the Constitution truly means also symbolizes a larger debate about what the idea of India means.[70]

National identity is about national self-determination and how a society perceives and defines itself.[71] A national identity is fundamentally multidimensional; it can never be reduced to a single element.[72] However, it is limited by its history and the way it is shaped by its history.[73] As British political theorist and academic Bhikhu Parekh puts it, national identity 'cannot be defined in the abstract but only in the light of the country's history, present circumstances and self-understanding, hopes for the future, and its assessment of the kind of world that is beginning to emerge and with which it has to cope'.[74] Like personal identity, the construction of national identity entails a judicious balance of continuity and change. When a constitution seeks to separate the future from the past in a manner that engenders transformative change, it leads to a transformation in national identity as well.[75] While constitutional identity is influenced by the peculiarities of a country, the constitution or its interpretation can in turn, shape collective self-identity.[76]

In India, the acceptance of heterogeneous identities and diverse ways of life through constitutional enactments and discourse has made the concept of citizenship more 'inclusive' and 'representative'. An example of change brought in through constitutional enactment is the decentralization of power through the Seventy-Third and Seventy-Fourth Amendments, which granted constitutional status to rural and urban bodies of local governance. Through the Seventy-Third Amendment, the Panchayati Raj system became an integral part of the Indian federal system.[77] It has led to a three-tier system of government where authority is divided between the Central level, the federal units and about half a million village councils. With a quota for women and marginal social groups belonging to the Scheduled Castes and Scheduled Tribes, these bodies have broadened the social base of the modern state.[78] It has led to the devolution of power beyond the state and national level and given a much-needed impetus to grassroots politics.

The provision for representation of women in rural and urban local bodies is a significant step towards equalizing power relations. Rural women, whose voices and interests have so far been stifled by deep-rooted patriarchal notions, are now given a participatory role in the government. While the barriers of gender division of labour, women's low levels of mobility, seclusion, lack of information and negotiation skills and stereotypes have not disappeared overnight, reservations have provided an opportunity for women's entry into a non-traditional space and a possibility for erosion of traditional gender, caste, class roles and hierarchy.[79] Through these enactments, the constitution, identity and reach of electoral politics has been altered.

The Constitution also accommodates the regional and linguistic diversity in India. Language not only expresses identity, but it also constructs it. Language was a basic marker of national and regional identity and a contentious subject in pre-Independence debates. In light of India's incredible linguistic diversity, instead of adopting a national language, a category of 'official languages' was adopted in which public business could be conducted. Alongside Hindi and English, India has a schedule which recognizes twenty-two languages. Further, even the status of English and Hindi has been subject to parliamentary review every ten years, so that these languages are not granted an irrevocable status in a country whose identity is constantly changing.

The Constitution tacitly provides that the regions comprising 'India' were not based on fixed or unalterable boundaries. These boundaries could be redrawn, which can be seen as recently as 2014 with the creation of Telangana. Regional identities were not required to be subsumed within an all-encompassing Indian identity—the Constitution enabled the creation of new regional identities and 'to accede to claims of various cultural groups for their own regional governments'.[80]

Sunil Khilnani,[81] a political scientist and public intellectual, argues that India's core framework as a democracy has enabled the emergence of diverse and often contrasting political identities—sometimes even those political identities that wish to limit the country's inherent diversity in the name of a narrower conception of what the nation represents.[82] But the working of the Indian democracy is also what limits these movements that envisage these narrow conceptions of Indian identity.[83] It allows not just the exploration of its propositional content but also an arbitration of contesting interpretations of the core values on which the nation's polity is based.[84] The working of the Indian Constitution has ensured that the question of the form and content of the Indian nation stays continuously in contention.[85] It is evident that some of the ideals are disputed and have become an integral part of political discourse—debated, discussed and contested in different political arenas.[86] Courts are also an important arena where contestation of these ideals takes place, and interpretation of these ideals by courts plays a crucial role in shaping the fabric of the nation.

Michel Rosenfeld, a constitutional law scholar, remarks that the establishment of a constitutional identity over time requires the weaving together of the 'past of the framers, one's own present, and the future of unborn generations'.[87] Since the past and future are both uncertain and open to conflicting possibilities, unearthing threads of continuity involves several complications. For even if the framers' actual intent were accessible, their relevance and binding character on posterity could always be disputed. Rosenfeld notes that since the framers' intent can be construed at several levels of abstraction, it provides room for the reinterpretation and reconstruction of one's constitutional identity.

Our body of constitutional law is fascinating in how it invokes fidelity to the original text, precedent and the founders' intent—elements rooted in the past—to dynamically reinterpret the

Constitution's ideals and its subjects, ensuring relevance amid societal change.[88]

The courtroom is a site where, in the words of Madhav Khosla,[89] an author and a professor of constitutional law at Columbia University, 'the Constitution is regularly made and unmade, interpreted and reinterpreted, and understood and misunderstood'.[90] Courts are not the only site where this happens; this is also done through the formal means of constitutional amendment.

We are witnessing a gradual emancipation of the individual in domestic and international law. This emancipation has translated to an increase in autonomy and personal freedom, which also includes the freedom of individuals to choose the multiple components of their identity—religion, nationality, profession, sexuality—and to form freely chosen affiliations. This development is not limited to Western society but has been driven by variables such as urbanization, the communications revolution, education and economic development. In this evolving context of individual autonomy and personal liberty, individuals increasingly select the components of their identity, choosing one or several from among multiple possible affiliations and questioning—even sometimes rejecting—the imposed or inherited forms of socialization. While these new identities are not based on geography and genetics, they nevertheless generate powerful new imagined communities that will affect the way we live, work and love.

Modalities of legal subjectivity, identity and citizenship are rapidly shifting in the context of contemporary globalization.[91] While state nationalism remains a strong force, there concurrently exist several other modes of connection that are shaping people's sense of personal and collective identities. This new range of legal relations is 'brought about by new labor markets, new industries and commodities, new forms of secular and religious violence, new cultural and sexual politics, new reproductive technologies, new materialist understandings of agency, and a rethinking of the autonomous subject/citizen with increasing attention being given to a blurring of conventional divides between the human and non-human'.[92]

Emerging changes in science and technology pose a challenge to our legal and constitutional values by disrupting conceptions of the very definition of personhood and identity.

Rosenfeld addresses the dilemma of how constitutional identity can distance itself sufficiently from identities against which it needs to forge its own distinct identity while, at the same time, engaging enough with these identities to remain viable within its own socio-political environment.[93] The burgeoning of multifaceted and intersectional identities, accompanied by an acknowledgement of the inherent fluidity in various identities, lends to the indispensable requirement of a Constitution that keeps pace with these identities.

In *Joseph Shine*,[94] the Supreme Court recognized the need to decimate antiquarian stereotypes associated with the identity of a married woman, which shackle her to a less than equal existence. In India, the delineation of public and private spaces is significant to the lives of women. The factum of marriage alters their identity in a way that the veneer of 'privacy' in marriage and other familial structures lends impunity to the patriarchal domination of women. Through her scholarly work, Catharine A. Mackinnon, American feminist legal scholar, activist and author, implores us to interrogate the treatment of women in the family sphere, termed 'personal', and view it as a 'crucible of women's unequal status and subordinate treatment sexually, physically, economically, and civilly'.[95] It was imperative for constitutional discourse to engage with this dichotomy and reinvent discourse about the identity of a married woman, which has a significant bearing on both the public and private lives of women.

In *Navtej Singh Johar*,[96] the differential impact of identities was evident when we recognized that for individuals who fall outside the framework of the heteronormative, even the conception of a 'private space' is utopian. The home is often reduced to a public space, as heteronormativity within the family relegates their identity to closets. In one sense, the case concerned the subjugation of adults engaging in consensual intercourse. In another sense, the case required us to interrogate the limits of citizenship envisaged by the Constitution, which includes the metaphors of 'inclusion' and 'belonging'.

In observing the multiple institutions—social, legal and political—at play to relegate the identities of these individuals into obscurity and oblivion, the case required a recognition of the identity of the Constitution as deeply committed to pluralism, to preserving diversity and being morally committed to enabling individuals as holders of rights to define their vision of equal citizenship. Recognizing a deeply polyvocal identity of the Constitution enabled us to question the straightjacket 'order of nature' formula employed to create binaries and enforce gender stereotypes. At a deeper level, then, the question in *Navtej Singh Johar* was a recognition of the Constitution's commitment to the protection of minorities in their struggle for self-determination and expression.[97]

> The Constitution admits to its imperfections and compromises. It preserves stability and allows for change. We say that the Constitution is the supreme law, but it is important for us to access it, engage with it and interrogate its meaning from time to time. Its entrenchment and progress are marked less by a perfection of consensus than by a refinement of debate.[98] Protection on the basis of identity groups has unintended side effects. Can a state empower its citizens by classifying them? Or does categorization of citizens reinforce the very categories they are meant to eradicate? As judges, the task of adjudication becomes particularly complex when we try to apply these oversimplified categories in complex social situations. Judges and administrators are less fortunate than social scientists: they must at some point draw lines between rival claimants, rewarding one and sending the other home empty handed.[99]

In the *Sabarimala Temple Entry* case,[100] we were confronted with a conflict between religious practices and the claim of dignity for women in matters of faith and worship. The Constitution recognizes both individual rights and group rights. But the question in the case required the court to interrogate the role of the individual in the identity of the Constitution.

In *Sabarimala Temple Entry* case, we recognized that inherent to the identity of our Constitution is the equality of individuals to find liberation in worship. Inherent in this identity was the notion that though the Constitution provided for group and community rights, liberty in matters of belief, faith, and worship must produce a compassionate and humane society marked by the equality of status among all its citizens. In interrogating the boundaries of religion, the Supreme Court recognized the aspiration of the drafters for a society marked by not just the equality of all *men*, but of all *individuals*. In recognizing that the stigma around menstruation subjugated women to a 'patriarchal order', the judgment presented an opportunity to recognize the unravelling of deeply entrenched social structures as envisaged by the framers and integral to the identity of an ameliorative Constitution.

Law represents a dichotomy that can both limit the expression of individual and group aspirations and simultaneously provide powerful resources for marginalized groups to assert their interests, to articulate their claims and to reconfigure their identities.[101] Viewing law as a set of symbols and norms that are integral to the constitution of relations among citizens draws our attention to how ordinary people (re)create law in their everyday lives.[102] But it is important to acknowledge that law is merely one facet of how individuals negotiate their daily interactions and instigate social change.[103] Social and political contexts and the particularities of history and culture play equally important roles in mobilizing individuals and groups to contest or affirm legal norms.[104]

I had the occasion to deal with the issue of identity in the present-day technological era in the *Aadhaar* case.[105] In my opinion, the Aadhaar Act subsumed all characteristics of a person to merely their biometric data. The myriad forms of expressing identity were pigeonholed into just biometric information. The concept of identity was 'flipped' so that identification through identifiers became the only form of identity in the time of database governance. This involved a radical transformation in the position of the individual. In holding the Aadhaar Act to be unconstitutional, I held that identity includes the right to determine the forms through which identity is expressed and the right not to be identified. When the Constitution protects our right to be and to be what we are, it creates a space where the individual is sheltered from interference. By recognizing our liberty as autonomous persons, the Constitution recognizes our ability to preserve and shape our identities in interactions with others.

But in my opinion, the *Aadhaar* case was not merely about the conflation of identity and identification; there was also a larger question of institutions, the functioning of which was crucial to our constitutional identity. According to me, superseding the authority of the Rajya Sabha by passing the Aadhaar Bill as a money bill was in conflict with the constitutional framework and the legitimacy of democratic institutions. Passing of the Bill as a money bill, when it does not qualify for it, in my view, damages the delicate balance of bicameralism, which is envisaged as a part of the basic structure of the Constitution. Similarly, the interplay of technology and freedom in the *Aadhaar* case was about a much larger question of the balance between the power of the State and the rights of its citizens—one of the fundamental tenets of constitutionalism.

In the *Aadhaar* judgment, I also referred to Amartya Sen's analysis of choice and reason in the domain of identities:

> Each of us invokes identities based on context—identities are thus contextual and have relevance depending on the context. The point he says is not whether we are free to choose any identity, but that we have choices over alternative identities or combination of identities, and perhaps more importantly whether we have some freedom in deciding what priority to give the various identities that we may simultaneously have.[106]

In the context of a living constitution, constitutional identity is the product of a dynamic process that is always open to further elaboration and revision.[107] The approach of transformative constitutionalism must go beyond 'who we are' to 'who we can be', both to ourselves and to each other and how we can use constitutional morality as a transformative power to address the myriad forms of inequalities that divide all of us.[108]

The prescient words of philosopher and writer Kwame Anthony Appiah come to my mind:

> There's no dispensing with identities, but we need to understand them better if we can hope to reconfigure them and free ourselves from mistakes about them that are often a couple of hundred years old. Much of what is dangerous about them has to do with the way identities— religion, nation, race, class, and culture—divide us and set us against one another. They can be the enemies of human solidarity, the sources of war, horsemen of scores of apocalypses, from apartheid to genocide. Yet these errors are also Central to the way identities unite us today. We need to reform them, because at their best, they make it possible for groups large and small to do things together. They are the lies that bind.[109]

While we acknowledge the inescapability of identities and their immense potential, both constructive and destructive, in shaping the course of our lives, we must always remember that these identities are not set in stone. We live in a world of changing identities, constructed and reconstructed by ideas of religion, gender and politics. In a country teeming with these evolving and often conflicting identities, the invention and reinvention of constitutional identity assume great significance. It must be so imagined, that it embraces these differences and gives them a meaningful existence.

11

A Borrowed Constitution

Fact or Myth?[1]

It is my distinct honour to be present before this august gathering to celebrate the birth centenary of the 'Courtroom Genius'.[2] Nani Palkhivala is a man who needs no introduction; however, do accept my humble attempt this evening.

As the story goes, Palkhivala was an academically bright student with a deep love for literature. Early on in his life, he wanted to become a lecturer in literature and held a BA and MA in the area as well. As fate would have it, however, he was passed over for the position, and he finally relented to the wishes of his father and began his study of law. It is a true testament to the power of fate, that the greatest lawyer of India was one by accident.

When he began his legal practice, he found unparalleled success, especially considering his young age and the fact that his family had no legal background. Over the years, his practice broadened to include areas of labour law, and he went on to represent India at various international tribunals and courts, such as the International Court of Justice and the International Civil Aviation Organization.

He was widely known for his expertise on taxation law and wrote the famous book titled *Law and Practice of Income Tax* with J.B.

Kanga, one of the doyens of the illustrious Bombay Bar.[3] The book was such a success that it had a permanent place in the court of Chief Justice M.C. Chagla of the Bombay High Court, who referred to it as 'the Book'. However, apart from educating the legal community, he felt a sense of greater responsibility towards educating the general citizenry about the law that governs them. In his early thirties, Nani started his Budget Speeches, where he simplified the Annual Budget of the Central government, sans the legalese, for the understanding of the common man. The speeches, which started from a small hall in a hotel, moved to the famous Brabourne Stadium in Mumbai as the spectators grew larger in number. However, he is most fondly remembered for his contribution to constitutional law. Palkhivala's fidelity to the Constitution is unmatched. He firmly believed that the Constitution was supreme, as is seen from his written submissions in *Kesavananda Bharati*,[4] where he argued that:

> Ours is a controlled 'Constitution' *par excellence*. All institutions, including the Parliament, are merely creatures of the Constitution and none of them is its master.[5]

He dedicated a large part of his life to the protection of this 'ideal' of the Constitution, which he believed was crucial for the development of modern India. Such was his passion that when the hearings, which sought to review *Kesavananda Bharati*, concluded, Justice H.R. Khanna commented:

> It was not Nani who spoke. It was Divinity speaking through him. Later I asked some of my brother judges for their reaction, and all of them were of the same opinion.[6]

Through the course of his legal career, he appeared in many cases of constitutional significance: *R.C. Cooper v. Union of India*,[7] where the court upheld the right of the government to nationalize banks; *Madhav Rao Scindia v. Union of India*,[8] where the Supreme Court struck down the presidential order, which derecognized all rulers across the country; *Bennett Coleman & Co. Ltd v. Union of India,*[9] where the Supreme Court struck down the newsprint control policy as violative of Articles 14 and 19(1)(a); *Kesavananda Bharati v. State of Kerala,*[10] where the 'basic structure' doctrine was evolved; *Minerva Mills Ltd. & Ors v. Union of India & Ors,*[11] where the amendments made to Article 31C through the Forty-Second Constitutional Amendment were struck down, to name just a few.

It is Palkhivala's contribution to our constitutional landscape, and its role in shaping the social fabric of modern India that has led me to choose the topic for today's lecture. Today, I shall attempt to debunk the oft-quoted myth that our Constitution is a 'borrowed' one, and that our Constituent Assembly did nothing more than to stitch together parts from different constitutions. The allegations of our Constitution being heavily borrowed are as old as the Constitution itself. Some of the members of the Constituent Assembly were, in fact, very vocal in expressing their concerns. One member called it 'Music of a Western Band' as opposed to 'Veena or Sitar'.[12] Another called it 'slavish surrender to the West'.[13] These allegations duly received a reply by Dr Ambedkar, who said:

> There is nothing to be ashamed of in borrowing. It involves no plagiarism. Nobody holds any patent rights in the fundamental ideas of a Constitution.[14]

Before I embark on this task to dispel the myth that our Constitution is a borrowed one, let me briefly address the question as to why the 'uniqueness' or the 'Indianness' of our Constitution is even relevant to begin with. To understand this, we must ask ourselves: What role does a constitution play in our society?

Michel Rosenfeld, a leading scholar in comparative constitutional law, posits that constitutions often take people as they are, and yet seek to make something more out of them by ascribing to them an identity through their text.[15] Often, the identity is created by referring to narratives of sameness and selfhood, along with offering a common aspiration for the future.[16] Hence, it would not be amiss to say that a constitution such as ours, which was created as an outcome of political struggle and a revolutionary freedom movement, was important in bringing about unity and stability to a young nation. However, while this Constitution serves as the base upon which we find our identity as 'We, the People' of India, it is equally imperative that we are able to identify our Constitution as 'Indian' too.[17] With this in mind, I begin with my task of taking you through the history of some of our provisions.

Any discussion of this nature must begin by addressing the claim that the concept of fundamental rights in Part III of our Constitution has been borrowed from the American Bill of Rights. However, one would not have to travel too far to realize that the idea of a set of inviolable justiciable rights, which are fundamental to every citizen, had been vehemently argued for throughout our freedom struggle, and the ultimate list of protected rights had grown organically.

This organic exercise in the creation of our fundamental rights began with the Constitution of India Bill of 1895, believed to have been inspired by Lokmanya Tilak. It set forth a 'variety of rights including those of free speech, imprisonment only by competent authority, and of free state education'.[18] This was followed by the Commonwealth of India Bill of 1925, which was authored by Annie Besant. Within it were seven provisions for fundamental rights, stating that individual liberty, freedom of conscience, free expression of opinion, free assembly and equality before the law were to be guaranteed.[19] Ultimately, the fundamental rights contained in our Constitution were in large part derived from the Fundamental Rights Chapter of the Nehru Report of 1928, a product of the Forty-Third Annual Session of the Indian National Congress.[20] Taken together, these documents highlight how the concept of guaranteed fundamental rights for all citizens of India was almost fifty years in the making when the Constituent Assembly considered it.[21]

Furthermore, if one needed more proof that the rights framework in Part III has evolved from the debates within our freedom movement and can be seen as distinct from the American Bill of Rights, one would only have to look at the 'due process' clauses in both the constitutions. While discussing the grounds for restriction, the present Article 21, the Constituent Assembly was at a crossroads between the phrase 'due process' (found in the Constitution of the United States) and 'procedure established by law' (found in the Japanese Constitution). To find an answer, B.N. Rau (adviser to the Constituent Assembly) visited Justice Felix Frankfurter, a sitting US Supreme Court judge. Justice Frankfurter advised Rau that the due process provision has resulted in the striking down of several beneficial legislations in the US and is a hindrance in the welfare schemes of the government.[22] Therefore, given the nascent stage of the Indian economy, they deemed it fit to incorporate 'procedure established by law', so as to protect beneficial legislations from unnecessary challenges. The social and economic needs of the country played an important role in deciding the course here.

Of course, our Supreme Court ultimately did move away from this understanding, which I shall address a little later in this lecture.

A second and related set of provisions which have been alleged to be borrowed are the Directive Principles of State Policy in Part IV of our Constitution. It is argued that they were borrowed from the Irish Constitution. However, it was the Karachi Resolution, adopted by a session of Congress in March 1931, which first extended the sphere of rights from purely negative rights to an articulation of positive obligations to provide the masses 'with the economic and social conditions in which their negative rights would have actual meaning'.[23] The Karachi Resolution can be seen as the 'spiritual' and 'direct' antecedent of the Directive Principles.[24] Furthermore, it was the Sapru Report of 1945, which helped outline the fundamental distinction between 'justiciable' and 'non-justiciable' rights, which came to be embedded in Part III and IV of the Constitution.[25] Hence, we find that discussions about the nature of positive non-justiciable rights took place in the Indian freedom movement long before the Constituent Assembly came into existence.

Moving on, if one were to look at concepts such as secularism and federalism, their interpretation in India is unique. The Indian model of secularism is distinct from the US model, which advocates a bilateral exclusion of the State from religion and vice versa, and also the French model, which advocates a one-way exclusion. Rather, it is rightly asserted by Professor Rajeev Bhargava that the Indian State exhibits a duality of both respect and disrespect for religion, instead of a singular disinterest. Thus, the Indian State can, and indeed does, interfere with religion when undertaking a reformation of its negative aspects, which infringe upon the fundamental rights of its citizens.[26]

It is also alleged that the makers of the Indian Constitution borrowed heavily from our own colonial oppressor. It is argued that many of the administrative provisions in the Constitution find their roots in the colonial administrative structure which was created by the Government of India Act, 1935. However, before our Constitution succumbs to this allegation, we must understand the unique context in which it was drafted. While our Constitution was similar to the likes of the American Constitution, inasmuch as it was the result of a freedom struggle against our colonial oppressor, and was influenced by the event of Partition and the transgressions that took place during this period.

Political scientist Sandipto Dasgupta aptly describes the circumstances in which the Constituent Assembly found itself in the following words:

> The nature of the anticolonial struggle that led to independence, and the material conditions of Indian society at large, meant that there was no existing consensus on the nature of a new political or social order . . . Therefore, the framers had to be attendant simultaneously to both the creation of the Constitution and the conditions that make such a creation viable. Their task could hence be defined as crafting a constitution that brings about the conditions of its own possibility.[27]

Hence, the Constituent Assembly was faced with a duality in its own role: of drafting the new constitution of the country and of also administering it in the interim, in order to be able to foster a system where the new constitution could be effectively utilized. One must remember that our Constituent Assembly consisted of many leaders who had gained from their experiences as administrators under the British Rule. So, it is unsurprising that they chose to continue with an administrative apparatus similar to the British in order to maintain administrative stability. However, it is argued by Dasgupta that continuing with such an apparatus did not mean ignoring 'the most fundamental shift in the nature of the two regimes—from an absolutist to a democratic one'.[28]

This shift can be seen very clearly from a speech Jawaharlal Nehru delivered to a new cadre of officers joining the Indian Police Services in 1952. He insisted that since an 'enormous break' had occurred from a non-democratic colonial regime to a democratic postcolonial one, it also necessitated a shift in the orientation of the executive.[29] He said that:

> [The police] have not only to deal with crime . . . and disorder in a general sort of way, but the real additional duty of the police, as of all of us, is that of dealing with human beings in the mass, not as something to be commanded or ordered about but as something to be won over and persuaded and guided.[30]

Having now taken all of you through the history of some of our constitutional provisions, I hope I have been able to, if not discharge the 'myth' that ours is a 'borrowed' Constitution, at least make us question its foundation. While undoubtedly our Constituent Assembly may have 'borrowed' certain concepts from foreign constitutions, it firmly made them unique to India before incorporating them.

But while we all know that the text of the Constitution often forms the clearest representation of its identity, it is not coterminous with it.[31] The identity of the Constitution has evolved through judicial interpretation. This is seen most obviously from the line of cases I had referred to earlier, which ended up incorporating the 'due process' guarantee in Article 21 similar to that of the Constitution of the United States, even though the drafted text may have suggested otherwise.[32] Similarly, the scope of Article 21 has been broadened to include multiple rights. One of the most recent cases is *K.S. Puttaswamy*,[33] where the Supreme Court read in the right to privacy in our Constitution under Article 21. Cases such as this go on to reflect the role our courts continue to play in developing the identity of our Constitution. Indeed, Palkhivala had once said the following words about our courts:

> So long as the Constitution endures, these Courts must exist. They decide the fierce controversies which in other countries are determined by the arbitrament of force; they maintain the most fundamental equilibriums of our society; they are the agency of a sovereign people to expound the Constitution and to ensure that its mandates are respected.[34]

A common factor noticeable in many cases that have broadened the scope of the rights available under Part III is their reliance on foreign jurisprudence in order to substantiate their reasoning. And this brings me to the second part of my lecture, which is about judicial borrowing from foreign courts.

Before I begin to justify this form of 'judicial borrowing', it is imperative for me to state one commonly held view: that many of our core Constitutional provisions, such as the ones on fundamental rights, are often drafted in abstract terms in order to facilitate their growth with the changes in the society around them. Therefore, I believe that when judges engage in constitutional interpretation of these rather abstract principles, it is quite useful to look at how other judges in foreign jurisdictions have similarly considered such problems.[35]

Eminent scholar Gary Jacobsohn argues that 'borrowing' of foreign constitutional material is useful in closing the gap which arises between the aspirations of a society and the actual constitutional rules in place.[36] His thesis is one that arises from a 'contextualist' approach to judicial borrowing, which tries to place the foreign legal norms within the context of a country's unique situation before using them.[37]

On the other hand, Sujit Choudhary, a constitutional law scholar and academic, recommends a 'dialogical' model of borrowing where comparative constitutional materials are interpretive foils or tools for constitutional self-reflection.[38] They help in identifying exactly what is special or distinctive about our constitutional order, since its uniqueness arises only in comparison to others.[39] Hence, when we engage with material arising from constitutions other than our own, we learn from their experiences in having dealt with situations similar to ours.[40] Through their experiences, we question the assumptions they have made, which in turn serve as *stimuli* for us to question our own assumptions about our constitutional order.[41] Therefore, such an engagement, according to Choudhary, is not really 'borrowing' but rather is using the foreign material to critically reassess our own constitutional ideas.

Now, if one were to start considering the objections to the use of foreign legal material, Justice Antonin Scalia of the US Supreme Court often held the strongest opposition. He argued that since such materials were not binding on the judges, they should not be used at all. He believed that there was no reason why the US, given its unique constitution and constitutional history, should even try to conform to the traditions of the rest of the world.[42]

Even in our own court, a similar objection to the use of foreign legal material was noted in the judgment of *Suresh Kumar Koushal*.[43] While overturning the judgment of the Delhi High Court in *Naz Foundation*,[44] there was a refusal to engage with the foreign jurisprudence cited by the Delhi High Court in order to understand the violation of the rights of the members of the LGBTQIA+ community under Articles 14, 15 and 21. It was argued that a decision of a foreign court, passed in a different context, could not be made applicable to ourselves. However, our court, while overturning the decision in *Suresh Kumar Koushal* and *Navtej Singh Johar*[45] relied upon a substantial amount of comparative material from other jurisdictions while coming to its conclusion. I believe that this form of 'judicial borrowing' is similar to the 'borrowing' done by our Constituent Assembly because, in engaging with such foreign legal material, we have not considered ourselves bound blindly by their reasoning. To the contrary, they have been used to broaden our own understanding of the rights individuals possess under our constitutional framework. Justice Albie Sachs of the South African Constitutional Court has aptly spoken:

> [When] I draw on statements by certain United States Supreme Court Justices, I do so not because I treat their decisions as precedents to be applied in our Courts, but because their dicta articulate in an elegant and helpful manner problems which face any modern court . . . Thus, though drawn from another legal culture, they express values and dilemmas in a way which I find most helpful in elucidating the meaning of our own constitutional text.[46]

In fact, if one were to look at the history of our Supreme Court, one would find that the use of foreign legal material has always been prevalent. The only opposition to it has been when they have been accepted uncritically and without thought to our own constitutional provisions.[47] It would also do us well to not forget that the origin of the 'basic structure' doctrine evolved in the *Kesavananda Bharati* case, was also from an article written by the German scholar Dietrich Conrad.[48]

Therefore, I find no hesitation in stating that judges can, and rather should, engage with materials from foreign jurisdictions while interpreting our Constitution. Doing so will not take away from the 'Indianness' of the Constitution's unique identity because the migration of ideas only contributes in its evolution without transplanting its soul.

It is important for us to remember that ultimately, the idea of any Constitution finds its deepest meaning in the role of people and their actions. The Constitution expects its citizens to fully realize its transformative potential. Why is the transformative potential so important after all? Because our framers, while adopting the

Constitution, were also aware of the immense social challenges lying ahead of their time. They knew that the real duty of transforming society would ultimately depend on citizens. History would not judge our constitution by the uniqueness it exhibited. Instead, it would judge them by the transformation that entailed. While the three wings of the government are tasked with their own constitutional mandates, the mantle of achieving the transformative ideals of our Constitution lies equally with citizens. Hanna Fenichel Pitkin, a leading scholar in political science, puts it beautifully in the following words:

> [C]onstitutions are made, not found. They do not fall miraculously from the sky or grow naturally on the vine; they are human creations, products of convention, choice, the specific history of a particular people, and (almost always) a political struggle in which some win and others lose. Indeed, in this vein one might even want to argue that our constitution is more something we do than something we make: we (re) shape it all the time through our collective activity.[49]

The task of realising the vision of the Indian Constitution falls upon every single citizen every day and in everything that we do. I am reminded of the prescient words of Nani Palkhivala himself. He said that:

> WE, THE PEOPLE OF INDIA, adopted, enacted and gave to ourselves the Constitution. We, the people, are also its only keepers . . . There is need in our time and land to remind ourselves that the Constitution is intended not merely to provide for the exigencies of the moment but to endure through a long lapse of years . . . The Constitution was meant to impart such a momentum to the living spirit of the rule of law that democracy and civil liberty may survive in India beyond our own times and in the days when our place will know us no more . . . Freedom cannot be inherited in the bloodstream. Each generation will

> have to defend it and fight for it then alone will it survive to be passed on to the next.[50]

Palkhivala had written two books titled *We, the People* and *We, the Nation*. When Palkhivala passed away, a poster regarding his demise described the loss most succinctly by saying, 'We the Nation, We the People, have lost a legend.' I would like to take the liberty to change that slightly to describe how I truly feel: 'We the Nation, We the People, were fortunate to have had such a legend amongst us.'

12

The Rules That Are India

From Plurality to Pluralism[1]

Justice Prabodh Dinkarrao Desai had the unique distinction of being appointed as a judge of the High Court of Gujarat when he was barely thirty-nine. Over a distinguished career, he functioned as the Chief Justice of three High Courts in succession: those of Himachal Pradesh, Calcutta and Bombay between December 1983 and December 1992. That a person who was appointed as a High Court judge so young and yet was overlooked by destiny or the higher powers (whichever way one looks at it) must remain another aberration in contemporary times when it comes to the process of judicial appointments. When the call for higher judicial office came, Chief Justice P.D. Desai preferred to retire from the Bombay High Court; so fiercely was he protective of his own independence and integrity.

There are vivid memories of my experiences as a young member of the bar who frequented his court unfailingly each day as a keen admirer of his court-craft and yearning for justice with an occasional brief. Administrative law flourished under his nuanced understanding just as labour law became the source of justice to unsung citizens. This was a unique amalgam: in administrative law, Chief Justice

P.D. Desai found an ally for the rigour of his intellectual discipline. In labour law, he found a bond for his compassion.

The Bombay High Court assembled at 11 a.m. in those days. Three-quarters of the first hour in his courtroom was a sight to witness. As young lawyers, we would remark that the durbar had assembled in PD's court. This was when he would list cases for mediation before him. The judge would use everything under his command, from persuasion to authority, to bring about just solutions. Chief Justice Desai could brook no excuse for unprepared counsel. His court had no place for the incompetent, and he could never tolerate a fool. But ironically, this strict disciplinarian was benevolent towards young juniors. Their immaturity was a challenge for him to overcome in finding true justice. Grooming them was his passion.

I had a unique opportunity to interact with him when he was a member of the inquiry committee set up as part of the impeachment process of a judge of the Supreme Court. I was to return home from New Delhi by an evening flight after attending a hearing in the Supreme Court. I had been tasked with the duty of delivering a sealed cover of the report to the residence of the Chief Justice. When I reached his residence at 9.30 p.m., he was waiting in his drawing room. He went inside the house and returned with a glass of tender coconut water. He was a different person, unfailingly kind, but distinctly proper.

Chief Justice Desai was a worthy successor in the traditions of the Bombay High Court, a court set in the post-Independence traditions of remedying injustices and sufferings. Towering behind the Chief Justice's seat in the Chief Justice's court are the portraits of Chief Justice Chagla and Sir Lawrence Jenkins. Looking over the shoulders of the Chief Justice, they would, I believe, invoke the message of the life of this great judge to say: 'This was indeed a judge in the path that we set.'

As a young boy, I remember having a toy called the Russian doll. They are also called Matryoshka dolls, dating back to 1890. The wooden doll has within it another smaller wooden doll, and this continues for ten iterations. When nested together one after the other, the doll is complete. However, if a single iteration is missed, the final form does not take shape. There is a deep lesson that the toy symbolizes—every iteration depends on and supports each other to take the final form. The doll is complete only when the inherent value of each part is recognized. In many ways, the Matryoshka doll is a metaphor for our country. India as a whole, boasts of significant diversity—heterogeneous along a number of intersecting dimensions, including race, class, religion and culture. This diversity is further defined across several axes: cultural, social and epistemic[2] and outlays diverse values, opinions and perspectives. In the plural mansion that is independent India, lies a population of over 1.3 billion people comprising several thousand communities.

At the framing of the Indian Constitution, questions arose on how independent India was to account for its heterogeneous polity. Uday Mehta, a political scientist, eloquently elucidates the immense range of social realities that the founding members were called upon to address and how the document they gave birth to sought to unify a divergent India by accommodating all people who called India their home. For the founders, the Constitution was premised on both a deep trust in the tolerant nature of its citizens and an unshakeable belief that our diversity would be a source of strength. As Mehta observes,[3] where the population was largely illiterate, the Constitution conferred Universal Adult Franchise. Where the population was diverse and assorted, the Constitution conferred citizenship without regard to race, caste, religion or creed. Where the people were deeply religious, the Constitution adopted the principle of secularism. Where the Indian State stood united, the Constitution created a federal democracy with all the political instruments necessary for local self-governance. Diversity within the strands of the Constitution is a reflection of the diversity of her people. One cannot exist without the other.

During the framing of the Constitution, the framers had to address two strands in political thought: liberalism and pluralism. Liberalism meant that people 'order their Actions . . . as they think fit . . . without asking leave, or depending on the Will of any other men'.[4] Thinkers from Locke to Rawls agreed on the fundamental liberal principle—that the burden of justification falls upon those who seek to interfere with liberty.[5] This entailed questioning the reason to obey monarchs and led to the idea that rulers are bound by a set of rules as encapsulated in the *Magna Carta*. The negative conception of liberty that emphasized the absence of interference was soon replaced with a positive conception—that liberty went beyond a guarantee of non-interference. It referred to the creation and sustenance of conditions conducive to the free *exercise* of rights.[6] It was then natural that pluralism—conceptualized as people pursuing a plurality of values, ends and cultural life[7]—would seem to conflict with the absolute exercise of freedom by every individual. Take, for example, a linguistic minority seeking to introduce their language as a compulsory subject in schools established by them. A student could argue against this, claiming an absolute freedom of choice.

The Constituent Assembly was tasked with expressing the equal worth of every individual,[8] as well as addressing the social reality of diversity along many axes. Another significant issue called for attention: How was the Indian State to protect cultural and group identity and ensure the prevention of disability that arose from membership of certain groups?

The rights encapsulated in Part III of the Constitution are a good starting point to understand the broad idealism of the framers in crafting a document that sought to balance these seemingly conflicting threads in political thought to ensure a delicate balance, in the guarantee of individual liberty and the protection of a plural polity. The rights are best understood in three broad senses:

The *first* set of rights articulates a commitment to individual liberalism. The right to equality,[9] the right to freedom of speech and expression,[10] the right to move freely throughout the territory of India,[11] and the right to life and personal liberty[12] ensured a fundamental commitment to individualism in a liberal democracy. Every individual was guaranteed the protection and the free exercise of individual rights for the fulfilment of any end considered to be of fitting value to them. The *second* set of rights is framed in terms of group rights. These include the right of religious denominations to establish and maintain institutions for religious and charitable purposes,[13] or the right of a 'section of the citizens' to conserve a distinct language, script or culture.[14] Another striking example of this is the power of the State to restrict the freedom to form associations or unions or move around freely throughout the territory of India, 'for the protection of the interests of any Scheduled Tribe'.[15] This demonstrates that the Indian Constitution recognizes certain groups as *direct* bearers of constitutional rights.[16] The location of groups as distinct bearers of rights was nested in the understanding that membership of groups had a unique role in crafting and determining individual identity.

It is the *third* set of rights that demonstrates a true understanding of the perceived tension between the liberal and plural strands of the Indian polity. While the framers were awake to the notion that the fulfilment of certain individual rights existed only in relation to groups, it was equally important for them to recognize that membership of certain social groups prevented the fulfilment of the liberal ideal that the Constitution sought to guarantee. This required the recognition that formal equality would only preserve the inequalities faced by individuals by virtue of their membership of groups. Take, for example, a religious group that prohibits the entry of women into institutions of worship grounded in their physiological characteristics. Here, inequality on the basis of sex is grounded in the membership of the group that seeks to prevent their entry. For this reason, the State was empowered to provide for social welfare and reform by throwing open Hindu religious institutions of a public character to all sections of Hindus. Similarly, the Constitution enacted a complete ban on untouchability and its practice in 'any form'. The Constitution also stipulates that no citizen is to be subject to any disability or condition with regard to access to public spaces and the use of public resources on the grounds of religion, race, caste, sex or place of birth and that the State is empowered to legislate special provisions for the advancement of any socially and educationally backward class of citizens.

In elevating groups as distinct rights holders as well as empowering State intervention to address historical injustice and inequality perpetrated by group membership, the framers located liberalism within the pluralist reality of India and conceptualized every individual as located at an intersection between 'liberal individualism and plural belonging'.[17] In the framing of the Indian Constitution, individual identity was constructed to maintain a delicate balance between the commitment to liberal notions of individualism as well as a pluralist conception that formed and shaped individual identity. While its framing demonstrated a remarkable commitment to liberal individualism, it did not ignore, but on the contrary, incorporated the force of a pluralist society in constituting individual identity. This was crucial, for then the provisions of the Constitution hold a significance larger than the sum of its parts, which is found in two distinct understandings of pluralism in Indian polity: an *ameliorative* dimension and a *constitutive* dimension. These two dimensions are crucial in disregarding misconceptions of the meaning of pluralism in Indian society and also in structuring the positive measures required for its protection.

In the *ameliorative* sense,[18] a commitment to pluralism did not imply non-interference, where group practices hinder the constitutional vision of an equal citizenship, premised on equal dignity, worth and liberty of every individual. The constitutional provisions on the freedom of religion best exemplify this. The individual right to the freedom of religion is not intended to prevail over but is subject to the overriding constitutional postulates of equality, liberty and personal freedoms recognized in the other provisions of Part III.[19] The scheme of Articles 25 and 26 of the Constitution does not disturb but strengthens the ethos of Part III of the Constitution, which is premised upon individual autonomy and dignity as the Central overarching values that infuse all fundamental rights with meaning. In the liberal promise of the Constitution, a balance was struck in relation to the position to be accorded to religion in the public sphere: essential but not impregnable. The Constitution went beyond the classical liberal commitment of disenabling people in power by enabling those who have traditionally been deprived of power.[20]

In the *constitutive* sense, the Constitution demonstrates an understanding that group identity and cultural difference play a significant role in shaping individual identity. One example of this is found in the linguistic diversity of our nation. Language is understood not merely as a tool for communication but an identity in itself. Thoughts are not abstract wisps of consciousness but are in fact, conceptualized and grounded in a particular language along with its unique characteristics. In other words, language and its idiosyncrasies fundamentally structure the way we think. Whenever I meet someone who speaks many languages, I sometimes ponder which language they think in. In a historically multilingual society like India, where language is so intrinsic to one's own self of history and identity, the plurality of languages is the plurality of thought itself. George Orwell, in his classic *1984,* highlighted the significance of language. In his dystopian world, the fictional language 'Newspeak' was a controlled language of restricted grammar and limited vocabulary. It was meant to be a vehicle of thought control, meant to limit personal identity, self-expression and free will.[21] For example, the only meaning of the word 'free' in Newspeak was to denote the absence of something—this field is *free* of weeds. Politically, the word was not envisaged to denote free will. Consequently, any such political notion was eliminated from society. Other words that were deliberately omitted from the Newspeak language included justice, science and democracy. Liberty and equality were reduced to a single word—'crimethink', which referred to thought that was considered not in line with the principles of society. This highlighted the political value of controlling language and diversity.

Our sense of group belonging is a significant factor in the formation of identity and provides members with a sense of individual as well as collective forms of identity.[22] We identify with and recognize one another as members of the same group on the basis of shared and divergent values, and have a more or less settled desire that the group should survive and flourish in the future.[23] This unique sense of constituting identity was well understood by the British, who attempted to make such diversity 'manageable'. For example, the notorious Vernacular Press Act of 1878, enacted by Lord Lytton, targeted 'certain publications in oriental languages'.[24] The *Amrita Bazar Patrika* in Calcutta had to convert itself into an all-English weekly within a week of the Act being passed.

Historian Ramachandra Guha in the epilogue to his book, *India After Gandhi*, titled 'Why India Survives' stated that the two cornerstones to the foundation of the Indian Republic are the pluralism of religion and language. He takes the example of our currency notes, which have denominations printed in Hindi and English along with fifteen other languages printed on the reverse side of the note.[25] With each language and each script, he says, comes a distinct culture and regional ethos, nesting within the idea of India as a whole.[26] Today, the Eighth Schedule houses twenty-two languages, which represent the mother tongue of 96.7 per cent of the Indian population.[27] The decision to shift Article 29, which includes the right to conserve distinct languages, from the Fundamental Duties chapter to the Fundamental Rights chapter also elucidates the effort that was taken towards the realization and not just a recognition of pluralism.[28]

This understanding of the role of group life is crucial for the recognition that cultural diversity and pluralism cannot be adequately addressed merely by a principle of non-interference. In the aftermath of the European wars of religion, reformation liberalism emphasized the virtue of *toleration*.[29] However, a commitment to true pluralism implies that the sources of diversity and the claims made by cultural minority groups today are not reducible to the early accounts of religious toleration, which aimed only to promote civil peace and order. Compared to the Western notions of pluralism and multiculturalism, which are limited to State-sponsored allocation of resources, the democratic inclusion and protection of a wide range of cultural minorities and diversity is premised on the inculcation of mutual respect between different communities and the creation of positive spaces for these identities to thrive. In moving beyond merely tolerance, celebrating and protecting diversity is linked with justice, equal concern and respect for every individual.[30]

How, then, does the Indian nation state ensure the creation and sustenance of spaces conducive to realizing the ideals of pluralism? I wish to highlight three things: *first*, the realization of the deliberative ideal; *second*, the continuous process of defining 'India'; and *third*, realizing the constitutional trust placed on every individual through a sense of fraternity.

An essential aspect of any successful democracy is its commitment to the protection of deliberative dialogue. Citizens manifest their equality not only by refraining from interference with the freedom of expression of others; they also do so by sustaining conditions conducive to free communication.[31] At the first level, this is nested within the institutional structures that give the country its laws. Deliberation within the legislature furthers a commitment to the fundamental liberal principles that political outcomes must be justified not by reference to self-interest and power but to *reason* and the ability to convince one another as to why a proposed course of action is beneficial. Beyond the rights-based procedures and goal-based outcomes of the Constitution is a commitment to a deliberation that incorporates the diverse views of all stakeholders concerned, including those who do not support a proposed law. The fine balance between majoritarianism and liberal democratic governance is marked by constitutional principles wedded to the rule of law, the guarantee of individual freedoms and ensuring freedom from discrimination. A democracy welded to the ideal of *reason* and *deliberation* ensures that minority opinions are not strangulated and ensures that every outcome is not a result merely of numbers but of shared consensus.

Where on the one hand due deliberation and consideration within institutional spaces underlines a commitment to pluralism, deliberation by individuals in public spaces, on the other hand, is of equal, if not more, importance. The true test of a democracy is its ability to ensure the creation and protection of spaces where every individual can voice their opinion without the fear of retribution. Inherent in the liberal promise of the Constitution is a commitment to the plurality of opinions. However, the litmus test of any claim of commitment to deliberation is assessed by the response of two key actors: the *State* and other *individuals*. If you wish to deliberate, you must be willing to hear all sides to the story. A legitimate government committed to deliberate dialogue does not seek to restrict political contestation but welcomes it.

As early as the nineteenth century, Raja Ram Mohan Roy protested against the curtailing of the press and argued that a state must be responsive to individuals and make available to them the means by which they may safely communicate their views. This claim is of equal relevance today. The commitment to civil liberty flows directly from the manner in which the state treats dissent. A state committed to the rule of law ensures that the State apparatus is not employed to curb legitimate and peaceful protest but to create spaces conducive to deliberation. Within the bounds of law, liberal democracies ensure that their citizens enjoy the right to express their views in every conceivable manner, including the right to protest and express dissent against prevailing laws. The blanket labelling of such dissent as 'anti-national' or 'anti-democratic' strikes at the heart of our commitment to the protection of constitutional values and the promotion of a deliberative democracy.

Protecting dissent is but a reminder that while democratically elected governments offer us a legitimate tool for development and social coordination, they can never claim a monopoly over the values and identities that define our pluralistic society. The employment of state machinery to curb dissent instils fear and creates a chilling atmosphere on free speech, which violates the rule of law and detracts from the constitutional vision of a pluralistic society.

The destruction of spaces for questions and dissent destroys the basis of all growth—political, economic, cultural and social. In this sense, dissent is the safety valve of democracy. The silencing of dissent and the generation of fear in the minds of people go beyond the violation of personal liberty and a commitment to constitutional values—it strikes at the heart of a dialogue-based democratic society that accords to every individual equal respect and consideration. A commitment to pluralism requires positive action in the form of social arrangements where the goal is 'to incorporate difference, coexist with it, allow it a share of social space'. [32] There is thus a positive obligation on the State to ensure that the deployment of its machinery to protect the freedom of expression is within the bounds of law and to dismantle any attempt by individuals or other actors to instil fear or chill free speech. This includes not just protecting free speech but actively welcoming and encouraging it.

An equal obligation to thwart attempts to curtail diverse opinions rests on every individual who may not agree with opposing views. Mutual respect and the protection of a space for divergent opinions is the process of viewing every individual as an equal member of a shared political community where membership is not premised on sharing a unanimous opinion. As Professor T.M. Scanlon puts it, toleration recognizes that common membership is deeper than conflicts and recognizes that others are 'just as entitled as we are to contribute to the definition of our society'.[33] When we look at each other, we do not just see fellow citizens entitled to our individual liberties. We perceive a mind and consciousness that is not our own, that has its own view of the world and its own account of how it should treat people who it sees as 'the other'. Taking democracy seriously requires us to respond respectfully to the intelligence of others and participate vigorously—but as an equal—in determining how we should live together. Democracy then is judged not just by the institutions that formally exist but by the extent to which different voices from diverse sections of the people can actually be heard, respected and accounted for. The great threat to pluralism is the suppression of difference and the silencing of popular and unpopular voices offering alternate or opposing views. Suppression of intellect is the suppression of the conscience of the nation.

This brings me to the second threat to pluralism—the belief that homogenization presupposes the unity of the nation. Alongside the ideals of securing to every individual justice, liberty and equality, the Constitution envisages the unity and the integrity of the nation. However, there is a belief that this ideal is achieved by the eradication of diversity and the assimilation of all identities. At the time of its birth, the nation was conceptualized as incorporating its vast diversity and not eliminating it. A member of the Constituent Assembly, Reverend Jerome D'Souza, described the conception of Indian pluralism when he said that:

> I do not think that the great majority communities of India or any of their most honoured representatives would be guilty of all that unfair overriding of privileges and safeguards; but by a genuine, though mistaken love of country and desire for unanimity and homogeneity, which it is not possible to have and which perhaps is not even necessary.[34]

As I have stated before, the framers demonstrated a commitment for the protection of India's pluralistic strands. For this reason, amendments to delete the right to propagate religion and to include a ban on dressing that identified with a religion were negatived in the Constituent Assembly. By negating these amendments, the Constituent Assembly asserted the place of plural expression in the public sphere and signalled a clear departure from the 'singular unification' model. Similarly, even though it was unanimously agreed that the freedom to propagate religion was included within the freedom of speech, the Constituent Assembly found it necessary to include a specific provision in Article 25, also stating that a heavy responsibility would be cast on the majority to see that minorities feel secure.[35]

A united India is not one characterized by a single identity devoid of its rich plurality, both of cultures and of values. National unity denotes a shared culture of values and a commitment to the fundamental ideals of the Constitution, in which all individuals are guaranteed not just the fundamental rights but also conditions for their free and safe exercise. Pluralism depicts not merely a commitment to the preservation of diversity, but a commitment to the fundamental postulates of individual and equal dignity. In this sense, pluralism furthers the basic postulates of the Constitution and nourishes and provides content to the goal of national unity.

In the creation of the 'imagined political community' that is India, it must be remembered that the very concept of a nation state changed from hierarchical communities to networks consisting of free and equal individuals. India, as a nation committed to pluralism, is not one language, one religion, one culture or one assimilated race. The defence for pluralism traverses beyond a commitment to the text and vision of the Constitution's immediate beneficiaries—the citizens. It underlines a commitment to protect the very idea of India as a refuge to people of various faiths, races, languages and beliefs. India finds itself in its defence of plural views and its multitude of cultures. In providing safe spaces for a multitude of cultures and the free expression of diversity and dissent, we reaffirm our commitment to the idea that the making of our nation is a continuous process of deliberation and belongs to every individual. No single individual or institution can claim a monopoly over the idea of India.

Defining the national identity in a collective and inclusive manner is crucial for, as Bhikhu Parekh, British political theorist and member of the House of Lords, UK, says: 'our sense of identity or who we think we are informs our values, guides our small and large choices, and gives our lives a sense of direction and coherence.'[36] The idea of a plural India guides and dictates how the institutions envisaged by the Constitution, as well as individuals in society, respond to diversity. In a polity committed to the protection of a plural identity, there is a positive obligation on every actor to create conditions conducive to the flourishing of diverse identities. These conditions must exist in the very structure of our institutions as well as the public sphere. This idea is put succinctly by Nobel laureate Amartya Sen when he states that 'our plural heritage is [thus] socially enriching as well as politically crucial'.[37]

Finally, the commitment to pluralism lies in the constitutional trust expressed by the framers in every individual. The Preamble to our Constitution sets forth the founding vision of securing to all its citizens justice, liberty and equality. However, the founders recognized that a commitment to pluralism went beyond its guarantee in the Constitution and in its institutions; it lay in how it was worked. In this sense, the guarantees of equality and liberty stipulated only a restricted pluralism. For this reason, the framers postulated that 'fraternity' presupposed the recognition of its ideals—a sense of brotherhood and sisterhood that went beyond the guarantee of equality and liberty. Dr Ambedkar put it eloquently when he said that 'without fraternity, liberty and equality could not become a natural course of things. It would require a constable to enforce them'.[38]

An example of this constitutional trust and obligation is evident in the divergent views of the relations between majorities and minorities upon India gaining independence. During the colonial rule, the Morley–Minto Reforms recommended separate electorates for 'minorities'. This recommendation for the first time introduced identity politics into the Indian regime by classifying groups as majority and minority. Minto justified the provision of separate electorates for Muslims because, according to him, they were 'a *separate community,* distinct by marriage, food and custom, and claiming in many cases to *belong to a race different from the Hindus*'. The emphasis was on the magnification of differences between different groups on the assumption by the British that a group will only protect its own interests. However, the Constituent Assembly dealt with the question of 'plurality' in a significantly different manner. When the Constituent Assembly was called to decide the fate of separate electorates in independent India, they decided that its inclusion was not essential to and even contrary to the requirements of a pluralistic society. They rejected separate electorates and dismissed the relevance of numerical disadvantage in a polity. The framers of the Constitution rejected the notion of a Hindu India and a Muslim India. They recognized only the Republic of India. As one member[39] of the Constituent Assembly said: 'we should proceed towards a compact nation, not divided into different compartments' but one where 'every sign of separatism should go'. As another member[40] said: 'There will be no divisions amongst Indians. United we stand; divided we fall.' The framers provided safeguards for the protection of individual identity as a part of a group and placed trust in future generations to create a common bond of what it meant to be Indian, embracing diversity without seeking homogeneity, and doing so in a way that unites rather than divides. It is that trust of the framers that we strive to live up to today.

Fraternity can only be realized when there exists a nation where different groups do not merely coexist but also share a common thread of tolerance, love, respect and affection. For example, the Rakhi/Raksha Bandhan protest called by Rabindranath Tagore[41] prevented the partition of Bengal with people exercising a token of solidarity and harmony. Historian Arnold J. Toynbee sums up this message when he says that we must learn to recognize and understand the different cultural configurations in which our common human nature has expressed itself. However, we must move beyond understanding them and value them and love them as being parts of mankind's common treasure and therefore being ours too.[42]

The transgender community in India has traditionally self-organized itself into a system of *gharana*s[43] and enjoys a vastly different form of *chosen* familial bonds, reflecting an age-old culture.[44] However, their lifestyle and culture have been treated as an aberration, and the community has faced systematic stigmatization. As a result, these communities are pushed to the fringes of society which affects their access to opportunities despite having received legal protection by the Supreme Court.[45] On the ground, these communities still suffer greatly. The judgments in *NALSA,* recognizing transgenders as a third gender, and in *Navtej Singh Johar,* decriminalizing consensual sexual activities between people of the same sex, do not directly translate to complete freedom and equality of members of the LGBTQIA+ community in India.[46] There is much to be done in fulfilling the project of fully integrating these communities in Indian society, the least of which is recognizing their entitlements to all civil rights.

The Constitution, in its reformative spirit, made major efforts to ameliorate the effects of the historic injustices founded in caste discrimination by making provisions for affirmative action, with the ultimate goal of giving meaning to the Constitution's promise of substantive equality. As one member of the Constituent Assembly said: 'If any kind of appeal to individual liberty and freedom is construed to mean an appeal to the continuation of the existing inequality . . . then you become static, unprogressive.'[47] Selection of socially and educationally backward classes for the purpose of affirmative action has been a continuing process,[48] and has increased the representation of these classes.[49] There is, however, a need to go beyond the mere representation of caste identities. A solution to deeply embedded forms of caste discrimination must come from within society. Dr Ambedkar advocated for inter-caste marriages,[50] which even today are resisted by the shackles of tradition. While the law makes stringent punishment for all acts of discrimination and the courts guarantee constitutional protection, the need is for an all-embracing social movement[51] to embrace, respect and empower people from all segments irrespective of ascribed identities. It is in our seeking answers to difficult questions that the true battle for a pluralistic India is waged.

Cultural values and political pluralism serve as a moniker to encompass the Indian idea of pluralism which cuts across religious, linguistic and regional differences. India, in keeping with her immense territorial diversity, contains within varying cultures that influence our ways of life, including food and lifestyle, non-religious beliefs and practices, which are not exclusive to any single religion or language. This shared sense of 'culture' is unique, for it is simultaneously distinct but also overlapping and lends itself to the idea of a layered 'Indianness', rather than a singular characterization.

This 'layered' conception has remained guarded and preserved through Indian history. It has, over the years, presented a rejection to calls for assimilation. To put it differently, this 'layered' identity, in itself, is what makes it 'Indian' and must be Central to our understanding of pluralism and efforts to foster it. We must endeavour to broaden the scope of the mainstream and bring forth voices that have often been sidelined or worse, been disapproved. The celebration of difference is not merely a step towards cultural tolerance. Going beyond tolerance, it forms the basis for equal treatment both socially and legally, in relation to opportunities and identities within the public sphere. We must embrace a participatory form of pluralism. Rather than being a mere acknowledgement of difference, it strives earnestly towards engaging and facilitating diversity in the public sphere.

What is of utmost relevance today is our ability and commitment to preserve, conserve and build on the rich pluralist history we have inherited. Homogeneity is not the defining feature of Indianness.

M.A. Kalam, a celebrated social anthropologist, wrote in a piece that: 'a visible, discernible, lively and successful engagement with diversity, is pluralism indeed'.[52] This definition calls upon us to look at each other and recognize that our differences are not our weakness. Our ability to transcend these differences in recognition of our shared humanity is the source of our strength. Pluralism should thrive not only because it inheres in the vision of the Constitution but also because of its inherent value in nation-building.

Today I have attempted to share with you the vision and spirit of pluralism that I believe has always defined India. India is a subcontinent of diversity unto itself. The mere mention of 'India' evokes in every person a different idea that they associate with the nation. Anybody truly conversant with Indian history will tell you that the single defining hallmark of 'ancient India' is its divergent, scattered and fragmented nature. It has been for centuries a land of vibrant diversity of religion, language and culture. Pluralism has already achieved its greatest triumph—the existence of India. The creation of a single nation out of these divergent and fragmented strands of culture in the face of colonial tyranny is a testament to the shared humanity that every Indian sees in every other Indian. The nation's continued survival shows us that our desire for a shared pursuit of happiness outweighs the differences in the colour of our skin, the languages we speak or the name we give the Almighty. These are but the hues that make India, and taking a step back, we see how altogether they form a kaleidoscope of human compassion and love surpassing any singular, static vision of India. Pluralism is not the *toleration* of diversity; it is its celebration.

13

Visualizing the Constitution Through Artistic Prisms

Stories of Aspiration and Emancipation[1]

I am honoured to speak at today's webinar organized by the Kalakshetra Foundation as a tribute to Constitution Day. It is often assumed that only the legal fraternity would see meaning in celebrating the day our Constitution was finished and adopted, as distinct from Republic Day, when the Constitution actually came into effect. This is far from the truth, as our legal systems are *constituted* by culture. Austin Sarat[2] and Jonathon Simon,[3] while analysing the role of cultural studies in legal interpretation, have noted that the process of attributing legal meaning is not one-directional, starting from what is enacted by Parliament to what is laid down by courts. Citizens, in their myriad social relationships, are consumers of culture. They use cultural means to advance their aspirations for a shared life.[4] Culture is a defining feature of identity.

An interdisciplinary study of law and culture tells us how professors and judges construct the law in their narratives, how ordinary people think about justice, how personal choices are governed by the law and how the law transforms it into a norm. Culture introduces a subjectivity into law, thereby expanding its learning.[5] With this thought in mind, I believe that there cannot be a better avenue to honour the crystallization of our founding commitments to a free and equal country, than in Rukmini Devi Arundale's halls of Gandharva Veda music and Bharatanatyam dance; she was no less than a revolutionary herself. I have heard several accounts about the serenity of the Chennai campus, and until I am fortunate enough to pay a visit, I will make do with my virtual presence today.

The world of fine arts, an avenue for entertainment and a break from the banality of day-to-day life, is also a minefield of progressive thought and action. I grew up in a (family) household of lawyers. Yet, my first inspiration to pursue law was built on my first childhood love—a love for literature. I resonate with what American academic Charles W. Eliot said: 'Books are the quietest of friends, wisest of counsellors and most patient of teachers.' Through the vicarious world of books, I have experienced the dangers of fascism and anti-Semitism with Anne Frank in Nazi Germany,[6] traversed through apartheid-ridden South Africa with Stephen Kumalo in Alan Paton's book *Cry, the Beloved Country*[7] and shared the intersecting indignities faced by a black queer woman, Celie, living in a southern state of the US in Alice Walker's *The Colour Purple*.[8] As a child, my life was shaped by books, as I belonged to a middle-class family, and my parents couldn't afford the costs of international travel. I learnt what I had to learn from the world of books and from home. Somerset Maugham's *The Moon and Sixpence* is partly based on the life of a French painter who left Europe and his family behind to live in Tahiti. Then came *The Good Earth* by Pearl S. Buck, which dramatized life in a Chinese village in the twentieth century; *The Lust for Life*, a biographical novel on Vincent van Gogh by Irving Stone; Ernest Hemingway's *The Old Man and the Sea* tells the story of a Cuban fisherman in Cayo Blanco who battles a giant marlin far out in the Gulf Stream. During the pandemic, I spent the last eight or nine months reading, apart from being in the virtual courts. I managed to read about fifteen books. A great sorrow I have is that I will be reading Priscilla Jana's *Fighting for Mandela* only a couple of months after she passed away. I was reading her obituary in the *New*

York Times last night. After almost two decades at the bar and another two at the bench, I believe that these stories indelibly transformed my world view and have had the most profound impact on my life, long before the study of law. My mother, Prabha, was a disciple of Gaan Saraswati Kishori Amonkarji, and my heart still resonates with the tunes of her *yaman* and *bageshri*. Even today, my heart is moved when I hear the 'Nirguni Bhajan' by Pandit Kumar Gandharva. My favourites include 'Jo Bhaje Hari Ko Sada' by Pandit Bhimsen Joshi and Pandit Jasraj's rendition of 'Om Namo Bhagavate Vasudevaya', which remains timeless to me. L. Subramaniam, the violin maestro, holds a special place in my heart. In Western music, I'm especially fond of the Eagles's 'Hotel California', Mark Knopfler's unmatched guitar work and Don McLean's 'Vincent (Starry, Starry Night)', which continue to resonate deeply.

Today, in honouring the framing of the constitutive document of our sovereign, I do not intend to assume the role of an academic to analyse the scope of constitutional freedoms and protections that guarantee free speech. There are excellent sources that have jurisprudentially analysed the role of artistic expression and may effectively serve that curiosity, better than the short time that I will be addressing you today. I will instead attempt to locate the role of art in Indian and global history as not just a cultural facet of human life but a fundamentally transformative medium for holding up a mirror to society.

Artists, irrespective of the nature of their medium, are the most vibrant thought leaders of our society. They foster engagement and debate at scales that are much higher than academic or political discourse. In my opinion, an artist's work is the closest human beings have been to achieving immortality. Van Gogh's magnum opus, *The Starry Night*, valued at almost nothing in his lifetime and today one of the world's priceless pieces of art, is currently being studied by medical researchers to understand psychosis. Sylvia Plath's semi-autobiographical work, *The Bell Jar*, preceded the second wave of feminism in the United States of America by over a decade, with its critical reflections on the cultural and social norms that defined and subjugated women. Shakespeare, renowned as the world's greatest playwright, writing between sixteenth and seventeenth centuries, is now also a subject of colonial studies. His play, *The Tempest*, is used to discern perceptions of the 'White Man's burden', which marginalized the natives (Caliban and Sycorax, in this case) as 'barbarians' with no legitimate claim to their land.

Art, politics and the law share a symbiotic relationship in any meaningful society that prides individual freedom and dignity. Today's books, cinema, museums, art galleries, theatres, songs, *nukkad natak*s (street plays), and even a grandparent narrating stories are all vectors of our civilization's history that simultaneously lay the seeds for our future. Often, there have been unfortunate times the world over, when artistic expression was policed and curbed by the excesses of the law. The Constitution of India was forged as a bulwark against censorship and subjugation that had pervaded British India. Its freedoms and State duties were meant to serve as an antidote to majoritarian tendencies that seek to silence what they cannot digest.

Our freedom struggle was a set of incremental victories that were achieved by mass mobilization and consequent deliberations with the British administration. Several Government of India Acts were promulgated with a view to devolving further powers to Indians, until the final Indian Independence Act of 1947. Sadat Hasan Manto, one of the finest Urdu writers, wrote a famous story titled 'The New Constitution/Naya Qanoon', where his protagonist, Ustaad Mango, was a tonga-driver in 1935, frustrated with the precarity and communal violence that had been perpetrated by British imperialist policies. Mango was elated after he heard of the Government of India Act, 1935, which promised self-rule and greater powers to Indians. Ustaad Mango assumed that this '*naya qanoon*' (which translates to 'new law') would mean liberation for all Indians. However, the story ends with him being dragged away by the British Police because while he had assumed that this '*naya qanoon*' would mean liberation from all of the colonial State's oppressive practices, including its brutal police powers and economic exploitation, it did little to change the status quo.[9]

The British Raj never recognized Indians as citizens who could stake a legitimate claim against their administration. Therefore, they went to great lengths to clamp down on all forms of free speech and artistic expression. This was considered necessary in order to sustain their economic domination over the Indian subcontinent. Oppressive legislations such as the Vernacular Press Act of 1878 could pre-emptively confiscate the machinery of vernacular newspapers that attempted to even loosely criticize their Raj.[10] Even outside the seemingly 'political sphere' of life, artistes were forced to adapt to Western tastes in order to retain patronage.[11] The Swadeshi movement was, therefore, popularized with the effort of Indian artists, who sought to revive folk traditions as a way of creating a shared cultural identity. Abanindranath Tagore (1871–1951) founded the Bengal School of Art with a view to reviving traditional forms of painting. Nandlal Bose was tasked with painting frescoes for the first Indian National Congress meeting in 1936 and the Exhibition at Haripura Congress that could convey the aspirational message of *poorna swaraj* (complete independence) through powerful images.[12]

Contemporaneously across the globe, art was evoked as the most powerful weapon to mould the collective conscience to validate the Universal Declaration of Human Rights of 1948, which enshrined norms of State sovereignty, life, liberty and equality. Subversive art, such as the multilingual plaque reading 'Never Again' at the Dachau Concentration Camp in Germany, infiltrated sites of the most gruesome oppression. They were a reminder to the world that some questions of human worth will never be up for debate again. The atomic bomb dome at Hiroshima is a stark reminder of the tragedies of war.

When we think about our Constitution and the freedom struggle that predated it, several events conjure up in our minds. Perhaps some of the prominent ones being that of Mahatma Gandhi marching to Dandi, Pandit Nehru addressing the Indian Parliament with his 'Tryst with Destiny', Bal Gangadhar Tilak coining the effervescent phrase 'Swaraj is my birth right and I shall have it' or Bankim Chandra Chatterjee's 'Vande Mataram', which sought to unify our country. Critical theory, particularly from the feminist and subaltern lenses, has begun probing these narratives to discover several marginalized voices that were equal forces in the fight for Indian independence, such as the working-class revolts against the feudalistic *jotedar* system, working women's protest against crippling land tax in the Bardoli Satyagraha and the tribal movements in Santhal Batidar, which were resisting the forceful usurpation of their lands and livelihood.[13] Uncovering marginalized narratives in history requires a critical effort at dissecting lives and interpersonal relations. One of the most important subjects for such an analysis has been cultural representations. What they omit becomes almost as important as what they retain.

Many of you may not know this, but the original copy of our Constitution, which was handwritten by calligrapher Prem Behari Narain Raizada, actually contained beautiful paintings. The beginning of every 'Part' or 'Chapter' of the Constitution was adorned by paintings created by the artists of Santiniketan's Kala Bhavan under the guidance of Nandalal Bose. These paintings were all in different styles that were prevalent across India, including the wall paintings of Ajanta, the book illustrations of Rajasthan, the Mughal and Deccani traditions, the sculptures of Konark, Amaravati and the Chola south. They depicted the history of our nation, right from the Harappan civilization until our Independence from the British Rule.[14]

Similar to this, the halls of our Parliament, too, are adorned by many murals that were commissioned right after Independence. The purpose of these was to capture the rich history of the nation, which could then be used to unify its constituents. These murals depict many important historical events, ranging from the court of Akbar to Mahatma Gandhi's march to Dandi.

However, while the beauty and artistry of these paintings and murals have been almost universally acknowledged, they have come under some criticism as well. The first of these criticisms has been about the choice of their artists, which often had little diversity. For instance, out of forty-three artists commissioned to paint the murals, only two were women.[15] A second criticism was the selection of the historical events considered for consecration through these paintings and murals. Now, I must acknowledge that a country like India has a very rich history, which is impossible to capture in its entirety for anyone. However, the criticism is focused on the lack of representation of common Indians, or the lack of subaltern voices and experiences in these paintings and murals. They tell the tale of India through its heroes who have come to dominate popular narratives, while leaving out the stories of its common people.[16]

All this said, it is important to remember that the Indian Constitution presented a marked shift in the people's lives from subjects under British India to citizens of a free country. People tend to pass hasty comments on the length and 'borrowed' nature of the Constitution to undermine its potential. However, it would be wrong for us to assume that nothing changed after Independence, just because we retained some of the administrative structures of the British and several frameworks of governance that were established by the preceding acts. The commitments to individual freedom and dignity, transcending divisions of class, caste, gender, religion and language, were engineered through the Constitution. After its promulgation, it became a State project to imbibe the Constitution's values and norms through school textbooks, pamphlets, public exhibitions and documentaries.[17]

Legal historians and political scientists have complained that not much attention was devoted to post-colonial India, and their efforts have been stymied by poor record-keeping.[18] In these gaps, and even otherwise, art has served as the emotional murals of our citizenry who were living in their brave new world. Vikram Seth, in *A Suitable Boy*, his fictional narrative of India in 1951–52, explored the complex realities of land distribution, class inequalities and communalism. Popular cinema caricatured the masses through a social and political analysis of a spectator negotiating the country's past and present.[19] Raj Kapoor singing '*Mera joota hain Japaani, yeh patloon Inglistaani, sar pe laal topi Rusi, phir bhi dil hain Hindustani*' as he migrated from a village to Mumbai in a Bollywood movie in 1955, became a national hymn that continues to evoke strong emotion. His infectious optimism for the future of our free country was emblematic of the times, as citizens navigated their relationship with an autochthonous state.

The nomadic communities of Putli-Bhatt in Gujarat and Rajasthan have been using their craft of *kathputli*s (wooden puppets) since the thirteenth century. These skilled craftspersons use the dexterity of their fingers to entertain audiences using sleek narrative, humour and music. Upon Independence, these folk legends were used by the State to communicate State messages of family planning, education and health to far-flung, rural areas.[20]

One can argue that the integration of art into the mainstream is predicated on its conformity to the dominant political consciousness of the time. While this may be largely true, the unique nature of artistic expression is such that it cannot be monopolized. Therefore, art from the fringes challenges society to reckon with its shortcomings and birth counter-discourse against oppressive manifestations of power and authority.

Even in times of constitutional crisis, such as the Emergency, the resilience and creativity of artists, in spite of being subject to pre-censorship and preventive detention, would illuminate our lives—like light entering through the cracks. One such tongue-in-cheek example was this obituary published in the *Times of India*, which nobody would have assumed would ever contain a political message. The obituary got past the censor's black pen soon after the Emergency was declared in 1975 and it wittily read: 'D'OCray -D.E.M., beloved husband of T. Ruth, loving father of L.I. Bertie, brother of Faith, Hope, Justicia, expired on June 26, 1975', which the clever Indian reader would be able to discern, meant 'Democracy, beloved husband of truth, loving father of liberty, brother of faith, hope, justice—died on the day the Emergency was proclaimed.'[21]

Therefore, art, in times of relative stability and also times of crisis, serves as a constant reminder of our founding commitments by bringing constitutional principles to life. Mahesh Elkunchwar, the prominent Marathi playwright and screenplay writer, wrote a play called *Party*, which was subsequently made into an eponymous movie by Govind Nihalani as part of what many called Bollywood's Parallel Cinema movement. Both the play and the film posed a Central question to their viewers in the form of a discussion between the elites of a city attending a 'party'. The question was: What is the value of art which does not challenge the political *status quo* of the era? It challenges people to ask themselves whether art would have any meaning to it if it were not being used to question the injustices around them and in helping uplift people. While all of us today will be left pondering on this question, we all cannot deny the powerful potential of art when it is used as a form of political contestation.

In talking about such art, one cannot help but begin by acknowledging the brilliant Dalit art forms that originated often due to the oppression faced by their communities. The father of our Indian Constitution, Dr Ambedkar, envisioned that the document would provide the necessary breaking ground for ensuring the abolishment of untouchability and equal status for Dalit communities. This vision is reflected in Articles 14, 15, 16 and 17 of our Constitution. However, I believe that while the Constitution does provide Dalit communities with a legal basis for equality of opportunity and dignity within India, it does not take away from the oppression they faced for years, and which is reflected in their art.

An example of this is the Mithila paintings, wherein women from the Mithila region of Bihar created their own form of the painting style native to that region, which was often practised by upper-caste women. Within this, Godna art became particularly popular. This art form was based on Godna tattoos, which were often created by Dalit women. These were in themselves a form of revolt against the upper-caste norms that forced these women to only wear jewellery of inferior metal. These paintings are created using colours made from mixing natural substances, such as cow dung with leaves, flowers and vegetables, and depict the daily lives of these Dalit women.[22]

Similarly, a new *genre* of art, colloquially termed as 'Protest Art', has been popularized, wherein one's art form becomes their means of protest, not just against entrenched political structures but even its dominant manifestations in art. Examples of protest art include street art and graffiti, which became a popular form of protest during the Arab Spring in countries such as Egypt. These art forms challenged their oppressive regimes.[23] Guerrilla Girls, a feminist collective operating in New York, challenged the prevalent sexism and racism of the world of art through their posters.[24] Their rebellion against museums, which may often represent the sensibilities of entrenched dominant consciousness, went a long way in ensuring that these sites of heritage begin to interrogate the power structures they unwittingly perpetuate. Resistance against social and cultural capital even birthed new styles of art, such as hip-hop dance, which emerged as a counter-cultural movement against the ghettoization of African Americans.

Closer home, art has served as an important tool for the preservation of a national collective memory. Scholars have argued that every nation goes through the process of nation-building, wherein the events of its past are used to form a collective conscience that can bind together all the varied identities.[25] Our Constitution aspires to be such a document, one that can provide common ground on which the identity of independent India could be forged.[26] While I do believe that our Constitution has been successful in building a collective 'nation', it is rather the individual communities' art that has preserved their place in our nation's collective memory. Art brings the stories and experiences of marginalized groups to the forefront while empowering communities to find a voice through these artistic expressions.

The first example that comes to my mind is Dancing Queens, which is India's first transgender dancing troupe. The troupe has been performing for nearly seventeen years now, and their shows often depict the stories of ordinary trans women while touching upon themes such as growing up different, discovering one's sexuality and facing difficulties like begging and prostitution. Their shows serve a dual purpose of providing a platform to transgender individuals for their artistic expression and also allowing the viewers to experience their story.[27]

Cinema is another medium through which the stories of marginalization and oppression often come to the forefront. In this context, the Marathi film *Fandry* (2013) is a prominent example. It tells the story of a young boy belonging to an untouchable community, trying to integrate himself into a caste-ridden society that is entirely unwilling to accept him. What is particularly moving about *Fandry* is its ending, which is not 'happily ever after', much like the lived realities of many Dalits. It ends with our young protagonist coming to realize his untouchability and his anger over it. He tries to give action to that anger by throwing a stone at the screen, consciously aimed even at the viewer. This forces the viewer to introspect upon their own lives.

Another film that comes to my mind is the Tamil film *Asuran* (2019), directed by Vetrimaaran. It tells the story of a Dalit family facing oppression from their upper-caste landlord, who seeks to take away their land. Not unlike *Fandry*, the film ends with our protagonist's family defeated on account of caste-based victimization. The father of the family, about to be sent to jail, poignantly tells his son not to chase acquisition of material prospects like land, which the oppressive classes can take away from their community, and instead pursue education, which will always be their own.

Art can also be used to acknowledge the history of oppression, often as a reminder of what has happened and why it must not be repeated. It forces us as a nation and as a community to not only acknowledge the horrors of what has come before but also develop empathy for those who have suffered during them.

In this vein, Rohinton Mistry's *A Fine Balance* highlights the Emergency-era policies, which were prominent factors that affected its characters' lives in Mumbai. Another such project is the Partition Museum, located in Amritsar, Punjab, which serves as a repository of the lived experiences of many whose lives changed overnight when India and Pakistan partitioned after Independence.

Globally, it is in this spirit that Marjane Satrapi created *Persepolis*, a graphic novel depicting her experiences as a young girl growing up in Iran and Austria during the Islamic Revolution. The beauty of the graphic novel lies not only in its ability to tell the story of a nation affected by a revolution, but also in keeping the reader engaged with its honest understanding of what it means to be a female child growing up in such a tumultuous time.

Such acknowledgement can often also be symbolic, as one can see from the architectural choices of the Constitutional Court of South Africa. The hall that houses the court was created using the bricks from the Awaiting Trial Block of their jail. This was done almost as a reminder of the nature of the apartheid Regime, which affected South Africa prior to the formation of its constitutional court and the duty of the court to ensure that this history was never repeated.

When considering art, especially public art, we must remember that one of the most fundamental disputes will often be about what art we choose to put at the forefront and at what opportunity cost. This contestation of public space is a widely acknowledged phenomenon across the globe.[28] Hence, in a country as diverse as India, it is inevitable that not all art has been provided a meaningful space. To counter this, many of the artists from traditionally marginalized communities have taken to the streets.

The prime example of this in my mind is the numerous pride parades that happen across the country. These parades serve as a safe space for members of the community to celebrate their sexuality and gender. Even more so, it allows members of the community to express themselves through some of the loveliest posters and clothes one can imagine. Another project I would like to mention is the Aravani Art Project, a Bengaluru-based collective. Its members are largely part of the transgender community and use their artistic talents to paint murals all across the city. These murals often depict scenes from their life and help spread a message of equality for their community. This allows for their lived experiences to see the light of day and reach a wider audience.

Finally, from my perspective as a member of the legal fraternity, I have also witnessed art being an instructive medium to acquaint citizens with the complexities of the judicial system. I fondly remember this one time, when I was on the bench in the Bombay High Court, and was surprised to notice Boman Irani, a popular Bollywood actor, attending my courtroom as a spectator. On inquiry, I was told that this was his endeavour to prepare for a role in a film. It made me wonder how powerful popular art and cinema truly are as mediums, in their ability to communicate complex ideas and legal principles in a satiable form. As judges, the adversarial process compels us to look at issues from a detached lens in order to retain our ability to uphold the rule of law. Art depicting the legal system then serves as a refreshing reminder of the lives that are impacted and humanizes the individuals who approach us with their problems.

A foremost example of this for me is Chaitanya Tamhane's multilingual film *Court* (2014). The film, through its story, explores the trial of an activist-poet charged for the abetment of the suicide of a manual scavenger through his politically charged songs. The film not only draws attention to the realities of our justice system but also tries to highlight the lived experiences of all the individuals affected by it. This includes not only our poet and the family of the manual scavenger but also of the defence lawyer, the prosecutor and even the judge presiding over the case. The film forces its viewer to acknowledge the human lives at stake in these disputes, rather than looking at them as mere precedents of law.

Another example that comes to my mind is a recent Bollywood film, Hitesh Kawalya's *Shubh Mangal Zyada Saavdhan* (2020), which humorously and lovingly tells the story of a father coming to terms with his son's homosexuality. Interestingly, the film is set against the backdrop of the Supreme Court's hearings challenging the constitutionality of Section 377 of the Indian Penal Code, 1860. When the homosexual couple is about to be arrested by the police for a violation of Section 377, the father finally acknowledges his son's sexuality and requests the police to wait until the next morning, when the verdict is due. The film ends with everyone, including the police, gathered around to the point when the Supreme Court (or us) pronounced the judgment in *Navtej Singh Johar v. Union of India*,[29] (which decriminalized homosexuality), and the police gladly leaving the couple alone as they celebrate with their family. I must confess, I had a lot of thoughts going on in my mind when I pronounced such an important judgment, but never did I imagine that my work would become the plot point of a Bollywood film!

To end this webinar, let me briefly speak about a book quoted often whenever one wishes to describe a dictatorial dystopia. I am, of course, talking about *1984* by George Orwell. While many of you may be familiar with this, for those who are not, the book tells the story of a fictional nation that was ruled by a leader referred to only as the 'Big Brother'. It is the story of an oppressive State seeking full control over every aspect of its citizens' lives through constant surveillance.

While *1984* is always remembered for these aspects, many readers often skip its Appendix altogether. Therein, Orwell describes the 'Principles of Newspeak', which was a language created by Big Brother to replace colloquial English. Orwell hauntingly describes Big Brother's ultimate goal to replace all of English with Newspeak, which severely limits an individual's vocabulary. It ultimately hopes to diminish their capability to dissent, since there will be no vocabulary to express it. As part of this goal, the State even tries to rewrite all existing literature in Newspeak. However, interestingly, the Appendix ends by letting us know that this ultimate goal of Big Brother's failed and led to his downfall. Newspeak failed because there were certain documents it just could not translate. The example it offers us is the Declaration of Independence of the US, in which they could not translate the concept of liberty and freedom, which are essential to negotiating with one's government.[30]

It is my firm belief that the role language played in Orwell's dystopia is an analogy to the role art plays in our lives. While forms of art contain their own aesthetic beauty, they also carry within them the history of our lives and communities. As such, the art being created within our nation often stores within itself the salient principles of our Constitution. The art of today may be a window into our future tomorrow. It may challenge our world view or even make us uncomfortable. But if history has taught us one thing, it is that preserving a genuine marketplace for ideas will always leave us for the better. Art forms that once envisaged sovereignty and self-rule for India were brutally suppressed due to their audacity to question the culture of authority. Therefore, when we suppress art, we suppress progress. To quote the European Union Agency for Fundamental Rights: 'There is a human right to create art, to admire it, critique it, challenge it, be provoked by it, respond to it, and to ignore it.'[31]

Our Constitution is not merely a collection of words that lay out the rules of the nation's governance. It is also a document of aspiration and hope. It contains within itself a dream of a nation, united in its resolve to ensure the greatest of democratization, while preserving individual liberty and dignity at its very core. If we wish to live in the society that our Constitution envisaged for us, our progressive action would also demand collective duties to live by the principles that it holds in its highest regard. Should Manto's Ustaad Mango step into our world today, we must ensure he never feels the same dejection and betrayal towards our Constitution—today's 'naya qanoon'—as he did towards the Government of India Act, 1935. This is our collective imperative.

14

Why Representation Matters[1]

I am honoured to speak at today's webinar organized by Live Law to launch the pathbreaking initiative CEDE—Community for the Eradication of Discrimination in Education and Employment—on the day we commemorate the birth of the architect of the Indian Constitution, Dr Ambedkar. I am delighted to speak at this event on the invitation of my former judicial law clerk and co-founder of this initiative, Anurag Bhaskar. CEDE seeks to bridge issues of under-representation of Dalits, Adivasis, OBCs, women, transgenders, persons with disabilities, and other minorities and marginalized groups in the legal profession.

I have decided to deliver this lecture for two reasons. *First*, because Anurag is a distinguished former judicial law clerk of mine. I watch silently—and on this occasion not so silently—as Anurag makes rapid strides as a front-ranking legal scholar, committed to the realization of the rights of the marginalized. Anurag represents, I believe, the social conscience of changing India. *Second*, my own life since childhood has been deeply influenced by diverse individuals, who in their own diversity have been my friends, mentors, colleagues, interns and judicial law clerks. I have learnt from those who critique my work, from loved ones who question my assumptions and from the whispers of adversaries who do not share my philosophy. We must remain open in our minds, beliefs and ideas if we have to grow and evolve. The life of a judge can often be isolated, as propriety dictates that we maintain a distance from some aspects of society in order to maintain our neutrality. Merely having judicial law clerks from diverse genders, sexualities, castes and physical abilities has had a positive transformation on my outlook towards judging and my capabilities to push for reforms as a judicial officer. The evolution of my own thoughts on gender, sexuality, caste and marginalization has been influenced by an ardent feminist who is a life partner, spouse and my best friend.

Hence, when I speak of representation in my address today, I don't intend to assume the role of a saviour who sees tokenistic value in representation as proof of upliftment. Instead, in order to bolster the importance of an initiative such as CEDE, I will attempt to draw on my experiences that were enriched by diverse associations with representation, along with some historical and contemporary examples.

To begin with my thoughts on 'Why Representation Matters', it is imperative for me to first outline the nature of discrimination faced by those who belong to marginalized communities. The fact that they face discrimination is obviously no longer a question of debate. This is evinced by the presence of the fundamental rights in our Constitution, which offer stringent protection against this discrimination. However, the evolving nature of this discrimination merits a closer inspection in order to enhance our understanding.

The adoption of the Indian Constitution was a transformative moment in our polity. The Constitution was to become the great leveller in its abolishing of untouchability, disavowal of discrimination on the grounds of caste, sex, religion, race or place of birth and the promise of religious freedom for all. The promise of reservation for SCs and STs as reparation for centuries of oppression was to enable a seat at the table for members who systemically were denied education, housing and access to public utilities as a consequence of their birth in an insidious caste system that was upheld by endogamous patriarchy. Over seventy years after the Constitution came into force, many argue that caste-based discrimination no longer exists, merely because untouchability and other egregious caste atrocities have been outlawed. However, a close look at our society and its constitutive systems reveals the existence of entrenched structures that are also proxies for upholding casteist, ableist and gendered hierarchies. Discrimination is built into their operation. This may not play out directly as oppression and segregation, but it continues to perpetuate a similar effect. Hence, the overt discrimination has now become 'systemic'.

I explored and studied this issue in a judgment that we pronounced last month, *Lt Col Nitisha Kumar v. Union of India*.[2] The genesis of this case lies in another decision delivered by our court in 2020 in *The Secretary, Ministry of Defence v. Babita Puniya and Ors*,[3] where we had negatived discrimination that forbade women officers from availing an opportunity at a Permanent Commission in the army. We held, in no uncertain terms, that women officers were entitled to be considered for Permanent Commission in parity with their male counterparts.

However, even after our decision in *Babita Puniya*, a sizeable number of these women officers had to knock at the Supreme Court's doors again in *Nitisha Kumar* on the methodology through which Permanent Commission was to be granted to these women officers. Before us, the authorities argued that they were merely applying the same medical and evaluation criteria as applicable to the male officers. However, we found that a case of indirect discrimination was made out since the medical criteria were being applied to women officers in their forties and fifties when they were being belatedly considered for Permanent Commission. The male officers had to meet this same criterion in their youth, between the ages of twenty-five and thirty, when they are typically considered for Permanent Commission. The male officers were never subsequently held to that exacting medical standard, with the advancement of their age.

Stories of discrimination against visible minorities are hardly isolated incidents. The acknowledgement we see in constitutional courts barely scratches the surface, the world over. Patriarchy, ableism, racism and even casteism are universal trends that manifest equally, no matter how developed or progressive a nation. In 1997, the Canadian Human Rights Tribunal[4] was called upon to assess a claim of workplace discrimination against visible minorities (in terms of gender, race and physical abilities) in promotions. It attempted to holistically probe the workplace. There was no direct policy or practice that could be assailed for denying hiring opportunities or eligibilities for promotions. A metric of formal equality would consider this as sufficient and attribute the top tier of the organizational structure as one constituted by merit. However, the Human Rights Tribunal went one step further and conducted a holistic analysis of the organization by collating testimonies of workers in the organization and by engaging experts on statistical analysis and human resource management. The evidence of the experts on human resources was analysed to situate systemic issues, ranging from the ghettoization of minorities in Canada, translating into lesser encouragement for professional ambition. The societal impact of discrimination was evidenced in informal staffing decisions, providing a fertile ground for unconscious bias and a broader perception of visible minorities as unfit for management. This self-fulfilling prophecy is applicable to workplaces, educational institutions, places of worship and even the seemingly private sphere of family. Discrimination translates into inferior gender roles for women, underpaid and exploitative jobs for *bahujans* (literally 'the majority') and poverty, marginalization and isolation for persons with disabilities. The Supreme Court of Canada,[5] in analysing a similar claim of women who sought to work in the railways, noted the mental impact of discriminatory policies on these women. As subjects of discrimination, the court noted how, 'The discrimination is . . . then reinforced by the very exclusion of the disadvantaged group because the exclusion fosters the belief, both within and outside the group, that the exclusion is the result of "natural" forces',[6] for example that women "just can't do the job"'.

Professor Marie Mercat-Bruns, in her seminal analysis on systemic discrimination, had underscored the continuing ineffectiveness of traditional tools of direct and indirect discrimination in rapidly evolving workplace structures, which have now proliferated into freelancing, contract work, informal work and even remote work, which has introduced complexity in linear forms of management. In addition to the workplace structures that discriminate in and of themselves, she observed a 'second generation of discrimination' alongside subtler forms of direct and indirect discrimination, that tends to keep protected groups out of social networks, thereby leaving them underinformed of advancement opportunities.[7]

The legal fraternity, in its fragmented structure of professional service, is endemic to these forms of discrimination. Corporate law firms could still have some semblance of a formal hierarchy or structure that would enable some countermeasures to exist. However, their private forms and the lack of a comprehensive anti-discrimination legislation in India render marginalized groups without enforceable recourse in law.

Having talked about the nature of systemic discrimination, it is imperative to also talk about another related type—discrimination under the guise of 'merit'. This discrimination is built into how we construct our pay scales, provide promotions, referrals and largely assess 'competence' arising out of a supposed objective assessment of 'merit'.

The barriers posed by the argument that 'they are simply not good enough' are real and formidable whenever marginalized groups assert that they have been denied equal opportunities. Michael J. Sandel, the author of the book *The Tyranny of Merit*, noted that in their minds, people who align themselves with meritocratic ideals tend to think, 'If I am responsible for having accrued a handsome share of worldly goods—income and wealth, power and prestige—I must deserve them. Success is a sign of virtue. My affluence is my due.'[8]

Nowhere is this thinking more clearly on display than when it comes to conversations surrounding reservations. Those who target reservations in public employment argue that reservations prevent the meritorious from getting their fair share, while the presumably 'un-meritorious' get it simply because of reservations and lower the standards and quality of institutions. However, arguments of this nature miss the point about what 'merit' truly means. If we define merit in an exclusionary sense, our answers will ensure the exclusion of the marginalized. If merit is defined as a value that promotes an inclusive society, our answers will ensure inclusion.

In my judgment in *B.K. Pavitra v. Union of India*,[9] often referred to as *B.K. Pavitra II*, we had the opportunity to re-characterize what 'merit' truly means. We achieved this aim in two ways. *First*, we underscored that looking at 'merit' as an ability to perform better at standardized tests would be insular and single-minded; rather, it was important to understand 'merit' in terms of what is beneficial for society at large. The reservation for SC, ST and OBC candidates could be considered more 'meritorious' since it fulfilled the constitutional goal of an inclusive society that can only be achieved by uplifting these communities. *Second*, we noted that Professor Marc Galanter has argued that three broad resources are required to perform well in standardized tests, which are usually considered as a measure of one's merit. These include (i) economic resources, (ii) social and cultural resources and (iii) intrinsic ability and hard work.[10] Two of these three resources, i.e., economic and social and cultural ones, lie outside of the control of any given individual. As such, any individual's merit could never entirely be just about themselves but would *always* depend on their position in society. Consequently, we held that reservations could not be considered as antithetical to the concept of 'merit', unless we understood 'merit' within a narrow compass that favours the already privileged.

To highlight the very tenuous understanding of merit while considering reservations, we should also note the words of Yashica Dutt, who, in her raw autobiography *Coming Out as Dalit*, has plainly remarked: 'Reservation for upper castes functions with connections, networks and contacts that go back decades.'[11]

Furthermore, it is also important to acknowledge that the establishment of a perfect meritocracy will still not change the pervasive attitude towards caste in India. Sociologist and author Satish Deshpande critically reflects on this attitude still prevalent in India through a form of a joke that became popular when the Ninety-

Third Amendment to the Constitution introduced reservations for OBCs. The joke goes as follows: When India decides to send a space exploration team to the moon, feverish negotiations begin immediately on the composition of the team. After much discussion, it is decided that the team will include nine OBCs, six SCs, three STs and, if there is any place left, two astronauts. Deshpande notes that the insight into the Indian attitude in this joke is that 'the "astronauts" are not identified by their caste but only by their qualifications (as astronauts), whereas the ["supposed"] quota-walas are identified only by their caste and not by their qualifications . . . [As such] upper-caste identity is such that it can be completely overwritten by modern professional identities of choice, whereas lower caste identity is so indelibly engraved that it overwrites all other identities and renders them illegible, along with the choices that they may represent'.[12]

This is a stark reminder for anyone who believes that the implementation of a proper meritocracy will erode the evils of a caste system, and that we could become 'casteless'. On the contrary, it is important to realize that this privilege of being 'casteless' will always remain available only to those belonging to the 'upper caste', since their caste never negatively affected them to begin with. In my dissenting opinion in *Abhiram Singh v. C.D. Commachen & Ors*,[13] I noted that:

> The Constitution is not oblivious to the history of discrimination against and the deprivation inflicted upon large segments of the population based on religion, caste and language. Religion, caste and language are as much a symbol of social discrimination imposed on large segments of our society on the basis of immutable characteristics as they are of a social mobilisation to answer centuries of injustice.

As such, any system that seeks to correct the evils of the caste system cannot succeed by denying its existence and effect. The only way to cure its negative effects is by first acknowledging its existence.

I cannot help but wonder how evident these forms of discrimination are in our legal profession, which thrives on the ability of a person to network, capitalizing on their existing family and social networks. The success of an individual is invariably determined by informal structures and networks, ranging from receiving quality mentorship, obtaining referrals from peers for clients, leading all the way up to designations as senior advocates or the collegium selections for the judiciary. To understand this phenomenon, it is important to consider for a moment how the legal profession is currently structured.

In its current avatar, the legal profession starts to create gradations between individuals even before they enter law school. As it stands today, entry into most of the top law schools offering the five-year integrated course is through competitive entrance examinations. These examinations are offered only in English, in addition to the language being a separate component of testing. This automatically favours those who are privileged enough to have access to a high-quality English-medium education. In contrast, students from underprivileged backgrounds are put at an obvious disadvantage. At a structural level, this excludes students whose education at the school level—primary, secondary and higher secondary—has been in any of the national or regional languages. Many students from such backgrounds aspire to join the judicial services. They are excluded from access to NLUs. In turn, the top-quality law schools churn out graduates who will compete for lucrative placements in private law firms. This has consequences as well for the legal education imparted to those who will join the district judiciary. The late Professor Shamnad Basheer saw this inequality for what it was, which inspired him to set up the Increasing Diversity by Increasing Access (IDIA) network, which aims to provide coaching assistance to underprivileged students and continuing support after their entry into law schools. He advocated for making these exams equitable and for them to take into account existing socio-economic inequalities.

Till last year, the examination papers also relied on some questions for determining logical reasoning capabilities that required the use of sight, thus discriminating against those who were visually challenged. Although the Common Law Admission Test (CLAT) consortium, the official body responsible for conducting the pan-India Centralized CLAT for admissions to NLUs across the country, has publicly assured us that this will not happen going forward, that commitment remains to be replicated in reality.

Even if a student manages to clear these competitive exams, they now face their second gradation—their choice of law school. It is no secret that there is often a real and perceived bias even between various NLUs, where the assumption persists that students belonging to certain 'top-tier' NLUs are better simply because of their law school affiliation. These 'meritorious' law schools are also expensive, and not all students are assured of long-term subsidies for their education. Even if scholarships or loan-based scholarships are present, they don't account for the wherewithal that is necessary to participate in activities and internships that students have to fund on their own. Hence, one exam given by an eighteen-year-old individual now becomes a means of differential treatment, since it determines their law school, experiences and life trajectories thereafter.

Even within law schools, a third gradation now exists in terms of who manages to thrive and succeed. The experience of law schools that have conducted representative surveys in this regard,[14] indicates that students from Dalit, Adivasi and other marginalized communities are often disproportionately affected. This reflects overtly through their academic grades, participation in extracurricular activities, such as moots, debates and college committees and internships as compared to their peers. However, many try to shrug this off by stating that it is simply a consequence of them not coping with the pressure. Sadly, this could not be further from the truth. It is important here to consider the kind of uphill battle students from these communities face while competing with their peers, who benefit from their natural privilege that manifests into confidence to participate and even seek appropriate training and mentorship. Unfortunately, this privilege is also reflected in the 'networks' within law schools, where support systems tend to benefit those who arguably need it the least—formed through social circles built on 'relatability' that are often shaped by gendered and caste-based dynamics. Other such prominent factors are an individual's cultural choice—such as the music, films or books that the individual partakes in—the access to which is obviously a consequence of one's privilege and the sociocultural admittance it provides.

The diversity reports of some law schools indicate a direct correlation between socio-economic status and grade point averages, and an inverse relationship in students who drop out or fail their exams. First-hand experiences of these students indicate how these students never receive enough peer or faculty support to cope with a high-pressure academic environment. They are deprived of the facility to set themselves apart by publishing and providing research assistance. Some of the internships that are considered to be of high value are often located in tier-I cities, which do not pay a living stipend to their interns. It is no surprise that students who don't belong to well-off families merely dismiss these opportunities as viable options for their professional advancement.

The CEDE initiative attempts to target this huge fissure in formal equality by consolidating a database of internship opportunities, which are otherwise disseminated through hierarchical networks and by guaranteeing a stipend to students from marginalized communities, so that the internships become realistic options.

Ultimately, these three gradations, if unaddressed, end up significantly affecting an individual's experience throughout law school. The presence of accumulated privilege already puts so many at such an advantage that by the time they enter the legal profession, they are provided an additional head start by a fourth gradation.

When seeking employment, many law students now look towards law firms. While the law firms are known for hiring based on 'merit' and 'grade point averages', we have already noted how tenuous our casual understanding of 'merit' is. Consequently, students from marginalized groups find themselves underrepresented in hiring. Many other law students seek employment with advocates and senior counsels, or even as law clerks to judges such as myself. Personally, my office does its best to assess every application we get and make a conscious effort to mitigate and account for the socio-economic location of a candidate. Hiring in lawyers' chambers is often based on informal references, which are a result of privileged networks from which the marginalized have been deliberately excluded over the years. There is an additional advantage if students belong to families with roots in the legal profession, which exponentially benefits their chances at success and minimizes their uncertainty in the gruelling years of initial practice. In more egregious cases, well-deserving candidates from marginalized communities are not offered employment because of active discrimination under the guise of 'merit'.

Let us now pause for a moment and reflect on this small journey I have described. At the end of that fourth gradation, a young lawyer would probably be between the ages of twenty-three and twenty-five. At such a young age and within such a short time of being in the legal profession, a young lawyer has already been knocked down four gradations from their peers, through no fault of their own. These accumulated roadblocks will continue to affect them in the future as well. They will only snowball over the years.

In the legal profession, women are constantly subjected to probing and pointed questions about their marriage and childcare plans, even when they enter the profession as fresh graduates, to determine whether an organization should invest in a candidate. The interviewer deduces whether she is apparently only pursuing a short-term career as a hobby. No one asks these questions of men. The statistics speak for themselves when women today seem to be joining the legal profession in equal numbers as men. This parity is, however, not noticed in the composition of persons who make partners in firms, are designated as senior counsel and even elevated as judges! The track record of institutions, even the Supreme Court, in terms of bahujans, Adivasis and persons with disabilities being in positions of power and responsibility is abysmal. We hear innumerable stories of people hiding their sexualities and conforming to their gender, no matter how overpowering the gender dysphoria, as they are acutely aware of how aligning with their true selves will relegate them to the margins of society; and that is the problem we are dealing with today. Their fears are compounded by contemporary examples.

It is because of this systemic discrimination at multiple levels that we need initiatives such as CEDE. The benefits of privilege may seem harmless to those who benefit from it; they, however, have a deleterious impact on those who are excluded. Initiatives such as CEDE not only make those in the profession question privilege but compel everyone to confront the role they may have been playing in upholding networks that support it. Further, they try to counter these all-pervasive privileged networks by granting information and access to those from marginalized groups who have been systemically excluded.

It is important to remember that representation in this way can serve multiple ends. The primary end is to benefit those who have been systematically excluded. But even more so, representation can have a positive effect by shattering the glass ceiling and ensuring that no one should ever have to think that they cannot do anything because someone like them has never done it before. A 2016 study conducted by researchers from the US's Carnegie Mellon University noted that reservations in higher education had a domino effect of spurring newer generations to educate themselves. The study found the Gross Enrolment Rate, which is a measure of the number or the percentage of actual enrolments in higher education, regardless of age, in a given academic year, of the between eighteen and twenty-three years of age eligible for higher education in that year, of STs doubling and SCs more than doubling in the period between 2000 and 2014.[15] To quote American actress Elizabeth Marvel, 'If you can see it, you can be it.'

It is also important to remember that offering these chances to those belonging to marginalized communities is not only required because the absence of such opportunities has negatively affected them but also because it is only through the representation of those belonging to marginalized communities that these existing practices that have come to be entrenched ways of doing things can be interrogated, modulated and completely dismantled. Let us take the example of an individual with a disability. A professor will never know that his practice of using slides without reading out the text contained in them excludes blind students in his class. Or that the habit of speaking extremely quickly will exclude a hearing-impaired student who relies on lip reading to communicate with others.

Judges and court administrators will never realize that their outmoded methods for filing and arguing cases are not disabled friendly until there are disabled people in the system pushing back against the unjust status quo. The existing status quo is often justified in the self-validating language of practicality and convenience, as well as avoiding complications. But it is only when discriminated groups find representation they can meaningfully push back at the slow process of changing institutions, which is followed by our hearts and minds.

However, this is easier said than done. A direct consequence of hierarchy-driven societies is that these members can rarely access the system, let alone change it. The way to break this cycle is by taking measures to open up institutions to those whom they exclude, such as proactive messaging and context-sensitive hiring. And, more importantly, never buying into the argument that a change in the system will only benefit a few marginalized members, at the cost of inconveniencing 'meritorious' members of the majority community for the reason why they are so few in the first place is often a direct consequence of the unjust way in which the system has worked to exclude them.

Dutt, in her autobiography *Coming Out as Dalit*, spoke about how her caste identity and composite gendered discrimination followed her even into the hallowed halls of St Stephen's College, one of the most prestigious institutions in India. For anyone who would consider presence at these institutions sufficient, her account indicated how her choices were shaped by her caste identity. Even as she chose to pursue her higher education abroad, she missed out on critical deadlines for scholarships, merely because she lacked the social circle that would keep her abreast with these opportunities.

Her account is not an aberration. Her mother could not sustain a successful business, even as she managed to put together a few funds, largely because her family and social circles were constructed around caste, where the knowledge or the acumen to run a business, which is socially inherited, was never passed on to her. As a woman earning her bread and butter, her mother's journey was unimaginably more difficult. Our news cycles are replete with stories of the marginalized dropping out of educational institutions or ending their lives at a disproportionate level. Quirk, the magazine run by the students of National Law School of India University, Bengaluru, published the chronicles of two bahujan students,[16] who shared their lived realities of discrimination in law school, which panned into novel forms of sexism, otherization on account of language, culture and most importantly, the lack of adequate mentorship. Before those with societal privilege scorn opportunities such as CEDE for their supposed handouts, it must be remembered that entry into the professional world, in the words of anti-racism activist Peggy McIntosh, is with an 'invisible package of unearned assets'.[17] Similarly, when the importance of representation is envisaged even in situations such as internships, it is but a mere tug to counteract the immensity of discriminatory societal forces that systemically disadvantage members of these vulnerable groups over a period of time. It is way past the time when the opaque structures of the legal profession and its institutions, both official and private, are opened up to ensure equal access and non-discrimination.

Before I conclude, I would also like to raise another important issue—of intersectionality. I have discussed how members of marginalized communities have been systemically excluded and why their representation matters. However, it is important to remember that there is often an intersection between an individual's numerous identities. An individual may simultaneously belong to many marginalized groups as a consequence of the multiple facets of their identities. The way in which systemic discrimination affects each individual will be unique, based on the facets of their identity. For example, the experience of a cis-heterosexual Dalit man will be very different from the experiences of a queer Dalit woman. Hence, while representation is important and it matters, it also has its limitations. Experiences of marginalization cannot be considered as a universal monolithic experience, whenever we attempt to check privilege and foster diversity in our communities.

Therefore, while we need to ensure adequate representation of members from marginalized communities, we must also be careful not to over-amplify its ultimate effect in curing the societal ills of systemic discrimination. When a woman is sexually harassed at her place of work, it is not just her dignity that is compromised but also her right to economic independence and work. When Dalit women are raped by upper-caste men as a means to exert dominance over the entire Dalit community, it doesn't remain in the domain of gendered violence alone. To rid our society of evils that are perpetuated by hierarchy, we also need to think about how to rebuild the existing structures and networks in a way that enables equal opportunity to all. I acknowledge that this is no small task because with great privilege comes greater insecurity. Those in positions of power due to these structures will want to cling on to them for as long as they can. However, it is up to the rest of us to think not only of ourselves but also about the larger societal goals when considering how to rebuild them. But before we do that, the first step is to begin by providing a platform and listening to those who are worst affected by it. Initiatives such as CEDE do exactly that. The project of bringing about societal change is a mission for everyone, not only for those who have been excluded.

We often wonder whether discrimination continues to exist over seventy years of Independence and a strong constitutional commitment to combat it. Every day in my life as a judge, I come across multiple forms of discrimination that strongly persist. Legal cases before the court are stories of real human suffering. They present themselves as caste atrocities, sexual violence or unreasonable difficulties in demanding reasonable accommodation. The list goes on. While my brothers and sisters on the bench attempt to do justice to the indignities highlighted before us, there are often moments when we are painfully reminded of how our interventions cannot offer a sweeping reform of discriminatory attitudes that govern all interactions in society, especially in the private realm of family and kinship.

In the *Indian Young Lawyers Association and Ors v. The State of Kerala and Ors* case (also referred to as the *Sabarimala Temple Entry* case),[18] I was one of the four judges who sought to strike down a religious practice that denied women in the menstruating age group the right to embark on the Sabarimala pilgrimage. In my opinion, I had probed the notion of menstruation and associated impurity from the transformative lens of abolishing of untouchability in the Constitution. Recently, I watched a Malayalam film titled *The Great Indian Kitchen* (2021), which was nominated for the Shanghai International Film Festival 2021. The film was situated in modern Kerala, where a newly wed bride was adjusting to her husband's household. In the latter half of the film, the men are shown to be preparing for their pilgrimage. The film charted out the compounding indignities that the bride faced, in her unpaid and thankless labour that was exerted in domestic chores and cooking, the denial of her ambitions to work a job of her choice and finally, the harsh isolation and associated untouchability when she was menstruating. The film poignantly engaged with the news of the Supreme Court judgement and juxtaposed it with the lived reality of this woman, who was not asserting a right to go on the pilgrimage but was fighting a much deeper battle as her existence was diminished by her gender. This was a stark reminder of how mere legislative or judicial interventions do not automatically upend the inequities that are entrenched in our society.

Even today, women struggle to achieve the most basic education and the right to economic independence, as they are forced to diminish their ambitions and toil thanklessly over domestic chores and caregiving, which society does not even recognize as labour that merits compensation. The Supreme Court may place an economic value on the work of a homemaker who dies in a motor accident to assess compensation to her heirs. The worth of her labour is recognized in death. Societal change requires more than a judgment. Homosexuality may not be punished by our statute books any longer, but society continues to punish them as they seek education, employment, advancement and housing. Scores of members of the LGBTQIA+ community continue to live in shame, and several are still oppressed by Section 377 of the IPC, 1860, even when the Supreme Court read it down in 2018. Transgender persons are still ostracized within families and seek out communities that survive on the fringes of society. With society washing their hands of someone who does not conform to their heteronormative standards, these persons are also excluded from law enforcement and are disproportionately victims of police brutality. Individuals with disabilities are often treated as unequal members of society or persons to be pitied. In a world as grossly unequal as ours, initiatives to bridge these fissures are not handouts. They are our modest attempts at creating a just world.

Adequate opportunities to flourish for every member of the society don't just benefit vulnerable groups but also enrich society the most. What would our Constitution have been like if Dr Ambedkar had not persevered and obtained his education? The examples of visible minorities having achieved great strides and changed our world are countless. In these overwhelming times of the pandemic, the world is thankful to Katalin Karikó, a Hungarian scientist, who struggled to persist in the sciences and has developed messenger ribonucleic acid (mRNA), which powers two effective Covid vaccines and could also potentially provide a vaccine against HIV/AIDS. Now more than ever, wouldn't we have been sorry if feminist advocates had not pushed for a woman's right to obtain education and the right to work, by liberation from gendered domestic labour in the household?

In a modern world, where working conditions are increasingly informalized and fragmented, visible minorities are further oppressed as their identities and disenfranchisement in society make them susceptible to dehumanizing wages and working conditions. It is no surprise that women, Adivasis, bahujans, landless farmers, Muslims and OBCs are over-represented in our migrant worker population who eke out an existence on bare minimum conditions. Hence, when I say that representation matters, it is not just to whet our moral appetite for an equal society but to confront the compounding precarities in our economy. In celebrating Ambedkar Jayanti and launching CEDE, it is my earnest hope that this platform, like many others, nourishes and mentors many who will follow the path of Dr Ambedkar tomorrow.

15

Speaking Truth to Power

Citizens and the Law[1]

It is an honour for me to have been invited to speak at this lecture organized in the memory of one of the greatest legal minds India has ever witnessed—Justice Mohammadali Carim Chagla. In no uncertain terms, Justice Chagla has profoundly influenced and impacted the development of law and the protection of civil liberties in India. He donned many roles during his lifetime, among them being that of a lawyer, judge, jurist, diplomat and cabinet minister. After studying at the University of Oxford, he joined the Bombay Bar in 1922 and practised as a lawyer for nineteen years in the High Court of Bombay before he was appointed as a judge and subsequently, the Chief Justice of the High Court of Bombay. Though he received an offer for appointment as a judge of the Supreme Court of India, he let the offer pass since he believed that he would be able to initiate more changes as the Chief Justice of a High Court than he ever would be able to as a *puisne* judge of the Supreme Court. After his retirement, he served as an ad hoc judge in the International Court of Justice, and as India's ambassador to the US and the UK, before taking oath as a cabinet minister, taking on the portfolio of education and then external affairs. Only a few others could possibly come close to the diversity of roles Chief Justice Chagla took on, and yet, unsurprisingly, he managed to excel in each of them.

Through all the various roles that he donned during his lifetime, he consistently upheld the rule of law, maintained an unbending faith in democracy and advocated his belief in civil liberties. He staunchly spoke out against the discrimination against Indians in South Africa; similarly, his voice was one of the most vocal when the national Emergency was imposed in India. Right at the beginning of the Emergency, addressing a gathering at the All-India Civil Liberties Conference, he said, 'I would rather have the Constitution abrogated than to pretend that she [referring to Mrs Indira Gandhi] is constitution[al], she is democratic and all that she has done is permitted by the Constitution. This is Constitutional dictatorship.'[2] In his autobiography, *Roses in December*, he defends the individuality of every citizen and states that he was opposed to the prohibition policy of the government and that 'it was no business of any Government to tell the people what they should drink and what they should not drink'.[3]

When the development of constitutional jurisprudence was in its nascent stage in India, Justice Chagla rested his interpretation of the Constitution on the principles of constitutional morality and constitutionalism. He believed that for the survival of a pluralistic society, it was important that the individual, irrespective of their social status or social class, is placed at the core of society. Speaking about Justice Chagla after his retirement from the Bombay High Court, eminent lawyer and jurist, Nani Palkhivala had, said, '[t]he law was to him no lifeless conglomeration of sections and decisions. He illumined justice and humanised the law'.[4] Similarly, my father, Chief Justice Y.V. Chandrachud, noted his contribution to the development of our young Constitution and stated that his 'innate sense of what is just and fair and the liberality of [his] social outlook enabled [him] to hold the scales of justice even between the rule of law and the liberty of the individual'.[5]

Justice Chagla believed that even though judges should not speak about certain political issues, they have a moral obligation to speak on others, as citizens of India.[6] Hence, it is an absolute honour for me to be delivering this lecture today in the memory of Justice Chagla, not only as a judge of the Supreme Court of India but also as a citizen of India.

Coming to the topic I have chosen for today, it is important to first ask ourselves: What does 'speaking truth to power' even mean? Defined in ancient Greek tradition as *parrhesia*, it refers to an act by a speaker to use truth to criticize someone more powerful than them.[7] In India, it would be akin to Mahatma Gandhi's philosophy of satyagraha, where truth is used as a form of non-violent resistance to those in power.[8] As such, 'speaking truth to power' aims to wield the power of 'truth' against the powerful, be it an imperial power or even an all-powerful State. Crucially, the assumption is that the act of speaking the 'truth' will counteract power and obviate a predisposition towards tyranny.

At the outset, then, it is important to consider why 'truth' is so important to democracy, which is the form of governance adopted to prevent the tyranny of the few. There is possibly no better way to do this, other than by first comparing the status of 'truth' in non-democracies.

In the Enlightenment Era in Europe, philosophers sought to challenge the domination of the Catholic Church and monarchies in public life because of their control over the 'truth'. Hence, the Renaissance was not merely a literary and artistic revolution but was also supposed to usher in an age where superstitions and dogma would give way to reason and evidence based on actual truth.[9] Similarly, philosopher Hannah Arendt associated totalitarian governments with their constant reliance on falsehood in order to establish dominance. She notes that this was so brazen that people often lost the bearings of their own selves in these States and living the actual 'truth' in itself became a political act.[10]

Even in early republics that served as precursors to democracies, truth was considered crucial in order to ensure the ethos of transparency and openness in the way of functioning.[11] Similarly, truth is important in modern democracies that have been described as 'spaces of reason', since any decision must be backed by adequate reasons and because a reason that is based on a falsehood would be no reason at all.[12] Truth is also important to instil a sense of public trust in democracies, that the officials in charge are committed to finding the 'truth' and acting by it.[13] Hence, it is no surprise that the national motto of India after its independence has been 'Satyamev Jayate' (Truth Shall Prevail).

Truth also plays an important role in creating a shared 'public memory' on which the foundations of a nation can be built in the future. It is because of this reason that many countries opt to establish truth commissions immediately on gaining independence from a totalitarian regime or after coming out of a period fraught with human rights violations. These commissions function to document, record and acknowledge the 'truth' of earlier regimes and violations for future generations, so as to not only provide catharsis to the survivors but also prevent any possibility of denial in the future.[14] In a different context, this role can also be played by courts that have the ability to document information from all the parties involved, after due process has been followed. In the suo motu cognizance of the COVID-19 pandemic taken by our Supreme Court, we have acknowledged this very role in the context of the pandemic.[15]

However, the relationship that truth shares with democracy is that of both a sword and a shield. The scope for extensive deliberation, particularly in the age of social media, exposes multiple 'truths', so much so that it seems like we live in an 'age of lies', and that shakes the very foundation of a democracy. The citizens should arrive at a consensus on at least the basic facts that are backed by both science and society to form collective decisions. Hence, if deliberations are censored by the State or if we either subconsciously or deliberately censor them, we would discern just one 'truth'—one that is not challenged by us. In contrast, deliberation by multiple groups with differing viewpoints will pave the way for the correction of errors in this 'truth'. Ideas will be aggregated and the entire process will help in the emergence of a creative solution that no one person could have thought of individually.[16]

Pre-legislative consultative process is an apt instance where deliberation between individuals has brought about impactful change. For instance, the draft bill for the Kerala Police Act, 2011, was published on the website of the state police, inviting feedback and suggestions. When the bill was introduced in the Legislative Assembly, it was referred to the Select Committee, and the Select Committee conducted a district-wide meeting. Around 400–500 people attended these meetings, and the necessary impact of such an extensive consultative process was the suggestion of 790 amendments to the draft bill after nearly four hours of extensive debate. Around 240 of those suggested amendments, most of which were centred on the public feedback, were ultimately accepted.[17] By contrast, in South Africa, pre-legislative consultation is a constitutional requirement, and any law that is enacted without pre-legislative consultation is deemed unconstitutional. In 2005, the Parliament of South Africa enacted legislation relating to the issue of reproductive healthcare. The Constitutional Court of South Africa, however, declared these laws unconstitutional since the National Council of Provinces did not fulfil its obligation of initiating public deliberation on the law.[18]

Hence, it is not difficult for one to understand why democracy and truth go hand in hand. Democracy needs the power of truth to survive. As such, once can consider 'speaking truth to power' as a right every citizen must have in a democracy, but equally as also the duty of every citizen. However, to understand how we can truly exercise this right of ours, it is important to first ask ourselves, what does 'truth' even mean?

To many of you, this must indeed be a very strange question to ponder upon since truth is often easily definable, in contrast to obvious falsehoods. For instance, the fact that I am wearing spectacles is the truth, while asserting to the contrary would be an abject lie. Hence, it may seem that the difficulty is then not in knowing what the 'truth' is, but only in identifying it. Indeed, Justice Chagla himself acknowledged that for him, the most challenging part of being a judge was to undertake the nearly impossible task of identifying the truth in the cases before him. According to him, a judge could get closer to identifying the truth only when contrasting arguments were put forth by the counsel representing the contending parties. He said that these deliberations, arguments and counterarguments then aided him in his pursuit of truth.[19]

However, I believe that while the identification of truth may be singularly at issue in judicial proceedings, the very nature of 'truth' can often be indeterminable in societies. Most commonly, truth is defined in terms of 'facts'. According to the 'correspondence' theory of truth proposed by Plato and Aristotle, a proposition is true if it corresponds to a 'fact'.[20] However, it is important to remember that even the most preliminary facts can be disputed. To this day, we continue to have a section of society that still disputes the phenomenon of global warming. However, a determination of what constitutes a 'true fact' is important since laws are enacted on the indispensable belief that the mischief the State seeks to rectify through them is in reality principally true and a fact. Hence, if the phenomenon of global warming were to turn out to be a lie, then the basis of many of our environmental laws would be farcical. Nevertheless, while it may continue to remain in dispute, the phenomenon of global warming is still a question for which we can have a scientifically determinable 'truth' through deliberation, thus allowing the State to proceed with its regulation.

A State does not seek to rectify merely mischiefs that are grounded in scientific truths but also those grounded in moral truths. Take, for instance, the Bonded Labour System (Abolition) Act, 1976, which was enacted, as the preamble of the statute notes, 'with a view to preventing the economic and political exploitation of the weaker sections of the people'. As such, the Act was enacted based on two premises: *first*, that the bonded labour system exploits people; and *second*, that such exploitation of people is principally wrong. A liberal rights philosopher who believes in the value and quality of life might argue that both these premises are true, while an economist studying the market and the methods to increase market output may not agree with them.

This then brings us to the 'pragmatic' theory of truth, which defines 'truth' in terms of 'opinions'.[21] It is in this context that

Sophia Rosenfeld, an eminent historian, notes that due to the increasing belief of people in the non-existence of impartial 'facts' and their legitimate sources, people's idea of 'truth' has become more instinctive, where 'truth' is whatever *feels* right to them. In essence, '"[t]ruth" has become personal, a matter of subjective feeling and taste and not much different from an opinion'.[22] However, a quick glance through history will teach that individuals sometimes tend to have opinions that may not be morally justifiable to others.

For instance, philosopher Jean-Jacques Rousseau considered women as a class to be naturally cunning and believed that they should be governed by constant fear and restricted, to be gazed at as objects of desire.[23] On the other hand, French judge Montesquieu regarded black Africans to be 'savage[s] and barbarians' who did not possess 'normal' human traits.[24] While these opinions were held by Rousseau and Montesquieu individually in the Enlightenment Era, they were also sometimes shared by the general public. As such, women and black Africans were not treated as citizens because they were—according to those who held power and could wield words—cunning, manipulative and weak. Hence, the very fact that these opinions are acknowledged today for their racist and sexist overtones lends credence to the argument that 'truth' cannot be akin to an opinion, since that would allow for personal prejudices to creep into its determination. It is in this vein that Daniel Patrick Moynihan, an American politician, sociologist and diplomat, said that 'everyone is entitled to [their] own opinion, but not [their] own facts'.[25]

However, I often wonder if facts are even considerably different from opinions in a plural society where there are varied lived experiences of different people. For instance, long before the decision of the Supreme Court in *Navtej Singh Johar,*[26] which decriminalized homosexuality, and long before a minuscule population of our country normalized homosexuality, Denmark had passed the Registered Partnership Act of 1989, which legalized same-sex marriage, subject to very few exceptions. Further, while India is currently transitioning towards normalizing same-sex relationships, more than ten countries around the world still prescribe capital punishment for homosexuality.[27] In considering another example, we can note that forty years after India legalized abortion in 1971, most of the Latin American countries are yet to legalize it. Hence, while for one part of the world, the 'truth' would be that a foetus is regarded to possess a right to life, yet for another, this would be a 'false' assertion.

As such, it was argued by philosopher Michel Foucault that different societies are engaged in different 'regimes of truth'. Even within such societies, different *sections* are governed by different truths, with often those in dominant positions imposing their version of the truth upon others.[28] Hence, facts and opinions cannot be confined to water-tight compartments when they overlap in various instances in their relationship with 'truth'. The opinion of a person is conferred the status of a 'fact' and subsequently 'truth' depending on the power they yield in society. This was also confirmed in a 1994 study by a historian of science Steven Shapin, when he noted that even at the height of the Scientific Revolution in seventeenth-century England, truth was closely linked to an elite culture of honour, wealth and civilized comportment and was not a universal standard.[29]

In India, since women, Dalits and others belonging to marginalized communities did not traditionally enjoy power, their opinions were not conferred the status of 'truth'. This is because since they did not enjoy the freedom to express their opinions, their thoughts were confined, crippled and caged. Even after these marginalized groups received the right to vote, their opinions were reckoned to be 'untrustworthy' because they were considered to be treacherous 'by nature'. In India, during the British Raj, when power was absolutely in the hands of a few powerful members of the Raj, the truth (and by necessary inference, the fact) was the opinion of the King or Queen and members of the Raj. After the abolition of the Raj, the truth then became the belief and opinion of upper-caste men. With progress in society and annihilation of the notions of patriarchy and caste supremacy, the opinions of women, Dalits and other marginalized communities are slowly but gradually starting to be regarded as 'truths' in India.

One way to address this problem is by broadening the scope of 'truth' itself, and for doing this, we can look at the example of the South African Truth and Reconciliation Commission, which defined four different kinds of truth.

The *first* of these was factual or forensic truth, which we would describe as 'scientific' truth since it is determined on the basis of facts and is the most commonly understood definition of 'truth'. However, it is the other three that were extremely peculiar. The *second* was personal or narrative truth, which was based on the cathartic benefit of storytelling, where every person who was affected by the apartheid regime could come forward and tell their story in public hearings. The *third* was social or 'dialogue' truth, which was defined by Justice Albie Sachs of the Constitutional Court of South Africa as 'the truth of experience that is established through interaction, discussion and debate'.[30] The basis of this truth often arose from the dialogue surrounding the work of the truth commission, which happened in an entirely public setting. And finally, the *fourth* was healing and restorative truth, where the truth commission offered an acknowledgement of the crimes committed against the survivors by putting the facts collected by them in their proper political, social and ideological context.[31]

These types of truth acknowledge that truth itself has varying dimensions and often plays different roles. Hence, when understood broadly, it has the capability to accommodate the world view of different individuals and also offer them the necessary catharsis. However, even within these broader conceptions of 'truth', the question of the standards for its identification, verification and validation still remains.

Rosenfeld notes that there are three very common means for the determination of 'truth' in democracies.[32] The *first* is obviously by the State, since it is the Central authority with access to all information that allows it to make decisions. Understandably, the State does not often adjudicate upon scientific truths, but it does provide them its tacit approval when it decides to form policies based on them. As such, all policies of the State can be assumed to have been formed on their basis of what the 'truth' of our society is. However, this by no means leads to the conclusion that the States cannot indulge in falsehood for political reasons, even in democracies. The role of the US in the Vietnam War did not see daylight until the *Pentagon Papers* were published. In the context of the COVID-19 pandemic, we see that there is an increasing trend of countries across the world who are trying to manipulate data on the COVID-19 infection rate and deaths. Hence, one cannot only rely on the State to determine the 'truth'.

The *second* means of determining the 'truth' is by 'experts' such as scientists, statisticians, researchers and economists who can verify knowledge. Because of their expertise in a given area, the citizens are often expected to bow down to their determination of the 'truth' since it does not suffer from the malaise of political bias. However, this is not always true because while experts may not have political affiliation, their claims are also subject to manipulation due to reasons such as ideological affinity, receipt of financial aid or personal malice. These 'experts' are also often employed by think tanks that conduct research to support specific opinions.[33]

I have mentioned earlier that the 'truth' of marginalized communities does not often see the light of day due to their position in society. Similarly, these communities are often never designated as 'experts' as they were prevented from accessing these positions through systemic oppression. As such, that takes away their opportunity to contribute to the determination of 'truth'. Since their perspective is never taken into account, the claims of 'experts' also suffer from the problem of their inherent biases.[34]

'Experts' also claim to base their opinion on concrete facts, which aims to make their conclusion the obvious 'truth'. However, postmodernist scholars have correctly noted that while the facts in themselves may be accurate, their selection, arrangement and the conclusions drawn from these are subject to the individual realities of the person making these determinations.[35] As such, the opinion of an 'expert' cannot really be considered as the objective 'truth' even when based on true facts because it is *one* possible opinion based on those facts, and not the *only one*. Arendt notes that this cherry-picking of facts in one's favour has given rise to 'spin', in which the citizens are not technically told a lie, but the facts are selected in a way to provide only a version of the 'truth',[36] which then helps manufacture the consent of the unsuspecting citizens.[37]

This leaves us with the *third* means of determination of truth, which is through deliberation and discussion by the citizens—by paralleling, combining and expounding the claims of truth in the public sphere. It is often argued that scientific truth, reliant on expert knowledge and withheld from public scrutiny due to state-imposed opacity, remains inaccessible and unverifiable to the common person, both because of the technical complexity involved and the lack of transparent information in the public domain. However, as responsible citizens, we should put these 'truth providers' through intense scrutiny and questioning to convince ourselves of the veracity of the claims made by them. For this, it is also equally important for those making truth claims to be transparent and conspicuous. We must together endeavour to create and encourage a culture that is conducive to the deliberation of truth, particularly because 'truth' dances on a fine balance between facts and opinions. However, this brings us to the question of who should be the citizens to take up this role?

Philosopher Immanuel Kant expected this role to be taken up by the European intellectual clerisy, the equivalent of modern-day 'public intellectuals', where they would mediate between the rest of the population and the State.[38] However, he took for granted that entry into this class was often barred by one's gender, access to education and wealth.[39] Similarly, Noam Chomsky, in his celebrated article 'The Responsibility of Intellectuals', written in the context of the United States's ongoing involvement in the war in Vietnam, noted that it was the duty of the 'intellectuals' to speak the truth and expose the lies of the State and its 'experts'. However, in contrast to Kant, he acknowledged that the intellectuals could only perform this function *because* of the power and privilege that their liberties granted to them, in contrast to other citizens.[40]

As such, it is important to remember that every person—rich or poor, male or female or belonging to a third gender; Dalit or Brahmin or otherwise; Hindu, Muslim or Christian or belonging to any other religion—has the inherent capacity to identify the truth and differentiate it from falsehood. This capacity to identify the truth stems from common knowledge, experiences in life, their individual struggles and much more. However, many of them are unable to participate in this process because of systemic oppression that either does not provide a platform for their voices or works to minimize their actual impact. Hence, while considering the role of citizens in determining the 'truth', we must keep in mind that this does not refer only to the elite, privileged class of intellectuals but includes everyone. Therefore, it is imperative for us to create an environment where this becomes possible.

This is also keeping in line with the ideas of philosopher John Stuart Mill, who in his seminal work *On Liberty* elucidated on the disadvantage of suppressing opinions and stated:[41]

> The peculiar evil of silencing the expression of an opinion is, that it is robbing . . . those who dissent from the opinion, still more than those who hold it. If the opinion is right, they are deprived of the opportunity of exchanging error for truth: if wrong, they lose, what is almost as great a benefit, the clearer perception and livelier impression of truth, produced by its collision with error.

As such, Mill was a firm believer in the 'marketplace of ideas', where, when given enough time, the truth would always prevail over falsehood. However, we must test the veracity of this claim in the present time, in what is now being called the 'post-truth' world.

To test this claim, we must therefore first define what a 'post-truth' world even means, for it could have two possible meanings: *First*, that it has become exceedingly difficult for citizens to find the 'truth' in this time and age; and *second*, which is the more disturbing possibility, is that having found the 'truth', they just do not care about it.

If we go by the first meaning, it is undeniable that the phenomenon of 'fake news' is on the rise. A pertinent example of this is that the World Health Organization (WHO) recently termed the current COVID-19 pandemic as also being an 'infodemic', due to the overabundance of misinformation online.[42] However, scholars have also noted that 'fake news' or false information is not a new phenomenon, having been in existence for as long as print media has existed.[43] But the rapid advancement in technology and the spread of internet access have undeniably exacerbated this problem.

It is often noted that even on the internet, the largest portion of the blame is often laid at the door of large corporations such as Facebook and X (formerly Twitter). Part of the problem is that while these social media platforms allow users to create their own networks and communities, this also leads to a homogeneity within those networks. After all, humans are social animals and have an increasing tendency to associate themselves with fellow humans with shared lived experiences or similar beliefs. This leads to the creation of 'echo chambers' or 'bubbles', where people are only exposed to the viewpoint they agree with while never coming into contact with an opposing one.[44] There is another issue that also relates to human nature—human beings are simply more attracted to sensational stories, which are often based on falsehood. As such, in a 2018 study, it was determined that lies dominated truth in every metric on Twitter, including reaching more people and doing so quickly.[45]

However, another problem has arisen due to what can only be described as our 'attention economy', which is to say that there is just so much information out there and we can only consume so little of it. Hence, everyone in the marketplace is constantly competing for our attention.[46] Leading First Amendment scholar Timothy Shiou-Ming Wu noted that because of this, the traditional methods of limiting free speech are being changed. He notes that when the First Amendment was introduced in the US, the State controlled the platforms of speech, and the First Amendment was designed to prevent the abuse of this power.[47] However, with the advent of the internet, the platform is no longer an issue, but rather it is about grabbing someone's attention. As such, while someone's speech may not be removed from the internet, it can be effectively drowned out by flooding the internet with massive amounts of information to the contrary. This will ensure that many people do not even read the original speech, or will be unconvinced of its truth.[48] Hence, it is easy to see why Mill's 'marketplace of ideas' approach to speech in order to uncover the 'truth' may no longer be an option. However, the internet and social media corporations are not the only ones to blame for this scenario.

This brings us to the second possible meaning of the 'post-truth' world, where 'truth' does not matter to people any more. While the advent of the internet may have played a part in this, too, it certainly cannot shoulder all the blame. It is important to acknowledge that we live in a world that is increasingly becoming divided along social, political, economic and religious lines. This also leads to increasing polarization of 'truth', where sections of the population contest on 'your truth' versus 'our truth' even on subjects that are unrelated to the common affinity that the group shares. This is particularly manifest when the political views of an individual interfere with the ability of that person to make an accurate assessment of 'opinion' that is unrelated to their political views. In a very interesting experiment conducted by researchers from the UK and the US, a group of participants were tasked with the categorization of shapes. However, before the task could start, they were given the opportunity to learn about the political views and skills on geometric shapes of their fellow participants. When the participants were given a free hand to form groups, it was found that they grouped themselves with those with whom they share close political affinity, though the task at hand was only to categorize shapes.[49] This tendency to exhibit 'epistemic spillovers' has led to the manifestation of multiple truths. No consensus is reached on the identification of '*the* truth' due to our tendency not to be able to accept or even consider the views of those whom we perceive as different from us. We subconsciously filter the 'truth' that does not align with our interest—we only read the newspapers that align with our beliefs, ignore books written by people who do not belong to our stream, and turn the TV on mute when someone furnishes an opinion contrary to ours. In sum, we do not truly care about the 'truth' as much as we do about being right. However, who is to blame for this?

Indeed, social media corporations can be afforded some of the blame because their interface and algorithms help increase existing polarization. But doing so only ignores the deeper underlying issues in our communities. People often have such differing conceptions of the 'truths' because their realities are very different to one another. This can be due to the difference in their gender, caste, religion or economic status; even within these, a combination of factors will give rise to differing lived realities. Indeed, if this is true, the question remains as to what can be done.

Of course, one possible way suggested by many scholars is to regulate the social media corporations. However, being a sitting member of the judiciary, it is not fit for me to comment upon that. Indeed, then, what can we do as *citizens* of India?

The first thing to do is to strengthen our public institutions. As citizens, we must strive to ensure that we have a press that is free from the influence of any kind, political or economic, which will provide us with information in an unbiased manner. Similarly, schools and universities need to be supported to ensure that they create an atmosphere where students can learn to differentiate truth from falsehood and develop a temperament for questioning those in power. Justice Chagla also sought to achieve these very aims during his tenure as the education minister of India.[50] Further, we also need to protect the integrity of our elections and look upon voting not only as a right but also as a duty. To do this, we need to ensure that all citizens are given a basic education and truly understand the value of their vote.

Second, we must not only acknowledge the plurality of opinions in a country as diverse as India but also celebrate it. This allows for more breathing space for all opinions and leaves room open for actual deliberation. In his autobiography, Justice Chagla states that 'kindness and gentleness are qualities which every human nature is capable of, and which every human nature appreciates and is moved by. These qualities require neither special training nor special equipment. They are present in every man—only they get overlaid by vanity and self-seeking'.[51] Hence, it is important for each one of us to be kinder to our fellow citizens and not be quick to judge them for their opinions. At the same time, we must work towards ensuring that barriers based on one's gender, caste, religion, language or economic status are removed, so as to bring everyone's realities as close as possible, in order to allow them to have similar notions about the 'truths' of our society.

Finally, as citizens of a democracy that is India, we need to commit ourselves to the search for 'truth' as a key aspiration of our society. I had mentioned earlier that our national motto is 'Satyamev Jayate' (Truth Shall Prevail). It is crucial that we etch this into all our hearts and work towards living up to it by developing the right temperament. We can do this by questioning the State, 'experts' and fellow citizens in order to determine the 'truth', and then speaking this truth to them, if they choose to ignore or deny it.

I know that what I may be saying right now may seem too idealistic a vision or may just seem impossible given the scale of democracy in India. To those of you, I wish to remind you of something Justice Chagla had said in his autobiography:[52]

> The democratic ideology is always willing to concede that there may be an element of truth in every belief held by any particular section of the public; it is not prepared to coerce a minority opinion by the brute force of numbers. It is ever ready to discuss and debate, and is more anxious to get the minority to acquiesce in the decision of the majority than coerce the minority into an unwilling submission. The democratic temper is also tolerant towards human frailty. A man may aspire to perfection, but he is made of clay, and more often than not, he deviates from

> the straight and narrow path. This deviation is partly due to his own weakness and partly to overpowering circumstances created by the society in which he is placed. His errors and his lapses are not always wholly of his making. We need a more sympathetic understanding of human frailty in the sphere of individual relations.

I will not deny that the challenge before us is tough and requires constant effort from all of us. I hope every single citizen of India does their bit in honouring the memory of the great Justice Chagla by speaking truth to power and working towards bettering our democracy!

16

Conceptualizing Marginalization

Agency, Assertion and Personhood[1]

It is an honour for me to have been invited to speak at this lecture organized in the memory of one of the greatest social revolutionaries India has ever witnessed—Dr Ambedkar. In no uncertain terms, Dr Ambedkar has profoundly influenced and impacted the development of law and social change in India. He gave us the Constitution and the rights that we so dearly hold on to.

I begin today's lecture by sharing a story from Dr Ambedkar's autobiography, *Waiting for a Visa*. As the story goes, in 1929, the government of Bombay had appointed a committee to study the injustice, oppression, subjugation and persecution faced by the untouchables in Bombay. Dr Ambedkar was appointed as a member of this committee. He visited Chalisgaon, located in the Jalgaon district in Maharashtra, to inquire into a case of social boycott that the members of the Dalit community in the village were facing. He had decided to stay the night with the Dalit community. The members of the community had arranged a horse carriage for him to travel from Chalisgaon. Shortly after embarking on the journey, the horse carriage in which Dr Ambedkar was travelling met with an accident. While investigating the cause of the accident, he was exposed to a tale of tyranny, domination and social ostracization. It came to his notice that no coachman was prepared to drive a Dalit passenger in the horse carriage. The coachmen were willing to lend the carriage on hire, but were not willing to drive a Dalit passenger. A member of the Dalit community of the village, who had no experience driving a horse carriage, had taken over the reins. In his autobiography, Dr Ambedkar recounts this incident by saying, 'To save my dignity, the Mahars of Chalisgaon had put my life in jeopardy. It [was] then [that] I learnt that a Hindu tongawalla, no better than a menial, has a dignity by which he can look upon himself as a person is superior to any untouchable, even though he may be a Barrister-at-law.'[2] In this account, there lies a melancholic tale of diminishing personhood. A well-educated barrister, who has been addressing the issue of untouchability at a high level, had to face ruthless and brutish humiliation by virtue of being a member of the Dalit community.

In the early 1900s, the discourse on the need to reduce the population in India was grounded on the alliance between eugenics and Malthusian ideas. Dr Ambedkar introduced a resolution in support of government-funded birth control in the Bombay Legislative Assembly. While introducing the resolution, he remarked, 'If men had to bear the pangs which women have to undergo during childbirth, none of them would even consent to bear more than a single child in their [sic] life.'[3] He steered the discourse away from the arguments of development and eugenics, where only the middle and the poor classes of the country were regarded to be contributing to the population explosion, by emphasizing the agency—or rather the lack of it—that women held in matters relating to bodily autonomy. In doing so, Dr Ambedkar highlighted the marginalization women faced, even in conversations about their own bodily autonomy.

Keeping in mind the spirit of the two incidents I recounted, I propose to speak about marginalization today. I will first speak about the members of the marginalized sections of society—on their struggles, loss of agency and personhood. I will then contextualize their marginalization as being not just a product of their existence as individuals but as a consequence of their membership of a group that is supposedly considered to be inferior to other social groups. Finally, I shall share some thoughts on what the law and society can do to remedy these concerns.

To begin, let us travel back to 1886. The US Supreme Court in *Santa Clara County v. Southern Pacific Railroad Co.*[4] held that the equal protection clause of the Fourteenth Amendment applies to corporations. It is important to remember that this decision came only about thirty years after the US Supreme Court's decision in *Dred Scott v. Sandford*[5] in 1857, where it ruled that blacks who reside in the country are not citizens of the country, and are hence not entitled to any rights. Thus, in the US, corporate entities acquired rights before the members belonging to the African American community did.

One of the greatest political acts of law is to define a legal person, i.e., define who can act in law, possess rights under the law and receive the protection of the law. The rights available under the Indian Constitution can be categorized into rights that are available to citizens and rights that are available to all persons—both citizens and non-citizens. While the right to equality under Article 14 of the Constitution is available to all persons, the right to freedom of speech and expression under Article 19 is available only to citizens. Therefore, a significant conversation that we must all engage in is on the identification of persons. Who are persons? Who identifies persons? What are the characteristics of personhood? And can personhood, once granted, be withdrawn?

Currently, there is abundant jurisprudential debate surrounding personhood. Questions have been raised on whether foetuses, animals and even artificially intelligent robots possess personhood. However, when I think about these complex questions, I find myself considering a preliminary question: Are even all human beings, who walk, live and breathe on the surface of the earth, conferred with personhood?

The criteria for the identification of personhood have evolved over time. One school of thought has defined personhood in terms of the entity that confers the right. They argue that a 'legal person' is any person who has the formal capacity to bear a legal right, and this person has no moral, social, political or historical character. Scholar F.H. Lawson terms this method of classification as 'mathematical equations', made for simplifying legal calculations.[6] The second school of thought defines personhood in reference to biological and metaphysical definitions of humanity. Under this categorization, a legal person is identified based on birth and death. The third school of thought uses the criterion of rationality for determining a legal person. This person is characteristically described in terms of their mental attributes, their ability to comprehend situations, their rationality and their ability to assume responsibility for their actions.[7] While all human beings would be considered a person by the first and the second schools of thought, the third school of thought excludes a sizable population of non-rational human beings from the category of 'persons'.

We ought to be wary of consolidating the ideals of citizenship and personhood. It is a general conception that citizenship is an evolving concept since it is a product of the law and political community in power, while personhood is universal and not *granted*.[8] Legal scholar and expert on the US Constitution, Alexander Bickel, in his book *The Morality of Consent* states, 'It has always been easier, it always will be easier, to think of someone as a noncitizen than to decide that he is a nonperson.'[9] It is indeed true that we experience an uncomfortable sensation while terming a human being as a non-person. While citizenship is a legal construction, personhood is both a legal and a moral construction. A person is a bearer of rights and has a moral standing in society. Citizenship and personhood are both different yet very similar conceptions. Both are granted and can be withdrawn, and are both historical and political constructions. However, while citizenship can only be formally withdrawn by the law, personhood can be diminished, contracted and moderated by non-legal tools as well. A class of society may be citizens in the eyes of the law of the country, yet their status of personhood could be withdrawn by the acts of the society they inhabit.

The Dalit community in India is by law recognized as persons and is also granted citizenship, since the Constitution came into force. The Constitution provides for their right to equality and prohibits discrimination on the ground of caste. In furtherance of the constitutional mandate of substantive equality, reservations in higher education and employment are granted to the Dalit and tribal communities. Parliament has also enacted the Scheduled Castes and Scheduled Tribes (Prevention of Atrocities) Act, 1989, to curb the commission of atrocities against members of the Dalit and tribal communities. However, are constitutional and legal mandates sufficient to protect the personhood of an individual belonging to such a marginalized group? Aruna Gogulamanda, a Dalit poet from Telangana, who weaves her poetry around the discrimination Dalit women face, has aptly described the life of Dalit women in India through her poetry. Her poem 'She Was Told!' goes as follows:[10]

> Her eyes two dry hollows bear silent witness
> Tell the tales of living through fears and years
> Of centuries and millennia of violations and deaths
> She was told that she was dirt and filth,
> In the sacred land of thousands of goddesses, she is called a Dalit.

Yashica Dutt, an Indian journalist, in her book *Coming Out as a Dalit*, speaks of the pain of a Dalit woman's soul living in the body of an upper-caste woman.[11] She speaks as a third-generation, educated Dalit woman who found it necessary to mask her 'Dalitness' to shield herself from social ostracization. Dalits in Chakwara, a village in Jaipur, Rajasthan, had launched a struggle to gain access to the pond in their village. After a prolonged struggle, the Dalits in the village were granted access to the village pond. The upper-caste community, arguing that the water in the pond was impure after the Dalits had utilized it, stopped using the water. In a desire to humiliate the Dalit community, they dug a channel that directly sent the sewage water into the pond.[12] Through this act, they sought to restrain the Dalit community's exercise of agency and impede their assertive capacity.

Further, though personhood, like citizenship, is also granted by the law, it need not necessarily be diminished only by the law.[13] For an individual to be recognized as a 'person', the components of externalization and internalization have to be fulfilled: *Firstly*, the society *and* the law must regard her as a person holding rights; and *secondly*, she must view herself as a person worthy of holding rights in the society. Thus, an action that affects both externalization and internalization would diminish personhood.

Marginalization embodies the principle of 'graded inequality'.[14] It is important to remember that humiliation is an integral part of an inherently dominant society that perpetuates marginalization. Humiliation means degradation and violation of their self-respect to bring down their image in their own eyes. It need not be direct and physical but can also be indirect and institutionalized.[15] Its direct effect is that a member of the marginalized community faces embarrassment, shame, indignity and disgrace while being shunned. When a person is humiliated, the 'outcast body becomes a stranger to itself'.[16] The members of the marginalized community are thus forced to live out of their bodies, where the soul is alienated from the body. In her work, feminist activist V. Geetha had focused on this dissociation that humiliation causes to the untouchables in India and stated that, 'This body in which the untouchable lives but does not inhabit is her prison-house even if she changes her vocation—through negotiation and struggle—her corporeal being precedes her. Forced to live out of a body that is its own ruin, the Dalit suffers a state of permanent dissociation.' Similarly, one of the arguments made by the African American community before the US Supreme Court in *Plessy v. Ferguson*[17] was that the segregation of transport based on race was degrading and humiliating. However, the court rejected their contention and observed that, 'We consider the underlying fallacy of the plaintiff's argument to consist in the assumption that the enforced separation of the two races stamps the coloured race with a badge of inferiority. If this be so, it is not by reason of anything found in the act, but solely because the coloured race chooses to put that construction upon it.'[18] Thus, the members of the African American community were humiliated with the policy of separate transportation because, in *effect*, the segregation was not by mutual consent but because the members of the privileged white community felt degraded in having any contact with the African Americans. Dalit scholar Bama, in her book *Karukku*, describes the residential segregation in her village. She recalls that the village had different settlements for every caste and that the Paraya (Dalit) settlement was right next to the village cemetery. She states that the Dalits would only go to the settlements of the other castes for work, and the upper castes would never visit the Dalit settlement because amenities such as a post office, school and milk depot stood in the upper-caste settlements. The residential segregation based on caste depicts the chasm between Dalits and the upper castes, where the members of the Dalit community are humiliated and denied their just entitlements. Enraged by the discrimination based on caste, Bama asks us all, 'Are Dalits not human beings? Do they not have common sense? Do they not have such attributes as a sense of honour and self-respect? Are they without any wisdom, beauty, or dignity? What do we lack? They treat us in whatever way they choose, as if we are slaves who don't possess human dignity.'[19] Author Sujatha Gidla breaks down the caste system for the American audience when she is questioned how the caste identity of a person is identified, since, unlike race, caste is invisible. She tells them that everybody in India knows everybody's caste identity because 'your life is your caste, your caste is your life'—it is an identity that cannot be shed, reversed or invisibilized.[20]

The Indian Constitution calls for the redistribution of material resources to further the constitutional ideal of substantive equality. However, we need to ask ourselves a very important question: Would redistribution of material resources, automatically and by itself, extend respect to the members of the marginalized community? Scholar and activist Suraj Milind Yengde has written in his book *Caste Matters*: 'A single Dalit success is taken as a sign of guaranteed success available to all Dalits. Dalits are not only hungry for economic and political emancipation but also for "identity, meaning and self-worth" . . .'[21] The access to the village pond did not extend recognition to the Dalit community in Chakwara, in Phagi tehsil in Jaipur district, Rajasthan. Formal equality requires recognizing all persons as equals, and substantive equality aims at equitable outcomes. However, without the fulfilment of the principle of recognition, the ideals of both formal and substantive equality would not be sufficient to address concerns of freedom. It is only through recognition that our existence as social beings is generated.[22] As scholar and philosopher Charles Taylor has emphasized, 'Due recognition is not just a courtesy we owe people. It is a vital human need.'[23]

An individual may be humiliated for her achieved status or her ascribed status. People may confer respect on an individual for her nature as a human being or for her professional achievements. An individual may be respected as a human being for her kind, humble or fierce nature; she may also be respected for her professional success. Many people of this country respect and admire P.V. Sindhu, Mithali Raj, Mother Teresa and Kalpana Chawla for their achievements in their respective fields. However, sections of the population are also either provided or denied respect based on the ascribed identity of a person—that is, based on caste, race, gender or sexuality. Indeed, it is this form of denial of respect that diminishes personhood. When a young Dalit homosexual woman is denied respect, she is humiliated for a feature of hers that she has no control over, unlike her nature or professional losses. When she loses respect in the eyes of others over an attribute that she has no control over, she distances herself from her metaphysical being.

At this point in the lecture, I must remind everyone that humiliation is perpetuated by two actors: institutions and society. Seventy-two years ago, we gave ourselves a Constitution, premised on justice, liberty, equality and fraternity of all. The text of the Constitution, in furtherance of the objectives in the Preamble, incorporated specific provisions providing the right to equality. However, it was only in 2005 that women by birth became coparceners in their own right; and it was only in 2018 that homosexuality was decriminalized by striking down Section 377 of the IPC. Thus, for nearly half a century of the Constitution's existence, a group of persons was denied its rights as equal members of this country.

The members of the marginalized communities can also be institutionally humiliated not merely by using the tool of law but also by establishments that further a conducive environment for discrimination and humiliation to be perpetuated. Even if a discriminatory law is held unconstitutional by the courts or is repealed by Parliament, the discriminatory behavioural pattern is not immediately overturned. The British Raj enacted the Criminal Tribes Act, 1871, through which a 'tribe, gang or class of persons addicted to the systemic commission of offences' were notified. Once a tribe was notified, all the members belonging to the tribe were required to register themselves. The Criminal Tribes Act was later repealed in 1952, once our Constitution was enacted, and the tribes were 'de-notified'. However, even after nearly seventy-three years since these tribes were de-notified, the members of the tribes continue to be subject to oppression and cruelty. Members of the de-notified tribes are still picked up by the investigating officers to cover up shoddy investigations. This court in *Ankush Maruti v. State of Maharashtra*[24] allowed a review petition filed against the conviction of six accused persons on rape and murder charges. The decision judicially recognized that the members of the nomadic tribes belonging to the lower strata of society are regularly harassed by investigating agencies by using the forces of criminal law.

The Constitution does not initiate change but only permits and accommodates the change. The Constitution was created in a social order dominated by hierarchical power structures. It tells us a story of freedom, liberty and independence. But it also tells us a story of subordination, subservience and lawlessness. The personhood conferred to members of the marginalized groups would be diminished unless we recognize and abolish, in spirit, the unequal power structures that facilitate their humiliation.[25]

Pertinently, the preamble of our Constitution begins with the phrase, 'We, the People of India.' But who are the 'People of India'? In 1990, the US Supreme Court in *United States v. Verdugo-Urquidez*[26] was concerned with an application seeking protection against unreasonable search and seizure under the Fourth Amendment. In that case, a Mexican national was arrested by the US officials and his residence in Mexico was searched by the officials. The majority judgment dismissed the argument by carving a class of 'people' from the class of 'persons'. It was observed, 'The people protected by the Fourth Amendment . . . refers to a class of persons who are part of the national community or who have otherwise developed sufficient connection with this country to be considered part of the community.' Thus, I often wonder if 'the people' referred to in the Preamble of the Constitution includes the tribes that were still recognized as 'notified tribes' when the Constitution came into force. Does it include homosexuals? Does it include women? The Dalit community, and the disabled?

Unlike the Western democracies, where the right to vote was granted in a gradational manner to different classes of people after a protracted political struggle, our Constitution granted universal adult suffrage to all Indian citizens from the date of its coming into force. However, this was not without its detractors, and the Constituent Assembly debates ought not to be ignored. Numerous voices in the Constituent Assembly echoed against the proposal to grant universal adult suffrage. Their arguments were centred on the supposed ignorance and lack of rationality of the members of certain communities. One of the members of the Constituent Assembly, Frank Anthony, in the context of universal adult suffrage, remarked, 'Democracy has always carried the postulate, the implication that at least the exercise of the franchise would be made, if not on an essentially rationalistic basis, would be made at least on a common-sense basis.'[27] Hence, some members of our Constituent Assembly were indeed of the opinion that certain classes or groups of people in India did not possess the rationality to make informed decisions and choices. As I had mentioned earlier, the externalization component of personhood requires both the law *and* society to recognize a person. Thus, personhood cannot be said to have been granted to members of the marginalized communities in India when the Constitution came into effect, in spite of including the provisions such as Articles 14, 17 and 326, when a segment of India did not, and probably still does not, recognize the ability of the marginalized sections to live as rational human beings who deserve their respect.

Google tells us that personhood is the 'quality or condition of being an individual person'. Such a characterization of personhood considers it as an individual and universal concept. However, I do not agree with this characterization of personhood. I think that personhood is a group right that is granted based on the political will of the powerful. Indeed, was personhood, ever in the history of mankind, granted to individuals? I cannot think of any such instance where an individual was granted personhood by the law and society. Personhood has always vested in groups or classes of people: Blacks, women, Dalits, tribes and homosexuals. It is the granting of legal and social recognition to individuals based on their membership of social groups. These groups were granted diminished personhood at some point in the history of mankind. Personhood is thus never granted to or taken away from one individual. Consequently, an individual's membership in these groups also becomes a part of their identity and who they are. These 'groups' or 'collectives' can take different shapes and forms. Some of these can be as basic as belonging to the same school or college, while others can over time become extremely complex institutions in themselves, such as religion, caste or race.

Having argued that the members of the marginalized groups possess diminished personhood because of social and institutional marginalization, an appropriate approach to tackle this problem needs to be ascertained. The assimilation or obliviousness of group identity would not rectify the problem of diminished personhood. Simply viewing people as individuals, without taking into account their differences or the groups choose to identify with and belong to, is a reductionist approach; in itself, insufficient to provide complete and truthful recognition to their personhood. For many, being part of those groups is a crucial and inviolable feature of who they are, shaped by their real-life experiences. Hence, members of the marginalized communities would be able to gain complete personhood only by assertion and recognition of their group identities. The international framework and the Indian Constitution facilitate this approach of identifying an individual as a member of the group to remedy marginalization.

Article 2 of the Universal Declaration of Human Rights provides that no one can be denied the benefits of the declaration on the basis of their membership of a particular race or sex or religion or a linguistic group. In principle, the requirement seeks to ensure that an individual's membership in a particular group does not disentitle her to the benefits of any rights she may have otherwise had. Such a requirement is also present in the International Covenant on Civil and Political Rights, wherein Article 26 explicitly lays down that no one can be discriminated against because of their membership of such a group. Within the international human rights framework, this ultimately culminates in the International Convention on the Elimination of All Forms of Racial Discrimination, which not only opposes discrimination based on an individual's racial identity but also places positive obligations upon States to combat it. A similar positive obligation is imposed upon States under Article 27 of the International Covenant on Civil and Political Rights, which mandates them to protect the rights of minority ethnic, religious or linguistic groups to preserve their own culture. Another positive recognition of 'group rights' in the covenant is in Article 1, which recognizes the ability of every group of individuals to determine its own future or their right to self-determination. All these examples highlight how the international human rights framework recognizes a duality inherent in the existence of an individual's 'group identity'. On the one hand, it seeks to protect against the negative consequences of belonging to a particular group, while on the other hand, it simultaneously protects the right to assert that very identity.

This duality is also traced to the provisions of the Indian Constitution. Articles 15(1) and (2), and Articles 16(1) and (2) recognize that individuals may be identified as belonging to a certain group due to their religion, sex or caste, amongst others. Further, it acknowledges that this membership or perceived membership may be the *basis* on which they are discriminated against. Finally, it then holds such discrimination to be unconstitutional. A very specific and abhorrent form of such discrimination, untouchability, is specifically declared unconstitutional through Article 17. However, at no point does the Constitution recommend that an individual should be considered as a *silo* or solely as themselves. It acknowledges the existence of group identity and membership, and that it may be used for a positive change as well. In this vein, Articles 15(3) to (6) and Article 16(3) to (6) protect the actions taken by the State to create beneficial legislation for the benefit of groups who have been historically discriminated against. Further, as we are all well aware, it legitimizes reservation in educational institutions and public employments for those who belong to the SCs, STs and OBCs. Examples of positive recognition of group identity and group rights in the Constitution also include the freedom of religion under Article 25, the freedom to manage religious affairs under Article 26, the protection of minority groups under Article 29 and the right of religious or linguistic minority groups to administer their own educational institutions under Article 30.

When I say that the approach in the Indian Constitution is through the assertion of group identity and not assimilation, I do not restrict my views to material disbursement of resources through reservation or other policies of affirmative action. What I mean is that the only way for the members of the marginalized communities to achieve personhood is through social mobilization as a collective against discrimination. Such mobilization should not be considered as 'politics of identity' but as a necessary means for redressing historical discrimination. The Supreme Court in *Abhiram Singh v. C.D. Commachen & Ors*[28] was tasked with determining if the electoral candidate is only prohibited from appealing for votes on the basis of '[her] religion, caste, community or language', or also on the basis of the voter's. The minority opinion by three judges held that the prohibition was limited only to the ascribed status of the candidate and not of the voters. Thus, in protecting the right of candidates to appeal to the constituent group identities of the voters, it was observed:

> Individual histories both of citizens and collective groups in our society are associated through the ages with histories of discrimination and injustice on the basis of these defining characteristics. In numerous provisions, the Constitution has sought to preserve a delicate balance between individual liberty and the need to remedy these histories of injustice founded upon immutable characteristics such as of religion, race, caste and language.

What is common to all these examples, however, is the Central idea that these groups exist and individuals recognize themselves as being a part of it, in order to seek the protection of the law. However, such a recognition is not only legal but also social and cultural. Indeed, an individual's inseparable link to her group identity is often strongly asserted when she belongs to a marginalized group. A leading scholar, Erving Goffman, has noted that reducing an individual's personal identity down to their membership of a particular marginalized group has the effect of 'disqualifying' her as a whole person on the basis of one characteristic.[29] Ralph Ellison, one of US's leading African American authors, had addressed these concerns in his work of fiction called *Invisible Man*.[30] The book tells a hauntingly real story of an African American protagonist who despite all his achievements and success, still remains invisible to the rest of the white elites except as a 'black man'. The story is one of alienation that is attached to this 'invisibility', and the feeling of futility that accompanies any achievement because one would always remain *only* a 'black man'.

Such a form of marginalization not only occurs to members from the lower castes or specific races but to those who belong to a particular gender or identify with a specific sexual orientation or are in other ways different from what is considered to be the 'norm'. This court saw this with respect to women when we had to adjudicate two cases in order to decide whether women officers could be granted Permanent Commission in the armed forces. In *Secretary, Ministry of Defence v. Babita Puniya & Ors*[31] and *Lt Col Nitisha v. Union of India,*[32] this court found that the armed forces were willing to overlook all military records and meritorious achievements of women officers when it came to granting them Permanent Commission, by effectively reducing their identity to being 'women'. Similarly, in *Navtej Singh Johar v. Union of India,*[33] this court noted that one of the effects of Section 377 was to reduce the identity of all members of the LGBTQIA+ community to their sexual relationships alone. While our judgments in all these cases have tried to improve the legal status of these groups, their impact on society continues to be limited. Members of the LGBTQIA+ community are still looked at with suspicion by society, and many times by their own parents. And even with the Permanent Commission having been granted to the women officers, our court continues to hear applications that seek to delay the process.

Having now spoken about the effect that group identity has on an individual's personhood, we must ask ourselves: What happens when an individual wishes to be considered only as who *she* is and not as a member of a marginalized group? Indeed, many members of the LGBTQIA+ community continue to remain 'closeted' due to the fear of the discrimination they may face. However, does our society allow every individual such a freedom, especially when their membership in a group is impossible to hide?

In relation to an individual's caste identity, Professor Satish Deshpande has located the answer to my question in a joke that became popular when the Ninety-Third Amendment to the Constitution was enacted which introduced reservations for OBCs. The joke goes as follows: When India decides to send a space exploration team to the moon, feverish negotiations begin immediately on the composition of the team. After much discussion, it is decided that the team will include nine OBCs, six SCs, three STs and, if there is any place left, two astronauts. Professor Deshpande notes that the insight herein being that:

> . . . the 'astronauts' are not identified by their caste but only by their qualifications (as astronauts), whereas the ['supposed'] quota-walas are identified only by their caste and not by their qualifications . . . [As such] upper caste identity is such that it can be completely overwritten by modern professional identities of choice, whereas lower caste identity is so indelibly engraved that it overwrites all other identities and renders them illegible, along with the choices that they may represent.[34]

To put it in simpler terms, while the professional achievements of upper-caste individuals are enough to wash away their caste identity, this can never be true for the lower-caste individuals. For them, their membership of this group will indelibly remain a part of their personhood forever. As Dr Ambedkar himself noted, he could have become a barrister-at-law, but to many, he was still no more than a lower-caste individual.

American philosopher Michael J. Sandel in his book *Tyranny of Merit* has noted that individuals with vast privilege can define their identity and success not as a consequence of their privilege but because of their belief that they have earned it through their 'merit'.[35] Hiding behind such a narrow conception of 'merit' only allows upper-caste individuals to mask their obvious caste privilege. At the same time, it allows them to relegate the achievement of Dalits and other reserved classes as being a consequence of caste-based reservation afforded to them. The Supreme Court, through its judgment in *B.K. Pavitra v. Union of India*,[36] however, has squarely rejected such a limited definition of 'merit'. Instead, it articulated a broader definition, which takes into account the accumulated caste privilege of the upper castes and the years of oppression suffered by the reserved castes. Re-framing this definition has allowed courts to approach the debate of reservation from a different point of view and it also changes the conversation surrounding reservation in the public arena. Alas, it remains to be seen whether this can positively change the mindset of every individual of this country as well.

Having now considered a situation where society continues to impose group identity upon individuals, we must consider when such an identity is taken away only to deny them the legal protection their group identity would offer. Our court saw a prime example of this in the case of *Vikash Kumar v. Union Public Service Commission*,[37] where a disabled individual was refused access to a scribe simply because his disability did not meet the requisite benchmark set by the examination committee. The examination committee's attitude herein highlighted how access to beneficial legislation is also sought to be limited only to those who are considered sufficiently marginalized within their own marginalized group.

When responding to such marginalization, it is often assumed that what needs to be addressed is the discrimination based on an individual's membership of a marginalized group. However, individual identities are extremely complex and they cannot often be reduced only to membership of certain groups. Pertinently, an individual's identity can be a combination of her membership in multiple groups. American writer and professor Audre Lorde acknowledged this problem when she noted that:

> . . . as a Black lesbian feminist comfortable with the many different ingredients of my identity, and a woman committed to racial and sexual freedom from oppression, I find I am constantly being encouraged to pluck out some one aspect of myself and present this as the meaningful whole, eclipsing or denying the other parts of self. But this is a destructive and fragmenting way to live.[38]

Hence, not only does membership in a marginalized group affect an individual's identity by reducing it to the membership alone, but it also forces individuals to make it the focal point of their lives when seeking to combat this marginalization. And when individuals belong to multiple such marginalized groups, this often is presented as a choice, in order for them to decide which part of their identity is responsible for their marginalization the most.

Feminist scholar Kimberlé Crenshaw introduced the concept of 'intersectionality' to counteract this very problem. She noted that the experience of marginalization suffered by Black women was inherently different to White women, and hence, a common theory of feminism could never address both of them. She called for an acknowledgement that individuals who belong to multiple marginalized groups can feel oppression on multiple axes, which has to be meaningfully considered as a whole.[39] In the Indian context, Dalit feminist scholar Shailaja Paik has similarly noted how a traditional feminist framework does not adequately capture the lived experiences of Dalit women, which ignores their caste oppression. Similarly, studies in caste oppression only focus on Dalit women's oppression from the upper castes while ignoring their specific position in society as Dalit women. Thus, she instead proposes the framework of 'womanist–humanist complex' along the lines of intersectionality, which acknowledges the unique location of Dalit women in society. Pertinently, she observes how Dalit women are often vulnerable to sexual exploitation due to their female identity, while at the same time losing all protection due to their Dalit identity.[40]

Intersectionality has thus become an important conceptual tool for all of us today, when numerous individuals are marginalized to different degrees due to their varying group identities. Therefore, any solution to this issue has to be one that does not force these individuals to choose between these multiple identities.

Since the core problem herein seems to be arising out of an individual's membership in marginalized groups, one would be remiss not to wonder why eliminating all these groups is not an appropriate solution. Indeed, some scholars have suggested that all such 'group identities' are nothing but human constructs or a myth created by humans to organize their behaviour.[41] If so, can human beings not easily eliminate them too? In the context of race, the answer to this question can be found within the texts of the

Critical Race Theory. Proponents of this theory do not wish to eliminate 'race' because they acknowledge that it is and will always remain a part of their life. Further, they highlight that after years of racial oppression, eliminating race will only serve the members of the privileged race, who have managed to convert their racial privilege into forms of social, political and economic capital in modern society. Hence, once it is acknowledged that race and racial discrimination exist, it makes it possible for the years of damage to be counteracted by positively uplifting the discriminated races.[42] A similar analysis also holds true for India with respect to caste, where 'castelessness' is a privilege that only the upper caste can afford because their caste privilege has already translated into social, political and economic capital. On the other hand, individuals who belong to the lower caste have to retain their caste identity in order to claim the benefits of measures such as reservation, which are in themselves a recognition of a historic harm.[43]

The question that then remains for us is: What can be done to rectify the diminished personhood of the marginalized communities? How do you rectify internalization that diminishes the personhood of the members of the marginalized communities?

First, the most obvious answer would be through legal means that provide them positive rights. However, as I have already highlighted from examples in this lecture, the presence of multiple such rights in our Constitution has not always led to a positive change in the society's perception of these marginalized groups and the individuals who belong to them. Would it then be fair to say that the groups and individuals should lose their faith in the framework of rights and try to claim their recognition through other means? Patricia Williams, a leading scholar of the Critical Race Theory, has eloquently conveyed the simultaneous mistrust of and reliance upon rights by African Americans by noting that:

> To say that blacks never fully believed in rights is true; yet it is also true that blacks believed in them so much and so hard that we gave them life where there was none before. We held onto

> them, put the hope of them into our wombs, and mothered them—not just the notion of them. We nurtured rights and gave rights life. And this was not the dry process of reification, from which life is drained and reality fades as the cement of conceptual determinism hardens round but its opposite. This was the resurrection of life from 400-year-old ashes; the parthenogenesis of unfertilized hope.[44]

Professor William's powerful words remind us that our rights framework is given meaning *only* due to the belief reposed on it by those who are the most marginalized. Anurag Bhaskar[45] in his award-winning paper titled '"Ambedkar's Constitution": A Radical Phenomenon in Anti-Caste Discourse?' succinctly explains how the Constitution and the rights framework is used by Dalits to mobilize, assert and reclaim their dignity. The rights provided in the Constitution constitute, in other words, a symbolic tool for the emancipation and empowerment for members of the marginalized communities.[46] Taking Bhaskar's thesis forward to fruition, it is important for our rights to constantly keep evolving in order to address the new forms of marginalization these groups face.

Second, though providing protective rights to the members of the marginalized community is empowering since it furthers internalization, it is in itself insufficient to confer personhood. It is important that we celebrate their identity, recognize their individual and group identities, and create conducive spaces for them to exercise their agency. The process of 'othering' and exclusion must be put to an end. There must be a transformation towards securing a communal vision premised on inclusiveness. It is necessary that the privileged members of society break free from the shackles of the past and confer respect and recognition on the members of the marginalized communities. German philosopher Axel Honneth, in his work titled *The Struggle for Recognition: The Moral Grammar of Social Conflicts*, emphasizes on the importance of self-confidence, self-respect and self-esteem for the development of personhood. He argues that each of these factors are dependent on the emotions conferred on them by 'others'.[47] Love and concern showered is a pre-requisite for self-confidence, one's sense of possessing rights for self-respect and viewing oneself as a 'special person' for self-esteem. These three forms of recognition would allow the members of the marginalized communities to claim holistic personhood from the continuous state of depletion.

In his final address to the Constituent Assembly on the eve of the Constitution's adoption, Dr Ambedkar also recognized these two methods when he acknowledged that our Constitution would only be as good as the people who implemented it. With an eye towards the future, Dr Ambedkar noted that:

> I feel, however good a Constitution may be, it is sure to turn out bad because those who are called to work it, happen to be a bad lot . . . The working of a Constitution does not depend wholly upon the nature of the Constitution. The Constitution can provide only the organs of State such as the Legislature, the Executive and the Judiciary. The factors on which the working of those organs of the State depend are the people and the political parties they will set up as their instruments to carry out their wishes and their politics . . . It is, therefore, futile to pass any judgement upon the Constitution without reference to the part which the people and their parties are likely to play.

Thus, with his parting words, Dr Ambedkar has squarely placed the responsibility upon each one of us to uphold the ideals behind our Constitution and give life to them through our actions. Combating something as prevalent and deep-rooted as marginalization is no easy task, and I admit to having no easy solutions. The only recourse available to us is to faithfully abide by and give life to the Constitutional ideals which Dr Ambedkar helped formulate, and use those to bring transformative change in the minds and perceptions of society.

17

Reconciling Rights and Innovation

Examining the Relationship Between Law and Technology[1]

It is my honour to deliver the Justice P.M. Mukhi Memorial Lecture, in the memory of late Justice Parsram M. Mukhi of the Bombay High Court. I thank his son, Professor Sunil Mukhi, for having invited me to deliver this lecture. The association between our families goes back a long way. Professor Mukhi's parents—Parsa and Sarla—as they were to my parents—were connoisseurs of Western classical music, heard on the gramophone on long-playing records, before the advent of cassette players and the modern digital age. My parents belonged to the genre of a traditional Maharashtrian family from Pune and loved to listen to and sing Indian classical music. The food on the Mukhis' dining table was a novelty to us. Mushrooms and paneer were unknown entities in our home until Sarla Aunty sent her cook over to give a culinary lesson to ours. My parents, and through them, I as a little child, were introduced to their eclectic tastes in music, food and culture. This perhaps, was my first engagement with a world view. A Diwali evening was spent happily on the terrace of Sunil Mukhi's apartment building on Mount Pleasant Road in Mumbai.

The story of Justice Mukhi's life is an inspiration in itself. After having been a civil judge in the Sindh region of Pakistan, he moved to Bombay during the horrors of Partition. Never one to let his circumstances bring him down, Justice Mukhi then restarted his legal career in Bombay. In the years to come, he made a name for himself as a litigator and was then appointed as a judge of the Bombay High Court in 1972. While his time on the bench of the Bombay High Court was limited, his judgments aimed at delivering justice to all members of society. During the internal Emergency of 1975, Justice Mukhi was unfortunately transferred to the Calcutta High Court since he spoke out against the then government's draconian measures. Sadly, it was in Calcutta that Justice Mukhi soon passed away. What then was a tragic departure from a life so well lived has since become a badge of honour for judicial independence. His memories and sense of justice still linger, with all of us who knew him and who share his commitment to using the law as a tool to help the less fortunate. During his reference speech, when he became a judge of the Bombay High Court, Justice Mukhi quoted my late father, Chief Justice Y.V. Chandrachud, and said, '[T]he cause of justice can only be helped by [our] participation. I believe that if the lawyer and the Judge can work together as a team, then many of the defects in the system as it exists today can be overcome. The material is there. We have only to work it.'[2] Through my lecture today, I hope I can do my part in honouring Justice Mukhi's legacy.

Today, I intend to address you, students, faculty and alumni of the Indian Institute of Science, Education and Research, on a topic that unites our seemingly disparate vocations—law and scientific advancement through technology. Through my lecture, I will attempt to demystify the relationship between law and technology. Traditionally, it is assumed that law and technology will be at odds, with the former favouring the protection of rights and the latter aiming to foster innovation. However, today I posit that law and technology have an interconnected relationship, which can achieve both: the protection of individual rights and the promotion of innovation in our society.

Let me begin by remembering the words of the noted science-fiction author H.G. Wells, in his last book titled *Mind at the End of Its Tether*, where he famously claimed that '[w]e [as in, us humans] live in reference to past experience and not to future events, however inevitable'. While his own intentions and contexts were slightly different, I keep going back to this quote as I begin thinking about our discussion today. People always assume that the relationship between law and technology is one where the former is invested in curbing the latter. Possibly, this is because of the presumption that a discipline that relies on history, and precedence will never understand, much less facilitate, a world that constantly seeks to re-imagine the future.

I find this presumption peculiar because the legal discourse has always found immense value in using technology. If you think about it, the legal discipline is rooted in documentation. In that regard, the very origins of computing have benefited the legal fraternity as much as anyone else. In fact, technology companies in the US began targeting law firms since the invention of the phonograph/voice recorder in the early 1950s. Likewise, the legal sector was revolutionized with the introduction of the red Ubiq terminal, an early model of a computer that enabled lawyers to access case laws online. The word processor, the fax machine, the personal computer, cloud computing and now blockchain technologies have all played a major role in the evolution of how law is practised around the world. It was only a few years back that Kathryn Haun, a federal prosecutor in the US, made use of the permanent nature of a blockchain trail to indict federal agents who had stolen bitcoins worth millions of dollars.[3]

Thus, the legal discipline has never shied away from technological innovation and its application. Yet, the presumption still exists. Now, one could argue that this premise has less to do with how technology is used by a few tech-savvy law firms and much more to do with how governments, bureaucrats and courtrooms approach this discussion. Even there, however, I believe that the relationship between law, governance and technology has often been considered to be one of complementarity. Let me explain this by considering the impact of one such technological change—that being the advent of the internet Age—on legal rights and governance structures.

To begin, it is often argued that the internet is a crucial tool that has vastly improved the work and relevance of the numerous human rights organizations that monitor human rights violations. In 1994, the Freedom Forum's Media Studies Centre noted that '[t]here appears to be a quality of inevitability to the marriage of a democratizing technology such as the internet with the world of humanitarian and human rights activities'.[4] Other scholars have similarly discussed how the internet can assist human rights organizations across the globe by improving the means of transmitting information in four ways: through increased *speed*, at reduced *cost*, with a wider *scope* and all the while allowing for greater *interactivity*. It is believed that this will allow the human rights organizations to more effectively record instances of human rights violations, which will provide for necessary evidence in prosecuting those who commit such crimes.[5]

Similarly, the impact of the internet on an individual's right to freedom of speech has also been substantial and meaningful. In her seminal article in 1998, Kathleen Sullivan, a leading constitutional law scholar in the US, has noted that, '[i]t is tempting to see the internet like First Amendment manna from heaven [the First Amendment to the United States Constitution being their guarantor of the right to freedom of speech] . . . [which] furnishes technological and organizational preconditions for considerable equality and competitiveness among speakers, and, accordingly, for an abundance of speech'.[6] Since her statement in 1998, it has been widely accepted that the influx of the internet Age has democratized speech for all individuals. Traditionally, the government has controlled the platforms through which individuals could make their speech heard to others. However, with the advent of the internet and social media, individuals can now be directly in control of these platforms.[7] An important example of this is during the Egyptian Revolution of 2011, where social media platforms were widely used by protestors to organize protests and to communicate with the outside world in order to highlight the human rights violations being committed by their government.[8]

In fact, global institutions such as the United Nations[9] and the UN Human Rights Council,[10] and courts such as the European Court of Human Rights[11] and the Inter-American Court of Human Rights[12] have all categorically held that an individual's right to freedom of speech and expression can be exercised through the internet. Even in India, the Supreme Court has recognized a citizen's fundamental right to speak, express and receive information through the medium of the internet.[13]

An individual's right to privacy on the internet has similarly been upheld by numerous global institutions and courts. Crucially, they all accept that without the guarantee of privacy on the internet, an individual's rights to health, education, freedom of movement, freedom of peaceful assembly and association, and freedom of expression will be compromised.[14] In India, in the case of *Justice K.S. Puttaswamy (retd) v. Union of India (I)*,[15] a bench of nine judges, including myself, held that the right to privacy is a fundamental right inherent in the Constitution. My reasoning was that reading the right to privacy as a fundamental right is imperative for the Constitution to protect our people in the digital age, where individual digital identities are equally important as their identities in the physical world.

The onset of the internet Age has also helped democratize elections by allowing candidates to harness the power of social media to easily reach out to their electorate without spending great amounts. It has also created avenues for information to be shared more freely, which is useful for preventing voter fraud and for creating more awareness among individuals about their right to vote.[16]

Till now, I have spoken of the impact of the internet on our most crucial constitutional rights, but judges like me are constantly called upon to interpret rights and obligations that are mediated by technology, not only in a constitutional sense, but even in seemingly routine functions. Hence, it is crucial for us to remain abreast with emerging technologies and their application to our existing systems.

Recently, I had to adjudicate upon the applicability of revised tariffs under the Customs Act, 1962, which had been digitally notified on the internet, thereby rendering to be determined with precision the timing of when the law came into effect and the bill of entry was submitted.[17]

I also believe that the use of technology and the internet has not only expanded the scope of an individual's rights but also their access to basic services that better help them realize these rights and liberties. Recently, we have been witnessing an increased reliance on Information Communication Technology by the Union and state governments for creating initiatives to improve governance, provide public services and strengthen accountability mechanisms. For instance, the Digital India programme of the Government of India aims to achieve inclusive growth by transforming India into a digitally empowered society and knowledge economy.

Similarly, on the part of the judiciary, there has also been an integration of technology and justice. As early as 2004, the Supreme Court of India established the e-Committee to adapt the administrative reforms in the judiciary to the information technology revolution. Since 2017, I have been serving as chairperson of the e-Committee, and I have gained valuable insights on how technology can be an enabler and a leveller.

The Indian legal system is currently steadfast on its path towards digitization due to the work of all the dedicated members of the e-Committee. We have sought to make a one-stop portal for the judiciary in India, through the National Judicial Data Grid, a repository of metadata holding court records of 40.3 million pending cases. This data also ensures greater transparency and accountability of our courts. Further, technology has not just been used as a facilitator of existing judicial processes but has also been used to transform the citizens' experience of the judicial process. For instance, the traffic courts dealing with ordinary traffic violations have received a substantial boost with the introduction of automatic settlement processes, which allow people to pay their dues without grappling with any litigation.

Surprisingly, the COVID-19 pandemic proved to be a spectacular accelerant to the virtual and digital courts project in India. Once the lockdown was imposed in 2020, the Supreme Court of India started conducting virtual hearings from 23 March. In the beginning, we had to mitigate the technological barriers that litigants faced in accessing justice. At the same time, there was a fear that the pandemic would increase the backlog. Thus, the immediate challenge at hand was to create a robust technology-enabled system that could effectively deal with fresh litigation and, concurrently, prioritize pending cases. Crucially, we had to ensure that the closing of the precincts of the highest constitutional court of the country did not mean that the doors to access justice were closed. We had to perform our duty to protect civil liberties, attend to cases of public importance and be available as the court of last resort. Slowly, the virtual court systems were also adopted by all courts across India. The cause of justice could not have been brought to a standstill due to the pandemic. Several courts, including many among the district courts with little to no infrastructure or experience with virtual systems, stood up to the task and are now making a transition to permanent avenues of hybrid hearing models.

The e-Committee's e-Courts project, which has been in its second phase since 2015, played an instrumental role in creating a technology-enabled judicial system that could withstand the novel challenges of the pandemic. Through the e-Courts project, we managed to create a system that was conducive to virtual courts, electronic filings and online payments. Let me give you a snapshot of what the e-Courts project was able to achieve in the past year. *First*, 3.54 billion electronic transactions were undertaken under the e-Courts project, which highlights the sheer reach of its services to the common citizens. *Second*, a total of 19.6 million cases were heard by courts through video conferencing. *Third*, out of the thirteen million cases registered, 8.3 million cases were disposed of, thus, achieving a disposal rate of over 60 per cent. *Finally*, in our endeavour to promote paperless filing, we also developed an e-filing software, using which over one lakh cases have been filed online in over 17,000 district courts and twenty-five different High Courts.

I truly believe that the silver lining of the COVID-19 pandemic has been the nudge faced by judges and lawyers to adapt to technology in their work in the legal ecosystem. During the virtual hearings, I have personally observed several lawyers, and evidently new mothers, arguing from the safety of their homes. This was a welcome change from the past, where women were unfairly forced to take a step back in their careers or steer away from barrister practice altogether, owing to its harsh and often gendered demands. A digital mode of e-filing and e-Courts also has the potential to address several of the inequities that are entrenched in the existing systems that hitherto served only the able-bodied. Technology is the great enabler in enhancing access to justice. On a personal note, I have taken this time to build on my technological skills and now exclusively rely on my laptop for all court-related matters.

Another necessary and welcome by-product of the transition to a virtual ecosystem was the increase in public access to our judicial systems. At the e-Committee, we saw this as an opportunity that could serve the cause of open justice.[18] Live-streaming was introduced in High Courts based on the model rules framed by the e-Committee. The High Courts of Gujarat, Karnataka and Orissa have begun live-streaming court proceedings in the Chief Justice's court. This was an attempt to demystify judicial processes, increase judicial accountability and disseminate information in cases of public importance.

Through the whole experience of the COVID-19 pandemic and the transition to virtual ecosystem, I understood that technology can tremendously empower, but *only if* our institutions are designed to enable such empowerment. Sadly, at the heart of the wonderful overnight transition to virtual courts during the pandemic also lay the unembellished fact that there exists a digital divide in the country.[19] The widespread shift to virtual platforms exposed the deep fissures in our society on access to the internet. It showed us that not everyone can afford to work or study from home, when high-speed internet, gadgets and electricity are not publicly guaranteed utilities.

The e-Committee and e-Courts project has been cognizant of the inherent inequalities that exist in our society, and how they stand to be reinforced with the switch being made to a virtual ecosystem. Hence, we created service centres that could consolidate all the essential facilities offered under the e-Courts project and make them available to litigants who lack digital access. These facilities include providing soft copies of judicial orders, facilitating e-filing of petitions, appending digital signatures, facilitating e-payments and guiding people on availing free legal services from legal aid authorities. We have also ensured that our online judicial processes protect the privacy of our litigants and provide data security. As a part of the e-Courts project, we also took steps to make our digital services accessible to persons with disabilities by adhering to the principle of reasonable accommodation.[20] We are also currently in the process of digitizing over thirty-one billion court records across India. Presently, we have launched this digitization project in five High Courts as a pilot. The standardization of digitization across the country will ensure interoperability between data repositories and is bound to make our justice delivery system more seamless and efficient. Digitization of court records will also expedite the dispute resolution process and particularly, it will advance the objective of efficient enforcement of contracts as sought to be achieved by our commercial courts. This will also improve the ease of doing business in India, in terms of the guidelines issued by the World Bank.

Another crucial lesson that the transition to virtual courts taught me is that digital reform should not be limited to merely automating our old ways of working and transposing the old physical infrastructures to a virtual environment. As Professor Richard E. Susskind argues, the COVID-19 pandemic has given us a springboard into a new world, and right now, we are just at the foothills.[21] While I believe that this is what the future should hold for us, transitions must be accompanied by a vision of access and inclusion. We have a long road ahead towards ensuring that technology can be meaningfully adopted in order to ensure greater access. This can only be achieved by democratic processes that are concerted in their aim to progress, but with an equal aim of leaving no person behind. To achieve this goal, the legal fraternity will have to work hand in hand with our scientific community.

Thus, we can now understand how the internet and technology have revolutionized the scope of our rights and our interactions with the government and the judiciary. The nature of efficiency and convenience that arise from the solutions in the digital age marks a profound shift from life just two decades ago. However, all solutions come with a cost.

The *first* kind of price that we seem to be paying is through the digital profiling of all persons. Every transaction of ours and every site that we visit leaves electronic tracks, generally without our knowledge. These electronic tracks contain powerful means of information that provide knowledge of the sort of person the user is and their interests. All of this data needs to be protected. In aggregation, this data may disclose the nature of an individual's personality: food habits, language, health, hobbies, sexual preferences, friendships, ways of dress and political affiliation. Privacy concerns are a serious issue in the information age, and our laws must evolve to address them.

The *second* kind of price is the nature of changes in our society due to the vast amount of information available through the internet. Characterized by scholars as an 'Attention Economy', all of us today are overwhelmed with the information we find online. This can have negative effects in multiple aspects of our lives—we can become susceptible to false information, we may be unable to verify the truth, or the information we receive may just become what is dictated by an algorithm, without any real choice on our part.[22] The vastness of this information can also have a numbing effect, where we become so used to hearing about issues that they no longer even affect us. Long back in 1996, a scholar eerily predicted that:

> [I]n an information age where satellite television broadcasts and internet appeals to address mass violations of human rights

> reach world populations on a daily basis, there is a danger that people will become callous to reports of difficulties everywhere in the world, that the limited human capacity for absorption, compassion, and responsive action will become spread so thin as to dilute popular outrage and forestall responsive action.[23]

Today, as I address engineers, data scientists and future harbingers of technological innovation among you, I am excited to see the strides that our society makes as a result of your contribution. However, I must warn you that it is important that steps towards improving artificial intelligence, automation and digitization must be mindful of the ways in which it would alter our social and economic relations. This brings me to the *third* kind of price we often pay. In his book *To Save Everything, Click Here*, Evgeny Morozov critiques what he calls 'solutionism'—the idea that given the right code, algorithms and robots, technology can solve all of humankind's problems, effectively making life 'frictionless' and trouble-free.[24] Techno-solutionism is problematic because its roots run deep and it is incredibly hard to weed out from public discourse once it has been introduced.[25] At its core, the issue with techno-solutionism is that it assumes that all ills can be cured by the right technology. In doing so, it ignores the economic, cultural, social, racial, classist and casteist problems that plague our society. I do not say this to suggest that technological solutions should not be sought for issues of governance. Rather, I say this to point out that their limitations in changing the mindset of society should be acknowledged. Some of these technological solutions may suffer from the same ills that plague society because they are ultimately a by-product of society itself.

For instance, while we think that algorithms are the key to the future, they can just as easily become gatekeepers of opportunity—deciding critical things such as who gets a job or quality of healthcare, and what communities get undue police scrutiny. A recent Netflix documentary called *Coded Bias* followed the work of Joy Buolamwini, a Canadian computer scientist, whose research exposed that facial recognition algorithms did not recognize the faces of black women as human beings.[26] The input images on which the various facial recognition algorithms were based comprised 80 per cent of images of white persons and 75 per cent of images of male faces. As a result, the algorithms had a high accuracy of 99 per cent while detecting male faces. However, the system's ability to recognize the faces of black women was significantly lower, at only 65 per cent. Facial recognition algorithms may serve as a form of policing and can be misused for surveillance. Hence, a combination of these ethical and policy concerns must be critical considerations for guiding innovation.

Similarly, we know that data is the key ingredient that makes machine learning possible. However, not all data is created equal, nor is it equally available across geographies and demographics. The biggest sources of risk for data-related discrimination are inadequate data availability and biased or error-ridden data. Therefore, diversity in the dataset becomes key to protecting human rights.[27] Caroline Criado-Perez, the author of the book *Invisible Women*, in which she investigates the absence of gender from data and its impact, has explained that if AI is based on 'bad' data, sourced predominantly from men and/or based on male profiles, it can have several unintended consequences. She speaks of examples as basic as seat belts, headrests and airbags in cars. In her research, she found how their designs are predominantly based on data collected from car crash dummy tests using the physique of men and their seating position. On the other hand, women's breasts and pregnant bodies don't fit into these seemingly 'standard' measurements. As a result, women are 47 per cent more likely to be seriously injured and 17 per cent more likely than a man to die in a similar accident.[28]

In today's world, the common perception is that raising concerns about these issues within the world of technology will kill innovation. The truth is quite the opposite. I believe that regulation, coupled with innovation, can result in marvels in society. Technology should be designed not with the solitary aim of efficiency but to serve the inherent value of every human being. An example of a potential solution to ensure that AI is responsive to gender considerations and other ethical concerns in the application of certification processes. Commercial considerations may overlook societal discrimination and caste, class and gender-based marginalization. Solutions such as obtaining an AI certification in certain regions across the world have been introduced to further distinguish companies and better position them in the investor and consumer markets.[29] Denmark has just launched the prototype of a Data Ethics Seal, which is backed by Danish companies that view the seal as an opportunity to gain a competitive edge.[30]

Another interesting example of the way in which the law can fundamentally alter the in-built design of technology comes from the EU's data protection law called the General Data Protection Regulation (GDPR). The law requires 'privacy-by-design', which means that companies must design products and services with the default assumption that they protect the privacy, data and information of data subjects.[31] It forces companies to consider not just new products and services but also the essence of their processes and take stock of whether they are privacy-friendly and privacy-centric.[32] A robust system of enforcement has established the EU as a model jurisdiction for data privacy and regulation.[33]

Scholars have argued that the future lies in the push for a 'human-rights-by-design' principle where the scientific community commits to designing tools, technologies and services to respect human rights by default, rather than allowing abuse or exploitation to be embedded within their business models.[34] This would, for example, prevent filtering companies from designing their technology with features that enable large-scale, indiscriminate or inherently disproportionate censorship capabilities—like the Netsweeper feature, which allows an internet service provider, colloquially called an ISP, to block an entire country's top-level domains.[35] Netsweeper, for the uninitiated, is a technology company that provides online filtering services to ISPs across the world. Choices made by Netsweeper have had a significant impact on the types of websites that users in a given country can ultimately access. Netsweeper's technology facilitates the blocking of digital speech.[36]

While it is important to improve the design of our technological solutions in envisaging a free and accessible digital sphere, it is equally crucial for us to reflect on the platform economy that has replaced traditional modes of employment. With the introduction of several mobile- or web-based apps, the labour market has fissured and the gig economy has had significant ramifications on the existing business models for food, clothing and groceries. App-based companies have alleged immunity from labour law obligations because these platforms are legally structured as aggregators and intermediaries. Their contract-based relationship with app-based workers does not fit within traditional definitions of employment, and the disaggregated nature of app-based work makes collective bargaining with platforms difficult. As a result, traditional labour law in India, which exists as a dispersed set of statutes, has not been effectively applied to most platforms.[37] How, for instance, do the labour law requirements of maintaining a crèche or statutory canteen or providing wages for overtime work translate in the emerging world digital spaces? These vexed issues are important for consideration across the domains of law, regulation, technology and policy.

Hence, a distinct blueprint of legal measures to effectively improve the conditions of app-based workers is urgently required. It is imperative that interventions cater to the distinct nature of app-based work, including ensuring autonomy for workers through increased transparency regarding fees earned and the ability to choose work. At the same time, it should clarify minimum obligations of platforms towards enhancing worker welfare, especially concerning health, safety and skill development.

Our world today has been transformed by technology, and we are living in the digital age, where data and information are the 'new oil'.[38] Intellectual property law is currently in the process of catching up and will soon have to remould itself to achieve its aim of maximizing human potential. Lawrence Lessig, a prominent scholar on the information age, has noted that 'the internet has unleashed an extraordinary possibility for many to participate in the process of building and cultivating a culture that reaches far beyond local boundaries', creating the possibility of markets that 'include a much wider and more diverse range of creators', if not stifled by incumbents who use intellectual property law to 'protect themselves against this competition'.[39]

To conclude, I would like to recount an interesting reference from Ari Ezra Waldman's book *Industry Unbound: The Inside Story of Privacy, Data, and Corporate Power*. Waldman wrote this book on informational privacy law after nearly four years of fieldwork in technology companies. He had gone to the office of one such company to speak to its employees. He caught up with a software engineer who had stepped out of a meeting. This person was a part of a team that was building a photo-sharing app. After a couple of questions about the project, including its interaction with Instagram, Waldman asked: 'When programmes have to talk to each other, are there privacy issues you have to deal with?' The software engineer quickly replied: 'That's really for someone else to do. I don't know. It gets done, I'm sure. But I don't do it.'

This is striking because here is this person who is working on an app involving copious amounts of data that includes the faces of the user, their friends, their family and their children. Questions of privacy were hardly an issue or a consideration while designing the code. This is concerning because the people who are at the frontline of protecting our privacy *and* human rights in the digital space do not necessarily sit in law schools, courtrooms or even parliaments, but right here in this room. The real power over the implementation of digital rights rests with technology companies, generally, and with engineers and designers, in particular. In effect, *you* are involved in translating human rights law into real life. Effectively, you are not just coding. You are invisibly rewriting the rules of our society, the menus from which our lives are being chosen. After all, in cyberspace, code *is* law.[40] And with this power comes the responsibility to interrogate the codes that are coming out into the products. This is where thinking about the law and power relations within society can help you, specifically as the architects of our digital world. In this era of technology revolution, it is my earnest hope that the legal system, in dialogue with the scientific community, is able to address these concerns and democratize these spaces.

18

Promoting Constitutional Morality Beyond Courtrooms[1]

It gives me a great honour to speak at the first convocation ceremony of the Maharashtra National Law University (MNLU). MNLU has, in a short span of time, become a centre of excellence. The university promotes interdisciplinary legal education and encourages its students to participate in co-curricular and extracurricular activities. The students at MNLU have made a name for themselves by winning accolades in debating, mooting and sporting competitions. The university also has a strong focus on research and boasts over fifteen research centres. I have also had the personal experience of engaging with students from MNLU at my chambers, where they have proved their mettle while interning under me. The students of MNLU were diligent, knowledgeable, and above all, grounded individuals.

Delivering a convocation address is always a difficult task. It marks an end and a beginning. Graduation invokes complex emotions—happiness, accomplishment, anticipation, nostalgia and also a little bit of sadness. You have to let go of the familiar. You will take with you the affection that you share for your friends, the admiration that you have for your faculty members and the shared experience of a time that has gone by, with all its adversities and joys. The journey of your batch was indeed tumultuous, with the pandemic overhauling our systems of education. But as Richelle E. Goodrich, an American novelist, says, 'Stand tall on the summit after a tedious climb. Take in the remarkable scenery and the exhilaration of accomplishment. But don't pause for long; there are greater mountains to climb while you still possess the drive and capacity to do so.'[2]

Graduation, as I said, also marks a beginning. Some of you may be joining a corporate law firm, some may be planning to pursue further education, some of you would be joining litigation, and it's even possible that some of you may be taking up film-making or a culinary course! All of them are worthwhile choices. There is no single way to use your law degree. There is no ideal linear trajectory to follow. As it is said, there is no curriculum to life; at every stage, it is an elective.

But there is one thing that I would want all of you to inculcate, and that is our 'constitutional morality'. You may have heard this phrase being used in judgments, but this principle has a wider import, beyond courtrooms. As Dr Ambedkar said, 'Constitution is not a mere lawyer's document, it is a vehicle of life, and its spirit is always the spirit of age.'[3]

The Constitution was not envisaged as a mere legal document but as a moral guiding force for citizens. Acharya J.B. Kripalani, a member of the Constituent Assembly noted that:

> What we have enunciated [in the Preamble] are not merely legal, constitutional and formal principles, but moral principles; and moral principles have got to be lived in life. They have to be lived whether it is private life or it is public life, whether it is commercial life, political life or the life of an administrator. They have to be lived throughout. These things, we have to remember if our Constitution is to succeed.[4]

As Ambedkar noted, constitutional morality is not a natural sentiment; it has to be cultivated. As you venture beyond the gates of your university, ask yourself, do you value the liberty, equality and dignity of every person? Do you believe in fraternity—that in a nation of 138 crore people, everyone has a share equal to yours? When I talk about fraternity, I am not talking about homogeneity but solidarity; that despite differences, we belong to this nation and this nation belongs to us. That difference should never be a ground for discrimination. Fraternity is an extremely important value that shapes the social life of a nation. Ambedkar once remarked, 'without fraternity, equality and liberty will be no deeper than coats of paint'.[5] Fraternity is also important in order to structure our democracy, to recognize and accept the plurality of people and interests, and the value of deliberation and not top-down imposition.

Democracy itself is more than the rule of majority, it is a 'system built on respect for the infinite dignity of each individual man and woman, on each person's moral striving for freedom, justice and truth . . . It is a "spiritual and moral possession". It is not just rules; it is a way of life. It encourages everybody to make the best of their capacities—holds that we have a moral responsibility to do so. It encourages the artist to seek beauty, the neighbour to seek community, the psychologist to seek perception, the scientist to seek truth'.[6]

But how does one live a life that imbibes constitutional values? Constitutional values can themselves be difficult to define; they are contested. Even judges differ on the meanings of these familiar phrases of liberty, equality and dignity. What is required is to decipher the underlying constitutional philosophy, or what we call constitutional morality? The Indian Constitution has been called a transformative document, which means that it not only sought to transfer the power from a colonial government to a democratically elected indigenous government, but it also aimed to bring substantive changes to the way society was structured. It is apparent that our Constitution promotes a tolerant and inclusive philosophy instead of an exclusionary one. Take the example of Article 15, which prohibits discrimination on the basis of race, caste, sex, place of birth and religion. What is common to these grounds is that they are personal characteristics that are either immutable or reflect the fundamental choice of an individual.[7] Another commonality is that many of these characteristics have been employed to historically discriminate against groups of people (such as Dalits, women, queer people and other minorities). The Constitution then prohibits discrimination against people who have been historically subjected to discrimination on the basis of these characteristics. It also recognizes that positive measures for the advancement of some of these marginalized groups need to be adopted by the State. This inclusive philosophy of the Constitution must be practised in our personal and professional lives.

Devoting one's life to social justice and rights litigation is a remarkable way to promote the values of our Constitution. However, I understand that pursuing such a career trajectory is not for everyone. In fact, for many, the low pay that accompanies such practice not only makes rights litigation an unlikely but an impossible choice. Many students come from impoverished backgrounds. They or their families may have taken loans to fund university education. They are compelled to take high-paying jobs to pay off their loans. Further, for many students from marginalized backgrounds, financially lucrative jobs bring social mobility. But one can promote constitutional values and social justice if one imbibes constitutional morality in the way one conducts your professional life.

Take, for instance, even if you are working at a corporate law firm, you can take up pro bono work. You can associate yourself with an NGO, or you can be a part of databases of lawyers that can support marginalized groups. There are many such databases online that have been created to cater to women, disabled and queer persons in need of legal counsel.

As transactional lawyers, you can support entrepreneurs who lack resources or who come from communities that are underrepresented in the economy.

Even small things like highlighting the lack of an effective, legally compliant anti-sexual harassment policy while conducting due diligence on a company that is to be acquired go a long way in promoting gender justice.

You can also review if the target company complies with its obligations under the Rights of Persons with Disabilities Act, 2016, and its rules. Private employers are required to frame an equal opportunity policy. Equal opportunity policies for establishments having more than twenty employees are required to include provisions relating to (i) appointment of liaison officers in establishments to look after the recruitment of persons with disabilities and provisions of facilities and amenities for such employees; (ii) identification of posts/vacancies for disabled persons; and (iii) provision of additional facilities and benefits for disabled persons. The Act also requires private establishments to conform to accessibility norms in their building plans. If private establishments have received incentives from the government, 5 per cent of their workforce must be comprised of disabled persons.[8] I note in my judgement in *Vikash Kumar v. Union Public Service Commission*[9] that:

> The role of the private sector in the market has increased manifold since the advent of liberalisation in India. The RPwD [Rights of Persons with Disabilities] Act 2016 recognizes that with the burgeoning role of the private sector in generating employment in India, an active responsibility has to be cast upon private employers to create an inclusive workforce by providing persons with disabilities equal opportunities in the job market. However, the guarantee of equal opportunity must be accompanied by the provision of reasonable accommodation.

The Transgender Persons (Protection of Rights) Rules, 2020, also impose obligations on private establishments to implement measures to prevent discrimination against transgender individuals. They are required to publish an equal opportunity policy for transgender persons, which should include details of (i) infrastructural facilities (such as gender-neutral washrooms); (ii) measures for safety and security (transportation and guards) and other amenities.[10]

If a manufacturing facility is a subject of a transaction, you can verify whether it complies with the safety provisions of the Factories

Act, 1948 and remuneration and retrenchment provisions of the labour codes.

These may not be red flags for your client not to enter the transaction, but it can be a good practice to start highlighting these compliances as a way to sensitize your clients.

In your litigation practice, you can make time for cases concerning rights and entitlements of marginalized groups. You can enrol yourself as a panel lawyer for legal aid authorities. Many universities and policy organizations also run weekly clinics for providing access to legal counsel and legal awareness to marginalized individuals. You can contribute to that.

If you have decided to pursue higher education or academia, you can make access to elite educational institutions more accessible by conducting free sessions for persons coming from marginalized backgrounds on admission and scholarship applications. Many of them do not have the cultural and social capital to pursue these opportunities. You can bridge this gap and make the admission processes more equitable.

One day, you will also be making hiring decisions for your own firms and chambers. I would urge all of you to be equal opportunity employers, to say the least. But you should go a step further and promote diversity in your workplaces. Justice Sonia Sotomayor, who is a judge of the US Supreme Court, came from poverty and a cultural background where her parents hardly spoke English. She has discussed how the affirmative action programmes at Princeton and Yale opened doors for her, enabling students like her from disadvantaged backgrounds to get a chance to succeed, calling herself a 'perfect affirmative action baby'.[11]

We must realize that the lack of accomplishments of a person coming from a marginalized background owing to their caste, gender, sexuality or disability is not reflective of their individual calibre but a product of their circumstances. With sufficient training and encouragement, people do bloom. This requires unlearning our own prejudices. Justice Sotomayor says in the context of gender discrimination:

> I found in my experiences that it's not that men are consciously discriminating against promoting women, but I do believe as people we have self-images about what's good. What's quote-unquote a 'good' lawyer, doctor, or whatever the profession is. And if you're a male who grew up professionally in a male-dominated profession, then your image of what a good lawyer is a male image.[12]

We must also promote constitutional morality in our homes. We must fight against casteism, patriarchy, homophobia and other harmful attitudes against minorities in our personal lives. The second wave of feminism popularized the slogan 'personal is political'. Let me discuss the origin of the slogan. The initial dominant liberal feminist thought did not specifically attack the assumption that the private sphere or the home belongs to the women. Its demands for equality were limited to the public sphere. However, the radical feminist thought that permeated the second wave of feminism aimed to target the social, cultural and political subordination of women in all aspects. It nudged the State to actively intervene in the private sphere that seeks to subordinate women. Indeed, the activities of the private sphere have a larger implication on the status of women. Confined to the domestic realm, women are assigned the toil of domestic labour. The discrimination and hierarchical set-up of the private realm often spills over to public life. Women are more likely to be relegated to feminized work roles and deprived of leadership positions, leading to workplace discrimination.

The rigid gender roles in the private sphere also promote the idea of oppositional and binary genders. Any deviation from gender norms in terms of gender presentation and sexuality is considered a deviance. This implicates the queer community where trans or non-binary persons and sexual minorities are termed as 'unnatural'.

We learn much of the casteist behaviour in our homes. This includes customs or traditions that reflect caste superiority or caste purity and the markers that upper-caste groups use to distinguish themselves from oppressed castes. This also includes the norms governing marriage, where marriages between upper-caste and oppressed-caste individuals are still looked down upon with prejudice in upper-caste households. This holds true even for inter-religious marriages. It is tragic when we allow social conformity to trump over personal autonomy. In *Shafin Jahan v. Asokan KM & Ors*,[13] the Supreme Court has observed, 'Our choices are respected because they are ours. Social approval for intimate personal decisions is not the basis for recognising them. Indeed, the Constitution protects personal liberty from disapproving audiences.'

Thus, our homes are not devoid of politics, and the onus is on us to give way to progressive practices in our personal lives. In this regard, Paula Rust, an American sociologist, has commented, '[O]ne should make personal choices that are consistent with one's personal politics; personal life and personal politics are indistinguishable.'[14]

Let constitutional morality be a guiding principle of how you conduct your lives in courtrooms and beyond. I have only shared a few ideas with you on how you can commit your life to social justice. It is my hope and belief that you all will come up with innumerable creative ways to work the Constitution. In parting, I will leave you with the words of American civil rights activist Maya Angelou:

> Look beyond your tasselled caps
> And you will see injustice.
> At the end of your fingertips
> You will find cruelties,
> Irrational hate, bedrock sorrow
> And terrifying loneliness.
> There is your work.

I wish all the graduating students the best of luck for their future endeavours.

19

Making Disability Rights Real

Addressing Accessibility and More[1]

August 2022 marks the third anniversary of Shamnad's tragic and untimely death. He was an illustrious scholar, a respected educator and a change maker par excellence. He was appointed as the professor of intellectual property law at National University of Juridical Sciences (NUJS), Kolkata, where he was beloved by the students, not only for his expertise on the subject but also because he took on the role of 'friend' and 'mentor'. SpicyIP, one of India's most widely read blogs on intellectual property law, was founded by Shamnad Basheer.

Beyond his academic achievements lies IDIA, or the Increasing Diversity by Increasing Access, programme—what many would term the crowning glory of Shamnad's achievements. As the audience is no doubt aware, IDIA was a movement that Shamnad spearheaded over two decades ago, with the aim of ensuring equitable access to legal education in the country. The legal profession boasted a centuries-old presence in India, but its higher echelons (or indeed, its lower ones) remained largely inaccessible to the common person. Although the advent of the National Law Universities challenged the notion that the legal profession was for the few and not for the many, legal education continued to remain the domain of the elite. IDIA, through its consistent efforts, has attempted to remedy this systemic flaw and has certainly succeeded in doing so! IDIA prepares young students from marginalized communities for law entrance exams, secures funding for their legal education, and mentors them through their five years at university. To influence the course of even a single person's life is a remarkable thing. That Shamnad influenced the trajectories of so many people's lives so positively is nothing short of extraordinary.

I had the pleasure of meeting Shamnad at IDIA's annual conference around four years ago, where I was invited to deliver an address on law and storytelling.

True to its name, IDIA's programmes targeted persons with disabilities as well. Of the eighty-six persons currently reading law in universities across India belonging to IDIA, fifteen are persons with disabilities.[2] Shamnad and others, working with IDIA's organizational team, have already put into action the theme of today's lecture: 'Making Disability Rights Real: Addressing Accessibility & More'. My congratulations to the IDIA team and all the IDIA scholars. I wish you continued success! By including persons with disabilities within the ambit of its outreach and training programmes, Shamnad as well as IDIA rightly recognized that persons with disabilities are just as deserving of and entitled to an education as the next person. It is not just any type of education that they ought to be able to access; they must have an equal shot at the best universities and most sought-after opportunities.

A person can either be born with a disability or become disabled later in life. These disabilities can take a variety of forms—they can be physical, mental, intellectual, learning-based or communication-based. Some disabilities are immediately visible, and others are invisible—you will not know about them unless the person in question chooses to tell you. Many chronic illnesses are also disabilities. The effect each disability has varies based on a multitude of factors.

When people encounter others with disabilities, there is a tendency to view them as being very different from able-bodied people, as being 'lesser than' them. By this, I mean that they are stereotyped as being less capable and less intelligent than their able-bodied counterparts. The stereotypes that persons with disabilities are burdensome or are defenceless victims also prevail. The differences between able-bodied people and persons with disabilities, both real and perceived, give rise to immense stigma in society. Children often bully their disabled classmates and friends, and adults with disabilities, too, are not treated with respect or empathy. It is also a very unfortunate fact that able-bodied persons discriminate against persons with disabilities and in many instances, commit violence upon them.

The prevalence of such harmful stereotypes has a pernicious effect and hinders access to educational spaces, public places, employment opportunities, as well as to free and full participation in society. Beyond hampering their access to those opportunities, which they are entitled to, such stereotypes also have the effect of dehumanizing each complex individual and reducing them to a fragment of all that they truly are. Such stereotypes are based on a denial of a person's rich inner life and their individuality.

Other, more material barriers also stand in the way of persons with disabilities. Despite laws mandating disability-friendly infrastructure, public transport, government and private buildings, hospitals, libraries, parks and a host of other spaces continue to be inaccessible to persons with disabilities. Some entities do not even pretend to comply with such laws, while others comply with them in a desultory fashion, and only with a view to getting their building and occupancy permits. I have noticed that some ramps are so steep that an able-bodied person cannot walk down without falling over, let alone a person who uses a wheelchair or crutches! This is just the tip of the enormous iceberg of problems with the implementation of disability-friendly policies.

I recently came across a story narrated by the famous disability rights activist Javed Abidi. Parts of this story were also reported by all the big media houses at the time. In 2001, Professor Stephen Hawking visited India to deliver a lecture. Abidi wrote to Professor

Hawking and requested him to help with the disability rights movement. Professor Hawking declined but informed Abidi that he was going to visit the Qutub Minar and other monuments in Delhi. Abidi and his colleagues promptly approached the Archaeological Survey of India (ASI) and requested them to install ramps at these historic sites that were on Professor Hawking's agenda. The ASI is reported to have refused, and the press picked this story up in no time. The ASI then sat up and took notice of Professor Hawking's visit, built ramps overnight and installed them at all the monuments. Professor Hawking, along with his wife Elaine, visited the Qutub Minar, where she put her arms around the iron pillar to make a wish. She was asked what she wished for, and she replied, 'I wished for the ramps to stay even after we leave.'

Abidi passed away in 2018, but his legacy endures, just like Shamnad's.

It is incumbent on all institutions, be they governmental or private, and all individuals to do their bit to ensure a more just world for persons with disabilities. Governmental or private entities must ensure that laws and policies are being complied with. This is of foremost importance. In our individual capacities, the least we can do is accord persons with disabilities the respect they deserve and treat them as equals.

The disability rights movement has always maintained that they do not want pity, and they do not want to be treated as inspirational figures for merely existing. Instead of being spoken to and treated in a patronizing fashion, persons with disabilities require equal access to opportunities at school and work, an equal chance at forging bonds of friendship, an equal chance to marry and have children if they wish to, and social acceptance. Persons with disabilities have asked to be treated like any other person.

This reminds me of the film *Margarita with a Straw*, where the protagonist Laila (played by Kalki Koechlin) is a young student who has cerebral palsy. To those who are yet to watch this movie, do not worry, for there are no spoilers ahead. In the film, Laila participates in a music competition, along with her band, and is delighted when the band is declared the winner. But her joy is short-lived. The judge of the music competition is quick to share that they awarded Laila's band the first place because Laila, a disabled person, had written the lyrics. The undertone is clear: The judge pities Laila, and the award is a consequence of the pity she feels. Of course, Laila is unhappy with the turn of events.

It is not out of the able-bodied's sense of pity that persons with disabilities require but to be treated as equals. We must also aim towards a just society that accounts for their needs and provides facilities to accommodate them. These facilities ensure that they are able to exercise their rights and enjoy their freedoms on an equal footing with able-bodied people. These facilities, which are known as 'reasonable accommodations' in legal terms, must not be viewed with contempt or derision. Some people ask, 'Why do they need *special* treatment?' The disability rights movement has long advocated against the position that they have *special* needs. They only have *human* needs, the fulfilment of which would enable them to participate in society on an equal basis with able-bodied or neurotypical persons.

Each one of us has needs. This is an undeniable facet of the human experience. What we need may vary based on our circumstances, but each of us requires something from society at some point in our lives. A few examples of able-bodied persons who commonly require some or other accommodation are pregnant women, babies and children, women who menstruate, elderly people, people with illnesses or single parents. By listing these examples, I do not mean to diminish the difficulties faced by persons with disabilities. Rather, I am making the limited point that to require accommodations is a *human* need and not a *special* need. The able-bodied adult male must not be classified as the standard or the norm, with all other groups thought of as the deviation. The spirit of our Constitution accounts for the rich tapestry of human experiences, and we must strive to do the same.

When we speak of disability rights, we cannot speak of them in silos. American advocate and scholar Kimberlé Crenshaw coined the term 'intersectionality' in the context of oppression. In this context, it means that various factors such as gender, sexuality, caste or class intersect with one another and result in unique forms of discrimination. Much closer to home, towering figures such as Dr Ambedkar applied an intersectional lens in their writings much before the term 'intersectionality' came into play.

Let us consider intersectionality in the context of disability. If a child with a disability is born into a rich family, the family will be able to afford expensive prosthetics if required, the best medical care and the resources to care for that child at home. Now consider a child who is disabled, in a much poorer family. How will the parents afford expensive treatments or schools that are equipped to teach the child? If both the parents of the child are working, how will they be able to afford full-time care for the child? If a public bus is not disability friendly, it is very likely that it will impact the child with lesser financial resources much more than it will impact the child whose parents can afford a car or a taxi!

How do we begin to address the various impediments to making disability rights real? Of course, a small but significant aspect is society's attitudes towards persons with disabilities, as I just mentioned. Institutional changes are necessary as well. In the context of the judiciary, sensitivity and empathy are of utmost importance. Judges would do well to remember that a person with a disability who may be before them is a person, first and foremost. Where the law contains provisions for persons with disabilities, they must be followed without exception. Section 164(5A) of the Code of Criminal Procedure, 1973 is a good example of a disability-friendly provision. This section permits the magistrate to take the assistance of an interpreter or special educator to record the statement of a person with a disability. Where such enabling laws do not exist, judges would do well to do what they can within the bounds of the law, in recognition of the needs of the person before them.

In a broader sense, Article 12 of the UN Convention on the Rights of Persons with Disabilities (CRPD) enshrines that persons with disabilities have equal recognition before the law. However, if we look at the legal history, we see that law restricts the legal capacity of persons with disability to make decisions about their body and life by appointing substitute decision-making regimes such as guardians or conservatorships. Such restrictions stem from the assumption that mental capacity is necessary to exercise legal capacity. Even presently, there are many laws in operation which deny legal capacity to persons with disabilities. The UN has urged that persons with disabilities have the same rights as able-bodied persons to make decisions about their lives.

The ability to hold rights and exercise them lies at the core of every individual. If this is the case, then arbitrary restrictions on the exercise of legal capacity deny persons with disabilities equal protection before the law. By doing so, the law deprives them of a whole host of rights, including civil, political, social, economic, sexual and reproductive rights. In *Suchita Srivastava v. Chandigarh Administration*,[3] the Supreme Court held that the State must respect the personal autonomy of women with mental disabilities to make reproductive choices, including the right to terminate her pregnancy. In case of persons with psychosocial or cognitive impairments, the State should refrain from taking decisions on behalf of persons with disabilities. Instead, the State should positively support persons with disabilities to exercise their rights to the fullest possible extent.

The Constitution protects full enjoyment of fundamental freedoms and rights of persons with disabilities. This protection is inherently grounded in the principle of dignity of the individual enshrined in the Preamble. Persons with disabilities have the right to life and personal liberty enshrined in Article 21 of the Constitution. This also includes all the concomitant sets of rights such as right to education, right to information, right to clean environment, right to livelihood and right to shelter, among others, which enable an individual to live life to its fullest extent possible. The exercise of all the rights and freedoms is necessary for social participation and enjoyment of citizenship by persons with disabilities. To live a dignified and independent life, persons with disabilities should be able to seamlessly participate in the community on an equal basis with others. Today, I wish to focus on two specific aspects integral to the full development of life: education and livelihood.

With a view to realize the right to education of persons with disabilities, the Rights of Persons with Disabilities Act, 2016 mandates reservation of at least 5 per cent of total seats for persons with benchmark disabilities in all government institutions of higher education and other higher education institutions receiving aid from the government. However, most schools and higher education institutions in India do not account for any reasonable accommodation that persons with disabilities might require. This puts additional strain on students with disabilities, who have to conform to the existing able-normative rules to succeed academically.

True realization of the right to education of students with disability is possible only in an inclusive and accessible education system. Lack of physically accessible schools, trained teachers and facilitators, and inadequate learning materials exclude students with disabilities from accessing education on equal terms with others. We as a society need to understand the educational needs of students with disabilities and address them in a collaborative manner to help them realize their right to education.

Similarly, the right to work is fundamental to recognizing other human rights, including the right to live with dignity and the right to livelihood. Indian law fosters greater participation of persons with disabilities in organized employment by providing them with reservations in government jobs. The law also mandates the government to provide incentives to employers in the private sector to hire persons with disabilities to compose at least 5 per cent of their workforce. The right to work of persons with disabilities should not be limited to their participation in the workforce. According to the CRPD, the right to work of persons with disabilities includes the right to gain a living by work freely chosen or accepted in labour market and a work environment that is open, inclusive, and accessible to persons with disabilities.[4]

The constitutional precepts of right to dignity and equality require public and private employers to do more to make their workplaces inclusive and accessible to persons with disabilities. An inclusive workplace entails creating an environment suited to the needs of persons with disabilities, where people feel welcomed and comfortable, not in spite of their disability, but because of their disability. Public and private employers must also ensure that persons with disabilities develop skills during their employment and have access to meaningful opportunities to progress in their careers.

Technology can play an essential role in creating inclusive and accessible workplaces. Emerging technologies such as artificial intelligence and the internet of Things can help persons with disability to effectively participate and engage in the workplace. However, along with the adoption of technology, we as a society should also introspect on the way our workplace functions. As a starting point, we could ensure that persons with disabilities are not ostracized in the workspace. We should make them feel that they 'belong' and are an integral part of the workplace.[5] Creating a sense of belonging in the work environment recognizes the right of persons with disabilities to work on an equal basis with others.

In the legal fraternity, we need to ask ourselves: Is the legal profession providing reasonable accommodations to persons with disabilities? Fostering an inclusive and accessible environment at courts will certainly trickle down to society, as courts at the end of the day are public spaces where society interacts and engages with its members. At the Supreme Court, our endeavour has been to make our processes and systems accessible to persons with disabilities. The e-Committee of the Supreme Court has been working to make the digital infrastructure of the Indian judicial system more accessible to persons with disabilities. We have introduced audio-captchas on the Supreme Court as well as High Court websites to ensure that visually impaired professionals face no hindrances in looking up the cause-list or the case status. We have also ensured that the case files are readable and screen-reader friendly to make them accessible to persons with disabilities. The e-Committee, in collaboration with the National Informatics Centre (NIC), has also created a judgment search portal accessible to persons with disabilities.

Through the initiative of the e-Committee, the High Courts of Odisha and Kerala have adopted the paperless courts system. The digitization of files and court records will ensure that courts remain accessible to persons with disabilities. We have also tried to make the Indian judicial services more inclusive by removing barriers to the entry of persons with disability. In *Vikash Kumar v. UPSC*,[6] we held that the exclusion of persons with over 50 per cent visual impairment from qualifying for judicial services was not in consonance with the 'reasonable accommodation' principle enshrined in the Rights of Persons with Disabilities Act, 2016. Of course, I will be the first to admit that much needs to be done to make our judiciary fully accessible to persons with disabilities. But I can say that at least we have taken the first steps in the right direction.

The legal arguments that take place in a courtroom are often backed by substantive legal research, which forms an integral part of any legal professional. Legal databases form an ineluctable part of the legal profession, both for academicians and professionals alike. However, we can see that most legal databases are inaccessible to persons with disabilities. The presence of access barriers such as unlabelled links, non-screen reader-friendly web pages and PDF files, and the absence of alternative text descriptions for images on websites and blogs casts a chilling effect on the ability of persons with disabilities to produce quality scholarship and practise law. As a fraternity, our failure to provide for reasonable accommodations to persons with disabilities invalidates their everyday struggles and conveys a message to them that they are unwelcome in the legal profession. This, in turn, shapes their social reality within which they are constrained to lead their professional lives. The physical barriers are often symptomatic of an ableist attitudinal mindset.

Ableism is systemic and rooted in the idea of preference for able-bodied and able-minded persons at the cost of discrimination and oppression of persons with disabilities. Disability is a social construct. The notions of normalcy and intelligence are deeply rooted in centuries of prejudice against persons with disability. We need to understand the experiences of persons with disability in order to change our own attitudes towards disability.

Ableism is widely prevalent in our everyday lives. In popular culture, disability is often essentialized to draw cheap humour. Treating disability in a cavalier fashion dehumanizes and stigmatizes persons with disability. Ableism can also take the form of inappropriate and harmful language. Language shapes the way we think. It has the power to define the way we interact and value others. Inappropriate or derogatory language can make persons with disability uncomfortable and act as a barrier to their full and meaningful participation in all aspects of society.[7] Therefore, a good starting point to fight against ableism is to unlearn our language by excluding the ableist slurs that often innocently slip from our mouths in everyday conversations.[8]

In the legal profession, particularly, law schools could take the lead in tackling ableist environments. If we truly believe that products of law schools have a role to play in guiding law and policy-making, we need to address the failure of our law schools and institutions to provide reasonable accommodations to persons with disability. This affects their ability to assert themselves and contribute effectively to the legal field, resulting in the creation of a legal fraternity that is largely under-inclusive. The invisibility of the identity of persons with disabilities within the legal fraternity is an affront to the constitutional guarantees of equality and non-discrimination enshrined in our Constitution.

It is often difficult for students with disabilities to avail internships with law firms or participate in international and national moot court competitions. This is essentially because most of their energies are spent in trying to overcome and interact with an ableist structure around them in order to fulfil their everyday necessities. The lack of reasonable accommodations constrains persons with disabilities to shape their entire lives within the interstices of an ableist environment. This can stifle their aspirations, too.

IDIA has launched the IDIA Disability Access Programme, through which it sensitized, trained and supported many students with disabilities. I am happy to note that multiple NLUs have collaborated with IDIA as part of their programme and are taking active steps to tackle accessibility barriers. I would particularly like to mention the Shamnad Basheer Accessibility Labs at NALSAR University of Law and The West Bengal National University of Juridical Sciences. The labs are a laudable effort to carry forward Professor Basheer's legacy by ensuring the creation of an enabling environment for students with disabilities.[9]

Before I conclude, I would like to extend my deepest gratitude to all the disability rights movements in the country and world over. It is due to their tireless work that I am able to speak about some of the themes discussed today.

20

Leveraging Technology Towards Dispute Resolution in Commercial Courts[1]

Though I would have loved to be a part of this excellent discussion physically in Sydney, I am constrained to attend the discussion virtually. A part of the reason for my inability to attend the discussion physically today is the ever-expanding workload of the Indian Supreme Court. As judges of the Supreme Court of India, we perform both judicial and administrative duties. Ours is not a strictly constitutional court. While we do hear matters of constitutional importance that have a far-reaching impact on the functioning of the Indian State and democracy, most of the work that we do (which I call the bread-and-butter work) comprises performing the functions of the court of last appeal in India. The seemingly routine matters tend to metamorphose into 'complex' issues by the time they reach the court thus. The Supreme Court of India, as the last court of appeal, hears abundant 'complex issues' or rather issues that have been made 'complex' by the hard and byzantine process situated at the levels below it.

Justice Sundaresh Menon, in the Goff Lecture, 2021, on 'the Complexification of Disputes in the Digital Age', argues that the complexity of disputes manifests itself in multiple ways. Such complexity may most commonly be due to the number of documents tendered, 'the number of witnesses or parties involved and ultimately in the sheer length of the trial'.[2] In such a case, the judge will need to sieve through dockets that run to thousands of pages in order to fetch the 'relevant information' buried therein. This form of complexity is referred to as 'information overload complexity'.[3]

The complexity problem is not only caused by the voluminous docket but also because of the complexity of the dispute itself. This is referred to as 'technical complexity'. With the advancement in science and technology, the ambit of disputes has widened. In my twenty-two years of experience as a judge, I have come to realize that regulatory and commercial matters are usually complex because these disputes involve the interplay of law and policy.

Another important cause of the complexification problem is an overburdened docket. Understanding and comprehending an enormous number of disputes in a short period of time is an arduous process. This form of complexification can be termed the 'overburdened complexity'. Let me take the example of the Indian Supreme Court to illustrate this complexity and the need for its consequent simplification. On Mondays and Fridays, which are designated as 'admission days', our dockets range from sixty to eighty fresh matters, with the average size of a file running into about 400 pages. On these two days, judges are required to decide within six hours, whether the Supreme Court ought to entertain such matters, i.e. whether it must admit for hearing and final disposal, the matters that have been filed before it.

I believe that technology can be used to resolve the complexities that I have outlined above. To some extent, we have tried to use technology at the Supreme Court of India to deconstruct the causes of the complexities.

Under the aegis of the e-Committee of the Supreme Court of India, an e-filing system has been developed which is a complete end-to-end solution for online filing of plaints, written statements, replies and applications. The digitization project of the e-Committee, of which e-filing is an important facet, was introduced to reduce the carbon footprint. Cases that were not filed through the e-filing route are digitized and circulated to the judges. While e-filing has not yet been made mandatory because of the lack of access to internet facilities for litigants and lawyers, the e-Committee is strongly pushing for the e-filing of cases. Various High Courts have been encouraged to consider making e-filing compulsory in taxation, arbitration and commercial disputes. The e-files are bookmarked, thus allowing us to easily navigate through the file on our devices. The computer committee of the Supreme Court has developed the Supreme Court of India interface software with features that simplify reading a voluminous file. For instance, the software notifies the judge every time a new inclusion, such as a counter-affidavit or status report, is made to the file. Thus, the digitization project, beyond ensuring an accessible, transparent, efficient and cost-effective judicial system, has also helped in engaging with the complexity problem that is caused by information overload.

Technology can be used not just to simplify voluminous documents but also to reduce the pendency of cases as much as possible. If the pendency of cases is reduced by deploying technological solutions, this will ultimately translate into a freer docket, allowing judges to dedicate more time to the matters before them, thus eliminating overburdened complexity. It would enhance the intellectual output of the judges by freeing up a significant chunk of their time to enable them to streamline their time in effectively deciding a lesser number of disputes that may be more complex or intellectually demanding. The e-Courts Mission Mode Project has developed virtual courts by relying on the use of AI. The concept is aimed at reducing footfalls in the courts by eliminating the physical presence of the violator or advocate in the court. For instance, on a pilot basis, virtual courts in India are being used for petty offences, such as traffic and transport challans. These are essentially cases where there is usually a proactive admission of guilt by the accused (such as running a red light) and a proactive compliance of the cause by the defendant on receipt of the summons in electronic form. The summons is sent in an electronic form, and after admission of guilt, the compensation/fine is also paid online.

Finally, I would like to address the question of whether technology could be used to simplify complexification that arises due to the inherently complex nature of the dispute itself, i.e. 'technical complexification'. Arbitration has been the most sought-after form of dispute resolution in complex commercial disputes. Time is of essence in commercial disputes. The long pendency and high cost, which are features of most of the litigation systems across the world, make arbitration a well-suited choice of dispute resolution in commercial disputes. The litigation system is constructed on the assumption that a full and exhaustive determination of facts is a necessity to deliver justice. However, the alternative forms of dispute resolution, such as arbitration, open us up to the idea that there is no one *conception* of justice. In commercial disputes, the resolution of the dispute in a quick and orderly manner is the ideal of justice. Technology can be interwoven in arbitration proceedings such as in the selection of an arbitrator to enable the selection of a bias-free arbitrator based on the preferences of the number, identity and qualifications indicated by the parties. Having said that, it would be amiss if I do not also acknowledge the fact that technology is a double-edged sword. Algorithms are not free of bias. Prominent AI researchers have written that the facial recognition software is less accurate in identifying women and people of colour because the software has predominantly been fed with pictures of white men. Similar concerns have also been raised in language algorithms, where racist and sexist language is used as the training data. This inherent bias in the algorithm would manifest as various forms of discrimination against the consenting parties.

Technology is a great enabler, but as judges, it is our ordained responsibility to ensure that it is not used to merely automate our old ways of working. Technology must be used as a tool to simplify and break down the complexities that are inherent in the process and form of dispute before the courts. To conclude, let me share with you the words of Professor Richard Susskind,[4] who has rightly observed that while the pandemic has ushered in an era of a technological judiciary, we are still at the foothills of this journey. Our onward and upward journey will involve a sustained effort to make judges adapt to technology, make them unlearn their existing ways of working with physical files and changing their mindsets.

21

Universal Adult Franchise

Translating India's Political Transformation into a Social Transformation[1]

An astute jurist, a fierce parliamentarian and a prolific writer, L.M. Singhvi was an encyclopaedia of knowledge on Indian history and culture. He played an important role in shaping Indian public life through his career as a lawyer and also as a distinguished parliamentarian. One of the most significant causes that Singhvi championed was the Panchayati Raj institution, with a focus on the importance of self-governance.

To honour Singhvi's commitment to the role played by citizens and their engagement with electoral democracy, I am speaking today on the topic 'Universal Adult Franchise: Translating India's Political Transformation into a Social Transformation.'

First, I will talk about the historical context in which we must reflect on the idea of Universal Adult Franchise. *Second*, I will discuss how this idea was deliberated and included in the constitutional discourse leading to the drafting of the Indian Constitution. *Third*, I will reflect on the impact of Universal Adult Franchise post-Independence and how it created social transformation. *Fourth*, I shall be talking about how the idea of Panchayati Raj, along with Universal Adult Franchise, led to the deepening of Indian democracy. *Fifth*, I will be reflecting on the connections between the principle of Universal Adult Franchise and the idea of participatory democracy. Lastly, I shall be reflecting on the Indian experiment with the Universal Adult Franchise.

THE HISTORICAL CONTEXT TO UNDERSTAND UNIVERSAL ADULT FRANCHISE

We must first reflect on the context in which we see the idea of Universal Adult Franchise. The context is not just of India but across the globe. History tells us that power was concentrated in the hands of a few. In many countries, power was used as a medium to control the behaviour of people. Even when the idea of democracy emerged, the exercise of power was kept limited only to the already powerful—whom we know as the so-called 'noble class'.

For instance, when the wave of democracy emerged in the world's oldest democracy, the US, the structures of democracy which were set up excluded marginalized and oppressed communities. African Americans were not even considered citizens of America when the Constitution of the United States was adopted.[2] In India, we find a historical social system in which power was concentrated in the hands of the upper class of society. The rights we now consider as universal were not universal all the time; they were denied to the oppressed communities.

This was the norm across the world. Those who did not hold power were subjected to several levels of oppression. Against this power hegemony, several social reformers led movements towards the distribution of power. These movements were to democratize the hold over power by a few communities.

When the structure of democracy was adopted by several countries in the eighteenth and nineteenth centuries, unfortunately, the exercise of democracy was used to retain power by the few. The right to vote was controlled and exercised by only those individuals who had already succeeded in society because of their social power.

For instance, the right to vote was exercised only by those who had certain properties or educational qualifications, which were the result of not their individual efforts but were a reflection of the influence and hegemony their communities had on society. As a result, the idea of democracy was controlled by the elites of society. In that sense, the structure and exercise of democracy were only retrenchments of social privileges and hegemony. Voting rights were denied to women and members of marginalized communities because the elites did not want to share the power with them, and neither considered them to be capable of exercising their wisdom.

It is in this history of injustice and exclusion that we must look at the idea of Universal Adult Franchise. The demand for equal voting rights and to become a part of the political process emerged from the marginalized communities across the world. Instances of this challenge can be found in the women's suffrage movement globally and the movement of the socially oppressed.

The emergence of social movements to gain voting rights was a simultaneous phenomenon in different parts of the world. People from different countries found inspiration and learned from each other how to claim an equal say in decision-making. If we take the example of the US, we see that the black community led the struggle to claim their humanity by asking for basic rights such as the right to vote. When the Thirteenth, Fourteenth and Fifteenth Amendments to the American Constitution were adopted because of the struggle of the American Black community,[3] we also found a resonance happening in India. It inspired our social leaders coming from marginalized communities.[4] These social reformers not only demanded equal citizenship for the oppressed communities but also started initiatives that could educate the masses about their rights.

For instance, the prominent social reformers Jyotirao Phule and Savitribai Phule started schools for girls to make them aware of the happenings in the world and also about their rights. In his book titled *Gulamgiri* (Slavery), Jyotirao Phule appealed to the upper-caste Indians that they should make way for the marginalized in the same way the Americans did by abolishing slavery through the Thirteenth Amendment of the Constitution of the United States.[5]

In that way, the negotiations against the colonial power of the British Government were not by a uniform stream of thought. While few Indians demanded a share in the administration, leaders such as Jyotirao Phule were laying down the ground for an alternate picture of providing the chance to become part of the administration to everyone.

When the negotiations to give rights to Indians and to draft their Constitution were happening in the twentieth century, our leaders, such as Dr Ambedkar, led a strong demand that the conception of a free India cannot happen without giving Universal Adult Franchise. According to Dr Ambedkar, the idea of a Universal Adult Franchise was non-negotiable. In his submissions before the Southborough Committee of 1919, which was constituted to draft the Government of India Act 1919, Dr Ambedkar categorically asserted that the right to become a part of the political system was interlinked with the idea of citizenship.[6] It was his belief that without exercising the right to vote, no one could claim to be a citizen. Babasaheb Ambedkar believed that adult suffrage would create a political conscience among the oppressed castes.[7]

Therefore, in that sense, the struggle for social change, which happened for several years from the 1920s till Independence, aimed at the distribution of power by claiming equal voting rights. The marginalized communities had to struggle every inch to claim equal rights. Therefore, the idea of Universal Adult Franchise is not just a political idea. The idea of Universal Adult Franchise is social at its core.

Our history tells us that society was regulated by denying power to certain communities and, therefore, the emergence of Universal Adult Franchise as a demand aimed at undoing the centuries of oppression. Furthermore, the idea of Universal Adult Franchise was also reflected in the political demand for freedom through documents such as the Nehru Committee Report of 1928, Karachi Resolution of 1931, etc. This evolution of Universal Adult Franchise was also seen in the debates and discussions of the Constituent Assembly.[8]

CONSTITUENT ASSEMBLY DEBATES

Under colonial rule, Indians were still confronted with a limited franchise and limited participation in the government. The Government of India Act, 1919, and the Government of India Act, 1935, reflected limited franchise qualified by property, income and education. Under the 1919 Act, women were categorically disqualified from voting. The 1935 Act, despite providing a broader franchise, could cover only one-fifth of the population.[9]

When Dr Ambedkar introduced the principle of universal adult suffrage in the Constituent Assembly on 16 June 1949, there were certainly apprehensions amongst the members of the assembly. Certain members opposed it on the ground that adult suffrage 'presupposes that the electorate is enlightened'[10] and believed that in a country with high levels of illiteracy and in a largely poverty-stricken republic, the experiment of universal adult suffrage would not be successful. Some even called it the 'greatest risk which the Constituent Assembly has taken'.[11] At the same time, there were members who considered adult suffrage to be a natural choice for India's freedom movement.[12]

After detailed deliberations, the Constituent Assembly decided to adopt Universal Adult Franchise and affirm political equality, marking the transformative character of our Constitution. The nation was shedding its colonial and pre-colonial shackles and evolving to adopt the system of parliamentary democracy based on equality of citizenship and Universal Adult Franchise. The Preamble of the Constitution beginning with the words 'We the People' made it abundantly clear that the will of the people of India was the source of sovereign authority and that India was to be constituted as a sovereign secular democratic republic. Universal Adult Franchise was set to bring in a five-fold increase in the electorate, extending it from three and a half crore voters to seventeen crore voters who were to participate in the first parliamentary elections of independent India.[13]

As Alladi Krishnaswamy Ayyar, a lawyer and former member of the Constituent Assembly of India, observed:

> . . . in spite of the ignorance and illiteracy of the large mass of the Indian people, the Assembly has adopted the principle of adult franchise with an abundant faith in the common man and the ultimate success of democratic rule and in the full belief that the introduction of democratic government on the basis of adult suffrage will bring enlightenment and promote the well-being, the standard of life, the comfort and the decent living of the common man . . .

The introduction of Universal Adult Franchise was a revolutionary act at a time when such a right had only recently been extended to women, people of colour and the working class in supposedly 'mature' Western democracies.[14] In this sense, our Constitution was a feminist document,[15] as well as an egalitarian, socially transformative document. It was a break from the colonial and pre-colonial legacy, the boldest move adopted by the Constitution that was truly a product of Indian imagination.

The drafters of the Constitution were cognizant of the fact that political equality would not suffice to weed out the inequality that existed in the social and economic spheres of Indian society. Even before the Constitution came into force, Dr Ambedkar offered a sobering reflection on the contradictions that would mark India's journey ahead. He cautioned that while the people of India would gain political equality through the right to vote, they would continue to live amidst deep social and economic inequality, a tension that could not be ignored if democracy was to truly thrive. He said, and I quote:

> On the 26th of January 1950, we are going to enter into a life of contradictions. In politics[,] we will have equality and in social

> and economic life[,] we will have inequality. In politics, we will be recognizing the principle of one-man[,] one vote and one vote, one value. In our social and economic life, we shall, by reason of our social and economic structure, continue to deny the principle of one man, one value.[16]

In light of these observations, the principle of 'one person, one vote' was adopted in the hope that political equality would gradually help overcome and diminish deep structural inequalities that plagued India. Universal Adult Franchise, enshrined in Article 326 of the Constitution, was committed to transforming a fractured society into a democratic, participatory and egalitarian society and translating India's political equality into social transformation, guided by the values of human dignity, liberty, equality, fraternity and social justice.

POST-INDEPENDENCE

As we see, Universal Adult Franchise was a solid determination of India's founding leaders to create a democratic State.[17] However, the translation of the right to vote being bestowed upon citizens and its realization has not been a simple journey. The Constituent Assembly Secretariat (CAS) started the preparation of electoral rolls in 1947 itself. It began issuing press releases, which allowed it to communicate with the public. In response to concerns, the precise method and procedure of creating the electoral rolls were published in the press. The Constitutional Adviser B.N. Rau himself oversaw these press releases. The press releases informed the public of the story of what happened next and any recurring alterations to the procedure. Israeli academic and author Ornit Shani, while describing the work of CAS, writes: 'In the same way an intimate address [in a novel] allows people to conjure up a uniquely vivid experience, the CAS's correspondence enabled people to conjure up a world of Universal Adult Franchise.'[18]

The preparation of the first electoral roll was also a momentous task, as the majority of the population (86 per cent) were illiterate and the new republic of India was grappling with the horrors of Partition, war and famines. While preparing the first electoral rolls, many women's names were missing, and instead, there was a description of the voter as X's mother or Y's wife. Young girls married off at an early age and forced to shift to a different matrimonial village found it extremely difficult to get their names enrolled in the electoral constituency of their husband's village. The Election Commission had to rectify this and redo the exercise.[19] It also took time to notify the reserved constituencies for SCs and STs, as relevant data was not available immediately.[20]

Furthermore, in order to increase its reach to the widest section of the population, the newly created Election Commission of India at that time innovated with outreach campaigns. It ran a documentary on the franchise and the duties of the electorate in over 3000 theatres to encourage the citizens. This was done to educate the masses about the election process. The Election Commission thus achieved the feat of preparing the first electoral rolls for 176 million Indians aged twenty-one years or more for deciding the fate of 4500 seats, including 500 for Parliament and 4000 for state assemblies.

Right from the very first elections of independent India, Indian citizens have demonstrated a lot of enthusiasm in participating in the electoral processes. Several constitutional commentators had believed that India would not be able to survive as a constitutional democracy.[21] But Indian citizens have proved such thoughts to be wrong.

Universal Adult Franchise helped establish a sense of belonging and responsibility amongst citizens as equal stakeholders in the country's progress. This sense of belonging and faith in democracy is best captured by the life of the late Shri Shyam Saran Negi, the first voter of independent India in 1951, who recently passed away on 5 November 2022, just three days after voting for the thirty-fourth time in the Uttarakhand state assembly elections.[22] He had, along the way, encouraged everyone to cast their votes and choose candidates after mindful deliberation.

It has to be ensured that everyone is able to participate in elections. For instance, the Election Commission has on multiple occasions set up polling booths for a single voter. During the 2004 General Elections, the commission set up a polling booth for just this one voter. In the same vein, the plight of the migrant workers must be considered, who most often are unable to effectively cast their vote in their constituency. Most migrant workers leave their hometowns and migrate to different cities, different states and different corners of the country in search of livelihood for themselves and their families.

One aspect we must emphasize is the participation in the electoral process by those communities who initially did not have the right to vote but were granted the right by the Constitution. Post-Independence history tells us that marginalized communities, such as Dalits, have considered the right to vote and the idea of Universal Adult Franchise as the sacrosanct feature of the Indian Constitution. The communities have shown a kind of ownership of the Constitution because they believed that it was the Constitution that gave them equal rights, as well as the power to exercise and claim those rights.[23]

Therefore, we must not look at the particular history of post-Independence from a solely political lens, but we must understand it is an interlinked phenomenon with the social emergence of democratic ideas. We see that the raising of political demands by the marginalized accompanied their demand to have equal rights and constitutional safeguards. Universal Adult Franchise in that sense acted as an equalizing force in shaping the future of India. Those who were denied the rights and powers now became a deciding force in selecting the composition of Parliament. This is an example of how political transformation through Universal Adult Franchise led to social transformation of Indian society. Universal Adult Franchise provided confidence to the oppressed communities, whose right to even believe in themselves was taken away by the oppressive structures and groups.

PANCHAYATI RAJ

Several years after Independence, it was felt that there must be decentralization of the constitutional structure. The idea was to deepen democracy and to make it further deliberative. Several individuals from the people's movement, as well as the leading lawmakers and jurists, including Singhvi, played a significant role in taking the idea of decentralization forward.

Singhvi chaired the committee for 'Revitalization of Panchayati Raj Institutions for Democracy and Development', popularly known as the L.M. Singhvi Committee.[24] The committee submitted its report in 1986 and identified Gram Sabhas as the incarnation of direct democracy and put forward the proposal of constitutional recognition of local self-government institutions. The report also focused on the importance of conducting panchayat elections without delay, provision of adequate financial resources to Panchayati Raj institutions and the establishment of the Panchayati Raj Judicial Tribunal, among others.

The most significant achievement of the L.M. Singhvi Committee was that it led to the constitutional recognition of Panchayati Raj institutions in 1992 through the Seventy-Third and Seventy-Fourth Constitutional Amendment Acts, leading to the insertion in Part IX of the Constitution. These amendments gave a new dimension to the entire concept of democratic decentralization of powers to the rural people in India.

These amendments had an effect on the conception of democracy, which is a basic feature of the Indian Constitution. The Supreme Court has held[25] that the Seventy-Third and Seventy-Fourth Constitutional Amendments enhanced the basic structure of the Constitution.

The court held that the structures of governance created through the said amendments have constitutionally entrenched participatory and representative democracy.

Furthermore, the extension of panchayats to tribal areas through the Panchayat Extension to Scheduled Areas Act, 1996, is a constitutional recognition of the legacy and culture of self-governance that the indigenous communities have.[26] It also tells us that the practise of democracy through Universal Adult Franchise is not just limited to Delhi but is happening in the remotest parts of India.

UNIVERSAL ADULT FRANCHISE AND PARTICIPATORY DEMOCRACY

Universal Adult Franchise is not limited to exercising the right to vote once every five years. Rather, the citizens engage with political processes all the time and reflect their choice through their votes later. Thus, the concept of Universal Adult Franchise is linked with the idea of participatory democracy.

The nine-judge bench[27] of the Supreme Court in 2017 has held, and I quote:

> . . . it must be realised that it is the right to question the right to scrutinize and the right to dissent which enables an informed citizenry to scrutinize the actions of government. Those who are governed are entitled to question those who govern, about the discharge of their constitutional duties including in the provision of socio-economic welfare benefits. The power to scrutinize and to reason enables the citizens of a democratic polity to make informed decisions on basic issues which govern their rights.

The exercise of the right to vote by citizens is an informed choice made by them. The actual realization of one's vote is to continuously participate in democracy in everyday life, to ask questions of the elected representatives and to keep the state accountable. Consultations, dialogues, debates and negotiations occur among diverse social groups, with participation not confined to elections but extending to larger political and public spheres to facilitate social transformation.

Citizens' ability to participate in electoral democracy and promote good governance was also enhanced through the tool of RTI. On a similar note, the Supreme Court of India recently inaugurated the online RTI portal, which further eases and facilitates the process for citizens to file RTI applications and access information.[28]

WHAT DOES THE INDIAN EXPERIMENT WITH UNIVERSAL ADULT FRANCHISE TELL US?

The Indian experiment with Universal Adult Franchise contradicts all myths against Universal Adult Franchise. It was believed that only a few had the wisdom to vote. Our experience tells us that even the most vulnerable have the political consciousness to choose the leader they want. It is imperative to repudiate any elitist conception of the democratic process that privileges education as the sole marker of sound decision-making. Such a view undermines the foundational premise of universal suffrage, that every individual, irrespective of formal education, possesses the capacity to participate meaningfully in shaping the destiny of the nation. Individuals, whom society has despised as being uneducated, have shown tremendous political acumen and awareness of local problems, which even the educated may not understand.

The elitist perceptions that only the educated or a few individuals should have the right to vote show contempt and distrust towards democracy. Since Independence, there are lakhs of examples of how individuals have used the power they received in the form of their right to vote to exercise political power beyond merely electing representatives, as they formed pressure groups and movements exerting and influencing the elected representatives to further the rights of individuals and engineer a social transformation.[29] This is truly reflective of participative democracy.

Electoral democracy has been an agent of pervasive change at the village and municipal levels. The reservation of seats for women and marginalized social groups in panchayats has given them the power to shape their own destinies. It is a silent revolution done by the Universal Adult Franchise. There are numerous examples of exemplary work done by women *sarpanchs* or all-women panchayats in different parts of India.[30] This also demonstrates the bottom-top approach of governance.

Lastly, Dr Ambedkar believed that universal adult suffrage would act as a stimulus that would help gradually transform India's political equality into social and economic equality.[31] The Indian experience has shown us the transformative potential of Universal Adult Franchise.

22

Law and Morality

The Bounds and Reaches[1]

Ashok Desai, or Ashok bhai, as he was known in the legal circles and beyond, was one of the doyens of the legal bar. Born and brought up in Mumbai, he completed his studies from Fergusson College, Pune and Government Law College, Mumbai. His peers at Government Law College included the who's who of the Indian legal fraternity—Fali Nariman, Anil Divan and Soli Sorabjee. They have fond memories of their law teachers: Nani Palkhivala, Justice Y.V. Chandrachud and Jal Vimadalal. Ashok bhai acknowledged their role in moulding his evolution as a legal thinker. He began his practice at the bar by joining the chambers of S.V. Gupte, a distinguished lawyer who later became the Attorney General of India. He had the distinction of working with H.M. Seervai and Nani Palkhivala.

During the Emergency, Ashok bhai played a vital role in defending the rights and liberties of political opponents. He also contributed significantly to the development of constitutional jurisprudence in India through cases such as *A.R. Antulay v. R.S. Nayak*[2] and *Piloo Mody v. Maharashtra*.[3] In 1989, he moved from Mumbai to Delhi when he was appointed as the solicitor general of India. In 1996, he had the distinction of being appointed the Attorney General of India. His towering legal intellect was recognized by the people of this country when he was honoured with the Padma Bhushan in 2001. In the later years of his life, Ashok bhai could still be found in courts, defending the rights and liberties of the marginalized sections of our society in pro bono cases.

One of the important cases in Ashok Desai's career was his defence of playwright Vijay Tendulkar's play *Sakharam Binder*, which unapologetically exposed the prudery of Indian society. In the play, Sakharam Binder rebels against the mores of society by providing food and shelter to women abandoned by their husbands. In return, the women had to satisfy his sexual urges. Because of its perceived violence and vulgarity, the play fell afoul of the Stage Performances Security Board of the Government of Maharashtra.[4] The first performance of the play was supposed to take place on a Friday evening. The legal team, led by Ashok Desai, anticipated police action against the play. The team drafted the petition overnight and filed a writ petition on Friday morning before the Bombay High Court, and was able to effectively stay any adverse action by the police.

Section 33 of the Bombay Police Act, 1951, allowed the police to make rules for prior scrutiny of theatrical performances by the board. Under the rules, the board had the power to refuse the grant of a suitability certificate to a performance on the grounds that the play is against public order, decency or morality, or in the interest of the general public. The board issued the certificate of suitability for the play, but with thirty-two conditions, which effectively destroyed the artistic essence of the play. Ashok Desai played an instrumental role in successfully challenging the validity of the action before the High Court. The efforts of the legal team led by Ashok Desai vindicated the theatrical and artistic freedom in India. In many ways, it could be said that Desai's commitment to free speech and expression convinced artists, journalists and writers that they could freely and confidently exercise their freedom of expression, because he had their back.[5]

During his long career, Ashok Desai deftly surfed the divide between law and morality. It is true that both law and morality play a vital role in channelling our behaviour. As all of you might be well aware, law is a definite body of rules enacted and enforced by the State.[6] Legal rules regulate human conduct by written rules, penalties and officials to interpret the laws.

The origins of law can be traced to morality. For example, in the beginnings of Roman law, adherence to contracts in good faith was left to the mores of the individual concerned rather than the law.[7] In this pre-legal stage, ethical customs governed human conduct. With the development of society, a need was felt to crystallize the codes of conduct by way of law for the sake of certainty. The difference between law and morals is often nebulous. Scholars from the time of Plato and Socrates to H.L. A. Hart and Lon L. Fuller have spent considerable ink trying to demystify the relationship between law and morality.

The theory of natural law asserts that there is a necessary relationship between law and morality.[8] According to natural law theory, natural law would prevail over human-made law if the two are in conflict. On the other hand, legal positivists like Hart argued that law and morality should be separate but have a very close connection.[9] Hart theorized that law must satisfy certain moral conditions to achieve its ultimate goal, which is to act as an instrument of social control. Hart argued that principles of impartiality, equality and non-retroactivity must be in-built in law. Thus, even legal positivists concede that law and morality interact with each other. Hart further explains that the influence of morality 'enter[s] into law either abruptly and avowedly through legislation, or silently and piecemeal through judicial process'.[10]

Having discussed the deep and intricate connection that law shares with morality, I ask myself other critical questions: What is the meaning of morality? What is the nature of morality? Is morality a unified and singular conception? Or does morality have multiple facets and compound meanings?

We use expressions of good and bad, right and wrong, often in our everyday conversations. Parents reprimand children when they think that their behaviour is inappropriate; discussions on the feasibility of a policy often take the route of whether it 'ought to be adopted'.[11] While law regulates external relations, morality governs the inner life and motivation. Morality appeals to our conscience and influences the way we behave. For example, we feel guilty if we fail to meet commitments made to our friends, or feel the prick of conscience if we appeal to falsehood. Similar to an individual, every society, every community, every village and every family has its own codes of morality.

Expressions of ethics, norms and morality are an inextricable part of our day-to-day conversations in public and private spaces. It is evident from the wide reach of the language of morality that it is a conception that is difficult, if not impossible, to define. We can all agree that morality is a system of values that prescribes a code of conduct. But do all of us principally agree on the content of morality? Is it necessary that what is moral for me ought to be moral to you as well?

I recall a news article that was carried out by the American magazine *Time*, on a ghastly incident of honour killing in Uttar Pradesh in 1991. It is a story of a fifteen-year-old girl who eloped with a boy of twenty belonging to the lower caste. The young boy and his friend who tried to help the couple elope were murdered, and their parents were forced to hoist the children on a banyan tree. Robert Deliège, in his book *The Untouchables of India*,[12] described the thoughts and convictions of the people of the village after the murder as follows:

> In fact, when the police arrived on the scene, no one sought to avoid responsibility. The villagers openly admitted their deed and were quite proud of themselves. Mangtu Ram, the leader, gave the police a detailed account of the execution. Convinced they were in the right, he stressed that they had no choice: 'If we had not been harsh', he added, not without insight, 'our entire community would have been disgraced. No one would have married our daughters.'

According to Mangtu Ram, his actions were acceptable and justified because they complied with the code of conduct of the society. However, is this the code of conduct that would have been put forth by 'rational people'? If this is not a code of conduct that would have been put forth by 'rational people', why did Mangtu Ram assume that his actions were morally justified? In the course of my address today, I aim to provide answers to these hard questions on the indissoluble link of law, morality and group rights.

Philosophers often use two approaches to define morality—the descriptive approach and the normative approach.[13] According to the descriptive approach, morality is a code of conduct that is put forward by a society or a group. According to the normative approach, morality is a code of conduct that *would* be put forth by 'rational people'. The descriptive and normative approaches to the definition of morality denote three important characteristics of morality: *First,* morality has multiple facets; *second,* morality is usually defined from the point of view of 'groups'; and *third*, there is a purported difference in actions that are considered moral while using the descriptive and normative approaches. The code of conduct that is put forth by society is not the same as that which *would* have been put forth by 'rational' people. If 'rational' people would have put forth an alternative code of conduct, who would establish the current code of conduct for society?

It is argued that though morality is relative and not unified, there are some constraints that are common across all groups. David B. Wong, in his book *Natural Moralities,* terms moral systems that meet both universal and context-specific standards as 'adequate moralities'.[14] The descriptive definition of morality encompasses 'adequate morality', which is the standard of morality that the members of society, across different groups, agree upon. To reach this standard of adequate morality, the inhabitants partake in a bargain. The groups, while negotiating to reach common ground, attempt to reconcile conflicting ideas. However, power differences affect the negotiation process and the outcomes that are reached pursuant to such a bargain. When two unequal parties negotiate, the stronger party undeniably has an advantage over the weaker.

While discussing the bargaining question in the context of adequate morality, we should not be concerned with the number of people who assented to the moral code. We should rather inquire and be inquisitive about how their consent was generated. Professor Sonia Sika in her research paper titled 'Moral Relativism and the Concept of Culture' argues that while discussing dominant cultural norms we 'need to ask not only whether most people in a society in fact assent to the [moral code], but also how they were generated, under what social arrangements, with what aims, and by whom. We need to ask ourselves 'how does it arise and whose interest does it serve'.[15] Thus, groups that have traditionally held positions of power in the socio-economic-political context of society have an advantage over the weaker sections in this bargaining process to reach adequate morality. So much so that very often, adequate morality coincides with the morality of powerful dominant groups trumping the interests of the weaker sections of society. Adequate morality is the morality of men, the upper castes and able-bodied persons.

I must not be mistaken to mean that only members of the dominant groups were consulted in the process of reaching 'adequate morality'. The argument that I am trying to build is that vulnerable groups are placed at the bottom of the social structure, such that their consent, even if attained, is a myth. For example, German sociologist Max Weber argues that Dalits have never rebelled against the system of caste oppression because they have internalized its values.[16] Michael Moffatt, an American social anthropologist and scholar, argues that because Dalits replicate the caste system by abiding by the rule of subdivisions within their castes, they have 'accepted' their placement and the culture of the dominant group.[17] Such an understanding of the Indian social context is rickety and fragile. The members belonging to the marginalized community have little choice but to submit to the 'dominant' culture. For example, even if a section of menstruating women believe that they should not enter religious premises, the question that we need to ask ourselves is whether this 'acceptability' of the culture and morality is independent of the morality of dominance represented by the sections that hold social and political power.

Vulnerable sections of society are unable to generate a counter-culture because of humiliation and suppression at the hands of the dominant groups. The counter-culture, if any, that the vulnerable groups develop is employed by the dominant groups to further alienate them.

Scholars often seek to distinguish between etiquette and morals. Hobbes uses the phrase 'small morals' to describe 'etiquette'. He states that etiquette consists of the 'decency of behaviour, as how one man should salute another, or how a man should wash his mouth or pick his teeth before company' and distinguishes them from those qualities of mankind that concern living together in peace and unity.[18] He argues that 'adequate morality' or 'common morality' does not consist of 'etiquettes'. I disagree with this understanding of the (ir)relevance of etiquette in creating a moral code of conduct. The significance of 'etiquettes' in a plural society is softened by philosopher Thomas Hobbes. Etiquettes—that is, how a person dresses or her food preferences—are usually group-specific and are the building blocks of counter-culture. These seemingly 'small morals' on food habits and clothing choices enable the creation and the sustenance of group identity. Dominant groups, by attacking the etiquettes of the vulnerable groups prevent them from creating an identity that is unique for themselves.

For example, clothing was one of the tools employed by dominant castes to alienate the Dalit community. It was a widespread norm that the members of the Dalit community must wear marks of inferiority for the public to identify them.[19] Dalits were denied their right to wear clean clothes, and silver and gold ornaments. The legend of Nangeli depicts the siren call of the unfair social order and the role of dominant castes in suppressing the identity and culture of the lower castes. The legend of Nangeli is a story of a Ezhava woman who lived in the early nineteenth century in the erstwhile princely state of Travancore. The story goes that the rajas collected 'breast tax' from Dalit women. Traditionally, no shame was attached to bare-chested women. Both men and women were bare-chested. However, in the early eighteenth century, clothing and in particular upper clothing were a symbol of social identity.[20] One such day, when the raja's men were doing the rounds to collect breast tax, Nangeli cut her breasts off and placed them on the banana leaf as the 'tax'. When Nangeli offered her breasts on a plantain leaf to the raja's men, it was not a call for modesty but a cry of anguish against social stratification.[21] And that is why when Dr Ambedkar dressed in a three-piece suit—in a blue blazer and a red tie, he was making a revolutionary statement. He crushed the code of conduct that was prescribed by the dominant castes through his clothing choices to reclaim his community's identity in society.

I am sure many of you are now reflecting on whether discussion on moral relativism is relevant to the discourse on law and morality in a constitutional democracy that is premised on the values of equality, liberty and fraternity. It must be remembered that the constitution is a behavioural code that determines the rules of behaviour of the citizens and the State. When the Constitution was adopted in 1950, it did not reset an 'original position' as advocated by American political philosopher John Rawls, where the members of society are placed behind a veil of ignorance unaware of their social position.[22] While drafting the Constitution, the members of the Constituent Assembly recognized the existing social stratification and then sought to redress the evils in society. Equality is one of the basic features of the Constitution. Article 14 guarantees non-discrimination, and Article 15 imposes positive obligations on the State to create enabling affirmative action policies to uplift women and lower castes. However, the principles of non-discrimination and substantive equality do not create an original position. For an original position to exist, social stratification must be ironed out to create a truly equal society.

Even after the framing of the Constitution, the law has been imposing 'adequate morality', that is, the morality of the dominant community. In our parliamentary system of democracy, laws are passed by the vote of the majority. Therefore, the discourse around public morality often finds its way into law. We see that differential moral concerns often creep into law. Such moral concerns reflect categorical preferences for and against certain social orderings and outcomes within society.

The English novel *Lady Chatterley's Lover* by D.H. Lawrence was banned in India on grounds of obscenity. The book depicted the story of a woman who pursues an affair with a lower-class worker. I ask myself this question often: Was the book regarded to be obscene because of the depictions of the sexual relationship or because of the depiction of a sexual relationship *between an upper-class woman and a lower-class man*?

The morality of the dominant classes plagued the Indian system yet again in 2005 when the Maharashtra Legislative Assembly banned the performance of dance, 'of any kind or type, in any eating house, permit room or beer bar'. However, the provision excluded the performance of dance in hotels that are three-star or above from the ban. The counsel for the state of Maharashtra submitted before the court that the classification between the exempted establishments and prohibited establishments is based on the 'degree of harm'. It was submitted (I quote) 'the type of crowd that visits banned establishments is also different from the crowd that visits the exempted establishments'. The Government of Maharashtra, by exempting hotels that are three-star and above from the purview of the ban, reinforced the morality of the dominant community that members belonging to the lower classes are sexually irresponsible.

Madhavi Menon, in her 2021 book *The Law of Desire*,[23] brings to light the morality of law in a constitutional democracy that is still skewed towards the vulnerable sections. She states, 'If obscenity is described in the law as something that is lascivious, prurient, depraved, and corrupt, then every one of these terms also gets class-coded. Despite not being defined, obscenity names a threat to the status quo of gender, religion, and class.'

When James Joyce first published his magnum opus *Ulysses* in 1922, he would not have imagined that the novel would be banned for its apparent lasciviousness. The novel traces the journey of Leopold Bloom, an advertising agent, through the city of Dublin on 16 June 1904. During the course of his journey, Bloom sees a young girl named Gertie displaying her legs on the beach. When the novel was first serialized in the American magazine *Little Review* in 1921, an American businessman complained to the officials that the magazine was mailed to his teenage daughter. Subsequently, it was banned in the US for its allegedly obscene content.

This ban continued in effect until 1932, when Judge John M. Woolsey of the district court ruled that the book was not obscene. Judge Woolsey devoted many weeks to reading the novel, which he described as 'not an easy book to read or understand!' In his opinion, the judge observed that the novel contains many words that might seem dirty or vulgar. However, he opined: 'I have not found anything that I consider to be dirt for dirt's sake. Each word of the book contributes like a bit of mosaic to the detail of the picture which Joyce is seeking to construct for his readers.'[24]

The real danger in *Sakharam Binder*, *Lady Chatterley's Lover* or *Ulysses* was not the depiction of obscenity but the moral outcry against the depiction of the characters exploring sexual pleasures outside their marriages. These artistic works questioned the very institution of marriage itself. They questioned the public morality that reinforced the sanctity of marriage and the importance of 'family values'.[25] But above all, they questioned the very nature of human conduct in public as well as private spheres. Under the garb of protecting morality, the State tried to use the repressive power of law to restrain freedom of expression, which is a constitutionally guaranteed right. Thus, even in societies governed by the rule of law, we find that morality has always influenced how the law is interpreted and enforced.

An individual is not always a part of solely one group, and it cannot be assumed that an individual would only reflect the culture or morality of one group. Individuals identify with multiple group constructs, and in that case, an exposition that their morality would be specific to one group is a misnomer. While discussing group-specific culture, concerns of intersectionality cannot be ignored. A Dalit who identifies as queer would follow a culture that is unique. Intersectional identities are multiple, and that is why justifications for moral judgments relative to one group have their fallacies. To counter the social morality of dominant groups imposed under the garb of common morality, there is a need to shift the conversation towards constitutional morality.

To rephrase the literary polymath George Steiner, our Constitution is an endeavour to enclose within its bounds of rational disclosure, the sum of human experience, our shared recorded past, present conditions and future expectations. The Constitution of India infused a new imagination based on a new social, political and economic order in our society. This new paradigm was inevitably rooted in the values of justice, liberty, equality and fraternity as in the Preamble.

Our Constitution was not only designed for people as they were but also how they ought to be. If you read the Constitution closely, you will find that it is not altogether devoid of public morality. The Directive Principles of State Policy lay down certain fundamental principles and mandates for the State to apply in enacting laws. Some of the principles of policy include the creation of social security, the redistribution of wealth, the prohibition of intoxicating drinks and the enactment of a Uniform Civil Code, among others. Thus, even our Constitution is a testament to the fact that there can really be no strict separation between law and morality. However, the enforcement of morality through legal means is subject to the overarching constitutional principles and values.

During the Constituent Assembly debates, Dr Ambedkar quoted classical historian George Grote to describe constitutional morality as:

> . . . a paramount reverence for the forms of the constitution, enforcing obedience to authority and acting under and within these forms.[26]

Under the Constitution of India, it is the individual who is the bearer of fundamental rights. In a constitutional democracy such as ours, it is the duty of both the State as well as individuals to advance and promote the constitutional order of values. Our Constitution is a living and breathing document because we, through our actions and conduct, put force into that parchment. The values and principles enshrined in our Constitution permeate every aspect of our personal and professional lives. It empowers us, motivates us, guides us, restrains us, and most importantly, allows us to live our lives in a manner we choose for ourselves, without any unreasonable external interference.

Eminent lawyer Ashok Desai was a firm believer in the ethos of our Constitution. He believed in the right of every human being to live a life of equality, liberty and dignity. This motivated him to appear pro bono in a batch of petitions challenging Section 377 of the Indian Penal Code (IPC) before the Supreme Court of India in *Navtej Singh Johar v. Union of India*.[27] In *Navtej Singh Johar*, the Supreme Court read down Section 377 of the Indian Penal Code to exclude consensual sexual relationships between adults of same-sex or otherwise. Thereby, the court decriminalized same-sex relationships and affirmed the rights of members of the LGBTQIA+ community in India.

Section 377 of the IPC was based on a conception of public morality, which approved heteronormativity and castigated homosexuality. In *Navtej Singh Johar*, the Supreme Court used the language of constitutional morality to effectively counter the impulses of public morality underlying Section 377. The Supreme Court observed:

> The conception of constitutional morality is different from that of public or societal morality. Under a regime of public morality, the conduct of society is determined by popular perceptions existent in society. The continuance of certain symbols, labels, names or body shapes determine the notions, sentiments and mental attitudes of the people towards individuals and things. Constitutional morality determines

> the mental attitude towards individuals and issues by the text and spirit of the Constitution. It requires that the rights of an individual ought not to be prejudiced by popular notions of society. It assumes that citizens would respect the vision of the Framers of the Constitution and would conduct themselves in a way which furthers that vision. Constitutional morality reflects that the ideal of justice is an overriding factor in the struggle for existence over any other notion of social acceptance.[28]

The courts have effectively used constitutional morality to counter public morality. The best example of this is the decision of the Constitution bench of the Supreme Court in *Joseph Shine v. Union of India*, where the court struck down Section 497 of the IPC which criminalized adultery. While countering the impulses of public morality underlying Section 497,[29] the court observed:

> A woman's 'purity' and a man's marital 'entitlement' to her exclusive sexual possession may be reflective of the antiquated social and sexual mores of the nineteenth century, but they cannot be recognised as being so today. It is not the 'common morality' of the State at any time in history, but rather constitutional morality, which must guide the law . . . A commitment to constitutional morality requires us to enforce the constitutional guarantees of equality before law, non-discrimination on account of sex, and dignity, all of which are affected by the operation of Section 497.

Constitutional morality does not only serve as a counter-force to the differential moral concerns or biases enunciated in our laws; it also serves as a guiding force for all of us. They convey that our personal and professional lives are not divorced from the Constitution; that our actions and thoughts should be attuned to the high ideals of our Constitution. That our individual morality should be subsumed within constitutional morality, and that our own individual biases should be subjected to introspection and correction.

I hope that my exposition on morality and its interplay with the law has kindled questions in your mind, questions that enable us to rethink our actions and biases. Ashok bhai spoke the tune of constitutional morality and was a staunch believer that society must not crumble in the hands of popularly conceived morality. He believed in the power of love and kindness. I would like to end my speech by quoting Vikram Seth's poem 'Through Love's Great Power'.[30] Coincidently, Ashok bhai quoted this very poem while he was arguing against the criminalization of homosexuality. The poem goes as follows:

Through love's great power to be made whole
In mind and body, heart and soul—
Through freedom to find joy, or be

By dint of joy itself set free
In love and in companionhood:
This is the true and natural good.
To undo justice, and to seek
To quash the rights that guard the weak -
To sneer at love, and wrench apart
The bonds of body, mind and heart
With specious reason and no rhyme:
This is the true unnatural crime

23

Law, Justice and the Heart

Cultivating Empathy in Legal Education[1]

Right from the moment I entered the campus this morning, I could sense a feeling of joy among everyone present. I know that this joy is not only of the achievements of your classmates and of reliving the memories of your campus life as you reconnect with the faculty and the staff of the university.

Dear students, as you are on the cusp of your legal career, I cannot help but feel a sense of nostalgia for my own law school graduation. I too sat like you sit today, eager to embark on a life of service to the law and to the people it serves.

In convocation addresses, it is generally expected that the visiting speaker share words of wisdom with the graduating students. But I belong to a different school of thought. I believe that students gather their own wisdom while embarking on their journey in law school and later on in their careers. Hence, I will share a few of my thoughts today only with the intention that they may benefit the younger ones in shaping their own journey.

As you chart a new course of your life, do remember everyone who directly and indirectly contributed to your journey. While we think of universities, we generally think of the faculty and the students, but a university also runs because of the labour of the support staff and workers. Your own life in the hostels was made easy because of the labour of the helpers and auxiliary staff. We must also acknowledge their labour in building an institution like a university. This shall be the true meaning of dignity, which the Supreme Court has recognized as a facet of the right to life under Article 21 of the Constitution.

In an era of *Avengers*[2] and Marvel-DC movies, I may be lagging behind in popular pop culture. However, I have always believed that movies, or any art form, have a significant impact on our thinking. Sometimes, a line in a book might remain in our minds throughout our lives. So, as you graduate, do not let your creative side fade away. In our profession, creativity has led to landmark constitutional judgments. Your life as a lawyer is also enriched by your explorations outside the law. In my own life, I made it a habit to read literature other than law textbooks, and I can share that it has helped me in my career, firstly as a lawyer and then as a judge. As the Chief Justice of the Supreme Court, I often revert to what Atticus Finch, the protagonist in Harper Lee's classic *To Kill a Mockingbird*, said:[3]

> But there is one way in this country in which all men are created equal—there is one human institution that makes a pauper the equal of a Rockefeller, the stupid man the equal of an Einstein, and the ignorant man the equal of any college president. *That institution, gentlemen, is a court*... Our courts have their faults, as does any human institution, but in this country our courts are the great levellers, and in our courts all men are created equal. (Emphasis added)

Justice Elena Kagan, a judge of the US Supreme Court, once quoted a line from the movie *Spider-Man* in her judgment, which goes like this: '[I]n this world, with great power there must also come great responsibility.'[4] Thus, while your graduation brings a feat of happiness and joy, there must also be a realization of self-responsibility that wherever you go, you strive towards healing the world and the lives of people around you.

The National Academy of Legal Studies and Research (NALSAR) is celebrating its silver jubilee. It is an achievement for the institution to have shaped the lives of so many students over the years. I congratulate the leadership of the university on this impressive achievement. Institutions of every kind play a crucial role in society. Running a university is about shaping the future of the country, as we train young minds.

The silver jubilee moment also gives us a chance to reflect on the larger issues concerning our higher education institutions. There may be many issues in terms of policy decision-making on higher education. But I wish to reflect on the state of higher education from a philosophical perspective—from the lens of *empathy*. I have chosen this lens because I believe that empathy is an essential ingredient in the law, and it is what separates a just society from an unjust one. It is a critical component of justice and facilitates in promoting a compassionate view of justice. For instance, the Supreme Court deals with a number of cases arising out of Motor Accidents Claims. The judges often look at the human side of the case through a lens of empathy, while balancing the technical requirements. In that sense, empathy is not a luxury but a necessity. Empathy can help break down barriers towards justice. That is why we must also understand education through the lens of empathy.

In our educational institutions, we tend to focus a lot on excellence. We are taught that our lives can be better only if we excel in our studies or professional life. However, education can only be complete if we nurture the values of empathy and compassion. Our educational institutions must not limit themselves to promoting competition among students but also shape their outlook towards life, where empathy is a crucial element. Excellence cannot go without empathy.

Lack of empathy in educational institutions has an adverse effect on students. I have been placing emphasis on the mental health of lawyers, but equally important is the mental health of students. Not only must our educational curriculum inculcate a sense of compassion among students, but academic leaders must also be sensitive to the concerns of students. When students leave their homes, it becomes the responsibility of educational institutions to establish a bond of institutional friendship with the students.

We must also realize that different students face different challenges. Only recently, I read the news about the suicide of a Dalit student at IIT Bombay.[5] It reminded me about the suicide of an Adivasi student in NLU, Orissa, last year.[6] My heart goes out to the family members of these students. But I have also been wondering where our institutions are going wrong, so that the students are forced to give up their precious lives. Incidents of suicides of students from marginalized communities are becoming common. These numbers are not just statistics. These are stories, sometimes of centuries of struggle. I believe that if we wish to address this issue, the first step is to acknowledge and recognize the problem. Sukhadeo Thorat, one of the senior-most educationalists of the country, has noted that if almost all those who have died by suicide in particular situations are Dalits and Adivasis, then it shows a pattern,[7] which we must question.

In our journey of seventy-five years since Independence, we have been focusing on creating 'Institutions of Eminence'. But more than that, we need 'Institutions of Empathy'—a term I read in a news article.[8] Some of you may be wondering why the Chief Justice is speaking on this issue. Well, because I think the issue of discrimination is directly linked to the lack of empathy in institutions. Furthermore, judges cannot shy away from social realities. Instances of judicial dialogues are common across the globe. When the Black Lives Matter movement emerged in the US after the murder of George Floyd, all nine judges on the Washington Supreme Court—the highest court in the state of Washington in the US—released a joint statement addressed to the judiciary and legal community on the 'degradation and devaluation of Black lives' in the US.[9] Furthermore, Harvard Law School Professor Michael Klarman notes that history tends to forget the equally groundbreaking work that several civil rights lawyers did outside the courtroom in educating the Black community about their rights under the Constitution.[10] In similar ways, judges in India have a crucial role in making a dialogue with the society, inside and outside the courtrooms—to push for social change. As Chief Justice, apart from my core judicial work and administrative duties, my effort is also to throw light on structural issues affecting our society.

Therefore, promoting empathy must be the first step that educational institutions ought to take. Nurturing empathy can end the culture of elitism and exclusion. This can be done by starting with small steps. Hostel allotments based on entrance exam scores often lead to caste-based segregation. Publishing students' marks along with their social categories, or publicly singling out Dalit and Adivasi students to ask about their scores, can be deeply humiliating. Mocking their spoken English or appearance, branding them as incompetent, ignoring incidents of abuse and bullying, cutting off scholarships or fellowships, and failing to provide emotional or academic support only deepens their isolation. Even casual jokes that reinforce harmful stereotypes contribute to an environment of exclusion. These are not small oversights; they are daily indignities that no student should have to face. Every educational institution has a duty to end such practices and foster a space that respects and uplifts all students.[11] In other words, practising empathy requires institutional changes.

In that sense, I believe that empathy can allow us to reflect on the state of legal education in a much broader way. When we approach the law with empathy, we recognize that the people who come before us in the legal system are not just names on a docket or numbers in a statistic. They are real people, with real lives and real struggles. We understand that their circumstances and experiences may be different from our own, and we try to see the world from their perspective. That such an understanding should be at the foundation of legal education was the idea behind the creation of NLUs. It was to promote an interdisciplinary learning based on a clinical education model, which would allow human interaction with the study of law. To what extent we succeeded is the foremost question today.

In my view, the experiment with NLUs was to create accessible institutions focused on quality legal education, and not to create elite institutions. However, the NLUs have been struggling to be accessible to a wide section of society. Concerns are continuously raised about the entrance exam pattern of NLUs, which acts as an access barrier for students not well acquainted with English. Furthermore, any efforts taken in revitalizing the entrance exam would be futile if the internal structures in law universities are not conducive for students coming from non-metropolitan or marginalized backgrounds. Along with this, the financial barriers are also a serious issue. Law universities and governments need to work together on the same to ensure financial accessibility.

I would also take the opportunity to highlight that the idea behind the creation of NLUs was not to leave behind traditional law universities or Central universities. A majority of judges on the bench are a product of what we now think of as traditional universities. Therefore, the outlook of legal education must be to improve the quality of law colleges across the country, and not just a few institutions. Further, the sense of entitlement that NLUs are better than other institutions leads to unnecessary wastage of energy. Instead, NLUs should be leaders in the field of legal education, which could help other smaller law colleges grow academically. NLUs ought not to work in a field of isolation. Law students studying in NLUs must not look down upon their counterparts from other law schools. After all, the legal profession is such that we are constantly learning and teaching each other.

The clinical legal model of education would be realized only when we are able to involve law students directly with the legal aid services. In other countries, law students are guided by clinical faculty work on real-life cases. This not only provides exposure but also inculcates a sense of responsibility among them. Our law schools also need to think in this way. Academic leaders, bar council representatives, and members of the bar and judiciary need to sit together and reflect on the state of clinical education in India.

It is by reshaping our legal education model that we will be able to make empathy a core value of our legal system. We must work to address the structural inequalities that are built into our legal system and to create a system that truly reflects our shared values of justice. I am aware of the fact that a fresh law graduate stepping into the profession faces many challenges, starting from getting into the chambers of good offices, the tendency of established lawyers and law offices to pay off meagre salaries even lower than the minimum wages, and extremely high fees for registration for state bar councils, to name a few. If we, as the legal profession, have to grow, we have to change our approach. We would have to move past the mindset that we are reaping as we had sown, i.e., justifying earlier practices as the norms for the future. We must ensure that the practice of law is done in a fair and equitable manner, without regard to a person's race, caste, gender, religion, disability or sexual orientation.

In the context I just narrated, my tenure as the Chief Justice has focused on improving the accessibility in legal education and the profession. The Supreme Court has now launched an e-version of the Supreme Court Reports (eSCR), which allows everyone to freely access around 34,000 reportable judgments of the Supreme Court from 1950 to 2023. As a result, young graduates will not have to spend a penny on accessing judgments and conducting legal research as they join the profession.

The court started live-streaming and hybrid court hearings, which allow any lawyer to argue a case sitting anywhere in the country. This has addressed the concern that only a few lawyers were able to reach the Supreme Court. During the pandemic, a number of women lawyers were able to actively participate in court proceedings.

Furthermore, I am laying stress on the increasing use of technology to not only increase access to justice but also to take it as an opportunity to make the judicial system an epitome of transparency. With the said goal in mind, most recently, we have started auto-transcription of court proceedings by employing AI and high-tech tools. By doing this, our court can become a court of record in the fullest sense of the term. The record of conversations between the bench and the bar shall act as an important medium of education, where students can learn about the art of arguing and what type of questions to expect from the bench. In that way, legal education can become more practice-oriented.

I have also been emphasizing diversity and inclusion. Recently, I approved in principle a proposal sent by the National Commission for Scheduled Tribes to have thirty-six law graduates from the ST community come and work at the Supreme Court as fellows and get first-hand experience of the working of the Supreme Court of India. These students whom we mentor today shall become successful lawyers and judges of the future.

Furthermore, to ensure that technological developments in courts do not leave behind persons with disabilities, I constituted a committee on accessibility, which is headed by Justice Ravindra Bhat, and is doing an accessibility audit of the court premises and functioning. Based on their report, we will be taking efforts to ensure that courts become disability-friendly.

However, before I leave, I wish to highlight that while the Supreme Court initially adopted technological infrastructure to meet the challenges of the pandemic, the same is being retained and developed further to ensure that everyone is now able to access the court from any part of the country and without any difficulty. I believe that our legal education must also evolve in the same way. That is to say, while online education during the pandemic provided us with the opportunity to easily interact with researchers and scholars across the globe, it also raised concerns about the inaccessibility to these very resources that students from rural or marginalized backgrounds face. Thus, the evolution of online-hybrid infrastructure must be done in such a way as to ensure that the marginalized and underprivileged are not left behind.

Today, we see a number of YouTube channels producing videos on legal concepts in a simplified form. The number of views on these videos indicates the level of curiosity which our citizens have towards legal discourse, and it is our job to make our citizens aware of the laws that govern them and the rights they possess. Therefore, I think technology can allow us to take legal education to the level of the masses, so that law does not remain a field or profession of the elites. Teaching modules or study resources can be made available online publicly to students, even if those students are not enrolled in the law school. This can encourage quality learning everywhere.

It is my sincere belief that with collective efforts, we shall be able to change the approach of legal education and the legal profession. We must use the law to create a society that is truly just, where everyone is treated with dignity and respect, and where everyone has the opportunity to thrive. We must work together to shape the law in a way that reflects our shared values of fairness, equality and justice.

So, dearest students, as you experiment with law after your graduation and chart your trajectories in this noble profession, do so with a sense of compassion towards the world around you.

24

A Prescription for Justice

Quest for Fairness and Equity in Healthcare[1]

I deem it a matter of pleasure and privilege to be called upon to deliver the address at the nineteenth Sir Ganga Ram Oration and extend my sincere appreciation to the organizers. The journey of Sir Ganga Ram Hospital from its humble beginnings as a fifty-bedded hospital in the 1950s to a multispecialty hospital with a capacity of more than 600 beds is reflective of the hard work and dedication of its community.

Each and every member of the hospital ecosystem has a critical role to play in providing healthcare justice. This became writ large during the time of the pandemic—whether it was the management's decision to keep the hospital functioning during COVID-19, the services of doctors and nurses who provided untiring medical and emotional care when the patients were alone in isolation, or the work done by the paramedical and support staff, including technicians, ambulance drivers and so many countless others. The hospital could not have functioned without the essential services provided by the hospital cleaners, who had the daunting duty of disposing of the medical waste, or the security guards, who had to manage the crowds. The vision of the pioneers of Sir Ganga Ram Hospital to provide quality healthcare with a humane touch has indeed come true.

When I received the invitation, I initially thought for a moment about what I, as someone belonging to the legal fraternity, should discuss with members of the medical profession. People often remark in a lighter vein that two persons from whom one should never keep secrets are one's doctor and lawyer. So many people join medicine and law with an aim to alleviate the suffering of our fellow human beings and provide service to humanity.

The important role played by medical professionals is captured beautifully in the words of our Hon'ble President Droupadi Murmu—while delivering the valedictory address at the Constitution Day Celebrations, she said, '*Gaon ke log teen logon ko bhagwaan maante thai: teachers, doctors and lawyers.*' In her village in Mayurbhanj district in Odisha, villagers consider teachers, doctors and lawyers as representatives of God. People approached doctors and lawyers when they were under immense stress and were facing problems in their lives.

It is easy to believe that the paths of law and medicine run in parallel to each other, never interacting or intersecting. However, as we all know, these two paths often intersect. The interaction between law and medicine has forged new dimensions.

To give an obvious example, doctors are often called upon as expert witnesses in criminal cases to give evidence and their opinion on technical issues that confound the courts. However, testifying in judicial proceedings often ends up being a time-consuming exercise, hampering a medical professional's duty. As the chairperson of the Supreme Court's e-committee, it is my endeavour to equip all courts in India with a video conferencing remote point to facilitate tele-evidence for doctors. This would result in saving time of the doctors, which could be utilized for patient care, medical education and research. A 2020 study conducted in Post Graduate Institute of Medical Education & Research, Chandigarh, revealed that through the facility of tele-evidence, more than 4900 summons have been attended in a period of five years, resulting in financial savings, reduced carbon footprint and timesaving.[2]

Another avenue where law and medicine meet can be seen in laws setting standards for conduct of medical professional practice; laws governing the sale, storage of drugs and medication; and laws dealing with management of emergencies, medicolegal cases and all aspects related thereto.

Sometimes, the Supreme Court also had to intervene even before a student embarks on her professional study in medicine. Several cases challenging National Medical Commission's decisions or cases dealing with National Eligibility cum Entrance Test (NEET) have found their way to my bench at the Supreme Court. Often, courts cannot enter the policy domain, and it is the duty of the State to listen to the representations made by the students. However, whenever injustice is done, it becomes our bounden duty to intervene. The sheer volume of litigation arising out of the NEET examination before us is indicative of the hopes and aspirations of millions of students. It is proof that medicine is one of the most sought-after professions in India. Yet, the litigation is also symbolic of the need for reforms in medical education in India.

At a more fundamental level, principles of justice underline the practice of both law and medicine. Both these fields are concerned with fairness, equality, and the well-being of individuals and communities. In the legal field, justice requires the rule of law, where people are treated impartially and fairly, as opposed to arbitrariness or the rule of any individual. In the field of health, justice requires that healthcare services and resources be distributed fairly and equitably. As caregivers, it becomes the solemn duty of healthcare providers to ensure health justice to whoever comes before them.

One of the most prominent examples where health and justice coincided is the struggle of the LGBTQIA+ community for aspiring to live their life with dignity, freedom and equality. Before 2018, the law in the guise of Section 377 of the Indian Penal Code 1860, criminalized homosexual activity, making the LGBTQIA+ community vulnerable to contracting HIV/AIDS. It tended to drive underground many of the people at risk of infection, pushing them out of the public health system. India has the world's third-largest population living with HIV—2.1 million people. About three in ten gay men and four in ten transgender people living with HIV do not know their medical prognosis.[3] Members of the LGBTQIA+ community who were susceptible to HIV/AIDS were faced with the dilemma of going untreated or facing ridicule and discrimination after coming out. One of the first steps to decriminalize homosexuality was initiated by a petition by an NGO called AIDS Bhedbhav Virodhi Andolan in 1994, out of a growing concern over male sexual health and the HIV/AIDS epidemic. The battle against Section 377 finally culminated in the 2018 decision of *Navtej Singh Johar v. Union of India*.[4] I was fortunate to have been a member of the bench that delivered this judgment.

The journey which began as a public health struggle against the prevalence of HIV/AIDS, among the 'key populations' of the LGBTQIA+ community due to their socio-economic status, has now catapulted into a larger struggle to demand freedoms and equality in all spheres of life, including the home, the workplace, education, healthcare and public places. One key hope which remains now is that the medical community sensitizes itself about the rights of the LGBTQIA+ community, and provides them with healthcare services without prejudice, discrimination and stigma.

UNDERSTANDING HEALTH THROUGH THE LENS OF CAPABILITY APPROACH

Before we delve into discussing what we mean by healthcare justice, it is essential that we understand the true significance of health.

As the World Health Organization (WHO) explains, the definition of health is related to a broad state of biopsychosocial well-being and is not merely the absence of disease. Health is the nucleus of all activities of life—physical, social, spiritual or any other conceivable human activity. At the very least, a life that is focused solely on survival is one that lacks many of the facets of life. By being free from ailments, people get a fair and equal chance to participate in different activities. It is good health that is often needed as the first step to escape the position of social disadvantage.

I remember coming across a newspaper article in November last year, in which the doctors of Ganga Ram Hospital had successfully performed a complex gender reaffirmation surgery by the state-of-the-art micro-surgical technique of tissue transfer.[5] After thirty-four years of the patient's life, the surgery gave him an opportunity to transition to his true, authentic self, become a member of society capable of pursuing and achieving good health, while also retaining individual freedoms to make alternative choices. It furthered the individual's capability to engage in meaningful interpersonal relationships.

Indian economist and philosopher Amartya Sen describes this as the capability approach. Sen argues that to evaluate how well-off people are, we need to look at an individual's capability to reach their full potential.[6] By capabilities, he means the substantive freedoms a person has to live a life he has a reason to value. Under this approach, while poverty is understood as deprivation of basic capabilities rather than merely low income, development is understood as expansion of capability. By providing healthcare and enabling citizens of this country to live a life that they want, each and every medical professional, in this sense, also plays a part in the nation-building project.

Inequalities in Health

However, growing socio-economic inequalities in India disproportionately affect the health outcomes of marginalized groups. People belonging to marginalized communities are perpetually faced with barriers in accessing healthcare. Social determinants of health, i.e. factors outside the healthcare system such as class, caste, gender and regional location often determine the health status of an individual. Injustice in healthcare becomes evident when one looks at the people not merely by the means of a stethoscope but by understanding their social determinants of health.

To give an example, while air pollution affects everyone in Delhi, the burden is shared unequally. The 2018 installation at Ganga Ram Hospital of a 3D model of artificial human lungs depicting the hazardous impact of Delhi's air pollution was a wake-up call for all of us.[7]

I want to share with you a *New York Times* article in which the newspaper shadowed two kids, named Monu and Aamya, living in two different parts of Delhi to measure their exposure to pollution for a day and see the impact of inequality.[8] Aamya resides in Greater Kailash II (GK II), dreams of becoming a musician and has a working air purifier at home, whereas Monu lives in a slum near the Yamuna River, uses a wood-burning stove for cooking and cycles to school with the dream of being an Indian Army officer. By the end of the day, Monu was exposed to about four times as much pollution as Aamya.

Dr Sheila Zurbrigg, in one of her books titled *Rakku's Story*,[9] lays bare the everyday struggles of the majority of the Indian population living below the poverty line in accessing healthcare. The book chronicles the story of Rakku, a daily-wage labourer who is often forced to leave her infant son in the care of her young daughter, while she is trying to make ends meet. In the absence of any framework for maternal care or any other social support, the baby develops diarrhoea and dehydration. After local remedies fail, she is compelled to borrow money from the moneylender for the bus fare to the nearest treatment centre in the city. In the process, she has to forego her daily wages, increasing her debt and uncertainty regarding her family's next meal. The story ends with the tragic death of the baby in the early morning, despite him getting the much-needed IV glucose.

Rakku's story is not unique. It reflects how low-quality housing, sanitation, unclean water and health-seeking behaviour determined by social and economic capital of a family can lead to poor health. Cases of tuberculosis afflict at a higher rate among the poor and undernourished. The risk of dying with tuberculosis while being treated is three times higher if undernourished.[10] The inequality of outcome is a reflection of social fault lines. Every year, developing countries like India have to face the brunt of infectious diseases. Within India, outbreaks of dengue, chikungunya and malaria are commonplace among the urban poor. Unplanned and uncontrolled urbanization, which pays scant regard to water drainage and sanitation, has led to the growth of urban slums where infectious disease outbreaks are quite common.

I am sure that everyone present here is probably even more cognizant of these harsh realities through their everyday outpatient department (OPD) practice. More than 4000 cases of dengue were reported in the national capital in 2022, with the death toll reaching nine cases.[11] It is a sad reality that at a time when these diseases are preventable and curable with medicine reaching newer scientific heights, neglect of social roots cripple the effectiveness of our healthcare system. Healthcare justice involves an understanding that it is not just the individual but social determinants that impact a person's health and absence of illness.[12]

WHAT DOES JUSTICE IN HEALTHCARE ENTAIL?

An important part is played by institutions like Sir Ganga Ram Hospital, which continues to uphold the charitable vision of its founder—whether it is by organizing regular OPD facilities for the poor and needy patients, or by being committed to making available 20 per cent of total bed strength for admission for indigenous and financially weaker patients.

However, Rakku's story and similar stories of millions of Indians make it clear that we as a society need to counteract structural and policy constraints that prevent access to good-quality healthcare in order to achieve healthcare justice. Rakku's story is a critique of the government's stress on medical treatment as the magic bullet to achieve healthcare justice, despite the reality being that access to core necessities like food, water, sanitation and housing are prerequisites to combat ill health. The capabilities framework allows for recognition of structural barriers to achieving health: constrained choice, lack of information or poverty—affecting an individual's capability to achieve good health.

Due to an overburdened healthcare system coupled with the increasing commercialization of healthcare, mistrust and suspicion in the medical services has become the narrative surrounding healthcare. The fiduciary nature of the patient–doctor relationship struggles when either side fails to recognize that the other side is also a person. The simmering anger of the public against injustice in healthcare is aggravated when either a patient treats the doctor as an infallible service provider, who mechanically provides services, or when a doctor looks at a patient merely as a medical issue which needs to be solved. This dehumanization of healthcare has often resulted in violent confrontations between the citizens and hospitals, with medical professionals being caught in the crossfire. This puts the lives of medical professionals at risk and creates a hostile environment for them to work in. This violence ends up hampering the delivery of medical services, which can have serious consequences for patients.

What might amount to justice in healthcare? Equality and fairness are prime factors that should permeate the healthcare system to facilitate justice. One way of understanding justice in healthcare is that there should be 'health equity'. This means that each person has a fair, just and equal opportunity to be healthier. Another component of healthcare justice includes the ethical principles that govern the interaction between medical professionals and patients, with a view to giving primacy to patient care and a patient's bodily integrity and autonomy. Ultimately, the goal is to achieve fairness, promote dignity, and ensure people have similar capabilities to lead healthy lives and contribute to society.

Viewing health from the perspective of rights and the social justice framework, law is increasingly being employed to address questions of inequalities in access to healthcare. Under the Indian Constitution, the right to life under Article 21 includes the right to lead a dignified and meaningful life, and the right to health is an integral facet.[13] In India, the right to health includes the right to emergency medical care and the right to the maintenance and improvement of a basic level of public health.[14]

To fulfil the constitutional goal of the right to health, the state capacity to finance health care is an important consideration. In the year 1946, the Bhore Committee Report[15] envisioned that the 'state should assume full responsibility for all measures, curative and preventive, which are necessary for safeguarding health'. It is imperative that the state policy is committed to improving people's overall health and ensuring that quality health services are available to vulnerable sections. Health needs to be on the financial policy radar to promote the productive potential of India's population. However, the finitude of economic and human resources is a pressing issue across the world.

The unfortunate reality is that there is a significant shortage of skilled health workers in India.[16] A 2021 study, led by a professor at the Indian Institute of Public Health, revealed that the density of the active health workforce in India is just a little over one-fourth of the WHO's recommended threshold.[17] The shortfall of medical professionals in rural areas is further exacerbated. The Rural Health Statistics 2021 showed that while 66 per cent of India's population lived in rural areas, only 27 per cent of doctors are available.[18] This can detrimentally affect the availability of both general and specialized care for patients, especially in rural areas, where the health infrastructure is often underdeveloped.

In the 2023–24 Union Budget, the government plans to open 157 new nursing colleges. However, incentives would still be needed to ensure that an increase in the number of medical colleges transforms into more medical professionals practising in rural areas. Along with medical professionals, the role played by Accredited Social Health Activist (ASHA) workers in fortifying primary healthcare in India needs to be recognized and economically supported.

To make healthcare more accessible to disadvantaged groups, it might be beneficial that culturally cognizant environments are created to cater to these groups. Increasing diversity in recruitment of staff members can be an important step towards healthcare equity.[19] Sensitivity to different cultures, patient-centred care and community engagement spearheaded by senior medical professionals would go a long way. In the *Neil Aurelio Nunes* case,[20] the Supreme Court recognized the importance of diversity in medical education by reconceptualizing the meaning of 'merit'. The court observed that 'merit cannot be separated from the function of the existing inequalities in society'. Special provisions (including reservations) are methods to ameliorate the structural inequalities. Fortitude required to uplift oneself from conditions of deprivation is reflective of individual merit and calibre.

The need of the hour is for healthcare providers, community leaders, lawmakers and policymakers to work together to identify possible initiatives and solutions that promote equitable access to healthcare.

CONCLUSION

I would be seriously remiss if I do not briefly touch upon how the pandemic has transformed us. The COVID-19 pandemic was a reality check for the government in India and exposed the fragility of India's public health. Nonetheless, the pandemic was prolific with stories of resilience and hope in the midst of adversity. Frontline workers toiled day and night, often sacrificing their own time and keeping their own well-being on the back burner, at a huge risk to their own and their family's health. Even today, 'the enormity of the moral mission of medicine'[21] lends a severe gravity to the everyday decisions a medical professional has to take, which impinges on the life and death of another human being. The demand on healthcare workers continues to be relentless and unpredictable, often leading to stress, burnout and mental health issues.

Just like every doctor present here must have prescribed 'plenty of rest' to their patients, I hereby order everyone gathered here today to pause, take a break and cultivate a 'rest ethic' in your professional lives. Caring for ourselves and providing the space for our juniors to self-care is a sign of strength. It is my hope that we are able to make those much-needed structural and institutional changes to implement this order.

I would like to conclude with the words of Dr Rudolf Virchow, also known as the father of modern pathology: ‘Should medicine ever fulfil its great ends, it must enter into the larger political and social life of our time; it must indicate the barriers which obstruct the normal completion of the life cycle and remove them.’

25

Free Speech

Identity, Expression and Self-Realization[1]

It is indeed a great pleasure to be delivering the second Soli Sorabjee Memorial Lecture at the Twenty-Third Commonwealth Law Conference today. I am happy to see distinguished dignitaries from across the globe in attendance. Sadly, the immense workload of the office I hold did not permit me to extend my stay in Goa to deliver the address in person. Having closely interacted with Soli Sorabjee both on a personal and professional front, I am happy to be a part of this occasion virtually. To me personally, Soli was a mentor, guide, friend and compass.

Soli Sorabjee, over the course of his illustrious career, brought a sense of dignity and ingenuity to the profession. His legal acumen and his wit should not surprise us. His legal acumen came second only to his versatility. The field of drama, mimicry and jazz suffered a great loss when Soli decided to pursue the law. When asked if he would prefer being Chief Justice or Benny Goodman, he said, 'I would any day play like Benny Goodman, which I'm doing in fantasy land now.' Soli defied the expression jack of all trades and master of none; he was a master of all trades, be it the field of law, jazz, poetry or simply mimicry. His ability to make a spoof on the high, mighty and the powerful ensured that the enormous weight of the roles he donned and the offices which he held did not affect his sensibilities. Soli truly spoke truth to power.

Two of the most prominent cases Soli Sorabjee appeared in as an advocate were *S. Rangarajan v. P. Jagjivan Ram*[2] in 1988 and *Shreya Singhal v. Union of India*[3] in 2015. In S. *Rangarajan*, the Madras High Court revoked the 'U' certificate (signifying suitability for unrestricted public exhibition) that was granted to a film criticizing the reservation or affirmative action policy of the government. In *Shreya Singhal*, section 66A of the Information Technology Act, 2000, punishing a person for sending any information through a computer resource or communication device that is grossly offensive or knowing that it is false were under challenge. In both these cases, Soli advocated for the expansion of the right to freedom of speech and expression. He argued that free speech and expression extended to controversial opinions, and such opinions must be evaluated through debate and discussion in the public forum and not in courts. Only such an interpretation, he argued, would be in tune with the liberal spirit of the Constitution. Along the same vein, he argued that free speech cannot be restricted based on the subjective notions of those who feel offended by speech. Soli understood the importance of free speech in terms of the value that it holds in a democratic society.

Today, I will speak about these values of freedom of speech and expression that Soli embodied. I will not focus on freedom of speech within the rights framework or how courts have more often than not been placed in a difficult position of balancing the competing claims of free speech and hate speech. Instead, I will focus on the inherent value of free speech in a democratic, multicultural polity.

According to Professor Thomas Emerson, the American law professor and one of the foremost First Amendment scholars of the twentieth century, society seeks to ascribe certain values in protecting the right to free speech. These values are assurance of individual self-realization, attainment of truth, individual participation in social and political decision-making, and maintaining a balance between stability and change in society.[4] Freedom of speech is intrinsically linked to freedom of thought and opinion. The ability to think and express freely is an important aspect of our identity and personhood, necessary to achieve the values Professor Emerson spoke about. Justice Thurgood Marshall, a civil rights champion and a judge of the US Supreme Court, opined that the 'human spirit demands self-expression [and] such expression is an integral part of the development of ideas and a sense of identity'.[5] Speech—whether it be verbal or non-verbal, expressed through alphabets or emojis—is an attempt to forge an identity.

Identity is an individual's perception of who they are. An individual's identity is both personal and social. In the personal sense, an identity implies an individual's set of attributes, beliefs, desires or principles that form the basis of their dignity or self-respect.[6] In the social sense, an identity implies a relationship with a wider social group—for example, a national identity, a cultural identity or a gender identity.[7] The Indian Constitution seeks to protect both personal and social identity.

The Constitution under Article 19 enumerates a bundle of rights such as free speech and expression, freedom of movement of residence and the practice of any profession or trade, among others. These enumerated rights enable a meaningful existence by guaranteeing an individual's identity and dignity. Similarly, the Constitution seeks to protect an individual's social identity by prohibiting discrimination on the grounds of religion, race, caste or sex. The entrenchment of the right to the freedom of religion, as well as cultural and educational rights in the Constitution has served to protect and nurture the social or group identity of individuals.

For centuries, markers of identity such as caste, religion, language and gender were used to structurally and institutionally marginalize vast sections of our population from the mainstream of society. However, with the advent of a constitutional democracy after independence from colonial rule, these very markers of social identity have become a site for the marginalized to organize themselves and fight for the rights of their communities. Expression is an assertion of identity.

Freedom of speech recognizes the autonomy of individuals to participate in public dialogues and cultural conversations. In one of my dissenting opinions, I observed that the integrity of our nation is based on a framework of mutual recognition of social identities and characteristics. I observed:

> Our Constitution recognises the position of religion, caste, language and gender in the social life of the nation. Individual histories[,] both of citizens and collective groups in our society[,] are associated through the ages with histories of discrimination and injustice on the basis of these defining characteristics. In numerous provisions, the Constitution has sought to preserve a delicate balance between individual liberty and the need to remedy these histories of injustice founded upon immutable characteristics such as of religion, race, caste and language. The integrity of the nation is based on a sense of common citizenship.[8]

For more than a century, the LGBTQIA+ community in India was oppressed and marginalized by the operation of Section 377 of the Indian Penal Code 1860, which criminalized consensual sexual conduct of same-sex adults. In *NALSA v. Union of India*, the Supreme Court noted that gender identity and sexual orientation are integral to one's personality and are a basic aspect of self-determination, dignity and freedom.[9] This was reiterated by the Constitution Bench of the Supreme Court in *Navtej Singh Johar v. Union of India*, which read down Section 377 of the IPC[10] to exclude sexual relationships between adults of the same gender. However, even before these decisions of the Supreme Court, the LGBTQIA+ community in India had been valiantly marching on the streets, with pride and rainbow flags, to assert their identity and to make a strong and collective point to bystanders that they have a right to equal participation and the right to live with dignity in society. To openly and bravely assert your gender identity, when the closet is an option, is to serve as a symbol for others.

Freedom of speech contains within itself the seeds of social and political liberty. Speech in itself is powerful, but it acquires social and political power only when it is articulated in public. For example, in the 1970s, a new literary movement spearheaded by Dalit writers burst forth in India. These Dalit writers verbalized their collective experience in prose and poetry replete with anger and resistance against the caste hierarchy.[11] These writers publicly articulated the practices, burdens and struggles of Dalits and thereby introduced society to their hitherto unknown and unimagined reality.

One of the primary motives of Dalit literature was to assert the Dalit identity and to develop a sense of fraternity within the Dalit community. In penning down their life stories, Dalit writers sought a sense of belonging to their own people and culture. The Dalit writers, inspired by narratives of their historical struggle, wrote songs of unity and upliftment. I would like to quote a few lines by poet Mangal Rathod, where he evokes Babasaheb Dr Ambedkar, the architect of the Indian Constitution:

O Babasaheb!
The first sip of water you drank
Quenched our thirst of ages.
We learned the taste of life!
We can never forget you
for your memory lingers
in each step we ascend.[12]

This poem refers to the historic satyagraha by Dr Ambedkar at Mahad in the year 1927. Such Dalit writings are an important site of dissemination of Dalit struggles and their cultural identity. In today's day and age of social media, the form of Dalit expression has undergone significant change. For example, today we have Dalit rappers who are taking on issues of Dalit identity through their songs and reels, one beat at a time.[13] The point that I want to emphasize here is that it is free speech that has enabled the Dalits to articulate their identity in public. And such public articulations have helped them participate in social and political decision-making.

Another important value in protecting freedom of speech is the assurance of individual self-fulfilment or self-realization. According to Rabindranath Tagore, our existence is meaningless if we can never expect to realize the highest point of perfection of our potentialities as human beings.[14] We often understand our character and potential only through self-realization. Self-realization is the development of our mind through the expression and exchange of ideas and opinions.

Author E.M. Forster queried, 'How can I tell what I think till I see what I say?'[15] We often articulate our thoughts in order to grasp and preserve their meaning. Often, this is just the first step in a series of interactions with society. Expression helps us become part of a process whereby we converse and debate and are often intellectually challenged by others. However, it is this very process which imbibes in us a greater awareness of the world.

In 2012, after the gruesome gang rape and murder of Nirbhaya in Delhi, thousands of protestors took to streets of the national capital demanding better safety for women and more stringent punishments for offenders.[16] This protest was a manifest expression of rage and anger against widespread instances of sexual violence against women in India. The protests compelled the general public, as well as legislators, to introspect on the efficacy of legislation dealing with crimes against women. The result was that in 2013, the penal law was amended to make it more stringent. Since the 2013 amendments, commentators have argued that a stringent law is not really the answer to eradicate crime against women. Such diverse opinions lead to a healthy discourse to identify the model that would best work for society. The Nirbhaya protests forced men to evaluate how they treat women who are part of their lives and even beyond. In the UK and Europe, we are witnessing young men and women protesting against the unrestrained use of fossil fuels, which is a significant contributor to climate change. These protests have forced the world to take cognizance of climate change and take immediate mitigating steps. This self-realization, which comes through a free expression of opinions and ideas, is what will ultimately spur us in the direction of justice.

Our Constitution grants every citizen the right to speech and expression. We should use this freedom to stand up for the voiceless and marginalized and use our privilege for the betterment of others. In doing so, we become more self-aware about our own role in society and recognize the social realities of the world we inhabit. Exercise of free speech is the first step towards understanding others and coming to terms with our human essence. The power of words and actions is an ally in the fight against collective vice and apathy towards the marginalized communities.

Baba Amte, a well-known social reformer from Maharashtra, devoted his life to serving leprosy patients and fighting the stigma associated with the disease.[17] Amte started Anandwan—a care centre for treatment and rehabilitation of leprosy patients in Chandrapur in Maharashtra. To fight the stigma around leprosy, Amte injected himself with bacilli from a patient to show that the disease itself was not contagious. It was through such efforts that Baba Amte broke the social stigma associated with leprosy and helped leprosy patients live a life of dignity. Baba Amte's life is a great example of how exercise of speech can be used to effectively enhance human freedom and offer a direct contribution to the quality of life of the neglected and the marginalized.

In 1963, Martin Luther King Jr delivered a monumental speech on the steps of the Lincoln Memorial. He said:

> We cannot be satisfied as long as the Negro's basic mobility is from a smaller ghetto to a larger one. We can never be satisfied as long as our children are stripped of their selfhood and robbed of their dignity by signs stating: for whites only.
>
> We cannot be satisfied as long as a Negro in Mississippi cannot vote and a Negro in New York believes he has nothing for which to vote.

> No, no, we are not satisfied, and we will not be satisfied until justice rolls down like waters, and righteousness like a mighty stream.[18]

Martin Luther King Jr's momentous speech caused a ripple effect within the Black community in the US and across the globe. It spearheaded the civil rights movement in the second half of the nineteenth century. Speech rouses emotions and opens up our minds. It stimulates our worries and sorrows. Speech is the medium through which we express happiness and joy. It is this power of speech that has aided in the aspiration for social change.

Closer home, in the Indian state of Andhra Pradesh, women led a mass uprising against the production and sale of arrack, a country liquor.[19] This movement was a product of the mass literacy programmes that were organized in the state. Women got together in groups and freely expressed their agonies as spouses, mothers and children subjected to domestic violence. This led to women expressing that cheap illegal manufacturing of alcohol was the source of their domestic woes.

These two illustrations indicate that free speech and expression of the marginalized communities is a formidable weapon to effect socio-political change.

In the second half of my lecture, I will focus on the intricate link between free speech and expression, and equality. While doing so, I will attempt to tackle an important question: What value does speech and expression hold for the marginalized groups? Does free speech serve a heightened purpose for marginalized and disadvantaged communities?

Free speech and equality share an integral link.[20] They are mutually reinforcing and are not, as some would like to argue, in conflict. The interrelationship of these two concepts, which are entrenched as fundamental rights in numerous constitutions of the United States, has undergone a four-stage evolution. In the first stage, restrictions on free speech of communities create and entrench marginalized groups. Communities are treated unfairly by limiting their access to free speech and expression. It is this unequal access to choices of expression that creates a stratified society. In the first stage, restriction on free speech and expression is the cause for marginalization. The restriction could be manifold. It could be a restriction on the expression of identity, or the expression of food and clothing choices, or it could be in the form of a limitation on the opportunities that the community would have liked to explore. All these restrictions on expression cumulatively create a marginalized community.

Most southern states in the US protected the freedom of expression, including freedom of the press. However, southern legislators and Congressmen enforced the 'slaver's veto' by adopting draconian laws against the exercise of free speech by the Black community. To put this in perspective, in 1776, Virginia approved the Declaration of Rights. But a Virginia law in 1836 criminalized publications intent on 'persuading persons of colour . . . to rebel, or denying the right of masters to property in their slaves, and inculcating the duty of resistance to such right.'[21] When David Walker, a free Black man, published an anti-slavery pamphlet, titled 'Appeal to the Colored Citizens of the World', the legislature responded by imposing the death penalty for the 'circulation of pamphlets of evil tendencies'.[22]

In India, until the Supreme Court decriminalized homosexuality a few years back, homosexuals were penalized for expressing their identity. Similarly, women are disadvantaged because their choices of expression are stifled and curbed in a patriarchal society. The restriction of expression could be attached to basic civil rights such as voting, or it could extend to the freedom to partake in recreational activities or even the freedom to play a sport of choice. Women in most parts of the world did not have the right to vote until the 1900s. In 1921, the English Football Association banned women, stating that the 'game of football is quite unsuitable for females and should not be encouraged'.[23] This ban was followed by many other countries across the globe, such as Belgium, Brazil and Denmark. In 1955, the German Football Association also imposed a ban on women's football claiming that the 'roughness of the sport would damage women's fertility and health' and that 'in the fight for the ball, female grace disappears, body and soul are inevitably damaged, and the public parading of the body is offensive and indecent'.[24] These rules and laws restricting the expression of choices of a community marginalizes them because access to free expression is vital for the development of the human self, both in terms of individual identity and group identity.

In the second stage, mostly through the Constitution, the law undoes all the restrictions on choices by communities. The law recognizes the discrimination and unequal treatment faced by marginalized communities and issues a call for equality and grants all citizens the same access to free speech and expression. On 26 January 1950, when the Indian Constitution was adopted, we gave ourselves a new order based on the rule of law and shed away the colonial baggage and the heavy-handedness of the State. The Constitution expressly abolished untouchability and conferred women with equal rights. Any rule that restricts access to the expression of marginalized communities is then struck down by the courts based on the constitutional principles of equality and freedom of free expression.

In the third stage, we are concerned with the operation of general restrictions on free speech and expression. Constitution framers across the globe disagreed with the old nursery rhyme, 'sticks and stones may break my bones, but words will never hurt me'. The Indian Constitution expressly limited free speech and expression on substantive grounds of 'sovereignty and integrity of the nation, the security of the State, friendly relations with foreign States, public order, decency or morality, contempt of court, defamation or incitement to an offence'.[25] Further, the penal statute in India—the Indian Penal Code 1860—criminalizes hate speech, defamation, sedition and obscenity. These substantive grounds of limitation are vague and not defined precisely, which allows for greater discretion in restricting free speech. The Delhi High Court, while vindicating M.F. Husain, an Indian artist, of the charges of obscenity, asserted that 'beauty lies in the eyes of the beholder and so does obscenity'.[26]

If anything, this depicts the vagueness that is inherent in the phrase 'obscenity', which is a statutory limitation on free expression.

Though the limitations are applicable to all citizens, in effect, they do not equally apply to all persons across group identities. These restrictions disproportionately impact members of marginalized communities. In the recent past, I have witnessed situations in which Dalit literature is sought to be censured and banned. Calls for a ban were issued against Dalit activist Perumal Murugan's book, *One Part Woman*. Officials coerced an unconditional apology out of the author in the form of a peace settlement order. Perumal Murugan instituted proceedings before the Madras High Court contending that the settlement was not binding on him. The Madras High Court allowed the petition observing that 'if you do not like the book, simply close it'.[27] He won the battle in the courtroom but lost the battle outside the courtroom. Perumal Murugan issued a statement on Facebook committing literary suicide. He claimed that 'Perumal Murugan—the writer is dead.' He became, he said, 'a walking corpse'.[28] The case of Perumal Murugan depicts the disproportionate impact of restrictions on freedom of speech and expression on the identity of members of the marginalized communities. His strong words depict the intensity of emotional devastation that he would have undergone.

In Florida's Polk County, Nobel laureate for literature Toni Morrison's novels *The Bluest Eye* and *Beloved* were taken off the shelves in public school libraries. While the books were sought to be taken off the shelves for the depiction of sex and racism, scholars have noticed that other books with similar depictions authored by whites have not been challenged.[29]

In 2005, the Legislative Assembly in the state of Maharashtra banned the performance of dance, 'of any kind or type, in any eating house, permit room or beer bar'. However, the provision excluded the performance of dances in hotels that bore three stars or above. The counsel for the state submitted before the court that the classification between the exempted establishments and prohibited establishments is based on the 'degree of harm'. It was urged [I quote] 'the type of crowd that visits banned establishments is also different from the crowd that visits the exempted establishments'. Scholars have argued how the ban was unjustified and reflected a restrictive social morality, which found problems with the bar-dancing activities of women from vulnerable communities like Bedia and Nat.[30] Furthermore, the state, by exempting hotels that are three-star and above from the purview of the ban, reinforced the morality of the dominant community that the members belonging to the lower strata are sexually perverted. The state class-coded the provision penalizing obscenity.[31]

That leads to the fourth stage, where we are concerned with the degree of protection required for speech and the expression of marginalized communities. The identity of marginalized communities is under threat due to the increasing tendency to homogenize culture such as food habits and clothing. In addition to the threat to identity, there are stigmas attached to their identity. Marginalized communities carry the baggage of the threat to identity and bear the scars of discrimination. Because of the manifold forms of discrimination, speech on biased ideas about protected identities, such as race, gender and caste, causes a higher degree of emotional and psychic harm. The Indian legal framework recognizes the higher degree of harm when the expression targets protected identity. The Scheduled Caste and Scheduled Tribe (Prevention of Atrocities Act), 1989, penalizes anyone who 'intentionally insults or intimidates with an intent to humiliate a member of the Scheduled Caste or Scheduled Tribe in any place within public view'. A corollary to this argument is whether speech by members of protected groups requires a higher degree of protection because of the historical and continuing forms of harms suffered by them. Would they not need stronger forms of expression to communicate their sufferings? I leave this question open and request all of you to ponder upon it.

The aim behind elucidating the four stages of evolution of the interlink between freedom of speech and equality is to explain how the concepts of speech and equality are joined at the hip. While formal restrictions on the freedom of expression of marginalized communities may have subsided, it is a reminder that for an equal society, care must be taken to nurture all forms of expression of marginalized communities.

Before concluding my speech, I would like to briefly speak about an important value that is essential in public discourse: civility and sensitivity. Having served as a judge for the past twenty-two years, I have noticed an increasing degradation of the values of tolerance and respect. Is this the new normal in our post-truth societies? We choose our friends carefully. We like to interact with like-minded people. This feeling of affinity towards like-minded people has led to a situation where the views of diverse sections of the population are insulated from us. We only interact with people who speak the same tongue with the same undertones. There is nothing wrong with liking to be surrounded by like-minded people to discuss politics and life and share happiness and sorrow. However, a society that is culturally diverse depicts a plurality of worldviews. In a culturally diverse society, it is important to *first* be open to contrarian social and political views and *second* to be civil and sensitive during such conversations. We need to inculcate the value of interacting with persons from diverse backgrounds. Associating with and understanding their stories and struggles is a step towards an inclusive existence.

In today's lecture, I have argued that free speech has a certain value and purpose in a democratic society. Free speech is the expression of our innermost being. It is an integral part of the development and assertion of identities. Such expression of ideas and opinions leads to revelation and self-realization. In today's world, speech takes many forms, but what is important is that we use our agency and autonomy to speak up for what is right and just. Through our expressions and with every word and emoji, we have the ability to differentiate between that which is just and unjust, between the good and the evil. Our speech has embedded in it the ability to give voice to the voiceless, mainstream the discourse on marginalization and bring gender to the canvas of equal rights. Expression sustains the eternal quest for the greater good of humanity.

Bob Dylan could encapsulate the essence of a long address in a few lines of verse titled 'Chimes of Freedom':

'Tolling for the aching ones whose wounds cannot be nursed
For the countless confused, accused, misused, strung-out ones
an' worse
An' for every hung-up person in the whole wide universe
An' we gazed upon the chimes of freedom flashing'.[32]

26

Journalism in the New Age

Challenges, Responsibilities and Excellence[1]

At the very outset, I extend my heartiest congratulations to the winners in all the categories of the awards presented today. Earlier today, I was browsing through the categories in which awards are presented as well as a few stories by previous winners. I must say that I am tremendously impressed by the depth and breadth of the reportage that journalists in our country engage in. To those journalists who have not won today—you are no less a winner in the game of life, for yours is a noble profession. To have chosen it at all (especially when more lucrative options are available) and to continue to pursue it despite the many difficulties which arise, is admirable indeed.

As I was reflecting on the profession of law and that of journalism, it occurred to me that journalists and lawyers (or judges, as in my case) share some things in common. Of course, persons of both professions are fierce believers of the aphorism that the pen is mightier than the sword. But they also share the occupational hazard of being disliked by virtue of their professions—no easy cross to bear. But members of both professions keep at their daily tasks and hope that one day the reputations of their professions will receive a makeover.

The magnitude of the task that journalists face in their careers was well described by philosopher and author G.K. Chesterton, who said, 'Journalism largely consists in saying "Lord Jones is dead" to people who never knew Lord Jones was alive.' Journalists are constantly engaged in the endeavour of simplifying complex information for the consumption of the public, which is frequently unaware of even the most basic facts underlying the issues sought to be exposed. This simplification of information must not be at the cost of accuracy, which further complicates the journalist's job. This is true world over.

The media sparks debates and discussion, which are the first step towards action. All societies inevitably become dormant, lethargic and immune to the problems that plague them. Journalism (in all its forms) is one of the key aspects which prods us out of this collective inertia. The media has always played and continues to play an important role in shaping the course of current events, and by extension, the course of history itself. Recently, the #MeToo movement was sparked in part by the publication of stories concerning the accusations of sexual harassment against prominent figures in the film industry in the USA. The #MeToo movement had cascading effects all across the world and was a watershed moment in history. In India, the media's coverage of the gang rape of a twenty-three-year-old medical student, or Nirbhaya, by certain men in Delhi resulted in widespread protests and, later, in reforms to criminal law. Even on a day-to-day basis, some news stories prompt questions and discussion in Parliament and in the legislative assemblies of states.

The media is the fourth pillar in the conception of the State, and thus an integral component of democracy. A functional and healthy democracy must encourage the development of journalism as an institution that can ask difficult questions to the establishment—or as it is commonly known, 'speak truth to power'. The vibrancy of any democracy is compromised when the press is prevented from doing exactly this. The press must remain free if a country is to remain a democracy.

India has a great legacy of newspapers that have acted as catalysts of social and political change. Prior to Independence, newspapers were run by social reformers and political activists to raise awareness and also as a means of outreach. For instance, Dr Ambedkar launched several newspapers, such as *Mooknayak*, *Bahishkrut Bharat*, *Janata* and *Prabuddha Bharat*, to create awareness about the rights of the most neglected communities in India. The newspapers and other publications of pre-Independence India also give us a picture of the detailed history of those times. These newspapers are now a source of knowledge, a historical record of the times when courageous men and women acted against the colonial rulers and fought fiercely for our independence. The newsprint voiced the aspiration of the soul—a yearning for freedom.

On a summer evening in 1919, in the aftermath of a massacre in Amritsar, India was holding its breath. The dead lay uncounted. The colonial censors were hard at work. But amidst this carefully manufactured silence, one editor refused to be quiet.

The editor of the *Bombay Chronicle*, Benjamin Guy Horniman,[2] circumvented the repressive regulations imposed by British officials, defied the risk of being arrested and was eventually deported for smuggling out images and eyewitness reports of the Jallianwala Bagh massacre.[3] Yet, what he achieved was far more powerful than a headline. He stirred the conscience of two nations—India and Britain—with the truth that power sought to suppress.

Journalism, in that moment, was not an industry. It was a human act of courage that altered the course of history. A revolt of the pen against the gun.

A hundred years later, we may not face colonial censorship in the same form. But truth is still embattled. Facts are still fragile. And silence, often, is more deadly than noise. Journalists must have the courage to challenge complacency rather than follow trends. To serve memory, not to seek spectacle. When the Emergency was declared on 25 June 1975, many news establishments were shut down for a few days. When the *Indian Express* came back with its edition on 28 June 1975, it issued a front-page apology for being out of print for two days and reported the mass political arrests by the government. But what spoke louder than words was its blank editorial as a protest against the presence of the censor. Ashok Mahadevan, a journalist, inserted a short twenty-two-word obituary in the *Times of India* which read: 'O'Cracy, D.E.M., beloved husband of T. Ruth, loving father of L.I. Bertie, brother of Faith, Hope and Justicia, expired on June 26.' The insert escaped the attention of a ham-handed censor and communicated a powerful thought.

As Anton Chekhov wrote in his short story 'The Bet',[4] 'The State is not God. It has not the right to take away what it cannot restore.' The statement, which was spoken in reference to the death penalty, which was part of a bet in the novel, also highlights journalism's unspoken compact with the public: to not damage what it cannot assist and to not denigrate what it cannot raise. Journalism that is not guided by humility and humanity becomes indistinguishable from power.

Modern-day India, too, has witnessed journalism of tremendous courage. You are all undoubtedly aware of Gauri Lankesh, who was the editor of *Lankesh Patrike* (Kannada word; pronounced as pa-thri-kay) and later of the *Gauri Lankesh Patrike*. That she was gunned down in her own home a few years ago is tragic and reflective of the danger that journalists face. Gauri is not alone. Many journalists, both in our country as well as across the world, work in difficult and unfriendly conditions. But they are relentless in the face of adversity and opposition. It is precisely this quality which must not be lost. As citizens, we may not agree with the approach that a journalist has adopted or the conclusions that they reach. I, too, find myself disagreeing with many journalists. After all, who amongst us agrees with all other people? But disagreement must not distort into hatred, and hatred must not be permitted to evolve into violence. As you must be aware, the Supreme Court of India has emphasized on the rights of journalists in a number of judgments. In one such judgment that I had the privilege of authoring, the Supreme Court held: 'India's freedoms will rest safe as long as journalists can speak truth to power without being chilled by a threat of reprisal.'[5]

Initially, the outreach of journalism was limited to print media, but this expanded with the introduction of television. I was taking a flight to the US in 1982 to pursue a master's degree in law from Harvard University. Coincidentally, it was the day of the launch of colour television in India. In the recent past, social media has been a game changer for journalists in more ways than one. Online platforms have provided an opportunity to individuals to launch their own online media channels. In that way, online platforms have led to the democratization of the media. Years ago, it was the paucity of space which was a constraining factor. Now perhaps it is the paucity of readers' patience. Readers have short attention spans. News is reduced to shorts on YouTube or reels on Instagram.

Our attention spans have seen a steady decline with the advent of social media. It is now the norm for short titbits of information to be conveyed through 280 characters or in a few seconds. This is, however, an unsatisfactory replacement for long-form or investigative pieces. In fact, there can be no replacement for such reportage. It is also proving to be a challenge for journalists to penetrate the echo chambers that social media has created and illuminate the truth.

The modern journalist faces a much more formidable foe: exhaustion. Not only information exhaustion but emotional and ethical fatigue. We are constantly confronted with crises from around the world, each of which briefly appears on screens before disappearing into the next.

Journalism, in such a world, must evolve; not just to report the problems but to constructively frame possibilities. We are urged to transcend the logic of indignation by the concept of constructive journalism—which involves embracing solutions, nuance and dialogue, rejecting increasing tabloidization, sensationalism and negativity bias.[6] It serves as a reminder that journalism's job is to map what can be fixed, not only reflect what is broken.

A free press, according to the 1947 report of the Hutchins Commission on the freedom of press, must also be responsible, that is, it must inform, contextualize and assist society in making decisions without giving in to fear, prejudice or the trivialization of facts. This kind of journalism was referred to as being in the public interest, not for profit or power, but for the people.

Over seventy-five years after the release of *A Free and Responsible Press*—the report of the Hutchins Commission[7]—we are facing a problem that is both uncannily similar to and possibly more complicated than the one that the Hutchins Commission considered.[8] Public confidence in the media is at a nadir. We now differ on fundamental facts rather than just policy because political divisions are so irreconcilable. Digital platforms, which were intended to democratize debate, have frequently turned into forums for propaganda, disinformation and half-truths. The press is also shrinking, its resources are being exhausted and its editorial independence is increasingly at risk.

Constructive journalism is not naive optimism. It is hope with facts. It is criticism with compassion. It is represented by Anton Chekhov's prisoner in 'The Bet', who, after fifteen years of voluntary confinement, realizes the futility of materialism and writes:

> I despise your books; I despise wisdom and the blessings of this world. It is all worthless, fleeting, illusory, and deceptive, like a mirage. You may be proud, wise, and fine, but death will wipe you off the face of the earth as though you were no more than mice burrowing under the floor, and your posterity, your history, your immortal geniuses will burn or freeze together with the earthly globe.

And yet, he walks away not bitter but awakened. That is what great journalism can do; it can awaken us, not just alarm us. It can make us not only better informed but more conscious.

Local or community-based journalism has played an important role in encouraging social cohesion and political activism. It has the ability to not only educate citizens but also to raise the little-known concerns and set the agenda for debate on those issues at the policy level. Local journalism shines a bright light on local issues, people and causes that many times may not get covered by the media at the national level. As several studies have shown, the composition of mainstream media is not representative of all communities;[9] community journalism opens the avenues for the members of marginalized communities to be a voice for their own issues. The emergence of social media enabled them to create their own space and come up with independent media platforms.

The relevance of the media was best highlighted during the period of the COVID-19 pandemic. Electronic, print and social media facilitated the State to disseminate relevant information to the general public at large even during the lockdown. The citizens were constantly reminded of the various precautionary as well as preventive steps which they were expected to take in order to ensure their well-being. The media highlighted administrative loopholes and excesses. Various High Courts and the Supreme Court of India relied on news reports in taking *suo motu* cognizance of instances of violations of people's rights during the pandemic.[10]

I was recently asked which newsperson I followed with keen interest. My answer did not name a newsperson but a cartoonist—the famed late R.K. Laxman. Although he was not a journalist, he succeeded in accomplishing the core of the journalist's mission by holding a mirror up to the powers that be. I am sure most of India will join me in considering R.K. Laxman's cartoons to be incisive and witty commentaries. He was what we call an 'equal opportunity offender'—everyone stood the risk of being the subject of his cartoons, and most took it in good spirit when they were ridiculed. My favourite anecdote about him was that he thought that the famous UK cartoonist David Low was actually David Cow because of the manner in which Low penned his signature!

I also joked that my favourite journalist (so to speak) was the one in the Hindi movie *Nayak*, which was a remake of the Tamil film *Mudhalvan*. Those who have watched either of these know that the protagonist is a journalist who is invited to take the place of the chief minister for a single day. He becomes wildly popular after doing this and becomes a politician. I see some young faces in the audience today, and I hope that they have not taken up journalism after watching this movie in their youth!

In recent years, we are also witnessing a rising interest in legal journalism. Legal journalism is the storyteller of the justice system, shedding light on the complexities of the law. However, selective quoting of speeches and judgments of judges by journalists in India has become a matter of concern. This practice has a tendency to distort the public's understanding of important legal issues. Judges' decisions are often complex and nuanced, and selective quoting can give the impression that a judgment means something entirely different from what the judge actually intended. It is, thus, essential for journalists to provide a complete picture of events, rather than presenting a one-sided view. Journalists have a duty to report accurately and impartially.

As with every institution, journalism is facing its own challenges. Fake news poses a serious threat to the independence and impartiality of the press in the current society. It is the collective responsibility of journalists as well as other stakeholders to weed out any element of bias or prejudice from the process of reporting events. A comprehensive fact-checking mechanism should be in place to verify all news items before reporting. Media houses are expected to act cautiously while publishing news. Fake news can misguide millions of people at once, and this will be in direct contradiction with the fundamentals of democracy, which form the bedrock of our existence. Across the globe, fake news has the capability to create tensions between communities by misleading people. Therefore, to save the democratic values of fraternity, which can be damaged, if not destroyed, through biased reporting, there is a strong need to bridge a gap between truth and lie.

Another issue affecting the media is that of legitimacy. A diverse and representative newsroom is essential for media institutions to provide well-researched and complex stories that explore a multiplicity of perspectives and voices. Maintaining a diverse workforce is imperative for the longevity of any media platform. This is not just about providing different perspectives and viewpoints. Media institutions need to ensure that their newsroom culture reflects the diverse news content they are producing. Otherwise, audiences may question their authenticity. Journalism ought not to be elitist, exclusionary or, for that matter, a selective profession.

A major issue that has percolated our system is trial by media. The presumption of innocence postulates that a person is presumed innocent until found guilty by a court of law. This is one of the core tenets of law and legal processes. However, there have been instances when the media has carried narratives that make a person guilty in the eyes of the public, even before the court finds them guilty. This can have long-lasting repercussions on the life of the affected individuals, as well as on due process. The media has the responsibility of preventing the distortion or forgetting of facts in a constitutional democracy. Several Supreme Court rulings have cautioned that 'media trials', no matter how well-intentioned, cannot replace judicial authority. In *State of Maharashtra v. Rajendra Jawanmal Gandhi*,[11] the court observed:

> A trial by press, electronic media or public agitation is the very antithesis of the rule of law. It can well lead to miscarriage of justice. Responsible journalism can shine a light on the blind spots within our judicial system. Yet, when reporting slips into unchecked sensationalism, it doesn't just distort perception; it risks clouding judgment and eroding the very ideals of justice it seeks to uphold.

According to the Madrid Principles on the Relationship Between the Media and Judicial Independence, it is the job of the media to 'convey information to the public and to comment on the administration of justice, including cases before, during and after trial, without violating the presumption of innocence'.[12]

Responsible journalism is the beacon of truth that can guide us to a better tomorrow. It is the engine that drives democracy forward, based on the quest for truth, justice and equality. As we navigate the challenges of the digital age, it is more important than ever for journalists to maintain standards of accuracy, impartiality and responsibility in their reporting.

27

The Relationship Between Constitutional Rights and Constitutional Structure

Delicate Balances and Overarching Considerations[1]

I am deeply honoured to have been invited to deliver the 2023 Annual Lecture organized by the Cambridge Pro Bono Project. I would like to begin the lecture by recalling the poem *Odyssey* by Homer.[2] Ulysses, the protagonist, upon his return from the Trojan War, encounters sirens who are beautiful creatures of the sea. Their mesmerizing voice has the capability of bewitching sailors and luring them to death. Ulysses, who is aware of this, asks his men to tie him up to the mast of the boat so that he does not succumb to the dangerous charm of sirens. When Ulysses asks to be tied, he does so not to be deprived of his freedom but rather to gain it, and to overcome the temptation.[3]

But what if the rope that binds Ulysses realizes its power to impose restraint and exerts too much pressure, choking Ulysses in the process? Should the rope not have a restraint on the power that it exerts? In this metaphorical story, Ulysses represents a citizen and the rope represents the State. In the course of my lecture, I will attempt to discern the relationship between the State and the citizens by referring to the relationship between constitutional structure and constitutional rights. I will do so by focusing on four key aspects of this relationship—*constitutional processes*, *institutional arrangements of governance*, *the scrutiny of actions as envisaged by and implicit in constitutions*, and *participation of the citizenry in a democracy.*

Similar to Ulysses, citizens across the world handed over a few rights to create a State. In doing so, they diminished their right to be free citizens untrammelled by external forces. In exchange, the State is reposed with the duty to protect the life, liberty and property of its citizens. In today's world, this agreement between citizens and the State is entrenched in the form of a constitution. However, constitutions do not merely recognize the rights that citizens hold but also ascribe the rights that they *ought* to hold in modern civilization. The Indian Constitution is an example of an aspirational constitution. It recognizes the rights that citizens held before the adoption of the Constitution. In addition to this, the Constitution, by creating an aspirational socio-political order, confers additional rights upon them. For example, the practice of untouchability was prevalent when the Constitution of India was framed in 1950. The Indian Constitution overhauled the existing socio-political order that was entrenched in the vices of discrimination and arbitrariness to create a new order embedded in the ideals of justice, liberty, equality and fraternity.

Another example of an aspirational or what is otherwise called a transformative constitution is the South African Constitution. The patterns of social, political and economic life in South Africa were influenced by apartheid. Access to public areas, permissible relationships and political participation, among others, was restricted based on the colour of skin. Much like the Indian Constitution, when the South African Constitution was adopted, it sought to shape a new socio-political order. A plethora of rights that were not available earlier were recognized. It includes the right to equality, the right to fair labour practices and the right not to be subjected to slavery or forced labour. The injustices of the past were sought to be cured by the adoption of the Constitution. In fact, the rights framework in both the Indian and the South African constitutions is elaborate because the injustices that traced every aspect of a citizen's life were sought to be cured by the Constitution.

The chapter on fundamental rights is for this reason often referred to as the soul of the Constitution. However, the mere recognition of fundamental rights is not sufficient for its effective protection because values are not self-enforcing. Articles 14 and 21 of the Indian Constitution recognize the right to equality and the right to life and liberty respectively. However, on the adoption of the Indian Constitution in 1950, Indian society did not miraculously wake up to an equal social order. On 26 January 1950 (the day that the Indian Constitution was adopted), Indian society was as stratified as it was the day before. Sati, untouchability and female infanticide still plagued society. Political dissenters were still imprisoned for exercising their right to free speech. However, with the adoption of the Constitution, the State was entrusted with the duty to create a society premised on the principles of social, economic and political justice. The State became an instrument for realizing the values entrenched in the Constitution. By the very nature of the duty placed on the State for realizing constitutional values, the State loses the face of neutrality. The State is *expected* to act in accordance with the Constitution, which has already charted out a specific plan for the attainment of social, political and economic justice. The Constitution, by espousing certain values, goads the State towards their fulfilment.[4]

But how does the State give effect to these constitutional values? Is it sufficient if the Constitution grants rights to citizens and places a corresponding duty on the State to enforce such rights? George Orwell's fable *Animal Farm* throws light upon the issue that I am attempting to elucidate. In the fable, the animals in Manor Farm rebel against their human owner. After a successful revolution overthrowing the humans, they adopt the seven commandments. One of the commandments is that: 'All animals are equal'. However,

Napoleon, the pig, establishes an authoritarian regime. Napoleon demands that the hens hand over their eggs to be sold. When the hens deny, they are starved and later slaughtered. Similarly, though it was the idea of Snowball, another pig, to establish a windmill to ease the workload of the animals, Napoleon takes credit for the idea, thus distorting the truth. Orwell ends the fable with the message, 'All animals are equal but some animals are more equal than others.' Why were the 'seven commandments' not sufficient to protect the rights of the animals? The governance in Manor Farm fell apart because there were no entrenched rules or institutions for governance. The lack of such rules led to an arbitrary exercise of power, radically altering the very content of rights itself. My argument is that the rights regime in the Constitution, similar to the seven commandments, would only be, as Justice Antonin Scalia of the US Supreme Court calls it, 'a parchment guarantee', if the Constitution does not establish a structure that effectively checks the exercise of power and abuse of it.

That is why, for the Constitution to stand the test of time, it is necessary that alongside assigning a duty to the State to protect fundamental rights, it must also establish other institutions to create a system of governance. The system of governance envisaged in a constitution is as important a component of constitutionalism as much as the rights framework is because it places checks to ensure that the State exercises its power fairly. The expansion of the rights framework would be insignificant if the Constitution prescribes a weak form of governance that does not ensure that the State exercises its power astutely. Or, if the judiciary interprets constitutional silences and interpretative gaps in a manner that would weaken the system of governance.

Constitutional theorists on the heels of Montesquieu opined that a strict separation of powers between different institutions of governance is the best method of assembling power. Scholars belonging to this school of thought believe that Parliament is supreme and that the courts do not have the power to strike down legislation. The institution that enacts the law, the institution that enforces the law and the institution that interprets the law were demarcated into specific functional spheres. It soon came to be understood that the possession of power does not necessarily mean that it would be exercised judiciously. And so, another school of thought arose which propounded that checks must be placed on the exercise of power to ensure that power is not exercised in a mala fide manner or that it is not clothed with personal attributes. Because those who hold power are human as well. And to be human is to err. As King Henry in *Henry V* says, 'I think the king is but a man, as I am. The violet smells to him as it doth to me. The element shows to him as it doth to me. All his senses have but human conditions. His ceremonies laid by, in his nakedness he appears but a man.'[5]

Thus, the two components that ensure constitutionalism are a guarantee of rights and a system of governance that checks the exercise of power of other institutions. The system of governance in turn has two components—constitutional processes and institutions of governance that are vested with powers and duties. The existence of a guarantee of rights and a system of governance have been understood to infuse the principle of constitutionalism as early as the seventeenth century. In 1776, the town of Concord, Massachusetts, resolved that a 'Constitution in its proper idea intends a system of principles established to secure the subject in the possession and enjoyment of their rights and privileges against any encroachment of the governing part.'[6] Similarly, Article 16 of the French Declaration of the Rights of Man and of the Citizen of 1789 stated that any society in which the guarantee of rights is not assured, nor the separation of powers determined, has no Constitution.[7]

The Indian Constitution is structured along the two ideals recognized above. Part III of the Constitution recognizes the rights of citizens and persons. The rest of the provisions of the Constitution outline the distribution of power among numerous institutions. The Constitution demarcates the scope of power of the executive, the legislature and the judiciary. Each institution places a check on the exercise of power by other institutions. The judiciary has the power to strike down legislation for violation of fundamental rights or infringement of any other constitutional provision. Executive actions are also amenable to judicial review. The executive is collectively responsible to the Lower House, that is, the House of People.

The Election Commission of India is a constitutional body entrusted with superintendence and control over elections. It prevents the interference of the ruling faction in the electoral process. Similarly, the Constitution prescribes a decentralized model of governance, which is a bottom-up approach towards governance. The Constitution creates panchayats, municipalities and co-operative societies, which are local bodies of governance where posts are filled by direct election. The local bodies of governance democratically decentralize power from the centre to locally elected authorities to encourage the involvement of the public in governance. A greater involvement in governance creates a field of greater accountability. In this way, the Constitution divides power and creates a system of accountability to minimize the misuse of power. The entrenchment of local bodies of governance in the constitution symbolizes the checks that are introduced by the Constitution on the exercise of power from the grassroots to the highest levels of governance.

The division of power between different institutions and the substantive checks on the exercise of power are not the only constitutional arrangements to prevent the misuse of power. The Constitution inhibits mala fide exercise of power and safeguards against the violation of constitutional values by introducing procedural guarantees. Procedural guarantees serve two purposes. *First*, it prevents the seepage of bias and unfairness in the process of decision-making. A decision that is reached after following procedural rules is expected to be fair; and *second*, fair procedure is not only a means to the end of achieving a fair outcome but is an end in itself. Procedural requirements create a stumbling block on the free exercise of power. Such stumbling blocks are necessary because it suggests that power is not unrestrained and it must be exercised with circumspection. Article 21 of the Constitution, which guarantees the right to life and liberty, introduces the facet of procedural guarantees. So does Article 22, which inculcates the principle of natural justice.

Recently, the Supreme Court of India in the case of *Subhash Desai*[8] expounded on the importance of legislative procedure for the furtherance of democratic ideals. Article 122 of the Indian Constitution states that the validity of proceedings in Parliament shall not be challenged on the ground of alleged 'irregularity of procedure'. The issue before the court was related to the scope of judicial review of procedural infringements. The court recognized that legislative procedure serves two objectives. *One*, it enables deliberation on the floor of the house, and such deliberation produces better outcomes that are more compatible with constitutional values, and *two*, it creates a system to check the power exercised by the incumbent government. Writing for a five-judge bench, I held that a violation of a procedure that serves one of the objectives recognized above and that is necessary for the sustenance of democracy would render the action invalid, and that the bar in Article 122 shall not apply to such cases.[9] Thus, it is imperative that procedural requirements entrenched in the Constitution or otherwise must be understood in terms of the broader purpose that it serves—of safeguarding constitutional values and checking abuse of power.

Further, constitutions also introduce stringent procedures to safeguard higher constitutional values. A gradation in the rigorousness of the procedure indicates that procedural guarantees do indeed aid in checking the abuse of power. A more stringent procedure is prescribed to check the abuse of 'higher' constitutional values. For example, Article 368 of the Constitution, which prescribes the procedure to amend the Constitution, stipulates that an amendment to the provisions of the Constitution shall require a two-thirds majority in both houses of Parliament. However, an amendment to certain provisions that deal with the scope of legislative power and executive power of the States, or the power of the judiciary, requires a special majority, that is, a majority of two-thirds of the members of Parliament and ratification by the legislature of at least one-half of the states. The Constitution introduces a stringent amending procedure to safeguard the autonomy of states, which is an important facet of federalism.

Another example of constitutional entrenchment of stringent procedure to safeguard constitutional principles is traceable to the ordinance-making power of the President. The President and the Governor have the power to promulgate a law on the aid and advice of the council of ministers when either of the houses of the legislature is not in session. The ordinance-making power of the executive is a departure from the principle of parliamentary form of governance and representative democracy, which are chief values of the Constitution. However, the Constitution circumscribes such power. The provision prescribes that the ordinance promulgated shall cease to operate on expiry of six weeks from the reassembly of Parliament. A limit on the operation of the ordinance is prescribed to prevent the misuse of ordinance-making power, which would subvert parliamentary accountability and weaken democratic functioning.

Having discussed the broad framework of arrangement of power among various institutions in the Constitution, it is important that we understand the role of courts in this constitutional structure. Through judicial review, courts primarily engage in the function of scrutiny, that is to say that they are tasked with scrutinizing the actions of legislatures and the executive. We can all agree that the job of the court is to interpret the law. But how should courts interpret the law, particularly in situations where there are interpretative gaps or in cases of constitutional silences?

Courts in India and all over the world do not solely rely on a single method of constitutional interpretation. Constitutional courts are generally eclectic in their interpretation. If you ask a student of law to start colouring a well-reasoned judgment of a constitutional court, you will soon discover that judgment is actually a rainbow—different colours fuse together to represent different interpretative approaches. This fusion of interpretative approaches helps a judge interpret a constitution as the time changes. As Justice Benjamin Cardozo, noted American lawyer and jurist, says, 'a constitution states or ought to state not rules for the passing hour, but principles for an expanding future'.[10]

The text of a written constitution is often inadequate, and does not and *cannot* deal with a multitude of situations that may arise. Words like 'human dignity', 'liberty' and 'freedom' contain within themselves a range of meanings. The text can also be ambiguous, vague or silent. Even a detailed Constitution such as the Indian Constitution may be found to be insufficiently explicit on particular contestations of power. The Indian courts were initially captivated by the idea that the written text or the black letter of law was the only guide to constitutional interpretation. Gradually, we moved beyond the plain text. Rather than focusing on a singular textual provision, we began looking at all parts of the Constitution together and their relation with each other; the values it espouses and the purpose it serves.

The courts have expansively interpreted fundamental rights by reading derived rights into the Indian Constitution. For example, the right to speedy justice, the right to environment, the right to livelihood and the right to health have been read into Article 21. The Indian courts have recognized that the right to life and liberty can be effectively protected only when an umbrella of other rights that it encompasses is recognized.

In 1973, the Indian Supreme Court in the prominent case of *Kesavananda Bharati*[11] held that Parliament does not have unbridled power to amend the Constitution, and that the 'basic structure', that is, the values of the Constitution that form the basis of the Constitution, cannot be abrogated by amendments. However, in spite of the decision in *Kesavananda Bharati*, the Indian courts have been rather reluctant to interpret provisions that deal with structural arrangements of power based on constitutional values. I assume that one of the reasons for this relative reluctance is the understanding that the Constitution is primarily a document that protects the rights of citizens, and thus it is only acceptable to branch beyond the text to interpret the rights regime. However, as I discussed earlier, the structural arrangements of power within the Constitution are as important a component of a constitution, as is the rights regime. It is, thus, imperative that courts interpret constitutional silences across various provisions relating to structural arrangements of power based on values of the Constitution.

In simple terms, let me use the example of a rope to elucidate the importance of constitutional values. A rope is manufactured by twisted strands of hemp or nylon. Each strand joins forces with the other to give shape and form to the rope. The form of the rope would not remain the same even if one of the strands of the rope is detached. Similar to how the numerous strands of thread form the rope, the numerous values entrenched in the provisions form the constitution. An alteration, which includes an alteration through interpretation, that is contrary to even one of these numerous values would render the Constitution unrecognizable. It is beyond the scope of my lecture today to delve into how the courts must identify these values. I will instead focus on how the courts have safeguarded constitutional structure and, in turn, constitutional rights by adopting an interpretation that furthers the values of the Constitution.

Before discussing a fairly recent judgment of the Supreme Court of India where it has adopted such an approach, I think it is necessary that I touch upon the decision of the Supreme Court of the United Kingdom in *R. v. Prime Minister* and *Cherry v. Advocate General for Scotland (Miller II)*.[12] In *Miller II*, the Supreme Court of the United Kingdom set aside the proclamation proroguing Parliament issued by Her Majesty the Queen on the aid and advice of the council of ministers. The Supreme Court held that the prorogation had the *effect* of preventing the ability of Parliament to carry out its constitutional functions as a legislature and as the body responsible for the supervision of the executive. That is, the prorogation frustrated the principles of parliamentary sovereignty and executive accountability. The Supreme Court of the United Kingdom in *Miller II* used core constitutional values to test the validity of the actions of the executive. By doing so, the court did not dislodge the structural arrangement of power in the UK polity. Rather, it re-established the principle of limited government.

Let me now discuss the decision of the Supreme Court of India on the ordinance-making power of the executive through the president and Governor, which is an exception to the rule that laws are enacted by the legislature which constitutes the representatives of the people. In *Krishna Kumar Singh II*,[13] the Supreme Court rejected a textual reading of the provisions, which provided that ordinances would have the same 'force and effect' as an Act of Parliament. While interpreting these words, the court reasoned that the ordinance power was not a prerogative power of the executive but was subject to a condition precedent and condition subsequent, provided in the text. The condition precedent requires the executive head to be satisfied that such an action was 'necessary' in the circumstances, and an 'immediate action' needs to be taken. These phrases contributed to the court's understanding that ordinance power must be exercised only when certain narrowly circumscribed conditions existed. If these conditions are not met, the exercise of the ordinance-making power would be invalid. The court restricted the ordinance-making power since it is an *exception* to Parliament's exclusive competence to enact laws, and since it dislodges the principle of representative democracy. The conditions were understood to strictly circumscribe the power of the executive to make laws in a parliamentary democracy, where the executive is collectively responsible to the legislature.

As I mentioned, the judicial process enables a scrutiny of the actions of the legislature and the executive. However, the process of scrutiny is not the domain of courts alone. The values prescribed in the Constitution are in numerous instances potentially conflicting. For example, the Indian Constitution is riddled with rights or conceptions of rights that conflict with one another. On the one hand, the right to equality of every citizen is recognized by the Constitution. On the other, marginalized sections of society, such as women and those belonging to the backward castes are granted reservations in education and government employment. Prima facie, it conflicts individual rights and group rights. In fact, the issue of whether reservation policy is an exception to the right to equality or is a facet of it has plagued the Indian polity since the 1950s. But it is not always necessary for the courts to be the first site of resolving these potential conflicts. Every institution of governance has a responsibility towards promoting the values of the Constitution and resolving the conflicts between these values in a manner that promotes the identity of the Constitution. The court's ability and its enthusiasm to adjudicate these issues must not diminish the democratic space available to citizens or usurp the functions of other democratic mechanisms.[14]

While courts enforce rights on a case-by-case basis, or in class action suits, the judicial system is not designed to be a panacea. Moreover, legal truth—or the position discerned by courts on the basis of the rules of evidence—must not be confused with social truth. Although they may overlap, social truths can exist even when they cannot easily be proved in a court of law. Courts are therefore a very effective tool in the quest to realize constitutional rights, but their field of impact is often laser-focused and is limited in scope.

Everyone here will agree with me when I say that to be equal is not only to be equal in the eyes of the law (although that is no doubt an important facet of equality) but to be *treated* as equals by our fellow citizens. The indignity of inequality often comes not in the form of a policy or a law but in the form of, say, exclusion from informal workplace gatherings or even social groups in school and university due to gender, caste or race. One of the biggest challenges we collectively face is how we surmount issues of this nature, where there is no violation of a legally enforceable right in the traditional sense. Certainly, judicial institutions were neither meant to tackle such problems nor are they equipped to.

The issue with framing all social and political issues in the language of rights and resorting to the courts to resolve these issues is that it reduces the constitutional space envisaged for other democratic mechanisms. The Constitution envisions other methods through which abuse of power can be legitimately checked. This includes debates and discussions inside and outside the legislature on crucial issues. The executive can be held accountable for its actions by Parliament inside the house, and outside by courts and citizenry.

The final component necessary for the effective realization of rights is the role ascribed to an individual in a constitutional democracy. The Constitution envisages a unique role for the individual, whose engagement with the other institutions I have spoken of is crucial to the realization of rights.

Pre-legislative consultative process is an apt instance that an informed citizenry can place an effective check on legislative functions. For instance, public comments were called on the draft bill for the Kerala Police Act, 2011. When the bill was introduced in the House, it was referred to the select committee, and the committee conducted a district-wide meeting. Around 400 to 500 people attended these meetings, and the necessary impact of such an extensive consultative process was the suggestion of 790 amendments to the draft bill after nearly four hours of extensive debate. Around 240 of those suggested amendments, most of which were centred on the public feedback, were ultimately accepted.[15]

The South African Constitution recognizes pre-legislative consultation process as a crucial aspect of structural arrangements of power. A pre-legislative consultation process is entrenched in the Constitution itself and a law that is enacted without pre-legislative consultation is unconstitutional. In 2005, Parliament of South Africa enacted a legislation relating to reproductive healthcare. The Constitutional Court of South Africa declared these laws to be unconstitutional because the National Council of Provinces (the upper house of South African Parliament) did not fulfil its obligation of initiating public deliberation on the law.[16]

It is, thus, very important for citizens to engage in a dialogue with each other and with the legislative and executive arms of the State. The practice of constitutional values and the organic reorientation of societal practices is essential to achieving the constitutional vision. Active participation by the citizenry in the democratic process in ways that are not expressly mentioned in the Constitution but are nonetheless implicit in its structure is indispensable to realizing constitutional rights. In this way, it is not only the judiciary that engages in scrutinizing the state of affairs but also the citizenry.

Every branch of the government bears allegiance to the structures and processes delineated in the Constitution. Each and every constitutional authority, be it a judge, a member of Parliament, a police officer in your locality or a civil servant, assumes control over the enforcement of constitutional law. Beyond constitutional authorities, it is individuals and communities themselves who play an indispensable role in the aim to achieve constitutional rights. It is only by valuing both constitutional structures and constitutional rights that an enduring constitution is created.

28

Reformation Beyond Representation

The Social Life of the Constitution in Remedying Historical Wrongs[1]

The theme for this year's edition of the International Conference on the Unfinished Legacy of Dr B.R. Ambedkar is 'Law, Caste and the Pursuit of Justice'. As the theme revolves around law, this may be the reason that I have been invited today to deliver the keynote address of the conference. I must say that I am delighted to be invited to deliver this keynote address—more so, as the conference in a way pays a tribute to the legacy of Dr B.R. Ambedkar, whom we all see as a guiding light.

I share a personal connection with Dr Ambedkar. When my father, late Chief Justice Y.V. Chandrachud, was a young lawyer, he would often go to a café called The Wayside Inn (Kala Ghoda) in Mumbai. He always saw a man sitting there the entire afternoon, writing down his thoughts and making notes. That man was none other than Dr Ambedkar. Back when he was a practising lawyer, my father also appeared against Dr Ambedkar in a case involving an electricity dispute.

The title of my keynote address is 'Reformation Beyond Representation: The Social Life of the Constitution in Remedying

Historical Wrongs'. In my address, I shall largely be referring to the Indian Constitution, but I will be making references to the American Constitution wherever necessary.

Before proceeding, I will briefly outline the contours of my address today. I intend to begin by discussing what we understand by 'historical wrongs'. I shall discuss what the role of the law was in the era of historical wrongs. I will then talk about how leaders such as Dr Ambedkar conceptualized an alternative framework of emancipatory constitutionalism to address the historical wrongs. I will discuss how the idea of *representation* was an essential ingredient of remedying historical wrongs. However, representation is only one way of remedying historical wrongs. Today, I want to look beyond representation. There has been a constitutional discourse on social reformation apart from the idea of representation. I shall discuss how the courts play a crucial role in this regard. At the end, I shall discuss why the discourse on reformation must not be limited to courtrooms and must be considered in light of larger social discourse on equality.

HISTORICAL WRONGS

Throughout history, marginalized social groups have been subjected to horrendous wrongs, often stemming from prejudice, discrimination and unequal power dynamics. From the brutal transatlantic slave trade that forcibly uprooted millions of Africans to the Native American displacement, to the caste inequalities in India affecting millions of backward—though Bahujan—castes, to the oppression of indigenous Adivasi communities in India, to the systemic oppression of women, LGBTQIA+ individuals and other minority communities, the annals of history are stained with instances of profound injustice. These wrongs have caused immeasurable suffering and have left lasting scars on these communities, underscoring the urgent need for societal reflection, reconciliation and efforts to rectify past injustices in the ongoing quest for a more equitable and inclusive world.

What sets these wrongs apart is that they deny that core truth of human equality. Reasonable people, governments and courts can disagree over various aspects of human rights such as questions of privacy and personal liberty. However, the historical wrongs I discuss deny individuals their right to participate and reap the benefits of living together in society based on the *identity* of the individual. Bahujan castes were denied access to public spaces, and slaves were denied their very liberty based on nothing beyond who they were. Such wrongs pertain not to what rights people have, but rather who constitutes the demos capable of claiming rights from society. Thus, when I say 'historical wrongs', it is not just about individual bad actions of a few individuals, but social systems and arrangements of identity-based exclusion that go against the idea of human equality and what may be considered a just and fair society.[2]

Unfortunately, the legal system has often played a pivotal role in perpetuating historical wrongs against marginalized social groups. Like in the United States, slavery was legalized in certain parts of India.[3] P. Sanal Mohan, in his book titled *Modernity of Slavery: Struggles against Caste Inequality in Colonial Kerala*,[4] highlights experiences of several oppressed castes, who were enslaved in the erstwhile Indian princely state of Travancore and other states. This slavery was only abolished in 1855. Even before that, the laws in ancient and medieval India had sanctions against the communities, whom we now call the Dalits or the Scheduled Castes.[5] Dr Ambedkar himself highlighted how the policies of the Peshwa regime discriminated against the oppressed castes.[6] The colonial rule was no better in India. The colonial era's Criminal Tribes Act, 1871, criminalized indigenous tribes, several castes and transvestites/transgender persons by declaring them as 'born criminals'. The British colonial courts refused to rule in favour of oppressed castes when it came to matters of personal law and religious customs.[7]

In the US, from the codification of discriminatory laws that supported the institution of slavery to the Jim Crow laws enforcing segregation in the American South,[8] to the forced assimilation policies targeting indigenous peoples,[9] the legal framework has frequently been weaponized to systematically oppress and marginalize certain communities.[10] The judgments of the Supreme Court of the US were regressive on several instances, including *Dred Scott v. Sandford* (1857),[11] *Plessy v. Ferguson* (1896)[12] and *Korematsu v. United States* (1944).[13] Furthermore, both in the US and India, the oppressed communities were denied voting rights for a long time, albeit in India, the Constitution introduced universal adult suffrage from the time it was enacted.

In that way, law as an institution was used to maintain existing power structures and to institutionalize discrimination, leaving a lasting legacy of injustice that continues to shape the lives of these groups. Even when these laws have been eventually overturned or repealed, the legacy of their harm can persist for generations, underscoring the complex and enduring relationship between law and historical wrongs committed against marginalized social groups.

These historical wrongs perpetuate injustice by creating a social system where the marginalized communities are not allowed to rise above their oppression. It creates a kind of self-perpetuating and hierarchical structure of society, which leads to normalization of injustice towards certain groups. This normalization can creep up to the instances where alienation of these communities makes them the *other* in societies.[14] Otherness can create a rift of violence and exclusion of these communities as well.[15]

For instance, historical marginalization leads to exclusion in accumulating resources or capital that ought to be equally distributed in the society. This exclusion leads to difficulty in overcoming marginalization even if there has been a recognition of historical wrongs. Consequently, it becomes imperative for the institutional setup of constitutional democracies to make sure that safeguards to these communities are upheld, and policies are made for the upliftment of these communities. Recognizing these historical injustices underscores the crucial role of legal reform and the need for a just and inclusive legal system to address past wrongs and work toward a more equitable society.

EMANCIPATORY CONSTITUTIONALISM

Remedying historical wrongs ought to be the goal of any constitutional system. This has been emphasized by leaders from the oppressed communities, who interpreted constitutionalism through the lens of social change. Indeed, using the British Constitution at the time and contemporary State constitutions as a baseline, Akhil Amar, a leading scholar of American constitutional law and originalism, outlines the methods through which the American Constitution rejected historical bases for wielding power and exercising franchise, such as hereditary titles and property ownership that were the norm at that time.[16] However, the framers of the United States Constitution failed to remedy the issue of slavery. This was questioned by Frederick Douglass, American abolitionist and social reformer. In a speech before the Scottish Anti-Slavery Society in Glasgow, Scotland, on 28 March 1860, Douglass outlined his views on the American Constitution, and stated:

> I . . . deny that the Constitution guarantees the right to hold property in man and believe that the way to abolish slavery in America is to vote such men into power as well use their powers for the abolition of slavery.[17]

In India, the constitutional imagination of equality was done by Dr Ambedkar. He envisaged a form of constitutionalism that was deeply rooted in democratic principles, social justice and the protection of individual rights.[18] His vision for the Indian Constitution was shaped by his commitment to ending the deeply entrenched social injustices and discriminations prevalent in Indian society.[19] In several of his writings, he advanced a transformative constitutionalism that aimed to address the historical injustices and systemic discrimination faced by the marginalized and oppressed communities in India. His vision was rooted in the principles of equality, social justice and the protection of fundamental rights. In his classic yet undelivered address, which he later published as *Annihilation of Caste* in 1936, he stated: 'If you ask me, my ideal would be a society based on Liberty, Equality, and Fraternity.'[20] Later, Dr Ambedkar brought these values into the language of the Constitution.[21]

Dr Ambedkar tried to institutionalize *social revolution through law*. He believed that a just and inclusive society could be achieved through a robust legal framework that would safeguard the rights and dignity of all citizens, particularly those from historically disadvantaged backgrounds. That is the reason why he held a different approach with the other leaders of Indian independence, who focused on political freedom without addressing social freedoms.[22] He wrote: '[P]olitical reform cannot with impunity take precedence over social reform in the sense of the reconstruction of society . . . [T]he makers of political constitutions must take account of social forces.'[23] Thus, in Dr Ambedkar's conceptualization, the idea of a constitution goes beyond its traditional role as a mere set of rules and principles. It extended the constitution's capacity to liberate and empower marginalized and oppressed groups. The 'emancipatory' idea of the Constitution, which Dr Ambedkar advanced, sought to address historical injustices, challenge systems of discrimination and advance the cause of emancipation and equality.

Furthermore, Dr Ambedkar's constitutionalism aimed at creating a robust framework of checks and balances, where the Constitution would serve as a bulwark against potential abuses of power, ensuring the protection of the rights of all citizens. One of the key aspects of Dr Ambedkar's constitutionalism was the inclusion of affirmative action measures, known as reservations in India, to uplift historically disadvantaged groups. For several decades, he advocated for incorporation of mandatory affirmative action provisions into the Constitution.[24] He believed that such measures would help rectify historical injustices by providing opportunities and representation to the marginalized. He called mandatory affirmative action a form of 'separation of power'.[25]

Today, non-discrimination and affirmative action are often differentiated by references to a negative and a positive form of liberty. Arguments that the state ought to *abstain* from discriminating are distinguished from a positive command or mandate to uplift individuals who have suffered from historical wrongs. It is also argued that affirmative action is fundamentally contrary to the idea of equality, or colour blind equality at the least. In countries such as India where affirmative action is actively pursued, non-discrimination and affirmative action are also differentiated through institutional roles between Parliament and the judiciary. It is argued that it is the court's duty to enforce non-discrimination norms, but mandates for affirmative action are left as questions for elected officials.

However, Dr Ambedkar did not view equality and affirmative action as contradictory. This is because he conceived equality and liberty as intrinsically connected norms.

Notions of negative freedom contemplate freedom *from* interference. However, as republican scholars have argued for centuries, the idea of freedom as the absence of State restrictions fails to recognize the difference between being free *from* interference and being free *to* act.[26] Using the classical Republican example, a slave may never be put in a cage or beaten, but that does not make them free to act. Negative conceptions of freedom characterise liberty as the absence of *episodic* interference, for after all, interference is inherently temporal. When a person is imprisoned, they are not free; when they are released, they are free. However, such negative conceptions of freedom ignore the ongoing deprivations that can arise out of dominating relationships or societal arrangements outside of episodic interferences with liberty. An individual may not be imprisoned, but the social, legal and economic structures that govern their lives may lead to domination on the site of caste, race, gender, disability or economic well-being.

I would submit that Dr Ambedkar took aim at precisely such forms of dominating relations and societal arrangements when seeking to secure freedom. In *Annihilation of Caste*, he characterizes liberty as 'the destruction of the dominion which one man holds over another'. He argued that '[i]f the source of power and dominion is, at any given time or in any given society, social and religious, then social reform and religious reform must be accepted as the necessary sort of reform'.[27] That is, even where domination is the result of actions by non-State actors or structural societal arrangements, liberty is at risk and must be remedied by the State. After all, liberty does not mean liberty to discriminate.

By characterizing liberty as *relational*, not episodic, Dr Ambedkar conceived of liberty and equality as two sides of the same coin. For him, ensuring liberty required ensuring that every person in a society had sufficient standing that they were not dominated, whether that be through economic, social or religious power. Unlike narrower conceptions of liberty that seek solely to prevent episodic State intervention, conceiving of freedom as non-domination allows the very site of State intervention to be liberty-*generating*, by eradicating sources of dominating power. Thus, Dr Ambedkar conceived of a reformative movement that was simultaneously interventionist yet liberty-enhancing.

This is not to say that Dr Ambedkar ignored the risks of excessive State intervention. His vision also encompassed the establishment of an independent judiciary that would serve as a guardian of the Constitution, interpreting and upholding its principles. He famously called Article 32, which grants citizens the right to approach the Supreme Court for enforcement of their fundamental rights, as the 'heart and soul of the Constitution'.[28]

While his vision of constitutionalism emphasized the protection of fundamental rights, it regarded the pursuit of social equality and justice as crucial to India's democratic framework. The Indian Constitution in 1950 incorporated a set of fundamental rights, such as the right to equality, the right to freedom from discrimination and the right to equal protection under the law. Apart from affirmative action, the most important impact of Dr Ambedkar's formulation was Article 17,[29] which abolishes untouchability and was placed in the chapter on fundamental rights, along with the provisions of equality and non-discrimination. It was hoped that these provisions would break the shackles of caste-based discrimination and untouchability, fostering a more equitable and harmonious society.

After its adoption, the Indian Constitution has interacted with the society in different ways.

THE IMPACT OF THE INDIAN CONSTITUTION

The 'social life' of a constitution refers to how a constitution functions within a society, its impact on the daily lives of citizens, how citizens perceive it, and its adaptability to changing social, political and cultural dynamics. The phrase 'social life' recognizes that a constitution is not just a static legal document, but a living framework that interacts with and shapes the social and political environment in which it operates. In essence, the social life of a constitution is about how the constitution functions within the broader context of a society, impacting not only the legal and political spheres but also the cultural, economic and social aspects of citizens' lives. It reflects the dynamic and evolving nature of constitutional governance as it responds to the needs and values of the people it serves.

The adoption of the Indian Constitution was seen as a moment of tectonic shift in Indian history. American historian Granville Austin travelled to India to document the process of drafting India's Constitution. In his classic book *The Indian Constitution: Cornerstone of a Nation*, Austin termed the Indian Constitution 'a social revolutionary statement', '*by its very existence*'—'a modernizing force'.[30] Austin narrated, and I quote:

> Representative government with adult suffrage, a bill of rights providing for equality under the law and personal liberty, and an independent judiciary were to become the spiritual and institutional bases for a new society—one replacing the traditional hierarchy and its repressions. Other constitutional provisions were designed to spread democracy by protecting and increasing the rights of minorities, by assisting underprivileged groups in society to better their condition, and by ending the blatant oppression of the Scheduled Castes and Tribes. These

> provisions have brought into, or closer to, the mainstream of society individuals and groups that would otherwise have remained at society's bottom or its edges.[31]

In that sense, the Constitution attempted to replace fundamental wrongs with fundamental rights. Affirmative action and representation were crucial components of constitutional foundations laid down in India. As mentioned earlier, Dr Ambedkar fought tooth and nail to get the provisions on affirmative action incorporated into the Indian Constitution. It was Dr Ambedkar's belief that the oppressed should have their own representation, and that representation would develop political conscience among these communities.[32] Dr Ambedkar stated that if British colonial rule over Indians was morally wrong, then in the same way, the rule of oppressor castes over the oppressed was equally wrong.[33] This again highlights Dr Ambedkar's idea of freedom as relational. He saw no difference between the actions of a colonial power in jailing political prisoners and the denial of access to public resources by oppressor castes. What mattered was the dominating relationship between the two individuals concerned. While the British departed in 1947, the dominating effects of caste oppression subsisted.

Since Independence, affirmative action policies in India have offered crucial support to oppressed social groups by providing them with opportunities for education, employment and representation that might otherwise be inaccessible due to deeply entrenched inequalities. As noted in the judgment of the Supreme Court of India in *Indra Sawhney v. Union of India*:[34] 'Objective was to change the social face as it shall advance public welfare, by demolishing rigidity of caste, promoting representation of those who till now were kept away thus providing status to them, restoring balance in the society, reducing poverty and increasing distribution of benefits and advantages to one and all.'

In theory as well as in practice, these policies serve as a means to level the playing field, granting access to opportunities that may have been systematically denied in the past. By actively including underrepresented individuals in education and employment sectors, affirmative action helps break down barriers. It develops a psychological assurance that individuals from marginalized backgrounds have a shot at achieving their full potential and contributing to the collective well-being of the community.

Looking at the statistics, the representation of constitutionally protected social groups (called Scheduled Castes and Scheduled Tribes) has increased in the government services under the various categories during the last seven decades. At the dawn of Independence, the representation of Scheduled Castes and Scheduled Tribes in services was very little.[35] As per available information, as on 1 January 1965, the representation of SCs in Groups A of government services (which are top-level bureaucratic) was just 1.64 per cent, which has increased to 13.21 per cent as on 1 January 2022. Likewise, while representation of STs as on 1 January 1965 in Group A was 0.27 per cent, it has increased to 6.01 per cent as on 1 January 2022.[36] This is the direct impact of the Constitution. The presence of marginalized communities in services, education, etc., is in itself realization of the constitutional mandate.

This is how the social presence of oppressed communities demonstrates the success of the social life of the Constitution, in the way that it is being implemented. Furthermore, the oppressed communities in India used the vocabulary of the Indian Constitution, with the focus on equality and affirmative action, to mobilise and reclaim their sense of dignity.[37] The Constitution of India legitimized the obvious personhood of the oppressed communities.

This was one way to facilitate and empower individuals from marginalized backgrounds to break free from cycles of oppression and helps in rectifying historical injustices. Moreover, it sends a clear message that society is committed to correcting systemic biases and working towards greater equality, ultimately fostering a more just and inclusive environment for all.

LIMITS OF DEBATES AROUND AFFIRMATIVE ACTION

However, mere presence of members of oppressed groups in government services must not be seen as the only parameter to analyse the power structures of society. Let's take the example of a press release, which stated: 'the representation of Scheduled Castes, Scheduled Tribes . . . in the posts and services under the Central Government, as on 01 January 2016, was 17.49%, 8.47% . . . respectively. Representation of SCs and STs is more than the prescribed percentage of reservation (15% and 7.5%, respectively).'[38] However, this press release does not mention how many SCs are in top decision-making positions in government and how many in lowest-level positions. The real question, therefore, is what the representation of SCs and STs in top positions is. The statistics show that out of a total of 322 officers currently holding the posts of joint secretaries and secretaries, which are top-level bureaucratic services, in different ministries/departments under Government of India, only sixteen belong to SCs, which is 4.9 per cent of total posts, and only thirteen belong to STS, which is only 4 per cent.[39] These statistics show that focusing only on the total number of employees, rather than examining how many SCs and STs hold top positions, is misleading. Reformation beyond representation entails ensuring that marginalized and underrepresented communities not only have a seat at the table but also have a meaningful voice in decision-making processes.

There is also a concern that in spaces where representation is not legally mandated, representation must not be confused with diversity. It has been stated by scholars that the sole focus on diversity can lead to tokenism, where individuals from under-represented groups are viewed as symbols of diversity rather than being valued for their skills and qualifications. This can undermine their professional and personal growth. Ellen Berrey, through his book *The Enigma of Diversity: The Language of Race and the Limits of Racial Justice*,[40] has struck a chord of caution that the invocation of 'diversity' must not be reduced to tokenism. She argues that 'diversity advocates' efforts to minimize group divisions and expand the bounds of social membership have focused on symbolism more than on social causes. Much discourse on diversity leaves advocates without a language for talking about inequality.'[41] Diversity therefore needs to be understood from the perspective of representation and social discrimination. Institutions need to be more diverse because communities that have been subjected to historical discrimination are underrepresented. Thus, as in India, historical wrongs form an independent justification for affirmative action irrespective of considerations of diversity.

The idea of representation through affirmative action must be facilitated by discourse on broader systemic issues, such as unequal access to quality education for everyone. Affirmative action in itself cannot solve the issue of universal education; rather, it is connected to the latter. When a greater number of people from oppressed groups would gain education, their presence in institutions through affirmative action will increase. That is when the full potential of affirmative action would be seen. Thus, social reformation involves dismantling systemic barriers and addressing structural inequalities. This could encompass reforms in education, healthcare, criminal justice and economic systems that have historically disadvantaged certain groups.

Furthermore, even the slightest success of affirmative action is used by the caste elites to dismiss the issues around caste inequalities. Arguments are advanced that just because affirmative action is being provided, structural issues of discrimination don't exist anymore. Such binary narrations must be rejected. Affirmative action and prevention of caste discrimination in India or racial discrimination or remedying different forms of injustices are complementary to each other. They are not different poles; rather, they are intersecting phenomena. That is to say, social transformation requires several different measures at the same time. Therefore, apart from emphasizing solely on affirmative action and representation, the constitutional and social discourse must also engage in reflecting on a wider range of methods to remedy historical wrongs.

Reformation beyond representation means that the mere presence of diverse groups within a political or administrative system is not enough. That it extends to a deeper transformation of power dynamics, policies and social structures is what matters. It emphasizes the need for substantive change in the way societies and governments operate. It is in this context of reformation that the Constitution plays a crucial role.

POTENTIAL OF THE CONSTITUTION

A broader framework of constitutionalism underscores the transformative potential of constitutional law to promote social justice and human rights. This approach often involves interpreting and applying constitutional provisions in ways that actively work to correct historical wrongs and to promote a more inclusive and equitable society, thereby serving as a vital tool for social progress and the realization of fundamental rights.

After Independence, there are several judgments of the Supreme Court of India, which challenge structural barriers. I would like to mention a few recent judgments. The court in *Navtej Singh Johar v. Union of India*,[42] decriminalized consensual sexual conduct between individuals of the same sex. The court noted that '[t]he ability of a society to acknowledge the injustices which it has perpetuated is a mark of its evolution'. It was further held that '[f]or those who have been oppressed, justice under a regime committed to human freedom, has the power to transform lives', and that the Constitution 'has within it the ability to produce a social catharsis'.

In another important judgment in *Indian Young Lawyers Association and Ors v. The State of Kerala and Ors*,[43] while deciding a case of exclusion of women from the Sabarimala Temple due to a long-standing religious practice, the court held that discriminatory practices cannot be allowed merely due to it being a custom. Even though the case has been pending for reconsideration, it is important to note that the judgment acknowledged that the Constitution of India is the 'end product' of not just struggle against colonial rule, but also a struggle of social emancipation going on for centuries that still continues. This struggle of emancipation, the court noted, 'has been the struggle for the replacement of an unequal social order' and 'a fight for undoing historical injustices and for righting fundamental wrongs with fundamental rights'.

A challenge to an affirmative action policy was adjudicated in *B.K. Pavitra v. Union of India*.[44] In deciding the case, the court observed that '[f]or equality to be truly effective or substantive, the principle must recognize existing inequalities in society to overcome them', and that reservations or affirmative action policies are 'the true fulfilment of effective and substantive equality by accounting for the structural conditions into which people are born'.

In another case titled *Babita Puniya v. Secretary, Ministry of Defence*,[45] the Supreme Court of India ruled in favour of granting Permanent Commission to women officers in the Indian Army at par with their male colleagues. Pursuant to the judgment, the Indian Army applied the same physical evaluation criteria that a male officer would have to pass to get Permanent Commission to women officers. This was challenged before the Supreme Court in the case of *Lt Col Nitisha v. Union of India*.[46] The court held that applying identical physical evaluation criteria to both women and men constituted indirect and systemic discrimination against women officers. The court held that 'a systemic view of discrimination, in perceiving discriminatory disadvantage as a continuum, would account for not just unjust action but also inaction' and that '[s]tructures, in the form of organizations or otherwise' ought to 'be probed for the systems or cultures they produce that influence day-to-day interaction and decision-making.' It was held that '[t]he duty of constitutional courts' is 'also to structure adequate reliefs and remedies that facilitate social redistribution by providing for positive entitlements that aim to negate the scope of future harm'.

Taking note of the oppression against the Scheduled Castes and Scheduled Tribes, the court in *Hariram Bhambhi v. Satyanarayan*,[47] while adjudicating a bail matter of a person who was accused of committing caste-based violence, held that:

> Atrocities against members of the Scheduled Castes and Scheduled Tribes are not a thing of the past. They continue to be a reality in our society even today. Hence the statutory provisions which have been enacted by Parliament as a measure of protecting the constitutional rights of persons belonging to the Scheduled Castes and Scheduled Tribes must be complied with and enforced conscientiously.

These judgments show the transformative potential of the constitution and the active role of courts. However, it would not be wrong to say that judgments such as the above are not always the case. Some of the judgments have been criticized for being regressive and have been overturned for the right reasons.[48]

SOCIAL LAW V. CONSTITUTIONAL LAW

The arguments in courtrooms also demonstrate that there is a constant tussle between constitutional aspects of the law and entrenched social practices. We can understand this as the gap between the aspirational values of the Constitution and the social realities of the day. Dr Ambedkar had termed 'social practices' as a *law within itself*, imposing social sanctions and violence on those who do not comply.[49] Thus, in addition to the constitutional and legal sovereignty that governs people, there also resides a governing power in various social and cultural institutions that determines how people live their lives.

While constitutional principles often embody ideals of justice, equality and human rights, deeply ingrained social norms and practices can sometimes run counter to these principles. This clash is particularly evident in cases involving issues like gender equality, religious freedom and caste discrimination. For instance, despite constitutional guarantees of gender equality, deeply rooted patriarchal customs may persist, leading to gender-based discrimination and violence. Similarly, despite legislations prohibiting caste-based discrimination, incidents of violence against the protected communities are on the rise.[50]

Courts and legal systems often find themselves at the centre of this tension, as they must interpret and apply the law in a manner that respects constitutional principles. This challenge calls for a nuanced approach, including legal reforms, public education and advocacy efforts, aimed at shifting societal norms in alignment with constitutional ideals. It is an ongoing struggle to ensure that constitutional principles are upheld even in the face of deeply entrenched practices that may hinder progress towards a more just and equitable society.

CONSTITUTION OUTSIDE COURTROOMS

For social reformation to happen, the discourse needs to extend beyond the courtrooms and judges. This is why the topic of my address contains the phrase 'social life of the Constitution'. Of course, the Constitution is 'a terrain of struggle'.[51] But, lawyers arguing in courts are not saviours in themselves or operate in a vacuum. They build upon the work of the scholars, community leaders and activists, and all other stakeholders. The role of the citizens in constitutional adjudication has to be highlighted.

As Issa G. Shivji, a Tanzanian author and expert in law, notes, it must be acknowledged that: '[L]egal struggles are only one front of the social struggles of the working people. Therefore, they cannot be waged in isolation from other battlefronts.'[52] He adds that other sites of struggle include mobilization among people.[53] Constitutional historian and scholar Michael Klarman notes that several civil rights lawyers did work outside the courtroom in educating the African American community about their rights under the American Constitution.[54]

In India, right from the adoption of the Constitution, the people of India have engaged with it in different ways. While one set of elites critique the Constitution as a document of foreign inspirations, the oppressed social groups have used the language of the Constitution to demand their rights.[55]

The social life of the Constitution in that sense is not in courtrooms, but in how the values of the Constitution are perceived by society. For instance, the enormous amount of literature produced by writers from Dalit or Adivasi communities takes the constitutional discourse to the masses. In this regard, I would like to mention some of the writings.

Prominent Dalit women authors, such as Urmila Pawar and Babytai Kamble, have highlighted the struggles of their communities, providing a foundation for understanding the complexities of caste, class, gender and power structures in Indian society. Contemporary Tamil writer Bama, in her autobiographical novel *Karukku* (1992), has chronicled the joys and sorrows experienced by Dalit women in Tamil Nadu. In that way, these writers have shown a mirror about how discrimination works.

A scholar from America and later settled in India, Gail Omvedt documented the movement of Dalits in a constitutional democracy.[56] Baburao Bagul shared his lived experiences as a Dalit in his Marathi book called *Jevha Mi Jaat Chorli Hoti* (translated in English as *When I Hid My Caste*, 1963). A significant work has been of Om Prakash Valmiki, whose autobiography is titled *Jhoothan*. The word 'jhoothan' refers to scraps of food left on a plate, destined for the garbage or animals. India's oppressed castes, who were treated as untouchables, were forced to accept and eat jhoothan for centuries, and the word in Valmiki's book encapsulates the pain, humiliation and poverty of a community forced to live at the bottom of India's social pyramid. Although untouchability was abolished in 1949, Dalits continue to face discrimination, economic deprivation, violence and ridicule. This is what has been narrated by Valmiki, when he describes his life as untouchable.[57]

The writings, as mentioned above, present a lived experience of constitutionalism, as the experience of law is not in a vacuum. The writings show the constant clash between the social realities and the aspired experience of equality under the Constitution.

Several Indian movies have also portrayed references to the Indian Constitution and its principles, reflecting its significance in the country's social and political fabric. Such films touch upon various aspects of Indian society and its relationship with the Constitution, highlighting the ongoing dialogues and struggles that revolve around constitutional principles and values.[58] They offer a thought-provoking perspective on how the Constitution influences the lives of ordinary citizens and the complexities of its implementation in the diverse Indian context.

However, for reformation to happen, the initiative is needed not from those who have been oppressed, but from those who have been oppressors. The society therefore needs a collective agenda, where the power of the historical oppressors is constantly questioned. In the context of the Constitution, this involves a scrutiny of legal practices, which perpetuate discrimination and discrimination.

A RADICAL AGENDA OF CONSTITUTIONALISM

The society must therefore adopt a radical agenda through constitutional means, where structures of discrimination are targeted. We already have certain theoretical frameworks to analyse the broader structures of inequalities.

In the US, scholars of critical race theory (CRT) have rejected the philosophy of 'colour blindness'. They have highlighted the persistence of 'stark racial disparities' in the US, despite decades of civil rights reforms. They raise structural questions about how racist hierarchies are enforced, even in seemingly neutral institutions. According to Kimberlé Crenshaw, one of the founders of CRT, history and social reality show that racism operates in American law and culture in many aspects.[59] Devon Carbado, a CRT scholar, argues that racial progress is not linear; rather, there have been setbacks that undo that progress. According to Carbado, 'CRT repudiates the view that status quo arrangements are the natural result of individual agency and merit.' He argues, 'We all inherit advantages and disadvantages, including the historically accumulated social effects of race. This racial accumulation—which is economic (shaping both our income and wealth), cultural (shaping the social capital upon which we can draw), and ideological (shaping our perceived racial worth)—structure our life chances. CRT exposes these inter-generational transfers of racial compensation.'[60]

Similarly, in India, there has been an attempt by scholars to conceptualize the framework of 'critical caste studies'. Anthropologist and historian Gajendran Ayyathurai argues, 'In Critical Caste Studies, the history of caste hegemony and the archives of the oppressed as well as caste-free and anti-caste memories and histories of Indian societies are a Central concern.'[61] Historian and theorist Shailaja Paik conceptualizes an anti-caste 'critical pedagogy', which centres the interconnections between caste, class, 'public' institutions such as education, and 'private' realms like the family, gender, desire, marriage and sexuality from the vantage point of stigmatized Dalit women.[62]

Another scholar has argued, 'Dr Babasaheb Ambedkar's writings provide a framework to understand the pre-colonial foundations that led to colonial and post-colonial criminalisation of certain communities.'[63] Dr Ambedkar had focused on the value of 'Fraternity', which he termed as 'another name for democracy'. Fraternity means mutual respect for each other. Fraternity can only be achieved, if the dignity of everyone is recognized. India has enacted several legislations which aim to protect the dignity of the oppressed communities.

Such frameworks are necessary for expanding the discourse on constitutionalism. In that sense, the social life of the Constitution is about fostering a culture of inclusion, equity and empathy. It encourages society to challenge stereotypes and prejudices and cultivate a more profound understanding of the experiences of all its members. It is a call to action to actively combat discrimination, bias and exclusion in all aspects of life, promoting a more just and harmonious society that transcends mere numerical representation to create a genuinely equitable and inclusive future. Contemporary notions of justice emphasize equitable distribution of resources, inclusivity, and the protection of marginalized groups.

CONCLUSION

In conclusion, I would refer to the philosophy of Dr Ambedkar. His idea of constitutionalism was instrumental in transforming Indian society by dismantling the deeply entrenched caste hierarchy and promoting social, economic and political empowerment for marginalized groups. His legacy continues to shape the constitutional values of modern India, serving as a beacon for social reform and the pursuit of justice for all. As a corollary, the social life of any constitution goes beyond tokenism and necessitates active engagement, active listening, and taking the perspectives and concerns of oppressed communities seriously. It means acknowledging the unique experiences and challenges faced by these groups and incorporating their input into policy development and implementation.

As Dr Ambedkar said, 'However good a Constitution may be, it is sure to turn out bad because those who are called to work it, happen to be a bad lot. However bad a Constitution may be, it may turn out to be good if those who are called to work it, happen to be a good lot.'[64]

I hope that the conversation on combating inequalities continues, and we all collaborate to make it happen.

29

Revisiting Penal Philosophy

Reformative Justice in India[1]

I am delighted and honoured to speak on the occasion of the birth anniversary of Justice V.R. Krishna Iyer. In many ways, Justice Krishna Iyer represents the indomitable spirit of India—a spirit that speaks truth to power, looks out for the underprivileged, gives voice to the voiceless and is conscious of social hierarchies and prejudice. Justice Krishna Iyer was a person of many hues. He carried the rich legacy of having been an MLA, a Cabinet minister, a member of the Law Commission, a judge and a social activist.

But these titles only tell you what Justice Krishna Iyer did; *they don't tell you why*. Growing up in colonial India, Justice Krishna Iyer learnt two things from his father—(i) to think of the community around him; and (ii) to use the law for the benefit of those who needed it the most.[2] His life is an embodiment of these principles.

> Our legal system, including the police is anti-Dalit, and anti-poor . . . The law barks at all but bites only the poor, the powerless, the illiterate, the ignorant.[3]

His courage and commitment to justice cannot be divorced from his understanding of the people of India and its marginalized citizens.

When I was invited to deliver this lecture, I thought about the remarkable life that Justice Krishna Iyer lived and the topic that might befit his rich contributions to law and society. Naturally, his contributions cannot be summarized in one lecture. However, the theme of social justice and emancipation runs through every stage of Justice Krishna Iyer's life.

Justice Krishna Iyer contributed to the development of constitutional law, labour laws, personal laws and criminal law in India. In my opinion, one of his important contributions is his strong commitment to reformative justice which brimmed through his judgments and personal philosophy. In his book *Access to Justice: A Case for Basic Change*, Justice Krishna Iyer said that:

> The criminal law in India is not victim oriented and the suffering of the victim, often immeasurable, is entirely overlooked in misplaced sympathy for the criminal. Though our modern criminal law is designed to punish as well as reform the criminals, yet it overlooks the by-product of crime i.e. the victims.[4]

Reformative justice has championed the cause of victims like no other approach to criminal justice. It asks questions like: What is the harm? What was the impact of that harm? How can that harm be remedied? These questions require a response from the person who has been harmed before the process can move forward. The person who suffers harm shapes the restorative conversation by defining the harm and the needs arising from that harm.[5]

However, our attitude towards crime has been unfortunate. Crime in its most normative sense is a morally reprehensible act, which is punishable by law. This sense of morality, however, is socially constructed and allows the prejudices of our society to percolate into law. We can see examples of this throughout our legal history—from criminalization of nomadic tribes and transgender persons under the Criminal Tribes Act, 1871, to anti-sodomy law and adultery provisions under the Indian Penal Code. These provisions trespassed over the dignity and autonomy of people under the name of criminal statute.

Reformative justice allows us to reimagine the possibilities of a society where we retain our humanity and that of a person who has committed a crime. At its core, it is built on *informality and flexibility*, offering a compelling alternative to our traditional criminal justice system. As Professor of Philosophy Linda Radzik suggests, adopting a restorative justice paradigm allows us to establish a moral advantage over the conventional criminal justice system.[6] It acknowledges that the wrongdoers possess moral responsibilities, affirming their status as agents and not mere objects. This is fundamental to treating them with the respect that all humans inherently deserve.

Although it is crucial to integrate restorative justice into our legal system, the real challenge emerges after offenders are released, as they struggle to reintegrate into society. They often lack self-respect, economic opportunities and face the social stigma of imprisonment, increasing the risk of recidivism. One example of this is the fact that there are express rules and regulations denying government jobs to those who have been previously convicted for a crime. Some of these rules even deny opportunities to those who are undergoing trial. Such is the tragedy of our prejudice against criminals that, in effect, we penalize innocent citizens who are undertrials and convicted criminals who have paid their dues under the law.

This also reminds me of a poignant moment from the movie *The Shawshank Redemption*, where a character, Brooks Hatlen, is released from prison after spending five decades behind bars. Despite his freedom, he finds himself overwhelmed by the outside world, unable to cope with the changes and feeling like a stranger in a society that has moved on without him. Like Brooks, many released prisoners face an uphill battle when they attempt to reintegrate into a world that has transformed during their time in confinement. The current punitive model, with its emphasis on punishment rather than rehabilitation, often fails to address the complex needs of these individuals. Restorative justice, with its focus on reformation and reintegration, offers a more promising approach to help these individuals regain their place in society and become contributing members once more. By addressing the root causes of criminal behaviour and offering support for rehabilitation, we can pave the way for a more just and inclusive society.

In this context, it is essential that we shift our perspective from solely focusing on the past actions of convicts to prioritizing their future and reformation. This future-oriented approach is at the heart of restorative justice. We have two methods to respond to crime: one is to maintain a hostile attitude towards the offender and punish them; while the other recognizes the social and individual breakdown that may have contributed to the offence and seeks to rebuild lives for a better future. The former is simply the old wine of retribution in a new bottle, while the latter, restorative justice, is a genuine and reformative approach.

Albert Eglash describes justice as 'the first mile', involving punishment or reparations, but this does not fully redeem the situation.[7] The 'second mile', represented by restorative justice, encompasses a complete restoration of goodwill and harmony. Restorative justice encourages offenders to empathize with the victim, make amends and embark on comprehensive rehabilitation, emphasizing personal freedom and social recognition. It invites them to become contributing members of society, fostering a sense of redemption crucial for lasting change.

Justice Krishna Iyer was far ahead of his time in espousing these techniques and verbalizing them in his judicial thought. The profound influence of his formative years shaped the doyen of civil liberties that we know today. As a young advocate in Malabar, he protested against police torture during interrogations. Consequently, he was imprisoned for a month on a fabricated charge of providing legal assistance to communists.[8]

These experiences shaped Justice Krishna Iyer's understanding of bail, imprisonment of undertrials and victim compensation. He truly believed that 'the issue of Bail is one of liberty, justice, and public safety, all of which require a developed jurisprudence of and a socially sensitised judicial process.'[9] The case *State of Rajasthan v.*

Balchand[10] etched his judicial philosophy in India's law on bail by declaring that 'bail is the rule, and jail is the exception'. On the same lines, Justice Krishna Iyer believed in the humanity which inheres in all people and believed parole to be a surety to the reformation of a convict. In *Rattan Singh v. State of Punjab,*[11] he allowed prisoners' temporary release and demonstrated a commitment to facilitating their social reformation.

One can identify the constitutional beginnings of victimology in Justice Krishna Iyer's perspective. Victimology, in the context of restorative justice, is the study of the experiences, needs and rights of victims within the criminal justice system. This field delves into understanding how the justice system can better respond to the needs of victims, fostering a more inclusive and compassionate approach.

Emilio Viano, a renowned scholar, in his book *Critical Issues of Victimology*[12] has passionately argued for a victim-centred approach, emphasizing that the justice system should prioritize the rights and well-being of victims above all else.[13] On the other side of the debate, Professor Marc Groenhuijsen, a scholar of victimology, has advocated for a more balanced perspective, arguing that restorative justice should seek a fair reconciliation of interests between victims and offenders.[14] He contends that while victims' rights and needs are crucial, a restorative framework should also consider the rights and potential for rehabilitation of the offenders.

This brings into focus another element of restorative justice—victim compensation. The Supreme Court has been instrumental in introducing victim compensation into Indian criminal law from the time when there was no specialized legislation for victim restitution in India. It incorporated the principles of restorative justice and compensation to the victims of crime. In the case of *Rudul Sah v. State of Bihar*,[15] the Supreme Court set a significant precedent by affirming its power to award compensation for violations of fundamental rights. It awarded Rs 35,000 as compensation to Rudul Sah, who had been held in jail for fourteen years, even after his acquittal on the grounds of insanity.

In this context, it is essential to connect the earlier discussion on victimology and the debates surrounding it with the introduction of victim compensation in the legal system. Scholars such as Andrew von Hirsch have debated the role of victim compensation in restorative justice.[16] Some argue that it can be a valuable tool for acknowledging the harm done to victims and promoting their healing and recovery. However, others raise concerns about whether compensation is a sufficient response to the harm caused and whether it can truly restore the victim's sense of agency and participation in the justice process. Balancing the rights and needs of victims with the rights and potential for rehabilitation of offenders remains an ongoing challenge in the implementation of victim compensation within a restorative justice framework.

In *Sarwan Singh v. State of Punjab*,[17] the Supreme Court held that factors such as the accused's capacity to pay, the nature of the crime and the extent of the victim's suffering ought to be considered while awarding compensation. Recently, in regard to the gruesome rape case that took place in Hathras, we were confronted with a special leave petition (SLP) challenging the judgment of the Allahabad High Court, which ordered the state government to consider giving a job to a family member of the victim and to relocate the family from Hathras.[18] The High Court had propounded a reformative approach by prioritizing the needs of those who have been directly harmed by a criminal act. We therefore had no choice but to dismiss the SLP at the threshold.

Compensation should not be seen as an alternative to conviction but necessarily as an additional measure. This approach acknowledges the evolving legal landscape in India, which seeks to strike a balance between addressing the needs of victims and the goals of restorative justice for the offender.

Justice Krishna Iyer was also a staunch critic of the death penalty. His critique aligned with his recommendation that meditation methods of Yoga should be practised by prisoners as a means to reform and restore them from criminal tendencies. In *Rajendra Prasad Etc. Etc. v. State of UP*,[19] he highlighted the constitutional culture's benevolent shift away from the death penalty, and stated that:

> Yoga in its many forms seems to hold splendid answers. Meditational technology as a tool of criminology is a nascent—ancient methodology. The State must experiment. *It is cheaper to hang than to heal, but Indian life—any human life—is too dear to be swung dead,* save in extreme circumstances.[20]

This thought brings to mind an interaction that I heard of a prison official who shared a fascinating story. A group of prisoners attempted to incorporate yoga into their daily routine within the prison walls. One day, during their meditation session, a mischievous squirrel found its way into the room and created quite a commotion. It scurried around, causing the prisoners to break their serene silence with fits of laughter. This incident served as a reminder that even in the most unexpected places, a touch of humour can lighten the path to reform and restoration. As Professor Albus Dumbledore from the Harry Potter series said, 'Happiness can be found, even in the darkest of times, if one only remembers to turn on the light.' We only have to create conditions for them to find it.

In *Dalbir Singh & Ors v. State of Punjab*,[21] Justice Krishna Iyer presciently noted that the interface of the constitutional culture with sentencing practices resembled Cinderella. He observed:

> . . . [T]he jurisprudence of sentencing in Free India has been a Cinderella and the values of our Constitution have not adequately humanized the punitive diagnostics of criminal courts, which sometimes, though rarely, remind us of the torturesome and trigger-happy aberrations of the Middle Ages and some gory geographic segments, soaked in retributive blood and untouched by the correctional karuna of our constitutional culture.

Justice Krishna Iyer passionately urged for the embrace of a humane spirit by the legal system; a spirit which values human life and rejects the notion that human beings are dispensable in the name of justice.

We have made many strides in the recent past at the Supreme Court. In 2014, in *Mohd. Arif @ Ashfaq v. Supreme Court of India*,[22] the court laid down that only a bench of three judges shall hear a death penalty appeal before the Supreme Court. Further, review petitions arising out of death penalty cases must be afforded an oral hearing in open court.

The peculiar history of the death penalty, its disproportionate effect on people from the marginalized communities and its irreversibility have made it imperative that the death penalty is placed under the careful gaze of the courts. In *Manoj v. State of MP*,[23] the court made it mandatory for trial courts to call for psychiatric and psychological evaluation reports of the accused before awarding capital punishment. We also cannot alienate a convict's criminality with their conduct in jail, and their previous and current family background. Crime is a social construct. While its impacts and brutalities are felt in material terms, we have an obligation to mitigate the convicts' conduct against their circumstances.

I vividly recall a case that came before us in March 2023, where we exercised our review jurisdiction in open court to commute the death penalty given to a person convicted of kidnapping and murdering a seven-year-old.[24] This case was undeniably gruesome, but it reiterated the principle that the death penalty should only be granted when there is no possibility of reformation in a criminal. Justice Krishna Iyer's wisdom and insights continue to guide us in our pursuit of a more compassionate and humane criminal justice system.

In India, there is also a concerted effort to integrate reformative ideals into our criminal justice system, reflecting a notable shift towards rehabilitative approaches and the exploration of alternatives to custodial sentences. The formal legal system in India has witnessed a growing emphasis on alternative dispute-resolution mechanisms, such as mediation, conciliation, arbitration, negotiation and Lok

Adalats. These mechanisms have gained prominence within our legal system, aiming to reach mutually beneficial solutions through informal settings, circumventing the intricacies of conventional court proceedings.

Interestingly, this journey towards restorative justice is not a new concept. It has been a part of the Indian social fabric for centuries, albeit informally. One fascinating example is the role of gram panchayats in villages, where community leaders and elders come together to mediate and resolve disputes. These grassroots institutions play a pivotal role in promoting reconciliation and rebuilding relationships within the community. This informal tradition serves as an early example of restorative practices in India, emphasizing the importance of community involvement in resolving conflicts.

A well-founded criticism of these systems is that these replicate the prejudices of our society. We still hear of biased statements being made to victims from marginalized communities and women. The process itself might be unsafe, giving those who have done harm access to their victims to do further physical or emotional damage. The likelihood of an unsafe process is exacerbated if the restorative facilitator lacks training and sensitivity. In one case, I was appalled to learn that the abuser who had committed sexual assault was asked to tie a *rakhi* (a thread signifying a fraternal bond) to his victim as a sign of goodwill. This clearly neither holds the abuser accountable nor does it allow the victim to reclaim her agency.

However, reformative justice can also facilitate better reconciliation to the victim by listening to their voice, empowering them, lending them a community and ultimately dismantling oppressive structures of patriarchy, casteism and homophobia, to name a few. As John Braithwaite, the emeritus professor at Australian National University of criminology and restorative justice, writes in *Restorative Justice and Responsive Regulation*, '[A]n underestimated way restorative justice might confer power upon the disenfranchised is simply by listening to their stories and taking them seriously.'[25]

Attiya Khan, maker of the documentary *A Better Man* (2017), recounted her experience confronting her abuser from intimate partner violence. Khan describes the meeting:

> The feeling of being able to tell him 'You hit me and you strangled me and you dragged me on the floor. You [are] the reason my knee has a scar' . . . It was huge.[26]

Now, I want to acknowledge that the adoption of restorative justice is not without its debates and challenges, even from a feminist perspective. Prominent feminist scholars have raised critical concerns regarding the application of restorative justice, particularly in cases of sexual violence.[27] They argue that this approach may inadvertently pressure victims into reconciliation, potentially compromising their autonomy and justice.[28]

Catherine MacKinnon, noted feminist theorist and law professor, for example, has highlighted the power imbalances in many gender-based violence cases and has expressed concerns about re-traumatizing survivors through face-to-face encounters with their offenders.[29] Kathleen Daly, another scholar, has stressed the need for restorative justice to acknowledge the systemic nature of gender-based violence and the importance of holding offenders accountable in a manner that does not undermine the survivor's experience.[30]

These debates within feminist perspectives add nuance to the discussion surrounding restorative justice, underscoring the need for careful consideration and adaptation to ensure that the approach is sensitive to the unique challenges of addressing violence.

When we consider the application of restorative justice to domestic violence victims in India, we find that it's a particularly complex issue. In a country where domestic violence remains a pervasive problem, restorative justice offers a potential avenue for healing and resolution. However, it must be approached with great care. The UN Office on Drugs and Crime in its *Handbook on Restorative Justice* highlights the challenges and complexities involved in using restorative justice in cases of intimate partner violence.[31]

This study points out that the dynamics of intimate partner violence create particular challenges for the practice of restorative justice, especially concerning safety and voluntary participation.[32] In cases of domestic violence, ensuring the safety and autonomy of survivors is paramount. Therefore, it is crucial to adapt restorative justice principles to the specific needs of domestic violence victims in India, all in a manner that aligns with international best practices.

For restorative justice to be effective in this context, it should prioritise the safety and autonomy of survivors while ensuring that offenders are held accountable for their actions. In this process, there is a need to involve skilled facilitators who can navigate the complexities of power dynamics and emotions involved in domestic violence cases. The goal should be to empower survivors, allowing them to make informed decisions about their own healing and justice.

So, while the debates and challenges surrounding restorative justice, especially in cases of gender-based violence, are complex, they underline the importance of an adaptable and survivor-centred approach. When applied sensitively and with a deep understanding of the unique challenges faced by victims, restorative justice can play a crucial role in fostering healing, empowerment and justice for survivors of domestic violence in India.

As we transition towards a restorative justice system in India, it is imperative to lay the groundwork for these transformative changes. This involves a reassessment of our legal framework in the realm of criminal justice, including the re-categorization of crimes and the process of decriminalization, aligning our approach with the principles of rehabilitation and reconciliation.

I would like to emphasize that the path towards a more restorative justice system in India is not without its hurdles and debates. However, it is a path worth treading. As we stand at the crossroads of tradition and transformation, let us remember that the true measure of a just society is how it treats its most vulnerable members. It is a path where the values of empathy, reformation and victim-centredness guide us towards a more humane and compassionate criminal justice system.

As we continue to explore and apply these values in different areas of the law, we have the potential to create a more just and harmonious society. There could be no better tribute to the likes of Justice V.R. Krishna Iyer than to create such lasting and meaningful difference.

Justice Krishna Iyer lived a fulfilling life of 100 years. He touched the hearts of millions of Indians and continues to inspire us even today from beyond the stars. One can only aspire to walk in the footsteps of this great patriot and social activist.

30

Upholding Civil Liberties in the Digital Age

Privacy, Surveillance and Free Speech[1]

It is my distinct honour to deliver the Fourteenth Justice V.M. Tarkunde Memorial Lecture. The previous thirteen speakers who graced this platform with their wisdom and insights are eminent public intellectuals—individuals I deeply respect and admire.

Justice Tarkunde was a man I had the pleasure of not just interacting with and briefing as a lawyer, but also looking up to as a legal luminary. His dedication to civil liberties inspired me as a young lawyer and continues to inspire me as I serve as a judge of a constitutional court. That Justice Tarkunde is regarded as the 'father of the civil rights movement' is no surprise. In every role he donned—as a senior advocate, High Court judge and activist—he was steadfast in his commitment to democracy, radical humanism and civil liberty.

As a member of the bar, I had the unparalleled honour of briefing Justice Tarkunde on a variety of cases, including *Sodan Singh & Ors v. New Delhi Municipal Committee*,[2] a dispute about the right of pavement hawkers in New Delhi to carry on their occupation. Each time I briefed this extraordinary man, I left his chamber with new insights and a fresh perspective of the law. His range of legal knowledge, foresight and ability to ground legal issues in their larger social context was nothing short of remarkable.

In addition to his legal acumen and deftness, Justice Tarkunde was an iconoclast—in the true sense of the term. Professor Shamnad Basheer, an illustrious scholar who was an ardent advocate of privacy and digital rights, described the term 'iconoclasm' as 'A streak that challenges established wisdom time and again; a streak that refuses to stoop to the powers that be; a streak that thinks nothing of being attacked for attacking cherished beliefs!'[3]

Throughout his life, Justice Tarkunde challenged established wisdom about his professional career and refused to stoop to the metaphorical 'powers that be'. Justice Tarkunde served as a political worker, followed by a legal practitioner, a Judge of the Bombay High Court and, finally, went back to legal practice again. He was an ardent advocate of M.N. Roy's philosophy of 'radical humanism' that sought a balance between revolutionary change and humanistic values. He founded the Indian Radical Humanist Association and was also an editor of the *Radical Humanist*—a weekly journal. M.N. Roy conceptualized 'radical humanism' with the belief that 'freedom is the supreme value because the urge for freedom is the essence of human existence'.[4] He aimed to create a society that values individual freedom, social justice and scientific inquiry while recognizing the dignity and potential of every individual. Justice Tarkunde, in no uncertain terms, exemplified this ideology throughout his life and work.

In 1974, in collaboration with Jayaprakash Narayan, Justice Tarkunde started an organization called Citizens for Democracy (CFD) to defend and strengthen democracy in India. In 1976, during the Emergency, he formed one of India's oldest civil liberties organizations called the People's Union of Civil Liberties (PUCL), setting the stage for India's deep traditions of civil liberty activism that continue to date.

No book, academic article or chronicle of the Emergency imposed in the 1970s is complete without a reference to Justice

Tarkunde's spirited defence of personal liberty and democracy, both inside and outside the courtroom. Legal luminaries have hailed the courage of Justice Tarkunde, for standing his ground against the internal emergency declared in the country. During this period, Justice Tarkunde played a significant role in defending civil liberties. He took up numerous cases related to punitive detentions under the Maintenance of Internal Security Act (MISA), 1971, jail conditions of the detenues and freedom of the press. At the time, there were very few advocates who were willing to do this work. Importantly, Justice Tarkunde took up these cases without charging any fees. One of the first legal victories during this period was the release of Kuldip Nayyar, a journalist with the *Indian Express*, who was detained under MISA. Justice Tarkunde argued the habeas corpus petition before the Delhi High Court and successfully got relief for Nayyar. Even outside the courtroom, Justice Tarkunde was a vociferous critic of the Emergency and wrote several articles that inspired the challenge to the Emergency.[5]

That Justice Tarkunde has been at the cornerstone of India's older traditions of civil liberties activism is uncontested. Justice Tarkunde, unfortunately, passed away in 2004, when the digital age in India was relatively nascent. Today, however, there are emerging initiatives and civil society groups that aim to tackle issues such as online censorship, mass surveillance and internet shutdowns. These initiatives run advocacy campaigns, both inside and outside the courtroom. They represent a contemporary form of protest and activism, which is rooted in Justice Tarkunde's tradition of safeguarding citizens' liberties. In many ways, the 'digital liberties activism' of today's internet age is a way of upholding the pre-existing traditions of civil liberties activism—a new wine in an old bottle.

The core emphasis of the civil liberties movement that Justice Tarkunde championed is mirrored by digital rights activism today. The aim is to curb the abuse of State power and create a space for dissent and democracy to prosper. Not only are the aims of digital activism similar, but they share a deep-rooted bond on the ground as well.[6] The People's Union for Civil Liberties (PUCL), one of the oldest civil liberties organizations in the country, with whom Justice Tarkunde was closely associated during his lifetime, secured one of the first landmark decisions of the Supreme Court regarding online censorship. PUCL petitioned the court for the repeal of Section 66A of the Information Technology Act, 2000, to safeguard the expression of dissent online. The provision criminalized what was termed as 'offensive speech' on the internet and was being widely used by various governments to stifle voices of opposition. Ultimately, the Supreme Court, in *Shreya Singhal v. Union of India* authored by Justice Nariman, invalidated the provision and set the stage for legal activism in the digital space.[7]

In the film *The Social Network* (2010), the character portraying Sean Parker, the first president of the social media platform Facebook, famously said, 'We lived on farms, then we lived in cities and now we're going to live on the internet!' As we strive to uphold the legacy of Justice Tarkunde today, it would be fitting to explore a theme that, while beyond his lifetime, his philosophy continues to steer. Indeed, discussing a theme that contemplates the future aligns with honouring the legacy of a man who was ahead of his times.

I will speak on the topic 'Upholding Civil Liberties in the Digital Age: Privacy, Surveillance and Free Speech'. I will engage with the discussions around privacy, exploring how a society transitioning into the digital age can strike the delicate balance between progress and the right to privacy. To this effect, I will locate privacy in its historical context, lay down an overview of Indian and global jurisprudence on digital privacy, and the interplay between mass surveillance and privacy. Finally, I will address the unique theoretical challenges that the right to free speech and expression poses in the context of the internet.

In this ever-evolving digital era, the preservation of civil liberties has transcended the confines of mere legalities; it has emerged as the very essence of our democratic ethos. This crucial juncture demands a delicate equilibrium between privacy, surveillance and free speech, especially in the vibrant tapestry of India, where the implications hold profound significance.

India's journey through the corridors of the digital realm resonates with the indomitable spirit portrayed in the Bollywood blockbuster *3 Idiots* (2009). I would like to reminisce about the scene where the protagonists find themselves faced with the unexpected challenge of assisting a woman in labour, stranded in a remote location with no immediate access to medical help. In this raw and vulnerable moment, the characters showcase not only wit and ingenuity but also a deep resilience in the face of adversity. This scene serves as a metaphor for India's journey in the digital realm—a nation faced with unforeseen challenges yet exhibiting a collective spirit to adapt, innovate and triumph. Just as the characters in *3 Idiots* ingeniously work together to bring new life into the world, India, too, is birthing a new era—one defined by technological innovation, connectivity and an unwavering spirit to overcome hurdles.

From the bustling streets of Mumbai to the tranquil landscapes of rural India, we see stories of ordinary individuals from various walks of life embracing unified payments interface (UPI) for seamless transactions. It is not just street vendors; it is the homemaker in Kanpur purchasing groceries, the small-town artisan selling handmade crafts in Madurai, and the tech-savvy college student ordering a meal online in Pune—all contributing to the democratization of financial access. This adoption of digital payment solutions resonates far beyond a specific demographic; it underscores the pervasive impact of technology in reshaping how we engage in commerce, transcending geographical and socio-economic boundaries.

In witnessing this widespread integration of digital tools into the fabric of everyday life, we find ourselves at the nexus of progress, and at a critical juncture where the very essence of individual privacy comes into focus. As we navigate this digital landscape, where financial transactions seamlessly traverse our devices, questions arise about the safeguarding of our personal information. The narratives of convenience and accessibility converge, but this cannot be detached from the necessity to protect the sanctity of individual privacy. Privacy, in the digital age, is not just a matter of data protection; it's a fundamental right that we must actively champion. The stories of individuals navigating the digital realm, from rural artisans to urban professionals, highlight the myriad ways in which personal data becomes intertwined with our daily interactions.

As we delve into the complexities of privacy concerns, it's essential to recognize that the digital era is a realm where information is both currency and vulnerability. The same technology that facilitates seamless transactions and connects us across distances also opens avenues for potential exploitation. It beckons us to reflect on how we can harness the benefits of a digitized society while safeguarding the very essence of what makes us individuals—our autonomy, personal narratives and the right to control the narrative of our lives.

The profound insights of Warren and Brandeis in their article titled 'Right to Privacy' in the *Harvard Law Review* resonate with the contemporary, globalized world shaped by the dominance of the internet and information technology. They argue that the principle protecting personal writings and other personal productions is not merely a safeguard against theft and physical appropriation, but an affirmation of an inviolate personality.[8] This embodies a core tenet of freedom and liberty—an assertion of the inviolable nature of the human personality. The technology that initially prompted the need for privacy preservation, photography, served as a catalyst for articulating the right to be free from intrusion. Warren and Brandeis's reflections on the impact of technology remain prescient, especially in an age dominated by the internet, where the boundaries of privacy are continuously redefined.

While contemporary accounts often attribute the modern conception of the 'right to privacy' to Warren and Brandeis, history points to Thomas Cooley, who, in his *Treatise on the Law of Torts*, employed the phrase 'the right to be let alone'. Cooley, in discussing personal immunity, underscored the right of an individual as one of complete immunity—a right to be alone.[9] This historical context emphasizes the enduring nature of the concept and its evolution over time.

Privacy, as understood through this lens, emerges as a natural right—an inherent aspect of an individual's control over their personality. Rooted in the belief that certain rights are natural and inseparable from human personality, privacy becomes a fundamental and inalienable aspect of life. Philosopher John Locke's observations in the seventeenth century, asserting that the lives, liberties and estates of individuals are a private preserve by natural law, set the stage for the concept of a private preserve-creating barrier against external interference. William Blackstone, in 1765, further articulated the concept of 'natural liberty', identifying absolute rights vested in the individual by the immutable laws of nature. These absolute rights, categorized into personal security, personal liberty and property, emphasized the legal and uninterrupted enjoyment of life, limbs, body, health and reputation—an early acknowledgement of the multifaceted nature of privacy.

As we navigate the complexities of a digital age, these historical perspectives on privacy as a natural right remind us that the preservation of individual autonomy and the sanctity of the human personality are enduring principles that transcend time and technological evolution.

The intricate interplay between surveillance by the State and an individual's right to privacy has been a subject of compelling debate within Indian jurisprudence. The first case that dealt with privacy was *R. Rajagopal v. the State of Tamil Nadu.*[10] The court determined that a magazine possessed the right to publish an autobiography penned by a prisoner, even in the absence of the prisoner's consent or authorization. Despite efforts by prison officials to hinder the publication by compelling the prisoner to request its non-publication, the court underscored the need to maintain a delicate equilibrium between press freedom and the right to privacy. The court concluded that the state and its officials lacked the authority to impose prior restraints on materials that could potentially defame the state.

In the landmark case of *People's Union for Civil Liberties v. Union of India*,[11] the court unequivocally held that telephone tapping infringes the guarantee of free speech and expression under Article 19(1)(a) unless authorized by Article 19(2). Drawing from international legal instruments, the judgment emphasized the protection of privacy under Article 17 of the International Covenant on Civil and Political Rights. This protection, the court asserted, must serve as an interpretative tool for construing the provisions of the Indian Constitution. The judgment in *PUCL* is significant not only for its stance on telephone tapping but also for its construction of the right to privacy as a constitutionally protected right. This interconnected interpretation recognized that wiretapping infringes privacy and, by extension, other fundamental rights.

The evolution of the right to privacy reached a watershed moment in 2017 with the judgment in *K.S. Puttaswamy (Retd) v. Union of India*.[12] The Supreme Court recognized privacy as an expansive right covering not only physical invasion but also the realm of the mind, decisions, choices and information. The court overruled earlier judgments in *M.P. Sharma and Others v. Satish Chandra, District Magistrate, Delhi and Others*[13] and *Kharak Singh v. State of Uttar Pradesh*,[14] firmly establishing the right to privacy as a fundamental right. While acknowledging that the right to privacy is not absolute, the judgment delineated a stringent standard of judicial review for cases of State intrusion, emphasizing the principles of legality, need, proportionality and procedural guarantees against abuse.

In navigating the complex terrain of privacy and state surveillance, Indian jurisprudence has continually grappled with striking a balance between individual rights and legitimate State interests. The nuanced approach taken by the courts reflects an evolving understanding of privacy as a dynamic and multifaceted right, adapting to the challenges posed by advancements in technology and the expansive reach of State actions. For instance, India and Sweden, despite their geographical and cultural differences, find themselves grappling with similar privacy concerns in the digital age. In India, the debate around the implementation of Aadhaar, a biometric identification system, raised questions about the balance between individual privacy and the State's interest in ensuring efficient service delivery. Similarly, Sweden's population registry system has raised similar concerns, as it consolidates vast amounts of personal data.

In our exploration of the intricate dance between privacy and state surveillance, it's imperative to broaden our lens and glean insights from international jurisprudence. Three striking cases from the Supreme Court of Estonia, the South African Constitutional Court and the European Court of Human Rights (ECHR) underscore the global struggle to safeguard individual privacy in the face of advancing surveillance technologies.

In a case heard by the Supreme Court of Estonia,[15] the court articulated a crucial principle that as the invasion of privacy intensifies, oversight measures must be correspondingly detailed and effective. The case dealt with the covert surveillance authorized by the codes of criminal procedure in Estonia. The court, recognizing the intensive violation of fundamental rights with covert surveillance, underscored the need for an oversight mechanism. It deemed the absence of such oversight as rendering a specific provision of the Code of Criminal Procedure in Estonia (CCPIA)[16] unconstitutional.

A few years later, the South African Constitutional Court, in the landmark case of *Amabhungane Centre for Investigative Journalism v. Minister of Justice and Minister of Police*,[17] delivered a judgment against the Regulation of Interception of Communications and Provision of Communication-Related Information Act, 2002 (RICA). This legislation, governing interceptions of communications, faced constitutional scrutiny as it lacked crucial safeguards to protect the right to privacy. A journalist, upon discovering that his communications had been intercepted, challenged the law alongside an investigative journalism centre. The court's unequivocal declaration that elements of RICA were unconstitutional emphasized the critical need for oversight and accountability. The court noted that the veil of secrecy shrouding the interception regime hindered any challenge to surveillance orders, escalating the risk of abuse and violating the right to privacy.

Turning our gaze to the ECHR, the case of *Big Brother Watch and Others v. The United Kingdom*[18] engaged with the intersection of electronic surveillance programs and fundamental human rights. The Grand Chamber of the ECHR found sections of the UK's Regulation of Investigatory Powers Act (RIPA) to be in violation of the European Convention on Human Rights. The case scrutinized electronic surveillance programmes operated by the government communications headquarters, highlighting deficiencies in authorization and oversight. The court's judgment underscored the necessity for robust safeguards, emphasizing that the absence of such safeguards violated the convention's guarantees of privacy and freedom of expression. These rulings serve as illustrations of nations grappling with the delicate balance between state surveillance and individual rights, asserting the paramount importance of robust legal frameworks with built-in safeguards.

In examining various international perspectives on privacy and state intrusion, it becomes evident that the struggle to protect privacy is a global endeavour. Courts worldwide grapple with challenges posed by technological advancements, highlighting the crucial need for legal frameworks prioritizing accountability, transparency and the fundamental right to privacy. Drawing from this global perspective, I will now explore specific facets of privacy infringement, beginning with facial recognition technology (FRT).

FRT represents a marvel of technological innovation, but its application raises significant privacy and discrimination concerns.[19] It is often contended that the right to privacy is 'a privilege of the few' and an individual must make a choice between the right to privacy and the welfare entitlements provided by the state. Studies reveal inherent biases within FRT algorithms, especially in identifying darker-skinned women, ethnic minorities and transgender individuals. For instance, a study by Massachusetts Institute of Technology (MIT) Media Lab found higher error rates for darker-skinned females in commercial FRT systems.[20] These inaccuracies gain significance when integrated into the criminal justice system, disproportionately affecting vulnerable groups. The COVID-19 pandemic accentuated these concerns with controversies surrounding FRT's use in health data management. Therefore, I would like to dispel the claim that economic status and access to welfare entitlements are more important than civil and political rights for socio-economically disadvantaged communities. All individuals, regardless of their socio-economic status, are deeply impacted by violations of the right to privacy, autonomy and intimacy.

In the realm of AI, we find that the unchecked algorithms used by tech giants compound privacy concerns. The movie *Minority Report*, directed by Steven Spielberg, envisions a future where a specialized police department apprehends criminals based on foreknowledge provided by three psychics called 'precogs'. The movie raises ethical questions about the potential misuse of predictive technologies, illustrating a dystopian society where privacy is virtually non-existent. The precognitive nature of AI depicted in the film poses profound dangers to personal privacy, as individuals are targeted for crimes they have not yet committed, challenging the very fabric of autonomy and individual rights.

The dual nature of technology is apparent as a catalyst for progress harbouring inherent privacy risks. Surveillance analytics, despite its benefits in healthcare and crime prevention, prompts substantial privacy concerns. Practices such as web cookies and social media data harvesting have raised alarm bells. The General Data Protection Regulation (GDPR) implemented by the European Union sets a global standard, prioritizing individual privacy rights. However, debates persist, exemplified by conflicts between the US government and tech companies like Apple over encrypted data access, highlighting the security versus privacy conundrum.

The *Puttaswamy* judgment introduced a stringent proportionality test, yet its operational complexities pose challenges, particularly in evaluating modern surveillance programmes. Examining the constitutionality of global surveillance programmes reveals significant challenges due to limited information on their operational aspects. The lack of clarity hampers comprehensive evaluations of their adherence to constitutional standards. A collaborative effort between policymakers, technology companies and informed citizens is imperative. Robust oversight mechanisms, stringent authorization protocols and increased public awareness, without compromising ongoing investigations, constitute the way forward.[21]

A pertinent example is the UK's Investigatory Powers Tribunal, which functions as a judicial body overseeing surveillance activities, ensuring compliance with legal standards and protecting individual rights. The delicate equilibrium between technological progress and privacy preservation mandates a careful, synergistic approach. It necessitates legislative precision, transparent oversight and an informed populace to ensure that technological strides do not come at the cost of fundamental rights.

Finally, the last aspect of civil liberties in the digital age that I seek to address is upholding the constitutionally protected right of free speech on the internet. Here, the traditional understanding of civil liberties can be distinguished from digital rights activism in two major ways. Firstly, the unprecedented proliferation of disinformation and hate speech on the internet has offered a serious challenge to the traditional ways of understanding free speech in a democracy. Secondly, in traditional civil rights activism, there was a classic state–activist–corporation relationship that played out in most struggles. Today, however, large social media corporations don't play the stereotypical role of being an entity that needs to be constrained or viewed as complicit with the state.

When it comes to content moderation of online speech, there is a complex moral dilemma that arises in attempting to balance two key values: (1) the upholding of freedom of expression; and (2) the prevention of harm caused by misinformation. There has been a plethora of discussion in recent times about the consequences of disinformation, the need for a regulatory mechanism and the free-speech concerns raised by such legislation or policies. Most criticisms of global 'anti-fake news' legislation are based on concerns that such legislation is overbroad and prone to misuse, thus restricting legitimate speech as well. Such issues about how to define disinformation and prevent selective misuse are essential; however, they put the cart before the horse.

All liberal democracies purport to protect the right to 'free speech and expression'—however, what remains contested is the application of this principle to concrete situations. The presence of laws against, inter alia, defamation, incitement to violence and contempt of court indicates that the free-speech protection does not extend to all acts of communication. In deciding the contours of this protection, therefore, courts and lawmakers are applying a certain theoretical understanding of free speech. Where can disinformation be located in these theories?

Before getting into the nitty-gritty details of how to tackle disinformation, we must ask ourselves a more fundamental question: is disinformation protected by traditional free speech theories and constitutional jurisprudence under Article 19 of the Indian Constitution? I believe that demonstrably false facts are not protected by traditional free speech theories.

The oft-quoted theory of free speech is the concept of a 'marketplace of ideas', which has found its way into Indian jurisprudence from the First Amendment in the US. The Supreme Court has relied on this understanding of free speech in several landmark cases like *Shreya Singhal* and *Bennett Coleman*.[22] This theory of free speech, which can be traced from Justice Holmes's dissent in *Abrams v. United States*,[23] is based on the frictionless exchange of ideas. It postulates the concept that just like a free market of goods, where consumer demand helps the best products rise to the top, a democratic public sphere with the free exchange of ideas will let the best ideas prevail. The usual presumption, therefore, is that under this theory, disinformation is a part of the marketplace of ideas and the only way to counter it is with more speech.

However, several scholars like Ari Waldman argue that false facts are not a part of this 'marketplace of ideas'. The marketplace can only exist when there is agreement on the veracity of basic facts. There is no marketplace of facts. In fact, the goal of fake news is to create one, to erode the stability of foundational elements of society—namely, truth. In this way, tolerating the proliferation of fake news erodes the free and open debate that democracy intends to protect. If we cannot agree on the veracity of basic facts, debate stops, partisanship hardens and social solidarity breaks down.[24]

A study conducted by MIT, which studied 1,26,000 false stories on social media, found that false news spreads faster, deeper and wider than the truth in all informational categories. These false stories were retweeted from three million accounts, approximately 4.5 million times.[25] Simply by virtue of the scale of dissemination, fake news drowns out true information, replacing the character of discourse from truth-seeking to the loudest voice. Disinformation, therefore, has the power of impairing democratic discourse forever, pushing a marketplace of free ideas to the point of collapse under the immense weight of fake stories. A cursory glance at the newspaper every day will bring to the fore instances of communal and vigilante violence fuelled by fake rumours and targeted disinformation campaigns. Across the globe—be it Libya, the Philippines, Germany or the US—elections and civil society have been tarnished by the proliferation of fake news.

The purpose of the metaphor of a 'marketplace of ideas' was to promote an exchange of ideas premised on the agreement of basic facts. Oliver Wendell Holmes Jr's dissent was in the context of persecuting anti-war activists for their speech—thus, what was being freely exchanged were radical 'ideas' about existing facts and not the veracity of the facts themselves. For example, whether a religious site was desecrated or not, whether a speech was *actually* delivered, whether COVID-19 is caused by a virus or bacteria are all facts and not ideas or opinions, with many possible answers. I remember that while the country was faced with the tragic COVID-19 pandemic, the internet was rife with the most outrageous fake news and rumours—a source of comic relief in difficult times but also forcing us to rethink the limits of free speech on the internet.

Traditionally, freedom of speech and expression was deemed to be an essential part of civil rights activism because of the fear that the government would prevent certain kinds of speech from entering the marketplace. With the advent of troll armies and organized disinformation campaigns across different social media platforms, the fear is that there is an overwhelming barrage of speech that distorts the truth. This 'epistemological battle' of sorts was explained eloquently in the *New York Times*, 'the spewing of falsehoods isn't meant to win any battle of ideas. Its goal is to prevent the actual battle from being fought.'[26] Therefore, we cannot fall back on traditional notions of free speech and must find new theoretical frameworks to locate free speech with the advent of the internet.

The second point of distinction lies in the rupture of the traditional state–activist–corporation relationship. Civil rights activists no longer place the corporation within the traditional box of an entity whose power is to be restricted. In fact, to the contrary, they rely on social media corporations such as Facebook, Twitter (now X) and YouTube to expand their freedom of speech and expression, often in opposition to the government.

In her article 'Defending Digital Liberties', lecturer and scholar Ankita Pandey argues that in the past, civil liberties activists had clearly defined battles.[27] They opposed the government–corporate alliance that allowed corporations to breach certain standards in the name of progress. From the perspective of many civil rights activists, the political arena was sharply divided—government and private capital were on one side, while people and activists were on the other. Today, however, digital rights activism is intertwined with private platforms in an unprecedented way. Digital liberties are being fought for in a public space that is privately owned. Those looking for a form of resistance, unsullied by the presence of private capital, chase a nostalgic illusion today more than ever before. The basic principles of liberal and socialist politics remain the same—liberty, equality and justice—but they are being fought for in a new space and conducted via a new privately owned medium that transforms the character of the activism itself.

However, there is a flip side to adopting privately owned platforms as the medium for dissent, activism and expression of free speech. With corporations wielding such immense power, there is an immense amount of trust placed on them to act as the arbiters of acceptable and unacceptable speech—a role that was earlier played by the state itself. This can have disastrous effects. It has been widely reported and recognized by the UN that social media was used as a tool for ethnic cleansing in Myanmar by the military and members of civil society. Unlike state actors who are held accountable by the Constitution and the electorate, social media platforms are relatively unregulated. This is another novel challenge that digital liberties activists have to find unique solutions to.

In conclusion, while digital liberties activism, including the protection of privacy and free speech, has gained currency at an unprecedented pace, we are still in an early period of theorizing on it. The civil liberties movement, led by luminaries like Justice Tarkunde, acted as the precursor to a larger narrative, a narrative of digital rights. The very principles he ardently upheld are the guiding lights that beckon us in this era of digital transformation. This transformation is not just about technology; it is about the people and their rights. The torch that Justice Tarkunde carried for justice now illuminates our path towards safeguarding digital freedoms, ensuring that as we traverse through this landscape, we do so with the commitment to upholding the basic values of justice, equality and freedom. After all, as the world moves online, our battles to uphold civil liberty must also follow suit.

31

Democracy, Debate and Dissent[1]

As we are concluding an essay and debate competition, I thought it would be an opportune moment to talk about the relevance of debate and deliberation to our society and civic structure. Therefore, I will be speaking about *democracy, debate* and *dissent* today. Since, we are in the pristine state of Uttarakhand, which is also known as 'Dev Bhoomi', I thought we must pay tribute to the currents that the holy book of our nation—the Constitution—has cultivated. *First*, I will talk about the objective of a democratic society and the role that the aspirations of citizens play in it. *Second*, I will talk about how deliberation underlies our democratic foundations and why it must inform persistent engagement with the polity. Lastly, I will talk about the vitality of dissent and the direction of a democracy.

The Constitution was adopted in an atmosphere of expectation and idealism. The framers of the Constitution rooted this expectation in the nation's ideals and provided the institutions and processes for achieving them.[2] The Constitution was designed 'to break the shackles of traditional social hierarchies and to usher in a new era of freedom, equality, and justice'.[3] All this was to be achieved through a democratic spirit using constitutional and democratic institutions.[4]

Our country has a robust democratic heritage, which it has earned over the last seven decades through constant dialogue, experimentation and participation. But to truly appreciate this heritage, we must explore a primitive question about what purpose a democracy serves in our society. In Abraham Lincoln's famous words, 'democracy is a government of the people, by the people, for the people'. People, therefore, form the basis of a democracy. This sentiment has been universally echoed. Jawaharlal Nehru in his book *The Discovery of India* highlighted his interactions with people at public meetings where he would say that ultimately, what counted were the people of India. Mother India was essentially its millions of people, and victory to her meant victory to the people.[5]

But one could as easily ask who these people are and in what way democracy serves them. At its most basic, democracy ensures that people get to vote in periodic elections. That every person has one vote and every vote has one value. It is a way of constituting political relations such that the exercising state power receives popular authorization.[6] Democracy is messy and imperfect, but inherent in it are the postulates of justice, liberty, equality and fraternity.

Mere appeal to voting and governance by those elected through periodic elections will remain an incomplete endeavour in the democratic experiment without upholding these postulates. These postulates are upheld in two ways: *first*, by robust institutions that carry out democratic functions; and *second*, by introducing procedural guarantees, which prevent seepage of bias and unfairness in the process of decision-making. Additionally, democracy requires constant dialogue between differing opinions and civil society organizations to fulfil the aspirations of the people. Imagine an uninstructed cook, without utensils. Imagine also a cook who is completely unsupervised and procures ingredients and utensils but instead of using them, keeps them as personal gains. Both these scenarios would fail to achieve the end goals. But even if the chef were to have adequate tools and supervision, they would still fail to meet the expectations of the consumers if they received no feedback or instructions.

Democracy unleashes the aspirations to fundamentally reorder social relations in a completely new way. It is premised on the recognition that there is no natural source of authority that can exercise power over individuals. Therefore, people are presumptively free and equal.[7] This presumptive equality in a democracy hardly reflects the reality of our society. Dr B.R. Ambedkar, on the eve of the enactment of our Constitution, had addressed the Constituent Assembly and said that:

> [W]e are going to enter into a life of contradictions. In politics we will have equality and in social and economic life we will have inequality . . . How long shall we continue to live this life of contradictions? How long shall we continue to deny equality in our social and economic life? If we continue to deny it for long, we will do so only by putting our political democracy in peril . . .[8]

Democracy is contingent on certain minimum guarantees where free citizens can genuinely claim control over the circumstances of their own lives. First, it must routinely produce consensus decisions without arbitrary or unfair imposition of power. Second, citizens must participate in civil and political discourse and have an interest in it. This is a social world where their moral status of citizens is acknowledged, a world which is structured to enable their freedom and serve their interests. Third, citizens must associate with each other, not only as competitors but in a relationship of reciprocal recognition and mutual respect.[9]

However, these consensuses, discourses and associations can only happen where democracy acts towards the ends of uprooting social hierarchies and prejudices. For all citizens to feel free in a democracy, the state must side with the weaker population, which may be a numerical or a social minority. This may, at first, appear to be at odds with the democratic principle of majority rule. However, a mere rule by majority can be established by many forms of government. The beauty of a democracy is the sense of moral status with which all citizens can participate in a country and the consensus in its decision-making. In a democracy, the majority will have its way, but the minority must have its say.

To be equal is not only to be equal in the eyes of the law but also to be treated as equals by our fellow citizens. Laws are the most visible guarantors of, and impediments to, personal freedoms.[10] However, the indignity of inequality often comes not in the form of a policy or a law but in the form of, say, exclusion from informal workplace gatherings or even social groups in school and university due to religion, caste, gender or sexual orientation. One of the biggest challenges we collectively face is how we surmount issues of this nature, where there is no violation of a legally enforceable right in the traditional sense. Members of social minorities, who are unlikely to be represented through electoral democracy because of religion, class, sex or sexual orientation, are overrepresented before the courts in constitutional cases.[11] But certainly, judicial institutions were neither meant to tackle such problems nor are they equipped to in all cases.

The issue with framing all social and political issues in the language of rights and resorting to the courts to resolve these issues is that it reduces the constitutional space envisaged for other democratic mechanisms. The Constitution envisions other methods through which abuse of power can be legitimately checked. This includes debates and discussions inside and outside the legislature on crucial issues. The executive can be held accountable for its actions by Parliament inside the house and outside by the citizenry.

While the Constitution grants rights to citizens and places a corresponding duty on the State to enforce such rights, the real test of the Constitution is seldom in courts but in society. In *Lord of the Flies* by William Golding, a group of boys stranded on an island attempt to establish a civil society. They create rules and systems, but their small, civilized society soon falls apart in the absence of long-lasting institutions or legislation. The rule of law crumbles, power is concentrated in a small number of hands, and the lads are violent, savage and chaotic. As Golding poignantly writes, '*The world, that understandable and lawful world, was slipping away.*' It reflects how quickly order gives way when the foundations meant to preserve it begin to erode. This allegory reflects the perils that exist in the actual world; ideals and concepts, no matter how admirable, disintegrate if they are not supported by institutions that serve as checks on power. Even the best-intentioned rights, whether social or constitutional, can devolve into despotism or chaos in the absence of structure. George Orwell's *Animal Farm* offers a powerful allegory for the fragility of rights in the absence of checks on power. The animals of Manor Farm rise up against their human oppressors and adopt the ideal that 'All animals are equal'. But Napoleon the pig quickly takes over, starves and kills dissident chickens, and twists the facts to claim that Snowball came up with the idea to erect a windmill to lighten their load. Over time, the commandments meant to guarantee equality are twisted. The final one reads: 'All animals are equal, but some animals are more equal than others.' Principles by themselves were insufficient for the revolution to succeed. The promise of rights was replaced by authoritarian rule in the lack of long-lasting institutions or legislation to restrain authority. Orwell reminds us that rights are meaningless without context.

By its very nature, a democracy may be guided by the Constitution, but its force must be driven from the morality inherent in constitutionalism. The rights given by the Constitution are always at risk of becoming 'a parchment guarantee' if the Constitution does not establish a structure that effectively checks the exercise of power and abuse of it. It is imperative for citizens to engage in a dialogue with each other and with the legislative and executive arms of the State. The practice of constitutional values and the organic reorientation of societal practices is essential to achieving the constitutional vision. Active participation by the citizenry in the democratic process in ways that are not expressly mentioned in the Constitution but are nonetheless implicit in its structure is indispensable to realizing constitutional rights.

Essential to this are structures that enable the citizenry to participate. An informed electorate is a choosing electorate. Without such information, a lot of what we say about the power in the vote of the people would just be meaningless. Whether a citizen would be a contributor to the democratic process or a passive observer depends on their access to the relevant information and their ability to not only consume it, but to engage with it. This engagement and debate lie at the core of what we call a participative democracy.

A participative democracy simply entails a democracy that operates on and promotes deliberation. This deliberation emerges not only from the need to secure the right to speech and expression but also to publicly *engage* with the ideas and enable transformation. It is rooted in the very conception of democracy and it liberates a democracy from its majoritarian impulses. The 'argumentative tradition', to quote the inimitable Amartya Sen,[12] is connected with the onward march of an egalitarian democracy.

While the right to free speech entails truth discovery and self-fulfilment of the citizen, its primary purpose is critical interaction and debate. There are overlaps, but in the context of democracy, the relevance of free speech lies in deliberation with the uncomfortable aspects of our realities. If a democracy cannot safeguard discourse around the needs of all its people, it falls short of its promise. Thus, in order to resolve their discontents, a democracy must begin with hearing them.

For instance, India's official entry to the Oscars in the Best Foreign Language Film category for the 2018 Academy Awards, *Newton,* a film by Amit V. Masurkar, told the story of a junior-level government official, who is deployed in a remote insurgency-ridden village in Chhattisgarh on election duty. The story of his many manoeuvres to have people exercise a simple right to vote is an uncomfortable truth, as much as it is a creative exercise. What it also does is show that the heart of a democracy lies in people willing to participate and register their voices, and the framework that it takes for people to exercise this will.

While free speech is in and of itself a whole universe of discussion, I intend to speak of its discursive purpose in a democracy. As I said earlier, a democracy continues to remain one when the electorate is informed, and has both access to and influence over its governing bodies. A 'discursive democracy' creates fertile ground for deliberation that is inclusive and egalitarian. Its institutions must ensure that everyone can engage in a discourse on equal terms and 'no force except that of better argument' interrupts such engagement.[13]

I will elucidate this by tracing how deliberation underlines our democracy from its very inception in the Constituent Assembly. The framers of the Constitution were tasked with stitching together the fragments of the country, as they found it, into a democracy. The Constitution has endured over seven decades and has been internalized by both elites and masses. It has provided the basis for limitations on ambitious executives and provided a language of politics for various groups in society.[14] However, there were several imperfections in the conditions in which the Constitution was enacted.

First, the colonial legacy of poverty, illiteracy and social division left many to be sceptical of the survival of India as a pluralistic society governed by a liberal democratic constitution. The endurance of the Constitution to this day is thus quite uncharacteristic in a society like ours.

Second, the cause of this endurance can hardly be its perfect composition. The Constituent Assembly did include a diverse set of members, but it was predominantly a majoritarian, male, upper-caste, urban exercise. Achyut Chetan, in his book about the founding mothers of the Constitution, writes that while they did play a formative role in envisioning a modern universe for the women of the country, their narratives as well as the history of their contributions were largely subsumed by the dominant 'founding fathers' narrative—a term we almost subconsciously adopted in our gendered vocabulary to represent the framers of the Constitution.[15]

So, if not its inclusive composition, what exactly explains the continued relevance of the Constitution to our lives? The answer lies in its discursive foundation as well as discursive potential. Its composition aside, the process of its framing was an inclusive exercise, rooted in discursive democracy. The Constitution, owing to this inclusive process, resonated with the people of the country and created windows of engagement with its discontents. This is precisely the reason for its entrenchment—the ability to promote debate and deliberation.

Instances of debates from the Constituent Assembly demonstrate how deliberations that lead to decisions impact our lives just as much, if not more, than the outcomes. For instance, despite Mahatma Gandhi's insistence, local self-governance was not made a part of the governing structures of the Constitution but rather relegated to the non-enforceable Directive Principles of State Policy. This was the result of Dr Ambedkar's understanding of Indian society as deeply fragmented along the lines of caste—local self-governance in such a context would only have created a legal structure that was rooted in the social reality of inequality and discrimination. However, after the failure to meaningfully engage with our rural populations through many top-down efforts, the Seventy-Third Amendment to the Constitution fell back on the principles that were earlier considered unfit and reintroduced local self-governance. We can argue if this change was reflective of an altered social reality or merely responded to administrative inconvenience, and also whether Dr Ambedkar's fears were adequately addressed. But the point I make is simply that the outcome earlier discarded in one deliberative exercise was altered based on the debates that transpired earlier.

The Constitution, while firmly anchored in principles of social justice, responds to changing social realities. This is because we have a record of the debates that transpired in the process of its making. A legitimate debate, which proceeds from the desire to learn and to expand the public discourse on a subject, is relevant precisely for this reason. The process of reaching outcomes is far more important than the outcome itself. In the context of the Constitution, it is said that deliberative exercises such as these are bound to have relative winners and relative losers. But despite the loss, the relative losers, if we can call them that, know that these imperfect outcomes are not impervious to change. With social change, the framework of rights that a democracy guarantees will facilitate the change of these outcomes. What a certain group has lost in the present negotiation will be up for renegotiation, and the framework, such as the fundamental rights guaranteed in the Constitution, will facilitate such renegotiation. For instance, the Women's Charter of Rights and Duties drafted by Hansa Mehta—one of the foremost voices in the Constituent Assembly—contained several progressive demands such as women's rights to limit the size of their families, recognition of women's work as homemakers and demands for crèches for working women, among others.[16] While these were not made a part of the constitutional rights regime right away, they were later made a part of the various legislations on maternity benefits and workplace regulations.

The Constituent Assembly engaged even beyond the members of the Assembly itself. It was constantly flooded with postcards, representations and memoranda from all nooks and crannies of the country. The secretariat of the Assembly would acknowledge the representations and, in some cases, even offer a detailed reply.[17] Those who participated in the constitutional bargain had a stake in its successful implementation and also its endurance. Unlike constitutions of authoritarian regimes—such as the 1889 Japanese Constitution, which was announced as a 'gift' from the emperor to his people—democratic constitutions endure due to their continued relevance.[18]

Beyond the Constitution, to engage meaningfully in a discourse that is governed only by the merits of the arguments, we need to strike a delicate balance between diversity of opinion on the one hand and agreement to basic rules of engagement on the other. Deliberation thrives only in conditions that promote candid discussions among all—unmitigated by markers of status, caste and identity. A democracy, in order to be more than a mere approximation of majoritarian preferences, must engage with all its stakeholders. This engagement may or may not lead to an outcome right away but will definitely remain etched as a historical fact capable of being resurrected in the future.

This inclusion and diversity separate a deliberated outcome from a heckler's veto, and a genuine, even uncomfortable, deliberation from an echo chamber. Deliberation is the difference between a majoritarian decision that is foisted on an unwilling electorate and a decision that the people are willing to accept, engage with and hopefully alter one day.[19]

A deliberated outcome accords legitimacy to the institutions of governance. It is the difference between a defeated idea and a disenfranchised democratic participant. While the former may eventually erode with time, the latter militates against the very foundations of a deliberative, engaging constitution.

In a diverse democracy, it is quite likely that certain opinions are heftier for reasons other than their intrinsic merit. There will, of course, be outcomes that are favourable to some more than others. If we truly manage to incorporate all streams of ideas into our decision-making processes, that by itself will not lead to outcomes that are acceptable to every participant.

The answer lies in what these outcomes represent. According to scholar John S. Dryzek, 'deliberative democracy' entails the ability of all individuals subject to a collective decision to engage in authentic deliberation about that decision. While deliberation sustains a democracy, dissent nourishes it. 'If democracy means that the views of the majority prevail, then it necessarily implies that a deliberating and eventually, a dissenting minority. And this can at times be more powerful than a dumb, unthinking accepting majority, ruled by slogans.'[20] A servile and subservient population guarantees a weakened democracy. There is an Urdu couplet by Sarshar Sailani:

चमन में इख़्तिलात-ए-रंग-ओ-बू से बात बनती है,
हम ही हम हैं तो क्या हम हैं तुम ही तुम हो तो क्या तुम हो . . .

It means: 'The essence of a garden is formed by the mingling of diverse colours and fragrances. What good am I if it's only me and what good are you if it's only you?'

Dissent emerges from profound questions about the working of the society. Abolition of slavery, annihilation of caste, emancipation of gender minorities and religious harmony were all once dissenting opinions. However, these dissents hold the power to fundamentally restructure our society by sparking an important conversation. These dissents emerge not from thin air but from a democratic culture of fierce debates. Therefore, a society that does not encourage its citizens to critically think, question the powers that be and engage in non-conformist democratic discourse will fail to progress because it will fail to create dissenters.

While social harmony among citizens is a prerequisite to democracy, it cannot be manufactured by removing conditions under which dissent may be freely expressed. A society is often known by its great dissenters because dissenters inform us of the location and direction of a democracy. Dissenters like Justice John Marshall Harlan in the US Supreme Court case of *Plessy v. Ferguson*,[21] often called 'The Great Dissenter', presented a dissent that was an act of lonely courage. Justice Harlan was the lone dissenter in the opinion that upheld the racist 'separate but equal' doctrine in the US and affirmed the Jim-Crow laws. In our own country, Justice Khanna's lone dissent in *ADM Jabalpur v. S.S. Shukla*[22] warned against the perils of accepting executive excesses into the fundamental rights of citizens.

Ultimately, these dissents, like all dissents, were not only speaking to the times in which they were written; they were speaking to the future. Dissents in a democracy, even those that are unpopular and unacceptable, give us windows to the future. *Plessy v. Ferguson* was overruled in *Brown v. Board of Education*[23] and *ADM Jabalpur v. S.S. Shukla* was overturned in *K.S. Puttaswamy v. Union of India.*[24]

As we conclude this memorial event, I hope that the young minds that participated in this event continue to be committed to the values of the Constitution, which cultivate a culture of democracy, debate and dissent.

32

Navigating Discrimination in Public and Private Spaces

Constitutional Imperatives for the State[1]

Justice E.S. Venkataramiah was the nineteenth Chief Justice of India. He started his journey as a lawyer in Bengaluru. He went on to be elevated to the Karnataka High Court and eventually found his way to the Supreme Court, in whose service he spent over a decade. Though his legal journey is nothing short of inspirational, he would often quip that he went from 'SCC', i.e. the Small Cause Court, to 'SC', i.e. the Supreme Court. But anyone who knew him and his work would attest that he was a teacher and an academic before being a lawyer or a judge. His practice of the law was always accompanied by his academic endeavours.

When I think of his academic career, I am reminded of bookends, which is how his teaching punctuated his legal practice. He started teaching law in 1945—at the same time as he enrolled at the bar and was actively engaged in teaching law at various colleges throughout his career. After hanging his robes as a judge, he was appointed the M.K. Nambyar Chair for Constitutional Law here at National Law School of India University, Bengaluru. Teaching the law, in many ways, was his first and last love. Naturally, then, the many landmark judgments that he authored are impressed upon by his profound body of academic work touching upon a wide range of issues such as human rights, freedom of the press, federalism and citizenship.

In his judicial writing, we see an empath, an environmentalist and a champion of free speech. He was a fierce defender of judicial independence in *S.P. Gupta v. Union of India.*[2] We saw in him a champion of the freedom of the press in *Indian Express Newspapers (Bombay) v. Union of India,*[3] where he balanced the freedom of press with the taxing powers of the State, writing that 'as long as the court sits, newspapermen need not have the fear of their freedom being curtailed by unconstitutional means'. In *M.C. Mehta v. Union of India,*[4] he separated the financial capacity of the tanneries discharging effluents into the Ganga from their obligations towards the environment. He held that it was not merely a Directive Principles of State Policy under Article 48A of the Constitution to protect and improve the environment, but a 'fundamental duty' of the Central government to 'direct all educational institutions to teach at least one hour a week lessons relating to the protection and improvement of the natural environment including forests, lakes, rivers and wild life in the first ten classes'. As many of you would know, he was writing this judgment when environment law in the country was still in its early stages. He was thinking way ahead of his time for the environment and also for the future generation of the country. Justice Benjamin Cardozo, a former judge of the Supreme Court of the US and a scholar, wrote that it is a judge's inevitable duty to decide based on their 'experience, study and reflection'.[5] In Justice Venkataramiah, we find an exemplary judge who did just that.

A perfect blend of pedagogical and judicial acumen, Justice Venkataramiah's two worlds often collided. As his juniors in the profession, and also as citizens of this country, we had the distinct benefit of insight into his wonderful mind and its musings through his judgments and his published works.

The academic in him would approve of a lecture in his memory. I thank my sister judge and my friend, Justice B.V. Nagarathna, for organizing this lecture and having me. I have chosen for myself the theme of 'Constitutional Imperative of the State: Navigating Discrimination in Public and Private Spaces'. In choosing this subject, I draw inspiration from the words of his brother judge, Justice P.N. Bhagwati, in *S.P. Gupta v. Union of India.* Underpinning the importance of an independent judiciary, he cast a wide role for the courts of a society that is 'pulsating with urges of gender justice, worker justice, minorities justice, *dalit* justice and equal justice between chronic unequals'.[6] It makes one think whether as such a pulsating society we have succeeded in creating public and private spaces that are conducive to people across dividing lines. Whether the laws and policies we adopt further the objects of the Constitution in both these spaces alike.

In creating our public offices, our lawmakers assumed that these offices would come to be occupied by righteous persons who would exercise their discretion wisely. The law presumes, for instance, that the civil and criminal courts, which are vested with wide-ranging inherent powers, will exercise those powers to 'do complete justice'. But what is justice? Is my version and understanding of justice the same as one of yours? If there is only one form of justice, if it is a rigid singular concept, then why do we have overturning judgments? A person's sense of justice emerges from their conscience. A lot of factors contribute towards moulding a person's sense of justice, such as the interactions with certain people, through reading or, in a lot of cases, just by observing. For example, my sense of justice on issues of gender evolved with my interactions with my wife, and Justice Sujata Manohar, before whom I had the privilege of appearing as a lawyer. Our sense of justice evolves when we are ready and willing to open our minds beyond the assumptions that the society has taught us to hold. It is only when we have an open mind that we are likely to feel the need to deviate from some of these base assumptions to curate our own sense of justice. We often see this 'need to deviate' take the form of legal amendments and overruling of previous decisions that were perfectly valid until a point in time. The law, in that sense, responds to social change as the fundamental assumptions underlying it alter over time.

One such assumption is the difference between public spaces and private spaces. As a society, we ascribe certain roles to certain persons. These ascribed roles may not always be based on objective abilities or lack thereof but rather on certain subjective notions. Artificial markers of ability, aside from one's skills, such as gender, class, caste and disability, often come to define the roles we give to ourselves. For instance, purely on grounds of gender, women are often perceived as 'natural' caregivers who must tend to the domestic needs of the family, while the men must undertake remunerative activities and form the financial axis of the household.

Much as we have designated roles to genders, since these roles are location-sensitive, we have also demarcated, neatly, the public space and the private space where each of these must be performed. Our laws, as we shall see in due course, crystallized this narrative of what is public and what is private. Accordingly, our laws and policies choose to treat people based on the physical location of their actions. To instantiate, the IPC 1860 provides that when two or more persons by way of a brawl in a public place, disturb public peace, they are said to commit an offence of affray. We must note that a brawl between two people will be punishable only if its location is a 'public' place and not otherwise. The thrust of the law, therefore, is not only the inherent merit or demerit of brawls but on where they take place. While there may be some merit to this distinction in certain situations, a holistic constitutionally governed society must be willing to look beyond this binary.

This dichotomy between what is private and what is public has formed the basis of the feminist and economic critiques of our laws and policies for several years. For freedom of expression to truly exist, it must exist in both these spaces. It cannot exist in one and not in the other. Both these spaces do not exist in neat individual spheres like that of a Venn diagram. They often overlap. The same hierarchy that pervades the private seeps into the public and vice versa, making both spaces slightly less equitable. There is, therefore, a need to look beyond this binary and search for the grievances that underlie both these spheres. For instance, the household, which is understood as a private space, is a site of economic activity by a homemaker who is not remunerated for it. Similarly, in public spaces, women are consigned to distinctively feminine, service-oriented and often sexualized occupations.[7] Thus, both sites involve rights and their infringement. However, if the law chooses that it will interfere only in the latter, perhaps because of its visibility, the law would be unjust. The framers of our constitution did not envisage such a geographical application of the law.

There is increased percolation between these two locations, whose oppressive biases and prejudices have transcended the boundary between the public and the private. Therefore, fixating on the public–private rather than identifying both of their common problems furthers stereotypes about gender, ableism and many such identities. These stereotypes create a self-perpetuating loop of 'who belongs where' and entrench the unjust outcomes of both.

Having said that, I believe that this public–private paradigm and its underlying assumptions could serve as a framework for examining our institutions to some extent. This is, in a way, a furtherance of the critique of this divide—as the division between the two spaces evaporates, we must examine our preparedness to secure the rights of our people in this new realm, which is neither wholly public nor wholly private. With technology virtually ending the spatial constraints, we must examine how our laws and institutions can overcome the limitations of both public and private spaces.

Our laws and procedures must expand beyond this binary and identify the oppression and the oppressed, wherever they may be. Even beyond that, we must ask ourselves what happens when the conventional public and private spaces are inhabited by those not stereotypically associated with them, in situations that are uncharacteristic of that geography. When a private home is a site of employment for a domestic worker, does the law protect their economic and personal rights as much as it does the rights of a corporate office employee? The purpose of the law would have to be extended to safeguard the interests of the conventional and unconventional participants of both these situations.

GENDER DISCRIMINATION

Between an individual and State lies a whole litany of institutions that mediate and define the individual's existence with respect to the State. Institutions of family, marriages, religious institutions, educational institutions, healthcare organizations and NGOs form a part of the relationship that we have with our governments, with our courts and with each other. These institutions also influence our access to resources and opportunities, alongside social markers of identity such as gender.

For instance, a 2018 report on women in prisons by the Ministry and Women and Child Development[8] found that abandonment of women inmates by the members of their families is a frequent phenomenon. These women are left on their own to lead a solitary legal battle. The reasons could be social stigma, financial constraints to pursue legal remedies or the general dispensability of the individual to the continuance of the family itself. The inherent merits of our laws and our legal aid aside, the institution of family is critical to the inmate's ability to access the law for herself. Without such support, she may eventually be able to find her way to the courts on the strength of legal aid, and the void created by one institution of the family may eventually be filled in the form of legal assistance. But the woman stands on shakier and uncertain grounds until that happens.

Such is the influence of these institutions; they not only mediate a person's ability to access the law but also sometimes *prevail over* the legal rights of the individual themselves. Our courts have in the past, in fact, privileged these institutions over the individual. They have held that the need to preserve the institutions is greater than the need to protect the individual's rights. For instance, it was long held in the context of marriage laws and the scope of courts' intervention that introducing the tenets of constitutional law in the privacy of a home or a marriage would weaken the institution of marriages. The sensitive sphere was considered to be an intimate sanctuary, immune from the applications of the 'cold principles of Constitutional law'.[9]

In all fairness, this tendency to insulate private lives of individuals is well-founded, even if we may disagree with effects such as the ones I just mentioned. After all, privacy is but an extension of personhood and dignity. Beyond that, privacy as a right is a guarantee against the excessive intrusion of an individual's life by State and non-State actors and against excesses of the public and private authorities. It affords an effective barrier against surveillance and restrictions on expression.

What is then the harm in stopping law at the threshold of the household? The answer lies in the fact that the household, as much as it provides a private sanctuary to its inhabitants, is not simply, by that reason, an equitable space. Despite the general sense of security they offer, there is a fair chance these spaces may become unequal and unfair to some. It is not uncommon to hear of instances where the family, when faced with a financial choice between the education of a male child and a female child, will choose in favour of the former.

There are subtler versions of this inequality; for example, the pressures a woman faces when stepping out of the household for her education, profession or recreation do not exist for her male counterparts. If the hierarchies persist in private space, and the law looks the other way in the name of sanctity of the household or sanctity of the marriage, we would be failing in the promise of equal protection of law and qualifying it with a location caveat. This would be a diluted understanding of what privacy entails—it is not a cloak for infringement of the rights, away from the watchful eyes of the law. It is a guarantee against *excesses* and not against the very reach of the law and due process. Hierarchies, prejudices and stigmas travel beyond the public–private binaries. But fortunately for us, just like the problem, the solution is equally fluid. The gains of improving our private lives will reflect in our public life as well.

As we began to recognize that these private structures are not constitutional vacuums and injustices in private spaces are also indeed what they are—unjust—we were able to better assess their role in society. This did not happen overnight. The dissolution of the barrier between the public and private lives of women is what led to this change. Very recently, in *Deepika Singh v. Central Administrative Tribunal*,[10] the denial of maternity leave based on a woman's previous marriage circumstances was challenged. Interpreting Section 3 (c) of the Maternity Benefit Act of 1961 and correlating the definition of 'delivery' with the same, a bench of the Supreme Court, of which I was a part, held that the Act aimed at securing women's right to pregnancy, maternity leave and affording reasonable flexibility to live both as a mother and as a worker. It then took up the challenge to Rule 43 of the Central Civil Services (Leave) Rules 1972. The judgment clarified the distinction between childcare and maternity leave, ensuring civil servants have access to both. By rejecting stereotypical ideas of what a 'family' is, the court embraced inclusivity for diverse family structures. This decision reflected the evolving societal norms and the need to reimagine family concepts beyond conventional nuclear models.

In *Kriti v. Oriental Insurance*,[11] the Supreme Court held that in deciding the compensation for the loss of life in a motor vehicle accident, we had to account for the value of a homemaker's labour within the household. The fact that such labour is not economically measured by our society, could not be perpetuated and furthered by the court's refusal to interfere.

The basis of the public–private divide and the perception that courts and laws apply differently to both spaces is inaccurate. The aged notion that 'what men do is public, what women do is private' has no application in societies governed by constitutions. We have come to realize that these spaces cannot be appropriated by a particular class of people at the cost of the rest. Public spaces are for everyone who wants to access them and cannot be made prohibitively difficult to reach for some. Public spaces are more than mere 'containers of social action'. Public space is defined not by its use for the public alone. They are spaces that structure the very nature of discourse. It is, of course, unfortunate if our public spaces, in their actual form, do not represent the diversity of our country. But what is more concerning for us as sentient beings is the loss of discourse. How do we incorporate changes that make our institutions more inclusive without hearing the voices of the people whose representation we are talking about? Without such discourse, our policies would only have the benefit of the observed experiences of a select few rather than the benefit of the lived experiences of people. We cannot, despite our best intentions, walk in their shoes; we can merely pave the way for their effective participation in decision-making. We need *spaces* of representation for representation to truly happen.

This principle applies to public spaces just as much as it does to the private sphere. Public spaces and public lives, as historian and philosopher Hannah Arendt puts it, represent certain values; it is in these realms that 'men could show who they really and inexchangeably were',[12] she said. Public spaces to Arendt represented spaces that were premised on a certain equality of peers, where individuals purposely came together in their efforts towards improving the lives of people and consolidated the efforts against tyranny. The public space was thus the avenue of realization of personal and social goals. A democratic society, its laws and institutions are supposed to enable exactly this kind of congregation of minds for better social outcomes. Our constitution is a testament to what deliberations can offer. For that, in turn, our institutions must facilitate such plurality.

The challenges faced by women and other disadvantaged groups transcend mere visibility, weaving a complex tapestry within the public sphere. The glass ceiling, an elusive yet formidable barrier, encapsulates these challenges, impeding the progression of capable women in both professional and personal spheres. It obstructs the upward mobility of talented women, demanding a nuanced understanding to navigate a path toward dismantling these barriers.

I remember reading about India's first female physician, Rukmabai. She was an Indian woman who bravely challenged societal norms and patriarchal constraints in the late nineteenth century, such as the practice of child marriage. She became a symbol of resistance against regressive practices, setting a precedent for women to defy societal expectations and pursue their aspirations. The fact that she was herself married at the age of nineteen years did not stop her from championing the cause of other women who faced a similar destiny. Her efforts eventually led to the enactment of the Age of Consent Act of 1891.

This is not the story of Indian women alone. The movie *Hidden Figures* provides a resonating example as to how this is reflected on a global scale and affects all individuals. This cinematic piece provides a compelling portrayal of Katherine Johnson, an African American mathematician, and her colleagues, who played pivotal roles in NASA's space missions. In a poignant scene, Katherine confronts racial and gender biases as she asserts her expertise to calculate trajectories. This moment lays bare the systemic hurdles women of colour face in professional arenas, showcasing the resilience required to break through the glass ceiling.

The echoes of Katherine's struggles resonate with the pervasive nature of gender discrimination faced by women in various spheres of life. The challenges depicted are not confined to the realms of fiction; they mirror the battles waged by women in the public sphere. Delving into legal precedents further emphasizes the persistent nature of gender discrimination, unravelling a narrative that extends beyond the boundaries of the film set.

In *Anuj Garg & Ors vs Hotel Association of India & Ors*,[13] the constitutional validity of a provision of the Punjab Excise Act, 1914, restricting the employment women in establishments serving intoxicating substances was challenged. The court observed that the provision, being a pre-constitution law, needed review given changed societal conditions. It struck down the provision, asserting that it perpetuated sexual differences and restricted a citizen's right to be considered for employment. Subsequently, in *Charu Khurana v. Union of India & Ors*,[14] the Supreme Court decisively struck down the discriminatory by-laws of the Cine Costume Make-up Artists and Hairdressers Association of Mumbai. The by-laws of the association barred qualified female make-up artists from joining based on gender, violating their constitutional rights to equality, employment and livelihood. The court ruled that while fundamental rights usually apply to the State, a clause in a trade union's by-laws, accepted by a State authority, cannot breach the Indian Constitution.

These legal vignettes not only spotlight the intricacies of gender discrimination but also underscore the adaptability of legal frameworks in addressing contemporary challenges. The courtroom battles in cases like *Deepika Singh* reveal the dynamic nature of the law and its capability of responding to evolving societal norms. These legal victories serve as beacons, illuminating the path towards a more just and equitable society.

The transformative impact of legal interventions against gender-based discrimination is evident, heralding a new era of consciousness and accountability. However, as we celebrate these victories, the quest for true equity persists. Despite legal victories and societal movements, subtle forms of bias and discrimination persist. For instance, workplace discrimination, microaggressions and unequal opportunities continue to undermine the principle of equality. Another persistent challenge lurks behind the gender pay gap. This issue is particularly pronounced for Indian women, especially those belonging to marginalized communities.

Despite their significant contributions to various professional spheres, women continue to face disparities in remuneration compared to their male counterparts. Nobel Laureate Claudia Goldin proved with her Nobel-winning thesis that women are 'vastly underrepresented in the global labour market and, when they work, they earn less than men'[15]. The disconcerting reality of the gender pay gap in India illuminates a complex interplay of factors, including societal norms, cultural expectations and systemic *unconscious* biases. The pay gap widens as it intersects with other forms of discrimination, amplifying challenges for women who navigate both gender and racial biases.

It is a stark reminder that achieving true equity requires more than legal provisions; it demands ongoing advocacy and systemic changes to dismantle entrenched biases and ensure equal opportunities for all. Efforts to bridge the gender pay gap must address the intersection of discrimination faced by Indian women.

Advocacy should encompass not only gender-sensitive policies but also initiatives that recognize and rectify the unique challenges faced by women from diverse backgrounds.

DISABILITY RIGHTS

I would like to speak about the public–private divide in the realm of disability rights. Disability often becomes a barrier, denying individuals access to public opportunities due to societal biases that perceive disability as a limitation. Even when given a chance, essential accommodations might be missing, like offering a job to a person with a disability but lacking necessary workplace tools or infrastructure, hindering their success first-hand. Moreover, individuals with disabilities often encounter doubts about their capabilities after receiving opportunities, a result of ingrained ableism. I remember my former law clerk, who is visually impaired, telling me that they face scepticism especially in a job interview for tech-driven roles. This limits their growth due to biased assumptions about their abilities.

This can also be exemplified through the Oscar-winning film *Rain Man*. In the film, the main protagonist, Raymond, who has autism and savant syndrome faces scepticism rooted in ableism regarding his task abilities. This is akin to real-life scenarios where the skills of individuals with disabilities are doubted despite meeting requirements, perpetuating exclusionary biases.

The ratification of the Convention on the Rights of Persons with Disabilities (CRPD) in 2007 signalled a paradigm shift, aligning India with the social model of disability and human rights. This global commitment to inclusivity had a profound impact on subsequent legal interpretations and interventions. The legislative journey is a narrative of progress—from a charity-centric mindset to the acknowledgement of rights as inherent to every person. Post the ratification of CRPD, Indian courts creatively embraced principles emphasizing non-discrimination, reasonable accommodation and affirmative action while deciding issues that concern disability rights.

In *Jeeja Ghosh & Anr v. Union of India & Ors*,[16] the Supreme Court strongly condemned discrimination against Jeeja Ghosh, who was deboarded from an aircraft due to her disability, awarding damages and highlighting the impact of social barriers on disabled lives. In *Vikash Kumar v. Union Public Service Commission*,[17] the court observed that individuals with writer's cramp or dysgraphia, not recognized as benchmark disabilities in the Act, are entitled to a scribe in the civil services examination. This decision underscores the principle of reasonable accommodation under the Act, emphasizing the positive obligation of the State and private entities to provide support for full participation. It marks a significant shift from a medical to a human rights model of disability, aligning with the CRPD. This has been showcased in recent judgments such as *Ravindra Kumar Dhariwal v. Union of India*.[18] In this case, the Supreme Court revitalized Article 14 by invoking inclusive equality and reasonable accommodation. It addressed whether disciplining a Central Reserve Police Force (CRPF) assistant commandant, who developed a mental disability during employment, was discriminatory. The court emphasized the importance of 'dignity' and 'equality' under Section 3 of the Rights of Persons with Disabilities (RPwD) Act, highlighting the State's positive obligation to fulfil the rights of persons with disabilities. Section 20 of the RPwD Act expands the obligation to provide reasonable accommodation, leading the court to conclude that the scope of this obligation has significantly broadened.

Cases like *Akanksha Singh v. High Court of Delhi*[19] and *Disabled Rights Group v. Union of India*[20] also highlight a commitment to accessibility, expanding the scope of disability under the RPwD Act, 2016. The courts, in cases such as the former, rejected categorizing bipolar disorder as a sign of incapacity, emphasizing the capabilities of individuals with mental health conditions. The latter recognized and enforced the principle of accessibility, directing the University Grants Commission (UGC) to establish accessibility guidelines for higher educational institutions.

The judiciary, recognizing the intersectionality of gender and disability, has recognized the vulnerability of disabled women, emphasizing the potential for indirect discrimination they may face. The recent cases serve as illustrations of the judiciary's evolving role, not only in recognizing individual rights but in addressing the intricate intersections of *disability with gender and mental health*, further enriching the discourse on equality. This underscores that disability is a nuanced, individualized concept shaped by factors like mental impairment and personal circumstances, rejecting a one-size-fits-all approach. The legal framework emphasizes the need to avoid stigmatization and discrimination against individuals with mental health issues or disabilities, recognizing the impact on their sense of disability.

The judgment in *Anuj Garg* highlighted a critical aspect—public places and institutions can become ableist and exclusionary without legal safeguards. It emphasized the cyclical nature of exclusion, where insufficient facilities lead to a decreased presence of a particular group. This perpetuating cycle, as evident in the scarcity of women's washrooms due to fewer women in an office, necessitates legal intervention to ensure a healthy and inclusive society. This case and other cases like *Vikash Kumar* become a beacon for understanding the intricate relationship between law and societal inclusivity. The judgments not only address a specific case but also underscore the broader societal impact of seemingly neutral policies that perpetuate exclusion. These interventions highlight the need for legal frameworks that actively counteract systemic discrimination.

This imperative aligns with the concept of universal design, which embodies the essence of inclusivity by advocating for spaces that embrace and accommodate everyone irrespective of ability. Architectural access audits, such as those conducted by the Supreme Court Committee on Accessibility, play a crucial role in evaluating the accessibility of buildings and public spaces. These audits identify barriers and recommend modifications, ensuring spaces go beyond legal compliance to demonstrate a commitment to human rights, social responsibility, and fostering inclusivity and diversity.

The Supreme Court Committee on Accessibility's meticulous approach in its report[21] auditing the Supreme Court's facilities provides invaluable insights into the existing challenges. From physical accessibility issues like the absence of wheelchair-friendly amenities to functional challenges such as the lack of sign language interpreters, the report paints a comprehensive picture of the challenges to accessibility and inclusion. The identification of gaps in physical and functional accessibility is not merely an exercise in critique but a strategic move towards inclusive reform. The report's recommendations, ranging from introducing accessible route maps to overhauling restrooms for better accessibility, showcase a commitment to tangible solutions.

We are currently on the path to adopting the suggestions outlined in the report, which seeks to comprehensively address concerns about accessibility and inclusivity within the legal system. This involves physical improvements such as accessible routes and designated parking, along with the establishment of dedicated sections, mediation protocols and enhanced facilities like accessible restrooms and lactation rooms. Cases involving individuals with HIV have been prioritized and de-identification measures during legal proceedings have been implemented. Additionally, we use technology with tailored online resources for persons with disabilities, highlighting the importance of inclusive digital spaces.

Universal design, as both a concept and a practical approach, becomes a tool to break the cycle highlighted in *Anuj Garg*. It is not just about addressing existing barriers but ensuring that the design of spaces inherently considers the diverse needs of all individuals.

The recognition of the role of technology aligns with the principles of universal design, extending the reach of inclusivity beyond physical spaces to the virtual realm. The role of technology in shaping inclusive spaces extends beyond convenience—it becomes a democratic force, ensuring that access to information and legal processes is not a privilege but a right. The Supreme Court's e-Committee initiatives underscore this, emphasizing the need to make filings accessible to lawyers with visual impairment; ensuring proper placement of stamps/watermarks to promote accessibility through assistive technology; and making CAPTCHAs on the

Supreme Court and High Court websites accessible. Also, recently, the Supreme Court has begun providing sign language interpretation for lawyers with hearing impairments. This was demonstrated in a recent case, where a hearing-impaired advocate, Sarah Sunny, was allowed to argue virtually with the assistance of a sign-language interpreter.

As we navigate through these legal landscapes and policy considerations, the concept of Crip theory emerges as a revolutionary force. This theory, born within the realm of disability studies, stands as a powerful tool to explore the experiences of individuals with disabilities, acknowledging the historical exclusion and social barriers they face. Developed at the intersection of gender and sexuality, Crip theory forms an integral part of critical disability studies.

'Crip time', a profound aspect of this theory, challenges societal assumptions about time, energy and resources, shedding light on pervasive able-bodied perspectives. By highlighting the unique needs of individuals with disabilities, Crip theory prompts a re-evaluation of our understanding of tasks, accommodations and expectations in both life and work. Originating from Alison Kafer's work in *Feminist, Queer, Crip*,[22] this theory delves into queer temporal theory, encouraging exploration of intricate connections between time, marginalization and visibility. It challenges the conventional understanding of time and urges consideration of how individuals with disabilities navigate temporal aspects of their lives, acknowledging their diverse temporal experiences.

It challenges ableism, advocating for the dismantling of biases and the recognition of the richness and diversity that individuals with disabilities bring to our collective tapestry. This theory goes beyond the notion of accommodation; it calls for an active valuation and integration of unique perspectives. For instance, a school implementing Crip theory might emphasize not only providing ramps for wheelchair access but also fostering an inclusive curriculum that represents diverse perspectives, experiences and contributions of individuals with disabilities. This goes beyond meeting basic accessibility standards; it actively values and integrates the unique viewpoints of students with disabilities, creating a more enriching educational environment for everyone involved.

Extending this to the legal realm, Crip theory serves as a critical lens to analyse existing legal frameworks. By challenging our societal understanding of time, it unveils potential ableism within legal norms. Integrating Crip theory into legal discourse empowers us to advocate for more inclusive frameworks that genuinely consider and accommodate the diverse temporal experiences of individuals with disabilities. Thus, our goal is not only to meet basic needs but also to shape a legal landscape that celebrates the unique perspectives and contributions of individuals with disabilities. This urges us to move beyond mere accommodation and strive for an inclusive society where every individual's contribution is not just acknowledged but celebrated.

PRIVATE DISCRIMINATION

Now, I wish to explore the complex terrain of equality and justice, where we find ourselves confronting a formidable obstacle: the domain of private discrimination. This dimension, often concealed within the folds of societal interactions and private arrangements, demands our attention as we unravel the layers of inequality embedded within. I would like to begin by dissecting the jurisprudential origins of anti-discrimination law in India. A crucial dichotomy surfaces—'formal equality' and 'substantive equality'. Articles 14 and 15 of the Indian Constitution birthed these perspectives. Legal equality, grounded in equal application of the law, encounters its counterpart, substantive equality, which delves into the nuanced characteristics of groups, acknowledging the potential for indirect discrimination. While legal equality ensures uniformity in application, substantive equality recognizes the need to accommodate differences within the application of the law.

Articles 15(2) and 17 of the Constitution directly address discrimination by entities beyond the state. Article 15(2) prohibits disabilities, restrictions or conditions for citizens concerning access to places like shops, hotels, wells and 'places of public resort'. Article 17 abolishes untouchability, providing a constitutional shield against certain forms of private discrimination. However, these provisions, though crucial, are confined to specific places and practices, illustrating the constitutional recognition of the need to combat private discrimination.

The oversight in recognizing indirect discrimination as a form of injustice, coupled with the absence of proactive measures to address it, reflects fundamental assumptions about the nature of the right against discrimination. Transforming this paradigm necessitates a thorough examination of how laws impact the opportunities, freedoms and dignity of diverse societal groups. Drafting rules around indirect discrimination demands a nuanced exploration by the judiciary into differentiating it from direct discrimination, delving into the intricacies of both intention and effects. This intricate interplay between intention and effects, as illustrated by the Supreme Court, compels a holistic reassessment of the foundations of the right against discrimination.

I would like to ground this theoretical exploration in the harsh reality of housing discrimination, drawing attention to a glaring example from Vattavada Panchayat in Kerala. Here, members of the Chakkiliyan community, identified as Dalits, experienced the egregious denial of entry into local barber shops.[23]

This discrimination faced by Dalits has extended beyond barbershops and encompassed access to water—a poignant reflection of societal biases.[24] Dr Ambedkar's insight into the social and cultural implications of water was profound. He keenly recognized the intersection of water with caste dynamics, acknowledging its role in perpetuating complex hierarchies. Water wasn't merely a source of sustenance but a deeply contested entity entangled with caste-based exclusion. This manifested through denying Dalits access to water sources, monopolizing control over water bodies by upper castes, embedding caste biases in cultural and religious contexts related to water, silencing Dalit narratives and wisdom on water, and relegating discussions on caste and water as peripheral.[25] For Dalits, water was not just life-giving; it became a symbol of anguish and segregation.

To further grasp the pervasive nature of private discrimination, consider the plight of individuals facing bias in employment based on their sexuality. This is not a hypothetical scenario; it is a harsh reality faced by many individuals, shedding light on the urgency of dismantling discriminatory practices deeply ingrained in private spheres.

Moreover, another example came to my attention when one of my law clerks showed me an Instagram reel depicting the entrepreneurial journey of a determined young woman. Despite her innovative business ideas and evident merit, the reel revealed the systemic discrimination she faced in securing funding. Investors, influenced by gender biases, dismissively overlooked her proposals, exemplifying the pervasive challenges women encounter in entrepreneurship. Her resilience in the face of these discriminatory barriers served as a powerful testament to the urgent need for challenging and transforming biased norms *within private spheres*. These experiences collectively underscore the imperative of dismantling discriminatory practices and fostering inclusivity within the private spheres of our society.

The Supreme Court case of *Zoroastrian Co-Operative Housing Society Limited and Another v. District Registrar, Cooperative Societies*[26] comes to mind when we talk about discriminatory practices in the housing sphere. In this case, a Parsi cooperative housing society, guided by by-laws that explicitly restricted non-Parsis from becoming members, came under legal scrutiny. The society contended that it was a Parsi association exercising its rights under Article 19(1)(c), which guarantees the freedom to form associations, and argued that this right allowed them to exclude membership on the basis of religion. The court, accepting this argument, construed the issue as whether cooperative societies, essentially being associations, could legitimately discriminate. The court concluded that they could. This judicial stance raises profound and intricate questions about the delicate balance between individual freedoms and the imperative of combating discriminatory practices within private entities.

The judgment in *Indian Medical Association v. Union of India*[27] in 2011, however, further expanded the scope of constitutional protection against horizontal discrimination. By incorporating educational institutions within the meaning of 'shops' under Article 15(2), the court ensured fundamental rights protection for anyone facing discrimination in such establishments. This marks a constitutional response to horizontal discrimination, providing a potent tool for challenging exclusionary private covenants. This renewed interpretation calls for an exploration of other services considered 'public' in the relevant sense, opening avenues for challenging discriminatory practices across diverse sectors.

CRAFTING AN INCLUSION OF TOMORROW

As seen through the examples reiterated previously, the courts have recognized that a seemingly neutral law might be a tool of oppression for a particular group. To truly achieve substantive equality, the impact of its provisions must be understood in the context of social realities. Overcoming socially ascribed roles necessitates transcending artificial public–private dichotomies. Addressing power imbalances wherever they thrive becomes imperative.

Our laws are powerful tools in opening up our public spaces as well as curbing private discrimination. Equally important, if not more, are the mechanisms that mediate access to law. Even something as seemingly neutral as the cause lists published by courts across the country can, in practice, exclude certain individuals from effectively accessing the legal system. If a person with visual impairment is unable to access the cause list or is having to spend more effort and time than anyone else to peruse the contents of the cause list, the promise of equal law and equal protection of laws loses some heft. The Supreme Court's *State of the Judiciary Report* indicates that only 30.4 per cent of district court complexes have separate washrooms for persons with disabilities (PwDs), and other infrastructural support such as tactile paving and wheelchairs is available in less than 30 per cent of the court complexes. In preparing for their day in court, rather than sharpening their arguments and submissions, a lawyer or a litigant is forced to account for parking arrangements and spot washroom facilities outside the court complex. They have access to the law, and also to the court, but the hurdles placed in their way will impact the ability to actually benefit from this access. This immediately places them at a disadvantage compared to those who could spend more time with their files. Inadvertently then, we are telling our lawyers and litigants that it is not the law's concern to intercede between such hidden forms of discrimination.

To truly overcome stereotypical roles, the law and policies should transcend the public–private dichotomy and address power imbalances regardless of their location. This requires a comprehensive approach that considers the societal context, historical perspectives and the jurisprudence of discrimination law. By doing so, we pave the way for a society where equality is not a mere slogan but a lived reality for all its members. The legal landscape must evolve, weaving a tapestry that accommodates differences, eradicates biases and ensures substantive equality. Let us, as legal practitioners, scholars and advocates, pledge to be architects of change, contributing to a tomorrow where the rights of every citizen, regardless of ability or background are not just protected but celebrated, and excesses, regardless of the location, are interfered with.

33

Unveiling the Seventy-Fifth Year of the Supreme Court of India[1]

With the year 2024, the Supreme Court of India marks the commencement of the diamond jubilee year of the moment of its inception on 28 January 1950.

First and foremost, I thank the prime minister of India, who graciously agreed to be with us, address the audience and launch the new initiatives of the Supreme Court of India. I also extend my heartfelt gratitude to my esteemed counterparts from Bangladesh, Bhutan, Mauritius, Nepal and Sri Lanka for joining us and commemorating this occasion together. India has long-standing cultural bonds with them and the presence of the Chief Justices today strengthens India's ties with their nations.

A conversation about this court must be necessarily prefaced with a conversation about the Constitution of India. It was through the Constitution that the people of our country gave to themselves this court. The Constitution is not just a legal document. Its soul lies in the feeling which it engenders. A feeling of mutual respect towards fellow citizens. A feeling of responsibility in the institutions it creates. The constitutional ideals permeate the fabric of our nation, guiding the actions and interactions of both the governed and those who govern.

The Supreme Court was established with a sense of *idealism*—that laws would be interpreted by a constitutional court in accordance with the rule of law and not by colonial values or social hierarchies. It affirmed the belief that the judiciary should serve as a bulwark against injustice, tyranny and the arbitrariness. The Supreme Court is an institution of resolution and justice. The fact that people approach it in large numbers, speaks to how far we have succeeded in discharging that role.

Today is not only a celebration of the day when the Supreme Court came into being, it is also a celebration of the decades' worth of hard work by succeeding generations of judges and lawyers that went into making this a 'people's court'. In celebrating the history of this day, we must look back and look forward in equal measure.

Since the founding of the court, our actions have been guided by Mahatma Gandhi's profound words: 'Recall the face of the poorest and weakest man whom you have seen and ask yourself if the step you contemplate is going to be of any use to him.'[2] Our decisions both in the judicial and administrative realms, have been aimed at enhancing accessibility to the Indian judicial system for common citizens.

Through its judgments, the Supreme Court has enhanced the rights of citizens by diluting the standards of *locus standi* and by recognizing a set of new rights under Article 21 of the Constitution, such as the right to a speedy trial. On the administrative side, the Supreme Court has been identifying and eliminating as many barriers to justice—unequal access to legal resources, unfamiliarity of the English language, issues of physical accessibility of courts—in order to create procedural fairness.

EFFICIENCY, ACCESSIBILITY AND TRANSPARENCY

The e-courts project of the Supreme Court of India attempts to enhance accessibility and transparency of the justice delivery system. At the heart of these initiatives is the desire to transform the judicial system into a technology-enabled, efficient, accessible and environment-friendly institution.

Let me briefly summarize the achievements of the court in simplifying its process.

e-Filing of Cases

The front-desk experience of approaching courts has changed completely. As opposed to lawyers lugging trolley carts of papers, we now have the facility of filing cases at the click of a button. An upgraded version of the Supreme Court's e-filing platform was launched in May 2023. It offers a host of improved features that have made 24/7 filing of cases simpler, faster and convenient.

Nearly 1,28,000 e-filings have been done so far, with a consistent rise in the share of e-filings compared to physical filings. E-filings are available in twenty-five states. They have recorded over twenty-nine lakh case filings. With the immense support of the bar and the bench, we were able to swiftly shift to virtual hearings during COVID-19. Even after the pandemic, hybrid hearings continue to be a feature of our courts. That is, any Indian lawyer sitting in any part of the country, or the world can argue before this court through video conferencing. This has democratized access to the Supreme Court. It has opened the space for those who were unable to approach the Supreme Court due to physical distance. Even yesterday, one of the judges joined the bench through video conferencing for a special hearing. Till now, we have dealt with over five lakh cases through hybrid hearings. The live proceedings of the Supreme Court Constitutional Bench hearings are popular and speak to the genuine curiosity that people have towards our courts and procedures.

Focus on Scanning and Digitization

The Supreme Court of India today operates in a near-complete paperless mode, with almost all benches using digitized paper books. Judges are provided with scanned, bookmarked and digitally signed case records, which they access, read, annotate and preserve for their reference at their residence and in courtrooms. More than thirteen lakh legacy and live case records with approximately ten crore pages have been digitized.

FUTURISTIC COURTS

The Supreme Court has enabled 'futuristic court technology' in three courtrooms, and soon other courtrooms shall be equipped with such technology. This technology facilitates paperless proceedings, a comprehensive digital library for the bench and the advocates, state-of-the-art video conferencing, large video walls, smart monitors and document visualizers, all of which redefine the courtroom experience.

Office Automation

Adoption of e-Office has enabled the officers of the Supreme Court Registry to perform their routine work in paperless mode. Thirty-six branches have been onboarded on e-Office, and more than 4000 office files have been processed online so far.

SuSwagatam

Launch of the SuSwagatam portal has enabled visitors to generate entry passes online, in a paperless mode. A total of 1,23,000 entry passes have been generated so far using SuSwagatam.

MoU with IIT Madras

We are also transcribing oral arguments in matters before Constitution Benches, which can be accessed on the Supreme Court website. The Supreme Court has entered into an memorandum of understanding (MoU) with Indian Institute of Technology (IIT) Madras to explore areas that can be completely automated, and to leverage technology and AI for enhancing process efficiency. As we speak today, a team of generative AI (gen AI) researchers at a premier management institute has built an end-to-end demo of an actual open-source gen AI model trained in public domain motor accident cases. It is trained to automatically extract parameters from petitions, documents and files and give a recommended compensation figure.

Quadrangle of Transformation

Together, e-filing, digitization, paperless courts and e-office constitute the golden quadrangle of transformation within whose enabling perimeter the Supreme Court of India is set to uplift the experience of everyone who is either a part of the judicial system or who comes in contact with it.

THE FUTURE

The Supreme Court is soon going to migrate its digital data to a safe, secure and sovereign cloud. This would be a shot in the arm for the IT set-up of the court. Cloud storage would ensure privacy, integrity, high availability and secure accessibility of Supreme Court's domain data.

We are also on the verge of opening a war room equipped with technology that would enable the Supreme Court to monitor judicial data of the entire country in real time by using National Judicial Data Grid (NJDG) and iJuris, both of which are information-sharing platforms for the district judiciary. iJuris has been launched by the Supreme Court to monitor statistics of vacancies and infrastructure relating to the district judiciary.

INITIATIVES UNDER E-COURTS PROJECT

Facilitating free accessibility of judgments for citizens and litigants has always been a priority of the e-Courts project. As of today, 36,209 judgments are uploaded online on the e-SCR portal in English, out of which about 36,000 judgments are translated in Hindi, and around 11,000 judgments in other languages.

The virtual courts initiative has been a game changer in courtroom access and online dispute resolution. Implemented in twenty states, the initiative has received 4.37 crore challans, leading to a total collection of Rs 502.25 crore in fines. Interestingly, according to the electronic transaction analyser of the Government of India, in 2018, e-courts had surpassed even the Indian railways in terms of total electronic transactions.[3]

All 713 district court websites have been migrated to the S3WaaS framework of the National Informatics Centre, which offers a user-friendly interface, greater customization and compliance with the guidelines for Indian government websites, thereby ensuring better accessibility for differently abled users.

On the NJDG, a repository of nationwide judicial data, information on 3256 countrywide courts, the High Courts and the Supreme Court of India is now a click away.

CHANGING DEMOGRAPHICS

Just as we make our courts tech-savvy, we must also realize that India is going through a period of social and demographic transformation. Anyone who visits India will notice a striking feature of the changing demographics. Now, women can be seen in important positions. There is a focus on greater inclusion of the marginalized sections of society. Equally inspiring is the confidence of the younger population to succeed in their professional lives.

Traditionally, the legal profession was a profession of elite men. Times have changed. Women, traditionally underrepresented in the profession, now constitute 36.3 per cent of the working strength of the district judiciary. In the recruitment examination for junior civil judges conducted in several states, namely Andhra Pradesh, Arunachal Pradesh, Chhattisgarh, Delhi, Himachal Pradesh, Karnataka, Madhya Pradesh, Maharashtra, Odisha, Rajasthan, Sikkim, Uttar Pradesh and Uttarakhand, more than 50 per cent of the selected candidates were women. In the Supreme Court of India, we hire law clerks-cum-research associates to assist the judges, out of which 41 per cent candidates are women this year.

We as judges and administrators cannot be ignorant of these rising aspirations. Before the beginning of 2024, only twelve women were designated as 'senior advocates' in the history of the Supreme Court over the last seventy-four years. Last week, the Supreme Court designated eleven women, coming from different parts of the country, as senior advocates at one selection. Our legitimacy will endure from the inclusion of diverse sections of the population in our system. Therefore, we need to make more efforts to bring different sections of the society into the legal profession. For instance, the representation of Scheduled Castes and Scheduled Tribes is quite low both at the bar as well as on the bench.

In the near future, we must address the structural issues affecting the judiciary, such as pendency of cases, archaic procedures and the culture of adjournments. Our effort in our work as judges and administrators must be to ensure dignity to the district judiciary, which is the first point of contact for citizens. Our ability to remain relevant as an institution requires us to recognize challenges and begin difficult conversations:

- First, we must emerge out of the adjournment culture to a culture of professionalism;
- Second, we have to ensure that the length of oral arguments does not interminably delay judicial outcomes;
- Third, the legal profession must provide a level playing field for first-generation lawyers—men, women and others from marginalized segments who have the will to work and the potential to succeed; and
- Fourth, let us begin the conversation on long vacations and whether alternatives such as flexitime for lawyers and judges is possible.

The seventy-fifth year since the founding provides an opportunity to meet these challenges and step into the future with an honest assessment of our progress. We must reflect on the journey that we have traversed and renew our pledge to uphold the Constitution within and beyond the courtrooms.

Our mission to make the judiciary accessible to all would be incomplete without the support of our High Courts. I thank the judges and the staff of all the High Courts as I thank my own colleagues and staff in facilitating our initiatives, which are being launched today.

34

The Supreme Court at Seventy-Five

A Journey Through Law, Liberty and Justice[1]

The day 28 January 2024 marked a significant day in constitutional history. The inaugural sitting of the Supreme Court of India was held seventy-five years ago on this day. The six judges of the Federal Court, led by Chief Justice Shri Harilal J. Kania, assembled for the first sitting of the Supreme Court of India. The event took place without much fanfare in the Prince's Chamber of the building of Parliament from which the Federal Court functioned.[2] For many, it would have seemed like another day at the Federal Court because neither the composition nor the seat of the court was altered. On closer reflection, with the benefit of the hindsight of a succeeding generation, we see now that much has changed.

On 28 January 1950, the judges assembled as judges of the highest appellate adjudicatory body in the world's largest democracy with wide, almost unrestricted powers to do justice. India was a newly formed republic, which had overcome colonial oppression and navigated a period of incredible social, political and legal turbulence to successfully draft and adopt its own constitution. Upon its establishment, the Supreme Court, as the custodian of the Constitution, shouldered a heavy burden of ensuring the development of the nation by protecting individual and group rights. What was a burden has survived decades of trials and triumphs, challenges and critiques, accolades and assaults—all along creating a uniquely Indian jurisprudence rooted and grounded in the expectations of its citizens.

The Chief Justice's address at the inaugural sitting emphasized three principles that are necessary for the Supreme Court to function according to the constitutional mandate. The first is an independent judiciary, where the Supreme Court must be independent of the legislature and executive. The second is the judicial approach towards adjudication, which postulates that the Supreme Court must interpret the Constitution not as a rigid body of rules but as a living organism. The third principle is that this court must secure the respect of citizens for it to establish itself as a legitimate institution. The confidence of our citizens is determinative of our own legitimacy.

Much has changed in the seventy-five years since the inaugural. The Supreme Court itself and the legal regime in which it adjudicates have undergone extensive structural alterations. At its first sitting, the Supreme Court consisted of six judges. It now has a sanctioned strength of thirty-four judges. In 1950, this court sat *en banc*, in a bench of six, even at preliminary hearings. In 1950, 1215 cases were instituted before the Supreme Court. Judgments were pronounced in forty-three of those cases. The Supreme Court now sits in a bench of two judges unless the case has been referred to a constitution bench or a bench of three judges. Between January and October 2023, 45,495 cases were instituted, and judgments were pronounced in more than 1000 cases. With the Indian economy having undergone a radical transformation, new areas of law—telecommunications, insolvency and bankruptcy, and intellectual property—have emerged. Conventional forms of alternate dispute mechanisms have metamorphosed into avatars dictated by the need for speed and business efficacy. The Supreme Court now deals with cases beyond the traditional classification of civil, criminal and constitutional. Disputes have become increasingly complex as the emerging areas of science and communication have reshaped our lives. In an interconnected world, neither the genesis of disputes nor their resolution exists in silos.

However, despite the change in the world around us, the three principles highlighted during the inaugural sitting of this court continue to remain as relevant today to the functioning of an independent Supreme Court. This court has, in the last seventy-five years, faced old and new challenges in confronting the face of injustice and meeting the expectations of those at the receiving end of power. This court has, through the course of many years, charted its understanding of principles and developed innovative approaches to achieve the ideals of a democratic polity governed by the rule of law under a written constitution. We have received the baton in this long run from wise forebearers—judges and lawyers who walked through these portals—with fortitude and compassion. While much has changed in the world, the core of our ideals remains valid today as ever—our commitment to human dignity, liberty, equality and fraternity. We are inheritors of a commitment where the welfare of the nation walks in tandem with the well-being of her citizens.

The Constitution entrenches several institutional safeguards for an independent judiciary, such as a fixed retirement age and a bar against the alteration of the salary of judges after their appointment. However, these constitutional safeguards are not in themselves sufficient to ensure an independent judiciary. An independent judiciary does not merely mean the insulation of the *institution* from the executive and the legislative branches but also the independence of individual judges in the performance of their roles as judges. The art of judging must be free of social and political pressure and from the inherent biases human beings hold. Efforts are being made from within the institution to educate and sensitize judges across courts to unlearn their subconscious attitudes inculcated by social conditioning on gender, disability, race, caste and sexuality.

Over the course of years, this court has been called upon to navigate through the ambiguities of the law, resolve the conflict between individual and group rights and the tussle between economic development and social reformation. This court has in every such instance stood up to the test of time and adjudicated these complex questions based on constitutional principles. Over the years, the court has understood the Constitution not merely as a document establishing a nation state and delineating the role of institutions of governance in the State, but also as a document with a transformative potential to reform social and political relationships. Once the transformative potential of the Constitution was unlocked by courts, the scope of the judicial function also enlarged. For example, the judgments interpreting the mandate of reservation in Articles 15 and 16 as a facet and not as an exception to equality, the limits placed on Parliament's power to amend the Constitution through the basic structure doctrine and the dilution of the doctrine of political questions are important jurisprudential developments. Through them, this court has upheld core constitutional tenets by interpreting the Constitution as a living document. In none of those court terms were the answers to these questions as clear as the day. Multiple benches of this court agreed and disagreed to arrive at these celebrated jurisprudential developments. It is in this dialogical process between different benches that a conclusion closest to the constitutional framework is reached. In multiple voices, we speak both to the present and the future. We may be, as it is sometimes called, a polyvocal court. But the strength of our polyvocal nature lies in its ability to adapt dialogue as a processual instrument in bringing together a synthesis of ideas. The synthesis in our court brings together diversity and respects inclusion. That is the true social ethos of the court, its social conscience. In the many that wear its apparel, the court emerges as one soul that knits together the bar and the bench in our desire to ensure justice to our citizens.

The Constitution establishes the Supreme Court of India and confers on it wide-ranging powers to do justice. The court, as the highest appellate and constitutional court of the nation, derives but cannot rest its legitimacy solely on the Constitution. The legitimacy of this court is also derived from the confidence of citizens that it is a neutral and impartial arbiter of disputes, which would deliver timely justice.

This court has followed two approaches to enhance faith in its justice delivery mechanism. First, by not conferring permanence upon judicial decisions, this court is cognizant that the law is not constant but is ever evolving. The space for disagreement is always open. In fact, the strongest jurisprudential developments of this court have undergone multiple rounds of litigation over the course of years where the court has taken divergent views on questions of law. This court has gone about its task less attentive to its supremacy and more cognizant of the fact that the court, though final, is not infallible. It has not only opened itself up to critique but has also taken positive steps to create space for the critique of its work. The Supreme Court, for its golden jubilee celebration, published the book titled *Supreme but Not Infallible*, a compilation of essays written by leading practitioners celebrating and *critiquing* the work of the Supreme Court.

The second approach of the court to enhance faith in the justice delivery system has been to increase access to courts by diluting the procedural rules for the institution of cases. This court was opened to citizens in every corner of the nation irrespective of their social and economic status. In 1985, 24,716 letter petitions were received in English, Hindi and other regional languages. This number has since then undergone an exponential surge. In 2022, about 1,15,120 letter petitions were submitted to the Supreme Court, clearly indicating that the common person believes that they would be able to secure justice in these halls. These are letters of all hues—some fall within the ambit of the judicial function and others that do not. As judges, we need to know what lies within and outside the judicial function.

The increase in access to courts does not necessarily translate into access to justice. This court has, over the course of years, faced immense difficulty in keeping up with the surge in the institution of cases. Currently, a total of 65,915 registered cases are pending before the Supreme Court. Much as we would like to reassure ourselves that the mounting pile represents the faith of citizens in the line, we need to ask hard questions on what needs to be done. There has to be a radical change in the approach to decision-making. In our desire to ensure justice in each individual case, should we risk the court becoming dysfunctional? I believe that we must have a common understanding of how we argue and how we decide and, above all, on the cases we select for decision-making. If we do not make hard choices and take difficult calls to resolve these pressing issues, the euphoria generated from the past may well be short-lived.

In recent years, this court has taken a positive approach towards decreasing the pendency of cases. In 2023, 49,818 cases were registered; 2,41,594 cases were listed for hearing and 52,221 cases were disposed of, which is more than the number of cases registered. Technology has been a steadfast ally in decongesting pending matters. The electronic filing of cases has reduced the time between filing cases and curing defects. To address the pendency of old, miscellaneous, after-notice matters, directions have been issued to list on priority the 7430 miscellaneous after-notice matters that have been pending since 1993. Specialized benches for civil, criminal, direct and indirect tax matters, land acquisition, motor accident, personal law, labour and service cases have been constituted. Criminal cases in which the sentence of imprisonment is less than three years, and the convict has undergone half or more than half of the sentence, have been identified and are listed for disposal on priority. Pending constitution bench references that involve crucial questions about the interpretation of the Constitution are listed on priority. This is of particular significance also because it would reduce the pendency of numerous cases that are not disposed of because the questions of law are yet to be settled by the constitution bench.

This is where we are today. Before I end, it is worth reflecting on perhaps the oldest challenge of all. The Supreme Court of India was, at its very core, designed to ensure that the exercise of power under the Constitution is legitimate and in accord with the rule of law. The occasion may be the exercise of power by the State against an individual, by the Union against the states, by one state against another or even one individual or group of individuals against another. The court is not the sole guarantor, but it is the final arbiter that power may be used to liberate, emancipate and include, but never to oppress or ostracize. The novel challenges of today must never distract us from this most sacred duty of the court. The framers of the Constitution clothed the judges of the Supreme Court with immense power and independence and cast upon them the task of restricting the exercise of unbridled power.

These are solemn duties. Since its founding, this court has constantly striven to fulfil them and address the challenges that it has faced. We are indebted to the bar for the valuable support we receive in deciding cases. All too often, the rich jurisprudence evolved by this court is viewed as the work of craftsmanship of the judges who author these decisions. The sleepless nights and the incisive mind of each lawyer ought not to be glossed over under the pen of the judge. The celebration of the history of this court is complete as we recognize the contribution of advocates to this court's rich tapestry. The Supreme Court of India has a staff of 2148 persons. The unwavering dedication of every staff member, past and present, has been instrumental in ensuring the smooth, day-to-day functioning of the Supreme Court. Their quiet but essential contributions deserve our deepest recognition and appreciation.

Today is a day to celebrate this court's achievements, reflect on its deficiencies and aspire for its advancement. Introspection is the art of bringing the seemingly unattainable within the line of vision.

Acknowledgements

During the course of the eight and a half years I spent as a judge of the Supreme Court, including two years as the Chief Justice of India, I worked closely with brilliant young law clerks. Fresh out of law school, they gave me refreshing insights into law and life, beyond the isolated chambers of a judge. They were selected through a competitive process, which has since been institutionalized to ensure that judges' chambers provide equal opportunity and access to law researchers across the spectrum. My daily conversations with the law clerks over their work and my own were open, animated and often fierce. We discussed issues such as gender, marginalization and the preservation of fundamental liberties. While many of these conversations grew out of the cases on which we worked together, many of them transcended the formal environment of the courtroom. They were years of serious work and camaraderie, in a shared understanding that there are many truths and many paths to realizing truth and justice. My law clerks became friends and family. In sickness our home became their own. This book is a tribute to their belief that a just, inclusive and compassionate society is work in progress. They have been inspirational. This book would not have been possible without their inputs, research and ideas.

Anurag Bhaskar, a young Dalit scholar, met me first in Lucknow. He clerked with me at the Supreme Court before moving on to an LLM at Harvard Law School. Anurag is one of the foremost contemporary scholars on the philosophy, life and jurisprudence of Dr Babasaheb Bhimrao Ambedkar, the architect of the Indian Constitution. My conversations with Anurag gave me a close insight into the issues confronting marginalized communities. During my tenure as the Chief Justice of India, Anurag returned to work with me at the Centre for Research and Planning at the Supreme Court. It was he who suggested that my speeches be compiled into a book for a wider audience.

Maithili Pai, a gender activist to the core, led the conversation in our chambers on equal rights. She was a source of transformation for everyone in chambers, in attempting to change attitudes and mindsets. The brilliant trio—Karan Gupta, Sarthak Karol and Vasudevan Devadasan—worked relentlessly, sometimes for thirty-six hours on the trot. They voluntarily assumed these work schedules, with Sarthak redesigning the workspace in preference to a well-deserved summer recess. Karan pursued a BCL at Oxford, Sarthak an LLM at Cambridge and at Columbia, and Vasu is pursuing an LLM at Melbourne University. Each of them was fiercely protective and fearless in voicing their views in chambers.

Nivedhitha K (Nivy) worked initially as an intern. Barely into her internship, Nivy persuaded me into realizing that the view I was about to take on the law of pre-emption was in error. She stayed on for nearly three years as a law clerk, producing stellar pieces of research and analysis. She has met the most unrealistic of deadlines she set for herself in her own quiet and unassuming manner. Nivy is a Fulbright scholar at Harvard Law School for 2025-26.

Sonal Rawat has a repertoire that spans into public international law and environmental governance. She has been a source of amazing thoughts on issues as diverse as climate change and child marriage. Sonal is pursuing an LLM at New York University (NYU).

Aishwarya Singh and Nauman Beig have provided deeply personal insights into the aspirations of the queer community. Spoorthi Cotha has always had a fresh perspective on any issue she worked on. Anuna Tiwari (on a scholarship to Cambridge for an LLM) is gifted with producing that rare turn of phrase. Ankita Gupta has been brilliant on issues ranging from commercial to constitutional law. Pratik Dixit has brought a sense of balance when things were fraught.

Rahul Bajaj is a Rhodes scholar and his work on disability has helped in making real changes in the legal profession.

Aarushi Nargas, Aditya Garg, Dayaar Singla, Gayatri Gupta, Sharvari Kothawade and Suniti Sampath have each contributed immensely to the development of the ideas that find expression in this book.

From the Fullbright to the Rhodes Scholarship, across Harvard, Columbia, NYU, Oxford and Cambridge, my law clerks are shining stars in the firmament of the law. Numerous interns have contributed their research and analysis to this compilation, including Aaradhya Sethia and Neil Modi.

My sons Abhinav and Chintan Chandrachud are prolific authors and speakers. Each one of their books has inspired me to make my own debut. Their quest for academic excellence in the midst of busy professional careers—Abhinav as counsel at the Bombay High Court and Chintan, as barrister and door tenant at Brick Court Chambers in London—inspired me to write beyond my judgments. At the cost of their own professional advancement, they decided not to appear before the Supreme Court of India so long as I was a judge and later the Chief Justice of India. I owe an immense debt of gratitude to them for being ethical and principled in the pursuit of their professional careers. They have followed a family tradition—years ago, I had in deference to the wishes of my father commenced law practice after he retired as Chief Justice of India.

My spouse Kalpana is my best friend, critic and an abiding source of solace and companionship in challenging times. In many areas of life and liberty, she has chiselled at my own ignorance. A life in the law can induce complacency and a life in judging can breed isolation. Kalpana has ensured that mine does not follow that path. She has stood steadfastly in support of my work, enriching it with her own commitment to gender equality, rights and liberty. She has devoted herself and her time to bringing up our daughters Priyanka and Mahi. Mahi, Priyanka and Kalpana have led me by example into the pursuit of an ethical, vegan lifestyle and protecting animal rights. Priyanka and Mahi have an uncanny ability to come up with insights which lead me into an uncharted area of thought.

Radha and Disha have become daughters within the family. Our grandchildren—Uday, Aparna, Shloka and Yeshwant—bring joy in the simple things of life; through their poems, paintings, music, videos and one-liners.

My parents, Yeshwant and Prabha, would have been delighted to see this book in print. If my father were to write at the end of a long tenure on the bench between 1961 and 1985, it would have filled quite some library space. Much of his public speaking was extempore and apart from the memories of those who heard his brilliant oratory, there are only a few recordings of his speeches that remain. My father gave the family time even when he was a busy judge. My parents led by example without expecting conformity. Kalpana's parents, Prafulla Kumar Das and Urmila Das, truly made me their own, even accepting my spoken version of Oriya with a smile and uncritical affection.

Neema and Dilip—my sister and brother-in-law—were the ones who motivated me to challenge myself and encouraged me to apply for admission to Harvard Law School. Their consistent support, love and affection continue to provide balm to my shoulders.

My secretaries Anju Arora and Chetan Arora have provided dedicated support. Whether it was my unearthly early-morning work schedules or weekend travel, judgment writing or seminar speeches, they have been unflinching in their commitment. They have handled numerous engagements and the responsibilities of my office with care. To them, I owe a debt of gratitude. Atul Kurhekar, secretary general of the Supreme Court when I was the Chief Justice of India, Rakesh Kumar, registrar, Judges' Administration and International Relations, and Mahesh T Patankar, registrar, provided solid support in my work as the Chief Justice of India. Uma Narayan provided research assistance of a high order, initially as a librarian in the Bombay High Court and later as registrar (Judges' Library) in the Supreme Court.

I am deeply grateful to my publishers, Penguin Random House India, for agreeing to host this project. Milee Ashwarya has been patient and professional; kind yet firm in nudging me into meeting the schedule for publication. The entire team at Penguin has provided its expertise in areas of publishing into which I am gaining new insights, thanks to them.

Rachna Kalra as a publishing professional has brought her years of experience in ensuring that the publication sees the light of day. She has an amazing array of contacts in publishing. Rachna has ensured that her long years of friendship with Kalpana and me do not intrude into her professionalism.

My grateful thanks to Ameet Naik, the founder and presiding partner of Naik, Naik and Company. Ameet relieved me of overseeing the nuances of the contract; something which even a judge of twenty-five years of experience looked at with trepidation.

The publishers have graciously agreed that my part of the proceeds of this book be handed over to my alma mater, Campus Law Centre, Delhi University, to be utilized in memory of my distinguished law teachers, Professor Lotika Sarkar, Professor B. Sivaramayya and Professor Mool Chand Sharma.

Thanks to Aditi Jog for her assistance.

The errors and omissions are mine.

Notes

Introduction

1. Richard A. Posner, Introduction to *Oliver Wendell Holmes, Jr., The Essential Holmes* (Richard A. Posner ed., 1992).
2. Yehuda Berg, 'The Power of Words', HuffPost, 17 November 2011, available at: https://www.huffpost.com/entry/the-power-of-words_b_716183 (accessed on 22 July 2025).
3. 'By the Content of Her Character', Houghton University, 2024, available at: https://www.houghton.edu/news/by-the-content-of-her-character/ (accessed on 22 July 2025).
4. C.C. Francis, *'Quote of the Day - Happiness can be found even in the darkest of times, when one only remembers to turn on the light.' Albus Dumbledore'| Halcyon,"* Medium, 2020, available at: https://medium.com/halcyonpub/qotd-happiness-can-be-found-even-in-the-darkest-of-times-when-one-only-remembers-to-turn-on-the-light-5fa45386682c (accessed on 22 July 2025).
5. Ruth Bader Ginsburg, Mary Hartnett and Wendy W. Williams, *My Own Words* (Simon & Schuster, 2016).
6. Ruth Bader Ginsburg in pictures and her own words, BBC, 2020, available at: https://www.bbc.com/news/world-us-canada-54218139 (accessed on 22 July 2025).
7. Primary Sources, *Woodrow Wilson Asks 'What Is Progress?'* Vol. 4999, no. 1 (1912): 7.
8. Sri M. Hidayatullah, *Lest We Forget*, available at: https://www.allahabadhighcourt.in/event/LestWeForgetMHidayatullah.pdf (accessed on 31 July 2025).

9. Ibid.
10. John Locke, *Two Treatises of Government*, Vol. V (1823), 146.

Chapter 1: The Sounds and Silences of Our Constitution

1. Speech at Chief Justice M.C. Chagla Memorial Lecture, Government Law College, Mumbai, 11 March 2017.
2. Laurence H. Tribe, *On Reading the Constitution,* The Tanner Lectures on Human Values (1986).
3. B.R. Ambedkar, Constituent Assembly Debates, 4 November 1948.
4. Sir Ivor Jennings famously characterized the Indian Constitution as being a 'lawyers' constitution' for being 'too long, too detailed, too rigid'. See Fali S. Nariman, 'The Way Forward', Seminar, No. 615, 2010, available at: https://www.india-seminar.com/2010/615/615_fali_s_nariman.htm (accessed on 11 August 2025).
5. Sujit Choudhury, Madhav Khosla and Pratap Bhanu Mehta (eds), 'Locating Indian Constitutionalism', *The Oxford Handbook of the Indian Constitution* (Oxford University Press, 2016), 2.
6. H.L.A. Hart, *The Concept of Law* (Third edition, Oxford University Press, 2012), 130.
7. James Madison, 'Concerning the Difficulties of the Convention in Devising a Proper Form of Government', *The Federalist,* no. 37.
8. Philip Bobbitt, 'Constitutional Fate', *Texas Law Review*, Vol. 58, no. 4 (1980): 695.
9. *See* Thomas E. Baker, 'Constitutional Theory in a Nutshell', *William & Mary Bill of Rights Journal*, Vol. 13, no.1 (2004): 57.
10. Robert H. Bork, 'The Constitution, Original Intent, and Economic Rights', *San Diego Law Review,* Vol. 23 (1986): 823.
11. Antonin Scalia (Amy Gutmann ed.), *A Matter of Interpretation: Federal Courts and the Law* (Prince University Press, 1998), 38.
12. Antonin Scalia, 'Originalism: The Lesser Evil', *University of Cincinnati Law Review,* Vol. 57 (1988–89): 849.
13. *Missouri v. Holland,* 252 U.S. 416 (1920).
14. William H. Rehnquist, 'The Notion of Living Constitution', *Harvard Journal of Law and Public Policy,* Vol. 29, no. 2 (2006): 401.

15. *A.K. Gopalan v. State of Madras*, AIR 1966 SC 816.
16. Jack M. Balkin, 'Alive and Kicking: Why No One Truly Believes in a Dead Constitution', Slate, 29 August 2005, available at: http://www.slate.com/articles/news_and_politics/jurisprudence/2005/08/alive_and_kicking.html (accessed 9 March 2017).
17. Jack M. Balkin is the Knight professor of constitutional law and the First Amendment at Yale Law School. A leading scholar of constitutional theory, his work spans free speech, legal interpretation and the impact of technology on democracy.
18. *Supra*, note 16.
19. Hermann Hesse, *Siddhartha: An Indian Tale*, trans. Joachim Neugroschel (New York: Penguin Books, 2013), 25
20. Laurence H. Tribe, 'Soundings and Silences', *Michigan Law Review Online,* Vol. 115 (2016): 26, 32.
21. Ibid., 34–37.
22. *Krishna Kumar Singh & Anr v. State of Bihar & Ors*, (2017) 3 SCC 1.
23. Article 358(1), Article 359(1A), The Constitution of India.
24. *Supra, note 22*, 91.
25. *Zee Telefilms Ltd v. Union of India,* (2005) 4 SCC 649.
26. Article 254, The Constitution of India.
27. *State of Orissa v. M.A. Tulloch and Co.*, AIR 1964 SC 1284.
28. *Hingir-Rampur Coal Co, Ltd v. State of Orissa*, AIR 1961 SC 459.
29. *Supra*, note 20, at 40.
30. *A.K. Gopalan v. State of Madras*, AIR 1950 SC 27.
31. Ibid., 97.
32. *Rustom Cavasjee Cooper v. Union of India*, AIR 1970 SC 564.
33. *Ram Singh v. State of Delhi* [1951] 2 SCR 451; *Naresh Shridhar Mirajkar v. State of Maharashtra* [1966] 3 SCR 744.
34. *Sakal Papers (P) Ltd v. Union of India* [1962] 3 SCR 842; *Express News Papers (P) Ltd v. Union of India* [1959] 1 SCR 135.
35. *Nabam Rebia v. Deputy Speaker*, 2016 (11) SCC 673.
36. Ibid., 143.
37. *Kharak Singh v. State of Uttar Pradesh*, 1963 (2) Cri LJ 329.
38. *Gobind v. State of Madhya Pradesh*, AIR 1975 SC 1378.
39. On 24 August 2017, a nine-judge bench of the Supreme Court (of which Justice Chandrachud was a part), handed down the verdict

in *K.S. Puttaswamy v. Union of India* (2017) 10 SCC 1. In doing so, the court upheld the right to privacy as being a fundamental right under Article 21.

40. *People's Union of Civil Liberties v. Union of India*, AIR 1997 SC 568.
41. *Griswold v. Connecticut*, 381 US 479 (1965).
42. *Kesavananda Bharati v. State of Kerala* (1973) 4 SCC 225.
43. *Shankari Prasad Singh Deo v. Union of India*, AIR 1951 SC 458; *Sajjan Singh v. State of Rajasthan*, AIR 1965 SC 845.
44. *Golak Nath v. State of Punjab*, AIR 1967 SC 1643.
45. *Supra* Note 42, 1537(vii).
46. As envisaged in *Kesavananda Bharati*, basic structure included the supremacy of the Constitution, republican and democratic form of government, secular character of the Constitution, separation of powers, federal character of the Constitution, mandate to build a welfare state contained in the Directive Principles of State Policy, maintenance of the unity and integrity of India, sovereignty of the country, Essential features of individual freedoms, provision of social, economic and political justice, liberty of thought, expression, belief, faith and worship and equality of status and opportunity.
47. *Indira Nehru Gandhi v. Raj Narain & Anr*, AIR 1975 SC 1590.
48. *I.R. Coelho v. State of Tamil Nadu*, AIR 2007 SC 861.
49. *S.P. Gupta v. Union of India*, AIR 1982 SC 149.
50. *Supreme Court Advocates-on-Record Association v. Union of India*, (1993) 4 SCC 441.
51. *Supreme Court Advocates-on-Record Association v. Union of India*, W.P. (Civil) No. 13 of 2013, 16 October 2015.
52. *Introduction to the Study of the Law of the Constitution* (Eighth ed., 1915), 87.
53. *Miller & Another v. Secretary of State* [2017] UKSC 5 (Brexit Case) 277.
54. Ibid.,122.
55. Michael Foley, *The Silence of Constitutions: Gaps, 'Abeyances,' and Political Temperament in the Maintenance of Government* (London: Routledge, 1989).

Chapter 2: Indian Environmentalism

1. Keynote Address at the National Green Tribunal Regional Conference on Environment. Queens Garden, Pune, 7 October 2017.
2. Ramachandra Guha, 'The Past & Present of Indian Environmentalism', *The Hindu*, 27 March 2013, available at: http://www.thehindu.com/opinion/lead/the-past-present-of-indian-environmentalism/article4551665.ece (accessed on 12 July 2025).
3. DTE Staff, 'Looking Back at Stockholm 1972: What Indira Gandhi Said Half a Century go on Man & Environment', *Down to Earth*, 30 May 2022, available at: https://www.downtoearth.org.in/environment/looking-back-at-stockholm-1972-what-indira-gandhi-said-half-a-century-ago-on-man-environment-83060 (accessed on 13 July 2025).
4. Jairam Ramesh, 'The Two Cultures Revisited: The Environment-Development Debate in India', *Economic and Political Weekly*, Vol. 45, no. 42 (2010).
5. *Supra*, note 2.
6. Jairam Ramesh, 'Poverty Is the Greatest Polluter: Remembering Indira Gandhi's Stirring Speech in Stockholm', Wire, 19 November 2018, available at: https://thewire.in/144555/indira-gandhi-nature-pollution/ (accessed on 12 July 2025).
7. The extract forms part of the proclamation adopted at the UN Conference on Human Environment at Stockholm in June 1972. It has been quoted with approval by Justice E.S. Venkataramiah in *M.C. Mehta v. Union of India* (Kanpur Tanneries: 22-9-87), (1987) 4 SCC 463, in 4 of the judgment.
8. *Karnataka Industrial Areas Development Board v. Sri C. Kenchappa*, AIR 2006 SC 2038.
9. Bharat H. Desai and Balraj Sidhu, 'On the Quest for Green Courts in India', *Journal of Court Innovation*, Vol. 3, no. 1 (2010): 79.
10. 1986 (2) SCC 176.
11. 1996 (3) SCC 212.
12. AIR 1999 SC 812.

13. The National Green Tribunal Act, 2010 (Act 19 of 2010), Preamble
14. National Green Tribunal, available at http://www.greentribunal.gov.in/.
15. Ibid.
16. Shalaka Shinde, 'India's "go green" mission: National Green Tribunal, Pune sows landmark judgments', *Hindustan Times*, 20 June 2020, available at: http://www.hindustantimes.com/pune-news/india-s-go-green-mission-national-green-tribunal-pune-sows-landmark-judgments/story ax1DJE9cwc34pSIMVwgjPJ.html (accessed on 12 July 2025).
17. *M.C. Mehta v. Union of India* (M.A. No. 594/2017 and 598/2017) (Principal Bench, New Delhi).
18. Ibid.
19. *Praffula Samantra v. Union of India*, Appeal No. 8/2011 (Principal Bench, New Delhi)
20. *Ramdas Janardan Koli v. Secretary, Government of India, MISC.* APPLICATION No. 19/2014 (Western Zone [WZ]).
21. Application No. 2/2014 (WZ).
22. Ambient Air Quality | Department of Environment, Department of Environment Government of NCT of Delhi, available at: https://environment.delhi.gov.in/environment/ambient-air-quality (accessed on 13 July 2025).
23. OA 21/2014
24. *Betty C. Alvares v. State of Goa*, MISC APPLICATION NOS. 32 OF 2014 (WZ).
25. Misha Singh and Shekhar Singh, 'Transparency and the Natural Environment', *Economic and Political Weekly*, Vol. 41, no. 15 (2006).
26. Ibid.
27. Ibid.
28. Appeal No. 39 of 2012, Judgment dated 7 April 2016.
29. Shibani Ghosh, 'Case Note: Access to Information as Ruled by the Indian Environmental Tribunal: Save Mon Region Federation v. Union of India', *Review of European Community and International Environmental Law,* 6 August 2013.
30. Geetanjoy Sahu, 'Impact of the National Green Tribunal on Environmental Governance in India: An Analysis of Methods

and Perspectives', *Journal on Environmental Law Policy and Development* (NLSIU), Vol. 3, 2016.

31. Livelaw News Network, 'Appeal against National Green Tribunal orders can be heard by High Court', Live Law, 6 February 2014, available at http://www.livelaw.in/appeal-national-green-tribunal-orders-can-heard-high-court/ (accessed on 12 July 2025).
32. Rahi Gaikwad, 'Challenges to NGT orders in courts a growing concern', *The Hindu*, 23 March 2016, available at: http://www.thehindu.com/news/cities/mumbai/news/challenges-to-ngt-orders-in-courts-a-growing-concern/article8387736.ece (accessed on 12 July 2025).
33. Yukti Choudhary, 'Tribunal on Trial', *Down to Earth*, 15 November 2014, https://www.downtoearth.org.in/environment/tribunal-on-trial-47400 (accessed on 13 July 2025).
34. Ibid.
35. Ibid.
36. 'Shock waves: Managing the impacts of climate change on poverty', World Bank, available at https://openknowledge.worldbank.org/bitstream/handle/10986/22787/9781464806735.pdf (accessed on 12 July 2025).
37. See P. Sainath, *Everybody Loves a Good Drought* (New Delhi: Penguin, 2000).
38. 'Shock waves: Managing the impacts of climate change on poverty', *World Bank.*
39. Organization for Security and Co-operation in Europe, 'Gender and Environment: A Guide to the Integration of Gender Aspects in the OSCE's Environmental Projects', Organization for Security and Co-operation in Europe
40. United Nations Environment Programme, 'Gender and nature action', UNEP, published 3 December 2024, https://www.unep.org/topics/gender/gender-and-nature-action (accessed on 22 July 2025).
41. 'Protecting the Environment: Why a gender perspective matters', Swedish Society for Nature Conservation (3 November 2015) available at https://www.sei-international.org/mediamanager/documents/Publications/SEI-2015-Report-Segnestam-Protectin

gTheEnvironmentWhyGenderMatters.pdf (accessed on 12 July 2025).

42. Gregson et al. (1997), cited from Ibid.
43. L. Segnestam, Protecting the environment: Why a gender perspective matters (Stockholm: Swedish Society for Nature Conservation (Naturskyddsföreningen), 2015), 15.
44. Section K, Beijing Declaration and Platform for Action.
45. *Gender and Environment*, UN Environment, available at http://www.unep.org/gender/who-we-are/gender-enviroment.
46. *Gender and Environment,* Swedish International Development Cooperation Agency *available at* http://www.sida.se/English/?epieditmode=true.
47. Ibid.
48. Ibid.
49. Ibid
50. United Nations, *Beijing Declaration and Platform for Action*, Fourth World Conference on Women, 15 September 1995, A/CONF.177/20 (1995) and A/CONF.177/20/Add.1 (1995), accessed August 5, 2025, http://www.un.org/womenwatch/daw/beijing/pdf/BDPfA%20E.pdf. (accessed on 12 July 2025).
51. Section K, Beijing Declaration and Platform for Action.
52. *Gender and Environment,* Swedish International Development Cooperation Agency available at http://www.sida.se/English/?epieditmode=true (accessed on 12 July 2025).
53. Ibid.
54. Ibid.
55. The Johannesburg Declaration on Sustainable Development, 1 (2002), available at: https://wayback.archiveit.org/12090/20220917132144/https://ec.europa.eu/environment/archives/wssd/documents/wssd_pol_declaration.pdf (accessed on 22 July 2025).
56. The Economic & Social Council, *Future Programme, Organisation and Methods of Work of the Commission Draft decision by the CSD11 - submitted by the Chairperson,* available at: https://www.un.org/esa/sustdev/csd/csd11/draft_decision.pdf (accessed on 22 July 2025).
57. United Nations et al., 'Agreed conclusions 1997/1 Women and Environment', I 23 (1997), available at: https://www.

un.org/womenwatch/daw/csw/agreedconclusions/Agreed%20 conclusions%2041st%20session.pdf (accessed on 11 August 2025.

58. Organization for Security and Co-operation in Europe, 'Gender and Environment: A Guide to the Integration of Gender Aspects in the OSCE's Environmental Projects', Organization for Security and Co-operation in Europe, available at: http://www.osce.org/gender/36360?download=true=true.
59. Section K, Beijing Declaration and Platform for Action (1995).
60. Prahlad Shekhawat, 'The Real Challenges to Sustainable Development', *India Together*, 22 May 2015, available at: http://indiatogether.org/articles/challenges-to-sustainable-development-government/ (accessed on 12 July 2025).
61. Ibid.
62. Sunderlal Bahuguna, *Sustainable Development in India: Perspectives by - PDF*, SCRIBD, https://www.scribd.com/doc/48469539/Sustainable-Development-in-India-Perspectives-by-Sunderlal-Bahuguna.
63. Ibid.
64. Guy Ryder, 'A Greener Future Will Not Be Decent by Definition, but by Design', Wire, 5 June 2017, available at: https://thewire.in/143728/green-economies-decent-work/ (accessed on 12 July 2025).

Chapter 3: The Indian Legal Profession in the Age of Globalization

1. Keynote Address at the Book Launch of The Indian Legal Profession in the Age of Globalization, organized by Harvard Law School. Taj Mahal Hotel, New Delhi, 15 December 2017.
2. Words of N.R. Madhava Menon, founder of the National Law School of Bangalore (the first and top law school in the country).
3. David B. Wilkins, Vikramaditya S. Khanna and David M. Trubek, eds. *The Indian Legal Profession in the Age of Globalization: The Rise of the Corporate Legal Sector and its Impact on Lawyers and Society* (Cambridge: Cambridge University Press, 2017), 526
4. Ruth Bader Ginsburg in 'Pursuit of the Public Good: Lawyers Who Care University of the District of Columbia David A. Clarke School of Law Joseph L. Rauh Lecture April 9, 2001

- Supreme Court of the United States' (*Supreme Court of the United States*, 2001), available at: https://www.supremecourt.gov/publicinfo/speeches/viewspeech/sp_04-09-01a (accessed on 13 July 2025).

5. For reference, see P. Weir, L. Jones and N. Sheeran, 'Australian Lawyers' Experience of Exposure to Traumatic Material: A Qualitative Study', *Psychiatry, Psychology and Law*, Vol. 28, no. 3 (2020): 363–81. See also, Secrecy and Fear of Stigma Among the Barriers to Lawyer Well-Being, YourABA (December 2017); 'New Study on Lawyer Well-Being Reveals Serious Concerns for Legal Profession', American Bar Association, December 2017, available at: https://www.americanbar.org/news/abanews/publications/youraba/2017/december-2017/secrecy-and-fear-of-stigma-among-the-barriers-to-lawyer-well-bei/ (accessed on 24 July 2025); and Bernice Donald and Alex Bransford, 'Widening the Lens, Sharpening the Focus: Mental Health and the Legal Profession', *Fordham Law Review*, Vol. 89 (2021): 2497, available at: https://ir.lawnet.fordham.edu/flr/vol89/iss6/7 (accessed on 24 July 2025).
6. Adele J. Bergin and Nerina L. Jimmieson, 'Australian Lawyer Well-Being: Workplace Demands, Resources and the Impact of Time-Billing Targets', *Psychiatry, Psychology and Law*, Vol. 21 (2014): 427, available at: https://www.researchgate.net/publication/278107010_Australian_Lawyer_Well-being_Workplace_Demands_Resources_and_the_Impact_of_Time-billing_Targets (accessed on 13 July 2025).

Chapter 4: The Rule of Law in India: Past and Present

1. Speech delivered at the University of Hawai'i at Mānoa, William S. Richardson School of Law, Hawai'i, 4 June 2018.
2. In Hindu religious traditions, Shastras and Smritis are collections of texts that guide religious and social life. Shastras are treatises on specific fields of knowledge, while Smritis are remembered or recorded traditions, often dealing with law, ethics and conduct.
3. Ananta Kumar Giri, 'Rule of Law and Indian Society: Colonial Encounters, Post-Colonial Experiments and Beyond', *Jura*

Gentium (2005), available online at http://www.juragentium.org/topics/rol/en/giri.htm#29 (accessed on 18 June 2025).

4. André Beteille, *Democracy and Its Institutions,* Oxford India Paperbacks (2012), 172.
5. Ibid.
6. Ibid., 170.
7. *Supra*, note 3.
8. Beteille, *supra,* note 4, at 166.
9. Ibid.
10. Ibid., 178.
11. Ibid., 166.
12. M.P. Jain, *Indian Constitutional Law*, Seventh ed. (Nagpur: LexisNexis, 2017), 7.
13. Ibid.
14. Beteille, *supra,* note 4, at 178.
15. Beteille, *supra,* note 4. See also Granville Austin, *Indian Constitution: Cornerstone of a Nation,* Oxford University Press (1966).
16. Granville Austin, *Working a Democratic Constitution: A History of the Indian Experience,* Oxford University Press (1999).
17. Austin, *supra note 16*, xii.
18. Part III of the Indian Constitution.
19. Part IV of the Indian Constitution.
20. Austin, *supra note 16*, xiii.
21. Article 141 of the Indian Constitution.
22. *Bachan Singh v. State of Punjab*, AIR 1982 SC 1325; *State of Bihar v. Subhash Singh,* (1997) 4 SCC 430.
23. See http://judis.nic.in/supremecourt/chejudis.asp; see also https://wikis.fu-berlin.de/display/SBprojectrol/India; and https://wikis.fu-berlin.de/display/SBprojectrol/India.
24. (1973) 4 SCC 225.
25. AIR 1976 SC 1207.
26. Article 356 of the Indian Constitution.
27. *Additional District Magistrate, Jabalpur v. Shivakant Shukla*, AIR 1976 SC 1207 at 527.
28. 'Fading Hope in India', *New York Times*, 30 April 1976, available at https://www.nytimes.com/1976/04/30/archives/fading-hope-in-india.html (accessed on 19 June 2025).

29. *Justice K.S. Puttaswamy (Retd) v. Union of India*, AIR 2017 SC 4161.
30. *Indira Nehru Gandhi v. Raj Narain*, AIR 1975 SC 2295; *S.P. Gupta v. Union of India*, AIR 1982 SC 149; *State of Bihar v. Subhash Singh*, (1997) 4 SCC 430.
31. *Kalpana Mehta v. Union of India*, Writ Petition (Civil) Nos. 558 of 2012 and 921 of 2013 (Decided on 9 May 2018).
32. Upendra Baxi, 'The Rule of Law in India', *SUR: International Journal on Human Rights*, Vol. 6 (2007): 7.
33. *S.P. Gupta v. Union of India*, AIR 1982 SC 149.
34. Ibid.
35. *PUCL v. Union of India, 2001* (also known as the Right to Food Case). The Supreme Court had appointed Supreme Court's Commissioners' Office on Right to Food to monitor the implementation of its interim orders.
36. *Nilabati Behera v. State of Orissa*, AIR 1993 SC 1960.
37. *Supra, note 35.*
38. *Hussainara Khatoon v. State of Bihar*, AIR 1979 SC 1360.
39. *Olga Tellis v. Bombay Municipal Corporation*, (1985) 3 SCC 545.
40. *Supra, note 29.*
41. *Unni Krishnan v. State of Andhra Pradesh*, AIR 1993 SC 217.
42. *Parmanand Katara v. Union of India*, AIR 1989 SC 2039.
43. *M.C. Mehta v. Union of India*, (1987) 4 SCC 463.
44. *State of UP v. Raj Narain*, AIR 1975 SC 865.
45. *Nilabati Behera v. State of Orissa*, AIR 1993 SC 1960.
46. Upendra Baxi, 'The Rule of Law in India', *SUR 6* (2007), available at: https://sur.conectas.org/en/rule-law-india/ (accessed on 6 August 2025).
47. United Nations and the Rule of Law, available at: https://www.un.org/ruleoflaw/what-is-the-rule-of-law/ (accessed on 11 August 2025).
48. World Justice Project, Rule of Law Index 2017–2018, available at: https://worldjusticeproject.org/sites/default/files/documents/WJP-ROLI-2018-June-Online-Edition_0.pdf (accessed on 22 July 2025).

49. Devesh Kapur and Milan Vaishnav, 'Strengthening Rule of Law', available at https://vaishnavmilan.files.wordpress.com/2011/08/rule-of-law-final.pdf (accessed on 19 June 2025).
50. Ibid.
51. Burt Neuborne, 'The Supreme Court of India', *International Journal of Constitutional Law*, Vol. 1 (2003): 476.
52. Marc Galanter, 'The Displacement of Traditional Law in Modern India', *Journal of Social Issues*, Vol. 24 (1968): 65–91, available at: http://www.deepdyve.com/lp/wiley/the-displacement-of-traditional-law-in-modern-india-tccLnzbfWp (accessed on 13 July 2025).
53. *Supra note at* 182.
54. Suranjita Ray, 'Khap Panchayats: Reinforcing Caste Hierarchies', Mainstream Weekly, 22 July 2010, available at: https://www.mainstreamweekly.net/article2205.html (accessed on 19 June 2025).
55. J.W. Spellman, *Political Theory in Ancient India: A Study of Kingship from the Earliest Times to circa A.D. 300* (Oxford: Clarendon Press, 1964), 111.
56. Rajeev Bhargava, 'What the Ruler and the Ruled Owe One Another', *The Hindu*, 4 March 2018, http://www.thehindu.com/opinion/columns/what-the-ruler-and-the-ruled-owe-one-another/article22920270.ece (accessed on 19 June 2025).
57. Amartya Sen, 'The Idea of Justice' (The Belknap Press of Harvard University Press, Cambridge, Massachusetts, 2009), available at: https://studylib.net/doc/8854001/amartya-sen-the-idea-of-justice (accessed on 13 July 2025).
58. Tufail Ahmad, 'Democracy in India Part 4: Rule of law routinely trampled upon by politicians in power, who act like "new kings"', FirstPost, 3 May 2018, available at: https://www.firstpost.com/india/democracy-in-india-part-4-rule-of-law-routinely-trampled-upon-by-politicians-in-power-who-act-like-new-kings-4434975.html (accessed on 19 June 2025).
59. Rajeev Bhargava, 'What the Ruler and the Ruled Owe One Another', *The Hindu*, 4 March 2018, https://www.thehindu.

com/opinion/columns/what-the-ruler-and-the-ruled-owe-one-another/article22920270.ece

60. *Kalpana Mehta v. Union of India, AIR 2018 SC 2493.*
61. C. Raj Kumar, 'Democracy and the Rule of Law', *The Hindu*, 29 September 2016, available at http://www.thehindu.com/todays-paper/tp-opinion/Democracy-and-the-rule-of-law-in-India/article14838443.ece (accessed on 19 June 2025).
62. Constituent Assembly Debates, Volume XI.

Chapter 5: The Rule of Law in a Constitutional Democracy

1. Speech at the 19th Annual Bodh Raj Sawhney Memorial Oration, National Law University, New Delhi, 8 September 2018.
2. *Navtej Singh Johar v. Union of India*, AIR 2018 SC 4321.
3. Ibid., opinion of Dhananjaya Chandrachud J. at 380.
4. Lon L. Fuller (1964), *The Morality of Law. New Haven*, CT: Yale University Press. Lon Fuller developed a framework comprising of eight principles – being inner moral requirements - that every legal system needs to satisfy so as to be considered.
5. (2012) 6 SCC 613.
6. The Finance Act, 2012.
7. *State of West Bengal v. Anwar Ali Sarkar*, AIR 1952 SC 75.
8. *E.P. Royappa v. State of Tamil Nadu*, 1974 AIR 555.
9. *A.K. Gopalan v. State of Madras*, AIR 1950 SC 27.
10. *Kesavananda Bharati v. State of Kerala*, 1973 Supp. (1) S.C.R. 1.
11. *ADM Jabalpur v. Shivkant Shukla*, AIR 1976 SC 1207.
12. *I.C. Golaknath v. State of Punjab*, 1967 AIR 1643.
13. Bar Council Maharashtra v. M.V. Dabholkar, AIR 1976 SC 242.
14. Article 13, The Constitution of India, 1950.
15. *Krishna Kumar Singh v. State of Bihar*, 2017 (2) SCJ 136.
16. *A.K. Roy v. Union of India*, AIR 1982 SC 710.
17. (2018) 5 SCC 1.
18. *Justice K.S. Puttaswamy (Retd.) vs. Union of India*, (2017) 10 SCC 1.
19. *P.V. Narasimha Rao v. State (CBI/SPE),* (1998) 4 SCC 626.
20. *Kalpana Mehta v. Union of India*, AIR 2018 SC 2493.

21. *Government of NCT of Delhi v. Union of India*, 2023 SCC Online SC 606.
22. Amartya Sen, *Identity and Violence: The Illusion of Destiny* (New York: W.W. Norton & Company, 2006).
23. *National Legal Services Authority v. Union of India*, AIR 2014 SC 1863.
24. *Air India v. Nergesh Meerza*, AIR 1981 SC 1829.

Chapter 6: Feminist Lawyering and Feminist Judging

1. Speech delivered at the event organized by O.P. Jindal Global University at the India Habitat Centre, New Delhi, on 6 October 2018.
2. Erika Rackley, Rosemary Hunter and Clare McGlynn, *Feminist Judgments: From Theory to Practice* (Hart Publishing, 2010), 40.
3. Ibid., 7.
4. Ibid., 37.
5. Ibid., 38.
6. Erika Rackley is professor of law at the University of Birmingham, UK, and a leading scholar in feminist legal theory and judicial diversity.
7. Erika Rackley, 'What a Difference Difference Makes: Gendered Harms and Judicial Diversity', in *Schultz and Shaw* (2012), above note 1, 49.
8. Heather Douglas, Francesca Bartlett, Trish Luker and Rosemary Hunter (eds), *Australian Feminist Judgments: Righting and Rewriting Law* (Hart Publishing, 2014), 6.
9. Rackley, Hunter and McGlynn, *Feminist Judgments,* 31.
10. Rosemary Hunter,' Can *feminist* judges make a difference?' *International Journal of the Legal Profession*, Vol. 15, No. 1-2 (2008): 10.
11. Hunter, 'Can *feminist* judges make a difference?', 10–12.
12. Rackley, Hunter and McGlynn, *Feminist Judgments*, 32.
13. *Shafin Jahan v. Ashokan K.M.*, AIR 2008 SC 582.
14. Ibid.
15. Rackley, Hunter and McGlynn, *Feminist Judgments*, 33.

16. Heather, Bartlett, Luker and Hunter, *Australian Feminist Judgments*, 2.
17. Bridget J. Crawford, Kathryn M. Stanchi and Linda L. Berger, 'Feminist Judging Matters: How Feminist Theory and Methods Affect the Process of Judgment', *University of Baltimore Law Review*, Vol. 47 (2018): 15–19, available at: https://digitalcommons.pace.edu/cgi/viewcontent.cgi?article=2087&context=lawfaculty (accessed on 20 July 2025).
18. Crawford, and Berger, 'Feminist Judging Matters', 20.
19. Carol Smart, *Feminism and the Power of Law* (Routledge, 1989).
20. Rackley, Hunter and McGlynn, *Feminist Judgments,* 55.
21. Ibid.
22. Undergraduate Library Awards, 'Can and Should Judges be Feminists: An Analysis of Feminist Judging', available at: http://www.undergraduatelibrary.org/system/files/undergraduate_awards_submission_2.pdf (accessed on 20 June 2025), 1.
23. Linda L. Berger, Kathryn M. Stanchi and Bridget J. Crawford, 'Introduction to the U.S. Feminist Judgments Project', *Scholarly Works*, Paper no. 995 (2016), available at: https://scholars.law.unlv.edu/facpub/995 (accessed on 23 July 2025), 3.
24. The UK Feminist Judgment Project.
25. Ibid.
26. Kathryn M. Stanchi, Linda L. Berger, and Bridget J. Crawford, 'Introduction to the U.S. Feminist Judgments Project', in *Feminist Judgments: Rewritten Opinions of the United States Supreme Court*, ed. Kathryn M. Stanchi, Linda L. Berger, and Bridget J. Crawford (New York: Cambridge University Press, 2016).
27. Ibid.
28. Rackley, Hunter and McGlynn, *Feminist Judgments*, 31.
29. Undergraduate Library Awards, 'Can and Should Judges be Feminists: An Analysis of Feminist Judging', 1, available at: http://www.undergraduatelibrary.org/system/files/undergraduate_awards_submission_2.pdf (accessed on 21 June 2025).
30. Undergraduate Library Awards, 2.
31. Rosemary Hunter, 'Can feminist judges make a difference?', *International Journal of the Legal Profession* 15, no. 1-2 (2008): 9, https://www.tandfonline.com/doi/abs/10.1080/09695950802439759.

32. Ibid.
33. Baines, Beverley, 'Must Feminist Judges Self-Identify as Feminist?', *Gender and Judging*, Ulrike Schultz and Gisela Shaw (eds), Hart Publishing, Forthcoming; Queen's University Legal Research Paper No. 015-037 (3 August 2009), available at: https://ssrn.com/abstract=1443324 (accessed on 23 July 2025).
34. Ibid.
35. Hunter, 'Can *feminist* judges make a difference?', 9.
36. Rackley, Hunter and McGlynn, *Feminist Judgments*, 31.
37. Hunter, 'Can *feminist* judges make a difference?',10.
38. Heather Douglas et al., eds., *Australian Feminist Judgments: Righting and Rewriting Law* (Oxford: Hart, 2015), 9.
39. Rosemary Hunter, Clare McGlynn, and Erika Rackley, eds., *Feminist Judgments: From Theory to Practice* (Oxford: Hart, 2010), 24.
40. Hunter, 'Can feminist judges make a difference?'10–12.
41. Rosemary Hunter, 'More Than Just a Different Face? Judicial Diversity and Decision-Making', *Current Legal Problems*, Vol. 68, no. 1 (2015): 131, available at: https://academic.oup.com/clp/article/68/1/119/337616 (accessed on 21 June 2025).
42. Rackley, Hunter and McGlynn, *Feminist Judgments*, 31.
43. For reference, see Aparna Chandra, Jhuma Sen and Rachna Chaudhary, 'Introduction: The Indian Feminist Judgements Project', *Indian Law Review*, Vol. 5, no. 3 (2021): 261–64. doi:10.1080/24730580.2021.1996077.
44. Hunter, 'More than Just a Different Face?', 131.
45. Ibid., 130.
46. Berger, Stanchi and Crawford, 'Introduction to the U.S. Feminist Judgments Project', 15.
47. Ibid.
48. *K.S. Puttaswamy v. Union of India*, AIR 2017 SC 4161
49. *Aruna Ramchandra Shanbaug v. Union of India*, (2011) 4 SCC 454.
50. Ratna Kapur, 'The Spectre of Aruna Shanbaug', Wire, 18 May 2015, available at: https://thewire.in/law/the-spectre-of-aruna-shanbaug (accessed on 13 July 2025).
51. *Navtej Singh Johar v. Union of India*, (2018) 10 SCC 1.
52. *Anuj Garg v. Hotels Association*, AIR 2008 SC 663.
53. *Joseph Shine v. Union of India*, AIR 2018 SC 4898.

54. *Santhini v. Vijaya Venketesh,* (2017) SCC OnLine SC 1080.
55. Professor Margaret Davies is the Matthew Flinders Distinguished Professor of Law at Flinders University (Australia), a legal theorist specializing in critical and feminist jurisprudence as well as the philosophy of property and pluralism. A foundation staff member of Flinders Law School, she is a Fellow of the Academy of Social Sciences in Australia and the Australian Academy of Law.
56. Margaret Davies, 'The Law Becomes Us: Rediscovering Judgment', *Feminist Legal Studies*, Vol. 20, no. 2 (2012): 167–81.

Chapter 7: Justice as a Narrative

1. Keynote Address at the IDIA Annual Conference: Law and Storytelling. Indian Law Institute, New Delhi, 8 December 2018.
2. Lon L. Fuller, 'The Case of the Speluncean Explorers', *Harvard Law Review*, Vol. 62, no. 4, February 1949.
3. Ibid., 27.
4. Ibid., 10.
5. Gerald Torres, 'Translation and Stories', *Harvard Law Review*, Vol. 115, no. 5 (March 2002).
6. Anthony G. Amsterdam and Jerome Bruner, *Minding the Law: How Courts Rely on Storytelling, and How Their Stories Change the Ways We Understand the Law—and Ourselves* (Cambridge, MA: Harvard University Press, 2000), 110.
7. James Boyd White, 'An Old-Fashioned View of the Nature of Law', *Theoretical Inquiries in Law*, Vol. 12, no. 1 (2011): 381–402, at 381.
8. Martha C. Nussbaum, 'Poets as Judges: Judicial Rhetoric and the Literary Imagination', *University of Chicago Law Review*, Vol. 62, no. 4 (Autumn 1995): 1477–1519.
9. *Navtej Singh Johar v. Union of India*, AIR 2018 SC 4321.
10. Urvashi Butalia, *The Other Side of Silence: Voices from the Partition of India* (Penguin Random House, 1999), 2.
11. Kamla Bhasin and Ritu Menon, 'An Exchange of Women', *Outlook*, 7 February 2024, available at: https://www.outlookindia.com/society/an-exchange-of-women-news-203611 (accessed on 22 June 2025).

12. *Virendra Singh v. State of U.P.* (1955) 1 SCR 415, 28.
13. *Indian Young Lawyers Association v. State of Kerala,* (2017) 10 SCC 689.
14. Nandini Sundar, 'The Constitution as a Living Document', Wire, 26 November 2018.

Chapter 8: Why Does the Constitution Matter?

1. Speech at the K.T. Desai Memorial Lecture, Bombay High Court, 17 December 2018.
2. 'In those days, to be invited by Chief Justice Chagla was itself a distinction.' Available at YouTube at 45:34, https://www.youtube.com/watch?v=AuHtaWL9TaU (accessed on 23 July 2025).
3. Courtroom 46 at the High Court of Bombay bears the distinction of being the court room from where the chief justice of the Bombay High Court conducts court proceedings. As a commemorative mark, there is a plaque on the wall outside, being the courtroom that witnessed the historic trial of Lokmanya Tilak after which he was sent to Mandalay prison in 1908.
4. Carl Schmitt (translated and edited by Jeffrey Seitzer), *Constitutional Theory* (Duke University Press (2008), 125, 128.
5. Jason Mazzone, 'The Creation of a Constitutional Culture', *Tulsa Law Review*, Vol. 40, no. 4 (2005): 4, available at: https://digitalcommons.law.utulsa.edu/cgi/viewcontent.cgi?referer=&httpsredir=1&article=2494&context=tlr (accessed on 23, 6, 2025).).
6. Sujit Choudhry, Madhav Khosla and Pratap Bhanu Mehta (eds), Chapter 1, 'Locating Indian Constitutionalism', *The Oxford Handbook of the Indian Constitution* (Oxford University Press, 2016), 2.
7. Shivprasad Swaminathan, 'India's Benign Constitutional Revolution', *The Hindu*, 26 January 2013, available at: https://www.thehindu.com/opinion/lead/India%E2%80%99s-benignconstitutional-revolution/article12318419.ece (accessed on 23 July 2025).
8. Ibid.
9. Adam Shinar, Accidental Constitutionalism: The Political Foundations and Implications of Constitution-Making in Israel

(2013), 217. Available at https://papers.ssrn.com/sol3/papers.cfm?abstract_id=2347839 (accessed on 23 June 2025).

10. *United Mizrahi Bank v. Migdal Cooperative Village*, 49(4) P.D. 221 (1995).
11. *United Mizrahi Bank Ltd. v. Migdal Cooperative Village, CA 6821/93,* [1995] Israel Law Reports, 1
12. M.V. Kamath, *Nani A. Palkhivala: A Life* (Hay House, 2007).
13. AIR 1950 SC 124.
14. AIR 1950 SC 129.
15. Constitution (First Amendment) Act, 1951.
16. AIR 1950 SC 27.
17. Zachary Elkins, Tom Ginsburg and James Melton, 'The Endurance of National Constitutions', John M. Olin Program in *Law and Economics Working Paper* No. 51 (2010), 8.
18. Sudhir Krishnaswamy, 'Constitutional Durability', India Seminar, available at: http://www.india-seminar.com/2010/615/615_sudhir_krishnaswamy.htm (accessed on 15 December 2018).
19. (1973) 4 SCC 225.
20. Choudhry et. al, Chapter 52: 'Property', *Oxford Handbook of the Indian Constitution.*
21. Shreeja Sen, 'Ten significant constitutional amendments', *Livemint*, 26 January 2017, available at: https://www.livemint.com/Politics/65oMWSoBghr4w4e6KCtb8L/Ten-significant-constitutional-amendments.html (accessed on 23 June 2025).
22. *Kesavananda Bharti v. State of Kerala, AIR 1973 SC 1461*, 634.
23. Ibid., 475.
24. Chintan Chandrachud, 'Constitutional Interpretation' (18 November 2015), *The Oxford Handbook of the Indian Constitution* (2016), available at SSRN: https://ssrn.com/abstract=2692834
25. Robert Post, professor of law at Yale University, commenting on the *Oxford Handbook of Indian Constitution.*
26. Granville Austin, Introduction, *The Indian Constitution: Cornerstone of a Nation* (Oxford University Press, 1966).
27. Rajeev Dhavan, 'Religious Freedom in India', *American Journal of Comparative Law*, Vol. 35 (1987): 209.
28. Austin, Introduction, *The Indian Constitution: Cornerstone of a Nation.*

29. (1994) 3 SCC 1.
30. Professor Domenico Amirante, Investing on diversity: Indian federalism in comparative perspective, Sapienza Universita Di Roma, available at: https://disp.web.uniroma1.it/sites/default/files/AMIRANTE_INVESTINGONDIVERSITY_ROME_ (accessed on 23 June 2025).
31. Harihar Bhattacharyya, 'Multiculturalism in Contemporary India', *International Journal on Multicultural Societies*, Vol. 5, no. 2 (2003): 48–161.
32. Rocco Amirante, 'Investing on Diversity: Indian Federalism in Comparative Perspective' (Paper presented at Sapienza Università di Roma, Rome, June 9-10, 2014), https://disp.web.uniroma1.it/sites/default/files/AMIRANTE_INVESTINGONDIVERSITY_ROME_9_10JUNE2014.pdf.
33. Robert C. Post, Democratic Constitutionalism and Cultural Heterogeneity, *Australian Journal of Legal Philosophy*, Vol. 25, no. 22 (2000): 185.
34. On 5 August 2019 the Government of India revoked the special status, or autonomy, granted under Article 370 of the Indian Constitution to Jammu and Kashmir. As on date, it does not possess its own constitution and all the laws prevalent in the territory of India apply to the erstwhile state of J&K as a result.
35. Gary J. Jacobsohn, *Constitutional Identity* (Cambridge, MA: Harvard University Press, 2010).
36. Ibid.
37. Ibid., 110.
38. Eve Darian-Smith, 'The Constitution of Identity: New Modalities of Nationality, Citizenship, Belonging and Being', in Austin Sarat and Patricia Ewick (eds), *The Handbook of Law and Society* (Malden, MA and Oxford: John Wiley & Sons Ltd., 2015), 352.
39. *Navtej Singh Johar v. Union of India*, AIR 2018 SC 4321.
40. AIR 1970 SC 564.
41. Rajamani, Lavanya, 'Public Interest Environmental Litigation in India: Exploring Issues of Access, Participation, Equity, Effectiveness and Sustainability', *Journal of Environmental Law*, Vol. 19, no. 3 (2007): 294, available at https://doi.org/10.1093/jel/eqm020.

42. Usha Ramanathan is an Indian legal scholar and human rights advocate. She serves as the South Asia Editor of the Law, Environment and Development Journal, jointly published by the International Environmental Law Research Centre (IELRC) and SOAS University of London.
43. AIR 1982 SC 1473.
44. Upendra Baxi, *Outline of a Theory of Practice of Indian Constitutionalism* (New Delhi: Oxford University Press, 2008).
45. Ibid., 93, 111.
46. *Justice K.S. Puttaswamy (Retd) v. Union of India,* (2017) 10 SCC 1 at 182.
47. B.R. Ambedkar, Final speech in the Constituent Assembly, 25 November 1949, 331, in Dr Ambedkar's last speech in the Constituent Assembly (PDF), 330 (Government of India, National Archives).

Chapter 9: The Rainbow above Kala Ghoda

1. Speech delivered at the Kala Ghoda Arts Festival. David Sassoon Library, Mumbai, 9 February 2019.
2. *Dead Poets Society*, directed by Peter Weir (Burbank, CA: Touchstone Pictures, 1989)
3. Shyam Divan, 'Sec 377: SC Has Signalled a Fresh Phase in the Evolution of Rights Jurisprudence', *Hindustan Times*, 7 September 2028, available at: https://www.hindustantimes.com/analysis/sec-377-sc-has-signalled-a-fresh-phase-in-thc evolution-of-rights-jurisprudence/story-RoZrQMFJLlr6IPfmX0IwAJ.html (accessed on 25 June 2025).
4. Gautam Bhatia, 'Sec 377 Judgment: An Atonement for a Grievous Error, But a Gateway Towards Greater Freedom', *Hindustan Times*, 10 September 2018, available at: https://www.hindustantimes.com/analysis/sec-377-judgment-an-atonement-for-a-grievous-error-but-a-gateway-towards-greater-freedom/story-9yfZ4027NSJpPFxqEoETqM.html (accessed on 25 June 2025).
5. Ibid.
6. Ibid.

7. Pulapre Balakrishnan, 'Sexual Equality Affirmed: On the Section 377 Verdict', *The Hindu*, September 2018, available at: https://www.thehindu.com/opinion/op-ed/sexual-equality-affirmed/article24885395.ece (accessed on 23 July 2025).
8. Gautam Bhan, 'For All That We May Become: On the Section 377 Verdict', *The Hindu*, September 2028, available at: https://www.thehindu.com/opinion/lead/for-all-that-we-may-become/article24885398.ece (accessed on 23 July 2025).
9. Gary J. Jacobsohn, *Constitutional Identity* (Cambridge, MA: Harvard University Press), 2010.
10. *Oxford Handbook of the Indian Constitution*, 110.
11. E. Darian-Smith, 'The Constitution of Identity: New modalities of nationality, citizenship, belonging and being', RegNet Working Paper, No. 66, Regulatory Institutions Network.
12. Ibid.
13. AIR 2018 SC 4898.
14. *Navtej Singh Johar v. Union of India*, (2018) 10 SCC 1.
15. Michel Rosenfield, 'The Identity of the Constitutional Subject', *Cardozo Law Review*, Vol. 16 (1994–95): 1049.
16. Abhijit Naskar, *Either Civilized or Phobic: A Treatise on Homosexuality* (Createspace Independent Pub, 2017).
17. Kenneth L. Parst, Paths to Belonging: The Constitution and Cultural Identity, *North Carolina Law Review*, Vol. 64 (1986): 338.
18. 'Art and the Law', SLS Court Catalogue, Past Offerings, available at: https://law.stanford.edu/courses/art-and-the-law/ (accessed on 25 June 2025).
19. Ossie Davis, Charter for Compassion, available at: https://charterforcompassion.org/arts/arts/online-exhibits/americans-who-tell-the-truth/anti-war-and-human-rights-activists/ossie-davis.html (accessed on 14 July 2025).
20. Olafur Eliasson, 'Why Art Has the Power to Change the World', World Economic Forum, 18 January 2016, available at: https://www.weforum.org/agenda/2016/01/why-art-has-the-power-to-change-the-world/ (accessed on 25 June 2025).
21. Ibid.
22. Ibid.

23. Ibid.
24. Darren Walker, *Yes Justice, Yes Peace: The Role of Art in Confronting Inequality,* Ford Foundation, 2016, available at: https://www.fordfoundation.org/news-and-stories/stories/yes-justice-yes-peace-the-role-of-art-in-confronting-inequality/ (accessed on 14 July 2025).
25. Ibid.
26. Ibid.
27. Prachi Patankar, *Adivasi Movements in India: An Interview with Poet Waharu Sonavane*, Toward Freedom, 2012), available at: https://towardfreedom.org/story/archives/asia-archives/adivasi-movements-in-india-an-interview-with-poet-waharu-sonavane/ (accessed on 14 July 2025).
28. Olafur Eliasson, 'Why Art Has the Power to Change the World', The World Economic Forum, 18 January 2016, accessed August 5, 2025.
29. Masterpiece Mixers, https://www.masterpiecemixers.com/art-affect-culture-society/
30. Ibid.
31. Ibid.
32. Ibid.
33. Ibid.
34. A Complex Weave: Women and Identity in Contemporary Art, USC Fisher Museum of Art (2012), available at: https://visualartsource.com/index.php?com=exdetail&eID=a560a675d035be101&page=listings (last visited Jul 14, 2025).
35. 'The Art of Gender Fluidity: 9 Works That Show How Sexual Identity Has Evolved Over Art History', Artspace, 6 November 2015, available at: https://www.artspace.com/magazine/art_101/body-of-art/body-of-art-gender-fluidity-53246 (accessed on 25 June 2025).
36. Ibid.
37. Olafur Eliasson, 'Why Art Has the Power to Change the World', The World Economic Forum , 18 January 2016, accessed August 5, 2025.
38. Ibid.
39. Ibid.

40. Ibid.
41. Albie Sachs, Chapter 10, 'The Beginning and the End', in *The Strange Alchemy of Life and Law* (Oxford University Press, 2009).

Chapter 10: Inventing and Reinventing Constitutional Identity

1. Sixth M.K. Nambyar Endowment Lecture, Kolkata, 9 March 2019.
2. Soli J. Sorabjee, *From Gopalan to Golaknath, and Beyond: A Tribute to Mr M K Nambyar Indian Journal of Constitutional Law,* Vol. 1 (2007): 19.
3. AIR 1950 SC 27.
4. Ibid.
5. B. Sen, 'The Supreme Court Bench and Bar: Reminiscences of the Formative Years', in ed. B. N. Kirpal, Ashok H. Desai, Gopal Subramanium, Rajeev Dhavan and Raju Ramachandran (eds), *Supreme But Not Infallible: Essays in Honour of the Supreme Court of India* (Oxford University Press, 2001)
6. *Menaka Gandhi v. Union of India,* (1978) 1 SCC 248.
7. *Supra*, note 3.
8. 1967 SCR (2) 762.
9. (1973) 4 SCC 225.
10. *Madhav Rao Jivaji Rao Scindia v. Union of India,* (1971) 1 SCC 85.
11. Nani A. Palkhivala, 'Chief Justice J C Shah', in Palkhivala (ed.) *We, the People* (Strand Book Stall, 2002).
12. 1973 SCR (2) 757.
13. Rogers Brubaker and Frederick Cooper, 'Beyond "Identity"', *Theory and Society*, Vol. 29 (2000): 1.
14. Bhikhu Parekh, 'Defining India's Identity', *India International Centre Quarterly*, Vol. 33, No. 1 (Summer 2006), 1–15.
15. Rogers Brubaker and Frederick Cooper, 'Beyond "Identity"', *Theory and Society* 29, no. 1 (2000): 1–47.
16. Richard D. Parker, 'Five Theses on Identity Politics', *Harvard Journal of Law & Public Policy* Vol. 29 (2005): 53.
17. Margaret Davies and Nan Seuffert, 'Knowledge, Identity, and the Politics of Law', *Hastings Journal on Gender and the Law*, Vol. 11(2000): 259.

18. Tommaso Pavone, 'Constitutional Identity: An Overview and Some Conceptual Concerns', (2014): 1.
19. Michel Rosenfeld, 'Constitutional Identity', in Michel Rosenfeld and András Sajó (eds), *The Oxford Handbook of Comparative Constitutional Law*, (Oxford: Oxford University Press, 2012).
20. Grant Lopatriello, Book Notes: Constitutional Identity, by Gary Jeffrey Jacobsohn, *Osgood Hall Law Journal*, Vol. 49, No. 3, Article 9 (2012): 601.
21. Ibid.
22. A.V. Bogdandy, 'The European Constitution and European Identity: Text and Subtext of the Treaty Establishing a Constitution for Europe, *International Journal of Constitutional Law*, 3(2–3) (2005): 295–315.
23. Bhikhu Parekh, 'Defining India's Identity', *India International Centre Quarterly*, Vol. 33, no. 1 (Summer 2006): 3.
24. Sri Aurobindo, *India's Rebirth: A Selection from Sri Aurobindo's Writings, Talks and Speeches*. Edited by Institut de Recherches Évolutives and Mira Aditi Centre. Mysore: Mira Aditi, [year]. p. 292.
25. Sunil Khilnani, 'Politics and National Identity', in Niraja Gopal Jayal and Pratap Bhanu Mehta (eds), *The Oxford Companion to Politics in India*, , (New Delhi: Oxford University Press, 2010),192–204. ch. 13, p. 193.
26. Ornit Shani, *How India Became Democratic: Citizenship and the Making of the Universal Franchise* (Cambridge University Press 2018), 1.
27. Ibid., 2.
28. Ibid., 2 and 3.
29. Ibid., 3.
30. Ibid.
31. Sujit Choudhary, Madhav Khosla and Pratap Bhanu Mehta (eds), 'Locating Indian Constitutionalism', in *The Oxford Handbook of the Indian Constitution* (Oxford University Press UK, 2016), 7.
32. Ibid.
33. Bhikhu Parekh, 'The Constitution as a Statement of Indian Identity', in Rajeev Bhargava (ed.), *Politics and Ethics of the Indian Constitution* (Oxford: Oxford University Press, 2010), 43–61.

34. Shefali Jha, 'Democratic Constitutionalism in India', *Seminar* 642 (February 2013), available at: https://india-seminar.com/2013/642/642_shefali_jha.htm (accessed on 23 July 2025)
35. 'Babasaheb' Dr B.R. Ambedkar: Maker and conscience-keeper of modern India, Ministry of External Affairs, Government of India.
36. Soli. J. Sorabjee, 'Equality in the United States and India', in Louis Henkin and Albert Rosenthal (eds), *Constitutionalism and Rights: The Influence of the United States Constitution Abroad* (Columbia University Press, 1989), 97.
37. Jagat Narain, 'Constitutional Changes in India: An Inquiry into the Working of the Constitution', *International and Comparative Law Quarterly*, Vol. 17 (1968): 878.
38. 'The Foreign and the Indigenous in the Indian Constitution', Constitution Day talk by Arun Thiruvengadam, Centre for Law and Policy Research (CLPR).
39. Vinay Sitapati, 'Reservations', in Michel Rosenfeld and András Sajó (eds), *The Oxford Handbook of Comparative Constitutional Law* (Oxford University Press, 2012), 928.
40. (2017) 2 SCC 629.
41. Sitapati, *Reservations in the Oxford Handbook of Constitutional Law*.
42. Gary J. Jacobsohn, *Constitutional Identity* (Cambridge: Harvard University Press, 2010).
43. CLPR, The Foreign and the Indigenous in the Indian Constitution: Constitution Day talk by Arun Thiruvengadam.
44. Jacobsohn, 'Constitutional Identity', 126.
45. Subrata Mitra, 'The Limits of Accommodation: Nehru, Religion and the State of India', *South Asia Research*, Vol. 9, No. 2 (1989): 107.
46. Kenneth C. Wheare, *Federal Government*, 3rd ed. (London & New York: Oxford University Press, 1953), p. 28.
47. *S.R. Bommai v. Union of India,* (1994) 3 SCC 1 (India) at 276 (opinion authored by Justices B.P. Jeevan Reddy and S.C. Agarwal)
48. (1994) 3 SCC 1.
49. *S.R. Bommai v. Union of India,* (1994) 3 SCC 1 (India) at 99 (opinion authored by Kuldip Singh and Sawant JJ.)

50. *S.R. Bommai v. Union of India*, (1994) 3 SCC 1 (India) at 165 (opinion authored by Ramaswamy J).
51. Erwin Chemerinsky, 'Amending the Constitution', *Michigan Law Review*, Vol. 96 (1998):1561.
52. Richard Albert, 'Counter-constitutionalism', *Dalhousie Law Journal*, Vol. 31 (2008): 1.
53. Michel Rosenfeld, 'The Identity of the Constitutional Subject', *Cardozo Law Review*, Vol. 16 (1994): 1049.
54. Ibid.
55. Ibid.
56. Ibid.
57. Ibid.
58. Ulrich K. Preuss, 'Constitutional Powermaking for the New Polity: Some Deliberations on the Relations between Constituent Power and the Constitution', *Cardozo Law Review*, Vol. 14 (1992–93): 639.
59. *Minerva Mills Ltd v. Union of India and Ors*, AIR 1980 SC 1789, 1798.
60. Sudhir Krishnaswamy, *Democracy and Constitutionalism in India: A Study of the Basic Structure Doctrine* (Oxford University Press, 2010).
61. Gautam Bhatia, Basic Structure II: 'The Argument from Democracy' Constitutional Law and Philosophy (blog), 4 November 2013
62. P.P. Rao, 'Basic Structure of the Constitution', in Alladi Memorial Trust, Alladi Memorial Lectures (1999), 176.
63. H.M. Seervai, *Constitutional Law of India* (Universal Law Publishing, 2001), 3161–62.
64. Jacobsohn, 'Constitutional Identity', 78.
65. Norwegian Constitution, Article 121, para 1, sentence 2 states: 'Such an amendment must never, however, contradict the principles embodied in this Constitution, but solely relate to modifications of particular provisions which do not alter the spirit of the Constitution, and two-thirds of the Storting must agree with such an amendment.'
66. French Constitution, Article 89, 5.
67. Ivo D. Duchacek, 'National Constitutions: A Functional Approach', *Comparative Politics*, Vol. 1, No. 1 (1968): 91–102.

68. Jon Elster, *Ulysses and the Sirens: Studies in Rationality and Irrationality* (Cambridge University Press, 1979).
69. Gautam Bhatia, Basic Structure II: 'The Argument from Democracy', Constitutional Law and Philosophy (blog), 4 November 2013.
70. Madhav Khosla, *The Indian Constitution* (Oxford India Short Introductions; New Delhi: Oxford University Press, 2012), 216 .
71. Bhiku Parekh, 'The Constitution as a Statement of Indian Identity' *in* Rajeev Bhargava (ed.), *Politics and Ethics of the Indian Constitution* (Oxford University Press, 2008).
72. Anthony D. Smith, National Identity, 14.
73. Parekh, 'The Constitution as a Statement of Indian Identity'.
74. Bhikhu Parekh, 'Defining India's Identity', *India International Centre Quarterly*, Vol. 33, no. 1 (2006): 1–15.
75. Jacobsohn, 'Constitutional Identity', 10.
76. Monika Polzin, 'Constitutional Identity as a Constructed Reality and a Restless Soul', *German Law Journal*, Vol. 18, no. 7 (2017):1595–1616.
77. Subrata K. Mitra, *Politics in India, Structure, Process and Policy*, Second Edition (Abingdon & New York: Routledge, 2017), wrote approximately 332–354 pages depending on the format.
78. Ibid.
79. Nirmala Buch, 'Women's Experience in New Panchayats: The Emerging Leadership of Rural Women', Centre for Women's Development Studies (CWDS), Occasional Paper No. 35, 2000.
80. Sunil Khilnani, 'Politics and National Identity', in Niraja Gopal Jayal and Pratap Bhanu Mehta (eds), *The Oxford Companion to Politics in India* (New Delhi: Oxford University Press, 2010), 192–205.
81. Sunil Khilnani is a political scientist and public intellectual, known for his work on Indian political thought and modern Indian history. He is the author of *The Idea of India* and was the founding Director of the India Institute at King's College London.
82. Ibid.
83. Sunil Khilnani, *The Idea of India* (London: Penguin, 2012), 193.
84. Rajeev Bhargava (ed.), *Politics and Ethics of the Indian Constitution*, Introduction (Oxford University Press, 2009).
85. Khilnani, 193.
86. Ibid.

87. Michel Rosenfeld, 'Constitutional Identity', in Michel Rosenfeld and András Sajó (eds), *The Oxford Handbook of Comparative Constitutional Law* (Oxford: Oxford University Press, 2012).
88. Pratap Bhanu Mehta, Sujit Choudhry and Madhav Khosla, *Our 'un-Indian' Constitution*, Live Mint (2016), available at: https://www.livemint.com/Leisure/bnC8qC7qe1mUpagf3CUzgI/Our-unIndian-Constitution.html (accessed on 15 July 2025).
89. Madhav Khosla, PhD (Harvard University 2017), LL.M. (Yale Law School 2010), and BA, LLB (Hons) (National Law School of India University 2008), is associate professor of law at Columbia University. A former junior fellow at the Harvard Society of Fellows, his work focuses on constitutional theory and comparative public law.
90. Madhav Khosla, *The Indian Constitution* (Oxford India Short Introductions (New Delhi: Oxford University Press, 2012)
91. E. Darian-Smith, 'The Constitution of Identity: New Modalities of Nationality, Citizenship, Belonging and Being', RegNet Working Paper, No. 66, 2015. Regulatory Institutions Network.
92. Ibid.
93. Michel Rosenfeld, 'The Identity of the Constitutional Subject', *Cardozo Law Review*, Vol. 16 (1994): 1049.
94. *Joseph Shine v. Union of India,* (2019), 3 SCC 39
95. Catharine A. MacKinnon, 'Sex Equality Under the Constitution of India: Problems, Prospects, and "Personal Laws"', *International Journal of Constitutional Law*, Vol. 4, no. 2 (2006): 181–202.
96. *Navtej Singh Johar v. Union of India*, (2018) 10 SCC 1.
97. Ibid.
98. Clifford Geertz, *The Interpretation of Cultures*, revised ed. (New York: Basic Books, 2000), 29.
99. Kevin R. *Johnson, Mixed Race America and the Law: A Reader*. New York University Press, 2002, p. 320.
100. *Indian Young Lawyers Association v. State of Kerala,* (2017) 10 SCC 689.
101. Lisa C. Bower, 'Queer Acts and the Politics of "Direct Address": Rethinking Law, Culture, and Community', *Law & Society Review,* Vol. 28, no. 5 (1994): 1009–33.
102. Ibid.

103. Ibid.
104. Ibid.
105. *Justice K.S. Puttaswamy (Retd) v. Union of India*, (2017) 10 SCC 1 (India) (Justice Chandrachud dissenting).
106. Amartya Sen, *The Argumentative Indian: Writings on India: Writings on Indian History, Culture and Identity* (Penguin UK, 2006).
107. Kenneth L. Parst, Paths to Belonging: The Constitution and Cultural Identity, *North Carolina Law Review*, Vol. 64 (1986): 338.
108. Gautam Bhan, 'For all that we may become: on the Section 377 verdict', *The Hindu*, 7 September 2018.
109. Kwame Anthony Appiah, *The Lies That Bind: Rethinking Identity* (New York: Liveright/Norton, 2018).

Chapter 11: A Borrowed Constitution: Fact or Myth?

1. Lecture at Nani Palkhivala Centenary Celebrations Lecture, *The Indian Society of International Law*, New Delhi, 29 March 2019.
2. Soli P. Sorabjee and Arvind P. Datar, *Nani Palkhivala: The Courtroom Genius* (LexisNexis Butterworths Nagpur, First Edition 2012).
3. J.B. Kanga and Nani Palkhivala, (Arvind P. Datar, ed.), *The Law and Practice of Income Tax* (LexisNexis; 11th Edition, 2020).
4. *Kesavananda Bharati v. State of Kerala,* (1973) 4 SCC 225.
5. Sorabjee and Datar, *Nani Palkhivala,* 376.
6. M.V. Kamath, *Nani A. Palkhivala: A Life* (Nani A. Palkhivala Memorial Trust, 2007), 198–99.
7. (1970) 2 SCC 298.
8. (1971) 1 SCC 85.
9. (1972) 2 SCC 788.
10. *Kesavananda Bharati v. State of Kerala,* (1973) 4 SCC 225.
11. (1980) 3 SCC 625.
12. Constituent Assembly Debate (CAD) *XI,* 4; 616.
13. CAD *VII,* 2; 242.
14. *CAD VII, 4; 38.*
15. Michel Rosenfeld, *The Identity of the Constitutional Subject* (Routledge, 2010), 11.

16. Ibid., 29.
17. Gary Jeffrey Jacobsohn, *Constitutional Identity* (Harvard University Press, 2010), 7.
18. Granville Austin, *The Indian Constitution: Cornerstone of a Nation* (Oxford University Press, 1999), 52–53.
19. Ibid., 54.
20. Ibid., 55.
21. Manoj Mate, 'The Origins of Due Process in India: The Role of Borrowing in Personal Liberty and Preventive Detention Cases', *Berkeley Journal of International Law*, Vol. 28, no. 1 (2010): 216.
22. Austin, *The Indian Constitution,* 104–06.
23. Ibid., 54–55.
24. Ibid., 56.
25. Ibid., 55–58.
26. Rajeev Bhargava, 'The Distinctiveness of Indian Secularism', in T.N. Srinivasan (ed.), *The Future of Secularism* (Delhi: Oxford University Press, 2006), 20–53.
27. Sandipto Dasgupta, '"A Language Which Is Foreign to Us" Continuities and Anxieties in the Making of the Indian Constitution', *Comparative Studies of South Asia, Africa and the Middle East*, Vol. 34, no. 2 (2014): 229.
28. Ibid., 236.
29. Quoted in Dasgupta, '"A Language Which Is Foreign to Us" Continuities and Anxieties in the Making of the Indian Constitution', 236.
30. Jawaharlal Nehru, 'Speech to the UP Police Officers, Lucknow, November, 1952', in B.N. Mullik (ed.), *Nehru on Police* (Palit and Dutt, 1951), 51.
31. Gary Jeffrey Jacobsohn, *Constitutional Identity* (Harvard University Press 2010), 78.
32. Manoj Mate, 'The Origins of Due Process in India: The Role of Borrowing in Personal Liberty and Preventive Detention Cases', *Berkeley Journal of International Law*, Vol. 28, no. 1 (2010): 216.
33. *K.S. Puttaswamy v. Union of India (Privacy-9 J.)*, (2017) 10 SCC 1.
34. Nani A. Palkhivala, 'The Supreme Court and High Courts as Guardians of Liberty', in *Our Constitution Defaced and Defiled* (Macmillan 1974), 77.

35. Jeffrey Goldsworthy, 'Questioning Migration of Constitutional Ideas', in Sujit Chowdhary (ed.), *The Migration of Constitutional Ideas* (Cambridge University Press 2006), 129.
36. Gary L. Jacobsohn, 'The Permeability of Constitutional Borders', *Texas Law Review*, Vol. 82 (2004): 1763, available at: http://www.la.utexas.edu/users/gjj69/docs/Permeability_borders.pdf (accessed on 26 June 2025).
37. Mark Tushnet, 'Some Reflections on Method in Comparative Constitutional Law', in Sujit Chowdhary (ed.), *The Migration of Constitutional Ideas* (Cambridge University Press 2006), 76.
38. Sujit Chowdhary, 'Migration as a New Metaphor in Comparative Constitutional Law', in Sujit Chowdhary (ed.), *The Migration of Constitutional Ideas* (Cambridge University Press 2006), 22.
39. Ibid.
40. Sujit Chowdhary, 'Migration as a New Metaphor in Comparative Constitutional Law', in Sujit Chowdhary (ed.), *The Migration of Constitutional Ideas* (Cambridge University Press 2006), 23.
41. Sujit Chowdhary, 'Living Originalism in India? "Our Law" and Comparative Constitutional Law', *Yale Journal of Law & the Humanities*, Vol. 25, no. 1, Article 2 (2013): 7.
42. A Conversation between US Supreme Court Justices (2005), International Journal of Constitutional Law, Vol. 3 (2005): 519.
43. *Suresh Kumar Koushal v. Naz Foundation,* (2014) 1 SCC 1.
44. *Naz Foundation v. Government of NCT of Delhi*, (2009) SCC OnLine Del 1762.
45. *Navtej Singh Johar v. Union of India*, (2018) 10 SCC 1.
46. S. *v. S.V. Lawrence, S v. Negal, S v. Solberg* (4) SA 1176, 1223 (South Africa 1997). Quoted by Gábor Halmai, 'The Use of Foreign Law in Constitutional Interpretation', in Michel Rosenfeld and András Sajó (eds), *The Oxford Handbook of Comparative Constitutional Law* (Oxford University Press, 2012), 1333.
47. Arun K. Thiruvengadam, 'Forswearing 'Foreign Moods, Fads or Fashions'? Contextualising the refusal of Koushal to engage with foreign law', *National University of Juridical Sciences Law Review,* Vol. 6, No. 4 (2013): 604.
48. A.G. Noorani, 'Behind the "Basic Structure" Doctrine', *Frontline*, Vol. 18, no. 9 (28 April–11 May 2001), available at: https://

frontline.thehindu.com/static/html/fl1809/18090950.htm (accessed on 26 June 2025).

49. Hanna Fenichel Pitkin, 'The Idea of a Constitution', *Journal of Legal Education*, Vol. 37, no. 2 (June 1987): 167–69.
50. Nani A. Palkhivala, *Our Constitution Defaced and Defiled* (Macmillan, 1974), vii.

Chapter 12: The Rules That Are India: From Plurality to Pluralism

1. Justice P.D. Desai Memorial Lecture 2020. Gujarat High Court, 15 February 2020.
2. James Bohman, 'Deliberative Toleration', *Political Theory*, Vol. 31, no. 6 (2003): 760.

> . . . Here was a document which granted Universal Adult Franchise in a country that was overwhelmingly illiterate; where, moreover, the conditionality of acquiring citizenship made no reference to race, caste, religion, or creed . . . which committed the state to being secular in a land that was by any reckoning deeply religious; which evacuated as a matter of law every form of prescribed social hierarchy under extant conditions marked by a dense plethora of entrenched hierarchies; that granted a raft of fundamental individual rights in the face of a virtually total absence of such rights . . . [and] most importantly, the Constitution created a federal democracy with all the juridical and political instruments of individual, federal, local, and provisional self-governance, where the nearest experience had been of imperial and princely authority.

3. Uday S. Mehta, 'History and the Social Problem: The Case of India', Proceedings of the Seventh Annual Gilder Lehrman Center International Conference at Yale University (27–29 October 2005), available at: https://glc.yale.edu/sites/default/files/files/justice/mehta.pdf (accessed on 26 June 2025).
4. John Locke, *The Second Treatise of Government in Two Treatises of Government* (Peter Laslett, ed.) (Cambridge University Press, 1960), 287.

5. Liberalism, Stanford Encyclopedia of Philosophy, revised on 22 January 2018, available at https://plato.stanford.edu/entries/liberalism/https://plato.stanford.edu/entries/liberalism/ (accessed on 3 February 2020).
6. Berlin, I. Isaiah, 'Two Concepts of Liberty', 1969, in I. Berlin, *Four Essays on Liberty* (London: Oxford University Press. New ed. in Berlin 2002); See also Jean-Jacques Rousseau, *The Social Contract* (Victor Gourevitch, ed.), Cambridge University Press (1997).
7. Isaiah Berlin, *The Proper Study of Mankind* (London: Chatto and Windus, 1997), 9.
8. Chakravarthi Ram-Prasad, 'Pluralism and Liberalism: Reading the Indian Constitution as a Philosophical Document for Constitutional Patriotism', *Critical Review of International Social and Political Philosophy*, Vol. 16, no. 5 (2013): 681.
9. Article 14, Constitution of India.
10. Article 19(1)(a), Constitution of India.
11. Article 19(1)(d), Constitution of India.
12. Article 21, Constitution of India.
13. Article 26(a), Constitution of India.
14. Article 29(1), Constitution of India.
15. Article 19(5), Constitution of India.
16. Gautam Bhatia, 'Freedom from Community: Individual Rights, Group Life, State Authority and Religious Freedom under the Indian Constitution', in *Global Constitutionalism*, Vol. 5, no. 3 (2016).
17. Chakravarthi Ram-Prasad, 'Pluralism and Liberalism', 681.
18. Gary Jeffrey Jacobsohn, *The Wheel of Law: India's Secularism in Comparative Constitutional Context* (Oxford University Press, 2003), 94.
19. *Indian Young Lawyers Association v. State of Kerala and Ors*, Indian Supreme Court, (2018) SCC OnLine 1690 (4-1 decision) (Indu Malhotra, J., dissenting), opinion of Dhananjaya Chandrachud at 219.
20. Rajeev Bhargava, *Politics and Ethics of the Indian Constitution* (Oxford University Press, 2008), 15.
21. 'George Orwell Explains How "Newspeak" Works, the Official Language of His Totalitarian Dystopia in 1984', Open Culture, 25

January 2017, available at: http://www.openculture.com/2017/01/george-orwell-explains-how-newspeak-works.html (accessed on 3 February 2020).

22. Stephen May, 'Misconceiving Minority Language Rights: Implications for Liberal Political Theory', in Will Kymlicka and Alan Patten (eds), *Language Rights and Political Theory* (Oxford University Press, 2003).
23. Alan Patten, 'Political Theory and Language Policy', *Political Theory*, Vol. 29, no. 5 (2001): 697.
24. Abhinav Chandrachud, *Republic of Rhetoric* (Penguin Viking, 2017), 49.
25. Reserve Bank of India, Bank Notes, available at https://www.rbi.org.in/scripts/ic_languagepanel.aspx (accessed on 3 February 2020).
26. Ramachandra Guha, *India after Gandhi: The History of World's Largest Democracy* (Macmillan, 2007), 752.
27. G. Seetheraman, 'Why Does the Census of India Focus on Mother Tongues? How Does It Make Linguistic Minorities Invisible?' *Economic Times*, 5 May 2019, available at: https://economictimes.indiatimes.com/news/politics-and-nation/why-does-the-census-of-india-focus-on-mother-tongues-how-does-it-make-linguistic-minorities-invisible/articleshow/69178250.cms?from=mdr (accessed on 3 February 2020).
28. B. Shiva Rao, *The Framing of India's Constitution* (Sweet & Maxwell), 281. However, this is just a first step. The right to conserve distinct languages is distinct from their active promotion. For example, Article 6 of the South African Constitution stipulates that the 'state must take practical and positive measures to elevate the status and advance the use of these languages'. In addition, a 'Pan South African Language Board' must 'promote and ensure respect for' all languages commonly used by communities in South Africa, which includes, amongst others, Gujarati, Hindi, Tamil, Telugu and Urdu, and Sanskrit.
29. Monique Deveaux, 'Toleration and Respect', *Public Affairs Quarterly*, Vol. 12, no. 4 (1998): 407–09.
30. *John Rawls, Political Liberalism* (1993), 122.
31. James Bohman, 'Deliberative Toleration', *Political Theory*, Vol. 31, no. 6 (2003): 760.

32. Ibid, 758.
33. T.M. Scanlon, *The Difficulty of Tolerance: Essays in Political Philosophy* (Cambridge University Press, 2003), 193.
34. Rev. Jerome D'Souza, Constituent Assembly of India Debates (PROCEEDINGS), 21 January 1947, Vol. 2, 6
35. Statement by Hukam Singh, Constitutional Assembly Debates, 8.92.15 (26 May 1949).
36. Bhargava, *Politics and Ethics of the Indian Constitution*, 43.
37. Ibid.
38. Rahul Rao, 'Test of Faith: The CAA Protests Shake the Old Bounds of Indian Secular Morality', *Caravan*, 30 January 2020, available at https://caravanmagazine.in/politics/caa-protests-shake-old-bounds-indian-secular-morality (accessed on 5 February 2020).
39. Hukam Singh, Speech in the Constituent Assembly, 8.92.14.
40. Tajamul Hussain, Speech in the Constituent Assembly, 8.92.50.
41. Deepanjan Gosh, 'In Bengal, the Bond of Rakhi Once Symbolised Eternal Protection Between Hindus and Muslims', Scroll.in, 7 August 2007, available at https://scroll.in/magazine/846275/in-bengal-the-bond-of-rakhi-once-symbolised-eternal-protection-between-hindus-and-muslims (accessed on 4 February 2020).
42. Arnold Toynbee, *A Study of History in Approaches to Islam in Religious Studies* (Richard C. Martin, ed.) (Oxford: Oneworld Publications, 2001), 105.
43. 'Gharanas' refer to traditional kinship-based houses or lineages within the Indian transgender community. Each gharana functions like a chosen family, led by a senior member called a guru, who mentors and supports the younger members or *chela*s (disciples). This system provides social structure, identity, livelihood support and emotional bonds outside the conventional family system.
44. Gee Imaan Semmalar, 'Unpacking Solidarities of the Oppressed: Notes on Trans Struggles in India', *Women's Studies Quarterly,* Vol. 42, no. ¾ (2014): 286–91.
45. *National Legal Services Authority v. Union of India*, (2014) 5 SCC 438.
46. Zainab Patel, 'The Long Road to LGBTQIA+ Equality in India', UNDP India, 17 May 2019, available at: https://www.in.undp.

org/content/india/en/home/blog/lgbtequalityindia.html (accessed on 4 February 2020).

47. Parliamentary Debate, XII, 16 May 1951.
48. Frank de Zwart, 'The Logic of Affirmative Action: Caste, Class and Quotas in India', *Acta Sociologica*, Vol. 43, no. 3 (2000): 235–49.
49. Press Trust of India, 'Representation of SCs, STs in Government Jobs Above Prescribed Percentage', *Hindustan Times*, 18 July 2019, available at: https://www.hindustantimes.com/education/representation-of-scs-sts-in-government-jobs-above-prescribed-percentage/story-9PWz5wqf2cdkdRxcwLQdII.html (accessed on 4 February 2020).
50. Bhalchandra Mungekar, 'Annihilating Caste', *Frontline*, Vol. 28, no. 15 (2011): 16–29.
51. Suhas Broker, 'How to Be Free of Caste in India', *The Hindu*, 13 April 2016.
52. M.A. Kalam, 'Towards Genuine Pluralism', The Hindu Centre for Politics and Public Policy (2017), available at: https://www.thehinducentre.com/the-arena/current-issues/towards-genuine-pluralism/article64931325.ece (accessed on 15 July 2025).

Chapter 13: Visualizing the Constitution Through Artistic Prisms: Stories of Aspiration and Emancipation

1. Speech delivered at the Constitution Day Celebrations organized by Kalakshetra Foundation (Virtual Event). 28 November 2020.
2. Austin D. Sarat is the William Nelson Cromwell Professor of Jurisprudence and Political Science at Amherst College. A renowned interdisciplinary scholar, he holds a J.D. from Yale and a PhD from the University of Wisconsin. Sarat has authored and edited over a hundred books exploring law, culture, capital punishment and legal humanities.
3. Jonathan Simon is the Lance Robbins Professor of Criminal Justice Law at UC Berkeley School of Law, where he specializes in criminal law, punishment, governmentality and risk. He holds a J.D. and PhD from UC Berkeley and previously taught at Michigan and Miami. Simon is acclaimed for his scholarship on mass incarceration and penology.

4. Austin Sarat and Jonathan Simon, 'Beyond Legal Realism: Cultural Analysis, Cultural Studies, and the Situation of Legal Scholarship', *Yale Journal of Law and the Humanities*, Vol.13, no. 3 (2001):19–20.
5. Ibid., 8.
6. Anne Frank, *The Diary of a Young Girl*, trans. B. M. Mooyaart-Doubleday (New York: Doubleday, 1952).
7. Alan Paton, *Cry, the Beloved Country* (Vintage Classics, 2002).
8. Alice Walker, *The Color Purple* (Weidenfeld & Nicolson, 2014).
9. Sadat Hasan Manto, 'Naya Qanoon', available at: https://www.rekhta.org/stories/nayaa-qanoon-saadat-hasan-manto-stories?lang=hi (accessed on 27 June 2025).
10. Bipin Chandra, *India's Struggle for Independence* 1857–1947 (New Delhi & New York: Viking/Penguin, 1988), 205–20.
11. Natasha Eaton, *Swadeshi' Color: Artistic Production and Indian Nationalism, Ca. 1905–Ca. 1947 95,* The Art Bulletin 4 (2013): 623–41.
12. Ibid.
13. 'Marginalised Narratives of the Indian Freedom Movement', *Economic and Political Weekly*, 14 August 2019, available at: https://www.epw.in/engage/article/independence-day-2019-marginalised-narratives (accessed on 27 June 2025).
14. Naman Ahuja, 'Can the Historic Art of Our Constitution Look to the Future?' *Mint*, 25 January 2020, available at: https://www.livemint.com/mint-lounge/features/can-the-historic-art-of-our-constitution-look-to-the-future-11579885322689.html (accessed on 27 June 2025).
15. Shirin M. Rai, 'Political Aesthetics of the Nation: Murals and Statues in the Indian Parliament', *Interventions: International Journal of Postcolonial Studies*, 2014.
16. Ahuja, 'Can the Historic Art of Our Constitution Look to the Future?'; Rai, 'Political Aesthetics of the Nation'.
17. *See* Srirupa Roy, *Beyond Belief: India and the Politics of Postcolonial Nationalism* (Duke UP, 2007); The Constitution of India, enacted 1950.
18. Rohit De, *A People's Constitution: The Everday Life of Law in the Indian Republic* (Princeton University Press, 2018), 22.

19. Ashis Nandy, *Indian Popular Cinema as a Slum's Eye View of Politics* (Oxford University Press, 1998), 8.
20. Hiren Gandhi and Saroop Dhruv, 'Puppetry: Re-establishing the Folk Art', *Economic and Political Weekly*, Vol. 46, No. 30 (2011): 10–11.
21. 'When a Smartly Worded Obit Exposed the Death of Democracy', *Times of India*, 26 June 2015, Available at: https://timesofindia.indiatimes.com/india/When-a-smartly-worded-obit-exposed-the-death-of-democracy/articleshow/47823701.cms (accessed on 27 June 2025).
22. Aditi Narayani, 'Mithila Paintings: How Dalit Women Have Used Art to Reclaim Their Identity and Their Stories', DailyO, 18 August 2018, available at: https://www.dailyo.in/variety/dalit-mithila-paintings-bihar/story/1/25978.html (accessed on 27 June 2025).
23. Walid El Hamamsy and Mounira Soliman, 'The Aesthetics of Revolution. Popular Creativity and the Egyptian Spring', in Walid El Hamamsy and Mounira Soliman (eds), *Popular Culture in the Middle East and North Africa: A Postcolonial Outlook* (New York: Routledge, 2013), 246–59.
24. Melena Ryzik, 'The Guerrilla Girls, After 3 Decades, Still Rattling Art World Cages', *New York Times*, 5 August 2015, available at https://www.nytimes.com/2015/08/09/arts/design/the-guerrilla-girls-after-3-decades-still-rattling-art-world-cages.html (accessed 27 June 2025).
25. Susan A. Crane, 'Writing the Individual Back into Collective Memory', *American Historical Review*, Vol. 102, No. 5 (1997): 1372–85.
26. Gary Jeffrey Jacobsohn, *Constitutional Identity* (Harvard University Press, 2010), 7.
27. Priti Salian, 'What India's First Trans Women-Led Dance Troupe Wants eople to Know', *World*, 19 June 2018, available at: https://www.pri.org/stories/2018-06-19/what-indias-first-trans-women-led-dance-troupe-wants-people-know (accessed on 27 June 2025).
28. Linda Berg and Anna Sofia Lundgren, 'We Were Here, and We Still Are: Negotiations of Political Space Through Unsanctioned

Art', in Alm E. et al. (eds), *Pluralistic Struggles in Gender, Sexuality and Coloniality: Challenging Swedish Exceptionalism* (Palgrave Macmillan, 2020) 49–80.

29. (2018) 10 SCC 1.
30. Laura Frost, 'You Probably Didn't Read the Most Telling Part of Orwell's "1984"—The Appendix', Quartz, 19 June 2013, available at: https://qz.com/95696/you-probably-didnt-read-the-most-telling-part-of-orwells-1984-the-appendix/amp/ (accessed on 27 June 2025).
31. *'Exploring the Connection Between Arts and Human Rights'*, Report of High-level expert meeting Vienna, European Union Agency of Fundamental Rights, 6 (29–30 May 2017), available at: https://fra.europa.eu/sites/default/files/fra_uploads/fra-2017_arts-and-human-rights-report_may-2017_vienna.pdf (accessed on 27 June 2025).

Chapter 14: Why Representation Matters

1. Speech delivered at the event organized by the Community for the Eradication of Discrimination in Education and Employment (CEDE) (Virtual Event). 14 April 2021.
2. (2021) 15 SCC 125.
3. *Secretary, Ministry of Defence v. Babita Puniya,* (2020) 7 SCC 469.
4. *National Capital Alliance on Race Relations v. Canada (Health & Welfare)* 1997 28 C.H.R.R.D./179 (Canadian Human Rights Tribunal).
5. *Action Travail des Femmes v. Canadian National Railway Company* (1987) 1 S.C.R. 1114.
6. See *Canadian National Railway Co. v. Canada* (Human Rights Commission) and *Action Travail des Femmes* (1987) 1 S.C.R. 1114 ('Action Travail des Femmes').
7. Marie Mercat-Bruns, 'Systemic discrimination: Rethinking the Tools of Gender Equality', *European Equality Law Review*, Vol. 2 (European Commission, 2018): 5–18.
8. Micheal J. Sandel, *The Tyranny of Merit: What's Become of the Common Good?* (Farrar, Straus and Giroux, 2020).
9. (2019) 16 SCC 129.

10. Marc Galanter, *Competing Equalities: Law and the Backward Classes in India* (Universal, California Printed Edition, 1984).
11. Yashica Dutt, *Coming Out as Dalit: A Memoir* (New Delhi: Aleph Book Company, 2019), 67.
12. Satish Deshpande, 'Caste and Castelessness', *Economic and Political Weekly*, Vol. 48, no. 15 (2013): 32.
13. (2017) 2 SCC 629.
14. IDIA, 'IDIA Diversity Survey Report, 2018–2019', available at: https://www.idialaw.org/wp-content/uploads/2020/04/diversity-survey-2018-19.pdf (accessed on 28 June 2025); Chirayu Jain et al., 'The Elusive Island of Excellence: A Study on Student Demographics, Accessibility and Inclusivity at National Law School 2015–16 (2016). Available at: SSRN: https://ssrn.com/abstract=2788311 or http://dx.doi.org/10.2139/ssrn.2788311 (accessed on 28 June 2025).
15. Surendrakumar Bagde, Dennis Epple and Lowell Taylor, 'Does Affirmative Action Work? Caste, Gender, College Quality, and Academic Success in India', *American Economic Review*, Vol. 106, no. 6 (2016): 1495–521.
16. Manisha Arya, 'Graduating as an Upper-Class Bahujan Woman', Quirk, 18 April 2020, available at: https://nlsquirks.in/graduating-as-an-upper-class-bahujan-woman/ (accessed on 28 June 2025); Abhishek Asha Kumar, 'Learning at Law School – Of High Tables and Floors', Quirk, 9 May 2020, available at: https://nlsquirks.in/learning-at-law-school-of-high-tables-and-floors/ (accessed on 29 June 2025).
17. Peggy McIntosh, 'White Privilege: Unpacking the Invisible Knapsack', 1989, Wellesley College Center for Research on Women.
18. *Indian Young Lawyers Association v. Union of* India, (2019) 11 SCC 1 (popularly known as the 'Sabarimala' verdict).

Chapter 15: Speaking Truth to Power: Citizens and the Law

1. Sixth Justice M.C. Chagla Memorial Lecture, 2021 organized as a virtual event on 28 August 2021.
2. M.C. Chagla, *Roses in December: An Autobiography* (K.V. Gopalakrishnan Printers, 1973), 561.

3. Ibid., 154.
4. Ibid., 548.
5. Ibid., 540.
6. Ibid., 153–54.
7. Michel Foucault, 'Discourse and Truth: the Problematization of Parrhesia, 6 lectures given by Michel Foucault at the University of California at Berkeley, CA, Oct–Nov 1983', available at: https://foucault.info/parrhesia/ (accessed on 27 August 2021).
8. John Kenneth Galbraith, *The Anatomy of Power* (Houghton-Mifflin Trade and Reference, 1983), 80.
9. Sophia Rosenfeld, *Democracy and the Truth: A Short History* (University of Pennsylvania Press, 2018).
10. Hannah Arendt, 'Truth and Politics', *New Yorker*, 17 February 1967, available at: https://www.newyorker.com/magazine/1967/02/25/truth-and-politics (accessed on 27 August 2021).
11. Sophia Rosenfeld, *Democracy and the Truth: A Short History* (University of Pennsylvania Press, 2018).
12. Michael P. Lynch, 'Democracy as a Space of Reasons', in Jeremy Elkins and Andrew Norris (eds.), *Truth and Democracy* (University of Pennsylvania Press, 2012), 115.
13. William A. Galston, 'Truth and Democracy: Theme and Variations', in Jeremy Elkins and Andrew Norris (eds.), *Truth and Democracy* (University of Pennsylvania Press, 2012), 130.
14. Audrey R. Chapman and Patrick Ball, 'The Truth of Truth Commissions: Comparative Lessons from Haiti, South Africa, and Guatemala', *Human Rights Quarterly*, Vol. 23, no. 1 (2001).
15. *In Re: Distribution of Essential Supplies and Services During Pandemic*, Suo Motu Writ Petition (Civil) No. 3 of 2021, Order dated 30 April 2021.
16. Cass R. Sustein, *Infotopia: How Many Minds Produce Knowledge* (Oxford University Press, 2006).
17. Anirudha Nagar, 'Laws by the people, for the People', *The Hindu*, 24 February 2014, available at: https://www.thehindu.com/opinion/op-ed/laws-by-the-people-for-the-people/article5719578.ece (accessed on 27 August 2021).
18. *Doctors for Life International v. Speaker of the National Assembly*, [2006] ZACC 11.

19. Chagla, *Roses in December*, 70.
20. Richard L. Kirkham, *Theories of Truth: A Critical Introduction* (MIT Press, 1995).
21. Ibid.
22. Sophia Rosenfeld, *Democracy and the Truth: A Short History* (University of Pennsylvania Press, 2018).
23. Mary Wollstonecraft, *A Vindication of the Rights of Woman* (London: Johnson, 1796), pp. 47–48, 71.
24. Paul Gordon Lauren, *The Evolution of International Human Rights* (University of Pennsylvania Press, 2011) 33.
25. 'An American Original', October 2010, *Vanity Fair*), available at: https://www.vanityfair.com/news/2010/11/moynihan-letters-201011 (accessed on 27 August 2021).
26. *Navtej Singh Johar v. Union of India*, AIR 2018 SC 4321.
27. Max Bearak and Darla Cameron, 'Here are the 10 countries where homosexuality may be punished by death', *Washington Post*, 16 June 2016, available at: https://www.washingtonpost.com/news/worldviews/wp/2016/06/13/here-are-the-10-countries-where-homosexuality-may-be-punished-by-death-2 (accessed on 27 August 2021).
28. Michel Foucault, 'Truth and Power', in Colin Gordon (ed.), *Power/Knowledge: Selected Interviews and Other Writings, 1972–1977* (1980, Pantheon),133.
29. Steven Shapin, *The Social History of Truth: Civility and Science in Seventeenth-Century England* (University of Chicago Press, 1994).
30. A. Sachs, 'Four types of truth', Peace Magazine, Vol. 15, no. 1 (1999): 6. Available at: https://gangporemirror.wordpress.com/2017/09/18/the-4-different-kind-of-truth/.
31. *Supra* at note 13.
32. Sophia Rosenfeld, *Democracy and the Truth: A Short History* (University of Pennsylvania Press, 2018).
33. Eric Lipton and Brooke Williams, 'How Think Tanks Amplify Corporate America's Influence', *New York Times*, 7 August 2016, available at: https://www.nytimes.com/2016/08/08/us/politics/think-tanks-researchand-corporate-lobbying.html (accessed on 27 August 2021).

34. Alfred Moore, *Critical Elitism: Deliberation, Democracy, and the Problem of Expertise* (Cambridge University Press, 2017).
35. Stanley J. Grenz, *A Primer on Postmodernism* (William B. Eerdmans Publishing Company, 1996), 7–8.
36. Hannah Arendt, 'Lying in Politics: Reflections on The Pentagon Papers', *NY Review of Books*, 18 November 1971, available at: https://www.nybooks.com/articles/1971/11/18/lying-in-politics-reflections-on-the-pentagon-pape/ (accessed on 27 August 2021).
37. Hannah Arendt, 'Truth and Politics', *New Yorker*, 17 February 1967, available at: https://www.newyorker.com/magazine/1967/02/25/truth-and-politics (accessed on 27 August 2021).
38. Immanuel Kant, 'An Answer to the Question: What Is Enlightenment?' trans. James Schmidt, in James Schmidt (ed.), *What Is Enlightenment? Eighteenth-Century Answers to Twentieth-Century Questions* (University of California Press, 1996), 59.
39. Sophia Rosenfeld, *Democracy and the Truth: A Short History* (University of Pennsylvania Press, 2018).
40. Noam Chomsky, 'The Responsibility of Intellectuals', *NY Review of Books*, 23 February 1967, available at: https://www.nybooks.com/articles/1967/02/23/a-special-supplement-the-responsibility-of-intelle/ (accessed on 27 August 2021).
41. John Stuart Mill, *On Liberty* (J.W. Parker & Son, 1859).
42. 'Managing the COVID-19 infodemic: Promoting healthy behaviours and mitigating the harm from misinformation and disinformation - Joint statement by WHO, UN, UNICEF, UNDP, UNESCO, UNAIDS, ITU, UN Global Pulse, and IFRC' (23 September 2020, *WHO*) available at: https://www.who.int/news/item/23-09-2020-managing-the-covid-19-infodemic-promoting-healthy-behaviours-and-mitigating-the-harm-from-misinformation-and-disinformation (accessed on 27 August 2021).
43. *Supra* at note 8.
44. Cass R. Sunstein, *#Republic: Divided Democracy in the Age of Social Media* (Princeton University Press, 2017).
45. Robinson Meyer, 'The Grim Conclusions of the Largest-Ever Study of Fake News', *Atlantic*, 8 March 2018, available at: https://www.theatlantic.com/technology/archive/2018/03/largest-study-

ever-fake-newsmit-twitter/555104/ (accessed on 27 August 2021).

46. Tim Wu, *The Attention Merchants: The Epic Scramble to Get Inside Our Heads* (Knopf, 2016).
47. Tim Wu, 'Is the First Amendment Obsolete?' *Michigan Law Review*, Vol. 117 (2018): 547.
48. Ibid.
49. David Burkus, 'Stop Talking about Politics at Work', *Psychology Today*, 13 August 2019, available at: https://www.psychologytoday.com/us/blog/creative-leadership/201908/stop-talking-about-politics-work (accessed on 27 August 2021).
50. M.C. Chagla, *supra* note 2, at 345–46.
51. Ibid., 475.
52. Ibid., 86–87.

Chapter 16: Conceptualizing Marginalization: Agency, Assertion and Personhood

1. Thirteenth B.R. Ambedkar Memorial Lecture, organized by the Indian Institute of Dalit Studies, New Delhi, delivered on 6 December 2021.
2. Dr B.R. Ambedkar, *Waiting for a Visa* (People's Education Society, 1990), Section 3 ('Pride, Awkwardness and a Dangerous Accident in Chalisgaon'), 18.
3. Prakshi Saha, *Babasaheb Ambedkar: How Come His Feminism Is So Unacknowledged?*, Breakthrough Trust (2019), available: https://inbreakthrough.org/ambedkar-feminist-politics/ (accessed on 17 July 2025).
4. 118 US 394 (1886).
5. 60 US 393 (1856).
6. F.H. Lawson, 'The Creative Use of Legal Concepts', *New York University Law Review*, Vol. 32 (1957): 915.
7. Ngaire Naffine, 'Who Are Law's Persons? From Cheshire Cats to Responsible Subjects, *Modern Law Review*, Vol. 66, no. 3 (2003): 346.
8. Linda Bosniak, 'Persons and Citizens in Constitutional Thought', *International Journal of Constitutional Law*, Vol. 8, no. 1 (2010): 21–24.

9. Alexander Bickel, *The Morality of Consent* (New Haven and London: Yale University Press, 1975), chapter 2, 53.
10. Aruna Gogulamanda, 'A Dalit Woman in the Land of Goddesses', Firstpost, 13 August 2017, available at: https://www.firstpost.com/long-reads/a-dalit-woman-in-the-land-of-goddesses-3919861.html (accessed on 24 July 2025).
11. Yashica Dutt, *Coming Out as a Dalit: A Memoir* (Aleph Book Company, 2019).
12. Prakash Louis, 'Dalit utpeedan: Chakwara se Jhajjar tak', *Hindustan,* 29 October 2002.
13. Bosniak, 'Persons and Citizens in Constitutional Thought', 7.
14. Dr B.R. Ambedkar described the Indian caste system as one of 'graded inequality', where each caste is ranked hierarchically with unequal status and privileges, creating a complex system of discrimination and oppression. He argued that this system, with its rigid social order and deep social divisions, prevented unity among the oppressed and perpetuated upper-caste dominance.
15. Bhikhu Parekh, 'Logic of Humiliation', in Gopal Guru (ed), *Humiliation: Claims and Context* (Oxford University Press, 2009), 27.
16. Geetha V., 'Bereft of Being: The Humiliations of Untouchability', in Gopal Guru (ed), *Humiliation: Claims and Context* (Oxford University Press, 2009), 97.
17. 163 US 537 (1896).
18. Ibid., 551.
19. Bama, *Karukku,* translated from the Tamil by Lakshmi Holmström (Oxford India Paperbacks, 2014).
20. Sujatha Gidla, *Ants Among Elephants* (Farrar, Straus and Giroux, 2017).
21. Suraj Milind Yengde, *Caste Matters* (Gurugram: Penguin Random House India, 2019), 239–40.
22. Parekh, 'Logic of Humiliation'.
23. Charles Taylor, 'The Politics of Recognition', in Amy Gutmann (ed.) *Multiculturalism and the Politics of Recognition* (Princeton University Press, 1994). See Nancy Fraser and Axel Honneth, *Redistribution or Recognition? A Political-Philosophical Exchange* (Verso Books, 2004).
24. (2009) 6 SCC 667.

25. See Carole Pateman, *The Sexual Contract* (Stanford University Press, 1988), where she provides a feminist critique to the social contract theory.
26. 494 US 256 (1990).
27. Constituent Assembly Debates, Vol. XI, 25 November 1949 speech by Frank Anthony, available at: https://www.constitutionofindia.net/debates/25-nov-1949/.
28. (2017) 2 SCC 629.
29. Erving Goffman, *Stigma: Notes on the Management of Spoiled Identity* (Englewood Cliffs, NJ: Prentice-Hall, 1963).
30. Ralph Ellison, *Invisible Man* (New York: Penguin Random House, 1952).
31. (2020) 7 SCC 469.
32. (2021) 15 SCC 125.
33. (2018) 10 SCC 1.
34. Satish Deshpande, 'Caste and Castelessness', *Economic and Political Weekly*, Vol. 48, No. 15 (2013): 32.
35. Michael J. Sandel, *The Tyranny of Merit: What's Become of the Common Good?* (Farrar, Straus and Giroux, 2020).
36. (2019) 16 SCC 129.
37. (2021) 5 SCC 370.
38. Audre Lorde, 'Age, Race, Class, and Sex: Women Redefining Difference', in *Sister Outsider: Articles and Speeches* (Crossing Press, 1984).
39. Kimberlé Crenshaw, 'Mapping the Margins: Intersectionality, Identity Politics, and Violence Against Women of Color', *Stanford Law Review*, Vol. 43 (1991): 1241.
40. Shailaja Paik, 'Dalit Feminist Thought', *Economic and Political Weekly*, Vol. 56, No. 25 (2021).
41. Goffman, *The Presentation of the Self in Everyday Life* (Pelican, 1959).
42. Darren Lenard Hutchinson, 'Progressive Race Blindness: Individual Identity, Group Politics, and Reform', *UCLA Law Review*, Vol. 49 (2002): 1455.
43. Deshpande, 'Caste and Castelessness'.
44. Patricia J. Williams, 'Alchemical Notes: Reconstructing Ideals from Deconstructed Rights', *Harvard Civil Rights-Civil Liberties Law Review*, Vol. 22 (1987): 401.

45. Anurag Bhaskar [B.A. LL.B. (Hons.), Dr Ram Manohar Lohiya National Law University, Lucknow and LL.M., Harvard Law School] is a legal scholar and advocate. He has been awarded the Bluestone Rising Scholar Award by Brandeis University, USA, for his paper on understanding the founding and the evolution of the Indian Constitution through an anti-caste lens. He began his professional journey as a law clerk with me during 2017–18 at the Supreme Court of India.
46. Anurag Bhaskar, 'Ambedkar's Constitution: A Radical Phenomenon in Anti-Caste Discourse', *CASTE: A Global Journal on Social Exclusion*, Vol. 2, no. 1 (2021): 109–31.
47. Axel Honneth, 'The Struggle for Recognition: The Moral Grammer of Social Conflicts' translated by Joel Anderson (1949 MIT Press).

Chapter 17: Reconciling Rights and Innovation: Examining the Relationship Between Law and Technology

1. Address at the Justice P.M. Mukhi Memorial Lecture (virtual event). 9 April 2021.
2. Parsram M. Mukhi - In Memoriam, available at: https://theory.tifr.res.in/~mukhi/PMM/pmm.html (accessed on 1 July 2025).
3. How the US government is using blockchain to fight fraud | Kathryn Haun | TEDxSanFrancisco, available at: https://www.youtube.com/watch?v=507wn9VcSAE (accessed on 1 July 2025).
4. Freedom Forum Media Studies Centre, *Communicators of Conscience: Humanitarian and Human Rights Organizations' Use of the internet* (1994), 28.
5. Jamie F. Metzl, 'Information Technology and Human Rights', *Human Rights Quarterly*, Vol. 18, No. 4 (1996): 705.
6. Kathleen M. Sullivan, 'First Amendment Intermediaries in the Age of Cyberspace', *UCLA Law Review*, Vol. 45 (1998):1653.
7. Tim Wu, 'Is the First Amendment Obsolete?' *Michigan Law Review*, Vol. 117, no. ¾ (2018).
8. Zeynep Tufekci, *Twitter and Tear Gas: The Power and Fragility of Networked Protest* (Yale University Press, 2017).

9. UNGA, 'Report of the Special Rapporteur on the Promotion and Protection of the Right to Freedom of Opinion and Expression, Frank La Rue' (2011) UN Doc A/HRC/17/27.
10. HRC, 'General Comment 34', 12 September 2011) UN Doc CCPR/C/GC/34.
11. *Fatullayev v. Azerbaijan*, App no 40984/07 (ECtHR, 22 April 2010).
12. IACHR, 'Freedom of expression and the internet' (31 December 2013) OEA/Ser.L/V/II.
13. *Anuradha Bhasin v. Union of India*, (2020) 3 SCC 637.
14. UNGA, 'The Right to Privacy in the Digital Age: Report of the United Nations High Commissioner for Human Rights', 2021, A/HRC/48/31.
15. (2017) 10 SCC 1.
16. 'Technology, Data and Elections: A Checklist on the Election Cycle', 17 July 2019, Available at: https://privacyinternational.org/advocacy/3093/technology-data-and-elections-checklist-election-cycle (accessed on 1 July 2025).
17. *Union of India v. G.S. Chatha Rice Mills*, SLP (C) 3860/2020 (23 September 2020).
18. Cunliffe Emma, *Open Justice: Concepts and Judicial Approaches, Federal Law Review*, Vol. 40 (2012): 385; *See also*, *Swapnil Tripathi v. Supreme Court of India,* (2018) 10 SCC 639.
19. Statista, *internet penetration rate in India from 2007 to 2021*, available at: https://www.statista.com/statistics/792074/india-internet-penetration-rate/ (Accessed on 21 on November 2021).
20. Accessible features such as increase/decrease the contrast and text, screen reader access, accessible calendar and audio captcha are available on the websites of High Courts. Modifications have been done to allow access to judgments/orders, case status and cause list using screen reader software.
21. Brett Milano, 'Online Courts: Reimagining the Future of Justice', *Harvard Law Today*, 4 December 2020, available at: https://today.law.harvard.edu/online-courts-reimagining-the-future-of-justice/ (accessed on 24 November 2021).
22. Tim Wu, *The Attention Merchants: The Epic Scramble to Get Inside Our Heads* (Knopf, 2016).
23. Jamie F. Metzl, 'Information Technology and Human Rights', *Human Rights Quarterly*, Vol. 18, no. 4 (1996): 705.

24. Samantha Floreani, 'Techno solutionism—very few things actually need to be an app', Digital Rights Watch, 24 March 2021, available at: https://digitalrightswatch.org.au/2021/03/25/technosolutionism/ (accessed on 1 July 2025).
25. Christine Rosen, 'Technosolutionism Isn't the Fix', *Hedgehog Review*, Fall 2020, available at: https://hedgehogreview.com/issues/america-on-the-brink/articles/technosolutionism-isnt-the-fix (accessed on 1 July 2025).
26. 'Center for Humane Technology | Your Undivided Attention Podcast Bonus: Coded Bias, available at: https://assets-global.website-files.com/5f0e1294f002b1bb26e1f304/609200a29aff7edbad663ce2_CHT%20Undivided%20Attention%20Podcast%20Bonus%20Coded%20Bias.pdf (accessed on 1 July 2025).
27. 'How diversity could solve for algorithmic bias', Ikigai Law (2021), available at: https://www.ikigailaw.com/article/387/how-diversity-could-solve-for-algorithmic-bias (accessed on 24 July 2025).
28. Carmen Niethammer, 'AI Bias Could Put Women's Lives at Risk: A Challenge For Regulators', *Forbes*, 27 May 2020, available at: https://www.forbes.com/sites/carmenniethammer/2020/03/02/ai-bias-could-put-womens-lives-at-riska-challenge-for-regulators/?sh=30d13ac7534f (accessed on 1 July 2025).
29. Ibid.
30. Dataethics, 'Danish Companies Behind Seal for Digital Responsibility', 11 June 2019, available at: https://dataethics.eu/danish-companies-behind-seal-for-digital-responsibility/ (accessed on 1 July 2025).
31. Xiuyan Shao and Harri Oinas-Kukkonen, 'How Does GDPR (General Data Protection Regulation) Affect Persuasive System Design: Design Requirements and Cost Implications', University of Oulu Repository,4 March 2019, available at:http://jultika.oulu.fi/files/nbnfi-fe2019050714579.pdf (accessed on 1 July 2025).
32. 'Privacy by Design: GDPR's Sleeping Giant', IAPP, 15 June 2020, available at: https://iapp.org/news/a/privacy-by-design-gdprs-sleeping-giant/ (accessed on 1 July 2025); Sylvain Magdinier and Claire Walsh, 'Using Privacy by Design to Build GDPR Resilience in Existing Business Systems', Thomson Reuters, 13 February 2019, available at: http://in-houseblog.practicallaw.com/using-

privacy-by-design-to-build-gdpr-resilience-in-existing-business-systems/ (accessed on 1 July 2025).

33. Japanese Attorney at Law - Bengoshi L.L., *Five Years On: GDPR Enforcement Trends, Major Fines, and the Role of the EDPB*, (2025), available at: https://japancompliance.com/five-years-on-gdpr-enforcement-trends-major-fines-and-the-role-of-the-edpb/ (accessed on 17 July 2025).
34. Sara Gustavsson, 'An Assessment of Privacy by Design as a Stipulation in GDPR', 24 June 2020, available at: http://www.diva-portal.org/smash/get/diva2:1446745/FULLTEXT01.pdf (accessed on 1 July 2025).
35. Lex Gill and Ronald J. Deibert Jonathon Penney, Sarah McKune, *Advancing Human-Rights-By-Design in the Dual-Use Technology Industry | Columbia, Journal of International Affairs* (2018), https://jia.sipa.columbia.edu/news/advancing-human-rights-design-dual-use-technology-industry (accessed on 24 July 2025).
36. *Ibid.*
37. Aniruddh Nigam and Trisha Jindal, 'Devising Legal Protections for App-Based Workers', Vidhi: Centre for Legal Policy, available at: https://vidhilegalpolicy.in/blog/devising-legal-protections-for-app-based-workers/ (accessed on 1 July 2025).
38. Amol Mavuduru, 'Is data really the new oil in the 21st century?' Towards Data Science. Available at: https:// towardsdatascience.com/is-data-really-the-new-oil-in-the-21st-century-17d014811b88.
39. Lawrence Lessig, *Free Culture: How Big Media Uses Technology and the Law to Lock Down Culture and Control Creativity* (Penguin Press HC, 2004), 19.
40. Lawrence Lessig, *Law and Other Laws of Cyberspace* (1999, Basis Books).

Chapter 18: Promoting Constitutional Morality Beyond Courtrooms

1. Address at the First Convocation Ceremony of Maharashtra National Law University (Maharashtra Judicial Academy, Thane, 2 July 2022).

2. Richelle E. Goodrich, *Making Wishes: Quotes, Thoughts, and a Little Poetry for Every Day of the Year* (Createspace Independent Publishing Platform, 2015).
3. Muhammed Rafi K.P., *Constitution: A Living Vehicle of Life and the Spirit of the Age*, Reflections (2023), https://reflections.live/articles/12836/constitution-a-living-vehicle-of-life-and-the-spirit-of-the-age-an-article-by-muhammed-rafi-kp-11187-llatjqao.html (last visited Jul 17, 2025).
4. Constituent Assembly of India Debates (Proceedings), Volume X.
5. Ibid., Volume XI.
6. Thomas Mann, *The Coming Victory of Democracy* (Alfred A. Knopf, Inc., 1938).
7. Tarunabh Khaitan, 'Beyond Reasonableness - A Rigorous Standard of Review for Article 15 Infringement', *Journal of the Indian Law Institute*, Vol. 50, no. 2 (2008): 177–208, available at: https://papers.ssrn.com/sol3/papers.cfm?abstract_id=1246892 (accessed on 24 July 2025).
8. These obligations have been noted in the judgement of *Vikash Kumar v. UPSC*, (2021) 5 SCC 370.
9. Ibid.
10. Rule 12, available at *The Gazette of India*, https://translaw.clpr.org.in/wp-content/uploads/2020/10/222096-1.pdf (accessed on 2 June 2025).
11. 'Sotomayor says she was "perfect affirmative action baby", CNN Politics, available at: https://edition.cnn.com/2009/POLITICS/06/11/sotomayor.affirmative.action/index.html (accessed on 2 July 2025).
12. Ibid.
13. (2018) 16 SCC 368.
14. Paula C. Rust, *Bisexuality and the Challenge to Lesbian Politics: Sex, Loyalty, and Revolution* (New York University Press, 1995).

Chapter 19: Making Disability Rights Real: Addressing Accessibility and More

1. The Third Professor Shamnad Basheer Memorial Lecture 2022, Virtual Event, 24 September 2022.

2. IDIA Brochure (2021), available at: https://www.idialaw.org/wp-content/uploads/2021/07/idia-brochure-final-2021.pdf (accessed on 2 July 2025).
3. (2009) 9 SCC 1.
4. CRPD/C/GC/8: General comment No. 8 (2022) on the right of persons with disabilities to work and employment', UNHR, available at: https://www.ohchr.org/en/documents/general-comments-and-recommendations/crpdcgc8-general-comment-no-8-2022-right-persons (accessed on 2 July 2025).
5. Sandra L. Robinson and Kira Schabram, 'What to Do When a Colleague Excludes You', *Harvard Business Review*, 13 April 2017, available at: https://hbr.org/2017/04/what-to-do-when-a-colleague-excludes-you (accessed on 2 July 2025).
6. (2021) 5 SCC 370.
7. 'Disability-inclusive Language Guidelines', available at: https://www.ungeneva.org/sites/default/files/2021-01/Disability-Inclusive-Language-Guidelines.pdf (accessed on 2 July 2025).
8. Rakshitha Arni Ravishankar, 'Why You Need to Stop Using These Words and Phrases', *Harvard Business Review*, 15 December 2020, available at: https://hbr.org/2020/12/why-you-need-to-stop-using-these-words-and-phrases (accessed on 2 July 2025).
9. https://www.barandbench.com/news/lawschools/idia-accessibility-lab-launched-at-nujs-in-honour-of-prof-shamnad-basheer

Chapter 20: Leveraging Technology Towards Dispute Resolution in Commercial Courts

1. Keynote Address at the Fourth Full Meeting of the Standing International Forum of Commercial Courts (SIFoCC), Federal Court of Australia and the Supreme Court of New South Wales, Sydney (Virtual Event), 20 October 2022.
2. Justice Sundaresh Menon in the Goff Lecture, 2021 on 'the Complexification of Disputes in the Digital Age'.
3. *Ibid.*
4. Richard Susskind, *Online Courts and the Future of Justice* (Oxford: Oxford University Press, 2019).

Chapter 21: Universal Adult Franchise: Translating India's Political Transformation into a Social Transformation

1. Eighth Dr L.M. Singhvi Memorial Lecture, delivered at Dr Ambedkar International Centre, New Delhi, on 2 December 2022.
2. *Dred Scott v. Sandford* (1857) 60 U.S. 393.
3. *Civil Rights in America- Racial Voting Rights: A National Historic Landmarks Theme Study*, Produced by U.S. Department of the Interior Washington, D.C, 2009.
4. *Slavery: In the Civilised British Government under the Cloak of Brahmanism*, Exposed by Jotirao Govindrao Phule, available at: https://thesatyashodhak.com/wp-content/uploads/2020/05/Jotirao-Phule-Slavery-Government-of-Maharashtra-1991.pdf (accessed on 2 July 2025).
5. Ibid.
6. Dr. B. R. Dr B.R. Ambedkar, *Writing and Speech* Vol. 1 (2019), 256, Available at: http://drambedkarwritings.gov.in/upload/uploadfiles/files/Volume_01.pdf.
7. Ibid., B.R. Ambedkar cited this before the Southborough Committee on Franchise, 1919.
8. CAD, Vol. XI.
9. Government of India Act, 1935.
10. CAD, Vol. VIII, 16 June 1949, Brajeshwar Prasad.
11. CAD, Vol. XI, 17 November 1949, R.K. Sidhwa.
12. CAD, Vol. XI 23 November 1949, Alladi Krishnaswami Ayyar .
13. Ornit Shani, *How India Became Democratic: Citizenship: Citizenship and the Making of the Universal Franchise* (New Delhi: Penguin, 2018). Speech of Dr Sitaramayya in Constituent Assembly of India Debates (CAD).
14. Rohit De, *The Republic of Writs: Litigious Citizens, Constitutional Law and Everyday Life in India (1947–1964)* (Princeton, NJ, 2013), 9.
15. Mehal Jain, 'Constitution Itself Is Feminist', Justice Chandrachud On Transformative Constitution & Feminism', LiveLaw, available at: https://www.livelaw.in/constitution-itself-is-feminist-justice-chandrachud-on-transformative-constitution-feminism/ (accessed on 2 July 2025).

16. Bhimrao Ramji Ambedkar, Dr. *Babasaheb Ambedkar Writings and Speeches: A Ready Reference Manual*, ed. D.C. Ahir (Delhi: B.R. Publishing Corporation, 2008).
17. Ornit Shani, *How India Became Democratic: Citizenship and the Making of the Universal Franchise* (Cambridge: Cambridge University Press, 2017).
18. *Ibid*, 88.
19. Ornit Shani, 'The First Indian Election: Inclusion, Independence and the Making of "We, The People"', Wire, 18 February 2022, available at: https://thewire.in/history/the-first-indian-election-inclusion-independence-and-the-making-of-we-the-people (accessed on 1 July 2025).
20. *Report on First General Elections in India, 1951–52*, Published by Election Commission of India, 20 February 2020.
21. Ibid.
22. PTI, 'Shyam Saran Negi, Who Cast First Vote in Independent India, Dies at 106', Wire, 6 November 2022, available at: https://thewire.in/rights/shyam-saran-negi-first-voter-independent-india-dies (accessed on 1 July 2025).
23. Anurag Bhaskar, 'Ambedkar's Constitution: A Radical Phenomenon in Anti-Caste Discourse?' *CASTE: A Global Journal on Social Exclusion*, 2021.
24. 'Draft Concept Paper on Revitalisation of Panchayati Raj Institutions for Democracy and Development: Committee for the Concept Paper on Panchayati Raj Institutions (C.C.P.P.R.I)', Indian Culture, Government of India, available at: https://indianculture.gov.in/reports-proceedings/draft-concept-paper-revitalisation-panchayati-raj-institutions-democracy-and (accessed on 2 July 2025).
25. *NCT Delhi v. Union of India, (*2023) SCC OnLine SC 606 (Opinion of Justice D.Y. Chandrachud), (July 2018).
26. Radhika Bordia, 'A "*Jungli*" In The Constituent Assembly: Jaipal Singh Munda', NDTV, 26 January 2017, available at: https://www.ndtv.com/people/a-jungli-in-the-constituent-assembly-jaipal-singh-munda-1652949 (accessed on 2 July 2025).
27. *Justice K.S. Puttaswamy (retd) v. Union of India*, (2017) 10 SCC 1.
28. Bhumika Indulia, *Supreme Court launches online portal for RTI Applications*, SCC Times (2022), https://www.scconline.com/

blog/post/2022/11/24/supreme-court-launches-online-portal-for-rti-applications/ (accessed on 18 July 2025).

29. Rakesh Mohan Chaturvedi, 'Cabinet Approves Bill to Overturn Supreme Court Order on SC/ST Act', *Economic Times*, 2 August 2018, available at: https://economictimes.indiatimes.com/news/politics-and-nation/cabinet-approves-bill-to-overturn-supreme-court-order-on-sc/st-act/articleshow/65227734.cms?from=mdr (accessed on 2 July 2025).
30. Bhanupriya Rao, 'Why Ashubi Khan's Pioneering Run Ends Today', IndiaSpend, 16 January 2016, available at: https://www.indiaspend.com/why-ashubi-khans-pioneering-run-ends-today-13263/ (accessed on 2 July 2025).
31. *Supra* note 8; Dr B.R. Ambedkar cited this before the Southborough Committee on Franchise, 1919.

Chapter 22: Law and Morality: The Bounds and Reaches

1. Ashok Desai Memorial Lecture, delivered at the Bombay High Court on 17 December 2022.
2. *R.S. Nayak v. A.R. Antulay*, (1984) 2 SCC 183.
3. *Piloo Mody v. State of Maharashtra*, Miscellaneous Petition No 519/ 1974 (Unreported).
4. Ashok H. Desai, 'Long Before Padmawati: Remembering the Row over Vijay Tendulkar's Marathi Play Sakharam Binder', Scroll.in, 19 November 2017, available at: https://scroll.in/magazine/858300/long-before-padmavati-remembering-the-row-over-vijay-tendulkars-marathi-play-sakharam-binder (accessed on 3 July 2025).
5. Vikram Nankani, 'A Tribute to My Sat Guru, Ashok Desai', Bar and Bench, 15 April 2020, available at: https://www.barandbench.com/columns/a-tribute-to-my-sat-guru-ashok-desai (accessed on 3 July 2025).
6. Steven Shavell, 'Law Versus Morality as Regulators of Conduct', *American Law and Economics Review* 4, no. 2 (2002): 227–57, available at https://papers.ssrn.com/sol3/papers.cfm?abstract_id=293905 (accessed on 6 August 2025).
7. Roscoe Pound, 'Law and Morals—Jurisprudence and Ethics', *North Carolina Law Review*, Vol. 23, No. 3 (1945).

8. John Finnis, *Natural Law and Natural Rights* (Second edition, Oxford University Press, 2011).
9. H.L.A. Hart, 'Positivism and the Separation of Law and Morals', *Harvard Law Review*, Vol. 71, No. 4 (1958).
10. H.L.A. Hart, *Concept of Law* (1961).
11. B. Gert, 'The Definition of Morality', *Stanford Encyclopaedia of Philosophy*, https://plato.stanford.edu/entries/morality-definition/.
12. Robert Deliège, *Untouchables of India* (Berg Publishers 1999).
13. *Supra,* n. 11.
14. David Wong, *Natural Moralities: A Defense of Pluralistic Relativism* (Oxford University Press, 2006), 312.
15. Sonia Sika, 'Moral Relativism and the Concept of Culture', *Theoria: A Journal of Social and Political Theory,* Vol. 59, No. 133 (2012): 56–57.
16. Max Weber, *The Religion of India: The Sociology of Hinduism and Buddhism* (The Free Press, 1958), 122.
17. Michael Moffatt, *An Untouchable Community in South India: Structure and Consensus* (Princeton University, 1979), 222, 247 and 270.
18. Thomas Hobbes, *Leviathan* (Richard Tuck ed., Cambridge Univ. Press rev. student ed. 1996) (1651).
19. B.R. Ambedkar, *Annihilation of Caste* (Critical Annotated Ed., S. Anand ed., Navayana 2014) (1936).
20. Deepti Priya Mehrotra, 'Nangeli—The Forgotten Dalit Women Who Stood Up Against Travancore's Breast Tax', ThePrint, 8 March 2022, available at: https://theprint.in/pageturner/excerpt/nangeli-the-forgotten-dalit-woman-who-stood-up-against-travancores-breast-tax/862452/ (accessed on 3 July 2025).
21. Manu S. Pillai, 'The Women Who Cut Off Her Breasts', *The Hindu,* 18 February 2017.
22. John Rawls, *A Theory of Justice* (Belknap Press, 1971).
23. Madhavi Menon, *The Law of Desire: Rulings on Sex and Sexuality in India* (Speaking Tiger, 2021), 70–71.
24. *United States v. One Book Called Ulysses*, 5 F Supp. 182 (SDNY 1933).
25. Kevin Birmingham, 'James Joyce's Ulysses: A Classic Too Sexy for Censors', BBC, 16 June2015, available at: https://www.bbc.com/

culture/article/20150616-a-classic-too-sexy-for-censors (accessed on 3 July 2025).

26. Constitutional Assembly Debates: Official Reports Vol. VII, 4 November 1948, p. 38.
27. Mariam Faruqi, 'Ashok Desai: Former Attorney General of India and LSE alumnus – A tribute', 24 April 2024, available at:https://blogs.lse.ac.uk/southasia/2020/04/24/ashok-desai-former-attorney-general-of-india-and-lse-alumnus-a-tribute/ (accessed on 3 July 2025).
28. *Navtej Singh Johar v. Union of India*, (2018) 10 SCC 1, 598.
29. *Joseph Shine v. Union of India*, (2019) 3 SCC 39, 25.
30. Vikram Seth, 'Through Love's Great Power', Global Poetry, 9 April 2014, available at: http://www.globalpoetry.org/blog/2014/04/09/through-loves-great-power/ (accessed on 24 July 2025).

Chapter 23: Law, Justice and the Heart: Cultivating Empathy in Legal Education

1. Address at the Nineteenth Annual Convocation Address at NALSAR, Hyderabad delivered on 25 February 2023.
2. A superhero movie series.
3. *To Kill a Mockingbird*, Chapter 20. Atticus, in his address to the jury, portrays the courtroom as the great equalizer, a place where all individuals stand equal and justice prevails. He underscores the tension between moral integrity and the entrenched biases of the Maycomb community. In his appeal, he urges the jury to transcend societal prejudice and uphold the principles of fairness and equality that the court is meant to embody.
4. Maya Rhodan, 'The Supreme Court Just Quoted Spider-Man', TIME, 22 June 2015, available at: https://time.com/3930115/supreme-court-spiderman/ (accessed on 3 July 2025).
5. 'Student bodies protest, demand FIR in Darshan Solanki's death at IIT-B', *Indian Express*, 21 February 2023, available at: https://indianexpress.com/article/cities/mumbai/student-bodies-protest-demand-fir-in-darshan-solankis-death-at-iit-b-8456995/ (accessed on 3 July 2025).
6. Aaratrika Bhaumik, 'Law Student Belonging to ST Community Found Dead in NLUO Girls Hostel, Suicide Suspected',

LiveLaw, 5 April 2022, available at: https://www.livelaw.in/news-updates/law-student-belonging-to-st-community-found-dead-in-nluo-girls-hostel-suicide-suspected-195850 (accessed on 3 July 2025).

7. Sukhadeo Thorat, 'Discrimination on the Campus', *The Hindu*, 4 December 2021, available at: https://www.thehindu.com/opinion/lead/Rohith-Vemula-suicide-Dalit-and-higher-education-Discrimination-on-the-campus/article62116029.ece (accessed on 3 July 2025).
8. Sukanya Shantha, 'Dalit Student's Suicide Points to Well-Known – But Ignored – Caste Discrimination in IITs', Wire, 15 February 2023, available at: https://thewire.in/caste/iit-bombay-darshan-solanki-suicide (accessed on 3 July 2025).
9. Radhika Roy, 'Injustices Faced by Black Americans Not Relics of Past' : Washington Supreme Court Judges Issue Solidarity Statement', Live Law, 6 June 2020, available at: https://www.livelaw.in/foreign-international/black-lives-matter-washington-supreme-court-judges-issue-solidarity-statement-157942 (accessed on 3 July 2025).
10. Brett Milano, 'The Work of Pioneering Civil Rights Lawyers Evinces Hope and Resilience in Today's Political Landscape, Says Klarman', Harvard Law, 9 May 2019, available at: https://hls.harvard.edu/today/the-work-of-pioneering-civil-rights-lawyers-evinces-hope-and-resilience-in-todays-political-landscape-says-klarman/ (accessed on 3 July 2025).
11. Anurag Bhaskar, 'The Modern Form of Institutionalised Casteism', *Hindustan Times*, 15 January 2021, available at: https://www.hindustantimes.com/opinion/the-modern-form-of-institutionalised-casteism-101610716480748.html (accessed on 3 July 2025).

Chapter 24: A Prescription for Justice: Quest for Fairness and Equity in Healthcare

1. Address at the Nineteenth Sir Ganga Ram Oration, The Sovereign Hall, Hotel Le Meridien, New Delhi, delivered on 25 February 2023.

2. P. Arora, A.K. Gupta and S. Talati, 'Establishment of a Tele-Evidence Facility at the Post Graduate Institute of Medical Education and Research, Chandigarh: A Unique Initiative', *National Medical Journal India,* Vol. 32 (2019): 239–24,available at: https://pubmed.ncbi.nlm.nih.gov/32769248/ (accessed on 24 July 2024).
3. Press statement, 'UNAIDS Welcomes Ground-Breaking Decision by India's Supreme Court That Strikes Down Law Criminalizing LGBTI People', UNAIDS.org, available at: https://www.unaids.org/en/resources/presscentre/pressreleaseandstatementarchive/2018/september/20180906_India_section377 (accessed on 1 July 2025).
4. (2018) 10 SCC 1.
5. 'Penile Construction Surgery in Delhi Helps 34-Year-Old UP Resident Complete Transition to Man', *Indian Express,* 21 November 2022, available at: https://indianexpress.com/article/cities/delhi/penile-construction-surgery-delhi-transition-to-man-8281042/ (accessed on 1 July 2025).
6. 'Capability and Well-being', in Nussbaum and Sen (eds.), *The Quality of Life* (Oxford: Clarendon Press), 30–53.
7. Astha Saxena, 'In two days: Delhi's air can affect lungs, says doctors', *Indian Express*, 6 November 2018, available at: https://indianexpress.com/article/cities/delhi/in-two-days-delhis-air-can-affect-lungs-say-doctors-5435428/ (accessed on 1 July 2025).
8. Wu, et al., 'Who Gets to Breathe Clean Air in New Delhi?', *New York Times*, 17 December 2020, available at: https://www.nytimes.com/interactive/2020/12/17/world/asia/india-pollution-inequality.html (accessed on 1 July 2025).
9. Sheila Zurbrigg, *Rakku's Story: Structures of Ill-Health and the Source of Change* (Madras: Sidma Offset Press P. Ltd, 1984).
10. Yogesh Jain, 'Back to Basics', *Mandate for Health, Seminar* (2019), available at: https://www.india-seminar.com/2019/714/714_yogesh_jain.htm (accessed on 18 July 2025).
11. 'Delhi Records First Malaria Death in Two Years', *New Indian Express*, 6 January 2023, available at: https://www.newindianexpress.com/cities/delhi/2023/Jan/06/delhi-recordsfirst-malaria-death-in-twoyears-2535236.html (accessed on 1 July 2025).
12. Arkin Braveman P. et al. 'What Is Health Equity?', Robert Wood Johnson Foundation, 1 May 2017, available at: https://www.rwjf.

org/en/library/research/2017/05/what-is-health-equity-.html (accessed on 1 July 2025).

13. *Devika Biswas v. Union of India*, (2016) 10 SCC 726.
14. *C.E.S.C. Limited v. Subhash Chandra Bose*, (1992) 1 SCC 441; *Consumer Education and Research Centre v. Union of India*, (1995) 3 SCC 42; *Paschim Banga Khet Mazdoor Samity v. State of West Bengal*, (1996)4 SCC 37; *Society for Unaided Private Schools of Rajasthan v. Union of India*, (2012) 6 SCC 1; *Ibid*; *Common Cause v. Union of India & Ors*, (2018) 5 SCC 1.
15. Report of the Health Service and Development Committee (Calcutta: Government of India Press, 1946), available at: http://www.nhp.gov.in/sites/default/files/pdf/Bhore_Committee_Report_VOL.1.pdf (accessed on 24 July 2025).
16. Divyani Dubey, 'How True Is the Health Minister's Claim That India's Doctor–Population Ration Exceeds WHO Guidelines?', Scroll.in, 5 August 2022, available at: https://scroll.in/article/1029766/how-true-is-the-health-ministers-claim-that-indias-doctor-population-ratio-exceeds-who-guidelines (accessed on 1 July 2025).
17. Anup Karan et al, 'Size, Composition and Distribution of Health Workforce in India: Why, and Where to Invest?', *Human Resources for Health*, Vol. 19, no. 39 (2021). The recommended threshold is 44.5 skilled health workers per 10,000 population.
18. Ministry of Health and Family Welfare, Rural Health Statistics 2020–21, available at: https://main.mohfw.gov.in/newshighlights-90 (accessed on 1 July 2025).
19. Regis College website: https://online.regiscollege.edu/blog/social-justice-in-health-care/ (accessed on 1 July 2025).
20. *Neil Aurelio Nunes (OBC Reservation) v. Union of India*, (2022) 4 SCC 1.
21. Paul Kalanithi, *When Breath Becomes Air* (Delhi: Random House, 1990).

Chapter 25: Free Speech: Identity, Expression and Self-Realization

1. Address at the Second Soli Sorabjee Memorial Lecture, Twenty-Third Commonwealth Law Conference, Goa delivered on 9 March 2023.

2. *S. Rangarajan v. P. Jagjivan Ram*, 1989 (2) SCC 574.
3. *Shreya Singhal v. Union of India*, (2015) 5 SCC 1.
4. Thomas Emerson, 'Toward a General Theory of First Amendment', *Yale Law Journal*, Vol. 72, No. 5 (1963): 877–956.
5. *Procunier v. Martinez*, 416 U.S. 396 (1974).
6. James Fearon, 'What Is Identity (As We Now Use the Word)?' available at: http://www.web.stanford.edu/group/fearon-research/cgi-bin/wordpress/wp-content/uploads/2013/10/What-is-Identity-as-we-now-use-the-word-.pdf (accessed on 1 July 2025).
7. David Buckingham, 'Introducing Identity' *Youth, Identity, and Digital Media (*MIT Press, 2008) 1-24, Available at: https://tile.loc.gov/storage-services/master/gdc/gdcebookspublic/20/20/71/82/80/2020718280/2020718280.pdf.
8. *Abhiram Singh v. C.D. Commachen & Ors*, (2017) 2 SCC 629, at 111.
9. *NALSA v. Union of India*, (2014) 5 SCC 438.
10. *Navtej Singh Johar v. Union of India*, (2018) 10 SCC 1.
11. Umer Ali, 'Self-Actualization of Dalit Woman and Narration as a Strategy for Transition: An Analysis of Bama's Works', *International Journal of Health Sciences,* Vol. 6, No. S2 (2022). Available at: https://doi.org/10.53730/ijhs.v6nS2.8276 (accessed on 1 July 2025).
12. Mangal Rathod, *O Babasaheb*, Eklavyas with Thumbs: (2014), https://eklavyaswiththumbs.blogspot.com/2014/11/mangal-rathod.html (last visited Jul 18, 2025).
13. Manasi Shah, 'Apun Ka Time Ayegaa', *Telegraph*, 7 February 2021, available at: https://www.telegraphindia.com/culture/dalit-rappers-apun-ka-time-aayegaa/cid/1805899 (accessed on 1 July 2025).
14. Rabindranath Tagore, 'Sadhana: The Realization of Life', Terebess Asia Online (n.d.), available at: https://terebess.hu/english/tagore16.html (accessed on 1 July 2025).
15. E. M. Forster, (1927). Aspects of the Novel (Chapter 5). Edward Arnold.
16. Divya Arya, 'Nirbhaya 10 Years On: The Lives the Delhi Gang Rape Changed', BBC, 6 December 2022, available at: https://www.bbc.com/news/world-63817388 (accessed on 1 July 2025).

17. 'On His Birth Anniversary, Remembering Social Reformer Baba Amte', *Indian Express*, 26 December 2019, available at: https://indianexpress.com/article/cities/mumbai/on-his-birth-anniversary-remembering-social-reformer-baba-amte-6185408/ (accessed on 1 July 2025).
18. Martin Luther King, Jr, 'I have a Dream', available: https://www.npr.org/2010/01/18/122701268/i-have-a-dream-speech-in-its-entirety (accessed on 1 July 2025).
19. Dhwani S., The Anti-Arrack Movement: The Historical Women's Protest for Total Alcohol Prohibition , Feminism in India, 14 June 2019, available at https://feminisminindia.com/2019/06/14/anti-arrack-movement-women-andhra-pradesh/. (accessed on 1 July 2025).
20. Nadine Strossen, 'Freedom of Speech and Equality: Do We Have to Choose', *Journal of Law and Policy*, Vol. no. 25 (2016): 185, available at: https://brooklynworks.brooklaw.edu/jlp/vol25/iss1/7 (accessed on 1 July 2025).
21. Jacob Mchangama, *Free Speech: A History from Socrates to Social Media* (New York: Basic Books, 2022), 209.
22. Ibid.
23. Suzanne Wrack, 'How the FA Banned Women's Football in 1921 and Tried to Justify It', *Guardian*, 13 June 2022). https://www.theguardian.com/football/2022/jun/13/how-the-fa-banned-womens-football-in-1921-and-tried-to-justify-it.
24. Matthias Kaelberer, 'Gender Trouble on the German Soccer Field: Can the Growth of Women's Soccer Challenge Hegemonic Masculinity?', *Journal of Gender Studies,* Vol. No. 28 (2019). https://doi.org/10.1080/09589236.2018.1469973 (accessed on 1 July 2025).
25. The Constitution of India, Art. 19.
26. *M.F. Hussain v. Raj Kumar Pandey*, 2008 Cri LJ 4107.
27. S. Tamilselvan v. Government of Tamil Nadu, (2016) 4 CTC 561.
28. '"Author Perumal Murugan has died": Tamil writer withdraws all published work following protests', Scroll.in, 13 January 2015, available at: https://scroll.in/article/700217/author-perumal-murugan-has-died-tamil-writer-withdraws-all-published-work-following-protests (accessed on 1 July 2025).

29. Olivia B Waxman, 'Why Toni Morrison's Books are so often the target of book bans', *Time*, 31 January 2022, available at: https://time.com/6143127/toni-morrison-book-bans/ (accessed on 1 July 2025).
30. S. Mandal, 'Book review: Sameena Dalwai. 2019. Bans & Bar Girls: Performing Caste in Mumbai's Dance Bars', review of *Bans & Bar Girls: Performing Caste in Mumbai's Dance Bars*, by Sameena Dalwai, *Contributions to Indian Sociology* 55, no. 1 (2020): 142–45, https://journals.sagepub.com/doi/full/10.1177/0069966720979335 (accessed on 1 July 2025.
31. Madhavi Menon, *The Law of Desire: Rulings on Sex and Sexuality in India* (Delhi: Speaking Tiger, 2021), 70–71.
32. Bob Dylan, 'Chimes of Freedom', available at: https://www.bobdylan.com/songs/chimes-freedom/.

Chapter 26: Journalism in the New Age: Challenges, Responsibilities and Excellence

1. Keynote Address at the Fourth Ramnath Goenka Excellence in Journalism Awards, hosted by the *Indian Express* Group, Kamal Mahal, ITC Maurya, New Delhi on 22 March 2023.
2. Benjamin Guy Horniman (1873–1948), a British journalist and editor of the *Bombay Chronicle*, was known for his outspoken support of India's independence movement. Following India's independence in 1947, the famous gardens situated in the heart of Fort, South Mumbai (formerly called as 'Bombay Green') were renamed 'Horniman Circle' as a tribute to him.
3. Vijay Singh, Mumbai-based English Editor Brought Out Jallianwala Horror', *Times of India*, 9 April 2019, available at: https://timesofindia.indiatimes.com/city/mumbai/mumbai-based-english-editor-brought-out-jallianwala-horror/articleshow/68788547.cms (accessed on 29 July 2025).'
4. Anton Chekhov, 'The Bet' (1889) translated by Constance Garnett. In *The Schoolmistress and Other Stories* (New York: The Macmillan Company, 1918).
5. *Arnab Ranjan Goswami vs Union of India* AIR 2020 SC 2386; see also the *Indian Express* newspapers *(Bombay v. Union of India*, [1985] 2 SCR 2 287.

6. Karen McIntyre and Cathrine Gyldensted, 'Constructive Journalism: An Introduction and Practical Guide for Applying Positive Psychology Techniques to News Production', *Journal of Media Innovation*, Vol. 4 (2017): 20.
7. Commission on Freedom of the Press., *A Free and Responsible Press; A General Report on Mass Communication: Newspapers, Radio, Motion Pictures, Magazines, and Books* (The University of Chicago Press, 1947), available at: https://clio.columbia.edu/catalog/SCSB-10479941?counter=1 (accessed on 21 July 2025).
8. Michael Luo, 'How Can the Press Best Serve a Democratic Society?', *The New Yorker*, 2020, available at: https://www.newyorker.com/news/the-future-of-democracy/how-can-the-press-best-serve-democracy (accessed on 21 July 2025).
9. '90% Of Leadership Positions in Indian Media Occupied by Upper Caste Groups: Report', *The Hindu*, 14 October 2022, available at: https://www.thehindu.com/news/national/90-of-leadership-positions-in-indian-media-occupied-by-upper-caste-groups-report/article66010136.ece (accessed on 29 July 2025).
10. 'Why Is Gujarat Forcing Hospitals to Only Accept COVID-19 Patients Coming Through "108" Ambulances?', Scroll.in, 26 April 2021, available at: https://scroll.in/article/993285/why-is-gujarat-forcing-hospitals-to-only-accept-covid-19-patients-coming-through-108-ambulances (accessed on 29 July 2025); In Re: Regarding Closure of Mid-Day Meal Scheme, Suo Motu Writ Petition (C) No(S). 2/2020 ; In Re: Problems and Miseries of Migrant Labourers, Suo Motu Writ Petition (Civil) No. 6 of 2020; Suo Moto Writ Petition (C) No. 3/2021 In Re: Distribution of Essential Supplies and Services During Pandemic; 'Breaking: Allahabad HC Takes Suo Moto Cognizance Of Hathras Case; Says 'Incidents Have Shocked Our Conscience', *Live Law*, 1 October 2020, available at: https://www.livelaw.in/top-stories/allahabad-hc-takes-suo-moto-cognizance-of-hathras-case-says-incidents-have-shocked-our-conscience-163851 (accessed on 29 July 2025).
11. *State of Maharashtra v. Rajendra Jawanmal Gandhi,* (1997) 8 SCC 386, 37.

12. 'The Madrid Principles on the Relationship between the Media and Judicial Independence', International Commission of Jurists, 1 February 1994, available at: https://www.icj.org/the-madrid-principles-on-the-relationship-between-the-media-and-judicial-independence/ (accessed on 29 July 2025).

Chapter 27: The Relationship Between Constitutional Rights and Constitutional Structure: Delicate Balances and Overarching Considerations

1. Address at the Cambridge Pro Bono Project's Annual Lecture 2023, University of Cambridge, 30 May 2023.
2. Homer, 'The Odyssey', Rendered into English Prose by Samuel Butler.
3. John Elster, *Ulysses and the Sirens: Studies in Rationality and Irrationality* (India: Cambridge University Press, 1984).
4. Suhar Palshikar, 'The Indian State: Constitution and Beyond', in Rajeev Bhargava (ed.) *Politics and Ethics of the Indian Constitution* (New Delhi: Oxford University Press, 2008).
5. Shakespeare, *Henry V*, Andrew Gurr (ed.) (Cambridge University Press, 2005).
6. Lee Resolution, The Resolution for Independence, passed by the Second Continental Congress on 2 July 1776.
7. Declaration of the Rights of Man and of the Citizen 1789, reproduced in *Encyclopedia Britanica,* 9 December 2022.
8. *Subhash Desai v. Principal Secretary, Governor of Maharashtra,* (2024) 2 SCC 719.
9. Ibid.
10. Benjamin Cardozo, *The Nature of the Judicial Process* (Yale University Press, 1974), 83.
11. *Kesavananda Bharati v. State of Kerala,* (1973) 4 SCC 225.
12. (2019) UKSC 41.
13. *Krishna Kumar Singh v. State of Bihar,* (2017) 3 SCC 1.
14. M.J.C. Vile, *Constitutionalism and the Separation of Powers* (Second edition, Liberty funds, 1998), 13.
15. Anirudha Nagar, 'Laws by the people, for the People', *The Hindu,* 24 February 2014, available at: https://www.thehindu.com/opinion/

op-ed/laws-by-the-people-for-the-people/article5719578.ece (accessed on 27 August 2024).

16. *Doctors for Life International v. Speaker of the National Assembly* ZACC 11 (2006).

Chapter 28: Reformation Beyond Representation: The Social Life of the Constitution in Remedying Historical Wrongs

1. Keynote Address at the Sixth International Conference on the Unfinished Legacy of Dr B.R. Ambedkar, Brandeis University, delivered on 22 October 2023.
2. Arto Laitinen and Arvi Särkelä, 'Social wrongs', *Critical Review of International Social and Political Philosophy*, 2020, available at: 10.1080/13698230.2020.1853435 (accessed on 15 October 2023).
3. P. Sanal Mohan, *Modernity of Slavery: Struggles against Caste Inequality in Colonial Kerala* (Oxford University Press, 2015).
4. Ibid., 39.
5. A. Thorat and M. Aquil, 'Historic Legacy of Untouchability and Caste Enslavement: A Case of Reparative Justice', *Journal of Social Inclusion Studies*, Vol. 7, no. 2 (2021): 107–16, available at: https://doi.org/10.1177/23944811221084404 (accessed on 1 July 2025).
6. B.R. Ambedkar, 'Annihilation of Caste', *Babasaheb Ambedkar: Writings and Speeches,* Vol. 1, Vasant Moon ed. (Delhi: National Book Trust, 2011).
7. Marc Galanter, 'Law and Caste in Modern India', *Asian Survey,* Vol. 3, no. 11 (November 1963): 544–59; Marc Galanter, 'Untouchability and the Law', *Economic and Political Weekly,* Vol. 4, no. ½ (January 1969): 131–70; Bharat Patankar and Gail Omvedt, 'The Dalit Liberation Movement in Colonial Period', *Economic and Political Weekly,* Vol. 14, no. 7–8 (1979).
8. Michael Klarman, *Unfinished Business: Racial Equality in American History* (Oxford University Press, 2007).
9. M. Hibbard, 'Indigenous Planning: From Forced Assimilation to Self-determination', *Journal of Planning Literature*, Vol. 37, no. 1 (2022): 17–27; Katherine Ellinghaus, 'Indigenous Assimilation and Absorption in the United States and Australia', *Pacific Historical Review,* Vol. 75, no. 4 (2006): 563–85.

10. Klarman, *Unfinished Business.*
11. 60 U.S. (19 How.) 393 (1857).
12. 163 US 537 (1896).
13. 323 US 214 (1944).
14. Chris Greer and Yvonne Jewkes, 'Extremes of Otherness: Media Images of Social Exclusion', *Social Justice,* Vol. 32, no. 1 (2005): 20.
15. Ibid.
16. Akhil Amar Reed, *America's Constitution: A Biography* (Random House, 2005).
17. Frederick Douglass 'The Constitution of the United States: Pro-Slavery or Anti-slavery?', 26 March 1860, available at: https://civics.asu.edu/sites/default/files/2021-06/Q75%20Douglass%2C%20Is%20the%20Constitution%20Proslavery%20or%20Antislavery%2C%201860_CPTL.pdf (accessed on 1 July 2025).
18. B.R. Ambedkar, 'Evidence before the Southborough Committee', in Vasant Moon (ed.), *Babasaheb Ambedkar: Writings and Speeches,* Vol. 1.
19. B.R. Ambedkar, 'Waiting for a Visa', in Vasant Moon (ed.), *Babasaheb Ambedkar: Writings and Speeches,* Vol. 12.
20. Ambedkar, 'Annihilation of Caste', *Babasaheb Ambedkar,* Vol. 1.
21. Constituent Assembly Debates, 25 November 1949.
22. B.R. Ambedkar, 'Annihilation of Caste', in Vasant Moon (ed.), *Babasaheb Ambedkar: Writings and Speeches,* Vol. 1.
23. Ibid.
24. Sukhadeo Thorat and Narender Kumar (eds), *B.R. Ambedkar: Perspectives on Social Exclusion and Inclusive Policies* (Oxford University Press, 2009).
25. Anurag Bhaskar, 'Reservations, Efficiency, and the Framing of Indian Constitution', *Economic and Political Weekly,* Vol. 56, no. 19 (2021).
26. Philip Pettit, *On the People's Terms: A Republican Theory and Model of Democracy* (Cambridge University Press, 2012).
27. Ambedkar, 'Annihilation of Caste', *Babasaheb Ambedkar,* 45.
28. Constituent Assembly Debate, Vol. VII, 9 December 1948.
29. Article 17 of the Constitution of India.

30. Granville Austin, *The Indian Constitution: Cornerstone of a Nation* (Oxford University Press, 1966), xiii.
31. Ibid., xii–xiii.
32. B.R. Ambedkar, 'Evidence before the Southborough Committee', in Vasant Moon (ed.), *Babasaheb Ambedkar: Writings and Speeches,* Vol. 1.
33. Bhaskar, 'Reservations, Efficiency, and the Framing of Indian Constitution'.
34. *Indra Sawhney v. Union of India* AIR 1993 SC 477.
35. Government of India, available at: https://caomod.gov.in/DHTI/Literature%20for%20AFHQ%20Employees/Reservation%20in%20Services.pdf (accessed on 1 July 2025), 9.
36. Ibid; See also 'SC/ST representation at Secretary, Joint Secy level in Centre stands at 4% and 4.9%: Govt data in Rajya Sabha', *The Hindu*, 16 December 2022, available at: https://www.thehindu.com/news/national/scst-representation-at-secretary-joint-secy-level-in-centre-stands-at-4-and-49-govt-data-in-rajya-sabha/article66267048.ece (accessed on 1 July 2025).
37. Anurag Bhaskar, '"Ambedkar's Constitution": A Radical Phenomenon in Anti-Caste Discourse?', *CASTE: A Global Journal on Social Exclusion,* Vol. 2, No. 1 (2021): 109–31.
38. 'Representation of Reserved Categories', Press Information Bureau, Government of India, 17 July 2019, available at: https://pib.gov.in/Pressreleaseshare.aspx?PRID=1579065 (accessed on 1 July 2025).
39. 'SC/ST representation at Secretary, Joint Secy level in Centre stands at 4% and 4.9%: Govt data in Rajya Sabha', *The Hindu,* 16 December 2022.
40. Ellen Berrey, *The Enigma of Diversity: The Language of Race and the Limits of Racial Justice* (University of Chicago University Press, 2015).
41. Ibid., 8–9.
42. *Navtej Singh Johar v. Union of India* 2018 INSC 790.
43. *Young Lawyers Association v. State of Kerala,* 2018/INSC/908.
44. *B.K. Pavitra v. Union of India,* (2019) 16 SCC 129.
45. *Puniya v. Secretary, Ministry of Defence,* (2020) 7 SCC 469.
46. *Lt Col Nitisha v. Union of India,* (2021) 15 SCC 125.

47. *Hariram Bhambhi v. Satyanarayan*, AIR 2021 SC 5610.
48. *ADM Jabalpur v. Shivkant Shukla*, AIR 1976 SC 1207; *Suresh Kumar Koushal v. Naz Foundation*), (2014) 1 SCC 1; *Subhash Kashinath Mahajan vs. the State of Maharashtra* 2018/INSC/248.
49. Ambedkar, 'Annihilation of Caste', *Babasaheb Ambedkar.*
50. 'A Worrying Rise in Atrocities on Dalits', *Deccan Herald*, 31 August 2023, available at: https://www.deccanherald.com/opinion/editorial/a-worrying-rise-in-atrocities-on-dalits-2666912 (accessed on 1 July 2025).
51. Issa G. Shivji, 'Do Constitutions Matter? The Dilemma of a Radical Lawyer', *Journal of National Law University Delhi*, Vol. 6, no. 2 (2019): 79–83, available at: https://doi.org/10.1177/2277401720986004, accessed on 18 October 2023 (accessed on 1 July 2025).
52. Ibid.
53. Ibid.
54. Brett Milano, 'The Work of Pioneering Civil Rights Lawyers Evinces Hope and Resilience in Today's Political Landscape, Says Klarman', *Harvard Law Today*, 9 May 2019, available at: https://hls.harvard.edu/today/the-work-of-pioneering-civil-rights-lawyers-evinces-hope-and-resilience-in-todays-political-landscape-says-klarman/ (accessed on 1 July 2025).
55. Anurag Bhaskar, 'Ambedkar's Constitution', 109–31.
56. Gail Omvedt, *Dalits and the Democratic Revolution: Dr Ambedkar and the Dalit Movement in Colonial India* (New Delhi: Sage Publications, 1994).
57. Omprakash Valmiki, *Joothan: An Untouchable's Life* (Columbia University Press, 2008).
58. Lata Jha, 'Ten Indian Films on the Caste System', *Mint,* 23 July 2018, available at: https://www.livemint.com/Consumer/6nnJc915E2imyZKE0jkVtJ/Ten-Indian-films-on-the-caste-system.html (accessed on 1 July 2025).
59. Jacey Fortin, 'Critical Race Theory: A Brief History', *New York Times*, 8 November 2021, available at: https://www.nytimes.com/article/what-is-critical-race-theory.html (accessed on 1July 2025).
60. Carbado, Devon W., 'Critical What What Commentary: Critical Race Theory: A Commemoration: Afterword', *Connecticut Law Review* (2011): 127.

61. Gajendran Ayyathurai, 'It is time for a new subfield: "Critical Caste Studies"', LSE South Asia Centre, 15 July 2021, https://blogs.lse.ac.uk/southasia/2021/07/05/it-is-time-for-a-new-subfield-critical-caste-studies/ (accessed on 1 July 2025).
62. Shailaja Paik, 'What Dalit People Taught Us About Education and Why We Must Commit to It', Wire, 1 February 2022, available at: https://thewire.in/caste/what-dalit-people-taught-us-about-education-and-why-we-must-commit-to-it (accessed on 1 July 2025).
63. Disha Wadekar, 'Understanding civil liberties from an Ambedkarite perspective', *Leaflet*, 14 April 2022, available at: https://theleaflet.in/understanding-civil-liberties-from-an-ambedkarite-perspective/ (accessed on 1 July 2025).
64. Constituent Assembly Debates, 25 November 1949, available at: https://loksabha.nic.in/writereaddata/cadebatefiles/C25111949.html (accessed on 1 July 2025).

Chapter 29: Revisiting Penal Philosophy: Reformative Justice in India

1. Speech delivered at the *Hundred and Ninth Birth Anniversary Celebration of Justice V.R. Krishna Iyer*, Speaker's Lounge, Constitution Club, Rafi Marg, New Delhi on 4 November 2023.
2. D.K. Iyer and F. Kuriakose, 'Balancing Power: Analysing Socially Transformative Jurisprudence of V.R. Krishna Iyer through New Genre Leadership Theory' (July 2016).
3. Justice V.R. Krishna Iyer, speaking at the International Conference Against Death Sentence in Stockholm, 1976 (as quoted in *Outlook* India).
4. V.R. Krishna Iyer, *Access to Justice: A Case for Basic Change* (B.R. Pub. Corp., 1991).
5. S. Baliga, *Self-Identified Victims' Needs: Toward a Feminist Restorative Justice* (Atlanta: Emory University, 2008).
6. L. Radzik, 'Offenders, the Making of Amends and the State', in G. Johnstone and D.W. Van Ness (eds), *Handbook of Restorative Justice* (Cullompton, UK: Willan Publishing, 2007), 192–207.

7. S Maruna, 'The Role of Wounded Healing in Restorative Justice: An Appreciation of Albert Eglash', *Restorative Justice*, Vol. 2, no. 1(2014): 9–23.
8. Ministry of Law and Justice; Justice VR Krishna Iyer, available at: https://lawmin.gov.in/sites/default/files/2015-02-02%20-%20JUS%20VR%20KRISHNA%20IYER_0.pdf (accessed on 29 July 2025).
9. *Gudikanti Narasimhulu and Ors v. High Court of Andhra Pradesh* (1978) 2 SCR 371.
10. *State of Rajasthan v. Balchand,* (1977) 4 SCC 308.
11. *Rattan Singh v. State of Punjab* (1980) 1 SCR 846.
12. Emilio C. Viano, *Critical Issues in Victimology: International Perspectives* (Springer Publishing Group, 1992).
13. Emilio C. Viano, 'Violence, Victimization and Social Change: A Sociocultural and Public Policy Analysis', *Victimology,* Vol. 8, no. 3–4 (1983):150–87.
14. Marc Groenhuijsen, 'Victims' Rights and Restorative Justice: Piecemeal Reform of the Criminal Justice System or a Change of Paradigm?', in H. Kaptein and M. Malsch (eds), *Crime, Victims and Justice. Essays on Principles and Practice* (Aldershot: Ashgate, 2004).
15. *Rudul Sah v. State of Bihar*, (1983) 3 SCR 508.
16. Andrew von Hirsch, Anthony Bottoms and Julian Roberts, *Restorative Justice and Criminal Justice: Competing or Reconcilable Paradigms?* (Oxford and Portland: Hart Publishing, 2003), 348.
17. *Sarwan Singh v. State of Punjab,* (1978) 4 SCC 111.
18. Asian News International, 'Hathras Case: Supreme Court Rejects UP Government Plea Against High Court Order', NDTV, 27 March 2023, available at: https://www.ndtv.com/india-news/hathras-case-supreme-court-rejects-up-government-plea-against-high-court-order-3897085 (accessed on 1 July 2025).
19. *Rajendra Prasad v. State of UP,* AIR 1979 SC 916.
20. Ibid., at 114.
21. *Dalbir Singh v. State of Punjab,* AIR 1979 SC 1384.
22. *Mohd. Arif v. Supreme Court of India,* (2014) 9 SCC 737.
23. *Manoj v. State of MP,* (2022) SCC Online SC 677.
24. *Sundar @ Sundarrajan v. State*, (2023) SCC OnLine SC 310.

25. J. Braithwaite, *Restorative Justice and Responsive Regulation* (New York: Oxford University Press, 2002).
26. Anjelina Chapin, 'Why Would a Woman Want to Talk to the Man Who Abused Her?' The Cut, 5 May 2017, available at: www.thecut.com/2017/05/a-better-man-film-restorative-justice-and-domestic-abuse.html (accessed on 1 July 2025).
27. E. Zinsstag and M. Keenan (eds), *Restorative Responses to Sexual Violence: Legal, Social and Therapeutic Dimensions* (New York: Routledge, 2017), 108–40.
28. P.S. Anderson, 'When Justice and Forgiveness Come Apart: A Feminist Perspective on Restorative Justice and Intimate Violence', *Oxford Journal of Law and Religion*, Vol. 5, no. 1, (2016): 113–34.
29. C.Q. Hopkins and M.P. Koss, 'Incorporating Feminist Theory and Insights into a Restorative Justice Response to Sex Offenses', *Violence Against Women*, Vol. 11, no. 5 (2005): 693–723.
30. K. Daly, 'Sexual Assault and Restorative Justice', in H. Strang and J. Braithwaite (eds), *Restorative Justice and Family Violence* (Cambridge: Cambridge University Press, 2022), 62–67.
31. UNODC, *Handbook on Restorative Justice Programmes*, Second edition (2020), 73–75.
32. J. Stubbs, 'Restorative Justice, Domestic Violence and Family Violence', *Australian Domestic and Family Violence Clearinghouse Issues*, Paper no. 9 (2004); J. Stubbs, 'Beyond Apology? Domestic Violence and Critical Questions for Restorative Justice', *Criminology and Criminal Justice*, Vol. 7, no. 2 (2007): 171.

Chapter 30: Upholding Civil Liberties in the Digital Age: Privacy, Surveillance and Free Speech

1. Fourteenth Justice V.M. Tarkunde Memorial Lecture, delivered at the Multipurpose Hall, India International Centre, New Delhi, on 1 December 2023.
2. *Sodan Singh v. New Delhi Municipal Committee,* (1989) 4 SCC 155.
3. Shamnad Basheer, 'Igniting Iconoclasm', *Round the Clock Magazine,* 2014, available at: https://spicyip.com/wp-content/uploads/2014/11/The-Iconoclast.pdf (accessed on 2 July 2025).

4. M.N. Roy (1887–1954) | Humanist Heritage: Exploring the rich history and influence of humanism in the UK, Humanist Heritage, available at: https://heritage.humanists.uk/m-n-roy/ (accessed on 20 July 2025).
5. A.G. Noorani, 'The Judiciary and the Bar in India during the Emergency', *Law and Politics in Africa, Asia and Latin America*, Vol. 11, no. 4 (1978): 403–10.
6. Ankita Pandey, 'Defending Digital Liberties: Changing Contours of an Old New Civic Activism', *Economic and Political Weekly* (Engage), Vol. 58, no. 40 (7 October 2023).
7. *Shreya Singhal v. Union of India,* AIR 2015 SC 1523.
8. Samuel Warren and Louis Brandeis, 'The Right to Privacy', *Harvard Law Review,* Vol. 4, no. 5 (1890).
9. Thomas Cooley, *Treatise on the Law of Torts or the Wrongs Which Arise Independent of Contract,* Second Edition (Chicago: Callaghan and Company, 1888).
10. *R. Rajagopal v. the State of Tamil Nadu*, AIR 1995 SC 264.
11. *People's Union for Civil Liberties v. Union of India*, AIR 1997 SC 568.
12. *K.S. Puttaswamy v. Union of India,* (2017) 10 SCC 1.
13. *M.P. Sharma v. Satish Chandra,* AIR 1954 SC 300.
14. *Kharak Singh v. State of U.P.,* AIR 1963 SC 1295.
15. Constitutional judgment 3-4-1-42-13, Privacy Library (2014), https://www.riigikohus.ee/en/constitutional-judgment-3-4-1-42-13.
16. The Code of Criminal Procedure Implementation Act (CCPIA).
17. *Amabhungane Centre for Investigative Journalism v. Minister of Justice and Minister of Police,* ZACC 3 (2021).
18. *Big Brother Watch and Others v. The United Kingdom,* Application Nos. 58170/13, 62322/14 and 24960/15.
19. Anushka Jain, '#PrivacyofthePeople: The boom of facial recognition technology in private spaces', internet Freedom Foundation, 31 August 2022, available at: https://internetfreedom.in/facial-recog nitiontechnologyinprivatespaces/ (accessed on 2 July 2025).
20. Larry Hardesty, 'Study Finds Gender and Skin-Type Bias in Commercial Artificial-Intelligence Systems', MIT News, 11 February 2018, available at: https://news.mit.edu/2018/study-

finds-gender-skin-type-bias-artificial-intelligence-systems-0212 (accessed on 2 July 2025).

21. Jhalak Kakkar et al., 'The Surveillance Law Landscape in India and the Impact of Puttaswamy', Centre for Communication Governance, 2023, available at: https://papers.ssrn.com/sol3/papers.cfm?abstract_id=4624419 (accessed on 2 July 2025).
22. *Shreya Singhal v. Union of India, Supreme Court of India*, AIR 2015 SC 1523; *Bennett Coleman v. Union of India* (1973) 2 S.C.R 757.
23. *Abrams v. United States*, 250 U.S. 616.
24. Ari Ezra Waldman, 'The Marketplace of Fake News', *University of Pennsylvania Journal of Constitutional Law*, Vol. 20, NYLS Legal Studies Research Paper no. 3141373 (2018), available at: https://ssrn.com/abstract=3141373 (accessed on 2 July 2025).
25. S. Vasoughi, D. Roy and S. Aral, 'The spread of true and false news online', *Science*, Vol. 359, no. 63 (2018), available at: https://doi.org/10.1126/science.aap9559 (accessed on 2 July 2025).
26. Emily Bazelon, 'The Problem of Free Speech in an Age of Disinformation', *New York Times* (2020), available at: https://www.nytimes.com/2020/10/13/magazine/free-speech.html (accessed on 2 July 2025).
27. Ankita Pandey, 'Defending Digital Liberties: Changing Contours of an Old New Civic Activism', *Economic and Political Weekly*, Vol. 58, no. 40 (7 October 2023), available at: https://www.epw.in/engage/article/defending-digital-liberties-changing-contours-old (accessed on 2 July 2025).

Chapter 31: Democracy, Debate and Dissent

1. Speech at Justice Keshav Chandra Dhulia Memorial Essay Competition, delivered at the Forest Research Institute, Dehradun, on 2 December 2023.
2. Granville Austin, *The Indian Constitution: Cornerstone of a Nation* (Oxford University Press, 1966), xi.
3. Rajiv Bhargava (ed.), *Politics and Ethics of the Indian Constitution* (Oxford University Press, 2008), 15.
4. Austin, *The Indian Constitution*, xi.

5. Jawaharlal Nehru, *The Discovery of India* (Oxford University Press, 1985), 60.
6. Pratap Bhanu Mehta, *The Burden of Democracy* (Delhi: Penguin, 2003).
7. Ibid.
8. Constituent Assembly Debates, 25 November 1949, available at https://loksabha.nic.in/writereaddata/cadebatefiles/C25111949.html (accessed on 2 July 2025).
9. Mehta, *The Burden of Democracy.*
10. Gautam Bhatia, *Offend, Shock or Disturb: Free Speech Under the Indian Constitution* (Oxford University Press, 2016).
11. Rohit De, *A People's Constitution: The Everyday Life of Law in the Indian Republic* (Princeton University Press, 2018), 17.
12. Amartya Sen, *The Argumentative Indian* (Delhi: Penguin, 2006).
13. J.S. Habermas, *Between Facts and Norms: Contributions to a Discourse Theory of Law and Democracy* (Cambridge, Massachusetts: MIT Press, 1998).
14. Zachary Elkins, Tom Ginsburg and James Melton, *The Endurance of National Constitution* (Cambridge University Press, 2012).
15. Achyut Chetan, *Founding Mothers of the Indian Republic: Gender Politics of the Framing of the Constitution* (Cambridge University Press, 2022).
16. Ibid., 97.
17. Ornit Shani, 'The People and the Making of India's Constitution', *Historical Journal,* Vol. 65, no. 5 (2022), available at: https://doi.org/10.1017/S0018246X21000856 (accessed on 2 July 2025).
18. Elkins, Ginsburg and Melton, *The Endurance of National Constitutions.*
19. John S. Dryzek, *Deliberative Democracy and Beyond: Liberals, Criques, and Contestation* (Oxford University Press, 2000).
20. Ibid.
21. *Plessy v. Ferguson*, 163 U.S. 537 (1896).
22. *ADM Jabalpur v. S.S. Shukla* (1976) SCR 172.
23. *Brown v. Board of Education,* 347 US 483 (1954). This decision overturned the policy status of 'separate but equal' established by *Plessy v. Ferguson.*
24. *K.S. Puttaswamy v. Union of India,* (2017) 10 SCC 1.

Chapter 32: Navigating Discrimination in Public and Private Spaces: Constitutional Imperatives for the State

1. Justice E.S. Venkataramiah Memorial Lecture, at Jnyana Jyoti Auditorium Gandhi Nagar, Bengaluru on 17 December 2023.
2. (1982) 2 SCR 365.
3. AIR 1986 SC 515.
4. AIR 1988 SC 1037.
5. Benjamin N. Cardozo, 'The Nature of the Judicial Process', *Columbia Law Review,* Vol. 22 (1922): 384.
6. Supra, note 2.
7. Karen V. Hansen, 'Feminist Conceptions of Public and Private: A Critical Analysis', *Berkeley Journal of Sociology*, Vol. 32 (1987): 111.
8. Press Information Bureau, *Report on 'Women in Prisons' launched by the Ministry of Women and Child Development*, 2018, available at: https://www.pib.gov.in/Pressreleaseshare.aspx?PRID=1536513 (accessed on 21 July 2025).
9. *Harvinder Kaur v. Harmander Singh*, AIR 1984 Del 66 [Delhi High Court].
10. (2023) 13 SCC 681.
11. (2021) 2 SCC 166.
12. Hannah Arendt, *The Human Condition* (University of Chicago Press, second ed. 1998), 41.
13. (2008) 3 SCC 1.
14. (2014) SCC Online SC 900.
15. The Prize in Economic Sciences 2023 - Press release, The Nobel Prize (2023), https://www.nobelprize.org/prizes/economic-sciences/2023/press-release/ (last visited Jul 21, 2025).
16. *Jeeja Ghosh v. Union of India,* (2016) 7 SCC 761.
17. *Vikash Kumar v. Union Public Service Commission,* (2021) SCC OnLine SC 84.
18. *Ravindra Kumar Dhariwal v. Union of India,* (2021) SCC OnLine SC 1293.
19. (2021) SCC OnLine SC 3326.
20. (2018) 2 SCC 397.
21. Supreme Court Accessibility Report, *A Court for All: Paving the Way for Greater Accessibility in the Supreme Court for Persons with*

Disabilities, Women & Senior Citizen, October 2023, available at: https://main.sci.gov.in/pdf/LU/06112023_140650.pdf (accessed on 2 July 2025).

22. Alison Kafer, *Feminist, Queer, Crip* (Bloomington: Indiana University Press, 2013).
23. Abhish K. Bose, 'Govt-Run Barbershop for All Opens in Kerala Village After Dalits Were Denied Haircuts', News Minute, 14 September 2020, available at: https://www.thenewsminute.com/kerala/govt-run-barbershop-all-kerala-village-opens-after-dalits-were-denied-haircuts-133014 (accessed on 2 July 2025).
24. Exclusion of Dalits from wells and access to water continues till present. See Swarup Dutta, Sukanta Behera and Ashok Bharti, 'Access to Drinking Water by Scheduled Castes in Rural India: Some Key Issues and Challenges', *Indian Journal of Human Development,* Vol. 9, no. 1 (2015): 115, 118.
25. Mukul Sharma, 'Observing Water Day on Ambedkar's Birthday Is a Hollow Exercise If His Legacy on Water Is Ignored', Scroll.in, 14 April 2017, available at: https://scroll.in/article/834435/observing-water-day-on-ambedkars-birthday-is-a-hollow-exercise-if-his-legacy-on-water-is-ignored (accessed on 2 July 2025).
26. *Zoroastrian Co-Operative Housing Society Limited and Another v. District Registrar, Cooperative Societies,* (2005) 5 SCC 632.
27. *Indian Medical Association v. Union of India,* (2011) 7 SCC 179.

Chapter 33: Unveiling the Seventy-Fifth Year of the Supreme Court of India

1. Foundation Day Address, Supreme Court of India on 28 January 2024.
2. Pyarelal, *Mahatma Gandhi: The Last Phase*, Vol. II (Ahmedabad: Navajivan Publishing House, 1958), 65.
3. Case Management through CIS 3.0 (Case Information system 3.0), 2, available at https://cdnbbsr.s3waas.gov.in/s388ef51f0bf911e452e8dbb1d807a81ab/uploads/2020/08/2020082670.pdf (accessed on 2 July 2025).

Chapter 34: The Supreme Court at Seventy-Five: A Journey Through Law, Liberty and Justice

1. Speech delivered at the Ceremonial Bench to Commemorate Seventy-Five Years of the Supreme Court of India, Supreme Court of India, 28 January 2024.
2. B. Sen, 'The Supreme Court Bench and Bar: Reminiscences of the Formative Years', B.N. Kirpal, Ashok H. Desai, et al., (eds) *Supreme but Not Infallible: Essays in Honour of the Supreme Court of India* (Delhi: Oxford University Press, 2004).

Scan QR code to access the
Penguin Random House India website